Anthropomorphism in Islam

Edinburgh Studies in Classical Islamic History and Culture
Series Editor: Carole Hillenbrand

A particular feature of medieval Islamic civilisation was its wide horizons. In this respect it differed profoundly from medieval Europe, which from the point of view of geography, ethnicity and population was much smaller and narrower in its scope and in its mindset. The Muslims fell heir not only to the Graeco-Roman world of the Mediterranean, but also to that of the ancient Near East, to the empires of Assyria, Babylon and the Persians – and beyond that, they were in frequent contact with India and China to the east and with black Africa to the south. This intellectual openness can be sensed in many interrelated fields of Muslim thought: philosophy and theology, medicine and pharmacology, algebra and geometry, astronomy and astrology, geography and the literature of marvels, ethnology and sociology. It also impacted powerfully on trade and on the networks that made it possible. Books in this series reflect this openness and cover a wide range of topics, periods and geographical areas.

Titles in the series include:

Arabian Drugs in Early Medieval Mediterranean Medicine
Zohar Amar and Efraim Lev

The Medieval Western Maghrib: Cities, Patronage and Power
Amira K. Bennison

Keeping the Peace in Premodern Islam: Diplomacy under the Mamluk Sultanate, 1250–1517
Malika Dekkiche

Queens, Concubines and Eunuchs in Medieval Islam
Taef El-Azhari

Medieval Damascus: Plurality and Diversity in an Arabic Library – The Ashrafiya Library Catalogue
Konrad Hirschler

The Popularisation of Sufism in Ayyubid and Mamluk Egypt: State and Society, 1173–1325
Nathan Hofer

Anthropomorphism in Islam: The Challenge of Traditionalism (700–1350)
Livnat Holtzman

Making Mongol History
Stefan Kamola

Lyrics of Life: Sa'di on Love, Cosmopolitanism and Care of the Self
Fatemeh Keshavarz

A History of the True Balsam of Matarea
Marcus Milwright

Ruling from a Red Canopy: Political Authority in the Medieval Islamic World, From Anatolia to South Asia
Colin P. Mitchell

Conquered Populations in Early Islam: Non-Arabs, Slaves and the Sons of Slave Mothers
Elizabeth Urban

edinburghuniversistypress.com/series/escihc

Anthropomorphism in Islam

The Challenge of Traditionalism (700–1350)

Livnat Holtzman

EDINBURGH
University Press

To Malka and Giora Ashkenazi

Edinburgh University Press is one of the leading university presses in the UK. We publish academic books and journals in our selected subject areas across the humanities and social sciences, combining cutting-edge scholarship with high editorial and production values to produce academic works of lasting importance. For more information visit our website: edinburghuniversitypress.com

© Livnat Holtzman, 2018

Edinburgh University Press Ltd
The Tun – Holyrood Road
12 (2f) Jackson's Entry
Edinburgh EH8 8PJ

Typeset in 11/15 Adobe Garamond by
Servis Filmsetting Ltd, Stockport, Cheshire

A CIP record for this book is available from the British Library

ISBN 978 0 7486 8956 9 (hardback)
ISBN 978 0 7486 8957 6 (webready PDF)
ISBN 978 0 7486 8958 3 (epub)

The right of Livnat Holtzman to be identified as the author of this work has been asserted in accordance with the Copyright, Designs and Patents Act 1988 and the Copyright and Related Rights Regulations 2003 (SI No. 2498).

Contents

Preface and Acknowledgements vii

Introduction 1

1 The Narrator and the Narrative: A Literary Analysis of *Aḥādīth al-Ṣifāt* 21

Introduction 21

I. A Preliminary Remark on Hadith and Narratology 23

II. The Framing Narrative 25

III. The Embedded Narrative 33

IV. The Narrator and his Audience 38

V. The Motives of the Narrator 42

VI. The Narrator's Role 47

2 A Tale of Two Narrators: Some Historical, Geographical and Cultural Considerations 68

Introduction 68

I. Two Different Narrators 69

II. The Proliferation of the Abu Razin Narrative 82

III. Two Narrators and One Narrative: The Tribal Connection 87

IV. The Proliferation of the Jarir Narrative 93

V. The Jarir Narrative and the *Miḥna* 99

3 Gestures and *Aḥādīth al-Ṣifāt* 120

Introduction 120

I. The Prophet's Gestures: Iconic, Metaphoric and Deictic 122

II. 'The Instance of Narrating': The Narrator and his Audience 128
III. The Performing Trend 134
IV. The Ultimate Performer of *Aḥādīth al-Ṣifāt* 146
V. The Predicament of the Traditionalists 153

4 The Diversified Solution to the Challenge of Islamic Traditionalism: *Aḥādīth al-Ṣifāt* and *Bi-Lā Kayfa* **185**
Introduction 185
I. Drawing the Borderlines of the Traditionalistic Discourse 189
II. The Earliest Debate 206
III. Transmission, Censorship and Euphemisms 216
IV. The All-inclusive *Tanzīh*: The Ashᶜarite Solution 223
V. Expanding the Borders of the Traditionalistic Discourse 234

5 Iconic Books and Gestures: *Aḥādīth al-Ṣifāt* in the Public Sphere **267**
Introduction 267
I. The Iconicity of the Qadiri Creed 272
II. The Three Dimensions of *Kitāb al-Tawḥīd* 278
III. Fakhr al-Din al-Razi's Response to *Kitāb al-Tawḥīd* 294
IV. Ibn Taymiyya's *al-Ḥamawiyya al-Kubrā* and Two Iconic Gestures 313
V. Iconic Gestures and the Hashwiyya 328

Final Remarks and Conclusions **360**

Appendix I: Full Translations of Lengthy Traditions 371
Appendix II: Full Translation of 'the *Ḥadīth* of Allegiance' of Abu Razin 376
Appendix III: Chains of Transmission 383
Appendix IV: Chains of Transmission 366
Appendix V: Chains of Transmission 390
Bibliography 392
Index 420

Preface and Acknowledgements

The purpose of this study is to identify, characterise and contextualise the different approaches towards anthropomorphism (*tashbīh*, the literal meaning of the word is to make similar, compare, liken) in Islamic traditionalism. The period under review is from the eighth to the fourteenth centuries. The traditionalistic approaches towards *tashbīh* were crystallised during centuries of vehement debates about *aḥādīth al-ṣifāt*, the traditions that depict God and His attributes in anthropomorphic language. These debates were an intrinsic part of the discussions on the divine attributes and God's spatiality. As versatile scholars who mastered the entire spectrum of literary genres, the Arab polymaths documented these debates in a variety of literary works. This documentation was neither systematic nor comprehensive. Naturally, we find references to these debates in the vast theological literature: *kalām* manuals, theological treatises, compendia of heresiography and simplistic traditionalistic creeds (*ᶜaqāʾid*). However, other literary works also disclose the essence of the inner debates of the traditionalistic circles. Thus, we find fragments of information about these debates in the historical sources, mainly chronicles, and the professional literature for Hadith scholars, such as biographical dictionaries, Hadith manuals, exegeses (*shurūḥ*) of prominent Hadith compilations, and exegeses (*tafāsīr*) of the Quran.

When I started planning the research for this book, I assumed that I would focus on the theological writings of the leading Islamic thinkers. Ibn Qutayba, Abu Yaᶜla, Ibn al-Jawzi, and naturally Ibn Taymiyya and Ibn Qayyim al-Jawziyya, were the names that immediately came into my mind. However, in my reading of these scholars' works of theology, I found myself drawn more and more to other literary genres, mostly Hadith compilations and Hadith manuals. As a result, the task of conducting the research for this study was less tranquil than I had initially imagined and planned. First, the amount of literature relevant for this study turned out to be overwhelming. I found that almost every respectable thinker, whether Hanbalite, Ashᶜarite or otherwise, possessed an unrestrainable need to write a treatise about the divine attributes, the divine throne or God's spatiality, topics which are related to *tashbīh*. Furthermore, I soon realised that the true story of anthropomorphism in traditionalist Islam lies in the almost unexplored territory of *aḥādīth al-ṣifāt*. The task of contextualising the different approaches towards *tashbīh* required me to temporarily leave my 'territorial waters', namely the hard-core theological literature. I was forced to set sail in 'high seas' into the heart of a conglomerate of texts of all kinds in search of pieces of evidence that contained the inner debates about anthropomorphism in Islamic traditionalism. The magnitude of this task entailed several decisions. The first decision was to concentrate on *aḥādīth al-ṣifāt* and touch upon other related issues (such as the Ashᶜarite doctrine of the divine attributes) only briefly. The second decision was to pay attention to the ultra-traditionalists (the Hanbalites and their forerunners) and middle-of-the-road traditionalists (the Ashᶜarites and their forerunners). This decision necessarily entailed the exclusion of other groups that did not fall under the category of Islamic traditionalism such as the Kharijites, the Zahirites, the Kullabites and the Karramites. These groups, as well as the rationalistic groups (the Muᶜtazilites, the Ibadites, the Shiᶜites, and the Zaydites) are of course mentioned in the course of the discussion, but the focus is strictly on the traditionalists. The third decision acknowledged the need to avoid redundancy by excluding theological treatises that duplicated the arguments of previous texts that were already included in the book. The outcome of these three decisions influenced the focus of the book; this work does not encompass the entire range of relevant sources and topics. Instead, by focusing on *aḥādīth al-ṣifāt*, the traditionalists who discussed them, and reading a selection of theological treatises, I was able to see the woods rather than the trees, and to explore new trajectories.

I am privileged to acknowledge three milestones that marked my path while writing this book. First, in 2005, a year after the approval of my doctoral dissertation, Sabine Schmidtke, who then served as the editor of the

Theology and Philosophy section of the third edition of *The Encyclopaedia of Islam* (Leiden: Brill), asked me to write the entry 'Anthropomorphism'. This surprising assignment (as my dissertation had nothing to do with anthropomorphism) was in fact the first step towards writing this book. This is a golden opportunity to acknowledge my debt of gratitude to Sabine who consistently showed genuine interest and support in my scientific work. Second, in 2010, I was awarded a four-year research grant from The Israel Science Foundation for the project 'Defining Anthropomorphism (*Tashbīh*): The Challenge of Islamic Traditionalism during the 8th–14th Centuries' (grant no. 10/79). In the framework of this project, I established a research group which was active between October 2010 and September 2014. Eiman Abu-Kishek and Liron Nuna-Malka were the dedicated research assistants of this project. They diligently classified the anthropomorphic material in Hadith and pseudo-Hadith collections, and also detected relevant material in the historical chronicles and the biographical sources. Without exaggeration, I would not have been able to conduct the research for this book without their valuable help. Third, in September 2015, I took a year-long sabbatical to complete the book. My gratitude is extended to the Rector of Bar-Ilan University, Prof. Miriam Faust, and the Dean of the Humanities, Prof. Shifra Baruchson-Arbib, for both making this sabbatical possible and showing their support and interest in this project.

Throughout the years of working on this book, I greatly benefitted from conversations and correspondences with colleagues who generously shared their insights and knowledge with me. I wish to thank especially the following scholars: Christopher Melchert, Jon Hoover, Walid Saleh, Frank Griffel, Caterina Bori, Yossef Rapoport, Yahya Michot, Maribel Fierro, Camilla Adang, Ayman Shihadeh, Jens Scheiner, Abdessamad Belhaj, Amikam Elad, Abdelkader Al Ghouz, Steven Judd, Yaacov Lev, Tzvi Y. Langermann, Yohanan Friedmann, Ella Landau-Tasseron, Etan Kohlberg, Meir Bar-Asher, Amalia Levanoni, Michael Ebstein, Sara Sviri, Joseph Witztum, Daniella Talmon-Heller, Almog Kasher, Silvia Adler and Miriam Ovadia. I am also grateful to Christian Bailey, Jonathan A. C. Brown and James W. Watts who shared their articles with me, prior to or shortly after their publication. I wish also to thank the graduate students of the Department of Arabic at Bar-Ilan University who participated in three seminars that I conducted on theology, anthropomorphism and politics in 2011, 2014 and 2017. These seminars enabled me to present my ideas and struggle with the most challenging and difficult research questions. Often I have found myself dashing into my office at the end of a seminar session to write the ideas that emerged from the fruitful dialogues with my students. Special thanks from the bottom of my heart are due to my long-time friend and colleague, Birgit Krawietz, who was enthusiastic about this book and never failed to ask me difficult questions that forced me to rethink my arguments and refine them, thus leading me to plausible solutions.

This book would not have been written without two pillars of wisdom, my two special teachers to whom I owe my academic career. Binyamin Abrahamov opened for me the window to the fascinating world of Islamic theology. Since the completion of my dissertation until today, he has continuously provided me with his wise advice and I am grateful for his friendship. Isaiah Goldfeld (1934–2016) introduced me to the beauty of classical Arabic poetry. During our regular weekly meetings, which lasted for seven happy years, I shared with him my thoughts about this book. He in particular encouraged me to develop the connection between gestures and *aḥādīth al-ṣifāt*. May this book serve as a memorial to this gentle kind man and brilliant scholar!

My gratitude also extends to the professionals who facilitated the writing of this book. First is my editor, Yosef Mackler, who meticulously read several drafts of this book, commented on each and every word, and drew my attention to ambiguities in my train of argumentations. Second is the anonymous reviewer, whose wise comments helped me improve the book and expand the discussion on certain crucial points. Third is Dina Baum, the Librarian of the Arabic Seminar Library in Bar-Ilan University, who provided daily assistance with much grace and enthusiasm. I am indebted to Edinburgh University Press (EUP) and the wonderful people who work there. I am grateful to Carole Hillenbrand, Editor of 'Edinburgh Studies in Classical Islamic History and Culture' for choosing my manuscript for this series. I thank Nicola Ramsey, Commissioning Editor for Islam and Middle Eastern Studies at EUP, and her assistants, Ersev Ersoy and Ellie Bush, for their generous professional support throughout the long process of preparing the manuscript. I am also grateful to Rebecca Mackenzie from Production, Paul Smith who designed the beautiful cover, Susan Tricklebank who prepared the index, Sue Dalgleish who edited the manuscript, and last but not least Eddie Clark who guided me patiently through the final stage of copy editing.

Finally, I owe an immense debt of gratitude to my husband, Ronen Holtzman, for his practical advice and help, unconditional support and enduring interest in my work. Ronen and my family made this book possible in many ways. My gratitude and love go to them, and to my parents to whom this book is dedicated.

Introduction

Ahmad ibn Salman ibn al-Hasan ibn Isra'il ibn Yunus, also known as Abu Bakr al-Najjad (d. 960, at the age of ninety five), was a *muḥaddith* (a professional Hadith transmitter) in tenth-century Baghdad. As a Hanbalite, Abu Bakr al-Najjad belonged to the most dominant group in this vibrant city. Led by the ambitious preacher al-Hasan ibn ᶜAli al-Barbahari (d. 941), the Hanbalites of tenth-century Baghdad were characterised by their doctrinal enthusiasm and political activism. They enjoyed the unrestricted support of *al-ᶜāmma*, the masses; this support enabled the Hanbalites to instigate riots against their opponents and dominate the public sphere.

The Hanbalite dominance of Baghdad notwithstanding, the city hosted scholars from the entire spectrum of Islamic thought. Thus, at one end of the spectrum of theological trends were the ultra-traditionalistic Hanbalites, who perceived themselves as the proponents of the genuine heritage of the Prophet Muhammad and his followers. At the other end of the spectrum were the rationalistic Muᶜtazilites, the leading proponents of *kalām*, namely speculative theology. Between the rationalists and ultra-traditionalists, the middle-of-the-road traditionalists were situated. This group formed the majority of the traditionalists of Baghdad. The middle-of-the-road traditionalists were engaged with the study of Hadith, and some of them even expressed rationalistic views. As a political movement, the Muᶜtazila lost its power in the middle of the ninth century; however, prominent Muᶜtazilite thinkers thrived in Baghdad while their intellectual influence was wide and transcended the boundaries of the city. The Muᶜtazilite thought attracted Shiᶜites and Zaydites, and even influenced the development of Jewish systematic theology.[1] Tenth-century

Baghdad also witnessed the emergence of Ashᶜarism. The Ashᶜarites, a rising force in Baghdad, were traditional-rationalists: their thought combined reliance on the Hadith material (and from this respect, they were traditionalists) with the application of the principles of *kalām*. Last but not least, Baghdad hosted Aristotelian and Neoplatonic philosophers and intellectuals of different faiths (Christians, Jews and Buddhists).[2]

However, as far as Abu Bakr al-Najjad and his fellow Hanbalites were concerned, Baghdad was the most important centre of Hadith transmission in the Islamic world, and a stronghold of Islamic traditionalism. Like many of his fellow *muḥaddithūn*, al-Najjad followed the model of Ahmad ibn Hanbal (d. 855), the eponymous founder of the Hanbalite school. Ibn Hanbal lived in abject poverty while generously sharing the scarce food he had with the poor and needy of Baghdad. This ethos of asceticism, called *zuhd*, united the Hanbalite scholars and the masses. Al-Najjad, as his fellow Hanbalite scholars recounted, was such a role model of piety. Once he joined a group of Hanbalites who paid a visit to one of the most bashful *muḥaddithūn* in Baghdad, Bishr ibn Musa (d. 901, at the age of ninety eight), to hear Hadith from him. Al-Najjad drew the attention of his fellow Hanbalites because he carried his sandals in his hand and walked barefoot in the streets of Baghdad. When his compatriots asked him why he did not wear his sandals, al-Najjad replied: 'I prefer to walk barefoot while I am in quest after the aphorisms of the Messenger of God.' A later Hanbalite scholar, who quoted this anecdote, remarked that perhaps al-Najjad followed a Prophetic *ḥadīth* in which the Prophet informed the believers that on the Day of Resurrection, God would look attentively and benevolently on the Muslim who walked barefoot while performing charitable deeds.[3]

Al-Najjad was exceptionally popular among the students of Hadith in Baghdad: his Hadith classes were offered regularly every Friday at the mosque named after the caliph al-Mansur. In fact, he offered two kinds of classes: one class on Hanbalite jurisprudence (*fiqh*) that was held before the Friday Prayer, and one class that occurred after the prayer. The latter was dedicated to dictating (*imlāʾ*) the copious Hadith material that was at al-Najjad's disposal. This class was so crowded that the superintendents of the mosque were forced to close the doors that led to the court in which al-Najjad taught, to prevent more fervent students from entering.[4]

Abu Bakr al-Najjad's prestige as a *muḥaddith* emanated from his stature as the last disciple of the illustrious Hadith compiler, Abu Dawud al-Sijistani (d. 889).[5] The Hanbalites used to passionately claim that al-Najjad also heard Hadith from ᶜAbd Allah ibn Ahmad ibn Hanbal (d. 903), the son of Ahmad ibn Hanbal.[6] ᶜAbd Allah was responsible for compiling his father's oral teachings and Hadith material. He canonised Ahmad ibn Hanbal's teachings by creating the *Musnad*, the most important textual source for the Hanbalites. As far as the Hanbalites were concerned, al-Najjad's alleged proximity to ᶜAbd Allah was sufficient to establish al-Najjad's scholarly stature. Other scholars, however, were much less impressed by al-Najjad's scholarship. First, they did not mention ᶜAbd Allah as one of al-Najjad's teachers, which means that they did not consider him one of ᶜAbd Allah's disciples. Secondly, al-Najjad's name was somewhat tainted by allegations of plagiarism. For instance, the Baghdadian Hadith scholar, Abu 'l-Hasan al-Daraqutni (d. 995), who participated in al-Najjad's classes, claimed that al-Najjad used the Hadith material of other scholars, and attributed this material, which he was not entitled to teach, to himself. Al-Khatib al-Baghdadi (d. 1071), who cited al-Daraqutni's unflattering view of al-Najjad, tried to exonerate al-Najjad from this severe accusation: 'Al-Najjad became blind towards the end of his life – explained al-Khatib al-Baghdadi – so perhaps one of his students dictated in his name this material that al-Daraqutni mentioned'.[7] These allegations aside, al-Najjad was generally considered a reliable *muḥaddith*: *ṣadūq*, that is, truthful, is the epithet that the Hadith experts attached to his name.

Al-Najjad's expertise in Hadith, combined with his ultra-traditionalistic worldview and his modest lifestyle, made him a faithful representative of tenth-century Baghdadian Hanbalism.[8] His oral teachings and testimonies, which are scattered throughout the biographical dictionaries, are therefore important in reconstructing the views of the Hanbalites of Baghdad. An unusually lengthy passage preserved in the biographical dictionary of Hanbalite scholars written by the authoritative Hanbalite scholar Ibn Abi Yaᶜla (d. 1131), describes al-Najjad's intensive efforts to verify the authenticity of one particular *ḥadīth*. This brief *ḥadīth*, attributed to the *tābiᶜī* (pl. *tābiᶜūn*, lit. a successor, an epithet given to a disciple of the *ṣaḥāba*, the companions of the Prophet Muhammad) Mujahid ibn Jabr (d. between 718 and 722), reflected Mujahid's understanding of God's promise to Muhammad as uttered in the

Quran. Mujahid normally transmitted exegetical Hadith material on the authority of the *ṣaḥābī* ᶜAbd Allah ibn ᶜAbbas (d. 687–8), who is generally considered to be the founder of the science of Quran exegesis. However, in the case of this brief *ḥadīth*, Mujahid opined his own understanding of God's promise to Muhammad as uttered in the Quran. According to Q. 17:79, God promised Muhammad 'an honourable station' (*maqāman maḥmūdan*). Mujahid explained this phrase: '[God] will make [Muhammad] sit down with Him on His throne'.[9] Previous scholarship that discussed this *ḥadīth* focused on its authenticity and its connection to the hardships that the illustrious historian and Quran exegete, Abu Jaᶜfar Muhammad ibn Jarir al-Tabari (d. 923), suffered from the Hanbalites of Baghdad.[10] Relying on the relevant primary sources, the following discussion on the *ḥadīth* attributed to Mujahid adds to the previous research and highlights several points that the research neglected. Three of these points, namely the paraphrasing of the *ḥadīth* attributed to Mujahid, the addition of embellishments to this *ḥadīth*, and the performance of a bodily gesture that accompanied the recitation of this *ḥadīth*, demonstrate the most important features of the present monograph.

When Abu Bakr al-Najjad completed his thorough investigations about this *ḥadīth*, he issued a creed (*ᶜaqīda* pl. *ᶜaqāʾid*), a profession of faith which reflected the feelings of the Hanbalites on this matter:

> This is our profession of faith before God: We believe in the content of the *aḥādīth* that are attributed to the Messenger of God, but also to ᶜAbd Allah ibn ᶜAbbas (d. 687–8), and the scholars who succeeded him. These *aḥādīth* were transmitted from one great scholar to another, from one generation to the next generation, until the times of our great teachers. We wrote these *aḥādīth*, and meticulously investigated their content. These *aḥādīth* interpret the meaning of the Quranic verse [Q. 17:79] 'your Lord may exalt you to an honourable station'. According to these *aḥādīth*, 'the honourable station' means that Muhammad will sit with His Lord on His throne. Whoever rejects this interpretation and refutes it, expresses the views of the Jahmiyya (the Muᶜtazilites). One must avoid this person, turn away from him, and beware of him. Abu Bakr al-Khatib (d. 933) informed me that Abu Dawud al-Sijistani told him: 'Whoever rejects the *ḥadīth* attributed to Mujahid is a Jahmite (Muᶜtazilite)'.[11]

Al-Najjad concluded that the belief in Muhammad's noble virtue (*faḍīla*) of sitting with God on the throne was one of the cornerstones of the Hanbalite creed. To illustrate the strength of this belief, al-Najjad explained that hypothetically, a man who declared that God would make Muhammad sit down with Him on the throne and thereafter took the oath on pain of triple divorce[12] to strengthen his declaration, should have never feared that he needed to divorce his wife. If this man came to al-Najjad to seek his legal advice whether he should divorce his wife or not, the scholar would tell him:

> You declared the truth, your oath is valid, and your wife should remain safely in her position. Because this is our way, our religion, and our creed. This is the root of our conviction from which we emerged. We will adhere to this conviction until the day we die.[13]

Written in the middle of the tenth century, al-Najjad's creed paraphrased the *ḥadīth* on Mujahid's interpretation of 'an honourable station' and elevated it to the degree of an article of faith for the Hanbalites. By doing so, al-Najjad sealed the turbulent history of this *ḥadīth* and silenced all the voices that spoke against this *ḥadīth* or merely doubted its veracity. Al-Najjad's creed concluded the continuous controversy about this *ḥadīth* with a smashing victory over the middle-of-the-road traditionalists.[14] To correctly evaluate al-Najjad's creed, we need to examine the meaning of this *ḥadīth* and its history.

The *ḥadīth* on Mujahid's interpretation of 'an honourable station' was one of the conspicuous *aḥādīth al-ṣifāt*, the traditions on the divine attributes that included anthropomorphic descriptions of God. This *ḥadīth* was controversial in spite of the fact that it did not describe God in any physical way or form. When read literally, this *ḥadīth* implies that 'an honourable station' is an actual, physical place, and that God's sitting on the throne (with Muhammad next to Him) is accordingly an actual sitting of a physical body. This reading obviously led to *tashbīh*, namely comparing God to His creation and anthropomorphising Him. Laymen who heard this *ḥadīth* might have been led to visualise a majestic human figure on a throne, sitting next to a much smaller human figure. The implied description of God in this *ḥadīth* was unmistakably an anthropomorphic description. Alongside the circulation of this anthropomorphic *ḥadīth* in ninth-century Baghdad,[15] a 'sterilised' or 'mild' version of the *ḥadīth* proliferated in growing numbers among the traditionalistic circles in Baghdad and elsewhere, and dominated the traditionalistic discourse. This version, devoid of any anthropomorphism, was attributed to several Hadith authorities: the *ṣaḥāba* Abu Hurayra (d. 678) and Ibn ᶜAbbas, and a group of *tābiᶜūn*, among whom the name of Mujahid was also conspicuous. According to this mild version and its variants, Mujahid and the other persona explained 'an honourable station' as 'the intercession (*shafāᶜa*) of Muhammad on the Day of Resurrection', that is, it was not an actual place but the role that Muhammad played as an intercessor (*shafiᶜ*) for the Muslims facing their trial in the Final Judgement.[16] This version, therefore, could have led its readers and listeners to an abstract concept but also to a specific scene depicting Muhammad as an intercessor before God while presenting his arguments on behalf of the Muslims. This scene was devoid of the divine throne and God sitting on it, and did not require sophisticated explanations to expel any likening of God to His creation. Unsurprisingly, this mild and certainly more convenient version was attributed to reliable persona throughout its transmission process. The flawless chain of transmitters (*isnād*, pl. *asānīd*) attached to the mild version and its variants, and the fact that it was a 'massively transmitted *ḥadīth*' (*ḥadīth mutawātir*, a *ḥadīth* with multiple chains of transmission) facilitated the entry of this version into some of the more important (although not canonical) Hadith compilations.[17] The anthropomorphic version, on the other hand, was problematic also because of its chain of transmitters. Thus, it was not labelled as an authentic and reliable text (*ṣaḥīḥ*). Accordingly, the anthropomorphic version found its way into marginal Hadith compilations. In one of these marginal compilations, the author, the Hanbalite *muḥaddith* Abu Bakr al-Ajurri (d. 971), decided to reconcile the anthropomorphic and the mild versions. In his *Kitāb al-Sharīᶜa*, a book highly venerated by the Hanbalites, al-Ajurri dedicated an entire chapter to 'an honourable station'. In the brief introduction to this chapter, al-Ajurri explained that the 'honourable station' that God granted His Prophet would be both his role as an intercessor for all of God's creatures and the noble virtue (*faḍīla*) attributed to him of sitting on the throne. Before quoting the anthropomorphic version, al-Ajurri quoted the ruling of the luminaries of Hanbalism according to which the *ḥadīth* attributed to Mujahid (the anthropomorphic one) should be accepted in the Islamic canon instead of being refuted.[18]

From Abu Bakr al-Ajurri's statement, this particular anthropomorphic *ḥadīth* served as a hallmark of Hanbalism, but still struggled for its place in the traditionalistic discourse. We suggest that this *ḥadīth* achieved this dual stature even before the second half of the tenth century, when Abu Bakr al-Najjad started his investigations in order to establish the authenticity of the anthropomorphic version. This struggle apparently accompanied this *ḥadīth* from its inception. Prior to the emergence of the Hanbalites as a distinct group in the Baghdadian public sphere, this *ḥadīth* was the demarcation line between middle-of-the-road traditionalism and extreme traditionalism: the ultra-traditionalists (later to be identified with Hanbalism) who embraced this *ḥadīth*, believed that Muhammad's sitting on the throne next to God was one of his many noble virtues (*faḍīla*, pl. *faḍāʾil*). The traditionalists who rejected this *ḥadīth* claimed that it promoted a dualist worldview (*thanawiyya*), as Muhammad's depiction in it led to the understanding that he would assume a ruling position next to God, and even as God's equal.[19] The ultra-traditionalists declared that their fellow traditionalists were infidels for not having accepted the veracity of this *ḥadīth*. Thus, for example, the Baghdadian *muḥaddith* Yahya Abu Bakr (d. 889 at the age of ninety-five)[20] taught this *ḥadīth* to his disciples and added: 'Whoever rejects this *ḥadīth*, resists God. Whoever denies the noble virtue of the Prophet, is an infidel.'[21] The rationalists (the Muᶜtazilites), by the way, did not show any interest at all in this controversy, because they rejected almost the entire corpus (*mukhālafat al-sunna*) of *aḥādīth al-ṣifāt*, namely the traditions which depicted God in an anthropomorphic language.[22] The debate about the anthropomorphic version of the *ḥadīth* attributed to Mujahid was therefore an entirely internal matter of the traditionalists.

The ninth-century ultra-traditionalists who defended this *ḥadīth* and studied it, toiled a great deal to prove the antiquity of the text. Thus, a marginal *muḥaddith* by the name of Muhammad ibn ᶜAbd al-Malik al-Daqiqi (d. 876) declared: 'I heard this *ḥadīth* for the last fifty years, and I never heard anyone rejecting it. Only the heretics and the Jahmites deny its veracity.'[23] The traditionalists also decorated the *ḥadīth* with further details during their study sessions. The Hanbalite Abu 'l-Hasan ibn al-ᶜAttar (d. 881) reminisced about such a study session, conducted by the *muḥaddith* Muhammad ibn Musᶜab al-ᶜAbid al-Daᶜᶜaʾ (d. 843) from Baghdad:

> Once I heard Muhammad ibn Musᶜab al-ᶜAbid recount this *ḥadīth* which is attributed to Mujahid, namely '[God] will make [Muhammad] sit down with Him on His throne'. After transmitting this *ḥadīth*, Muhammad ibn Musᶜab al-ᶜAbid added: 'So all the creatures will see Muhammad's position at His Lord, and the respect that His Lord has for him. Thereafter, Muhammad will retire to his chambers, gardens and wives in Paradise, so God will remain alone in His ruling of the world.'[24]

The Hanbalites had a taste for *aḥādīth* embellished with pictorial scenes. This is why they warmly embraced Muhammad ibn Musᶜab's freestyle explanations and additions to the anthropomorphic version. Repeated by his disciples, Muhammad ibn Musᶜab's embellishments were admitted into the Hanbalite canon, but rejected by the overall traditionalist canon.

Alongside their vigorous efforts to promote this *ḥadīth* attributed to Mujahid, who was merely a *tābiᶜī*, the Hanbalites searched for additional ancient versions of this text. Thus, they found evidence that a similar version circulated in the eighth century. This version was considered more valuable than the *ḥadīth* attributed to Mujahid, because it was attributed to the *ṣaḥābī* ᶜAbd Allah ibn Salam Abu 'l-Harith al-Israᵓili (d. 663–4). This *ṣaḥābī* was a Medinese Jew who converted to Islam two years before the Prophet died, and became an overflowing source of Judaeo-Christian traditions. ᶜAbd Allah ibn Salam became one of the Prophet's closest friends and the first Muslim who was promised Paradise in his lifetime. In the second half of the eighth century, ᶜAbd Allah ibn Salam's name was connected to a *ḥadīth* which circulated in Basra and was quite similar to the anthropomorphic version attributed to Mujahid. According to this *ḥadīth*, ᶜAbd Allah ibn Salam said: 'On the Day of Resurrection, your Prophet will be summoned [to God], and will be asked to sit in front of God on his throne.' A prominent *muḥaddith* from Basra, Abu Masᶜud Saᶜid ibn Iyas al-Jurayri (d. 761–2), transmitted this *ḥadīth*. One of Abu Masᶜud al-Jurayri's disciples asked: 'Oh Abu Masᶜud, does this mean that by being on the throne, the Prophet will be actually with God?' Abu Masᶜud was annoyed by this question, and replied: 'Woe unto you! This is the most precious *ḥadīth* for me in the entire world.'[25] The Hanbalites of Baghdad perceived this anecdote about al-Jurayri as a reinforcement of their position in the debate about Muhammad's sitting on the divine throne. More importantly, they regarded the *ḥadīth* attributed to ᶜAbd Allah ibn Salam as precious, because it established the antiquity of the concept of Muhammad's sitting on the divine throne. However, as mentioned earlier, the textual evidence that the Hanbalites presented about the authenticity of the anthropomorphic version made no impression on the majority of the traditionalists. They preferred the mild version which had no anthropomorphism in it. The Hanbalites, however, promoted the anthropomorphic version which they cherished in different channels to a degree that this text became an icon of Hanbalism.

There were other *aḥādīth*, similar to the *ḥadīth* attributed to Mujahid that were considered texts of dubious origin. These texts were compiled by the Baghdadian *muḥaddith* Abu 'l-Qasim ᶜAbd al-ᶜAziz ibn ᶜAli al-Khayyat (d. 1052); however, his Hadith compilation about the divine attributes is no longer extant. One of the rare versions in al-Khayyat's compilation (quoted by a later source) was attributed to ᶜAᵓisha (d. 678), the beloved wife of Muhammad. According to this version of the *ḥadīth*, ᶜAᵓisha testified: 'I once asked the Messenger of God about the honourable station, and he replied: "My Lord promised me that I would sit on the throne."'[26] Another interesting version is attributed to the *ṣaḥābī* ᶜAbd Allah ibn ᶜUmar (d. 693). According to his avowal, Ibn ᶜUmar's interpretation of Q. 17:79 relied on the Prophet himself. Ibn ᶜUmar thus explained that the verse meant that God would make the Prophet sit with Him on the throne.[27]

The great canoniser of Ahmad ibn Hanbal's teachings, Ahmad ibn Muhammad Abu Bakr al-Marwazi (or al-Marrudhi, d. 888), was responsible for the transformation of the anthropomorphic version of the *ḥadīth* on the 'honourable station' from a marginal *ḥadīth* to an iconic text. Al-Marwazi and his fellow Hanbalites were concerned by voices within the community of the *muḥaddithūn* which expressed their serious doubts about the veracity of the anthropomorphic version and forthrightly preferred the mild version. Al-Marwazi and his colleagues were especially concerned by a certain *muḥaddith* who issued a letter denouncing the anthropomorphic version. The name of this *muḥaddith* was never clarified; the Hanbalite scholars merely referred to him as 'al-Tirmidhi', thus emphasising his Persian origin (al-Tirmidh is located in today's southern part of Uzbekistan).[28] 'Al-Tirmidhi' made his views against the anthropomorphic version known to the entire community of Hanbalite *muḥaddithūn* in response to their vigorous efforts to promote this *ḥadīth*. One of these Hanbalites, Yahya Abu Bakr (whom we mentioned earlier), received a letter from 'al-Tirmidhi' claiming that 'whoever transmits the *ḥadīth* attributed to Mujahid is a Jahmite (Muᶜtazilite) and a dualist'. Yahya Abu Bakr immediately sent the letter to Abu Bakr al-Marwazi, the most senior disciple of Ahmad ibn Hanbal.[29] The letter containing the shockingly heretical words of 'al-Tirmidhi' immediately brought to al-Marwazi's memory a conversation that he had had with Ahmad ibn Hanbal years before the incident. According to al-Marwazi's avowal, he asked Ahmad ibn Hanbal what would happen to someone who rejected one of the anthropomorphic traditions (*al-aḥādīth fī 'l-ṣifāt*). Ahmad ibn Hanbal's forthright reply was 'avoid him' (*yujfā*).[30] We note that Ahmad ibn Hanbal did not address the *ḥadīth* attributed to Mujahid in this brief conversation, probably because this *ḥadīth* was not known to him.

The meaning of Ahmad ibn Hanbal's reply was not to ignore this person, but to excommunicate him. Brushing up this long-forgotten reply by Ahmad ibn Hanbal drove al-Marwazi to an immediate act: he composed a book dedicated entirely to Muhammad's special virtue of sitting on the divine throne. According to later sources, al-Marwazi's book, which unfortunately no longer exists, contained all the possible variants of the *ḥadīth* attributed to Mujahid as well as a list of the scholars who vouched for the veracity of all these variants.[31] Parts of this book are preserved in *Kitāb al-Sunna*, authored by al-Marwazi's disciple Ahmad ibn Muhammad Abu Bakr al-Khallal (d. 923), himself an important Hanbalite theologian and jurisprudent. Judging from the available fragments of al-Marwazi's book, it contained dozens of declarations by Hanbalite *muḥaddithūn* who were active in the second half of the ninth century, in defence of the anthropomorphic version. These declarations also condemned 'al-Tirmidhi', describing him as a brilliant man who produced words of heresy. The Hanbalite *muḥaddithūn* forbade any association with 'al-Tirmidhi' and called for a ban of his Hadith classes.[32] There is no doubt then, that 'al-Tirmidhi' was in fact one of the *muḥaddithūn* and not a fully fledged Muᶜtazilite. We will reserve the inquiry about 'al-Tirmidhi's' identity for another time.[33]

Al-Marwazi promoted the anthropomorphic version attributed to Mujahid by another effective way: whenever he recited this *ḥadīth*, he used to stand up and then sit down. This gesture illustrated that Muhammad's sitting on the throne was an actual sitting. The Damascene Hadith scholar and historian Shams al-Din al-Dhahabi (d. 1348), who recounted this rare anecdote (we have not located it in any other source), remarked that al-Marwazi indeed exaggerated his demonstration of support of this *ḥadīth*.[34] Al-Marwazi's gesture was meant for the masses: the performance of gestures was the most powerful device that the *muḥaddithūn* used to excite their audience. More powerful than any word, al-Marwazi's gesture conveyed the message of the anthropomorphic version effectively.

Abu Bakr al-Khallal, al-Marwazi's disciple, continued his master's activism and also strove to keep the anthropomorphic version present in the public sphere. In 904, Abu Bakr al-Khallal, who spent several years in Tarsus (in today's southern central Turkey), learned that the followers of 'al-Tirmidhi' (*aṣḥāb al-Tirmidhī*) were expelled from Baghdad in circumstances that unfortunately we have no knowledge about. These followers settled in Tarsus and started publicising their views against the anthropomorphic version while denying Muhammad's virtue of sitting on the throne. Al-Khallal wrote to his fellow Hanbalites in Baghdad and asked them to issue a well-reasoned opinion about this *ḥadīth*. The leaders of the Hanbalites in Baghdad sent al-Khallal a lengthy essay, which is located in his *Kitāb al-Sunna*.[35] According to his avowal, al-Khallal conducted several public readings of the text throughout his long stay in Tarsus. His audience, no doubt supporters of Hanbalism, received the text with sheer joy.[36]

By the end of the ninth century, and certainly due to the activism of Abu Bakr al-Marwazi and Abu Bakr al-Khallal, the Hanbalites came to the point of declaring the anthropomorphic version as consensually accepted by the entire community of traditionalists. This declaration was wishful thinking, but as the dominant group in Baghdad they saw themselves entitled to coerce others to accept their opinion. We found that the Hanbalite *muḥaddith* Muhammad ibn Ishaq Abu Bakr al-Saghani (d. 903) declared that the traditionalistic consensus worldwide accepted the veracity of the *ḥadīth* attributed to Mujahid.[37] The Hanbalites were happy with al-Saghani's judgement, because he was known for his numerous travels and close connections with the leading scholars of the prominent centres of learning throughout the Muslim world.[38] If al-Shaghani unequivocally declared that the *ḥadīth* was accepted worldwide, no doubt he knew what he was saying. Al-Saghani's judgement of this *ḥadīth* was therefore accepted by the Hanbalites and other ultra-traditionalists as the absolute truth. While the Hanbalites, whose unabashed traditionalism was uncompromising, embraced this *ḥadīth* and defended it vehemently, other 'mild' traditionalists rejected it. Thus, Abu 'l-Hasan al-Ashᶜari (d. 935–6), the eponymous founder of the Ashᶜarite school who served as a spokesman for middle-of-the-road traditionalism, mentioned the anthropomorphic version as a work of forgery.[39]

The Hanbalite scholarship in defence of the anthropomorphic version included enthusiastic declarations supporting this *ḥadīth* and crowning it as authentic and valuable. Some Hanbalites went further and declared that this *ḥadīth* reflected the absolute truth, and should it be refuted, they would immediately divorce their wives.[40] The more reserved Hanbalites searched for Ahmad ibn Hanbal's opinion on this *ḥadīth*. We found evidence of his supposed opinion in *Ibṭāl al-Taʾwīlāt*, a thematic Hadith compilation authored by the Hanbalite theologian and qadi Abu Yaᶜla ibn al-Farraʾ (d. 1066; he was also the father of the biographer Ibn Abi Yaᶜla). Abu Yaᶜla dedicated a lengthy chapter in his book to the efforts of the Hanbalite *muḥaddithūn* to validate the *ḥadīth* attributed to Mujahid. Thus, the Hanbalites claimed that Ahmad ibn Hanbal himself ordered his disciples to transmit the anthropomorphic version attributed to Mujahid in the exact wording as it was received. The Hanbalites further claimed that Ahmad ibn Hanbal believed that the anthropomorphic version should have been attributed to Mujahid's teacher, the *ṣaḥābī* Ibn ᶜAbbas.[41] These two claims do not correspond with the fact that the *ḥadīth* attributed to Mujahid was not included in the *Musnad* of Ahmad ibn Hanbal, the canonical Hadith compilation of the Hanbalites. Furthermore, Ahmad ibn Hanbal is not mentioned in the list of some thirty early Hanbalite scholars who professed their support for the anthropomorphic version attributed to Mujahid. These names were assembled by Abu Bakr al-Marwazi himself.[42] It is reasonable to assume that if al-Marawzi thought that Ahmad ibn Hanbal had supported this *ḥadīth*, or merely acknowledged its existence, he would have mentioned Ahmad ibn Hanbal at the top of the list.[43]

The debate about the anthropomorphic version did not remain a theoretical issue. The *ḥadīth* became a major component in the political agenda of the Hanbalites. In the year 922 (this is an approximate chronology, as the historical sources do not provide specific details about the following occurrence), a group of Hanbalites attacked the illustrious historian and Quran exegete Abu Jaᶜfar Muhammad ibn Jarir al-Tabari (d. 923) in Baghdad. Al-Tabari, as one of the sources claimed, refused to accept the anthropomorphic version attributed to Mujahid and had the audacity to reject this *ḥadīth* in public.[44]

In his great exegesis of the Quran, al-Tabari implanted subtle references to his rejection of the *ḥadīth* attributed to Mujahid: he first established that 'the majority of the scholars' (*akthar ahl al-ᶜilm*) believed that the 'honourable station' was Muhammad's intercession for the people on the Day of Resurrection,[45] by quoting a dozen *aḥādīth* to prove his point.[46] In the next phase, al-Tabari remarked that 'others' (*ākharūn*) claimed that the 'honourable station' meant that God promised the Prophet that He would make the Prophet sit on the throne, next to God.[47] Thereafter, al-Tabari quoted ten anthropomorphic variants of the *ḥadīth* attributed to Mujahid.[48] As a rule, al-Tabari did not hesitate throughout his work of exegesis to accept certain *aḥādīth* as authentic and reject others. Nonetheless, he was extremely cautious in the case of the *ḥadīth* attributed to Mujahid: Al-Tabari declared that there is no way to refute the authenticity of the *ḥadīth* attributed to Mujahid, neither by locating some textual evidence (*khabar*) nor by applying rational reasoning (*naẓar*).[49] This saying is far from the enthusiastic declarations of the Hanbalites support for this *ḥadīth*'s veracity. We note that the Hanbalites declared that the sceptics who did not accept this *ḥadīth* were heretics. However, in the severe circumstances in which al-Tabari lived in Baghdad (he was forced to stay at home, while visitors were prevented from visiting him),[50] al-Tabari seemed to have no other choice but to issue his lukewarm support of this *ḥadīth's* authenticity.

In 929, strife arose between the Hanbalite supporters of Abu Bakr al-Marwazi and 'a group of commoners' (*ṭāʾifa min 'l-ᶜāmma*) in Baghdad. This strife, which soon escalated into riots (*fitna*) was ignited because of an argument about Q. 17:79, and 'an honourable station'. Relying on earlier sources, the Damascene historian Ibn Kathir (d. 1373) reported on these riots in his monumental chronicle *al-Bidāya wa'l-Nihāya*. Ibn Kathir's report is quite odd, because in it the 'commoners' claimed that 'an honourable station' was 'the great intercession', while the Hanbalites held their traditional position about Muhammad's sitting on the throne. According to Ibn Kathir, the riots resulted in the deaths of an unspecified number of rioters. Ibn Kathir adds his opinion that according to *Ṣaḥīḥ al-Bukhāri*, the canonical Hadith compilation, 'an honourable station' was indeed the great intercession.[51] It seems that by determining that there was only one possible interpretation of 'an honourable station', and that this interpretation was not the one favoured by the Hanbalites, Ibn Kathir (who was considered an indirect disciple of the Hanbalite Ibn Qayyim al-Jawziyya) expressed his reservation about the behaviour of the tenth-century Hanbalites and their choice of texts to venerate. Other authors of the Mamluk period, like the Shafiᶜite Ibn Hajar al-ᶜAsqalani (d. 1449), who in fact was inclined towards Ashᶜarite theology, accepted the *ḥadīth* attributed to Mujahid.[52] Ibn Hajar even harshly condemned a later rationalistic scholar who refuted this *ḥadīth*.[53] The admission of the anthropomorphic version to the traditionalistic canon was therefore fully accomplished in the fifteenth century.

The case of the *ḥadīth* attributed to Mujahid illustrates one of the major disputes in Islamic theology from the eighth to the fourteenth centuries: the problem of anthropomorphism (*tashbīh*). More than any other issue in Islamic theology, anthropomorphism stood at the heart of many theological debates, and was mostly discussed within the circles of traditionalist Islam. The way a traditionalistic scholar interpreted the anthropomorphic descriptions of God in the Quran, and even more so in the Hadith (for instance, God's hand, God's laughter or God's sitting on the heavenly throne), often reflected his political and social stature, as well as his theological affinity. We need to clarify that the Arabic term *tashbīh* is not equivalent to 'anthropomorphism'. In fact, the term *tashbīh* is wider than merely attributing human traits (both physical and behavioural) to God. In addition, the discussions about *tashbīh* included careful deliberations on spatiality, directionality (especially aboveness) and confinement. Any feature that implied God's resemblance to any created body (either animate or inanimate) was included in the discussions on *tashbīh*, although we often see the use of the term *tajsīm*, corporealism, inserted in the theological discussions. In the absence of an equivalent term for *tashbīh* in English, and because 'anthropomorphism' is the term selected for *tashbīh* in western scholarship, both *tasbīh* and 'anthropomorphism' are interchangeably used in this book.

This book examines the corpus of *aḥādīth al-ṣifāt* or *āthār al-ṣifāt* (literally, the traditions or reports about the divine attributes) and its role in shaping the traditionalistic definition of anthropomorphism. These traditions depict God in anthropomorphic and corporealistic language. Widely used by Hadith scholars, both terms refer to anthropomorphism in the widest sense of the word: these traditions describe God's place in the universe, His bodily organs, the dialogue that He conducts with humans and His actions. The descriptions of God in *aḥādīth al-ṣifāt* which are articulated in a simple language are meant to transmit a specific image of God, which is sometimes surprisingly detailed. *Aḥādīth al-ṣifāt* form a rich source of information about the development of anthropomorphic concepts, their transmission and their proliferation. However, only a limited amount of research has investigated *aḥādīth al-ṣifāt* and conceptualised them. This book examines closely these literary texts from phenomenological, literary, linguistic and historical perspectives.

This book, as a whole, offers a close, contextualised and interdisciplinary reading of Hadith compilations, theological treatises and historical sources. In addition, this book offers an evaluation and understanding of the traditionalistic endeavours in defining anthropomorphism during the most crucial and formative period of Islamic thought. The book is divided into two parts: the first part (Chapters 1, 2 and 3) presents an in-depth literary analysis of the textual and non-textual elements of *aḥādīth al-ṣifāt*. The second part (Chapters 4 and 5) focuses on the internal controversies in the major traditionalistic learning centres of the Islamic world regarding the understanding and interpretation of these anthropomorphic traditions. In Chapter 1, we present the methodology of literary analysis that we applied throughout this book through a close reading of three proto-types of *aḥādīth al-ṣifāt*. As the methodology of literary analysis has never been applied to *aḥādīth al-ṣifāt* before, this chapter aims to present the insights that can be reached by applying this methodology. We detect the typical features of *aḥādīth al-ṣifāt* and reveal hidden meanings in the texts while considering two styles of narration: mimesis and diegesis, or showing (performing) and telling (recounting). Chapter 2 offers a combined literary-historical approach to two versions of *ḥadīth al-ruʾya*, that is, the *ḥadīth* on the beatific vision. This chapter further considers the role of the narrator in shaping the narrative, identifies the geographical origin of this *ḥadīth*, and considers its role in the events of the *miḥna*, one of the major events in the history of Islamic traditionalism. Chapter 3 spotlights the gestures (*ishāra*, pl. *ishārāt*) performed by the *muḥaddithūn* in the process of transmitting *aḥādīth al-ṣifāt*. Gestures were a significant feature in the process of Hadith transmission in general. In the case of *aḥādīth al-ṣifāt*, the use of gestures entailed doctrinal and theological implications, and was in itself a matter of dispute. Chapter 4 examines the challenges that *aḥādīth al-ṣifāt* posed to the traditionalists, and the way these challenges were met through the implementation of the *bi-lā kayfa* formula. This formula either meant 'without asking further questions', 'without paraphrasing text' or 'without attributing physical characteristics' to God, depending on the scholar's level of traditionalism. The lion's share of Chapter 4 presents the problematic aspects of *aḥādīth al-ṣifāt* in the traditionalistic discourse through the case study of what is undoubtedly the most extreme text in the repertoire of *aḥādīth al-ṣifāt*, namely *ḥadīth ḥaqw al-raḥmān*, 'the *ḥadīth* about the loin of the Merciful'. Chapter 5 examines the ubiquitous presence of *aḥādīth al-ṣifāt* in the public sphere by focusing on four milestones in the theological debates on the anthropomorphic texts in the Hadith. The focus of this book is on Islamic traditionalism and *aḥādīth al-ṣifāt*: the ultra-traditionalists (the Hanbalites and their forerunners) and middle-of-the-road traditionalists (the Ashᶜarites and their forerunners). Other groups that contributed to the debates on anthropomorphism are mentioned in the book only in the context of their debates with the traditionalists. These groups are the Muᶜtazilites, the Ibadites, the Shiᶜites, the Zaydites, the Kharijites, the Zahirites, the Kullabites and the Karramites. Even without dedicating separate sections in this book to these groups, there remained several topics that touch upon anthropomorphism and Islamic traditionalism which we were forced to exclude from the present discussion. Thus, we reduced our deliberations on the various theories of the divine attributes and hermeneutics, and referred only to the concepts which are intrinsic to *aḥādīth al-ṣifāt*. Likewise, the convoluted Muᶜtazilite-Ashᶜarite controversy on the origins of language and the deliberations on the dichotomy of *ḥaqīqa* (the actual meaning of a word) and *majāz* (metaphor) that prevailed in the Ashᶜarite and Taymiyyan discourse were reduced to the absolute necessary minimum. These topics, in addition to the nuanced approach of the Hanbalite scholars Abu Ya^c^la and Ibn al-Jawzi to *aḥādīth al-ṣifāt*, remain for another opportunity. All the translations from the Arabic sources in this book are the product of this author, apart from a few texts where we duly refer to the translations we used. Throughout this book, we systematically used N. J. Dawood's translation of the Quran, *The Koran with a Parallel Arabic Text*, 1st edition 1956 (London: Penguin Classics, 2000), which is a personal favourite.

Notes

1. On this, see: Holtzman and Ben-Shammai, 'kalām'.
2. Kraemer, *Humanism in the Renaissance of Islam*, pp. 46–74.
3. Ibn Abī Yaᶜlā, *Ṭabaqāt al-Fuqahāᵓ al-Ḥanābila*, vol. 2, p. 14 (the biography of Abu Bakr al-Najjad).
4. Ibn Abī Yaᶜlā, *Ṭabaqāt al-Fuqahāᵓ al-Ḥanābila*, vol. 2, p. 14.
5. Al-Dhahabī, *Siyar Aᶜlām al-Nubalāᵓ*, vol. 15, p. 502 (the biography of Abu Bakr al-Najjad). Abu Dawud al-Sijistani studied Hadith with the luminaries of ninth-century traditionalism, like Ishaq ibn Rahwayh (d. 853) and Ahmad ibn Hanbal himself. His *Kitāb al-Sunan* is one of the six canonical Hadith compilations: al-Dhahabī, *Siyar Aᶜlām al-Nubalāᵓ*, vol. 13, p. 203 (the biography Abu Dawud al-Sijistani).
6. Ibn Abī Yaᶜlā, *Ṭabaqāt al-Fuqahāᵓ al-Ḥanābila*, vol. 2, p. 13 (the biography of Abu Bakr al-Najjad).
7. Al-Khaṭīb al-Baghdādī, *Tārīkh Madīnat al-Salām*, vol. 5, p. 312 (the biography of Abu Bakr al-Najjad).
8. Sadly, al-Najjad did not leave any written works, although al-Khatib al-Baghdadi claimed that al-Najjad indeed collected Hadith material and arranged it in two compilations: al-Khaṭīb al-Baghdādī, *Tārīkh Madīnat al-Salām*, vol. 5, p. 310.
9. Ibn Abī Yaᶜlā, *Ṭabaqāt al-Fuqahāᵓ al-Ḥanābila*, vol. 2, p. 14.
10. Ignaz Goldziher was the first scholar to address this *ḥadīth* and its consequences in both the public sphere (the 929 riots, al-Tabari's ordeals, etc.), and the role that Mujahid played in shaping this *ḥadīth*: Goldziher, *Die Richtungen der islamischen Koranauslesung*, pp. 101–11. Franz Rosenthal's informative introduction to his translation of al-Tabari's *Kitāb al-Rusul wa'l-Mulūk* focuses on al-Tabari's interpretation of Q. 17:79, and provides an interpretation of al-Tabari's discussion on the *ḥadīth* attributed to Mujahid: Rosenthal, 'General

Introduction', pp. 57–8, 69–78. Another illuminating discussion on al-Tabari's interpretation of Q. 17:79 is Claude Gilliot's. Gilliot also analyses a parallel passage authored by the Quran exegete Abu ᶜAbd Allah al-Qurtubi (d. 1272): Gilliot, *Exégèse, langue, et théologie*, pp. 249–54. Two indispensable discussions are Swartz, *A Medieval Critique of Anthropomorphism*, p. 249, footnote 358; and Ramadān, *Uṣūl al-Dīn ᶜinda 'l-Imām al-Ṭabarī*, pp. 23–33. The confrontations between the Hanbalites and al-Tabari are briefly described in Turner, *Inquisition in Early Islam*, pp. 145–8. Turner determines that '[t]he violent Ḥanbalī response to al-Ṭabarī is most clearly understood if their madhhab is seen as a new player competeing with al-Ṭabarī's madhhab, which was equally new': Turner, *Inquisition in Early Islam*, p. 146. A comprehensive study on the relationships between al-Tabari and the Hanbalites, including an illuminating discussion on al-Tabari's treatment of Q. 17:79, including a reference to the prominent Hanbalite sources, is Shah, 'Al-Ṭabarī and the Dynamics of the Tafsīr', pp. 105–10.
11. Ibn Abī Yaᶜlā, *Ṭabaqāt al-Fuqahāᵓ al-Ḥanābila*, vol. 2, pp. 16–17.
12. On the oath on pain of triple divorce (*ḥilf bi'l-ṭalāq thalāthan*), see Rapoport, *Marriage, Money and Divorce*, p. 92.
13. Ibn Abī Yaᶜlā, *Ṭabaqāt al-Fuqahāᵓ al-Ḥanābila*, vol. 2, pp. 17–18.
14. Al-Najjad's disciple, the influential *muḥaddith* and Hanbalite jurisprudent Ibn Batta (d. 997), also issued a creed. In this creed he clarified that Mujahid's *ḥadīth* is one of the cornerstones of the Hanbalite creed: Laoust, *La profession de foi d'Ibn Baṭṭa*, pp. 60–1, 113.
15. According to the ample evidence in al-Khallāl, *al-Sunna*, vol. 1, pp. 209–68.
16. The comprehensive collections of the anthropomorphic version and the mild version are located in al-Ṭabarī, *Jāmiᶜ al-Bayān*, vol. 15, pp. 42–54 (interpretation of Q. 17:79); al-Suyūṭī, *al-Durr al-Manthūr*, vol. 9, pp. 419–27 (interpretation of Q. 17:79).
17. For references to these Hadith compilations, consult the extremely informative footnotes in al-Ṭabarī, *Jāmiᶜ al-Bayān*, vol. 15, pp. 48–50.
18. Al-Ājurrī, *Kitāb al-Sharīᶜa*, pp. 517, 521.
19. Al-Khallāl, *al-Sunna*, vol. 1, pp. 215–16, anecdote 247.
20. See his biography in al-Khaṭīb al-Baghdādī, *Tārīkh Madīnat al-Salām*, vol. 16, p. 323 (the biography of Yahya ibn Abi Talib).
21. Al-Khallāl, *al-Sunna*, vol. 1, p. 215, anecdote 246.
22. Al-Shahrastānī, *al-Milal wa'l-Niḥal*, vol. 1, p. 92.
23. Ibn Abī Yaᶜlā, *Ṭabaqāt al-Fuqahāᵓ al-Ḥanābila*, vol. 2, pp. 16–17. See simi-

lar declarations by ninth-century traditionalists in al-Khallāl, *al-Sunna*, vol. 1, pp. 217–18, anecdote 250; p. 219, anecdote 253.

24. Ibn Abī Ya^clā, *Ṭabaqāt al-Fuqahā^ɔ al-Ḥanābila*, vol. 2, p. 14.
25. Al-Khallāl, *al-Sunna*, vol. 1, pp. 209–12, anecdotes 236–8.
26. Abū Yaʿlā, *Ibṭāl al-Taʾwīlāt*, p. 476, *ḥadīth* 441.
27. Abū Yaʿlā, *Ibṭāl al-Taʾwīlāt*, p. 476, *ḥadīth* 440.
28. Yahya Abu Bakr referred to al-Tirmidhi as 'this Persian' (*hādhā 'l-ʿajamī*): al-Khallāl, *al-Sunna*, vol. 1, p. 234, anecdote 268.
29. Al-Khallāl, *al-Sunna*, vol. 1, p. 234, anecdote 268.
30. Al-Khallāl, *al-Sunna*, vol. 1, pp. 246–7, anecdote 283.
31. Ibn Qayyim al-Jawziyya, *Badāʾiʿ al-Fawāʾid*, vol. 4, pp. 1380–1; Shah, 'Al-Ṭabarī and the Dynamics of the Tafsīr', p. 107.
32. Al-Khallāl, *al-Sunna*, vol. 1, pp. 234–69. Several passages of Abu Bakr al-Marwazi's book are preserved in the biography of Abu Bakr al-Najjad: Ibn Abī Yaʿlā, *Ṭabaqāt al-Fuqahāʾ al-Ḥanābila*, vol. 2, p. 14.
33. Joseph van Ess suggested that al-Tirmidhi should be identified with the respectable *muḥaddith* Muhammad ibn Ismaʿil ibn Yusuf al-Tirmidhi (d. 893); however, his suggestion was refuted by Michael Cook, who presented a well-reasoned argument which rejected this identification: van Ess, *TG*, vol. 2, p. 642; Cook, *Commanding Right*, p. 117, footnote 14.
34. Al-Dhahabī, *al-ʿUlūw*, p. 170.
35. Al-Khallāl, *al-Sunna*, vol. 1, pp. 224–32, anecdote 266.
36. Al-Khallāl, *al-Sunna*, vol. 1, p. 224, anecdote 266.
37. Al-Khallāl, *al-Sunna*, vol. 1, p. 233, anecdote 267.
38. Ibn Abī Yaʿlā, *Ṭabaqāt al Fuqahāʾ al-Ḥanābila*, vol. 1, pp. 374–5 (the biography of Muhammad ibn Ishaq Abu Bakr al-Saghani).
39. Al-Ashʿarī, *Maqālāt al-Islāmiyyīn*, p. 211.
40. Al-Khallāl, *al-Sunna*, vol. 1, pp. 256–7, anecdotes 307–8; pp. 258–9, anecdote 312.
41. Abū Yaʿlā, *Ibṭāl al-Taʾwīlāt*, p. 480, anecdotes 447–8; van Ess, *TG*, vol. 2, pp. 642–3.
42. Ibn Qayyim al-Jawziyya, *Badāʾiʿ al-Fawāʾid*, vol. 4, p. 1380.
43. See the illuminating analysis of Ṭāhā Muḥammad Najjār Ramāḍān, *Uṣūl al-Dīn ʿinda 'l-Imām al-Ṭabarī*, pp. 29–30, and the precise remark of Shah, 'Al-Ṭabarī and the Dynamics of the Tafsīr', p. 136, note 153.
44. Yāqūt, *Muʿjam al-Udabā'*, vol. 1, p. 2450.
45. Al-Ṭabarī, *Jāmiʿ al-Bayān*, vol. 15, p. 43 (the interpretation of Q. 17:79).

46. Al-Ṭabarī, *Jāmiᶜ al-Bayān*, vol. 15, pp. 43–7 (the interpretation of Q. 17:79); Gilliot, *Exégèse, langue, et théologie*, pp. 249–51; Shah, 'Al-Ṭabarī and the Dynamics of the Tafsīr', pp. 108–9.
47. Al-Ṭabarī, *Jāmiᶜ al-Bayān*, vol. 15, p. 47 (the interpretation of Q. 17:79).
48. Al-Ṭabarī, *Jāmiᶜ al-Bayān*, vol. 15, pp. 47–51 (the interpretation of Q. 17:79).
49. Al-Ṭabarī, *Jāmiᶜ al-Bayān*, vol. 15, p. 51 (the interpretation of Q. 17:79). Al-Tabari developed his implied rejection of the *ḥadīth* in a convoluted discussion on God's transcendence that he wisely inserted in other passages in his discussion of Q. 17:79: al-Ṭabarī, *Jāmiᶜ al-Bayān*, vol. 15, pp. 51–4. This discussion remains for another time.
50. Al-Khaṭīb al-Baghdādī, *Tārīkh Madīnat al-Salām*, vol. 2, p. 551 (the biography of Abu Jaᶜfar Ibn Jarir al-Tabari).
51. Ibn Kathīr, *al-Bidāya wa'l-Nihāya*, vol. 15, pp. 42–3 (the events of Hijri year 317). Cf. the reports of the historians Ibn al-Athir (d. 1233) and Shams al-Din al-Dhahabi (d. 1348): Ibn al-Athīr, *al-Kāmil fī 'l-Tārīkh*, vol. 8, p. 57 (the events of Hijri year 317); al-Dhahabī, *Tārīkh al-Islām*, vol. 23, p. 384 (the events of Hijri year 317).
52. Ibn Ḥajar al-ᶜAsqalānī, *Fatḥ al-Bārī*, vol. 8, p. 259, *ḥadīth* 4534 (*Kitāb Tafsīr al-Qurʾān, bāb qawlihi taᶜālā ᶜasā an yabᶜathaka rabbuka maqāman maḥmūdan*).
53. Ibn Ḥajar al-ᶜAsqalānī, *Fatḥ al-Bārī*, vol. 11, pp. 433–7, *ḥadīth* 6344 (*Kitāb al-riqāq, bāb ṣifat al-janna wa'l-nār*).

I

The Narrator and the Narrative: A Literary Analysis of *Aḥādīth al-Ṣifāt*

Introduction

This chapter provides a literary analysis of three prototypes of *aḥādīth al-ṣifāt* or *āthār al-ṣifāt* (literally, the traditions or reports about the divine attributes). What is the benefit in applying literary analysis to these colourful, animated and eventful texts? First, such an analysis has never been applied to *aḥādīth al-ṣifāṭ*. Neither researchers of Hadith nor researchers of Islamic theology have exhibited much interest in the literary aspects of this material.[1] In the field of Islamic theology, *aḥādīth al-ṣifāt* represented the point of departure for embarking on complex theological and hermeneutical debates. These debates frequently had minimal connection to the material that inspired them; the fact that *aḥādīth al-ṣifāt* served as textual evidence in these theological debates dictated an instrumental approach towards them. The Islamic theologians who frequently quoted these texts in their debates were first and foremost interested in the theological message that these texts conveyed. These theologians were also interested in the validity of *aḥādīth al-ṣifāt* as textual evidence for their argumentations. The literary value of *aḥādīth al-ṣifāt*, their potential to entertain, stimulate, provoke or frighten, their structure, style and language – all these factors were absent from the scholarly discourse. In addition, the beauty of the texts, the elegant flow of the narrative and its sophisticated structure, have to date failed to draw the attention of western research.

Second, the methodology of literary analysis is unfortunately still marginal in the field of Hadith studies. This marginality is clearly reflected in

Harald Motzki's seminal state-of-the-art survey of Hadith studies. Motzki, who is one of today's most prominent scholars in this field, names Daniel Beaumont and Sebastian Günther as the only scholars who have applied theories of literary analysis to Hadith material.[2] Neither Beaumont nor Günther, by the way, discussed *aḥādīth al-ṣifāt* or other theological traditions. As a historian, Motzki admits that '[i]n cases of traditions transmitted in variant versions, literary analysis may even help to trace the stages of the transmission process'.[3] In other words, Motzki is not bothered by the dearth of researchers that apply literary analysis on the Hadith material, because he sees literary analysis as an instrument that can potentially contribute to the major scholarly concerns of Hadith researchers, namely the process of oral transmission, the recording of the texts and the authenticity of the Hadith text units. However, as literary texts or 'narratives'[4] the *aḥādīth* deserve literary scrutiny detached from other considerations. As Sahair El Calamawy states correctly, a *ḥadīth* that represents an event (or a story) or a series of events (or stories) can be defined as a story, and as such it contains layers of fiction and imagination.[5] Applying literary analysis to these texts can therefore become an end in itself.

Literary examination of a single *ḥadīth*, namely a narratological text unit, enables us to separate the fictional content from the factual content. Such an examination enables us both to assess the text as a literary narrative and observe how its author invested considerable efforts in applying rhetorical and stylistic devices. These devices were used to make the *ḥadīth* authoritative, entertaining, frightening or thought provoking, without neglecting its purpose to morally educate its receptive audience. As demonstrated in this chapter and in the two subsequent chapters, literary analysis deciphers the design of the narrative and reveals the connection between the narrator and his recipients. This analysis thus contributes to our understanding of the gradual formation of the text. This topic of text formation has preoccupied Hadith scholars from the inception of ninth-century Hadith science until today. Literary analysis, and more precisely literary analysis that draws from narratology, opens a new venue for investigation.

Three prototypes of *aḥādīth al-ṣifāt* were selected from a large database of anthropomorphic Hadith accounts for literary analysis in this chapter. These are the *ḥadīth* of the beatific vision (*ḥadīth al-ruʾya*), the *ḥadīth* of the sacrifice (*ḥadīth al-fidāʾ*), and the *ḥadīth* of the divine fingers (*aṣābiʿ al-raḥmān*). By examining three building blocks of the narrative – the framing narrative, the embedded narrative and the narrator – this chapter sheds light on the literary aspects of *aḥādīth al-ṣifāt*. The goal here is to sketch the typical features of these texts, and to reveal hidden meanings in these representative case-studies.

I. A Preliminary Remark on Hadith and Narratology

Most fields of the humanities, including Classical and Biblical studies, enriched their discourse and benefitted from narratology. This term refers to 'the theory of narratives, narrative texts, images, spectacles, events; cultural artifacts that "tell a story". Such a theory helps scholars to understand, analyze, and evaluate narratives.'[6] In 1996, Daniel Beaumont offered a literary analysis of the *khabar* literature, while borrowing his terms of inquiry from Gérard Genette's *Narrative Discourse* (originally published in 1972, this work is considered the cornerstone of narratology).[7] In 1998, Sebastian Günther published a ground-breaking article entitled 'Fictional Narration and Imagination within an Authoritative Framework'. In this article, Günther applied methods of text analysis mainly developed by the German branch of narratological studies (*Erzähltheorie*) on Hadith text units. He defined these text units as 'fictional narrative' (as opposed to 'factual narrative').[8] Narratology provided Günther with analytical devices which enabled him to prove that fictional narrative is a separate category of Hadith. According to Günther, fictional narrative comprises a considerable corpus of traditions easily traceable within the two major traditional categories of *aḥādīth*: the *aḥādīth al-aḥkām* (texts of juridical nature) and the *maghāzī* or *al-sīra* (texts of historiographical nature that also include various subjects).[9] Günther established the idea that a definable category of *aḥādīth* which are small-scale literary works indeed exists. He further concluded that questions of historical factuality and authenticity in transmitting *aḥādīth* are simply irrelevant to *aḥādīth* which are 'stories'.[10] *Aḥādīth al-ṣifāt*, as demonstrated in this chapter, fall into this category of fictional narrative, to use Günther's definition.[11] However, as opposed to Günther's categorical conclusion, we believe that these texts also demand a thorough examination of their historical context.[12] Although this point is mentioned here in Chapter 1, it is axial to Chapters 2 and 3.

As Günther successfully demonstrated in his article, *aḥādīth* are the perfect text units to which to apply methods of literary criticism. First, *aḥādīth* fit the definition of 'narrative', because they tell a story.[13] They are relatively brief, and their language is heavily laden with symbols and codes that were known to the original audience to which these texts were orally transmitted. As we continue the reading process, we soon realise that these simple – if not simplistic – texts are complicated and raise many questions. For instance, we assume *sub silentio* that each singular text has its **audience**, when in fact there are several audiences for each text; sometimes these audiences are mentioned in the text, and at other times they are omitted. A more complex question concerns the **narrator**: a singular text unit provides several narrators for the same text, the *ruwāt* (the earliest links of the *isnād*, i.e. the *ṣaḥābī*, *tābiᶜī* and the *tābiᶜī*'s disciple) and the *muḥaddithūn* (the professional Hadith scholars who use the Hadith text units in their classes). The role of each narrator in shaping the narrative, the *matn*, is a matter that literary analysis can highlight. For instance, when reading the *ḥadīth* as a literary text, the question of the narrator who sometimes appears as an active protagonist in the narrative becomes crucial. Another complex question concerns the **coherence** of the text. Sometimes the single text unit, the *ḥadīth*, interprets itself; however, in most texts, no comment or explanation follows an enigmatic saying of the Prophet. Rarely, the elaborate exegeses (*shurūḥ*) of Hadith compilations which were composed from the late thirteenth century onward[14] provide clues or leads that help answer these questions. Should we infer from these lacunae that the 'implied' meaning of the codes and symbols enfolded in the texts faded away, or that their meaning was intrinsic to the receptive audiences and as a result required no further explanation? The answers to these questions are hidden in the texts.

As mentioned earlier, narratology is a field somewhat alien to Hadith studies, and certainly alien to the study of Islamic theology, which is the author's primary field of training. The use of narratology here is meant to advance the reading of *aḥādīth al-ṣifāt*; therefore, its use here is the means and not the end in itself. The author therefore has decided not to read the *aḥādīth* in close proximity to the narratological terminology as did Günther and Beaumont. Nonetheless, both these scholars' works indeed inspired the discussion in this chapter. Compared to the analysis offered by Günther and

Beaumont, our reading of the *aḥādīth* is more flexible and less committed to the various narratological doctrines. Accordingly, we present two sets of terminology: the terminology used in the classical science of Hadith and the terminology used in the modern field of narratology. Both terminologies are combined here into one set that complements our approach to the texts.

Since the wide selection of studies on narratology is dazzling, this chapter limited its scope to introductory works that offer accessibility to a comprehensive discussion. This discussion includes Seymour Chatman's *Story and Discourse* (1978), Mieke Bal's *Narratology* (2nd edn, 2007) and H. Porter Abbott's *The Cambridge Introduction to Narrative* (2nd edn, 2008). These three introductory works are indispensable to an understanding of the theories of Gérard Genette and Roland Barthes. Accordingly, the 'dosages' of narratology in this chapter are meagre and implicit, similar to a model presented by Stefan Leder in his stimulating article entitled 'The Literary Use of the Khabar: A Basic Form of Historical Writing'. Published in 1992, the article combines the historical and the literary approaches.[15]

II. The Framing Narrative

Although *aḥādīth al-ṣifāt* form a distinctive group, they vary in theme and style: *aḥādīth al-ṣifāt* range from brief dicta of the Prophet or a *ṣaḥābī*, to relatively lengthy texts. These lengthy texts comprise at least two narratives which are connected to each other. Their connection is similar to the connection between the 'framing narrative' (or 'primary narrative' or 'primary fabula') and the 'embedded narrative' (or 'embedded text').[16] The classic example of this narrative structure is the story cycle of *Alf Layla wa-Layala* (*The Thousand and One Nights*): the framing narrative presents the story of Shahrazad who was forced to recount stories to her husband, the king Shahriyar, to escape her death sentence. The stories which Shahrazad tells every night are the embedded narratives, which are more captivating and entertaining than the framing narrative, namely the story of her husband, his former wives and her own story.[17] The more complex type of *aḥādīth al-ṣifāt* is structured as a combination of framing and embedded narratives. However, before examining this combined narrative, it is worthwhile first to examine several aspects of *aḥādīth al-ṣifāt* that contain dicta, which are not considered narratives. These non-narrative dicta convey the basic theological message of the entire corpus of *aḥādīth al-ṣifāt*. It is therefore easier to present the theme of *aḥādīth al-ṣifāt* through the simple dicta. In addition, these dicta are sometimes combined in the text of the more complex forms of narrative.

Contentwise, *aḥādīth al-ṣifāt* are situated in close proximity to *āyāt al-ṣifāt*, the verses in the Quran that mention God, His attributes and His actions. One can locate clusters of *aḥādīth al-ṣifāt* in the *tafsīr* sections of the prominent Hadith compilations, and naturally in the works dedicated entirely to Quran exegesis. Most *aḥādīth al-ṣifāt* function as complementary texts to the Quranic verses: they either explain the content of the Quranic verse or extend the description of the divine beyond the description which the Quran provides. Hence, *aḥādīth al-ṣifāt* directly present or quote the dicta of the Prophet, one of his companions (*ṣaḥābī*) or one of the companions' followers (*tābiʿī*). For example, among *aḥādīth al-ruʾya*, the traditions that refer to the beatific vision in the afterlife, there is a cluster of *aḥādīth* that interprets Q. 10:26 ('Those that do good works shall have a good reward, and more besides'). This cluster merely quotes the words of the first caliph Abu Bakr (d. 634), the *ṣaḥābī* Ibn ʿAbbas (d. 687–8) or the words of Ibn ʿAbbas's disciple, ʿIkrima (d. 723–4).[18] The structure of these texts is identical to the following example:

> Zakariyyaʾ told us on the authority of Abu Ishaq. Abu Ishaq [related this *ḥadīth*] on the authority of ʿAmir ibn Saʿd al-Bajali, [who in turn related this *ḥadīth*] on the authority of Abu Bakr the truthful, regarding the Quranic verse 'Those that do good works shall have a good reward, and more besides': He (i.e. Abu Bakr) said: ['And more besides' means] seeing God's face.[19]

The concise wording of this text is typical of *aḥādīth* and *āthār* that interpret various Quranic verses, not necessarily those which contain anthropomorphic expressions. The most prominent bulk of these *aḥādīth* are the teachings attributed to Ibn ʿAbbas, the founding father of the science of Quran exegesis. In these texts, Ibn ʿAbbas conveyed his opinion without quoting the Prophet.[20] However, *aḥādīth al-ṣifāt* also include concise texts which are not immediately connected to a specific Quranic verse. These texts frequently quote sayings which are attributed either to the Prophet or to a prominent *ṣaḥābī* or *tābiʿī*. The quoted saying appears immediately after the *isnād* without any further introduction. The following quote is a typical example:

> On the authority of Abu Hurayra (d. 678) who said: The Messenger of God said: 'When you hit [someone], avoid [hitting] the face, for God created Adam in His image'.[21]

Dicta are not narratives because they lack events and most importantly they lack a time sequence.[22] According to Seymour Chatman, '[n]on-narrative text-types do not have an internal time sequence, even though, obviously, they take time to read, view, or hear. Their underlying structures are static or atemporal.'[23] Literary analysis, therefore, is impossible in this case of interpretive *aḥādith al-ṣifāt*.

Within the corpus of *aḥādīth al-ṣifāt* the complex *aḥādīth* are noticeable. These *aḥādīth* contain several layers of narrative and likewise, several layers of time. The purpose of these texts is to inform of actions, events and dicta of the Prophet and his companions; however, the information is served to us in a convoluted package: the *ḥadīth* does not merely contain the words of the Prophet as cited by a companion, but presents a sequence of events or stories (hence a narrative) that leads to a peak (mainly, a dictum of the Prophet). In his analysis, Günther explains that 'the lengthy or long *ḥadīths*' often describe the Prophet's actions and sayings in a reported speech.[24] This format means that 'the third party', namely the narrator, is present in the narrative as an illustrated character who acts within the narrative, and is not merely represented by his name in the formula 'on the authority of x who said y'. In other words, the narrator's story is also represented as part of the narrative of the complex *ḥadīth*. This observation is crucial when one tries to define the different layers of the narrative and to eventually identify the narrator. The first layer that requires examination is therefore the framing narrative, a narrative within which another narrative is embedded. In the complex *aḥādīth al-ṣifāt* and in other *aḥādīth* that adopt the same structure, the framing narrative is a part of the *matn* and serves as an introduction to the embedded narrative. The embedded narrative can be described as the 'kernel' or the 'peak' of the *matn*.

The framing narrative is usually brief: it contains no more than a sentence or two. Its purpose is to place the *rāwī* (the original narrator) in the *matn*, and by doing so to add to the credibility of the narrator's report.[25] The brief framing narrative often becomes almost unnoticeable in the reading process. A Prophetic *ḥadīth* mentions that God never sleeps and that He covers His face with a veil of fire. His face is veiled so that the majesty of His face will not burn the people who are fortunate to see His face. This *ḥadīth* begins with the following introduction by the *ṣaḥābī* Abu Musa al-Ashᶜari (d. *c.* 663):[26] 'The Prophet stood up when we were sitting (*qāma fīnā*) and told us five (or four) things.'[27] This opening statement places the narrator in the audience that witnessed the Prophet in a one-time event, without however providing additional details about this specific event (in this case, a gathering of the *ṣaḥāba*). In sum, the narrator is an eyewitness, and that makes his testimony precious.

Dull as this framing narrative may seem to us, even less descriptive framing narratives are frequent. In many other cases of *aḥādīth al-ṣifāt*, the narrator places the Prophet's dictum in a specific setting. The narrator – as a *ṣaḥābī* – was present at the event, although there is no textual indication that he attended. This minimalist style is probably the dullest form of the framing narrative; yet, this style is the most frequent form. Abu Hurayra's versions of *ḥadīth al-ruʾya* are a case in point:

> On the authority of Abu Hurayra: People asked: 'Oh, Messenger of God, shall we see our Lord on the Day or Resurrection?' The Prophet asked: 'Do you differ from one another about seeing the sun at midday when it is not covered with clouds?' They replied: 'No, oh Messenger of God.' He said: 'Do you differ one from another about seeing the full moon when it is not covered with clouds?' They replied: 'No, oh Messenger of God.' He said: 'So you will not differ one from another about seeing your Lord on the Day of Resurrection, just as you do not differ about seeing the sun and the moon.'[28]

The framing narrative in this case describes a scene: a group of people asked the Prophet a question and he answered them. The scanty details that Abu Hurayra provided about the setting almost encourage us, the readers, to fill in the gaps and recreate the framing narrative. In the same vein, the *ṣaḥābī* Suhayb ibn Sinan (d. 659) narrated extremely lengthy and detailed teachings of the Prophet on the beatific vision. However, unlike Abu Hurayra's narrative, the audience of *ṣaḥāba* who listened to the Prophet were not present in this narrative, as Suhayb only quoted the Prophet.[29] This structure seems to be the common procedure: in their versions of *ḥadīth al-ruʾya*, Abu Musa al-Ashʿari,[30] Ibn Masʿud (d. 652–3),[31] Ibn ʿAbbas,[32] Anas ibn Malik (d. 711)[33] and others quoted the exchange between the audience and the Prophet in direct speech. In his discussion on the *akhbār* literature, Stefan Leder points out that narration in direct speech was 'used to reduce the narrator's account and avoid any comment or interpretation'. Consequently, Leder claims that '[t]his form of narration reinforces the impression that these texts are narrative representations of events, not subject to the literary creativity of an author'.[34] This observation, although refuted by Beaumont,[35] is certainly applicable to *aḥādīth al-ṣifāt* in which the narrator's presence in the narrative is minimised to the role of a passive eyewitness.

Another conspicuous feature of *aḥādīth al-ruʾya* attributed to the prominent *ṣaḥāba* is that the narrators did not literally place themselves in any type of scene or setting. In fact, these *aḥādīth* fail to provide details about the setting. However, in the following example, the narrator is more present in the narrative. Umm Salama (d. 679 or 680), the last of the Prophet's wives to survive and the second female narrator of Hadith after ʿAʾisha, placed herself in the narrative of the following *ḥadīth* when she said:

> I heard the Prophet say: 'Every heart is held between two of the All-Merciful's fingers. If He wants to set it aright, He sets it aright. If He wants to cause it to deviate, He causes it to deviate.'[36]

True, the framing narrative in this case is also dull: we have no idea when and where Umm Salama heard the Prophet say these words. We can only assume that the Prophet said these words to Umm Salama alone. In another version of the same *ḥadīth*, which contains a slightly richer framing narrative, the Syrian *tābiʿī* Shahr ibn Hawshab (d. c. 719)[37] testified:

> I asked Umm Salama: 'What was the most frequent supplication that the Prophet uttered when he was with you?' And she answered: 'The hearts are held between two of the All-Merciful's fingers. Whatever He wishes, He sets it aright. Whatever He wishes, He causes it to deviate.'[38]

With the assistance of biographical sources, we soon realise that the framing narrative indeed presents a concrete setting. Shahr was a respectable *tābiʿī* who used to enthusiastically seek Hadith from the mouth of the prominent *ṣaḥāba*, and a frequent visitor in Umm Salama's house.[39] In this framing narrative, we actually see Shahr when interviewing the elderly Umm Salama. At the time of this interview, Shahr was between the ages of fifteen and twenty-six,[40] and Umm Salama was between eighty and ninety years old.[41]

The framing narrative is a double-layered story with a flow: first, Shahr asks the aged Umm Salama a question. Her answer is the second layer of the framing narrative: it is a recollection of herself as a younger albeit mature woman. Umm Salama depicts a situation in which, while in the intimate sphere of her private home, the Prophet used to utter this supplication, which is the embedded narrative. Shahr ibn Hawshab, the narrator of the framing narrative, placed himself in the framing narrative as the interviewer of Umm Salama. In contrast, Umm Salama placed herself in the background of her narrative as a passive observer. Her unique position as the only witness to the event that she described amplified the authenticity of the message that she conveyed. In addition, Umm Salama's version is unique compared to the testimonies of other *ṣaḥāba* about the same prayer; in all the other versions, the *ṣaḥāba* omit details about the occasion or the place in which the Prophet invoked his supplications. For example, Anas ibn Malik quoted the same prayer about the hearts being held between the two fingers of God, but he preceded his quotation with the following laconic remark: 'The Prophet used to say the following often (*kāna yukatthiru an yaqūla*)'.[42]

The most fascinating group of *aḥādīth al-ṣifāt* is the one that contains dynamic and elaborate settings. In this group of texts, the narrator is more often than not a marginal *ṣaḥābī*. In addition, he places himself in the setting as part of a calculated strategy to add to the credibility of his narrative. *Ḥadīth al-nuzūl*, which describes God's nocturnal descent to the lower heavens in various versions with different degrees of elaboration, is a case in point. The *ḥadīth*, in its different versions, was attributed to sixteen *ṣaḥāba*.[43] The most quoted version states:

> Each night, at the last third of the night, our Lord the Blessed and Sublime descends to the lower heaven and says: 'Who calls for Me [in his prayer] that I may answer? Who is in need of something that I may grant? Who is asking for My forgiveness, so I forgive him?'[44]

This *ḥadīth* has different framing narratives: the prominent *ṣaḥāba* are connected to the succinct ones, while the marginal *ṣaḥāba* are connected to the detailed ones. In the versions attributed to Abu Saᶜid al-Khudri (d. 683 or 694) and Abu Hurayra, the framing narrative is laconic and dull: both Abu Saᶜid and Abu Hurayra confirmed to the Kufan *tābiᶜī* al-Agharr Abu Muslim (death date unknown),[45] either together or separately, that they heard the Prophet describe God's descent.[46] In contrast, a marginal *ṣaḥābī*, Rifaᶜa ibn ᶜAraba al-Juhani (death date unknown), preceded the *ḥadīth al-nuzūl* with the following framing narrative:

> We were [travelling] in the company of the Messenger of God. When we arrived to [a well in the Hijaz] called al-Kadid or Qudayd,[47] some of us asked [the Prophet's] permission to leave and go back to their families, and he gave them his permission. Then [the Prophet] praised God for His grace, and said: 'After midnight – or after one third of the night passes – God descends to the lowest heaven and says: Only I address my servants, asking: Who asks for My forgiveness, so I shall forgive him? Who prays to Me, so I shall grant him his request?'[48]

The Hadith scholars pointed to Rifaᶜa's marginality as a *rāwī*: they did not provide any details about him except that he lived in Medina, and that the two traditions that were attributed to him circulated among the *muḥaddithūn* of the Hijaz.[49] These two traditions are combined into one narration in a less quoted version of *ḥadīth al-nuzūl* (see Appendix I). In this combined version, the elaborate framing narrative presents the Prophet and the *ṣaḥāba* as they return from one of their expeditions. Several of the Prophet's companions asked permission to return to their families, and when the permission was granted, they took their leave. Suddenly, the Prophet said: 'Why do you detest the side of this tree, which is adjacent to the Messenger of God, and not the other side of the tree?' The people, who immediately grasped the Prophet's words as a reproach, started to cry. Abu Bakr, the faithful deputy of the Prophet, hurriedly stated: 'Whoever asks for a permission to leave after hearing your words is a fool.' The Prophet stood up, praised the Lord, said the *shahāda* and commenced a lengthy speech about the place of the *ṣaḥāba* within the selected few who were promised to enter Paradise. In the concluding part of the speech, he described God descending every night to the lowest heaven.[50]

The detailed framing narrative of *ḥadīth al-nuzūl* merely serves as a literary introduction to the heart of the matter, which is the Prophetic dictum. Obviously, the details in the framing narrative were carefully inserted by the narrators. These seemingly minor details (a name of a place, a description of the Prophet's position while speaking to the *ṣaḥāba*, etc.) were meant to amplify the authenticity of the narrative.[51] By placing the narrative in a specific time and place, the narrators implicitly attested that the events that they described indeed occurred. However, if we take these *aḥādīth* simply as stories, we also realise that the point of these minor details is to create narrativity, which is 'the degree to which one feels a story is being told or performed'.[52] Every detail is meant to symbolise something that contributes to the overall design of the single *ḥadīth*. For example, a group of people is gathered outside the Prophet's house on the night of a full moon and awaits his words. This picture creates anticipation, maybe not for us as readers, but surely for the people who eagerly listened to this *ḥadīth* recounted by a local teacher or a *muḥaddith*. The picture also creates in the audience a sense of empathy and rapport with the generation of the *ṣaḥāba*: here we are, gathered in a mosque in eleventh-century Baghdad, or in a madrasa in fourteenth-century Damascus, exactly like the *ṣaḥāba* who gathered outside the house of the Prophet. Like them, we are about to hear a meaningful Prophetic message.

The elaborate framing narratives of *aḥādīth al-ṣifāt* have several common features. First, the setting is specific: most of the stories occur in Medina (inside Umm Salama's house, outside the Prophet's house or somewhere in the desert), with the exception of one that occurs in Mecca.[53] Second, the scene is specific: The Prophet speaks either to one person or to an audience. He often preaches to the *ṣaḥāba*, sometimes in response to a question posed by the *ṣaḥāba*. The narrator wisely links the external event in the setting with the message conveyed by the Prophet. For example, the narrator links the scene of the *ṣaḥāba* watching the full moon with the Prophetic promise of the beatific vision. In Rifaᶜa's narrative there is a drama of emotions: the Prophet sees the people take leave of him one by one to go to their families. He mutters something and stirs the emotions of his audience; the audience reacts by bursting into tears of shame and regret.

The framing narrative is meant to lead the audience to a sphere disconnected from the 'here and now', and transform the listeners from a group of individuals to one attentive, curious and intrigued entity. The framing narrative serves first and foremost the purpose of the narrator to seize the attention of his audience. The narrator then safely guides the audience through peaks of joy and terror, abysses of sadness and despair, and plateaus of contemplation and acceptance. This all occurs in the few minutes in which the story – for indeed, this is a story – lasts.

III. The Embedded Narrative

Aḥādīth al-ruʾya form a cluster of traditions describing the formidable events that the believers will experience on the Day of Resurrection. As part of the dramatic and often theatrical eschatological discourse, *aḥādīth al-ruʾya* are characterised by rich and detailed descriptions, more eventful than the *aḥādīth al-ṣifāt* that we surveyed heretofore. The traditions connected to the beatific vision are varied: there are in fact several dominant versions of *aḥādīth al-ruʾya*, while each version grows numerous variants.[54] One of the most quoted of the *aḥādīth al-ruʾya* is attributed to the influential *ṣaḥābī* and military leader Abu Musa al-Ashᶜarī (d. *c.* 663). This *ḥadīth*, which appears in two variants (with and without a framing narrative), was denounced as feeble (*ḍaᶜīf*) and unreliable by Hadith scholars. In parallel, this *ḥadīth* was excluded from the canonical Hadith compilations and was mostly quoted by Hanbalite scholars. This *ḥadīth* appears in Ahmad ibn Hanbal's (d. 855) *Musnad* and Abu Saᶜid al-Darimi's (d. between 892 and 895) *al-Radd ᶜalā al-Jahmiyya*,[55] two canonical works of early Hanbalism. In addition, this *ḥadīth* is preserved in the thematic Hadith compilations of Ibn Khuzayma's (d. 924) *Kitāb al-Tawḥīd* and Abu Bakr al-Ajurri's (d. 971) *Kitāb al-Sharīᶜa*. These works were also cornerstones in the traditionalistic curriculum.[56] Two extremely elaborate variants of the same story are attributed to the prominent *ṣaḥāba* Ibn Masᶜud and Anas ibn Malik.[57] These variants were also considered feeble or, at best, controversial. Nevertheless, another elaborate variant attributed to the *ṣaḥābī* Abu Saᶜid al-Khudri was widely accepted by the Hadith scholars and included in the two canonical Hadith compilations *al-Ṣaḥīḥān*.[58] This is the shorter version of *ḥadīth al-ruʾya* attributed to Abu Musa al-Ashᶜari:

> The Messenger of God said: When the Day of Resurrection comes God will bring all the nations together in the same plateau. And when He sees fit to

> separate between His creatures, He will present to each nation [the idol] that they used to worship. The people will follow their idols until they will be pushed into the fire. Then our Lord the Blessed and Exalted will come to us as we stand in a high place, and say: 'Who are you?' and we will say: 'We are the Muslims'. He will say: 'What are you waiting for?' They (i.e. the Muslims) will say: 'We are waiting for our Lord the Blessed and Exalted.' He will say: 'Will you recognize Him when you see Him?' They will say: 'Yes.' He will say: 'How will you recognize Him when you have never seen Him?' And they will say: 'He has no equal.' Then, He will be revealed to them laughing, and say: 'Rejoice, oh you Muslims! For I have already replaced each one of you destined to go to Hell with a Jew or a Christian.'[59]

This *ḥadīth* (henceforth, the abbreviated version or the abbreviated *ḥadīth al-ruʾya*) has several conspicuous features as a faithful representative of the eschatological narrative. First, the embedded narrative contains several anthropopathisms: God differentiates between His creatures when He sees fit (*fa-idhā badā lahu an yaṣdaᶜa bayna khalqihi*), God presents the idols to them (*maththala*), probably as sculptures, He comes to the Muslims (*yaʾtī*), and finally, He is revealed to them, laughing (*fa-yatajjalā lahum ḍāḥikan*). The second conspicuous feature of this *ḥadīth* is the composure that the Muslims hold in the middle of a supposedly chaotic and dreadful scene: around them, people are led to their horrific fate and pushed into the fire, while the Muslims stay serene and wait for God. The frightful atmosphere is the third feature of this text. In the eschatological *aḥādīth*, the introductory scene which represents the idolaters' dreadful fate is not chaotic. This scene presents an artificial hierarchy of sinners and heretics: each class of sinners receives a different horrible punishment. Instead of presenting chaos, this scene reflects an orderly arrangement of horrors, destruction and pain, while the description of the various punishments becomes more and more ornate.[60] Because the narrative of the abbreviated version of *ḥadīth al-ruʾya* is not fully developed, these embellishments are missing from the text.

This abbreviated version of Abu Musa al-Ashᶜari's *ḥadīth al-ruʾya* presents a meagre description of the misfortunes that befell the idolaters; however, this version succeeds in creating a sense of suspense. The *ḥadīth* begins with a static view of a waiting crowd gathered on one plateau. Although the picture presented here is invariable, the opening sentence creates a sense of anticipation and suspense by the mere mention of the Day of Resurrection. The suspense ('a curious mixture of pain and pleasure')[61] is disrupted by a sudden movement of the crowd as it divides into groups. Again, we sense the anticipation that dominates the narrative when each group follows the idol it worships. The scene of the idolaters being pushed into the fire is mechanical and almost routine. This scene does not arouse any interest or anticipation. From this shallow point in the story, the narrative reaches a sudden climax with the arrival of God. This major event, or the 'peak' of the narrative, guides the audience to positive feelings of joy and satisfaction.

The peak of the narrative is the dialogue between God and the Muslims. Prior to God addressing the Muslims, the narrative describes them as 'we'. In addition, the eventful (although mechanical and artificial) atmosphere of the idolaters pushed into the fire transitions to a calmer more peaceful rhythm: the Muslims, 'we', stand in a high spot, while obviously below them, the idolaters are thrown into the fire. God comes to the Muslims – of course the meaning of 'comes' is not explained or described – and an exchange of words occurs between Him and the Muslims. The words of God, somewhat similar to a dialogue between a father and his children, transmit warmth and affection to the people gathered in that high spot, waiting for Him. This scene is tranquil and naive. After the Muslims provide God with the correct answer (and there is no fear that they would not succeed), God is revealed to them, laughing,[62] and promises them that their place in Heaven is secured, at the expense of the Jews and the Christians. The laughter of God is benevolent and auspicious for the Muslims, and ominous for the others.

Similar to other eschatological *aḥādīth*, the narrative in its entirety is presented in the future tense.[63] Nonetheless, the effect of the future tense is diminished, because the dialogue between God and the Muslims occurs in the present tense: 'Who are you?', 'We are the Muslims', 'What are you waiting for?' and so forth. Likewise, the closing sentence depicts God in the present tense, although this sentence includes a promise for the future: 'Rejoice, you Muslims! For I have already replaced each one of you destined to go to Hell with a Jew or a Christian.' Note that the prophetic effect vanishes when we reconstruct or paraphrase the dialogue. This effect disappears because the narrative transforms from a future prophecy into a story, and a story is told in either the past or the present tense.[64]

In the lengthy version of this *ḥadīth* (henceforth, the lengthy version or the lengthy *ḥadīth al-ruʾya*), which is also attributed to Abu Musa al-Ashʿari, the embedded narrative is more dynamic and colourful. Here the anthropopathisms are reduced considerably, and the text retains a certain degree of ambiguity when it refers to God. The following paragraph is the full translation of the text:

> When the Day of Resurrection arrives, [the idols] that each nation used to worship in this world will be presented before them. Each nation will approach [the idol] that they used to worship in this world, and only the monotheists (*ahl al-tawḥīd*) will remain. Someone will then say to them: 'What are you waiting for, when everyone else has already gone?'[65] And they will answer: 'We have a lord whom we used to worship in the material world, but we have never seen him.' They will be asked: 'Will you know him when you see him?' They will say: 'Yes.' They will be asked: 'So, how will you recognize him, when you have never seen him?' They will answer: 'Because there is nothing similar to him.' Suddenly, the curtain will be drawn in front of them, and they will see God, the mighty and powerful. Immediately they will prostrate themselves on the ground – all, but a group of people who will want to prostrate themselves but will be unable to do so, because their backs will be stuck and erect like cattle's horns. This [scene] will be exactly as described in the Quranic verse: 'On the day when the dread event unfolds and they are told to prostrate themselves, they will be unable.'[66] So God will say to them: 'Raise your heads up, because for each and every one of you I marked a substitute who is either a Jew or a Christian, to be sent instead of you to Hell.'[67]

In this version, God does not approach the believers and speak to them; instead, a mysterious voice speaks to the believers. Only in the closing sentence of the embedded narrative, is the identity of the speaker revealed. The embedded narrative is double-layered: it retains the general structure of the narrative in the abbreviated *ḥadīth al-ruʾya* – albeit with a greater deal of elaboration – and it includes a reference to Q. 68:42 ('On the day the dread event unfolds and they are told to prostrate themselves, they will not be able'). Both this ambiguous Quranic verse and the exegetical discourse that evolved from it describe a group of heretics among the Muslims, a group that will be exposed on the Day of Resurrection. Contrary to the brief *ḥadīth al-ruʾya*, the lengthy version of this *ḥadīth* presents the credence that the Muslims (here, *ahl al-tawḥīd*) are not one homogenous group. According to this version, unidentified negative elements will exploit the believers and take refuge among them. This version does not name these elements; however, other *aḥādīth* connected to Q. 68:42 refer to them mostly as hypocrites (*munāfiqūn*) or heretics, 'those who worship in this world for the sake of appearances (*riyāʾ*) and maintain their reputation (*sumʿa*)'.[68] Other *aḥādīth* describe these elements as heretics (*kuffār*).[69]

The embedded narrative in the lengthy *ḥadīth al-ruʾya* presents a sequence of events in the future tense, a dialogue between the mysterious voice and the Muslims, and then the sudden appearance of God. However, unlike the abbreviated version, this lengthy version closely examines the reaction of the Muslims to the beatific vision and corroborates the entire scene with the above-mentioned Quranic verse. The narrative concludes with the divine promise of securing the place of every Muslim in Heaven.

The basic narrating line of the abbreviated version is duplicated in the lengthy version: the line retains the elements of suspense and surprise. The lengthy version also raises more questions than the abbreviated version. According to this version, the hypocrites could not prostrate themselves; therefore God's promise to replace each Muslim by a Jew or a Christian is supposedly addressed solely to the believers. But what if the text alludes to the replacement of Muslim hypocrites by Jews and Christians? And if so, on what grounds will these hypocrites be given their immediate absolution? Will they not be required to prove that they repented? These questions, no doubt, engendered many lengthy versions. One of these versions, attributed to ʿAbd Allah ibn Masʿud, clarified that indeed the Muslims who could not prostrate themselves will find their replacements in Hell in the form of a Jew or a Christian, but also that each of them will have to carry a lamp whose size symbolises the deeds that he performed in the material world.[70] Another version, attributed to Abu Saʿid al-Khudri, does not promise the replacement of Muslim sinners by Jews or Christians, but describes the ordeal these sinners undergo before they are allowed to enter Paradise 'not for any good deed they had performed'.[71]

Another version which competes with the abbreviated and lengthy versions of *ḥadīth al-ruʾya*, appears in the canonical *Ṣaḥīḥ Muslim.*[72] This version, also attributed to Abu Musa al-Ashʿari, is a much paler version free from anthropopathisms such as God's laughter or God having an intense dialogue with the believers:

> Abu Burda [recounted] on the authority of Abu Musa: On the Day of Resurrection, God will hand over a Jew or a Christian to every Muslim, saying: 'This is the sacrifice[73] that will redeem you from Hell.'[74]

This is entitled 'the *ḥadīth* of the sacrifice' (*ḥadīth al-fidāʾ*)[75] or 'the *ḥadīth* of the sacrifice in favour of the believer' (*ḥadīth fidāʾ al-muʾmin*).[76] Lacking time and motion, this 'sterilised' version cannot be considered a narrative, but a Prophetic dictum. The importance of *ḥadīth al-fidāʾ*, however, lies in its framing narrative as demonstrated below, in the following section.

IV. The Narrator and his Audience

The framing narratives of *ḥadīth al-ruʾya* and *ḥadīth fidāʾ al-muʾmin* accentuate the cardinal questions of the narrator, the audience and the coherence of the text, simply because these framing narratives record the effect of the embedded narratives on the receptive audience.[77] In this section, we first address the framing narrative of the lengthy *ḥadīth al-ruʾya* and then examine several elements in the framing narrative of *ḥadīth fidāʾ al-muʾmin*. This examination illustrates the following characteristics of the lengthy *ḥadīth al-ruʾya*: the audience's reaction to the embedded narrative, the narrator's intent in recounting the narrative, the place of the narrator in the narrative, and finally the coherence of the embedded narrative.

The framing narrative of the lengthy *ḥadīth al-ruʾya* (for the full translation, see Appendix I) comprises three parts: the *isnād* which identifies the narrator of this *ḥadīth*, a story that prefaces the embedded narrative and a closure of the story, which follows immediately after the embedded narrative. This triple-layered framing narrative in fact sheds light on the embedded narrative and the circumstances of its inception. According to the framing narrative, the first actual narrator (*rāwī*) of this *ḥadīth* was not Abu Musa al-Ashʿari (to whom this *ḥadīth* is attributed), but his son, Abu Burda (d. *c.* 721–3), who was a qadi in Kufa.

In the framing narrative, Abu Burda recounts in detail how he headed a delegation from Kufa which was sent to the caliph al-Walid ibn ᶜAbd al-Malik (r. 705–15) or to his successor Sulayman ibn ᶜAbd al-Malik (r. 715–17).[78] ᶜUmar ibn ᶜAbd al-ᶜAziz (r. 717–20), who later became a caliph, was appointed by the ruling caliph to handle the requests of the Kufan delegation. This event occurred sometime between 712 and 717. ᶜUmar, then in his early thirties, was attached to the caliphal court as an advisor after he was dismissed from his post as the governor of the Hijaz. Abu Burda, the narrator, claimed to be more than eighty years old when this event occurred, but according to the biographical literature he probably was in his seventies. According to Sufyan ibn ᶜUyayna (d. 813), who was not their contemporary, ᶜUmar asked Abu Burda for his age and the latter replied: 'I am twice the age of maturity (*ashuddān*).' Sufyan explained that *ashudd* is forty-four years;[79] hence, Abu Burda claimed to have been eighty-eight.

The encounter between ᶜUmar and Abu Burda occurred in ᶜUmar's humble residence in Damascus.[80] Abu Burda recounts:

> When I accomplished my mission, I came to ᶜUmar and bade him farewell. I then went on my way, when suddenly I recalled a *ḥadīth* my father had once told me, a *ḥadīth* he had heard from the Messenger of God. I wanted to recount it to ᶜUmar who kindly took care of my needs. So I returned to him. When he saw me, he said: 'The sheikh remembered that he needs something else, and that is why he returned.' I approached him, and he said: 'What made you come back? Have you not accomplished your mission?' I said: 'Yes, of course. However, there is a *ḥadīth* that I heard from my father, who in turn heard it from the Prophet, and I wished to recount it to you, because you were so kind to me.' He said: 'What is it?' And I said: 'My father told me that he heard the Messenger of God say…'.[81]

And Abu Burda told ᶜUmar ibn ᶜAbd al-ᶜAziz the lengthy version of *ḥadīth al-ruʾya*.

As indicated earlier, the embedded narrative of the lengthy version of *ḥadīth al-ruʾya* is followed by the closing section of the framing narrative. This closure raises several questions regarding the authenticity of the embedded narrative and the credibility of the narrator, Abu Burda:

> ᶜUmar ibn ᶜAbd al-ᶜAziz said: 'Allah, there is no god but Him! Did your father tell you this *ḥadīth*? Did he hear it from the Prophet?' [Abu Burda said]: At his request, I made an oath in his presence three times, and then ᶜUmar ibn ᶜAbd al-ᶜAziz said: 'I have never heard a *ḥadīth* about the monotheists that I loved better than this one.'[82]

This closure indeed ties loose ends left by the first part of the framing narrative. First, this ending explains why Abu Burda came back to ᶜUmar's residence after accomplishing his undisclosed mission. The story obeys an internal logic that gives the whole narrative additional meaning.[83] In this case, the narrator, Abu Burda, recounted the *ḥadīth* for a purpose, not just for the sake of transmitting a Prophetic dictum or telling a story. Reading the embedded narrative again, while considering that the *ḥadīth* or the embedded narrative is the object of the narrator's activity,[84] makes the reader wonder whether recounting this specific *ḥadīth* by a Kufan judge to an esteemed member of the caliphal court – a former governor and a future caliph – had a purpose in its own right. In other words, the simple immediate reading of the entire text assumes that Abu Burda wanted to repay ᶜUmar for his grace, and that the only valuable token at his disposal was this *ḥadīth*, allegedly recounted to him by his father. However, this reading of the text does not explain why this specific *ḥadīth* was chosen by Abu Burda as a gift and not another one. Certainly, Abu Burda could have told ᶜUmar one of the many *aḥādīth* that he transmitted on the authority of his father, Abu Musa al-Ashᶜari.[85] Assuming that this *ḥadīth* bears a significant message to the recipient, the way to expose it is by applying a combined reading in both the Hadith material and the historical sources.

Let us return to the framing narrative. The text implies that Abu Burda had never told this *ḥadīth* before his meeting with ᶜUmar. The details added to the lengthy version indeed raise the suspicion that Abu Burda was adorning and embellishing his tale to please the righteous ᶜUmar. ᶜUmar's response and the oath that Abu Burda was forced to take (three times!) indicate that this gift was accepted by the recipient with an obvious display of pleasure mixed with a pinch of a doubt. In a slightly different version of this *ḥadīth*, ᶜUmar took this story with a grain of salt, and sceptically exclaimed: 'By God! Did you really hear Abu Musa transmitting this *ḥadīth* on the authority of the Messenger of God?'[86]

Another version of the same *ḥadīth* indeed emphasises that ᶜUmar doubted whether Abu Burda was telling the truth. Two Kufan *muḥaddithūn,* Saᶜid ibn Abi Burda (who was Abu Burda's son; d. 756)[87] and ᶜAwn ibn ᶜAbd Allah ibn ᶜUtba ibn Masᶜud (who was ᶜAbd Allah ibn Masᶜud's great nephew; d. between 729 and 738), recounted the *ḥadīth al-ruʾya* attributed to Abu Musa al-Ashᶜari. When teaching this *ḥadīth*, they used to transmit only the closing statement: 'For every Muslim who dies, God sends a Jew or a Christian to replace him in Hell.' These two *muḥaddithūn* thereby disconnected this closing statement from the embedded narrative that we have seen in other versions of *ḥadīth al-ru'ya.* In other words, Saᶜid and ᶜAwn omitted the framing narrative and the lion's share of the embedded narrative. Both scholars testified that they were present in the meeting between Abu Burda and ᶜUmar, where they saw Abu Burda transmit the *ḥadīth* to ᶜUmar. However, only ᶜAwn addressed the obviously embarrassing part of the event: 'He (i.e. ᶜUmar) made him take the oath "there is no god but Him" and swear that his father indeed told him that he had heard the *ḥadīth* from the Prophet.' The following remark by Ahmad ibn Hanbal (d. 855) amplifies the embarrassment that Abu Burda must have experienced during that event: 'Saᶜid [ibn Abi Burda] never denied ᶜAwn's words that [ᶜUmar] made him take an oath.'[88]

Saᶜid's silence indicates that this story about his father was also a cause of embarrassment for the son: he probably did not want to make his father's embarrassment known. This is why Saᶜid, as well as other *muḥaddithūn*, did not teach the lengthy version of *ḥadīth al-ruʾya.* This version presented the immediate recipient of *ḥadīth al-ruʾya*, ᶜUmar ibn ᶜAbd al-ᶜAziz, as expressing doubt about the veracity of the *ḥadīth* that Abu Burda recounted, and demanding Abu Burda's triple oath before accepting the veracity of this *ḥadīth.* Saᶜid believed that the only course he could take to squash this embarrassing story was to ignore it. The fact that the version quoted from Saᶜid in fact sterilises the embedded narrative and preserves merely the Prophetic dictum, indicates that the lengthy version of *ḥadīth al-ruʾya* was perceived as problematic.

Even so, Abu Burda's authenticity as a *muḥaddith* was never questioned. He was unanimously considered reliable,[89] although the incident with ᶜUmar implies otherwise. Hadith scholars explained that this *ḥadīth* was excluded from the canonical Hadith compilations because of ᶜUmara al-Qurashi (death date unknown), an unknown member of the Kufan delegation to the caliph. ᶜUmara al-Qurashi, who was another eyewitness to the encounter between Abu Burda and ᶜUmar, transmitted this *ḥadīth* on the authority of Abu Burda.[90] Both the abridged and lengthy versions of this *ḥadīth* were in fact the only material ᶜUmara ever transmitted. Both versions were denounced by Hadith scholars as weak on the grounds of the dubious credibility of ᶜUmara and the transmitter who heard the *ḥadīth* from him.[91]

As mentioned earlier, the *ḥadīth* in its lengthy and abridged versions later became part of the ultra-traditionalist (mostly Hanbalite) curriculum. Ahmad ibn Hanbal's son, ᶜAbd Allah (d. 903), quoted the *ḥadīth* on the authority of his father in *Kitāb al-Sunna*. According to ᶜAbd Allah, Ahmad ibn Hanbal deemed all *aḥādīth al-ruʾyā* authentic. Ahmad compiled these *aḥādīth* in a book which he used in his classes without any reservation.[92] The lengthy version of the *ḥadīth* with the elaborated framing narrative was probably included in Ahmad's teachings: ᶜAbd Allah quoted an abridged version on the encounter between Abu Burda and ᶜUmar in the *Musnad*.[93] This version gained some circulation in Baghdad: Abd Allah testified that he heard it from two other *muḥaddithūn*, and not from his father.[94] However, the *muḥaddithūn* from outside the Hanbalite and ultra-traditionalist circles rejected Abu Burda's version of *ḥadīth al-ruʾya* not because of its colourful content (the trend of content criticism surfaced only decades later), but – as we indicated above – because of ᶜUmara al-Qurashi's lack of credibility.

The framing narrative of the lengthy *ḥadīth al-ruʾya* provided previously missing details about the narrator (Abu Burda), the audience (ᶜUmar ibn ᶜAbd al-ᶜAziz), and the method in which the embedded narrative was accepted. Several questions, however, remained unanswered: the narrator's motives, the exact scene in which the narrator told his narrative, and whether the message in the embedded narrative was successfully conveyed to the receptive audience. These questions are answered in the following section through a close examination of *ḥadīth al-fidāʾ*. The linkage between *ḥadīth al-fidāʾ* and *ḥadīth al-ruʾya* is also clarified in the following section.

V. The Motives of the Narrator

Ḥadīth al-fidāʾ, the 'non-identical twin' or the 'sterilised' version of *ḥadīth al-ruʾya*, enables us to reconsider Abu Burda's motives in recounting *ḥadīth al-ruʾya* to ᶜUmar. In *Ṣaḥīḥ Muslim*, the Prophetic dictum of this sterilised version is attached to the framing narrative of the lengthy version of *ḥadīth al-ruʾya*. This attachment suggests that Abu Burda merely told ᶜUmar a *ḥadīth* lacking drama and motion.[95] In addition, marginalised versions of this *ḥadīth* were recorded by the *muḥaddith* and historian Ibn ᶜAsakir (d. 1176) in *Tārīkh Dimashq*. These versions provide possible answers to some of the questions that we raised previously.[96] Ibn ᶜAsakir included these versions in the biographical entries of contemporaries of Abu Burda, who were present in the encounter between him and ᶜUmar. One of the versions was transmitted by Saᶜid, Abu Burda's son, while the other four versions were transmitted by other eyewitnesses to the encounter between Abu Burda and ᶜUmar. In these five additional versions in *Tārīkh Dimashq*, Abu Burda recounts to ᶜUmar the *ḥadīth al-fidāʾ* and not the *ḥadīth al-ruʾya*. These five texts indeed require special attention, but for the purpose of our discussion, we will briefly examine the three most relevant versions.[97]

According to his avowal, Saᶜid ibn Abi Burda accompanied his father in the delegation to the caliph al-Walid. As Ahmad ibn Hanbal remarked, Saᶜid never denied that ᶜUmar asked his father to swear on the authenticity of the *ḥadīth* that he recounted to him. Following the material in Ahmad ibn Hanbal's *Musnad* and Muslim's *Ṣaḥīḥ*, Ibn ᶜAsakir added that Saᶜid never denied nor affirmed this incident.[98] According to Saᶜid, after completing his business with ᶜUmar, Abu Burda awakened Saᶜid in the middle of the night and led him through the streets of Damascus. They arrived at ᶜUmar's house, which was situated between the vegetable market and the cheese market, and knocked on the gate of the house. The gatekeeper informed Abu Burda that ᶜUmar had already retired to bed, but Abu Burda insisted on informing ᶜUmar that he was waiting for him at the gate. Soon after, permission was granted for Abu Burda and his son to enter the house. 'Is something wrong, Abu Burda?' –asked ᶜUmar whose sleep was interrupted. 'Everything is fine' – answered Abu Burda. 'What is it that you want?' – asked ᶜUmar. Abu Burda explained: 'I finished my business, but I remembered a *ḥadīth* that my father had told me. And here it is: The Messenger of God said: When the people will be gathered for Judgement Day, a Jew or a Christian will be brought, and [a voice] will say: Oh believer! This is the sacrifice that will redeem you from Hell.'[99] ᶜUmar asked: 'Did you hear it from your father?'

Abu Burda confirmed this.[100] This version negates any possibility of the presence of witnesses to the event, other than Saᶜid. This version also retains Abu Burda's dignity: here, ᶜUmar did not question the veracity of the *ḥadīth*. On the other hand, perhaps due to the late hour at night, ᶜUmar's reaction to the *ḥadīth* seemed reserved.[101] This version, in spite of the realistic atmosphere of its framing narrative, is equally as ambiguous as the lengthy version of *ḥadīth al-ruᵓya*, because it does not explain why Abu Burda recounted this specific *ḥadīth* to ᶜUmar or why he bothered doing so in the middle of the night. In conclusion, the internal logic of the narrative remains inaccessible.

The second version, recounted by another member of the Kufan delegation to the caliph, suggests that it was ᶜUmar who specifically asked Abu Burda to transmit the Prophetic *aḥādīth* that he personally heard from the Prophet. In the presence of one of the family members of the prominent *ṣaḥābī* Talha ibn ᶜUbayd Allah (d. 656), Abu Burda recounted the *ḥadīth fidāᵓ al-muᵓmin*. ᶜUmar immensely enjoyed the *ḥadīth*, and he immediately ordered that ink and paper be brought to him, and the *ḥadīth* was recorded straightaway.[102] However, the emphasis in this narrative seems to be the historical bitter controversy on the recording of knowledge (*taqyīd al-ᶜilm*)[103] and not the recounted *ḥadīth* itself. This version merely contributes the name of another eyewitness to the event, but does not help decipher the story's internal logic.

The third version provides an alternative reading in the narrative. This version was recounted by Qudama ibn Hamata al-Dabbi from Kufa (death date unknown). Qudama was recognised as a reliable Hadith authority. Two of his sources were Abu Burda and ᶜUmar ibn ᶜAbd al-ᶜAziz.[104] Qudama provided a story that satisfies the expectations of the readers (or the audience) to receive a reasonable explanation of the behaviour of the main characters. In brief, Qudama's version provides a solution; whereas, all the other versions of either *ḥadīth al-ruᵓya* or *ḥadīth fidāᵓ al-muᵓmin* fail to do so.[105] Qudama's presence in the event is unquestionable, as we learn that he was one of the frequent visitors to ᶜUmar's premises when ᶜUmar was a governor in Medina. The narrative of Qudama retains a high degree of objectivity mainly because of the narrator's use of direct speech and his undisputable presence in the background of the narrative.[106] In this story, Qudama is comfortably situated in ᶜUmar's sitting room and observes the following scene:

> I was sitting at ᶜUmar ᶜAbd al-ᶜAziz's when suddenly Abu Burda, the son of Abu Musa came in, and told ᶜUmar ibn ᶜAbd al-ᶜAziz that he once heard his father tell the following *ḥadīth* on the authority of the Prophet, who said: 'In the Day of Resurrection, the Jew and the Christian will be brought, and a voice will say: "Oh Muslim, this is the sacrifice that will redeem you from Hell".' ᶜUmar ibn ᶜAbd al-ᶜAziz said to Abu Burda: 'Allah, there is no god but Him! Did you hear your father tell this *ḥadīth* on the authority of the Messenger of God?' [Abu Burda] said: 'Allah, there is no god but Him! My father indeed told me this *ḥadīth*, and he in his turn heard it from the Messenger of God.' [Qudama said]: I then saw ᶜUmar ibn ᶜAbd al-ᶜAziz prostrate himself in adoration three times.[107]

This version is definitely the most elegant narrative of the three. The narrative would have been even more elegant if instead of *ḥadīth fidāʾ al-muʾmin* it had included *ḥadīth al-ruʾya*: in this narrative, namely Qudama's narrative, ᶜUmar's reaction connects the framing narrative and the embedded narrative of *ḥadīth al-ruʾya*. With this connection, the inner logic of *ḥadīth al-ruʾya* is revealed. Apparently, the purpose of Abu Burda recounting the *ḥadīth al-ruʾya* in the lengthy version was to provide an illustrated explanation to Q. 68:42 ('On the day when the dread event unfolds and they are told to prostrate themselves, they will not be able'). This is why Abu Burda depicted in detail (in the lengthy version of *ḥadīth al-ruʾya* and not in *ḥadīth fidāʾ al-muʾmin*) the heretics who are unable to prostrate themselves, and remain seated with erect, immovable backs even after the call to prostrate was issued. The believers, as several other places in the Quran and especially Q. 32:15 ('. . . those who, when reminded of them, prostrate themselves in adoration') indicate, comply with the call and succeed in prostrating themselves. By prostrating himself three times, ᶜUmar signalled to Abu Burda that the message of his father's *ḥadīth* was clearly conveyed and fully comprehended. We now understand that Abu Burda paid ᶜUmar a cryptic compliment: Abu Burda wanted to tell ᶜUmar how pious and righteous he was compared to the people around him. ᶜUmar understood the *ḥadīth* as a compliment and reacted accordingly. This explanation also suggests that ᶜUmar's incredulous reaction to Abu Burda's story ('Did you hear your father tell this *ḥadīth* on the authority of the Messenger of God?') was not meant to doubt Abu Burda, but meant to conceal ᶜUmar's sheer enjoyment from Abu Burda's compliment. The story finally has a closure which connects the framing narrative to the embedded narrative.

The historical sources provide additional information on Abu Burda that helps accentuate his motives as a narrator. Abu Burda owed his appointment as a judge in Kufa and his frequent visits to the caliphal court to his noble origin and his ability to provide exclusive information about the Prophet from the mouth of a prominent *ṣaḥābī*, namely his father.[108] According to one anecdote, Abu Burda never tired of bragging about his father. One day, while sitting in a public assembly (*majlis ᶜāmm*), Abu Burda dominated the conversation and commenced a lengthy discourse in which he described his father's virtues and intimate companionship with the Prophet. Although the text does not explicitly state so, Abu Burda claimed – among other allegations – that Abu Musa once cupped the Prophet. The poet al-Farazdaq (died in Basra in about 728 or 730), who was present at the *majlis*, became annoyed at Abu Burda's never-ending stories and wished to belittle him. 'Had Abu Musa's only virtue been that he had the honour of cupping the Messenger of God, it would have been enough for him' – said al-Farazdaq. Abu Burda also was annoyed, and replied: 'You are quite right; however take notice that he never cupped anyone, not before the Prophet, and not after him.' Obviously, Abu Burda's purpose was to emphasise that his father, the military leader who never practiced cupping on a regular basis, was allowed to practice cupping on the Prophet probably in some special circumstances which unfortunately remained unrevealed. This made no impression on al-Farazdaq who sharply remarked: 'But surely Abu Musa knew better than to experiment his first cupping on the Prophet himself!' Al-Farazdaq's mocking astonishment infuriated Abu Burda, who was forced to keep silent.[109] This anecdote, combined with the fact that Abu Musa was never mentioned in the sources as one of the few people who cupped the Prophet, presents Abu Burda as a liar.[110]

Abu Burda was first and foremost a politician who exploited the Hadith he supposedly heard from his father on various occasions for different goals: to make a point, to win a discussion, to tell a story. When Yazid ibn Muhallab (d. 720) was appointed governor of Iraq and Khurasan, he offered Abu Burda an official post in his administration. Abu Burda politely requested an exemption. Yazid refused. Abu Burda then suggested: 'Oh, emir! Would you like me to tell you something that my father had once told me? He heard it from the Messenger of God.' Yazid replied in a somewhat rude manner: 'Let me have it!' Without further introduction, Abu Burda said: 'He told me that he heard the Messenger of God say: Whoever assumes a position while knowing that he is unfit for it, will have a chair reserved for him in Hell.' Yazid was not impressed. He replied cynically that Abu Burda's begging only made him, Yazid, even more enthusiastic to have Abu Burda for the job. He then ordered him to assume the position immediately. Abu Burda reluctantly complied. After some time, he came to Yazid's residence and asked his permission to approach him: 'Oh, emir! Would you like me to tell you something that my father had told me? He heard it from the Messenger of God.' Yazid nodded and Abu Burda continued: 'Damned is the man who asks something for the sake of God (*bi-wajhi Allāh*)! Damned is the man who is asked by someone to do something for the sake of God, and he refuses to grant that someone his wishes, especially when this request was not meant to mock or insult.' After quoting this saying of the Prophet, Abu Burda hurriedly added: 'Oh, emir, all I asked you – for the sake of God – was that I would be exempted from your service.' Yazid then acquiesced and released Abu Burda from his prior obligation.[111] Both statements that Abu Burda quoted on the authority of his father (and the Prophet) were never included in the canonical Hadith compilations, although they appear in other Hadith compilations and several theological treatises on the authority of Abu Musa and other *ṣaḥāba*.[112] This fact alone should have discredited Abu Burda as a *muḥaddith*; however, none of the Hadith scholars doubted his sources and his narration.

VI. The Narrator's Role

The relations between the 'framing narrative' and the 'embedded narrative' are one of the stylistic devices that empower the message of the narrative as a whole. Another stylistic device that helps empower the message of the narrative is the 'paratext', the 'material that lies somehow on the threshold of the narrative'.[113] Paratexts are intrinsic to the genre of Hadith: the chain of transmission, the *isnād*, consistently introduces the narrative, the *matn*. Consistently – because authors of theological treatises and exegeses of the Quran sometimes tended to skip the lion's share of the *isnād*, mention only the *ṣaḥābī* or another individual to whom they attributed the *ḥadīth*, and move forward to the *matn*. However in the classic Hadith compilations, where quoting the *isnād* was strictly maintained, the *isnād* indeed provides a necessary introduction to the text, or in other words, a paratext.

While dating a certain tradition by methods of *isnād* analysis has been the gold standard of Hadith studies for decades,[114] research in Islamic theology (with the exception of a few studies)[115] tended to ignore the *isnād* and the narrators. The reason for this disregard is the instrumental approach to Hadith in the theological discourse, which was mentioned earlier, at the beginning of this chapter. However, the case of Abu Burda and *ḥadīth al-ruʾya* no doubt proves that questioning the identity of the narrator, his position and his motives contributes to a fuller understanding of the text. In the following example, which is a conspicuous *ḥadīth* in the repertoire of *aḥādīth al-ṣifāt*, the *isnād* helps clarify the narrator's role in shaping the narrative. In the opening lines of the *ḥadīth*, a Jewish rabbi (*ḥabr* or *ḥibr*) comes to the Prophet and says:

> When the Day of Resurrection comes, God will place the heavens on one finger, the earth on one finger, the mountains on one finger, and all the creatures on one finger. Then He will shake His fingers and say: 'I am the king!'

As a sign of approval of the rabbi's words (*taṣdīqan lahu*), the Prophet laughed until his molars were revealed. Then the Prophet recited the following Quranic verse (Q. 39:67): 'They underrate the might of God. But on the Day of Resurrection He will hold the entire earth in His grasp and fold up the heavens in His right hand.'[116]

The different versions of 'the *ḥadīth* of the divine fingers' retain the same kernel in the framing narrative. In this narrative, the meeting of the Jewish rabbi and the Prophet is depicted without disclosing any details about the circumstances of their meeting. In several versions of this *ḥadīth*, the rabbi immediately starts lecturing without further introduction. In other versions, he either addresses the Prophet informally: 'Oh Muhammad', 'Oh Abu 'l-Qasim', or formally: 'Oh Messenger of God'.[117]

The prolific *ṣaḥābī* ʿAbd Allah ibn Masʿud (d. 652–3) claimed to have sat with the Prophet when a Jewish rabbi – 'one of the rabbis of the Jews' – approached the Prophet of his own accord. The rabbi sat in front of the

Prophet as a sign that he wished to commence a conversation with him. The Prophet then asked the rabbi: 'Tell us something' (*ḥaddithnā*). The rabbi's response was the description of God's fingers on the Day of Resurrection.[118] A version attributed to Ibn ᶜAbbas depicts the scene differently:

> A Jew once walked past the Prophet, while the Prophet was sitting. The Prophet said: 'Oh Jew, come and tell us something!' The Jew said: 'Oh Abu 'l-Qasim, what do you think about the day in which God placed the sky on this one, the earth on this one, the mountains on this one and the rest of creation on this one?' Thereafter God revealed the verse 'They underrate the might of God'.[119]

As for the rabbi's identity: one version does not attach the epithet *ḥabr* to the Jew; hence, he was not necessarily a rabbi.[120] Another version is unclear: the Jew appears to be one of the People of the Book, that is, a Jew or a Christian.[121]

Upon a general examination of the stylistic features of 'the divine fingers' the original narrator was supposedly ᶜAbd Allah ibn Masᶜud. Nonetheless, upon closer examination, we realise that the original narrator (*rāwī*) who was responsible for the final version of the text that reached us was actually ᶜAbida ibn ᶜAmr al-Salmani (d. between 691 and 693). This scholar was one of Ibn Masᶜud's disciples in Kufa. A competing version of this *ḥadīth* came from another disciple of Ibn Masᶜud, ᶜAlqama ibn Qays (d. between 681 and 692, at the age of ninety).[122] Apparently, the two competing versions reflect two different approaches to Hadith transmission. Let us first examine the framing narrative of these two competing versions: ᶜAbida's versus ᶜAlqama's (see Table 1.1).

The beginning of ᶜAbida's version reflects the narrator's momentary hesitation about the identity of the man who came to the Prophet. This hesitation signals that a considerable period of time passed between Ibn Masᶜud telling his story and ᶜAbida's narration: ᶜAbida is not certain whether Ibn Masᶜud described the 'man from the People of the Book' as a Jew or a Christian.[125] However, this hesitation is no doubt deliberate and functional: it is meant for the audience. With this brief hesitation, the narrator signals to his audience that he struggles to remember the details of a past event, and by doing so he indirectly builds the audience's trust in his narrative. In addition, the

Table 1.1

The framing narrative	ᶜAbida's version[123]	ᶜAlqama's version[124]
Opening section	On the authority of ᶜAbida [who recounted this *ḥadīth*] on the authority of ᶜAbd Allah who said: a man from the People of the Book came – [ᶜAbida] said: I think that he (i.e. ᶜAbd Allah ibn Masᶜud) said that he was a Jew or a Christian – to the Messenger of God, and said . . .	On the authority of ᶜAlqama [who recounted this *ḥadīth*] on the authority of ᶜAbd Allah who said: a man from the People of the Book came to the Messenger of God, and said . . .
Closing section	And the Messenger of God laughed until his molars were revealed, then he quoted the following verse: 'They underrate the might of God' (Q. 39:67)	And I saw the Messenger of God laugh until his molars were revealed, then he quoted: 'They underrate the might of God' (Q. 39:67)

narrator's hesitation creates an atmosphere of suspense which keeps the audience attentive.[126] As for the readers, the sentence 'I think that he said' signifies the authenticity of both layers of the framing narrative: the first layer is a story that Ibn Masᶜud originally told ᶜAbida, and the second layer is the same story as transmitted by ᶜAbida. ᶜAbida's version of Ibn Masᶜud's narrative is 'tainted' by the rhetorical device or the hesitation marker ('I think that he said . . .') which shifts the audience's focus to ᶜAbida, and also marks the narrative as ᶜAbida's, and not Ibn Masᶜud's. By contrast, ᶜAlqama's version is more 'sterile' in the sense that the narrator, ᶜAlqama, reduces his presence in the narrative to zero. The sterility of this version signals that it is a 'pure' Ibn Masᶜud narrative with no additions, embellishments or interpretations.[127]

The difference between the two framing narratives of the same *ḥadīth* is not only stylistic but reflects the way the narrator grasps his role: ᶜAbida obviously saw himself as an involved narrator, and a teacher who clarifies obscure points in Ibn Masᶜud's teachings. In addition, ᶜAbida is depicted both as a disciple who places himself in the narrative next to Ibn Masᶜud, and as a story-teller who strives to gain his audience's trust by using rhetorical devices. In contrast, ᶜAlqama saw himself strictly as a means of transmitting the teachings of the great scholar without adding anything to what he actually heard from Ibn Masᶜud. This typification of the two narrators is corroborated by the historical sources.

ᶜAbida and ᶜAlqama were two of ᶜAbd Allah ibn Masᶜud's five chosen disciples. As such, their seniority among the *tābiᶜūn* in Iraq is often emphasiszed in the sources.[128] Both ᶜAbida and ᶜAlqama participated in Ibn Masᶜud's titanic endeavours to educate the people of Kufa in the duties of their new religion.[129] The *muḥaddith* and dream-interpreter Muhammad ibn Sirin (d. 728), who was ᶜAbida's disciple, described Ibn Masᶜud's five disciples as handicapped, among whom ᶜAbida was marked as the one-eyed and ᶜAlqama as the lame.[130] Their contemporaries and successors often argued about the virtues of Ibn Masᶜud's five disciples (a familiar *topos* in the biographical literature) and particularly delved into the question: Who was more prominent, ᶜAbida or ᶜAlqama? Some preferred the scholarship of ᶜAbida, while others deemed ᶜAlqama more prominent.[131] Although both disciples achieved fame, apparently ᶜAbida toiled to earn his scholarly status, while ᶜAlqama won Ibn Masᶜud's affection without any struggle. In the long run, ᶜAlqama made a more positive impression on later generations than ᶜAbida. The *muḥaddith* and historian Shams al-Din al-Dhahabi (d. 1348) meticulously summarised and analysed hundreds of literary works of previous generations. He is a reliable source for reflecting the way his contemporaries and the entire establishment of *muḥaddithūn* evaluated the status of scholars of previous generations.[132] Al-Dhahabi described ᶜAbida as 'one of the luminaries' (*aḥad al-aᶜlām*), labelling him a prominent *muḥaddith* in Kufa, a qadi who issued legal opinions and an expert in *fiqh* and law.[133] In comparison, the opening of ᶜAlqama's considerably lengthy biographical entry in al-Dhahabi's *Siyar Aᶜlām al-Nubalāʾ* uses all the laudatory vocabulary that al-Dhahabi had at his disposal. According to al-Dhahabi, ᶜAlqama was the most prominent lawyer in Kufa, one of the greatest luminaries in scholarship, the most celebrated Quran teacher, imam, Hadith scholar, reciter of the Quran, and an eminent jurisprudent.[134] Elsewhere, ᶜAlqama is described as one of the scholars who possessed unique knowledge of God (*min al-rabbāniyyīn*).[135]

The relationship between these two disciples and Ibn Masᶜud is relevant to the framing narrative of the *ḥadīth* of the divine fingers. While ᶜAbida is mentioned in the sources as the student of both ᶜAbd Allah ibn Masᶜud and ᶜAli ibn Abi Talib,[136] ᶜAlqama is described as ᶜAbd Allah ibn Masᶜud's favourite disciple (although he had other teachers; in fact, more than eighteen *ṣaḥābī*-sources and teachers). After years of travelling in search of knowledge, and participating in wars (such as the battle of Siffin), ᶜAlqama accompanied Ibn Masᶜud 'until he became a leading authority in both Hadith and religious practice. The scholars acquired their knowledge from him, and his reputation reached far and wide.'[137] Ibn Masᶜud is quoted several times as holding ᶜAlqama's recitation of the Quran in high esteem. He actually appointed ᶜAlqama his teaching assistant.[138] The two scholars used to gather people outside the gates of the Kinda cemetery in Kufa, arranging them in two rows: Ibn Masᶜud was responsible for teaching the disciples in the first row, while ᶜAlqama was responsible for teaching the disciples in the second row.[139] No doubt, this arrangement indicates that Ibn Masᶜud saw ᶜAlqama as his successor and almost his equal.

So why then was ᶜAbida's version of the framing narrative of the *ḥadīth* of the divine fingers more appealing than ᶜAlqama's? Why is ᶜAbida more present in the narrative of this specific *ḥadīth* than ᶜAlqama? The obvious reason is the way each one understood his role: ᶜAbida was more inclined to *fiqh* and law, and was considered one of the two most knowledgeable qadis among the five disciples of Ibn Masᶜud.[140] While ᶜAbida demonstrated his skills in resolving legal cases independently, ᶜAlqama adhered to the exact wording of Ibn Masᶜud's sayings.[141] In addition, ᶜAlqama's loyalty to Ibn Masᶜud reached such an extent that he actually adopted his master's conduct and manners.[142] In fact, one of their acquaintances declared that seeing ᶜAlqama was as good as seeing Ibn Masᶜud, because ᶜAlqama's conduct was exactly as Ibn Masᶜud's.[143] These textual findings provide the best explanation for ᶜAlqama's dry narrative: he saw no reason to interpret Ibn Masᶜud or, God forbid, to add his wording to Ibn Masᶜud's *ḥadīth*, simply because he mirrored Ibn Masᶜud.

The less obvious reason for the difference between ᶜAbida's version and ᶜAlqama's is ᶜAbida's tempo and emotional baggage. The sources do not explicitly indicate a rivalry between him and ᶜAlqama.[144] However, they describe his complex personality. On the one hand, ᶜAbida was pious and strictly maintained moral conduct. On the other hand, he was a colourful type: bitter, constantly seeking recognition and stature, and perhaps desperately striving to demonstrate his proximity to Ibn Masᶜud. Both ᶜAlqama and ᶜAbida were labelled *tābiᶜūn* by later generations, although their proximity to the Prophet's times is frequently emphasised: ᶜAlqama was born in an unknown year, but during the lifetime of the Prophet.[145] ᶜAbida, who was probably ᶜAlqama's senior, converted to Islam while living in Yemen two years before the Prophet's death. Unfortunately ᶜAbida did not have the opportunity to be close to the Prophet, or even see him.[146] Although the sources do not indicate how old ᶜAbida was when he converted, it is clear that had he met the Prophet, he would have been considered a *ṣaḥābī*.

This failure to be a *ṣaḥābī* could serve as a legitimate explanation for ᶜAbida's thirst for recognition and stature, as reflected in the following anecdote: one day, a group of people who had a long-standing feud between them came to ᶜAbida and asked him to serve as their arbiter. ᶜAbida, who was both a qadi and the head (*ᶜarīf*) of his tribe, the Banu Murad,[147] refused to resolve the matter unless they appointed him as an *amīr*. The historian Ibn Saᶜd (d. 845), with a distinct disapproving note, remarked on this incident: 'It was as if he thought that an *amīr* has an advantage in this kind of business over a qadi or anyone else, for that matter.'[148] This criticism is however toned down by a handful of anecdotes depicting ᶜAbida as pious, modest and humble. When one of his tribesmen prophesised that ᶜAbida would be resurrected even before the Day of Resurrection, and would be seen carrying a banner and leading an army to unprecedented victory, ᶜAbida humbly replied: 'If God was to resurrect me twice and let me perish twice before the Day of Resurrection, He would not have wished me well.'[149] In other words, I thank you for the compliment, but it is inappropriate to attribute such stature to me. As depicted in the sources, ᶜAbida's personality is more energetic and colourful than ᶜAlqama's. Placing himself in the framing narrative, even as a mere observer, indeed served ᶜAbida's thirst for recognition. Compared to him, ᶜAlqama was a solemn and strict narrator who saw no reason to place himself in the narrative, because he believed that his duty was to faithfully narrate what he had heard.

ᶜAbida's and ᶜAlqama's are not the only versions of the *ḥadīth* of the divine fingers. Different versions of this *ḥadīth*, with different degrees of elaboration, were circulated through other channels of transmission (with *ṣaḥāba* like Ibn ᶜAbbas, Abu Hurayra and ᶜAᵓisha as first narrators); however ᶜAbida's and ᶜAlqama's versions were the most widely cited.[150]

Table 1.2

	ᶜAbida's version[151]	ᶜAlqama's version[152]
The framing narrative – opening section	On the authority of ᶜAbida, on the authority of ᶜAbd Allah who said: a man from the People of the Book came – [ᶜAbida] said: I think that he (i.e. ᶜAbd Allah ibn Masᶜud) said that he was a Jew or a Christian – to the Messenger of God, and said:	On the authority of ᶜAlqama, on the authority of ᶜAbd Allah who said: a man from the People of the Book came to the Messenger of God, and said:
The embedded narrative	On the Day of Resurrection, Allah, may His praise be high, will place **the sky and the earth** on one finger, **the mountains and the trees** on one finger, and **the water and the moist earth** on one finger, and say: I am the king. [ᶜAbida] said: I think that he (i.e. ᶜAbd Allah ibn Masᶜud) said this twice.	Oh, Abu 'l-Qasim! God created (*khalaqa*) **the sky** [so it is placed] on one finger, **the earth** [is placed] on one finger, **the trees** on one finger, **the moist earth** on one finger, and **the creatures** on one finger. Then He said: I am the king!
The framing narrative – closing section	And the Messenger of God laughed until his molars were revealed, then he quoted the following verse: 'They underrate the might of God' (Q. 39:67)	And I saw the Messenger of God laugh until his molars were revealed, then he quoted: 'They underrate the might of God' (Q. 39:67)

The difference between ᶜAbida's and ᶜAlqama's versions is also apparent in the embedded narrative (see Table 1.2).

The embedded narrative is actually quite unusual, because the person who transmits the theological message is not the Prophet. In ᶜAbida's version, the Jewish rabbi or the Christian priest assumes a position of a teacher, who lectures to the Prophet. In the closing section of the framing narrative we learn that the Prophet was familiar with the scene that this scholar described. The Prophet laughs as a sign that he recognised the transmitted content. The meaning of this laughter is explained in the narrative. One may think that the Prophet mocked the foreign scholar, because the verse that the Prophet quoted refers to the ignorance of the heretics regarding God's mightiness. However, the verse actually corroborates the description of the foreign scholar: 'But on the Day of Resurrection He will hold the entire earth in His grasp and fold up the heavens in His right hand.' (Q. 39:67; for more on the *ḥadīth* of the divine fingers, see Chapter 5).

ᶜAlqama's version does not refer to the Day of Resurrection, but to the creation of the world; however, quoting the verse in the closing section of the framing narrative connects it to the eschatological events. The verb *khalaqa*, 'created', seems out of place. No wonder, then, that another variation to ᶜAlqama's version replaces this verb with the verb *yumsiku*, 'holds': God holds the sky by one finger, the earth by another, and so on.[153] ᶜAlqama's version reflects a fully confident narrator: there is no sign of hesitation and the formidable picture is well-balanced and complete, because God is described as having five fingers. According to ᶜAbida, God has three fingers (or, at least, three fingers are described in this scene). However, there are apparently two additional later versions that are attributed to ᶜAbida. These versions correct the scene to include five divine fingers. In fact, these later versions are almost identical to ᶜAlqama's version.[154]

The difference between these almost identical versions again reverts to ᶜAbida as a narrator: ᶜAbida enriched the embedded narrative by describing the way in which God will shake the creation on the Day of Resurrection.[155] In an almost identical version, he explains the reason for the Prophet's laughter, quoting Ibn Masᶜud as saying: 'And I saw the Messenger of God laughing until his molars were revealed as a sign of his approval to his (the rabbi's) words (*taṣdīqan lahu*).'[156] Another version, which reflects ᶜAbida's personality as a narrator, contains explanatory sentences that interpret the Prophet's reaction to the audience:

> On the authority of ᶜAbida al-Salmani [who recounted] on the authority of ᶜAbd Allah ibn Masᶜud: a rabbi came to the Prophet and said: 'Oh Muhammad!' or [he said]: 'Oh Abu 'l-Qasim! On the Day of Resurrection, God will hold the skies by one finger, the layer of earth by one finger, the mountains and the trees by one finger, the water and the moist earth by one finger, and the rest of creation by one finger, **and then He will shake them** and say: I am the king! I am the king!' **Astonished from what the rabbi said**, the Messenger of God laughed. **[By his laughter], he confirmed and approved what the rabbi said**. Then he recited: 'They underrate the might of God. But on the Day of Resurrection He will hold the entire earth in His

grasp and fold up the heavens in His right hand. Glory be to Him! Exalted be He above their idols! (Q. 39:67)'.[157]

The *ḥadīth* of the divine fingers – with its different variants and two competing versions – demonstrates the complexity of the role of the narrator in the building of the narrative. A close reading of the different voices in the single narrative brings to the surface the issue of the narrator's role. The original narrator of this *ḥadīth* was presumably the *ṣaḥābī* ᶜAbd Allah ibn Masᶜud. In this framing narrative, Ibn Masᶜud narrates in the first person the event he witnessed during the lifetime of the Prophet. The use of the first person constructs the narrative as the reliable testimony of the historical ᶜAbd Allah ibn Masᶜud. The narrator also used the first person when he quoted the dialogue between a Jewish rabbi and the Prophet. The narrator cited the words of the Jewish rabbi in direct speech, described the Prophet's response (laughter until his molars were revealed) and concluded the narrative with the Prophet's words, which were in fact a citation of a Quranic verse. In the two versions of the present *ḥadīth*, ᶜAbd Allah ibn Masᶜud was both a narrator of and a witness to the event.

The narrator, we can easily agree, is the one who tells the story, and it is his voice that we hear.[158] In the case of the *ḥadīth* of the divine fingers, two different narrators, ᶜAlqama and ᶜAbida, claimed to faithfully transmit the narrative of the historical ᶜAbd Allah ibn Masᶜud. We find a similar transmission in Abu Musa al-Ashᶜari's *ḥadīth* of the beatific vision (*ḥadīth al-ruʾya*) and his *ḥadīth* of the sacrifice (*ḥadīth al-fidāʾ*), and Umm Salama's *ḥadīth* on the two fingers of the Merciful: Abu Musa al-Ashᶜari's son, Abu Burda, claimed to and even swore to have faithfully transmitted his father's story, while Shahr ibn Hawshab testified that he transmitted (accurately, we may presume) the story of Umm Salama. But is it indeed possible to accurately transmit someone's story?

By recounting Ibn Masᶜud's story, his disciples brought forward both his voice and their different voices. ᶜAlqama adopted Ibn Masᶜud's voice, so his narrative was possibly a faithful representation of Ibn Masᶜud's narrative. ᶜAbida, on the other hand, took a step forward, and placed himself in the narrative. ᶜAbida's narrative reflects hesitation about his recollection of what Ibn Masᶜud had actually said. This hesitation adds to the credibility of ᶜAbida as narrator, and we are willing to believe that he indeed was among Ibn Masᶜud's disciples when Ibn Masᶜud told them his story. ᶜAbida highlighted his position as a passive disciple as he observed Ibn Masᶜud recollect an event Ibn Masᶜud had witnessed. By conveying his hesitations and efforts in recollecting what Ibn Masᶜud had actually said, ᶜAbida offered a different style of transmission or narration than his colleague ᶜAlqama. While ᶜAlqama performed as Ibn Masᶜud, ᶜAbida distinguished himself from Ibn Masᶜud and presented himself as an 'intervening narrator', a narrator who sought to explain and expand, and who intentionally left his mark on the narrative.[159] ᶜAlqama and ᶜAbida are in fact two representations of the classical distinction between mimesis and diegesis, between showing and telling.[160] Still, both narrators, regardless of their involvement and presence in the text, are considered responsible for the shaping of the text.[161]

The Hadith scholar al-Darimi labelled the *ḥadīth* of the divine fingers as 'Ibn Masᶜud's *ḥadīth* about the five fingers'.[162] Al-Darimi used this title to differentiate it from the *ḥadīth* about the two fingers of the Merciful. By doing so, al-Darimi implicitly stated that Ibn Masᶜud, who is named in the narrative as the 'original' narrator, is indeed the creator of this literary text. The different versions of Ibn Masᶜud's two disciples suggested that the literary text of the *ḥadīth* of the divine fingers was shaped and formed, first and foremost, by his two prominent disciples. However, because later links in the *isnād* or later *muḥaddithūn* participated in the transmission process, we can assume that each link contributed to the re-shaping and re-forming of the narrative. The role of the narrator, the *rāwī*, and the question of re-shaping and processing the text accompany us in Chapter 2 of this book.

Notes

1. The almost single exception is Daniel Gimaret's *Dieu à l'image de l'homme*, which provides French translations to anthropomorphic *aḥādīth*. Divided into themes (God's hand, leg, throne, etc.), this book is practically a reproduction of thematic Hadith compilations. Gimaret does not provide literary analysis of the texts, but is satisfied with providing bibliographical notes on the Hadith transmitters and clarifying notes on theological terms.
2. Motzki, 'Introduction', p. li. One should also mention Stefan Sperl's literary

analysis of tales in the Hadith where he methodically uses Gérard Genette's terminology of 'shell' and 'core': Sperl, 'Man's "Hollow Core"', p. 477.

3. Motzki, 'Introduction', p. li.
4. This is the definition of H. Porter Abbott, *The Cambridge Introduction to Narrative*, p. 13.
5. El Calamawy, 'Narrative Elements in the *Ḥadīth* Literature', p. 309.
6. Bal, *Narratology*, p. 3.
7. Beaumont, 'Hard-Boiled', p. 5.
8. A concise version of the theoretical section of Günther's 1998 article is Günther, 'Modern Literary Theory', pp. 171–6.
9. Günther, 'Fictional Narration', p. 439.
10. Günther, 'Fictional Narration', p. 437, footnote 9.
11. Cf. Genette, *Fiction and Diction*, pp. 54–84.
12. The need for a combined approach towards Hadith was persuasively articulated by Recep Senturk in his *Narrative Social Structure (*2005). Senturk presents persuasive arguments against one of the trends in narratological studies: the insistence on isolating the narrative from its social context. Instead, Senturk offers a combined approach of examining narratives and social patterns: Senturk, *Narrative Social Structure*, pp. 73–93.
13. Abbott, *The Cambridge Introduction to Narrative*, pp. 12, 15.
14. Brown, *Hadith*, p. 53.
15. See especially Leder, 'The Literary Use', pp. 307–15.
16. Abbott, *The Cambridge Introduction to Narrative*, 25–7; Bal, *Narratology*, pp. 44–55. Note that Marston Speight uses the term 'circumstantial introduction' for 'framing narrative': Speight, 'Narrative Structures', p. 265. Speight's method of classifying Hadith (two-, three- and four-part narratives) is an exception to the general trends in literary analysis.
17. Bal, *Narratology*, pp. 52–5.
18. Al-Ājurrī, *Kitāb al-Sharīᶜa*, pp. 270–2, *aḥādīth* 584–91a.
19. Al-Ājurrī, *Kitāb al-Sharīᶜa*, pp. 271–2, *ḥadīth* 589.
20. For the role of the teachings attributed to Ibn ᶜAbbas in building a collective Islamic memory, see Berg, 'The *Isnād*', pp. 268–77.
21. Al-Ājurrī, *Kitāb al-Sharīᶜa*, p. 328, *ḥadīth* 721. Al-Ajurri quotes several versions. For a discussion on the *isnāds* of the various versions of this tradition, and a consideration of their authenticity, see Melchert, 'God Created Adam', pp. 114–18.
22. Günther defines the prototype of dicta as 'short *aḥādīth*': the words of the

Prophet transmitted by eyewitnesses or eavesdroppers without any interpretation or comment of the transmitter: Günther, 'Fictional Narration', p. 440.

23. As quoted in Abbott, *The Cambridge Introduction to Narrative*, p. 14.
24. Günther, 'Fictional Narration', p. 440.
25. For the presence of the original narrator in the *matn* of traditions from the *maghāzī* type, see Günther, 'Modern Literary Theory', p. 174. In the *akhbār* narratives, by contrast, the narrator is absent from the narrative: Leder, 'The Literary Use', pp. 307–9.
26. For the uncertainty of his death dates, see al-Dhahabī, *Siyar Aᶜlām al-Nubalāʾ*, vol. 2, pp. 397–8.
27. Al-Ājurrī, *Kitāb al-Sharīᶜa*, pp. 341–2, *aḥādīth* 760–3.
28. Al-Ājurrī, *Kitāb al-Sharīᶜa*, p. 274, *aḥādīth* 596–8.
29. Al-Ājurrī, *Kitāb al-Sharīᶜa*, pp. 276–7, *aḥādīth* 602–4.
30. Al-Ājurrī, *Kitāb al-Sharīᶜa*, p. 278, *ḥadīth* 607, p. 279, *ḥadīth* 609.
31. Al-Ājurrī, *Kitāb al-Sharīᶜa*, pp. 279–80, *ḥadīth* 610.
32. Al-Ājurrī, *Kitāb al-Sharīᶜa*, p. 280, *ḥadīth* 612.
33. Al-Ājurrī, *Kitāb al-Sharīᶜa*, pp. 280–1, *ḥadīth* 613.
34. Leder, 'The Literary Use', p. 308.
35. Beaumont, 'Hard-Boiled', pp. 14–17.
36. Al-Ājurrī, *Kitāb al-Sharīᶜa*, p. 331, *ḥadīth* 730.
37. Al-Dhahabi records the dispute regarding Shahr's year of death: al-Dhahabī, *Siyar Aᶜlām al-Nubalāʾ*, vol. 4, p. 378 (the biography of Shahr).
38. Al-Ājurrī, *Kitāb al-Sharīᶜa*, pp. 330–1, *ḥadīth* 729.
39. Shahr was present at Umm Salama's house when the news of the death of Husayn ibn ᶜAli reached her, shortly before her death: al-Dhahabī, *Siyar Aᶜlām al-Nubalāʾ*, vol. 3, p. 318.
40. Al-Dhahabi claimed that Shahr started studying Hadith in Hijri year 50 (AD 670): al-Dhahabī, *Siyar Aᶜlām al-Nubalāʾ*, vol. 4, p. 378. Shahr's date of birth is marked somewhere during the reign of ᶜUthman (between 644 and 655).
41. Al-Dhahabī, *Siyar Aᶜlām al-Nubalāʾ*, vol. 2, p. 210. This anecdote indicates that Shahr intended to systematically collect material from Umm Salama; yet, solely due to her advanced age the project did not come to fruition. This anecdote also explains why Umm Salama's material attracted no particular proponents. Cf. Lucas, *Constructive Critics*, p. 334.
42. Al-Ājurrī, *Kitāb al-Sharīᶜa*, p. 331, *aḥādīth* 731–2.
43. Al-Ājurrī, *Kitāb al-Sharīᶜa*, p. 321 (a summary of *aḥādīth* by Abū Bakr

al-Ājurrī). For the list of the *ṣaḥāba* who transmitted versions of *ḥadīth al-nuzūl*, see al-Dāraquṭnī, *al-Nuzūl*, pp. 84–5.

44. Al-Ājurrī, *Kitāb al-Sharīᶜa*, p. 321, *ḥadīth* 699. For a French translation, see Gimaret, *Dieu à l'image de l'homme*, pp. 90–102.
45. The traditions attributed to al-Agharr Abu Muslim were circulated only among the Kufan *muḥaddithūn*. Al-Agharr was Abu Hurayra's slave: Ibn Ḥajar, *Tahdhīb*, vol. 1, p. 185; vol. 2, p. 69.
46. Al-Ājurrī, *Kitāb al-Sharīᶜa*, pp. 322–3, *aḥādīth* 702–6; Ibn Khuzayma, *Kitāb al-Tawḥīd*, pp. 290–302, *aḥādīth* 1–17.
47. Both names (Qudayd and al-Kadid) appear in the sources: Ibn Manẓūr, *Lisān al-ᶜArab*, vol. 5, p. 3544 (*q.d.d*), p. 3834 (*k.d.d*).
48. Al-Ājurrī, *Kitāb al-Sharīᶜa*, pp. 323–5, *aḥādīth* 709–12.
49. Al-Baghawī, *Muᶜjam al-Ṣaḥāba*, vol. 2, p. 342.
50. Ibn Khuzayma, *Kitāb al-Tawḥīd*, pp. 312–15, *ḥadīth* 36. Three distorted versions appear in al-Ṭabarānī, *al-Muᶜjam al-Kabīr*, vol. 5, pp. 49–51, *aḥādīth* 4556–9.
51. The connection between narrativity and the illusion of authenticity is demonstrated in Leder, 'The Literary Use', pp. 307–9. See also Günther, 'Fictional Narration', p. 447.
52. Abbott, *The Cambridge Introduction to Narrative*, p. 193.
53. The only *ḥadīth al-ṣifāt* that depicts a scene that occurs in Mecca is the *ḥadīth* of the mountain goats (*ḥadīth al-awᶜāl*): al-Ājurrī, *Kitāb al-Sharīᶜa*, pp. 305–6, *ḥadīth* 665. This *ḥadīth* is discussed in Holtzman and Ovadia, 'On Divine Aboveness' (forthcoming).
54. Most of these versions (if not all of them) were meticulously collected by the Hadith scholar ᶜAli ibn ᶜUmar al-Daraqutni (d. 995): al-Dāraquṭnī, *Kitāb al-Ruʾya*, pp. 91–361.
55. Ibn Ḥanbal, *Musnad*, vol. 32, pp. 422–4, *ḥadīth* 19654; al-Dārimī, *Radd*, p. 92, *ḥadīth* 180. For a French translation, see: Gimaret, *Dieu à l'image de l'homme*, p. 268. Abu Saᶜid al-Darimi is mentioned in Ibn Abi Yaᶜla's *Ṭabaqāt al-Ḥanābila* as one of the early Hanbalites; however, it is more likely that he was not associated with the Hanbalites: Ibn Abī Yaᶜlā, *Ṭabaqāt al-fuqahāʾ al-Ḥanābila*, vol. 1, p. 312, biographical entry 298. Still, his treatises were extensively studied and quoted by later Hanbalites. See, for example, Ibn Qayyim al-Jawziyya and Ibn al-Mawṣilī, *Mukhtaṣar al-Ṣawāᶜiq*, p. 1743 (index).
56. Al-Ājurrī, *Kitāb al-Sharīᶜa*, p. 279, *ḥadīth* 608; Ibn Khuzayma, *Kitāb*

al-Tawḥīd, pp. 577–8, *ḥadīth* 340. For the place of *Kitāb al-Tawḥīd* in the traditionalistic curriculum, see Chapter 5.

57. Al-Ājurrī, *Kitāb al-Sharīᶜa*, pp. 279–82, *ḥadīth* 610, *ḥadīth* 612.
58. Muslim ibn Ḥajjāj, *Ṣaḥīḥ*, pp. 100–2, *ḥadīth* 302 (*Kitāb al-Īmān, bāb maᶜrifat ṭarīq al-ruʾya*); al-Bukhārī, *Ṣaḥīḥ*, vol. 3, p. 217, *ḥadīth* 4581 (*Kitāb al-tafsīr, bāb inna Allāh lā yaẓlimu mithqāla dharratin*), vol. 4, pp. 391–2, *ḥadīth* 7439 (*Kitāb al-Tafsīr, bāb wujūhun yawmaʾidhin nāḍiratun ilā rabbihā nāẓiratun)*.
59. Al-Ājurrī, *Kitāb al-Sharīᶜa*, p. 279, *ḥadīth* 608; Ibn Ḥanbal, *Musnad*, vol. 32, pp. 422–4, *ḥadīth* 19654; Ibn Khuzayma, *Kitāb al-Tawḥīd*, pp. 577–8, *ḥadīth* 340; al-Dārimī, *Radd*, p. 92, *ḥadīth* 180; Gimaret, *Dieu à l'image de l'homme*, p. 268.
60. An example of what is perhaps the longest eschatological narrative some parts of which correspond with Abu Musa al-Ashᶜari's *ḥadīth al-ruʾya* is a *ḥadīth* attributed to ᶜAbd Allah ibn Masᶜud: al-Suyūṭī, *al-Durr*, vol. 14, pp. 649–54 (interpretation of Q. 68:42); al-Ājurrī, *Kitāb al-Sharīᶜa*, pp. 279–80, *ḥadīth* 610. This material is analysed in Holtzman, 'Does God Really Laugh?', pp. 179–82.
61. Chapman, *Story and Discourse*, p. 59.
62. For the meaning of God's laughter, see Holtzman, 'Does God Really Laugh?', pp. 183–4.
63. In western literature, the future tense is regarded odd for narration; in religious discourse, much less so. Fludernik, 'Narratology and Literary Linguistics', pp. 90–3.
64. Fludernik, 'Narratology and Literary Linguistics', pp. 87–90.
65. *Wa-qad dhahaba al-nās* is a double entendre. It means 'the people went', but also 'the people were perished'.
66. On the translation of *yawma yukshafu ᶜan sāqin* (Q. 68:42) into English, see the Introduction to Chapter 5, note 11.
67. Al-Ājurrī, *Kitāb al-Sharīᶜa*, p. 278, *ḥadīth* 607. For a different version, see al-Ājurrī, *Kitāb al-taṣdīq*, p. 80; al-Ṭabarānī, *Al-Muᶜjam al-Kabīr*, vol. 9, p. 418.
68. A representative *ḥadīth* is attributed to the *ṣaḥābī* Abu Saᶜid al-Khudri: al-Suyūṭī, *Durr*, vol. 14, p. 642 (interpretation of Q. 68:42). For other *aḥādīth* in the same vein, see al-Suyūṭī, *Durr*, vol. 14, pp. 642–57.
69. Al-Suyūṭī, *Durr*, vol. 14, p. 643.
70. Al-Ājurrī, *Kitāb al-Sharīᶜa*, pp. 279–80, *ḥadīth* 610. The longest version of

this *ḥadīth* appears in al-Suyūṭī, *Durr*, vol. 14, pp. 649–54 (interpretation of Q. 68:42).

71. Al-Dāraquṭnī, *Kitāb al-Ruʾya*, pp. 91–4. The same version appears in Muslim, *Ṣaḥīḥ*, pp. 100–2, *ḥadīth* 302 (*Kitāb al-Īmān, bāb maʿrifat ṭarīq al-ruʾya*). Different parts of this *ḥadīth* appear in *Ṣaḥīḥ al-Bukhārī* in several places: al-Bukhārī, *Ṣaḥīḥ*, vol. 3, p. 217, *ḥadīth* 4581 (*Kitāb al-Tafsīr, bāb inna Allāh lā yaẓlimu mithqāla dharratin*), vol. 4, pp. 391–2, *ḥadīth* 7439 (*Kitāb al-Tafsīr, bāb wujūhun yawmaʾidhin nāḍiratun ilā rabbihā nāẓirathun*).
72. Muslim, *Ṣaḥīḥ*, p. 1107, *ḥadīth* 2766 (*Kitāb al-tawba, bāb qabūl tawbat al-qātil*). Abu Bakr al-Bayhaqi (d. 1066) compiled a substantial number of versions in *Shuʿab al-ʾĪmān*, vol. 1, pp. 579–86. For further reference to other Hadith compilations, see Ibn Ḥanbal, *Musnad*, vol. 32, pp. 230–3 (in the footnotes).
73. Sacrifice: *fidāʾ*. In another version: *fikāk*, that is, ransom.
74. Muslim, *Ṣaḥīḥ*, p. 1107, *ḥadīth* 2766 (49), (*Kitāb al-tawba, bāb qabūl tawbat al-qātil*); al-Bayhaqī, *Shuʿab al-ʾĪmān*, vol. 1, p. 579.
75. Al-Bayhaqī, *Shuʿab al-ʾĪmān*, vol. 1, p. 582.
76. Ibn Manjuwayh, *Rijāl Ṣaḥīḥ Muslim*, vol. 1, p. 247.
77. Al-Dārimī, *Radd*, p. 92, *ḥadīth* 180; al-Ājurrī, *Kitāb al-Sharīʿa*, p. 278, *ḥadīth* 607; ʿAbd Allāh ibn Aḥmad, *al-Sunna*, p. 252, *ḥadīth* 463.
78. Al-Dārimī, *Radd*, p. 92, *ḥadīth* 180; al-Ājurrī, *Kitāb al-Sharīʿa*, p. 278, *ḥadīth* 607; ʿAbd Allāh ibn Aḥmad, *al-Sunna*, p. 252, *ḥadīth* 463.
79. Al-Bukhārī, *Tārīkh*, vol. 6, p. 447 (the biography of Abu Burda).
80. Upon arrival to Damascus, ʿUmar lived in his modest house which was situated between the vegetable market and the cheese market: Ibn ʿAsākir, *Tārīkh Dimashq*, vol. 26, p. 43 (the biography of Abu Burda). In the year 717, the caliph Sulayman died and ʿUmar was proclaimed caliph. The influential advisor, Rajaʾ ibn Haywa al-Kindi, asked ʿUmar thereupon whether he planned to move in the palace. ʿUmar replied: 'The family of Abu Ayyub (Sulayman) still occupies it. My pavilion (*fusṭāṭ*) suffices until they move out.' He remained in his humble *fusṭāṭ* until the family of Sulayman left the palace: al-Ṭabarī, *Tārīkh*, vol. 6, p. 553 (the events of Hijri year 99).
81. Al-Ājurrī, *Kitāb al-Sharīʿa*, p. 278, *ḥadīth* 607.
82. Al-Ājurrī, *Kitāb al-Sharīʿa*, p. 278, *ḥadīth* 607.
83. On the term 'internal logic', see Bal, *Narratology*, p. 7.
84. On 'the object of the narrator's activity', see Bal, *Narratology*, p. 17.
85. Abu Burda's name is repeated dozens of times in Ahmad ibn Hanbal's *Musnad*,

and especially in volume 32, pp. 230–533, which quotes a collection of *aḥādīth* on the authority of Abu Musa al-Ashᶜari. Several anecdotes collected by Ibn ᶜAsakir describe Abu Burda writing a *ḥadīth* that he heard from his father. His father erased the material with water, and demanded that his son recite the Hadith by heart: Ibn ᶜAsākir, *Tārīkh Dimashq*, vol. 26, pp. 54–6 (the biography of Abu Burda). As a source of knowledge about the Prophet, Abu Musa was the most prolific Kufan after ᶜAbd Allah ibn Masᶜud and ᶜAli: Lucas, *Constructive Critics*, p. 337.

86. Al-Dārimī, *Radd*, p. 92, *ḥadīth* 180.
87. See Ibn Hajar's remark regarding his death date: Ibn Ḥajar, *Tahdhīb*, vol. 2, p. 8.
88. Ibn Ḥanbal, *Musnad*, vol. 32, p. 234. See also the same remark as transmitted by Qatada (d. 735): Muslim, *Ṣaḥīḥ*, pp. 1107–8, *ḥadīth* 2766. (*Kitāb al-tawba, bāb qabūl tawbat al-qātil*).
89. Ibn Ḥanbal, *Musnad*, vol. 32, pp. 231–2 (in the footnotes).
90. See his report in the first person in Ibn ᶜAsākir, *Tārīkh Dimashq*, vol. 43, p. 333.
91. Al-Dāraquṭnī, *ᶜIlal*, vol. 7, pp. 205–6. See also a detailed footnote by the editors Ibrahim al-ᶜAli and Ahmad al-Rifaᶜi in al-Dāraquṭnī, *Kitāb al-Ruᵓya*, pp. 153–4, *ḥadīth* 39; Ibn Ḥanbal, *Musnad*, vol. 32, p.423, footnote 4.
92. ᶜAbd Allāh ibn Aḥmad, *al-Sunna*, p. 229, *ḥadīth* 411.
93. Ibn Ḥanbal, *Musnad*, vol. 32, p. 425, *ḥadīth* 19655 (the *Musnad* of Abu Musa al-Ashᶜari).
94. ᶜAbd Allah heard this *ḥadīth* from the *muḥaddithūn* ᶜIsa ibn Salim Abu Saᶜid al-Shashiᶜ (d. 847) and Muhammad ibn Ishaq al-Daghani (d. 884): Abd Allāh ibn Aḥmad, *al-Sunna*, pp. 252–3, *aḥādīth* 463–4.
95. Muslim, *Ṣaḥīḥ*, pp. 1107–8, *ḥadīth* 2766 (50) (*Kitāb al-Tawba, bāb qabūl tawbat al-qātil*).
96. Ibn ᶜAsākir, *Tārīkh Dimashq*, vol. 21, p. 166; vol. 25, p. 134; vol. 26, p. 47; vol. 49, pp. 301–2; vol. 52, p. 25.
97. I do not discuss the following versions: Ibn ᶜAsākir, *Tārīkh Dimashq*, vol. 60, p. 103 (the biography of Muqatil ibn Hayyan) and Ibn ᶜAsākir, *Tārīkh Dimashq*, vol. 52, p. 25 (the biography of Muhammad ibn Ishaq).
98. Ibn ᶜAsākir, *Tārīkh Dimashq*, vol. 21, p. 166.
99. Ibn Ḥanbal, *Musnad*, vol. 32, pp. 375–6, *ḥadīth* 196000.
100. Ibn ᶜAsākir, *Tārīkh Dimashq*, vol. 26, p. 47 (the biography of Abu Burda).
101. Ibn Ḥanbal, *Musnad*, vol. 32, pp. 375–6, *ḥadīth* 19600.

102. Ibn ᶜAsākir, *Tārīkh Dimashq*, vol. 25, pp. 134–5 (the biography of Talha ibn Yahya Talha ibn ᶜUbayd Allah).
103. For a summary of the controversy, see Heck, 'The Epistemological Problem of Writing', pp. 85–114.
104. Ibn Abī Ḥātim, *al-Jarḥ wa'l-taᶜdīl*, vol. 7, pp. 127–8; Ibn Ḥabbān, *al-Thiqāt*, vol. 7, p. 341.
105. Abbott, *The Cambridge Introduction to Narrative*, pp. 58–66. Abbott also addresses the reading experience of a narrative that lacks a closure.
106. Leder, 'The Literary Use', pp. 307–9.
107. Ibn ᶜAsākir, *Tārīkh Dimashq*, vol. 49, pp. 301–2.
108. Judd, *Religious Scholars*, p. 169; Schacht, 'Abū Burda', *EI2*, vol. 1, pp. 693–4; Ibn ᶜAbd Rabbihi, *al-ᶜIqd al-Farīd*, vol. 6, p. 168; Ibn Khallikān, *Wafayāt*, vol. 3, pp. 10–12.
109. Ibn Khallikān, *Wafayāt*, vol. 3, p. 11; al-Ṣafadī, *al-Wāfī*, vol. 16, p. 337. Cf. Baron de Slane's translation in *Ibn Khallikan's Biographical Dictionary*, vol. 2, p. 3.
110. Usually, Abu Tayba, a client of Banu Haritha from *al-anṣār*, is named in the sources as the one who regularly cupped the Prophet: Ibn Saᶜd, *Ṭabaqāt*, vol. 1, pp. 381–5 (*dhikr ḥijāmat rasūl Allāh*).
111. Al-Dhahabī, *Siyar Aᶜlām al-Nubalāᵓ*, vol. 4, p. 345; Ibn ᶜAsākir, *Tārīkh Dimashq*, vol. 26, pp. 57–8.
112. See, for example, al-Ṭabarānī, *al-Muᶜjam al-Kabīr*, vol. 22, p. 377; Ibn ᶜAsākir, *Tabyīn*, p. 88. Shuᶜayb al-Arnaᵓut and Husayn al-Asad indicate that these *aḥādīth* were considered weak, and provide several references to historical sources and marginal Hadith compilations which quote them: al-Dhahabī, *Siyar Aᶜlām al-Nubalāᵓ*, vol. 4, p. 345, footnote 1 (the biography of Abu Burda).
113. Abbott, *The Cambridge Introduction*, p. 27. This is a word invented by Genette: Bal, *Narratology*, pp. 60–1.
114. Harald Motzki's *isnād-cum-matn* method requires the collection of all possible versions of a single *ḥadīth* in as many sources as possible, dissecting the narrative elements from these versions, reconstructing the earliest version, and identifying the responsible narrator (the 'Common Link'). For a description of this method, see Motzki, 'Dating Muslim Traditions', pp. 250–2. For a coherent implementation of this method, see Görke, 'The Historical Tradition', pp. 241–68.
115. See, for example, Josef van Ess's contextualised approach to *aḥādīth* on pre-

determination in van Ess, *Zwischen Ḥadīṯ und Theologie.* Wesley Williams' dissertation also applies a contextualised approach to anthropomorphic Hadith material. Two recently published articles of Christopher Melchert combine *isnād* analysis with the investigation of the theological doctrines: Melchert, 'God Created Adam' and 'The Early Controversy'.

116. Al-Ājurrī, *Kitāb al-Sharīᶜa*, p. 332, *ḥadīth* 736; al-Ṭabarī, *Jāmiᶜ al-Bayān*, vol. 20, p. 248 (commentary on Q. 39:67). The *ḥadīth* and its versions appear in all six canonical Hadith compilations and are frequently quoted in theological treatises on the divine attributes. See, for example, Muslim, *Ṣaḥīḥ Muslim*, p. 1121, *ḥadīth* 2786 (*Kitāb Ṣifat al-Qiyāma*). The first part of the quoted verse 'They underrate the might of God' also appears in Q. 6:91.
117. Al-Ājurrī, *Kitāb al-Sharīᶜa*, p. 333, *ḥadīth* 737; Ibn Khuzayma, *Kitāb al-Tawḥīd*, p. 896, *ḥadīth* 607.
118. Al-Ṭabarī, *Jāmiᶜ al-Bayān*, vol. 20, p. 248 (commentary on Q. 39:67).
119. Al-Ṭabarī, *Jāmiᶜ al-Bayān*, vol. 20, p. 249 (commentary on Q. 39:67).
120. Al-Ājurrī, *Kitāb al-Sharīᶜa*, p. 333, *ḥadīth* 738; al-Ṭabarī, *Jāmiᶜ al-Bayān*, vol. 20, p. 248.
121. Al-Ājurrī, *Kitāb al-Sharīᶜa*, p. 334, *ḥadīth* 739; Ibn Khuzayma, *Kitāb al-Tawḥīd*, p. 896, *ḥadīth* 607.
122. Al-Dāraquṭnī, *ᶜIlal*, vol. 5, pp. 177–82.
123. Al-Ājurrī, *Kitāb al-Sharīᶜa*, p. 334, *ḥadīth* 739.
124. Ibn Khuzayma, *Kitāb al-Tawḥīd*, p. 896, *ḥadīth* 607; Muslim, *Ṣaḥīḥ*, p. 1121, *ḥadīth* 2786 (*Kitāb Ṣifat al-Qiyāma*).
125. Al-Ājurrī, *Kitāb al-Sharīᶜa*, p. 334, *ḥadīth* 739.
126. Dupriez, *A Dictionary of Literary Devices*, p. 437.
127. In *Ṣaḥīḥ Muslim*, the version attributed to ᶜAbida does not contain the hesitation marker and is similar to the version of ᶜAlqama: Muslim, *Ṣaḥīḥ*, p. 1121, *ḥadīth* 2785 (*Kitāb Ṣifat al-Qiyāma*).
128. Ibn al-Athīr, *Usd al-Ghāba*, vol. 3, p. 546; al-Dhahabī, *Tadhkirat al-Ḥuffāẓ*, vol. 1, pp. 48, 50.
129. Al-Mizzī, *Tahdhīb al-Kamāl*, vol. 20, p. 304.
130. Al-Mizzī, *Tahdhīb al-Kamāl*, vol. 20, p. 304; al-Dhahabī, *Siyar Aᶜlām al-Nubalāʾ*, vol. 4, p. 56.
131. As quoted by Ibn Sirin: 'Some of ᶜAbd Allah [ibn Masᶜud]'s companions preferred ᶜAbida, while others preferred ᶜAlqama. However, all of them unanimously agreed that Shurayh [ibn al-Harith] lagged behind them': al-Dhahabī, *Siyar Aᶜlām al-Nubalāʾ*, vol. 4, p. 43.

132. Al-Dhahabi drew most of his information on ᶜAbida and ᶜAlqama from al-Khaṭīb al-Baghdādī's *Tārīkh Madīnat al-Salām* (ᶜAbida, vol. 12, pp. 422–5; ᶜAlqama, vol. 14, pp. 240–5).
133. Al-Dhahabī, *Siyar Aᶜlām al-Nubalāʾ*, vol. 4, pp. 40–1. On ᶜAbida's stance against writing Hadith, see Cook, 'The Opponents of the Writing', pp. 457–8, 479, 488, 504–5.
134. Al-Dhahabī, *Siyar Aᶜlām al-Nubalāʾ*, vol. 4, p. 53. On ᶜAlqama's stance against writing Hadith, see Cook, 'The Opponents of the Writing', p. 487.
135. Al-Dhahabī, *Siyar Aᶜlām al-Nubalāʾ*, vol. 4, p. 57; al-Mizzī, *Tahdhīb al-Kamāl*, vol. 20, p. 305. Cf. Q. 3:79 *kūnū rabbāniyyin*, 'Be devoted servants of God'. *Rabbānī* was also a Jewish rabbi, although this is the meaning of the word neither in the Quranic text nor in connection to ᶜAlqama. For a thorough discussion on the meaning of *rabbānī*, see also Ibn Qayyim al-Jawziyya, *Miftāḥ*, pp. 150–5.
136. Al-Dhahabī, *Siyar Aᶜlām al-Nubalāʾ*, vol. 4, p. 40.
137. Al-Dhahabī, *Siyar Aᶜlām al-Nubalāʾ*, vol. 4, p. 54.
138. Al-Dhahabī, *Siyar Aᶜlām al-Nubalāʾ*, vol. 4, p. 58.
139. Al-Dhahabī, *Siyar Aᶜlām al-Nubalāʾ*, vol. 4, p. 55.
140. The other one was Shurayh ibn al-Harith, the long-time qadi in Kufa (d. 697–8, at the age of 108): al-Dhahabī, *Tārīkh al-Islām*, vol. 5, p. 420.
141. Al-Dhahabī, *Tārīkh al-Islām*, vol. 5, p. 420.
142. Al-Dhahabī, *Siyar Aᶜlām al-Nubalāʾ*, vol. 4, p. 54.
143. Al-Dhahabī, *Siyar Aᶜlām al-Nubalāʾ*, vol. 4, p. 55.
144. Some of the members of Ibn Masᶜud's school followed ᶜAbida, while others preferred the scholarship of ᶜAlqama: Ibn Saᶜd, *Ṭabaqāt*, vol. 8, p. 214.
145. Al-Dhahabī, *Siyar Aᶜlām al-Nubalāʾ*, vol. 4, p. 53.
146. Al-Dhahabī uses the phrase *wa-lā ṣuḥbata lahu*, which is reserved for Muslims who converted during the Prophet's lifetime, but failed to meet him: al-Dhahabī, *Siyar Aᶜlām al-Nubalāʾ*, vol. 4, p. 40. Muhammad ibn Sirin testified that ᶜAbida told him that he had never seen the Prophet: Ibn Saᶜd, *Ṭabaqāt*, vol. 8, p. 213; al-Dhahabī, *Tārīkh al-Islām*, vol. 5, p. 482.
147. Ibn Saᶜd, *Ṭabaqāt*, vol. 8, p. 213. On the Banu Murad in Kufa, see Morony, *Iraq*, p. 242.
148. Ibn Saᶜd, *Ṭabaqāt*, vol. 8, p. 214.
149. Ibn Saᶜd, *Ṭabaqāt*, vol. 8, p. 215.
150. Al-Bayhaqī, *al-Asmāʾ wa'l-Ṣifāt*, vol. 2, pp. 164–74. Al-Bayhaqi enumerates

all the Hadith compilations and theological treatises known to him that cited these two versions.

151. Al-Ājurrī, *Kitāb al-Sharīʿa*, p. 334, *ḥadīth* 739.
152. Ibn Khuzayma, *Kitāb al-Tawḥīd*, p. 896, *ḥadīth* 607; Muslim, *Ṣaḥīḥ*, p. 1121, *ḥadīth* 2786 (*Kitāb ṣifat al-qiyāma).*
153. Muslim, *Ṣaḥīḥ*, p. 1121, *ḥadīth* 2786 (*Kitāb Ṣifat al-Qiyāma).*
154. Al-Ājurrī, *Kitāb al-Sharīʿa*, p. 333, *aḥādīth* 737, 738.
155. Al-Ājurrī, *Kitāb al-Sharīʿa*, p. 334, *ḥadīth* 739.
156. Al-Ājurrī, *Kitāb al-Sharīʿa*, pp. 332–3, *ḥadīth* 736.
157. Muslim, *Ṣaḥīḥ*, p. 1121, *ḥadīth* 2786 (*Kitāb Ṣifat al-Qiyāma).*
158. Abbott, *The Cambridge Introduction to Narrative*, pp. 238–9; Cuddon, *The Penguin Dictionary of Literary Terms*, pp. 572–3.
159. Chapman, *Story and Discourse*, p. 161.
160. Chapman, *Story and Discourse*, p. 32.
161. Günther, 'Modern Literary Theory', p. 174.
162. Al-Dārimī, *Radd*, p. 60.

2

A Tale of Two Narrators: Some Historical, Geographical and Cultural Considerations

Introduction

The lion's share of the previous chapter was dedicated to an examination of *aḥādīth al-ṣifāt* through the prism of narratology. In the last section of the chapter, we discovered that several narrators participated in shaping the narrative of 'the *ḥadīth* of the divine fingers'. Regarding this *ḥadīth*, we concentrated on the two first links of transmitters in the *isnād*, and the examination was purely literary. In this present chapter, we wish to expand upon the discussion on the narrator and his role, and combine other considerations that were not discussed in Chapter 1. In other words, Chapter 2 offers a combined literary-historical approach to the texts. We do not presume to set a chronology of the texts in question, but we believe that a patient close reading of both the *matn* and the *isnād* can clarify the channels through which the narrative was transmitted from generation to generation.

The two case studies in this chapter are thematically connected to *ḥadīth al-ruʾya*. We chose them because they present the two ends of 'the spectrum of narration', similar although not identical to the dichotomy between ᶜAlqama and ᶜAbida, that is, the difference between mimesis and diegesis, or between showing and telling. This is the starting point of the chapter. The beginning of the chapter provides a general literary analysis of the two versions of *ḥadīth al-ruʾya* and introduces the two narrators: the first narrator, Jarir al-Bajali, minimises his presence in the text to the degree of 'non-narrator'; the second narrator, Abu Razin al-ᶜUqayli, demonstrates an involved narrator who presents himself as the narrative's protagonist. In Section II, we examine the proliferation of Abu Razin's narrative, while combining historical, geographical and cultural considerations in the discussion. Section III presents the interface between Abu Razin and Jarir, while concentrating on the historical Jarir. Section IV discusses the *rāwī* who was responsible for the proliferation of the Jarir narrative. Finally, Section V illuminates the role that Jarir's version of *ḥadīth al-ruʾya* played in the *miḥna*, that is, the procedure of interrogation adopted by the caliph al-Maʾmun (reigned 813–33) and pursued forcefully by his successors, al-Muʿtasim Bi- 'llah (reigned 833–42) and al-Wathiq Bi-'llah (reigned 842–7), against the traditionalistic scholars.

The aim of this chapter is to monitor the paths of two almost identical versions of *ḥadīth al-ruʾya*, and to highlight the different historical, geographical and cultural aspects that are connected to the origin of this *ḥadīth* and its circulation. The focus in this chapter shifts from the supposedly original narrator, namely the *ṣaḥābī* to whom the specific version of *ḥadīth al-ruʾya* is attributed, to later narrators, who actively shaped the narrative, and the environment in which they operated.

I. Two Different Narrators

Questions play an important role in our everyday life; however, we rarely stop to contemplate their significance. We often take for granted that the best way to attain information is to direct questions to authorities of knowledge: yesterday these authorities were our parents and teachers; today it is Google. The American theorist Neil Postman wrote: 'Everything we know has its origin in questions. Questions, we might say, are the principal intellectual instruments available to human beings.'[1] In William Jordan's 1992 book on ancient philosophy, the author observes that 'asking philosophical questions is part of the human condition, and that philosophical questioning arises naturally in the context of everyday life'. He further argues that 'the nature of philosophical questions has not changed much down the ages . . . the main difference between ourselves and the ancients lies not in the questions that we ask . . . but in the answers that we return (or fail to return) to philosophical questions'.[2]

In ancient societies, the dynamics of questions and answers formed the most prominent mechanism of learning. This mechanism was refined and perfected in the discussions between scholars, disciples and even laymen, and was recorded in a variety of religious and didactic works such as polemics, dialogues and practical correspondences.[3] We can safely assume that the pattern of question-answer that appears in these literary works is not merely a rhetorical device, but a crystallised reflection of a real-life exchange of ideas between people.[4]

While asking questions – philosophical or otherwise – is part of the human condition, the great monotheistic religions showed ambivalence regarding questions. On the one hand and as part of their inherent didacticism, the scriptures of these religions presented numerous questions. On the other hand, they discouraged the believers from presenting questions that touch upon the realms of metaphysics and mysticism. An entire body of knowledge remained inaccessible to the laymen and was marked as the intellectual property of those who perceived themselves as the privileged custodians of this knowledge. Accordingly, the scriptures issued a comprehensive warning against meddling with theological issues. The author of the book of Sirach advises his son:

> Things too difficult for you do not seek, and things too strong for you do not scrutinize. The things that have been prescribed for you think about these, for you have no need of hidden matters. With matters greater than your affairs do not meddle, for things beyond human understanding have been shown to you. For their presumption has led many astray, and their evil fancy has diminished their understanding. (Sirach, 3:21–24)[5]

The same idea echoes in the Quranic description of the *mutashābihāt*, the ambiguous verses that mention theological and metaphysical matters, among others. The Quran subtly and indirectly suggests that delving in the meaning of the *mutashābihāt* is undesirable. The Quran describes those who 'observe the ambiguous part' of the scripture as people 'whose hearts are infected with disbelief'. The Quran warns that these people wish to create dissension, *fitna* (Q. 3:7). On the other hand, asking questions about the *muḥkamāt*, the verses which are precise in their meaning, was not mentioned as being problematic.[6] The classical interpretations of Q. 3:7, backed by the history of the politico-theological schisms in the early Muslim community, accentuated the difference between theological, legal and normative matters: theological issues are in general not a favourable topic for discussion, whereas legal and normative issues are constantly examined and questioned. Another Quranic verse that discourages the believers from asking questions is Q. 5:101, which states: 'Believers, do not ask questions about things which, if made known to you, would only pain you'.

As a natural continuation of the concept articulated by these two Quranic verses, the Hadith literature adopted the line that rejects asking questions. Although the dominant image of the early Muslim community (henceforth, the *Umma*) as reflected in the Hadith literature is that of a learning society which directed questions to the Prophet and other dominant figures,[7] the Hadith literature mainly articulates disapproval of questions raised by members of the *Umma* in the presence of the Prophet, even if these questions were directed to him in good faith. This dual disapproval first referred to the content of the questions that the Prophet was asked, and second referred to the questioners themselves. In the Hadith literature, this disapproval was also articulated in a specific prohibition to ask questions, a prohibition that followed the wording of Q. 5:101. *Ṣaḥīḥ al-Bukhārī* which contains a chapter entitled 'Dislike of asking too many questions about certain topics and dislike of asking questions that are not one's concern'[8] is one such example. The *aḥādīth* and historical anecdotes in this chapter correspond with Quran 5:101. Al-Bukhari (d. 870), for instance, quotes a letter that the influential *ṣaḥābī* al-Mughira ibn Shuᶜba (d. *c.* 668–71) sent to the caliph Muᶜawiya (d. 680). In this letter al-Mughira testified: 'The Prophet used to forbid *qīla wa-qāla* (idle talk, gossip) and the habit of asking too many questions.'[9]

The prohibition to ask questions was articulated also through the recounting of stories that linked the exchange of questions and answers with the tense relationships between the *munāfiqūn*, namely the hypocrites of Medina, and the Prophet. As dozens of anecdotes in the Hadith literature reveal, the Prophet quickly identified the evil intentions of these sceptics and latent heretics when they posed supposedly guileless questions. These questions were in fact deliberately meant to mock and insult the Prophet. The elaborate anecdotes about the questions that the *munāfiqūn* asked emphasise the gravity of the situation in which several people took the liberty of ridiculing (*istihzāʾan*) the Prophet during his sermons. They asked the Prophet questions about the hidden and unknown such as: 'Who is my father? Where is my she-camel?' These traditions described vividly the Prophet's anger at being addressed with these questions: He was either 'furious and red-faced' (*ghaḍbānu muḥmārrun wajhuhu*) or 'extremely annoyed' (*wa-ughḍiba ghaḍaban shadīdan*).[10] The Prophet's anger indicated that the questions directed at him were not merely the outcome of lightness and even stupidity, but that they were in fact deliberate provocations. The purpose of such questions was to expose the Prophet as a pretender, who did not know the hidden, and therefore was inferior to the pre-Islamic soothsayers (*kahana*). We do not know whether or not these anecdotes reflect events that actually occurred. However, their significance lies in portraying the Prophet's intolerance to questions.

The Hanbalite scholar Ibn Rajab (d. 1392), who quoted these anecdotes in his interpretation of Quran 5:101, mentioned the prohibition to ask questions (*masāʾil*, sing. *masʾala*) on subtle and difficult issues 'that God has deliberately concealed from His servants'.[11] Ibn Rajab claimed that the only people who were allowed to ask questions were mostly members of the Bedouin delegations who came to Medina to pledge their allegiance to the Prophet. These new converts posed questions about practice and faith which the Prophet tolerated. In contrast, 'the *muhājirūn* and *anṣār*, whose faith was solidly fixed in their hearts, were forbidden to ask subtle questions'.[12] This prerogative of asking questions was granted to the Bedouin converts because they lacked the finesse and sophistication of the *munāfiqūn* and *ahl al-kitāb*; therefore these converts could not cause any harm, such as casting doubt in the hearts of the believers or belittling the Prophet. Several new converts also appear in the sources as asking the Prophet questions that were accepted with grace.

No wonder, then, that the sauciest most impudent questions about God are presented in the Hadith literature as coming mostly from the lips of Bedouins and new converts. In the huge corpus of *aḥādīth al-ṣifāt* there is one interesting case of a Bedouin by the name of Abu Razin al-ʿUqayli (death date unknown) who inquired precisely about the forbidden topics; however, he received respectful and illuminating responses from the Prophet. Abu Razin's questions were recognised by later scholars as the almost exclusive source for Prophetic dicta on God's attributes and actions. The Persian Hadith scholar (and an expert on Sufism) Abu Nuʿaym al-Isfahani (d. 1038) observed that all the traditions transmitted by Abu Razin were based on the questions that he directed to the Prophet, and that most of these traditions were on matters of faith (*al-tawḥīd wa'l-uṣūl*).[13] Jarir al-Bajali (d. 671 or 674), another new convert (although not a Bedouin), was also permitted to ask questions that only Bedouins and the newly converted were allowed to ask, and others dared not.

As narrators, Abu Razin al-ᶜUqayli and Jarir al-Bajali represent two opposing styles of narration. In principal, both narrators transmitted versions of *ḥadīth al-ruʾya*. Their versions were similar in content, but different in their narrative presentation. Let us first consider Jarir's versions:

> The Messenger of God went out to meet us on the night of the full moon. He looked at the moon, and then he said: 'You will see your Lord as you see this moon. You will not draw yourselves together and sit closely together in order to see Him (*lā tuḍāmmūna fī ruʾyatihi*)'.[14]

In a more elaborate version, Jarir recounted:

> We were sitting at the Prophet's on a night of a full moon, and he (i.e. the Prophet) said: 'You will see your Lord as you see this moon. You will not differ one from another about seeing Him (*lā tuḍārrūna fī ruʾyatihi*).[15] So, if it is in your power to struggle with your difficulties and perform the prayer before the rising of the sun and the prayer before the setting of the sun, do so.'[16]

The *ḥadīth al-ruʾya* by Jarir appears in several additional versions;[17] all are schematic and dull. Although Jarir's narrative sets the Prophetic message in a concrete scene, the description is concise and brief. The audience in the narrative is a passive observer; no one from the audience asks the Prophet any questions. In the more elaborate version, the Prophetic message comprises two parts: the first informative yet sketchy part describes a scene from the Day of Resurrection; the second part is a directive regarding the two difficult prayers to perform: the morning prayer (*ṣalāt al-fajr*), the call for which is performed by the muezzin when the Muslims are asleep, and the afternoon prayer (*ṣalāt al-ᶜaṣr*), the call for which is performed when the Muslims are preoccupied with their everyday business. The performance of these prayers under such challenging circumstances is connected to the ultimate reward of seeing God's face in the afterlife, a reward which is reserved for the righteous.

Jarir was known as a narrator in the background: although he was –

according to his avowal – among the group of *ṣaḥāba* who sat outside the Prophet's house on the night of a full moon, in both narratives he blended into the audience. Jarir's narrative presents the Prophet as spontaneously mentioning the beatific vision, while the narrative implies that his words were generated by the sight of the full moon. However, parallel versions of other *ṣaḥāba* who supposedly witnessed the same event explicitly state that a question was indeed presented to the Prophet. The same *ḥadīth* with a more detailed framing narrative was transmitted on the authority of the prominent *ṣaḥābī* Abu Saᶜid al-Khudri (d. 683 or 694), later to become a mufti in Medina. Abu Saᶜid placed himself among the group of *ṣaḥāba* who sat outside the Prophet's house in Medina on the night of the full moon. In this version, contrary to Jarir's narrative, the audience is interactive with the Prophet:

> We asked: 'Oh, Messenger of God, will we see our Lord in the Day of Resurrection?' He answered: 'Do you differ one from another about seeing the sun on a cloudless noon?' We said: 'No.' He said: 'Do you differ one from another about seeing the moon on a cloudless night of the full moon?' We said: 'No.' He said: 'Well, then. You will not differ one from another about seeing Him, as you do not differ one from another about seeing the two of them.'[18]

Was it Jarir who asked the Prophet the question that set the dialogue in motion? Jarir ibn ᶜAbd Allah al-Bajali, a military commander and an exceptionally handsome man (al-Dhahabi called him 'the noble handsome emir', *al-amīr al-nabīl al-jamīl*) whom the Prophet was fond of,[19] was a likely candidate to ask this question, although none of the sources state this. The fact that the same scene was depicted by different narrators adds to the credibility of Jarir's story. Obviously, Jarir's version of the Prophet describing the beatific vision was worth saving because it corresponded to the versions of other *ṣaḥāba*. The multiplicity of these versions endowed the entire corpus of *ḥadīth al-ruʾya* with the label of 'massively transmitted *aḥādīth*' (*aḥādīth mutawātira*).[20] In addition, Jarir's version (at least in *al-Ṣaḥīḥān*) was classified under *aḥādīth* about the benefits of the morning and the afternoon prayers, and was often related to Q. 50:39 'Give glory to your Lord before sunrise and before sunset'. This classification demonstrates that both al-Bukhari and

Muslim (d. 875), the compilers of *al-Ṣaḥīḥān*, saw this tradition as a precious reminder of the performed rituals, and ignored its theological content.[21]

Two other versions of *ḥadīth al-ruʾya* are connected to the *ṣaḥābī* Abu Razin. The first version is almost identical to Jarir's narrative, although Abu Razin's version actually describes a dialogue between the Prophet and the narrator:

> On the authority of Abu Razin al-ʿUqayli who said: I asked: 'Oh, Messenger of God, will all of us see your Lord on the Day of Resurrection?' [The Prophet] answered: 'Yes.' I said: 'What is the sign for it in His creation?' [The Prophet] said: 'Oh Abu Razin, don't you all see the whole moon completely and at the same time (*mukhliyan bihi*)?'[22] I said: 'Yes.' He said: 'God is greater [than the moon].'[23]

This version of Abu Razin's *ḥadīth al-ruʾya* is one of several anecdotes that appear in the early Hadith compilation of the *muḥaddith* Sulayman ibn Dawud al-Tayalisi (d. 819 or 820) and in Ahmad ibn Ḥanbal's (d. 855) *Musnad*.[24] According to these brief anecdotes, a marginal *ṣaḥābī* by the name of Abu Razin al-ʿUqayli directed questions to the Prophet and received an immediate response. For instance, Abu Razin once asked the Prophet: 'Oh, Messenger of God! In what way does God bring the dead back to life?' The Prophet responded: 'Have you never walked in a dry ravine only to pass through it later and see it green and watery?' Abu Razin responded in the affirmative. 'Well, then – said the Prophet – this is exactly the case with the Resurrection.' In another version, the Prophet's response was: 'This is exactly how God brings the dead back to life.'[25] Other questions that Abu Razin posed were connected to the mysteries of the divine. When the Prophet described the horrors of the Day of Resurrection and determined 'Our Lord will laugh because of His servants' despair, and because He knows that soon He will change things', Abu Razin asked the Prophet whether God would really laugh.[26] On another occasion, assuming that God maintains an actual location in the physical world, Abu Razin asked the Prophet where God was situated before He created the heaven and earth:

> Abu Razin said: I asked: 'Oh, Messenger of God! Where was our Lord before He created the sky and the earth?' He answered: 'He was in lofty

> clouds (*ᶜamāᵓ*), beneath which was a vacuity (*hawāᵓ*), and above which was a vacuity. Then He created the throne above the water (*māᵓ*).'[27]

A more captivating version that raises many questions appears in Ahmad ibn Ḥanbal's *Musnad.* This version is a minor part of an extremely lengthy *ḥadīth* which appears to be a later patchwork. The lengthy *ḥadīth* comprises the same Abu Razin anecdotes which were otherwise distributed separately, and some additional material (for a full translation of this text, see Appendix II).[28] One of the passages of this text is a colourful version of the same dialogue that the Prophet and Abu Razin allegedly conducted:

> I said: 'Oh Messenger of God, how is it possible that in the Day of Resurrection we will look at Him and He will look at us, and there will be so many of us in the land while He is but one person (*shakhṣ wāḥid*)?' The Prophet answered: 'I will tell you by using a similar example from God's blessings. The sun and the moon are both signs from Him, and they are small. You see both of them and they see all of you at the same time, and you do not differ one from the other in seeing them. By your Eternal God! There is no doubt that He has more power to make you all see Him and see all of you than the sun and the moon have, and all the same, you see both of them and they see all of you at the same time, and you do not differ one from the other in seeing them.'[29]

Further in the dialogue, Abu Razin asked the Prophet: 'And with what will we see [our Lord]?' The Prophet answered: 'With the same [organ] you use today in order to see.'[30]

In the lengthy *ḥadīth*, the many questions that Abu Razin asked the Prophet are embedded in a unique framing narrative. According to this framing narrative, Abu Razin al-ᶜUqayli, also known as Laqit ibn ᶜAmir,[31] was a delegate of the Banu al-Muntafiq, a powerful tribe which occupied territories in al-Yamama.[32] Since Abu Razin's mission was to represent his tribe, the tribal affiliation and the tribe's affairs lie in the background of the framing narrative of the lengthy *ḥadīth*. The problem is that our only source about the visit of the delegation of the Banu al-Muntafiq at the Prophet's is the lengthy *ḥadīth* attributed to Abu Razin. The Shafiᶜite historian and Quran exegete Ibn Kathir (d. 1373), whose only source about the encounter between Abu

Razin and the Prophet is the lengthy *ḥadīth*, determined that Abu Razin was sent by his tribesmen to negotiate with the Prophet, and arrived in Medina at the end of month of Rajab, supposedly in Hijri year 9 (approx. 15 November 630). Ibn Kathir inserted the text in the chapter of Hijri year 9 (630–1 AD) in his *al-Bidāya wa'l-Nihāya* simply because all the tribal delegations came to the Prophet in the year 9. This year is called therefore 'the year of the delegations'. Ibn Kathir did not have any textual evidence indicating that this encounter indeed took place in the year 9.[33] The starting point of Abu Razin as a narrator is therefore rather shaky.

Considering Abu Razin as the narrator of the lengthy *ḥadīth* attributed to him, we soon realise that Abu Razin enumerated several goals that are reflected in the narrative. When this story was first recounted by Abu Razin, it was a detailed report to the tribe about the success of his mission. No doubt that Abu Razin wished to present himself to his tribesmen in a good light, because he went to the Prophet as an infidel and came back as a Muslim. However, the narrative that we have is a cleverly manipulated version of Abu Razin's initial report. The goal of the framing narrative of this lengthy *ḥadīth* clearly is to provide a positive representation of Abu Razin: he was the first of his tribe to convert to Islam, he established an intimate rapport with the Prophet, and he claimed that the Prophet recognised the outstanding merits of the Banu al-Muntafiq. According to Abu Razin, in the presence of the *muhājirūn* and the *anṣār,* the Prophet promised him that his tribe would inherit a piece of land between the east and the west. To confirm his words, the Prophet opened his clenched fist, spread his fingers and said: 'This land is yours. You will inhabit whichever territory you desire, and dwell in solitude, so if any harm is inflicted on you, it will come from your own hands.'[34] In agreement with this line, the emphasis in the framing narrative is on Abu Razin, and not on the Prophet. Abu Razin is depicted as a saucy clever Bedouin whose questions both amuse the Prophet and challenge his knowledge of the divine. Since the framing narrative of this *ḥadīth* recounts the story of Abu Razin's conversion to Islam and his pledge of allegiance to the Prophet, I will refer to it as 'the *ḥadīth* of allegiance' instead of 'the lengthy *ḥadīth*'.

But was Abu Razin the narrator of the *ḥadīth* of allegiance? An examination of the *isnād* reveals that the narrator was actually Dalham ibn al-Aswad (death date unknown). Al-Aswad was Abu Razin's great-nephew, who claimed to have quoted his great-uncle's exact version to an extraordinary event which would have otherwise remained obscure.[35] After an introductory sentence that presents Abu Razin in the third person, Dalham adopts the voice of Abu Razin and tells Abu Razin's story in the first person, through Abu Razin's eyes. A master storyteller, the narrator (either Dalham or the literary figure of Abu Razin) unfolds the following story: accompanied by his friend, Nahik ibn ᶜAsim (a completely anonymous tribesman who is mentioned only in this anecdote), Abu Razin arrived in Medina at the end of the month of Rajab. The two friends entered the Prophet's mosque shortly after the morning prayer and heard the Prophet preach to the worshippers:

> O people (*ayyuhā 'l-nāsu*), hear me well! I refrained from talking to you in the last four days. But hear me well! I am now going to speak to you. Hear me well! Is there someone whose tribe sent him [to me], saying: 'Tell us what the Messenger of God says?' Is there among you a person whose mind is diverted by his own thoughts or by what his friends say? Is there among you someone whose mind is diverted by misguidance? Hear me well! You can ask me [anything], have I not told you (*hal ballaghtu*)? Hear me well! Hear me well, so you will live.[36]

After this address, the Prophet ordered the worshippers, who probably wanted to pursue their daily routine, to remain seated in their places. Everyone obeyed. Abu Razin testified: 'The people sat down, and I and my friend stood there, until his (i.e. the Prophet's) mind opened to us and his eyes fell on us.'[37] The narrator uses here three devices to enhance the credibility of his narrative. First, the Prophet's address contains two phrases that echo the famous sermon of the Prophet in 'the farewell pilgrimage' (*ḥijjat al-wadāᵓ*): the opening 'O people' and the closing 'have I not told you'.[38] The narrative itself is shaped as the extremely detailed testimony of an active participant in the event, and we are bound to accept his words as truthful. The details enable the audience to reconstruct the scene and wait in suspense for further developments to evolve in the narrative.

The bold Abu Razin, having noticed that he drew the Prophet's attention, commenced his series of questions. Abu Razin asked ten questions about the divine and the hereafter, and the Prophet answered each question patiently, other than the tenth question. Abu Razin then asked the eleventh question, which reflected his complete submission to the Prophet and his conversion to Islam.[39] Thereafter, Abu Razin asked three more questions: about the status of his tribe and about the fate of those who died unbelievers. He meant to ask another question, question number fifteen, but refrained from asking. So he asked questions number sixteen and seventeen, and for them he received answers.[40] The Prophet's answers to Abu Razin's questions included several anthropomorphic and corporealistic descriptions of God on the Day of Judgement. God is described as strolling about the earth after the entire human race became extinct. The earth looks empty to Him (*wa-khalat ᶜalayhi 'l-bilādu*), so God orders the sky to shower with rain, and the rain comes from the vicinity of the divine throne in such force that all the graves on earth break apart and the dead emerge alive. This prophecy appears in the beginning of the dialogue between Abu Razin and the Prophet. Each question leads the Prophet to another description of God and his physical contact with the newly resurrected. For example, Abu Razin asked: 'Oh Messenger of God, what is our Lord going to do to us when we meet Him?' The Prophet answered:

> You will be presented to Him with your heads uncovered; no secret will be hidden from Him. He will then take a handful of water in His hand and moisten your faces. By God! Not a drop will miss your faces: the drop will make the Muslim's face as white as a piece of cotton, but it will leave the heretic's nose as black as a lump of coal.[41]

This part of the dialogue in particular assumes a physical connection between God and the resurrected, in line with God's description in other parts of the narrative as a substantial physical being that walks around the empty earth, or laughs at the despair of the resurrected Muslims.

The narrator Dalham, who is the voice of Abu Razin, supposedly transmitted faithfully the long conversation between the Prophet and Abu Razin. This is what the narrator wants us to believe. However, the fact that this narrative is a patchwork of short anecdotes about Abu Razin that were transmitted by another narrator (this point is elaborated in the next section of this chapter) may explain the inconsistencies in the narration. For example, the Prophetic dicta in the narrative, which are in fact prophecies on the future, are sometimes cited in the past tense. On the other hand, the narrative is rich and captivating. It is decorated by references to the Prophet's gestures while he spoke, Abu Razin's reactions to the Prophetic dicta, his inner thoughts and emotions, and even the behaviour of the audience. These occasional minutiae certainly help to create an atmosphere of credibility, and more importantly, they 'glue' the single anecdotes together and transform them into one coherent narrative. The narrative gradually leads Abu Razin from the position of a bold infidel to that of a humble believer. Two examples from the lengthy *ḥadīth* will suffice to demonstrate the narrator's mastery in the art of storytelling.

The first example is from the beginning of the event, immediately after Abu Razin and his companion entered the Prophet's mosque. With the attention of the Prophet drawn to the foreign Bedouins, the narrator gradually builds a narrative tension or anticipation. This tension is soon to be intensified by an extremely detailed account of the exchange between Abu Razin and the Prophet that begins with the first question that Abu Razin presented:

> I asked: 'Oh Messenger of God, what have you from the knowledge of the invisible (*ʿilm al-ghayb*)'? By the Eternal God! The Prophet laughed and shook his head, because he already knew that I wished to trick him. Finally, the Prophet said: 'God used keys to lock five secrets that only He knows.' The Prophet gestured with his hand the number five.[42]

As Abu Razin inquired about these secrets, the Prophet continued:

> He knows the destiny of each and every one of you, and you do not. He knows when the sperm enters the womb, and you do not.[43] He knows what will happen tomorrow, and what you will eat tomorrow, and you do not. He knows when the rain will fall. He watches you when you are wretched, afraid and long for compassion. And [all this time] He keeps on laughing, because He knows that the time for the change in your situation is near.[44]

Abu Razin, who started the conversation with the wish to trick the Prophet (perhaps to show that the Prophet was no different than any other tribal sorcerer), admiringly said: 'A Lord who laughs benevolently will never deprive us of His bounty.' To the five secrets known only to God, the Prophet added the sixth: 'He knows when the Day of Resurrection comes.'[45] Abu

Razin's poetic response marked his submission to the new faith. He asked the Prophet to teach him whatever he taught the believers, having complained to the Prophet that he belonged to a small group of people who wished to join the Prophet, but suffered from the mocking and the harassment of their own tribesmen and other powerful tribes.[46] At Abu Razin's request, the Prophet provided him valuable information about the Day of Resurrection and the afterlife.[47]

The second example of the narrator's mastery in storytelling appears at the end of the narrative where, after asking his twelfth question, Abu Razin and his friend prepared to take their leave. Remembering that he had yet another question to ask, Abu Razin approached the Prophet and asked about the fate of those people of the *Jāhiliyya*, who were kind and charitable. One of the Qurashites exclaimed: 'By God! Your ancestor, al-Muntafiq, is in Hell!'[48] Abu Razin recounts:

> I felt as if my skin, my face, and my entire body burnt because of what he said about my father in front of all these people. I almost cried: 'And what about your father, Oh Messenger of God?', but I thought about this matter for a while, and asked in a more polite manner: 'And what about your family, oh Messenger of God?'[49]

The provocation of the Qurashite was the outcome of burning envy, because before Abu Razin presented his twelfth question, the Prophet appreciatively described Abu Razin and his friend as pious, in fact 'two of the most pious of all people'.[50] Ignoring the Qurashite's provocation, the Prophet explained that since these people of the *Jāhiliyya* did not respond to his call to embrace Islam, they were considered misguided and hence doomed to inhabit Hell.[51] Although implied, the Prophet's response assured Abu Razin that all the people of the *Jāhiliyya* who died after the Prophet's advent shared the same fate, including the family of the Qurashite who insulted him. In one of the shorter anecdotes of Abu Razin, the same episode is described differently. In this anecdote, Abu Razin asked the Prophet: 'My mother was always kind to her kinship, taking care of them incessantly, but she died an infidel. Where is she now?' The Prophet responded: 'She is in Hell.' Abu Razin asked: 'Oh, Messenger of God! And where is your mother?' The Prophet responded: 'Rest assured that your mother is with my mother.'[52]

This episode, as described in the lengthy narrative, presents Abu Razin as self-restrained and polite, because he did not respond to the Qurashite's provocation, which no doubt humiliated him. However, it is not Abu Razin's self-restraint or piety, but his legendary skill to ask the Prophet questions that is emphasised in the *ḥadīth* of allegiance. This characteristic is highlighted in the following saying attributed to a handful of narrators, among whom were Abu Razin's son, ᶜAsim ibn Laqit, and one of his nephews, Wakiᶜ ibn ᶜUdus: '[Abu Razin] said that the Prophet disliked questions (*kāna yakrahu 'l-masāʾil*) and disapproved of people asking them; however, when Abu Razin posed a question, [the Prophet] was delighted with his question (*aᶜjabathu masʾalatuhu*) and he answered it.'[53] The word *masʾala* here denotes 'a subtle question' on philosophical and metaphysical matters which are dispensable.[54]

The inner logic of the *ḥadīth* of allegiance directs the readers to the conclusion that the Prophet's availability to Abu Razin and his questions in that formative event was not merely because of Abu Razin's Bedouin origin, but because the Prophet genuinely admired him. Indeed, there are several indications that once converted, Abu Razin became one of the Prophet's favourite companions.[55] The Prophet's promise to Abu Razin that they both would sit together in Paradise and drink the milk that never turned sour, could have served as an indication of the intimacy between the two, were it not set in a supposedly fabricated *ḥadīth*.[56] We will briefly discuss this report in the following section.

II. The Proliferation of the Abu Razin Narrative

As said before, the *ḥadīth* of allegiance is a patchwork of Abu Razin short anecdotes and additional material, and this patchwork is embedded in an extremely detailed framing narrative. According to ᶜAbd Allah ibn Ahmad ibn Hanbal (d. 903), who in fact compiled Ibn Hanbal's *Musnad*, the Medinese *muḥaddith* Ibrahim ibn Hamza al-Zubayri (d. 845) sent him a letter in which he included this lengthy *ḥadīth*. Ibrahim, a lineal descendant of the anti-caliph ᶜAbd Allah ibn Zubayr (d. 692)[57] claimed to have recorded the *ḥadīth* faithfully from one of his teachers.[58] In his letter, Ibrahim asked ᶜAbd Allah to transmit this *ḥadīth* to his disciples on Ibrahim's behalf, hence granting him a written permission to teach the material. The chain of transmission as quoted by ᶜAbd Allah indicates that in the eighth and ninth centuries this material circulated in Medina, and Ibrahim's letter to ʿAbd Allah expanded this *ḥadīth*'s circulation to include Baghdad (see Appendix II).

There is no reason to doubt ʿAbd Allah's declaration about the way this material arrived to him. One may suspect that at some point during the transmission in Medina, one of the scholars (probably Ibrahim himself) gathered the Abu Razin anecdotes and concocted a coherent and independent narrative, namely the *ḥadīth* of allegiance. In addition, it is unclear whether this material originated in Medina. On the contrary, we suggest that the anecdotes which comprise the *ḥadīth* of allegiance possibly originated in Iraq and circulated there prior to the ninth century, and even prior to its circulation among the scholars of Medina.

The Abu Razin corpus, namely the short anecdotes and the *ḥadīth* of allegiance, is a cluster of stories recounted by members of the Banu al-Muntafiq. Originally from al-Yamama, the Banu al-Muntafiq settled in the marshes of Kufa and Basra during the Arab conquest of Iraq.[59] The *ḥadīth* of allegiance in fact provides an indirect explanation of their sole domination in the marshes: the Prophet predicted that they would live far from any civilization, with no neighbours to harass them.[60] A close examination of the *isnāds* of the entire Abu Razin corpus (see Appendix III, chart 1a) reveals that it was transmitted via two different channels. The *isnāds* of the Abu Razin short anecdotes include Abu Razin, who recounted his stories to his nephew Wakiʿ ibn ʿUdus (or Hudus). Wakiʿ in his turn recounted the stories to the *muḥaddith* Yaʿla ibn ʿAtaʾ.[61] The *ḥadīth* of allegiance is recounted, as was previously mentioned, by Abu Razin's great-nephew, Dalham ibn Aswad.[62] Dalham testified that he had heard the story from his father, al-Aswad. Al-Aswad either heard the story directly from Abu Razin, or from Abu Razin's son, ʿAsim ibn Laqit. Dalham, in turn, recounted the story to the *muḥaddith* ʿAbd al-Rahman ibn ʿAyyash.[63] The *isnāds*, then, identify Abu Razin's nephew, Wakiʿ ibn ʿUdus, and his great-nephew, Dalham ibn al-Aswad, as the original narrators of the Abu Razin material.

There is an unexplained lacuna in the biographical sources regarding Wakiʿ and Dalham: their death dates are unknown and their whereabouts are a complete mystery. Dalham probably did not reside in Medina, although ʿAbd al-Rahman ibn ʿAyyash (death date unknown), the *muḥaddith* who transmitted the *ḥadīth* of allegiance on his authority was Medinese.[64]

The Hadith scholar Ibn Hibban (d. 965) remarked that ᶜAbd al-Rahman transmitted Hadith 'from the Medinese scholars and from Dalham ibn al-Aswad'.[65] This sentence conveys the notion that Dalham was not a scholar and that he did not live in Medina. Wakiᶜ, Abu Razin's second nephew, most probably lived in Iraq: the *muḥaddith* Yaᶜla ibn ᶜAtaᵓ (d. 738) who collected his short anecdotes came from al-Taif, but resided most of his life in al-Wasit, Iraq.[66] ᶜAbd al-Rahman ibn ᶜAyyash and Yaᶜla ibn ᶜAtaᵓ were professional *muḥaddithūn*. Their connection to Dalham and Wakiᶜ indicates that they collected tales from the Iraqi tribesmen of the marshes and transformed the material into Prophetic Hadith.

The material which was attributed to Abu Razin was subjected to manipulation, of which the Hadith scholars were aware. While the *Musnads* of al-Tayalisi and Ahmad ibn Hanbal preserved the *isnāds* which point to the tribal origin of the material,[67] a peculiar *isnād* was 'glued' to another anecdote attributed to Abu Razin, which contains two of his familiar anecdotes. According to this anecdote, the illustrious Ibn ᶜAbbas (d. 686–7) quoted Abu Razin recounting a dialogue he had with the Prophet. In the beginning of the dialogue, the Prophet promised: 'You and I, Oh Abu Razin, will drink milk that never turns sour.' Abu Razin asked the Prophet about the Day of Resurrection and the Prophet compared the act of resurrecting to the dry ravine that becomes green and wet. Then Abu Razin asked how he would know whether he was a believer or not. The Prophet responded that only a believer had a firm knowledge that his good and bad deeds would receive the appropriate recompense or the due punishment from God.[68]

As recorded in several historical sources, this *ḥadīth* was transmitted by Muhammad ibn Saᶜid ibn al-Tabari. He was also known as *al-maṣlūb*, 'the crucified', because in 767, during the reign of the second ᶜAbbasid caliph Abu Jaᶜfar al-Mansur (reigned 754–75), he was executed for heresy.[69] Ibn al-Tabari, who taught Hadith in Damascus, was known for having 100 names. Apparently, the *muḥaddithūn* of Damascus who wished to transmit Ibn al-Tabari's sensational Hadith material concealed their dubious source by changing the name of the narrator.[70] Ibn ᶜAsakir quoted the Abu Razin anecdote that Ibn al-Tabari transmitted in four different versions, with four different *isnāds*.[71] Elsewhere, he indicated that Ahmad ibn Hanbal quoted a *muḥaddith* who had met Ibn al-Tabari. According to that *muḥaddith*, Ibn al-Tabari admitted: 'Whenever I hear a nice story, I see no harm in inventing an *isnād* for it so it will be accepted and highly regarded.'[72]

Although Ahmad ibn Hanbal rejected the Abu Razin material which arrived through the channel of Ibn al-Tabari, there were other *muḥaddithūn* who were willing to accept it. The illustrious Quran exegete, Abu ᶜAbd Allah al-Qurtubi (d. 1272), quoted the same Abu Razin anecdote while mentioning Ibn al-Tabari as the source of the material, and added: 'Although the *isnād* of this *ḥadīth* is not strong, the content of the *ḥadīth* is sound.'[73] On the other hand, Shams al-Din al-Dhahabi, who was meticulous about his sources, declared that the Hadith compilation of Abu ᶜIsa Muhammad ibn ᶜIsa al-Tirmidhi (d. 892) was ranked (by al-Dhahabi, most probably) as less reliable than the *Sunan* of Abu Dawud al-Sijistani (d. 888) and the *Sunan* of al-Nasaᵓi (d. 915), because al-Tirmidhi quoted the material attributed to *al-maṣlūb*.[74]

In spite of Ahmad ibn Hanbal's reservations about some of Abu Razin's material, Abu Razin's status as the source of valuable material on the divine was secured in the Hanbalite circles. The history of the *ḥadīth* of allegiance attributed to Abu Razin is typical of the history of the more colourful *aḥādīth al-ṣifāt*: this literary work was incorporated in Ibn Hanbal's *Musnad* by ᶜAbd Allah ibn Ahmad and was considered valuable material by Hanbalite Hadith authorities. In fact, parts of the *ḥadīth* of allegiance were considered the cornerstone of their perception of God and His attributes.[75] In other circles, the *ḥadīth* of allegiance was regarded as controversial. While prominent Hadith authorities from Iraq and Khurasan such as Sulayman ibn Ahmad al-Tabarani (d. 971) transmitted this *ḥadīth* and included it in their writings, other Hadith authorities ignored it.[76] Muhammad ibn Ismaᶜil al-Bukhari (d. 870), for instance, studied Hadith from Ibrahim ibn Hamza al-Zubayri, the *muḥaddith* who introduced this lengthy *ḥadīth* to ᶜAbd Allah ibn Ahmad ibn Hanbal. Even so, al-Bukhari neither included this lengthy *ḥadīth* nor any other *ḥadīth* attributed to Abu Razin in his *Ṣaḥīḥ*. He merely quoted a tiny fragment from it in his biographical dictionary in reference to Dalham, Abu Razin's great-nephew.[77]

The great *muḥaddith* from Isfahan, Abu ᶜAbd Allah ibn Manda (d. 1005), also mentioned that this *ḥadīth* was read publicly in a gathering of the scholars of Iraq, among whom were ᶜAbd Allah ibn Ahmad ibn Hanbal and the

Baghdadian Hadith scholar Muhammad ibn Ishaq al-Saghani (d. 883–4) 'and none of the scholars rejected it or argued about its authenticity'.[78] Ibn Manda fiercely defended the authenticity of this *ḥadīth*:

> No one dared to reject this *ḥadīth* or argue about [the credibility of] its transmitters. On the contrary, they (i.e. the Iraqi and Persian *muḥaddithūn*) transmitted it while accepting it wholeheartedly. Only a heretic or an ignoramus or a transgressor of the Quran and the Sunna, rejects it.[79]

This ardent declaration, preceded by a list of the distinguished Iraqi and Persian scholars who taught this *ḥadīth*, indicates that the *ḥadīth* of allegiance was widely rejected; otherwise, such a statement in its favour would hardly have been required. This *ḥadīth* was also included in Ibn Khuzayma's *Kitāb al-Tawḥīd*.[80] *Kitāb al-Tawḥīd* and its author were highly esteemed in the circles of the ultra-traditionalists, but rejected by the Ashᶜarites (see Chapter 5).

The scholar who in particular strove to retrieve the *ḥadīth* of allegiance from the *Musnad* and include it in the traditionalistic curriculum was Ibn Qayyim al-Jawziyya (d. 1350), the disciple of the influential Ibn Taymiyya (d. 1328). Ibn Qayyim al-Jawziyya copied this *ḥadīth* verbatim from Ahmad ibn Hanbal's *Musnad* and discussed its content in three different works: his treatise on the divine attributes, *al-Ṣawāᶜiq al-Mursala ᶜalā al-Jahmiyya wa'l-Muᶜaṭṭila* (Thunderbolts Directed against the Jahmiyya and Muᶜattila),[81] his elaborate treatise on the hereafter, *Ḥādī al-Arwāḥ ilā Bilād al-Afrāḥ* (The Leader of the Souls to the Land of Joy) and his sophisticated biography of the Prophet, *Zād al-Maᶜād fī Hady Khayr al-ᶜIbād* (Provisions for the Afterlife, on the Teachings of the Best of All People).[82] In *Ḥādī al-Arwāḥ*, Ibn al-Qayyim decided to include this *ḥadīth* 'to decorate our book with it, because its majesty, awe and the light of prophethood that it contains attest to its veracity'.[83] Ibn Qayyim al-Jawziyya set this *ḥadīth* in a chapter that describes a controversy between the traditionalists as to whether sexual intercourse between the believers and their spouses in the hereafter would entail pregnancy. Since Abu Razin's tenth question touched the exact same topic, and the Prophet's answer assured Abu Razin that there would be no pregnancies in the hereafter, Ibn Qayyim al-Jawziyya thusly justified the inclusion of the *ḥadīth* of allegiance in *Ḥādī al-Arwāḥ*.[84] In *Zād al-Maᶜād*, however, the inclusion of this *ḥadīth* was more reasonable, because it appears in a chapter entitled 'the arrival of the delegation of the Banu al-Muntafiq' to the Prophet, that is, Ibn Qayyim al-Jawziyya used the *ḥadīth* as a historical source.[85] As indicated in Section I of this chapter, Abu Razin's testimony is the singular source which mentions the content of the Prophet's meeting with this delegation. Therefore, we find that the chapter in *Zād al-Ma^cād* discusses this *ḥadīth*, its vocabulary, authenticity and credentials, simply because there are no other sources about the delegation of the Banu al-Muntafiq to discuss.

Ibn Qayyim al-Jawziyya was eager to prove that this rather dubious *ḥadīth* was wide-spread (*mashhūr*) and hence acceptable in the eyes of the traditionalists. In his eagerness, he quoted a conversation he had with the great *muḥaddith* of Damascus, Abu'l-Ḥajjaj al-Mizzi (d. 1341). Ibn Qayyim al-Jawziyya testified: 'When I asked him about this *ḥadīth*, he said that the majesty of prophethood rests upon it (*^calayhi jalālatu 'n-nubuwwati*)'.[86] Al-Mizzi was just being polite: in his *Tuḥfat al-Ashrāf bi-Ma^crifat al-Aṭrāf* (The Gem of the Notables, about the Knowledge of the Abbreviated Content of the Hadith),[87] al-Mizzi quoted the beginning of the *ḥadīth* of allegiance and expressed his doubts about this *ḥadīth*. According to al-Mizzi, he found a shorter version – in fact, a version of one sentence – of this *ḥadīth* in a distorted copy of the *Sunan* of Abu Dawud al-Sijistani (d. 889). Al-Mizzi, who was not a Hanbalite, was afraid that this particular tradition was added to the copy of the *Sunan* by the Sufi *muḥaddith* Abu Sa^cid al-A^crabi (d. 952).[88] Al-Mizzi's concern regarding the authenticity of the *ḥadīth* of allegiance is further evidence that this *ḥadīth* was a part of the Hanbalite curriculum and that the other trends of Islamic traditionalism did not use or cite it.

III. Two Narrators and One Narrative: the Tribal Connection

A frequently quoted *ḥadīth* in theological treatises records a dialogue between the Prophet and a mysterious visitor, who arrived in Medina after a long journey in the desert; amazingly he was not dusty and tired as a traveller was expected to be. The mysterious visitor joined the circle of the *ṣaḥāba* and directed several questions to the Prophet, whom he familiarly addressed by his first name. During the dialogue between the two men, the Prophet informed the mysterious visitor about several topics, sketching the outline of the religion of Islam with its five pillars of performed obligations and its six articles of faith. The most commonplace version of this *ḥadīth* indicates that the mysterious visitor was 'Gabriel, who came to teach you the fundamentals of your religion', as the Prophet told the astonished ᶜUmar ibn al-Khattab (d. 644), a witness to the event.[89]

The most widespread version of the dialogue between Muhammad and the archangel Gabriel is attributed to ᶜUmar ibn al-Khattab, and it was transmitted by ᶜUmar's son, ᶜAbd Allah (d. 693).[90] ᶜAbd Allah recounted the story on several occasions as a response to the Qadarite views that were promoted by prominent public figures (including *muḥaddithūn* with Qadarite inclinations) in Iraq and Syria. Each time, ᶜAbd Allah emphasised that this *ḥadīth* was meant to prove that the belief in predetermination (*qadar*) was one of the six articles of faith in Islam. For example, Yahya ibn Yaᶜmar (d. 742), a Basrian *muḥaddith*, once performed the pilgrimage to Mecca with a friend hoping to meet one of the *ṣaḥāba*. Ibn Yaᶜmar and his friend wanted to consult with this *ṣaḥābī* about the trend of Qadarism in Basra and particularly about the harmful activities of the Qadarite Maᶜbad al-Juhani (executed in 703). By coincidence, the two pilgrims encountered ᶜAbd Allah ibn ᶜUmar who sat in his usual place in the mosque. They hurried to the respectable *ṣaḥābī*, caught hold of his arms, while Yahya presented the problem: 'Recently appeared among us people who recite the Quran and seek the Hadith, but claim at the same time that there was no such thing as *al-qadar*, namely predetermination and that nothing was preordained.' ᶜAbd Allah listened attentively and immediately declared that he disassociated himself from these people, adding: 'Suppose one of them gave a legendary amount of gold to charity, God would have never accepted it until he professed his belief in *al-qadar*.'[91] To corroborate his declaration, ᶜAbd Allah recounted the following story to the two Basrian pilgrims:

> My father ᶜUmar ibn al-Khattab told me: 'we were sitting at the Prophet's, when suddenly a man with extremely white clothes and extremely black hair, who did not seem at all exhausted from the journey, and whom none of us had known before, sat in front of the Prophet, made his knees lean on the Prophet's knees, and put his hands on the Prophet's thighs and said: 'Oh Muhammad! Inform me what Islam is!' [The Prophet] answered: 'You must testify that there is no god but God, and that Muhammad is the

> Messenger of God. You must perform the prayers, give alms, fast during the month of Ramadan and perform the pilgrimage if you are able to perform it.' Then [the man] asked: 'Inform me what faith is!' [The Prophet] answered: 'You must believe in God, His angels, His books, His messengers, and the Last Day. You must believe in predetermination, its good and its evil.' [The visitor said]: 'You are quite right.'[92]

The didactical structure of this *ḥadīth*, which enables the narrator to coherently convey the Prophetic message to the audience, was duplicated in other, less familiar, versions. The first version was attributed to Abu Razin, the Bedouin whose questions the Prophet welcomed. Instead of Gabriel, Abu Razin asked the Prophet to define faith, and the Prophet responded.[93] In fact, in Abu Razin's version, Gabriel does not appear in the text at all. The second version was attributed to the *ṣaḥābī* Jarir ibn ᶜAbd Allah al-Bajali (d. 671 or 674), the leader of the Banu Bajila tribe. Jarir's version sterilises the element of surprise in the story, as its opening sentence is 'Gabriel came to the Prophet in the form of a young man (*fī ṣūrat shābb*)'. The *ḥadīth* then presents the same dialogue between the Prophet and Gabriel that ᶜAbd Allah ibn ᶜUmar transmitted, including the closing statement by the Prophet, who addressed the witnesses to the event and said: 'This is Gabriel, who came to teach you the fundamentals of your religion.'[94]

Apart from the thematic resemblance, Abu Razin and Jarir al-Bajali's versions of the *ḥadīth* about Gabriel have several common features. First, both versions were almost exclusively preserved in the Hanbalite curriculum: Abu Razin's version was recorded in Ahmad ibn Hanbal's *Musnad*, while Jarir's version was recorded in Abu Bakr al-Ajurri's *Kitāb al-Sharīᶜa*. Accordingly, both versions were rejected by the majority of the Hadith scholars. Second, both versions circulated among the Banu al-Muntafiq and the Banu Bajila tribes in Iraq. Third, the source of the *ḥadīth* was a tribal *ṣaḥābī*, who was claimed to have maintained close relationships with the Prophet.

When the *isnād*s of both versions are closely inspected, another pattern emerges. It seems that the stories were disseminated by tribesmen whose expertise in Hadith and reliability as *muḥaddithūn* were dubious. The *muḥaddith* responsible for the distribution of Abu Razin's version of the *ḥadīth* was the mufti of Damascus, Sulayman ibn Musa (d. 737), who was held in low esteem by the Hadith scholars.[95] His recklessness in transmitting Hadith was recorded in Abu Razin's version of the *ḥadīth*: Sulayman allegedly quoted Abu Razin, whom he could have never met, as if he directly heard him recount this *ḥadīth*. The *isnād* of this *ḥadīth* is therefore broken (*munqaṭi*ᶜ) (see Appendix III, chart 2b).

The Jarir al-Bajali's version (see Appendix III, chart 2a), which circulated among the Banu Bajila, was mainly distributed by Khalid ibn Yazid ibn Khalid al-Qasri al-Bajali (death date unknown). Khalid al-Qasri was not a prominent scholar; in fact, later Hadith scholars regarded him as a 'weak' Hadith transmitter.[96] However, he was a member of the Banu Bajila, and more so, he was the grandson of Khalid ibn ᶜAbd Allah ibn Asad al-Bajali al-Qasri (d. 743–4), the governor of Iraq.[97] Therefore, Khalid ibn Yazid's grandfather was a distinguished member of the tribe – one of the notables among the *ṣaḥāba*[98] – a man whose wisdom and life experience people sought and obviously quoted. Abu Bakr al-Ajurri, who included Jarir al-Bajali's version of the *ḥadīth* of Gabriel in his *Kitāb al-Sharī*ᶜ*a* against the judgement of the Hadith scholars of his times, did so for two reasons: first, he needed the text to corroborate a theological statement. In theological treatises, the criteria applied on the Hadith material were not as strict as the criteria in legal writings. Second, al-Ajurri was enthusiastic about collecting rare material.[99]

Al-Ajurri's nature as an antiquarian is reflected in his painstaking arrangement of the material in his *Kitāb al-Sharī*ᶜ*a*: for example, he arranged more than fifty *aḥādīth* about the beatific vision in a chapter divided into sub-sections; each sub-section comprises the material attributed to a certain narrator.[100] In the chapter on the beatific vision, he quoted several versions of *ḥadīth al-ru*ᵓ*ya* attributed to Jarir al-Bajali.[101] As opposed to Abu Razin's material, which was almost exclusively studied by the Hanbalites and rejected by other traditionalists, at least four of the versions of *ḥadīth al-ru*ᵓ*ya* that were attributed to Jarir al-Bajali were unanimously accepted by Hadith scholars. As such, Jarir's *ḥadīth al-ru*ᵓ*ya* appears in the major Hadith compilations.[102] The obvious explanation for its acceptance is that this *ḥadīth* and its various versions enjoyed reliable chains of transmission and were therefore labelled *ṣaḥīḥ* by Hadith scholars. We can, however, consider several other factors that contributed to the preservation of Jarir's several versions of *ḥadīth* *al-ruʾya*. Some of the answers to the wide acceptance of this *ḥadīth* lie in the personality and political stature of the historical Jarir.

As stated earlier, the conspicuous Jarir was one of the Prophet's favourites. His relationship with the Prophet, which began towards the end of the Prophet's life, was warm and cordial. One day, in the month of Ramadan of the year 10 (December 631),[103] the Prophet, who sat with the *ṣaḥāba*, predicted: 'One of the finest Yemenites, an exceptionally fortunate man whose forehead was touched by an angel, will come to you through this door.'[104] Shortly afterwards, the handsome and tall Jarir,[105] who was the tribal leader of the Banu Bajila, entered the room with 150 of his men to profess Islam and pledge allegiance to the Prophet. The Prophet welcomed him with a memorable gesture: he spread his own mantle on the floor for Jarir to sit on. Jarir, deeply touched by this display of respect, prostrated on the mantle, and excitedly thanked the Prophet.[106]

What happened next is somewhat similar to the report about Abu Razin's conversion: like Abu Razin, Jarir informed the Prophet about the fertile lands which his tribe occupied,[107] and the Prophet gave the Banu Bajila his blessing. Like Abu Razin, Jarir asked the Prophet questions, although he was less inquisitive than Abu Razin: Jarir did not ask questions about the hereafter, but asked the Prophet to inform him about the creation of heaven and earth. The Prophet's answer, that the sky and the earth were made of smoke, foam and water, and that the earth was carried on the back of a whale, pleased Jarir to such a degree that he immediately stretched his hand and pledged allegiance to the Prophet.[108] A few months after the conversion, the Prophet appointed Jarir as governor in North Yemen.[109] According to Jarir's avowal, from that point onward, the Prophet used to smile warmly at him whenever they met.[110]

The Prophet died in the month of Rabiᶜ al-Awwal of Hijri year 11 (June 632), and Jarir's conversion occurred in the month of Ramadan of the previous year.[111] Therefore, the scene that Jarir depicted in the *ḥadīth al-ruʾya* occurred somewhere in the last seven months of the Prophet's life. This *ḥadīth* was distributed as an independent unit, separate from the reports on the solemn event of conversion, in which the Prophet asked Jarir to destroy the monumental idol that his tribe and several other Yemenite tribes worshipped.[112]

The prominent part of Jarir's career as a tribal leader occurred in Kufa, where the Banu Bajila settled during the Arab conquest.[113] In the unstable ethnographic landscape of Kufa, this tribe was part of the elite: the Banu Bajila was among the first tribes which came to Iraq in 635, and among the founders of Kufa in 638.[114] The Banu Bajila, like the other tribes who founded Kufa, were not nomads and pastoralists, but urbanised warriors.[115] Kufa was a town divided into separate tribal districts, one of them occupied by the Banu Bajila who, like other tribes, conducted a secluded communal life. They had their mosque in which they held their gatherings and they had their separate cemetery. Jarir and the tribe's notables (*ashrāf*) – like other prominent *ṣaḥāba* who resided in Kufa – owned private lots in the centre of Kufa.[116] Jarir, as one of the tribal leaders (*ashrāf al-qabāʾil*),[117] was part of the establishment: he guaranteed his tribe's loyalty to the caliphs and was highly esteemed by the caliphs ᶜUmar and ᶜUthman ibn ᶜAffan (d. 655).[118] As a sign of his loyalty to ᶜUmar, he fought in the battle of al-Qadisiyya in 636.[119] His loyalty to ᶜUthman was rewarded when the latter appointed Jarir governor in Hamadhan.[120]

Jarir's troubles began when ᶜAli ibn Abi Talib (d. 661) resumed the caliphal position after the assassination of ᶜUthman. In spite of the vigorous warnings from his advisor, ᶜAli assigned Jarir – at the latter's request – to go to his sworn enemy Muᶜawiya (d. 680) in Damascus and ask him to pledge allegiance to ᶜAli. Jarir entered Muᶜawiya's court with the certainty that he would succeed in persuading the latter to submit to the authority of ᶜAli. However, having witnessed Muᶜawiya presenting the bloody shirt of the slaughtered caliph ᶜUthman (Muᶜawiya's second cousin) to his men and blaming ᶜAli for ᶜUthman's murder, Jarir quickly grasped that he would not be able to complete his task. He went back to ᶜAli and reported about the heated atmosphere in Muᶜawiya's court and his failure to complete his mission. A vehement argument occurred between ᶜAli's advisor and Jarir, during which the advisor accused Jarir of treason.[121] This event occurred in 657 (before the battle of Siffin) and it marked the end of Jarir's court in Kufa. The offended Jarir left Kufa with his adherents and settled in Qarqisiyaʾ in al-Jazira, on the left bank of the Euphrates (formerly the important Roman town of Circesium).[122] This town which was governed by Muᶜawiya became, like several towns in al-Jazira, the asylum of Kufans and Basrians who supported ᶜUthman and were forced to leave their home towns when ᶜAli ascended the caliph's throne.[123] Jarir died either there or in the homeland of the Banu Bajila, in the mountains of al-Sarat[124] in Hijri year 51 or Hijri year 54 (671 or 674 CE).

Until the end of his life, Jarir was well known for his *iᶜtizāl*, that is, his choice to side neither with ᶜAli nor Muᶜawiya.[125] According to one of the reports, upon leaving Kufa Jarir declared: 'I will never reside in a town in which the name of ᶜUthman is abused.'[126] It is noteworthy that while Jarir left Kufa in anger, most of his family and adherents remained there. The Shiᶜite historian Nasr ibn Muzahim (d. 827) reported that shortly after Jarir and his tribe left Kufa, ᶜAli and his men tore down Jarir's estate and burnt his *majlis*. Jarir's beloved grandson, Abu Zurᶜa ibn ᶜAmr ibn Jarir al-Bajali, hurried to ᶜAli and said: 'May God give you health! In this court there are patches that belong to other people than Jarir.' ᶜAli then hurried to leave the place, and went to burn down the house of one of Jarir's adherents.[127] The grandson, who was raised by Jarir and even accompanied him to the appointment with Muᶜawiya, remained in Kufa and later became one of the town's most prominent *muḥaddithūn*.[128]

IV. The Proliferation of the Jarir Narrative

Contrary to Abu Razin's material, the entire corpus of some 100 *aḥādīth* attributed to Jarir[129] – among which is the *ḥadīth al-ruʾya* – enjoyed a wide circulation in Kufa, which was a major Hadith centre.[130] From Kufa, these *aḥādīth* spread rapidly to other Hadith centres such as Medina, Baghdad and Basra.[131] One may assume that the immediate reason for this wide circulation was Jarir's high profile as a charismatic leader. Many *muḥaddithūn* from the Banu Bajila, among them Jarir's grandson, enthusiastically cited his *aḥādīth*. We argue that the rapid circulation of the *aḥādīth* attributed to Jarir was mostly due to the vigorous scholarly activities of Ismaᶜil ibn Abi Khalid (d. 762–3). Ismaᶜil specialised in the Hadith material that was attributed to Jarir, although he never met Jarir. Moreover, we argue that this *muḥaddith* had political and personal considerations in spreading the material attributed to Jarir.

Jarir – unlike Abu Razin – was indeed an important *ṣaḥābī*.[132] As mentioned earlier, Abu Razin boasted of his intimate rapport with the Prophet.

Abu Razin's relatives made some efforts to preserve his supposed legacy, but other than the Hanbalites, nobody seemed to have remembered Abu Razin. Abu Razin sank into oblivion and his incredible story about the sixteen questions that he asked the Prophet was tagged as one of the many Hanbalite curiosities. Jarir on the other hand was a charismatic leader and an apparently gifted poet who was able to compose poetry in extempore.[133] However, Jarir's rhetoric skills – unlike Abu Razin's – were not reflected in the *ḥadīth al-ruʾya*. This *ḥadīth,* and in fact all the *aḥādīth* attributed to Jarir, was preserved mainly because it was a unifying factor for the Banu Bajila in Kufa. In other words, these *aḥādīth* provided essential support in the tribe's attempts to regain its political position in Kufa and to rehabilitate its name. Jarir – an esteemed member of the mythological Muslim community (*Umma*), beloved by the Prophet, a man of all caliphs – lost his status and was humiliated by ᶜAli.[134] Jarir's decline marked the decline of the Banu Bajila in Kufa: most of the tribesmen opposed ᶜAli and did not join his troops in the Battle of Siffin. Ousted from their former influential position in the local Kufan politics, the Banu Bajila recalled the splendid legacy of their tribe by retelling Jarir's maxims and recollections. The *ḥadīth* on the beatific vision was a good example of Jarir's proximity to the Prophet, although the narrative of this *ḥadīth* did not focus on Jarir at all (again, unlike Abu Razin's narrative).

The *tābiᶜī* who transmitted Jarir's material, among which are the *ḥadīth* of Gabriel and the *ḥadīth* on the beatific vision, was Qays ibn Abi Hazim al-Ahmasi al-Bajali (several death dates in the range between 703 and 716 appear in the sources). The sources describe Qays as a well-connected *muḥaddith*, who transmitted Hadith from the most prominent *ṣaḥāba*: political figures like the four righteous caliphs, military commanders such as Khalid ibn al-Walid (d. 642), and prominent *ṣaḥāba* who transmitted many *aḥādīth* (*mukaththirūn*) such as Abu Hurayra (d. 678) and ᶜAbd Allah ibn Masᶜud (d. 652–3).[135] Qays's reliability as a Hadith transmitter was almost undisputable: Ismaᶜil ibn Abi Khalid (d. 762–3), who frequently quoted (*akthara ᶜan*) Qays, awarded him the epithet 'the pillar' (*al-usṭuwāna*),[136] meaning that he was as trustworthy as one. The professional *muḥaddithūn* praised his legendary memory and awarded him the title 'reliable' (*thiqa*).[137] However, one of the leading Hadith scholars claimed that some of his material should be rejected (*munkar*).[138] The material quoted from Qays included mostly aphorisms that Jarir heard from the Prophet,[139] and ample historical and personal anecdotes.[140] In these anecdotes, unlike Jarir's pale version of *ḥadīth al-ruʾya*, Jarir the narrator recounted rich, detailed and captivating stories as befits the art of storytelling: these stories featured protagonists, and the narratives were characterised by action and suspense.[141]

The nature of Qays's relationship with Jarir is unclear. Although he was one of the most prominent sources for Jarir's material,[142] and fought next to him in the battle of al-Qadisiyya,[143] he did not join Jarir when the latter left Kufa. Qays was known to have fought with ᶜAli against the *khawārij* in Nahrawan,[144] a battle that took place in 658, two years after Jarir's self-willed exile from Kufa. This did not mean that Qays sided with ᶜAli in the events of the first *fitna*.[145] On the contrary, based on the testimonies of Qays's contemporaries, the historian al-Dhahabi remarked that Qays was 'a Kufi who supported ᶜUthman, which is rare'.[146]

The *ḥadīth al-ruʾya* appears with the *isnād* Jarir ibn ᶜAbd Allah – Qays ibn Abi Hazim – Ismaᶜil ibn Khalid, which is also one of the most common *isnād*s of the material attributed to Jarir (see Appendix III, chart 1b). This *isnād* has one feature that characterises most of the *isnād*s of Prophetic material from Kufa: all or most of its first three links (companion–successor–successor) died at the age of eighty and above. These long-lived *ṣaḥāba* and *tābiᶜūn* were known as *al-muᶜammarūn* (those whose lives God prolonged).[147] The Hadith scholars made efforts to establish the exceptional longevity of *al-muᶜammarūn*. Al-Dhahabi, for example, rejected an anecdote in which Qays testified that he was seven or eight when he first saw the Prophet preach in his mosque in Medina. Al-Dhahabi preferred another anecdote according to which Qays was a young man when he first came to Medina to pledge allegiance to the Prophet. However, upon his arrival he learned that the Prophet had already died; hence, he had never met the Prophet face to face.[148] This anecdote, although depriving Qays of the title of a lesser *ṣaḥābī* (*ṣaḥābī ṣaghīr*) but granting him the respectable titles *tābiᶜī* and *mukhaḍram* (because his lifespan extended from the *Jāhilyya* to Islam),[149] enabled al-Dhahabi to substantiate the reports according to which Qays died 'many years' after he reached the age of 100. This estimation of Qays's longevity was corroborated by Ismaᶜil ibn Khalid's first-hand report on Qays's last years as a pitiful senile.[150]

Isma^cil ibn Abi Khalid (d. 762–3) was not a *mu^cammar* (at least, the sources do not indicate at what age he died), but he was considered a *tābi^cī*.[151] A star student of the Kufan *muḥaddith* al-Sha^cbī (d. after 718), Isma^cil was also a miller, although the number of people who quote him indicates that his main occupation was probably transmitting Hadith, rather than carrying sacks of grain or operating a mill. Because of his conspicuous activity in Hadith transmission, he earned several sobriquets that expressed his mastery in this profession. He was, for example, referred to as the prominent *muḥaddith* in Kufa in his days (*muḥaddith al-Kūfa fī zamānihi*),[152] 'the scales' (*al-mīzān*) probably for his precision in transmitting his material,[153] and one of the four prominent *ḥuffāẓ* (the custodians of the Prophetic legacy) in Kufa.[154] Although there were other *muḥaddithūn* who transmitted Hadith on the authority of Qays, Isma^cil gained exclusivity, as the sobriquet *rāwiyat Qays*, 'the copious transmitter of the material of Qays', indicates.[155]

With his status as the undisputable and prominent transmitter of the material of Qays, came the role of a custodian of the legacy of the Banu Bajila. More appropriately, Qays served as a propagandist who transmitted material that was meant to build the tribe's self-esteem. Isma^cil was a *mawlā*, a client or protégé of al-Ahmas, one of the clans of Banu Bajila.[156] His source of tribal legacy, Qays, was a member of al-Ahmas, yet Isma^cil, who was probably a son of a Persian convert,[157] was of lower status.[158] Another indication of Isma^cil's foreign origin was his language: Ahmad ibn Hanbal held Isma^cil in high esteem for his reliability and accuracy in transmission; nevertheless, he did not conceal the fact that Isma^cil systematically spoke ungrammatical Arabic (*faḥish 'l-laḥn*).[159] In addition, there were claims that Isma^cil was illiterate.[160]

Isma^cil's insufficient knowledge of the Arabic language provides an explanation to the brevity of Jarir's *ḥadīth al-ru^ɔya*: lacking the embellishments of other transmitters, Isma^cil's dominant versions of this *ḥadīth* reflect rigidity in the wording that could be attributed to the transmitter's lack of confidence in the language. The two versions of Jarir's *ḥadīth al-ru^ɔya* that Isma^cil transmitted include two peculiar verbs (*tuḍāmmūna* and *tuḍārrūna*) that sound similar. According to one version, the Prophet promised: 'You will see your Lord as you see this moon. You will not draw yourselves together and straiten yourselves in order to see Him (*lā tuḍāmmūna fī ru^ɔyatihi*).'[161] According to the second version, the Prophet promised: 'You will see your Lord as you see this moon. You will not differ one from another in seeing Him (*lā tuḍārrūna fi ruʾyatihi*).'[162] The use of these two verbal forms was not necessarily wrong, grammatically speaking.[163] On the contrary, there are marginal versions of *ḥadīth al-ruʾya* attributed to Abu Hurayra and Abu Saᶜid al-Khudri that in fact combine these two forms in a single narrative.[164] However, referring to the two versions of Jarir's *ḥadīth al-ruʾya*, Ahmad ibn Hanbal remarked that the use of the almost identical, interchangeable and rare verbal forms *tuḍāmmūna* (draw yourselves together and sit closely together) and *tuḍārrūna* (differ from one another) reflected Ismaᶜil's uncertainty or doubt about the use of the correct expression.[165] Notwithstanding this apparent uncertainty in his Arabic, Ismaᶜil indeed made his mark on *ḥadīth al-ruʾya*. As indicated earlier, Jarir's versions of *ḥadīth al-ruʾya* were preserved in the canonical Hadith compilations. In the version recorded in *Ṣaḥīḥ al-Bukhārī*, Jarir concluded his description of the Prophet and the *ṣaḥāba* on the night of the full moon with the following sentence: 'and [the Prophet] recited: "Give glory to your Lord before sunrise and before sunset" (Q. 50:39).' To this conclusion, Ismaᶜil added his own input: 'Perform [these two prayers], and never miss them.'[166]

The Baghdadian Hadith scholar, Abu 'l-Hasan al-Daraqutni (d. 995), who diligently collected all the known versions of Jarir's *ḥadīth al-ruʾya*, mentioned 105 *muḥaddithūn*, who transmitted this *ḥadīth* directly from Ismaᶜil.[167] Among these *muḥaddithūn* one may find the names of his immediate disciples, those who studied regularly with him and transmitted most of the material attributed to him. Among these *muḥaddithūn* were the honourable and trustworthy Malik ibn Mighwal al-Bajali (d. 775 or 776) from Kufa,[168] Shuᶜba ibn Ḥajjaj (d. 776) from Basra,[169] Sufyan ibn ᶜUyayna (d. 813) from Kufa[170] and Wakiᶜ ibn al-Jarrah (d. 813) from Kufa (see Appendix III, chart 1b).[171] Others, such as Yahya ibn Hashim 'the middleman' (*al-simsār*; d. 840)[172] from Kufa, were notorious liars. In the case of Jarir's *ḥadīth al-ruʾya*, the huge number of *muḥaddithūn* from different places who claimed to have heard this *ḥadīth* directly from Ismaᶜil indicates that sitting in his Kufan abode, Ismaᶜil was a lodestone for *muḥaddithūn*. Among the many *muḥaddithūn* who visited and heard this *ḥadīth* directly from him was Abu Hanifa, al-Nuᶜman ibn Thabit (d. 767), the eponym of the Hanafite school. Muqatil ibn Sulayman (d. 767), the Quran exegete and an infamous anthropomorphist, also transmitted this *ḥadīth* directly from Isma^cil.[173]

In addition, al-Daraqutni mentioned five people who transmitted Jarir's version of *ḥadīth al-ru^ʾya*, which they heard directly from Qays. They were Kufans and four of them belonged to the Banu Bajila.[174] The four Bajalis were in close proximity: they all belonged to the al-Ahmas clan, which was also Isma^cil's clan. One of them, Jarir ibn Yazid ibn Jarir al-Bajali, was in fact one of Jarir's grandsons. In spite of his noble origin, later Hadith scholars labelled him *munkar al-ḥadīth*, namely 'a transmitter of objectionable material'.[175] Be that as it may, Jarir ibn Yazid was one of Kufa's notables, as an anecdote from his early childhood indicates.[176] The other three Bajalis who transmitted Jarir's version of *ḥadīth al-ruʾya* also were considered controversial *muḥaddithūn*.[177] Their versions of this *ḥadīth* are identical to Ismaʿil's versions; however, their versions did not meet the strictest standards of the prominent compilers of Hadith and were excluded from the important Hadith compilations.[178] Does this mean that they personally heard Qays tell this *ḥadīth*? Al-Daraqutni believed that they did not. In fact, he suggested that they merely duplicated Ismaʿil's versions (*bi-mutābaʿat riwāyat Ismāʿīl*) while attributing the material to themselves.[179] By this remark, al-Daraqutni re-established Ismaʿil's status as the most reliable transmitter of material attributed to Jarir, a Hadith transmitter who gained the trust of the majority of the scholars of Hadith. Nevertheless, the circulation of these additional versions of Jarir's *ḥadīth* among the Banu Bajila contributes to our suggestion that this *ḥadīth* was, as well as the entire Jarir corpus, part of the tribe's heritage and folklore.

G. H. A. Juynboll, who was the first to draw the attention of western scholarship to the material attributed to *al-muʿammarūn*, remarked that this material mainly originated in Kufa and was characterised by a 'single strand', namely a single *ḥadīth* that reverts to one single authority. This authority, the *ṣaḥābī*, transmitted the material to only one *tābiʿī*, and he passed the *ḥadīth* in turn to another *tābiʿī*.[180] From that point on, the second *tābiʿī* taught the material to numerous disciples, thus spreading the material in multiple chains of transmission in Kufa and elsewhere.[181] In other words, according to this pattern, the *ḥadīth al-ruʾya* by Jarir was supposed to be transmitted by Qays only to Ismaʿil, thus endowing Ismaʿil with exclusive access to material that other *muḥaddithūn* supposedly did not have.[182] Ismaᶜil therefore almost single-handedly transmitted Jarir's *ḥadīth al-ruʾya* to numerous disciples and was therefore responsible for its wide distribution.

V. The Jarir Narrative and the *Miḥna*

Due to the rapid distribution of Jarir's version of *ḥadīth al-ruʾya* and its inclusion in the major Hadith compilations, it was accepted by wider circles, unlike a lot of Abu Razin's narrative. This unanimous acceptance is a clear indication that the traditionalists, by and large, perceived this *ḥadīth* with its numerous transmitters as an irrefutable proof of the beatific vision.

Ibn Qayyim al-Jawziyya, who discussed Jarir's version of *ḥadīth al-ruʾya* in *Ḥādī al-Arwāḥ* (a discussion that generously relied on al-Daraqutni's data), emphasised the unequivocal stature of this *ḥadīth* in the traditionalistic discourse. He remarked that the rationalists who rejected this *ḥadīth* (and other *aḥādīth* in the same vein) accused the traditionalists of being the proponents of anthropomorphism and corporealism *(ahl al-tashbīh wa'l-tajsīm)*. Disregarding the dubious qualifications of some of the *muḥaddithūn* who heard this *ḥadīth* from Ismaᶜil ibn Abi Khalid, Ibn Qayyim al-Jawziyya enthusiastically declared:

> They all witnessed that they heard it from Ismaᶜil ibn Abi Khalid, and Ismaᶜil ibn Abi Khalid witnessed that he heard it from Qays ibn Abi Hazim, and Qays ibn Abi Hazim witnessed that he heard it from Jarir ibn ᶜAbd Allah, and Jarir witnessed that he heard it from the Messenger of God. It is as if you yourself heard the Messenger of God saying it and informing his *Umma* about it. There is nothing more precious to them than him (i.e. the Prophet).[183]

This ardent address should be read as a directive to the devout Muslims, instructing them to defend their belief in the beatific vision from the mockery of the rationalists. More specifically, Ibn Qayyim al-Jawziyya here explains how to defend the *ḥadīth al-ruʾya* transmitted through the chain Jarir–Qays–Ismaᶜil: the reliability of its transmitters is sufficient proof of the veracity of this *ḥadīth*.

Ibn Qayyim al-Jawziyya's fierce defence of this *ḥadīth* indicates that attacks were specifically directed at it. These attacks go back to the *miḥna*, in which this *ḥadīth* – according to some sources – played a fascinating role. The *miḥna*, which is probably the most prominent of all formative events of Islamic traditionalism, will not be discussed here.[184] Suffice it to say that during this procedure of interrogation adopted by the caliph al-Ma°mun (reigned 813–33) and pursued forcefully by his successors, al-Mu°tasim Bi-'llah (reigned 833–42) and al-Wathiq Bi- 'llah (regined 842–7), the leading *muḥaddithūn* and local leaders of Baghdad and other major cities were forced to accept the Mu°tazilite doctrine of the createdness of the Quran (*khalq al-qur°ān*). The story of Ahmad ibn Hanbal, a leading *muḥaddith* and jurist from Baghdad, who endured imprisonment and torture but did not capitulate to his Mu°tazilite interrogators, is one of the building blocks of the traditionalistic ethos.[185]

Despite the centrality of the *khalq al-qur°ān* doctrine in the *miḥna*, the question of *aḥādīth al-ṣifāt* and the anthropomorphic descriptions of God in the Quran and the Hadith also arose during the interrogations.[186] More specifically, Ahmad ibn Hanbal (and others) were asked to address the issue of the beatific vision.[187] According to Ibn Hanbal's testimony, as recorded by his cousin Hanbal ibn Ishaq (d. 886), his interrogators refused to acknowledge the veracity of the *aḥādīth* that he quoted (which unfortunately are not specified in the sources), claiming that 'these traditions are transmitted with various chains of transmission, and that they contain fantasies and fabrications'.[188] Apparently, Ibn Hanbal did not respond to the interrogators' accusations against the Hadith, and focused on the Quran 'on which we all agree', that is, he did not try to persuade his interrogators that the Hadith material is authentic and valid as textual evidence.[189] However, his interrogators soon disclosed that their reading of the Quran was different from his because they rejected the beatific vision.[190]

The claim of the interrogators regarding *aḥādīth al-ṣifāt* was typical of the rationalistic worldview. In particular, the rationalists focused on the legendary or mythical nature of these *aḥādīth*, and indeed saw them as fabricated stories.[191] However, the reports on the *miḥna* provide a unique perspective on another aspect in refuting *aḥādīth al-ṣifāt*: that of 'various chains of transmission' (*ikhtilāf asānīdihā*).[192] The key person in the story is °Ali ibn al-Madini (d. 849), a *muḥaddith* from Basra, who came to Baghdad where he quickly became a prominent member of the traditionalistic milieu. He was a close friend of Ahmad ibn Hanbal, an expert of *ᶜilm al-rijāl* (the science dedicated to Hadith transmitters, their biographies, qualities, etc.), an industrious teacher of Hadith, and a diligent author who was claimed to have produced 200 works (most of which were lost). One of his existing works is *al-ᶜIlal*, the earliest and most cited work of Hadith criticism.[193]

ᶜAli ibn al-Madini was also a dream interpreter. One day, a fellow *muḥaddith* visited him to find him silent and gloomy. 'What is the matter with you?' inquired the friend. Ibn al-Madini replied: 'I had a dream in which I preached on the pulpit of David, upon him be peace.' The friend exclaimed: 'But this is a good thing! You saw yourself preach on the pulpit of a prophet!' Ibn al-Madini sadly shook his head: 'I wish I would have seen myself preach on the pulpit of Job. That would have been a better sign for me, because Job was put to the test [and endured], while David was subject to temptation [and was tempted].'[194] The Basrian preacher and qadi Ghulam Khalil (d. 888) who told this anecdote explained that the dream indeed foretold what would happen to Ibn al-Madini during the *miḥna*. Al-Dhahabi discredited Ghulam Khalil because of his unreliability, but nonetheless quoted this tale.[195]

As his dream suggested, Ibn al-Madini was one of the *muḥaddithūn* who capitulated in the *miḥna*, declaring that the Quran was created by God.[196] Not only did he capitulate but he also collaborated with his Muᶜtazilite interrogators by providing them *aḥādīth* on the Quran. These *aḥādīth* helped the interrogators refute the textual evidence that Ibn Hanbal used against the doctrine of *khalq al-qurʾān*.[197] Ibn al-Madini was also requested to give his learned opinion on the *ḥadīth al-ruʾya* transmitted through the chain Jarir–Qays–Ismaᶜil. Apparently, during the second round of the *miḥna* in 835, the Muᶜtazilite qadi Ibn Abi Duwad (d. 854) disclosed an astonishing piece of information to the caliph al-Muᶜtasim: 'Oh, Commander of the Faithful! This one (namely Ahmad ibn Hanbal) claims that God will be seen in the afterlife. However, it is well-known that the eye can grasp only limited bodies, and that God has no limits.' Ahmad was brought to the caliph who asked him to prove his claim. In response, Ahmad quoted *ḥadīth al-ruʾya* in full, with the chain of transmission preceding the narrative. Al-Muᶜtasim asked Ibn Abi Duwad's opinion: after all, Ibn Hanbal provided a textual proof for his belief in the beatific vision! In response, the qadi Ibn Abi Duwad said that he would check the *isnād* of the *ḥadīth*, and quickly made his exit.[198]

Ibn Abi Duwad went to search for ᶜAli ibn al-Madini, the Hadith expert, in the streets of Baghdad. In those days, Ibn al-Madini was destitute, without a dirham to his name. The artful qadi paid the respectable scholar a visit, in which he first gave him 10,000 dirhams, an incredulous sum which was enough to provide him with all his needs for two years. 'This is a gift from the Commander of the Faithful to you' – said the qadi – 'he ordered that all your needs will be taken care of.' After the grateful Ibn al-Madini accepted the gift, Ibn Abi Duwad asked: 'Abu 'l-Hasan, how is the *ḥadīth* told by Jarir ibn ᶜAbd Allah about the beatific vision, evaluated?' The scholar immediately rejoined: 'This *ḥadīth* is *ṣaḥīḥ*.'[199]

The qadi was not satisfied with the answer and asked Ibn al-Madini whether he could find anything to discredit this *ḥadīth*. Ibn al-Madini begged the qadi to be exempted from this task, but the qadi continued imploring him, saying that 'this [task] (namely, discrediting this *ḥadīth*) is a pressing need (*ḥājat al-dahr*)'. More gifts were brought: clothes, perfumes and a fine, fully equipped stallion. Finally, Ibn al-Madini said: 'One of the transmitters in the *isnād* is a person whose conduct was not exemplary and his narrative cannot be taken as obligatory. His name is Qays ibn Abi Hazim. He was a Bedouin of no importance.' Here Ibn al-Madini used the figurative expression 'a Bedouin who frequently urinated on his heels' (*aᶜrābī bawwāl ᶜalā ᶜaqibayhi*). This strong language leaves no doubt that Ibn al-Madini discredited Qays as a source of Prophetic knowledge.[200]

The rejoicing qadi, whose mission was successfully accomplished, embraced Ibn al-Madini and kissed him. On the next day, the qadi hurried to the caliphal palace to use the argument that Ibn al-Madini provided him in the interrogation of Ahmad ibn Hanbal. He confronted Ahmad ibn Hanbal, repeating the charge that Qays was 'a Bedouin who frequently urinated on his heels'. Ahmad later recounted: 'When he presented this argument to me, I immediately knew that this was the deed of ᶜAli ibn al-Madini.'[201] Ahmad ibn Hanbal's judgement about Ibn al-Madini's role in this incident was crucial. Al-Khatib al-Baghdadi (d. 1071), from whom al-Dhahabi copied this story, remarked that this incident and several similar ones finally led to Ibn al-Madini's downfall.[202]

This entire incident was peculiar because, as a professional *muḥaddith*, Ibn al-Madini used to transmit material attributed to Qays. In addition, Qays's stature among the *tābiᶜūn* was – as Ibn al-Madini himself testified – secured, because of his unlimited access to nine of the ten prominent *saḥāba*, and many others.[203] No doubt, it presented Ibn al-Madini as a greedy *muḥaddith* who was ready to sell his professional integrity for money. This kind of story put the entire corpus transmitted by Ibn al-Madini in danger. This is why, given Ibn al-Madini's reputation as a Hadith expert, al-Khatib al-Baghdadi doubted the veracity of the story, and clarified that 'none of those who recounted the story of the *miḥna* ever mentioned that Ahmad [ibn Hanbal] was confronted with *ḥadīth al-ruᵓya*'.[204] In addition, al-Khatib al-Baghdadi suggested that what Ibn Abi Duwad quoted as Ibn al-Madini's unflattering opinion of Qays had its roots in the Hadith. Al-Khatib al-Baghdadi's intention was to exonerate Ibn al-Madini from the charge of defaming a respectable *tābiᶜī* and he therefore emphasised that Ibn Abi Duwad merely claimed that Ibn al-Madini provided him with this information. Unfortunately, Al-Khatib al-Baghdadi did not explain further, leaving this matter obscure.

The thread was picked up by al-Dhahabi. In his attempt to somehow clear Ibn al-Madini's name, al-Dhahabi speculated that Ibn al-Madini indeed provided an unflattering opinion on Qays, although this opinion was not his; he was just quoting what the Basran Hadith expert Yahya al-Qattan (d. 813) had said about Qays.[205] There is evidence that Yahya indeed tagged Qays as *munkar al-ḥadīth*, namely a transmitter whose material should be rejected, not because of *ḥadīth al-ruᵓya* but because of a historical anecdote that Qays recounted about an incident that happened to ᶜAᵓisha in the Battle of the Camel.[206] In a brilliant passage in which he analysed all the pieces of evidence at his disposal, al-Dhahabi suggested that once having learnt from Ibn al-Madini that Yahya al-Qattan had disregarded Qays, Ibn Abi Duwad fabricated the allegation against Qays and attributed it to Ibn al-Madini, while connecting this allegation to *ḥadīth al-ruᵓya*.[207] The attempts of al-Khatib al-Baghdadi and al-Dhahabi to clear Ibn al-Madini's name are supported by textual evidence: in his *al-ᶜIlal*, Ibn al-Madini dedicated a brief chapter to Qays, in which he verified Qays's direct connection with nine of the ten prominent *ṣaḥāba*.[208] Nowhere in his book did Ibn al-Madini defame Qays or discredit his credibility as a *muḥaddith*.

Al-Dhahabi's defence of Ibn al-Madini came six centuries too late. After the *miḥna*, Ibn al-Madini was subject to mockery and offensive poetry.

Numerous anecdotes about his opportunism suddenly appeared, while prior to the *miḥna* all the leading *muḥaddithūn* sang his praises.[209] Ibn al-Madini was dependent on the kindness of Ibn Abi Duwad, and therefore was excommunicated from the scholarly circle of the *muḥaddithūn*; some even refused to transmit his material. Others described that sheer fear drove him to behave the way he did in the *miḥna*. They therefore accepted his public expression of repentance in which he repudiated the doctrine of *khalq al-qurʾān*, and continued to teach Hadith they heard from him.[210]

Jarir's version of *ḥadīth al-ruʾya*, by the way, is connected to a later *miḥna* trial. In 846, Ahmad ibn Nasr al-Khuzaʿi, a popular leader of the masses in Baghdad, was interrogated by the caliph al-Wathiq (d. 847). During his interrogation, Ahmad ibn Nasr cited *ḥadīth al-ruʾya*. The caliph responded: 'Woe unto you! Do you mean that God will be seen just like any other thing which has its limits and shape? Does He occupy a space? Can a human glance encompass Him? I do not believe in a god who is described in such a way.'[211] Thereafter, al-Wathiq himself hit Ahmad ibn Nasr with his sword, and stabbed him in the stomach.[212]

The incident of Ahmad ibn Hanbal and Ibn al-Madini in the *miḥna* accentuates the role that *aḥādīth al-ṣifāt* played in theological and political controversies. The *miḥna* occurred in the ninth century, and the *ḥadīth al-ruʾya* of Jarir started circulating at the end of the seventh century (if we consider Jarir its original narrator and creator) or in the middle of the eighth century (if we take Ismaʿil as its original narrator). Perhaps this tradition was ingeniously recounted by Jarir out of a pure wish to record the Prophet's dicta and transmit them to his relatives and friends. However, soon after this tradition started circulating in Kufa, it was tainted by personal ambitions, tribal calculations and political disputes. Abu Razin's version of *ḥadīth al-ruʾya* also reflected tribal politics and personal ambitions, although its limited distribution (compared to Jarir's version) minimised its resonance to the circle of the Hanbalite *muḥaddithūn*, who practically embraced almost any rejected tradition from *aḥādīth al-ṣifāt*. In terms of theological content, both versions presented the traditionalistic acceptance of the beatific vision, but refrained from providing any anthropomorphic depiction of God. The following chapter presents traditions with more explicit anthropomorphic descriptions; however, the focus in Chapter 3 is not the anthropomorphic descriptions, but the manner in which these descriptions were conveyed.

Notes

1. Postman, *The End of Education*, p. 173.
2. Jordan, *Ancient Concepts of Philosophy*, pp. 2–3.
3. Cribiore, 'School Structures', p. 152.
4. See, for example, Holtzman, 'Debating the Doctrine'.
5. Wright, *Sirach*, p. 722.
6. 'It is He who revealed to you the Book. Some of its verses are precise in meaning – they are the foundations of the Book – and others ambiguous. Those whose hearts are infected with disbelief observe the ambiguous part, so as to create dissension by seeking to explain it. But no one knows its meaning except God. Those who are well-grounded in knowledge say: "We believe in it: it is all from our Lord." But only the wise take heed' (Quran 3:7). The discussion of the Malikite Quran exegete Abu ʿAbd Allah al-Qurtubi (d. 1272) of Q. 3:7 is extremely comprehensive and serves as a defining introduction to the topic of *al-muḥkamāt* and *al-mutashābihāt*: al-Qurṭubī, *al-Jāmiʿ*, vol. 4, pp. 7–14 (commentary of Q. 3:7).
7. Dozens of questions that the Prophet was asked appear in the form of *fatāwā* in the last section of Ibn Qayyim al-Jawziyya's *Iʿlām al-Muwaqqiʿīn*, vol. 6, pp. 209–603. For the structure of 'question and answer' in the Hadith, see Speight, 'Narrative Structures', pp. 266–7.
8. Al-Bukhārī, *Ṣaḥiḥ*, vol. 4, pp. 361–3 (*Kitāb al-Iʿtiṣām bi'l-Sunna, bāb mā yukrahu min kathrat al-suʾāl*).
9. Al-Bukhārī, *Ṣaḥiḥ*, vol. 4, p. 362, *ḥadīth* 7292.
10. Ibn Rajab, *Rawāʾiʿ al-Tafsīr*, vol. 1, pp. 448–9 (interpretation of Q. 5:101).
11. Ibn Rajab, *Rawāʾiʿ al-Tafsīr*, vol. 1, p. 450 (interpretation of Q. 5:101).
12. Ibn Rajab, *Rawāʾiʿ al-Tafsīr*, vol. 1, p. 451 (interpretation of Q. 5:101).
13. Al-Iṣbahānī, *Maʿrifat al-Ṣaḥāba*, vol. 5, p. 2418.
14. Al-Ājurrī, *Kitāb al-Sharīʿa*, pp. 273–4 (*ḥadīth* 595). The exact phrase appears in Lane, *Arabic-English Lexicon*, vol. 5, pp. 1775–6 (the entry *ḍārrahu*).
15. Lane, *Arabic-English Lexicon*, vol. 5, pp. 1775–6.
16. Al-Ājurrī, *Kitāb al-Sharīʿa*, pp. 272–3 (*aḥādīth* 592–4). 'To struggle with your difficulties' (*an lā tughlabū)* literally means 'to not be overpowered [by difficulties]'.
17. According to a different version, Jarir said: 'We were sitting in the Prophet's

house, and he gazed at the moon on the fourteenth of the month': al-Ṭabarānī, *al-Muʿjam al-Kabīr*, vol. 2, p. 295, *ḥadīth* 2227. Another version specifies that this event occurred during one of the Prophet's expeditions: al-Ṭabarānī, *al-Muʿjam al-Kabīr*, vol. 2, p. 296, *ḥadīth* 2233.

18. Al-Ājurrī, *Kitāb al-Sharīʿa*, pp. 275–6 (*aḥādīth* 600–1). Cf. the similar versions of Abu Hurayra: al-Ājurrī, *Kitāb al-Sharīʿa*, pp. 274–5 (*aḥādīth* 596–8). Abu Saʿid al-Khudri and Abu Hurayra used the verb *qāla* (said) to indicate both 'asked' and 'answered'.
19. Al-Dhahabī, *Siyar Aʿlām al-Nubalāʾ*, vol. 2, p. 530; al-Ṣafadī, *al-Wāfī*, vol. 11, p. 58.
20. Ibn Qayyim al-Jawziyya, *Ḥādī al-Arwāḥ*, p. 625.
21. According to al-Dhahabi, al-Bukhari and Muslim included the same eight *aḥādīth* by Jarir in their *al-Ṣaḥīḥān*. Al-Bukhari included two additional *aḥādīth* and Muslim included six: al-Dhahabī, *Siyar Aʿlām al-Nubalāʾ*, vol. 2, p. 537.
22. *Akhlā bi-* means 'he was in one empty place, in which no one pushed him': al-Fīrūzābādī, *Muḥīṭ*, p. 1280. According to Abu Razin's narrative, everyone will see the entire 'being' of God at the same time.
23. Al-Ājurrī, *Kitāb al-Sharīʿa*, pp. 277–8 (*ḥadīth* 605–6); al-Ṭayālisī, *Musnad*, vol. 2, pp. 418–19, *ḥadīth* 1190; Ibn Ḥanbal, *Musnad*, vol. 12, p. 481, *ḥadīth* 16130; vol. 26, p. 124, *ḥadīth* 16206.
24. Al-Ṭayālisī, *Musnad*, vol. 2, pp. 414–19; Ibn Ḥanbal, *Musnad*, vol. 26, pp. 100–20.
25. Al-Ṭayālisī, *Musnad*, vol. 2, p. 415, *ḥadīth* 1185; Ibn Ḥanbal, *Musnad*, vol. 26, pp. 112–13, *aḥādīth* 16192–4; pp. 115–16, *ḥadīth* 16196.
26. Al-Tayālisī, *Musnad*, vol. 2, p. 417, *ḥadīth* 1188; Ibn Ḥanbal, *Musnad*, vol. 26, p. 106, *ḥadīth* 16187.
27. Al-Ṭayālisī, *Musnad*, vol. 2, p. 418, *ḥadīth* 1189; Ibn Ḥanbal, *Musnad*, vol. 26, p. 108, *ḥadīth* 16188; pp. 117–18, *ḥadīth* 16200.
28. Ibn Ḥanbal, *Musnad*, vol. 26, pp. 121–35, 306-11. Shuʿayb al-Arnaʾut and the other editors of the *Musnad* denounced the lengthy *ḥadīth* as weak, if not mere fabrication: Ibn Ḥanbal, *Musnad*, vol. 26, p. 128, footnote 4.
29. Ibn Ḥanbal, *Musnad*, vol. 26, p. 124, *ḥadīth* 16206. The phrase 'so many of us in the land' (*wa-naḥnu milʾa l-arḍ*), literally is 'we fill the land', and the phrase echoes Biblical references (for example, Genesis 1:28: 'fill the earth and subdue it', *milʾū et ha-aretz ve-khivshuha*).
30. Ibn Ḥanbal, *Musnad*, vol. 26, p. 125, *ḥadīth* 16206. For a concise presentation

of the different views regarding the beatific vision, including the traditionalistic stance of seeing God with one's eyes, see Gimaret, 'Ruʾyat Allāh'.

31. There was much dispute among scholars about Abu Razin's identity, because he was identified as either Laqit ibn ʿAmir or Laqit ibn Sabira (or Sabara). Al-Tirmidhi testified that al-Bukhari identified both Ibn ʿAmir and Ibn Sabira as the same person, while al-Darimi said that they were in fact two different people: al-Nawawī, *Tahdhīb*, vol. 2, p. 72; see also Ibn al-Athīr, *Usd al-Ghāba*, vol. 5, p. 253, biography 5100.
32. Al-Qalqashandī, *Nihāyat al-Arab*, p. 75; Levi Della Vida, 'al-Muntafiḳ'.
33. Ibn Kathīr, *al-Bidāya wa'l-Nihāya*, vol. 7, p. 231.
34. Ibn Ḥanbal, *Musnad*, vol. 26, p. 127, *ḥadīth* 16206.
35. Ibn Ḥanbal, *Musnad*, vol. 26, p. 121. The story of the delegation of Banu al-Muntafiq is not mentioned in *Sīrat Ibn Hishām.* Dalham's account of this event, which appears in later historical sources, is the only source about this event.
36. Ibn Ḥanbal, *Musnad*, vol. 26, pp. 121–2, *ḥadīth* 16206.
37. Ibn Ḥanbal, *Musnad*, vol. 26, p. 122, *ḥadīth* 16206.
38. Cf. Ibn Hishām, *Sīra*, vol. 4, pp. 248–9.
39. Ibn Ḥanbal, *Musnad*, vol. 26, p. 127, *ḥadīth* 16206.
40. Ibn Ḥanbal, *Musnad*, vol. 26, pp. 127–8, *ḥadīth* 16206.
41. Ibn Ḥanbal, *Musnad*, vol. 26, pp. 124–5, *ḥadīth* 16206.
42. Ibn Ḥanbal, *Musnad*, vol. 26, p. 122, *ḥadīth* 16206.
43. Here there is an echo to Proverbs 30:18–19 ('Three things are too wonderful for me; four I do not understand: the way of an eagle in the sky, the way of a snake on a rock, the way of a ship on the high seas, and the way of a man with a girl').
44. Ibn Ḥanbal, *Musnad*, vol. 26, pp. 122–3, *ḥadīth* 16206. Cf. Ibn Ḥanbal, *Musnad*, vol. 12, p. 487, *ḥadīth* 16150. The Prophet's speech was probably accompanied by folding his fingers one after the other, in order to indicate the number of the revealed secret; however, the text lacks any indication of this gesture.
45. Ibn Ḥanbal, *Musnad*, vol. 26, p. 123, *ḥadīth* 16206.
46. Ibn Ḥanbal, *Musnad*, vol. 26, p. 123. Abu Razin mentioned the powerful tribes of Madhhij and Khathʿam as the source of his troubles.
47. Ibn Ḥanbal, *Musnad*, vol. 26, pp. 123–6. Among other things, the Prophet tells Abu Razin about drinking from the Prophet's pool (*ḥawḍ al-Rasūl*) and the purifying effect of the water on the believers, about the eight gates of

Heaven and the seven gates of Hell, about the rivers of Heaven, and about the pure wives who are promised for the righteous believers.

48. Ibn Ḥanbal, *Musnad*, vol. 26, p. 127, *ḥadīth* 16206.
49. Ibn Ḥanbal, *Musnad*, vol. 26, pp. 127–8, *ḥadīth* 16206.
50. Ibn Ḥanbal, *Musnad*, vol. 26, p. 127, *ḥadīth* 16206.
51. Ibn Ḥanbal, *Musnad*, vol. 26, pp. 127–8, *ḥadīth* 16206.
52. Al-Ṭayālisī, *Musnad*, vol. 2, p. 416, *ḥadīth* 1186; Ibn Ḥanbal, *Musnad*, vol. 26, p. 109, *ḥadīth* 16189.
53. Al-Ṭabarānī, *al-Muʿjam al-Kabīr*, vol. 19, pp. 208–9, *ḥadīth* 472; al-Nawawī, *Tahdhīb al-Asmāʾ*, vol. 2, p. 72; Al-Iṣbahānī, *Maʿrifat al-Ṣaḥāba*, vol. 5, p. 2418.
54. Lane, *Arabic-English Lexicon*, vol. 4, p. 1284.
55. There is a relatively long account on the authority of ʿAsim, Abu Razin's son, about Abu Razin's visit to ʿAʾisha's private residence. Abu Razin and his friend wanted to visit the Prophet. While waiting for him, ʿAʾisha gave the guests a modest meal of dates and porridge. When the Prophet entered the house, he inquired whether the guests had eaten. A few moments later, the shepherd who was responsible for the Prophet's herd brought him a newborn she-lamb. The Prophet immediately ordered that a male lamb be slaughtered and its meat prepared for the guests. The Prophet explained that the lamb was not slaughtered because of the guests, but because he kept his herd with only 100 sheep. While eating together, Abu Razin addressed two questions to the Prophet and consulted him about his wife's tongue-lashing. The Prophet advised him either to divorce her or educate her: Ibn Ḥanbal, *Musnad*, vol. 26, p. 309, *ḥadīth* 16384.
56. Ibn ʿAsākir, *Tārīkh Dimashq*, vol. 53, p. 72 (the biography of Muhammad ibn Saʿid ibn Hassan ibn Qays).
57. Al-Dhahabī, *Siyar Aʿlām al-Nubalāʾ*, vol. 11, pp. 60–1; al-Bukhārī, *Tārīkh*, vol. 1, p. 283.
58. The teacher is the Medinese *muḥaddith* ʿAbd al-Rahman ibn al-Mughira al-Hizami (death date between 816 and 826): al-Bukhārī, *Tārīkh*, vol. 5, p. 354.
59. Al-Qalqashandī, *Nihāyat al-Arab*, p. 75; Levi Della Vida, 'al-Muntafiḳ', *EI2*.
60. Ibn Ḥanbal, *Musnad*, vol. 26, p. 127, *ḥadīth* 16206.
61. Al-Ṭayālisī, *Musnad*, vol. 2, pp. 414–19; Ibn Ḥanbal, *Musnad*, vol. 26, pp. 100–20.
62. Ibn Ḥanbal, *Musnad*, vol. 26, p. 121, *ḥadīth* 16206.
63. This *isnād* is considered weak by the Hadith scholars: Ibn Ḥanbal, *Musnad*, vol. 26, p. 128, footnote 4.

64. Al-Bukhārī, *Tārīkh*, vol. 5, pp. 335–6 (the biography of ʿAbd Allah ibn ʿAyyash al-Ansari).
65. Ibn Ḥibbān, *al-Thiqāt*, vol. 7, p. 71.
66. Yaʿla ibn ʿAtaʾ's material was transmitted by Kufan *muḥaddithūn* like al-Shaʿbi (d. c. 718) and Sufyan al-Thawri (d. 778), and by the Basran *muḥaddith* Hammad ibn Salama (d. 784): al-Bukhārī, *Tārīkh*, vol. 8, p. 415 (the biography of Yaʿla ibn ʿAtaʾ).
67. Cf. al-Tabarani, *al-Muʿjam al-Kabīr*, vol. 19, pp. 204–17, *aḥādīth* 459–83.
68. Ibn ʿAsākir, *Tārīkh Dimashq*, vol. 53, p. 72 (the biography of Muhammad ibn Saʿid ibn Hassan ibn Qays).
69. Al-Dhahabī, *Tārīkh al-Islām*, vol. 9, p. 270. For a summary of sources about Ibn al-Tabari, see van Ess, *TG*, vol. 1, pp. 136–7. Van Ess suggested that the execution took place in 770, during al-Mansur's visit to Damascus: van Ess, *TG*, vol. 1, p. 136.
70. Ibn ʿAsākir, *Tārīkh Dimashq*, vol. 53, p. 74 (the biography of Muhammad ibn Saʿid ibn Hassan ibn Qays).
71. Ibn ʿAsākir, *Tārīkh Dimashq*, vol. 53, pp. 72–3.
72. Ibn ʿAsākir, *Tārīkh Dimashq*, vol. 53, pp. 72–3.
73. Al-Qurṭubī, *al-Jāmiʿ*, vol. 1, pp. 136–7 (interpretation of Q. 2:9).
74. Al-Dhahabī, *Tārīkh al-Islām*, vol. 9, p. 270. The only *ḥadīth* attributed to Ibn al-Tabari that we managed to locate in *Sunan al-Tirmidhī* is accompanied by a warning from al-Tirmidhi that Muhammad ibn Hassan (Ibn al-Tabari) was unreliable: al-Tirmidhī, *Sunan*, p. 805, *ḥadīth* 3549 (*Kitāb al-Daʿwāt, bāb fī duʿāʾ al-nabī*).
75. Watt, *Islamic Creeds*, p. 37; Holtzman 'Does God Really Laugh?', p. 184.
76. For a list of scholars from Iraq and Khurasan who taught this *ḥadīth* between the ninth to the eleventh centuries, see Ibn Qayyim al-Jawziyya, *Zād al-Maʿād*, p. 51. Ibn al-Qayyim relied heavily on an unknown text by the Isfahani *muḥaddith* Abu ʿAbd Allah Ibn Manda (d. 1005).
77. Al-Bukhārī, *Tārīkh*, vol. 3, p. 249 (the biography of Dalham).
78. Ibn Qayyim al-Jawziyya, *Ḥādī al-Arwāḥ*, p. 536.
79. Ibn Qayyim al-Jawziyya, *Zād al-Maʿād*, p. 51.
80. Ibn Khuzayma, *Kitāb al-Tawḥīd*, pp. 460–76.
81. The *ḥadīth* appears in the abridgement of the *Ṣawāʿiq*: Ibn Qayyim al-Jawziyya and Ibn al-Mawṣilī, *Mukhtaṣar al-Ṣawāʿiq*, pp. 1170–86.
82. Ibn Qayyim al-Jawziyya, *Ḥādī al-Arwāḥ*, pp. 530–7; Ibn Qayyim al-Jawziyya, *Zād al-Maʿād*, vol. 3, pp. 48–56.

83. Ibn Qayyim al-Jawziyya, *Ḥādī al-Arwāḥ*, p. 536.
84. Ibn Qayyim al-Jawziyya, *Ḥādī al-Arwāḥ*, p. 537. For Abu Razin's tenth question, see Ibn Ḥanbal, *Musnad*, vol. 26, p. 126, *ḥadīth* 16206.
85. The same material was used verbatim by Ibn Kathir (d. 1373) in *al-Bidāya wa'l-Nihāya*, vol. 7, pp. 332–9. This material does not appear in the classical biography of the Prophet authored by Ibn Hisham. Ibn Kathir also used Abu Razin's *ḥadith* of allegiance in his commentary of Q. 47:14–15: Ibn Kathīr, *Tafsīr al-Qur'ān al-ᶜAẓīm*, vol. 7, pp. 313–14.
86. Ibn Qayyim al-Jawziyya, *Ḥādī al-Arwāḥ*, p. 536.
87. *Tuḥfat al-Ashrāf* is an index to the six canonical Hadith compilations arranged in *aṭrāf*, namely the abbreviated content of the *aḥādīth*. On this work, its arrangement and importance, see Juynboll, *Encyclopedia of Canonical Hadith*, pp. xvii–xviii.
88. Al-Mizzī, *Tuḥfat al-Ashrāf*, vol. 7, pp. 583–4. For the full text of this one line *ḥadīth*, see Abū Dāwūd, *Sunan*, p. 368, *ḥadīth* 3266 (*Kitāb al-Aymān wa'l-Nudhūr, bāb fī 'l-qasam hal yakūnu yamīnan*).
89. Al-Ājurrī, *Kitāb al-Sharīᶜa*, pp. 108–11, *aḥādīth* 205–8; pp. 195–6, *ḥadīth* 378; *Musnad*, vol. 1, pp. 434–6, *ḥadīth* 367 (*Musnad ᶜUmar ibn al-Khaṭṭāb*). The *ḥadīth* opens *Ṣaḥīḥ Muslim*: Muslim, *Ṣaḥīḥ*, p. 36, *ḥadīth* 1 (*Kitāb al-Īmān, bāb bayān al-īmān wa'l-islām wa'l-iḥsān*). For references to other Hadith compilations, see Ibn Ḥanbal, *Musnad*, vol. 1, p. 436, footnote 1.
90. For the most known version of this much circulated and translated *ḥadīth*, see Ibn Ḥanbal, *Musnad*, vol. 1, pp. 434–6 (*Musnad ᶜUmar ibn al-Khaṭṭāb, ḥadīth* 367). For references to this specific *ḥadīth* in the prominent Hadith compilations, see ibid. p. 436, footnote 1.
91. Al-Ājurrī, *Kitāb al-Sharīᶜa*, p. 109; Muslim, *Ṣaḥīḥ*, p. 36.
92. Al-Ājurrī, *Kitāb al-Sharīᶜa*, p. 109; Muslim, *Ṣaḥīḥ*, p. 36.
93. Ibn Ḥanbal, *Musnad*, vol. 26, pp. 113–14, *ḥadīth* 16194; Ibn al-Athīr, *Usd al-Ghāba*, vol. 4, p. 492 (the biography of Abu Razin, Laqit ibn ᶜAmir).
94. Al-Ājurrī, *Kitāb al-Sharīᶜa*, p. 196, *ḥadīth* 380. Another version attributed to Jarir with an extremely elaborate framing narrative appears in Ibn al-Athīr, *Usd al-Ghāba*, vol. 6, p. 401 (the biography of Jarir).
95. Al-Dhahabī, *Siyar Aᶜlām al-Nubalā'*, vol. 5, pp. 433–7. In this case, his source is unknown, because he directly quoted Abu Razin.
96. Ibn ᶜAsakir summarised the opinions of the Hadith experts about Khalid ibn Yazid in the latter's short biographical entry: Ibn ᶜAsākir, *Tārīkh Dimashq*, vol. 16, pp. 285–8.

97. For Khalid ibn ᶜAbd Allah al-Qasri al-Bajali's biography and especially his activities against heretical movements, see Hawting, 'Khālid b. ᶜAbd Allāh al-Ḳasrī', *EI2*. Morony seems to misidentify him: Morony, *Iraq*, p. 671 (Khalid al-Qasri and Khalid ibn ᶜAbdullah ibn Asid indicated in Morony's index are actually the same person).
98. Al-Dhahabī, *Siyar Aᶜlām al-Nubalāᵓ*, vol. 2, p. 530.
99. See, for example, the rare material that al-Ajurri collected about the uncreatedness of the Quran and the pro-Shiᶜite material that takes the lion's share of the book: al-Ājurrī, *Kitāb al-Sharīᶜa*, pp. 81–102, 714–821.
100. Al-Ājurrī, *Kitāb al-Sharīᶜa*, pp. 264–91.
101. Al-Ājurrī, *Kitāb al-Sharīᶜa*, pp. 272–4.
102. Al-Bukhārī, *Ṣaḥīḥ*, vol. 1, p. 190, *ḥadīth* 554 (*Kitāb Mawāqīt al-Ṣalāt, bāb faḍl ṣalāt al-ᶜaṣr*); vol. 1, p. 96, *ḥadīth* 573 (*Kitāb Mawāqīt al-Ṣalāt, bāb faḍl ṣalāt al-fajr*); vol. 3, p. 296, *ḥadīth* 4851 (*Kitāb al-Tafsīr, bāb wa-sabbiḥ bi-ḥamdi rabbika*); Muslim, *Ṣaḥīḥ*, p. 249, *ḥadīth* 211 (*Kitāb al-Masājid, bāb faḍl ṣalātay 'l-ṣubḥ wa'l-ᶜaṣr*); al-Tirmidhī, *Sunan*, vol. 4, p. 687, *ḥadīth* 2551 (*Kitāb Ṣifat al-Janna, bāb mā jāᵓa fī ruᵓyat al-rabb*); Ibn Māja, *Sunan*, p. 47, *ḥadīth* 177 (*bāb fīmā ankarat al-jahmiyya*); Ibn Ḥanbal, *Musnad*, vol. 31, pp. 526–30 (*Musnad Jarīr*).
103. This report is according to al-Waqidi (d. 822), as quoted by Ibn Jarir al-Tabari (d. 923): al-Ṭabarī, *Tārīkh*, vol. 3, p. 158 (the events of the year 10). Cf. Donner, *Early Islamic Conquests*, p. 201.
104. Al-Dhahabī, *Siyar Aᶜlām al-Nubalāᵓ*, vol. 2, p. 532.
105. ᶜUmar ibn al-Khattab compared Jarir's good looks to those of the Biblical Joseph: al-Dhahabī, *Siyar Aᶜlām al-Nubalāᵓ*, vol. 2, pp. 534–5.
106. For different versions of this story, see Ibn Kathir, *al-Bidāya wa'l-Nihāya*, vol. 7, pp. 324–8.
107. Jarir's description of the tribal lands in rhymed prose (*sajᶜ*) is an indication of his poetic skills: al-Ṭabarānī, *al-Aḥādīth al-Ṭiwāl*, p. 20.
108. Al-Ṭabarānī, *al-Aḥādīth al-Ṭiwāl*, pp. 19–21.
109. Al-Ṭabarī, *Tārīkh*, vol. 3, p. 187 (the events of Hijri year 11); Donner, *Early Islamic Conquests*, p. 201. Al-Baladhuri reports on a controversy between scholars: whether the Prophet assigned Jarir to fight the rebel al-Aswad al-ᶜAnsi in Yemen or not: al-Balādhurī, *Futūḥ al-Buldān*, p. 146.
110. Al-Dhahabī, *Siyar Aᶜlām al-Nubalāᵓ*, vol. 2, p. 531; Ibn Kathīr, *al-Bidāya wa'l-Nihāya*, vol. 7, pp. 326.
111. Al-Ṣafadi quotes a statement by Jarir that his conversion occurred forty days

before the Prophet's death: al-Ṣafadī, *al-Wāfī*, vol. 11, p. 58 (the biography of Jarir).

112. Ibn al-Jawzī, *Al-Muntaẓam*, vol. 3, p. 383; Ibn Kathīr, *al-Bidāya wa'l-Nihāya*, vol. 7, p. 328. For further references, see Fahd, 'Dhu 'l-Khalaṣa', *EI2*, vol. 2, pp. 241–2; Watt, 'Badjīla', *EI2*; Donner, *Early Islamic Conquests*, p. 68.

113. For the role of Jarir and the Banu Bajila in the conquest of Iraq, see Donner, *Early Islamic Conquests*, pp. 196–202. Jarir negotiated with ᶜUmar ibn al-Khattab regarding a piece of land that was promised to his tribe for their participation in the battle of al-Qadisiyya. He later relinquished his claim: Morony, *Iraq*, pp. 239–41; Donner, *Early Islamic Conquests*, pp. 242, 260.

114. Morony, *Iraq*, pp. 236–7. From its inception, Kufa was dominated by Medinese politics. For the establishment of the social order in Kufa, the system of stipends and the distribution of land, see Hinds, 'Kūfan Politics', pp. 348–9.

115. Morony, *Iraq*, p. 239.

116. Morony, *Iraq*, pp. 242–3; Donner, *Early Islamic Conquests*, p. 228; Djaït, 'al-Kūfa', *EI2*.

117. Hinds, 'Kūfan Politics', pp. 346–7. On Jarir's involvement in the inner politics of Kufa, see ibid. pp. 353–4.

118. Morony, *Iraq*, pp. 240–1.

119. Al-Ṭabarī, *Tārīkh*, vol. 3, pp. 576–7 (the events of Hijri year 14).

120. Al-Ṭabarī, *Tārīkh*, vol. 4, p. 561 (the events of Hijri year 36).

121. Al-Ṭabarī, *Tārīkh*, vol. 4, pp. 561–2 (the events of Hijri year 36); al-Dhahabī, *Tārīkh al-Islām*, vol. 3, p. 538 (the events of Hijri year 37).

122. Al-Ṭabarī, *Tārīkh*, vol. 4, p. 562.

123. Naṣr ibn Muzāḥim, *Waqᶜat Ṣiffīn*, p. 12.

124. Al-Sarāt is a chain of mountains that run from the Gulf of ᶜAqaba to the Gulf of Aden: Donner, *Early Islamic Conquests*, p. 68; Grohmann [van Donzel], 'al-Sarāt', *EI2*.

125. Al-Khaṭīb al-Baghdādī, *Tārīkh Madīnat al-Salām*, vol. 1, p. 545. For a description of the Jarir–ᶜAli relationship in a wider context, see Hinds, 'Kūfan Politics', pp. 362–7.

126. Ibn ᶜAsākir, *Tārīkh Dimashq*, vol. 72, p. 74 (the biography of Jarir).

127. Naṣr ibn Muzāḥim, *Waqᶜat Ṣiffīn*, p. 61; Lecker, 'Ṣiffīn', *EI2*. On the ascription of this work to Naṣr, see Leder, 'The Literary Use', pp. 293–301.

128. Al-Dhahabī, *Siyar Aᶜlām al-Nubalāᵓ*, vol. 5, p. 8.

129. Al-Dhahabī, *Siyar Aᶜlām al-Nubalāᵓ*, vol. 2, p. 537.

130. Juynboll provides a general survey on Kufa as a centre of Hadith: Juynboll,

Muslim Tradition, pp. 58–62. As far as we know, a study on Kufa as a centre of Hadith transmission is yet to be written. See the remark of Scott Lucas about the prominence of Kufa as a Hadith centre: Lucas, *Constructive Critics*, p. 355.

131. Al-Dāraquṭnī, *Kitāb al-Ruʾya*, pp. 192–249; Ibn Qayyim al-Jawziyya, *Ḥādī al-Arwāḥ*, pp. 634–7.
132. Jarir was among the few *ṣaḥāba* to whom sub-chapters concentrating on their merits were dedicated in the important Hadith compilations: Lucas, *Constructive Critics*, p. 256.
133. A verse Jarir composed on the battlefield in al-Qadisiyya is quoted by al-Tabari: al-Ṭabarī, *Tārīkh*, vol. 3, p. 577 (the events of Hijri year 14). More impressive is the rhymed and metered speech that Jarir gave to his adherents in his court in Hamadhan, in which he explains why they all should pledge allegiance to ʿAli: Naṣr ibn Muzāḥim, *Waqʿat Ṣiffīn*, pp. 18–19.
134. Jarir's privileged status was recognised by the Hadith experts Ibn Abi Shayba (d. 849), al-Bukhari (d. 870), Muslim (d. 874) and ʿAbd Allah ibn Ahmad ibn Hanbal. All four experts included Jarir in the list of the twenty-three most esteemed *ṣaḥāba*. Jarir is the only late convert recorded in this list: Lucas, *Constructive Critics*, p. 259.
135. Al-Khaṭīb al-Baghdādī, *Tārīkh Madīnat al-Salām*, vol. 14, pp. 464, 467.
136. Al-Khaṭīb al-Baghdādī, *Tārīkh Madīnat al-Salām*, vol. 14, p. 467.
137. Ibn ʿAsākir, *Tārīkh Dimashq*, vol. 49, p. 463.
138. Al-Dhahabī, *Siyar Aʿlām al-Nubalāʾ*, vol. 4, pp. 199–200 (the biography of Qays). The Hadith expert is Yahya al-Qattan (d. 813).
139. Al-Ṭabarānī, *al-Muʿjam al-Kabīr*, vol. 2, pp. 290–9.
140. The most conspicuous anecdotes are those from the Battle of al-Qadisiyya: al-Ṭabarī, *Tārīkh*, vol. 3, pp. 576–80.
141. See, for example, an anecdote in which Jarir remembered that he heard mysterious Yemenites foretell the Prophet's death: Ibn Kathīr, *al-Bidāya wa'l-Nihāya*, vol. 8, pp. 169–70.
142. Al-Ṭabarānī, *al-Muʿjam al-Kabīr*, vol. 2, pp. 293–312.
143. Al-Ṭabarī, *Tārīkh*, vol. 3, p. 576 (the events of Hijri year 14); al-Khaṭīb al-Baghdādī, *Tārīkh Madīnat al-Salām*, vol. 14, pp. 464–5.
144. Al-Khaṭīb al-Baghdādī, *Tārīkh Madīnat al-Salām*, vol. 14, p. 464.
145. See a quote by the Hadith expert ʿAli ibn al-Madini (d. 849) that Qays did not participate in the Battle of the Camel: al-Khaṭīb al-Baghdādī, *Tārīkh Madīnat al-Salām*, vol. 14, p. 466.
146. Al-Dhahabī, *Tārīkh al-Islām*, vol. 6, p. 458 (the biography of Qays).

147. Juynboll, 'The Role of *Mu*ᶜ*ammarūn*', pp. 155–6, 165.
148. Al-Dhahabī, *Siyar A*ᶜ*lām al-Nubalā*ᵓ, vol. 4, p. 201 (the biography of Qays); al-Dhahabī, *Tārīkh al-Islām*, vol. 6, p. 458 (the biography of Qays).
149. Ibn Ḥajar, *Hady al-Sārī* (the introductory volume to *Fatḥ al-Bārī*), p. 458.
150. Al-Dhahabī, *Siyar A*ᶜ*lām al-Nubalā*ᵓ, vol. 4, p. 201 (the biography of Qays ibn Abi Hazim); al-Dhahabī, *Tārīkh al-Islām*, vol. 6, pp. 459–60 (the biography of Qays).
151. Juynboll, *Muslim Tradition*, p. 58, note 215. Juynboll argues that Ismaᶜil was considered a *tābi*ᶜ*ī*, or claimed the title of a *tābi*ᶜ*ī*, because Qays – his source – was a *mu*ᶜ*ammar*.
152. Al-Dhahabī, *Siyar A*ᶜ*lām al-Nubalā*ᵓ, vol. 6, p. 176 (the biography of Ismaᶜil ibn Abi Khalid).
153. Al-Dhahabī, *Siyar A*ᶜ*lām al-Nubalā*ᵓ, vol. 6, p. 177 (the biography of Ismaᶜil ibn Abi Khalid); Ibn al-ᶜImād, *Shadharāt al-Dhahab*, vol. 2, p. 208 (the events of Hijri year 145).
154. Lucas, *Constructive Critics*, pp. 375–6 (a clarification on the title *ḥāfiẓ*). References to Ismaᶜil ibn Abi Khalid: ibid. pp. 343, 346.
155. Al-Dhahabī, *Tārīkh al-Islām*, vol. 9, p. 69 (the biography of Ismaᶜil ibn Abi Khalid).
156. Ibn Saᶜd, *Ṭabaqāt*, vol. 8, p. 463 (the biography of Ismaᶜil ibn Abi Khalid); al-Dhahabī, *Siyar A*ᶜ*lām al-Nubalā*ᵓ, vol. 6, p. 176; al-Dhahabī, *Tārīkh al-Islām*, vol. 9, p. 68.
157. The sources disagree about his father's name; some sources suggested that he was called Hurmuz: Ibn Saᶜd, *Ṭabaqāt*, vol. 8, p. 463; al-Dhahabī, *Siyar A*ᶜ*lām al-Nubalā*ᵓ, vol. 6, p. 176; al-Dhahabī, *Tārīkh al-Islām*, vol. 9, p. 68.
158. On the inferior status of non-Arabs in the Umayyad society, see Crone, *Roman, Provincial and Islamic Law*, pp. 40–2, 55.
159. Ibn Ḥanbal, ᶜ*Ilal*, vol. 1, pp. 347–8 (*bāb fī al-laḥn*), vol. 2, p. 249.
160. Ibn Ḥajar, *Tahdhīb*, vol. 1, p. 148 (the biography of Ismaᶜil ibn Abi Khalid).
161. Al-Ājurrī, *Kitāb al-Sharī*ᶜ*a*, pp. 273–4 (*ḥadīth* 595).
162. Al-Ājurrī, *Kitāb al-Sharī*ᶜ*a*, pp. 272–3 (*aḥādīth* 592–4).
163. The various readings of *tuḍammūna* and *tuḍarrūna* are neatly presented by Abu Muhammad al-ᶜAyni (d. 1451) in ᶜ*Umdat al-Qārī*, vol. 5, p. 61 (*Kitāb Mawāqīt al-Ṣalāt, bāb faḍl ṣalāt al-*ᶜ*aṣr*).
164. Al-Dāraquṭnī, *Kitāb al-Ru*ᵓ*ya*, pp. 98–9, 112–13.
165. Ibn Ḥanbal, *Musnad*, vol. 31, p. 541, *ḥadīth* 19205 (the *Musnad* of the People of Kufa).

166. Al-Bukhārī, *Ṣaḥīḥ*, vol. 1, p. 190, *ḥadīth* 554 (*Kitāb Mawāqīt al-Ṣalāt, bāb faḍl ṣalāt al-ᶜaṣr*).
167. Al-Dāraquṭnī, *Kitāb al-Ruʾya*, pp. 192–249. Ibn Qayyim al-Jawziyya conveniently arranged the names of the 105 *muḥaddithūn* in a list: Ibn Qayyim al-Jawziyya, *Ḥādī al-Arwāḥ*, pp. 634–7. The directness in transmission is designated by the transmission terms 'I heard' (*samiᶜtu*), 'he reported to us' (*ḥaddathanā*) and even the ambiguous *ᶜan*, 'on the authority of' that link Ismaᶜil ibn Abi Khalid and each of the 105 *muḥaddithūn*.
168. Al-Dāraquṭnī, *Kitāb al-Ruʾya*, pp. 214–15; Ibn Qayyim al-Jawziyya, *Ḥādī al-Arwāḥ*, p. 634; al-Dhahabī, *Siyar Aᶜlām al-Nubalāʾ*, vol. 7, pp. 174–6.
169. Al-Dāraquṭnī, *Kitāb al-Ruʾya*, p. 208; Ibn Qayyim al-Jawziyya, *Ḥādī al-Arwāḥ*, p. 6350; al-Dhahabī, *Siyar Aᶜlām al-Nubalāʾ*, vol. 7, pp. 174–6.
170. Al-Dāraquṭnī, *Kitāb al-Ruʾya*, p. 198; Ibn Qayyim al-Jawziyya, *Ḥādī al-Arwāḥ*, p. 634; al-Dhahabī, *Siyar Aᶜlām al-Nubalāʾ*, vol. 8, pp. 454–6 (his biography extends more than thirty pages).
171. Al-Dāraquṭnī, *Kitāb al-Ruʾya*, pp. 210–11; Ibn Qayyim al-Jawziyya, *Ḥādī al-Arwāḥ*, p. 634; al-Dhahabī, *Siyar Aᶜlām al-Nubalāʾ*, vol. 9, pp. 140–68.
172. Al-Dāraquṭnī, *Kitāb al-Ruʾya*, p. 233; Ibn Qayyim al-Jawziyya, *Ḥādī al-Arwāḥ*, p. 636; al-Dhahabī, *Siyar Aᶜlām al-Nubalāʾ*, vol. 10, pp. 160–2. Yahya was known to be the last disciple of Ismaᶜil.
173. Al-Dāraquṭnī, *Kitāb al-Ruʾya*, pp. 222–3, 248; Ibn Qayyim al-Jawziyya, *Ḥādī al-Arwāḥ*, pp. 636–7.
174. Al-Dāraquṭnī, *Kitāb al-Ruʾya*, p. 244; al-Dāraquṭnī, *al-ᶜIlal*, vol. 13, p. 453. The four Bajalis mentioned by al-Daraqutni are: Bayan ibn Bishr al-Bajali, Tariq ibn ᶜAbd al-Rahman al-Ahmasi, Jarir ibn Yazid ibn Jarir al-Bajali and ᶜIsa ibn al-Musayyib.
175. Ibn Ḥajar, *Tahdhīb*, vol. 1, p. 298.
176. See the anecdote in al-Dhahabī, *Siyar Aᶜlām al-Nubalāʾ*, vol. 4, p. 309 (the biography of al-Shaᶜbi).
177. Bayan ibn Bishr al-Bajali was considered 'reliable' (*thiqa*): al-Dhahabī, *Siyar Aᶜlām al-Nubalāʾ*, vol. 6, p. 124 (the biography of Bayan). Mujalid ibn Saᶜid al-Kufi al-Hamadhani was controversial; most scholars did not approve of his versions: al-Dhahabī, *Siyar Aᶜlām al-Nubalāʾ*, vol. 6, pp. 284–7 (the biography of Mujalid). The scholars also could not agree on Tariq ibn ᶜAbd al-Rahman al-Bajali al-Ahmasi's reliability: Ibn Ḥajar, *Tahdhīb*, vol. 2, p. 233. ᶜIsa ibn al-Musayyab al-Bajali was considered 'weak' (*ḍaᶜīf*): Ibn Ḥajar, *Līsān al-Mīzān*, vol. 6, p. 280.

178. The versions of these five transmitters were rejected because of flaws in the chains of transmission: al-Dāraquṭnī, *Kitāb al-Ruʾya*, p. 245–9. Bayan ibn Bishr's version appears in the thematic compilations, like al-Ājurrī, *Kitāb al-Sharīʿa*, p. 273, *ḥadīth* 595 and Ibn Khuzayma, *Kitāb al-Tawḥīd*, p. 412, *ḥadīth* 239. For further references, see al-Dāraquṭnī, *Kitāb al-Ruʾya*, p. 245.
179. Al-Dāraquṭnī, *Kitāb al-Ruʾya*, p. 244. Ibn Qayyim al-Jawziyya duplicated al-Daraqutni's remark in *Ḥādī al-Arwāḥ*, p. 637. For the meaning of *mutābaʿa*, see Juynboll, *Encyclopedia of Canonical Ḥadīth*, p. xxvii.
180. 'Single strand', coined by Juynboll, is in fact parallel to the traditional *khabar al-wāḥid*: Juynboll, *Encyclopedia of Canonical Ḥadīth*, pp. xviii, xxiv.
181. See the chart in Juynboll, 'The Role of *Muʿammarūn*', p. 156.
182. This is the core of Juynboll's argument that Ismaʿil invented Qays, Jarir and the traditions that he allegedly transmitted on their authority. This hypothesis appears also in Juynboll, 'The Role of *Muʿammarūn*', pp. 155–6, 165 and 'Munkar', *EI2*. We do not embrace Juynboll's sceptic view. That said, we found Juynboll's other observations most helpful for our discussion.
183. Ibn Qayyim al-Jawziyya, *Ḥādī al-Arwāḥ*, p. 637.
184. For informative and illuminating analysis of the *miḥna*, one should consult Madelung, 'The Origins of the Controversy' and Shah, 'Trajectories in the Development of Islamic Theological Thought'.
185. Melchert, *Ahmad ibn Hanbal*, pp. 8–18.
186. Turner, *Inquisition in Early Islam*, p. 92.
187. Al-Khatib al-Baghdadi doubted whether Ahmad ibn Hanbal was interrogated about the beatific vision during the *miḥna*: al-Dhahabī, *Siyar Aʿlām al-Nubalāʾ*, vol. 11, p. 54.
188. Ḥanbal, *Dhikr*, p. 52; Cooperson, *Classical Arabic Biography*, p. 122.
189. Ḥanbal, *Dhikr*, p. 52.
190. Ḥanbal, *Dhikr*, p. 53.
191. Holtzman, 'Anthropomorphism', *EI3*.
192. Ḥanbal, *Dhikr*, p. 52; Cooperson, *Classical Arabic Biography*, p. 122.
193. Dickinson, *The Development*, pp. 49–53; Lucas, *Constructive Critics*, pp. 49, 75 (esp. footnote 40); Hurvitz, *The Formation*, p. 151.
194. According to the exegetical tradition of the Quran, Job (Ayyub) was put to the test by Satan, but remained faithful to God. After eighteen years of suffering, God rewarded him by restoring to him his property and family: al-Ṭabarī, *Jāmiʿ al-Bayān*, vol. 20, pp. 109–11 (interpretation of Q. 38:41–4). The exegetical tradition of the Quran also mentions the tale of David (Dawud),

Uriah and Bathsheba: al-Ṭabarī, *Jāmiᶜ al-Bayān*, vol. 20, pp. 58–61, 64–9 (interpretation of Q. 38:24).

195. Al-Dhahabī, *Siyar Aᶜlām al-Nubalāᵓ*, vol. 11, pp. 51–2 (the biography of ᶜAli ibn al-Madini). The same biography, with slight changes, appears in al-Dhahabī, *Tārīkh al-Islām*, vol. 17, pp. 276–81. For al-Dhahabi's judgement of Ghulam Khalil as an unreliable *muḥaddith* who fabricated his material, see al-Dhahabī, *Siyar Aᶜlām al-Nubalāᵓ*, vol. 13, pp. 282–5 (the biography of Ghulam Khalil). Al-Dhahabi copied the anecdote from al-Khaṭīb al-Baghdādī, *Tārīkh Madīnat al-Salām*, vol. 13, p. 431.
196. Melchert, *Ahmad Ibn Hanbal*, p. 17; Hurvitz, *The Formation*, p. 151; van Ess, *TG*, vol. 3, p. 464. On Ibn al-Madini's capitulation and the humiliation that followed it, see al-Dhahabī, *Siyar Aᶜlām al-Nubalāᵓ*, vol. 11, pp. 54–6.
197. Al-Khaṭīb al-Baghdādī, *Tārīkh Madīnat al-Salām*, vol. 13, pp. 434–5; Ibn al-Jawzī, *Manāqib*, p. 526; al-Dhahabī, *Siyar Aᶜlām al-Nubalāᵓ*, vol. 11, p. 54.
198. Al-Khaṭīb al-Baghdādī, *Tārīkh Madīnat al-Salām*, vol. 13, p. 432; Ibn al-Jawzī, *Manāqib*, pp. 526–7; al-Dhahabī, *Siyar Aᶜlām al-Nubalāᵓ*, vol. 11, p. 52. Al-Dhahabi and Ibn al-Jawzi in fact copied the entire story about *ḥadīth al-ruᵓya* in the *miḥna* from al-Khatib al-Baghdadi (d. 1071).
199. Al-Khaṭīb al-Baghdādī, *Tārīkh Madīnat al-Salām*, vol. 13, p. 432; Ibn al-Jawzī, *Manāqib*, p. 527; al-Dhahabī, *Siyar Aᶜlām al-Nubalāᵓ*, vol. 11, pp. 52–3.
200. Al-Khaṭīb al-Baghdādī, *Tārīkh Madīnat al-Salām*, vol. 13, p. 432; Ibn al-Jawzī, *Manāqib*, p. 527; al-Dhahabī, *Siyar Aᶜlām al-Nubalāᵓ*, vol. 11, p. 53. The expression 'a Bedouin who frequently urinates on his heels' (*aᶜrābī bawwāl ᶜalā ᶜaqibayhi*) is not recorded, as far as I know, in any of the classical dictionaries. However, a *ḥadīth* on an argument between two *muḥaddithūn* about the marriage of the Prophet to Maymuna Bint al-Harith (d. 681) clarifies this expression. The two *muḥaddithūn* argued whether the Prophet married her when he was in a state of ritual consecration (*muḥrim*) or not (*ḥalāl*). One of the *muḥaddithūn* brought Ibn ᶜAbbas's words as evidence that the Prophet was *muḥrim* when he married her. The other *muḥaddith* brought Yazid ibn al-Asamm's (d. 720 or 722) words that the Prophet was *ḥalāl*, and added: 'She (i.e. Maymuna) was Yazid's maternal aunt.' The first *muḥaddith* exclaimed: 'Do you compare a Bedouin urinating on his heels with Ibn ᶜAbbas? She was also the maternal aunt of Ibn ᶜAbbas!': al-Bayhaqī, *al-Sunan al-Kabīr*, vol. 9, p. 497, *ḥadīth* 9231 (*Kitāb al-Ḥajj, bāb al-muḥrim lā yankuḥu wa-lā yunkaḥu*). Since Yazid transmitted *aḥādīth* from both Maymuna and Ibn ᶜAbbas, the intention of the speaker was to indicate Yazid's insignificance as a source of knowledge.

201. Al-Khaṭīb al-Baghdādī, *Tārīkh Madīnat al-Salām*, vol. 13, p. 433; Ibn al-Jawzī, *Manāqib*, p. 527; al-Dhahabī, *Siyar A*ᶜ*lām al-Nubalā*ᵓ, vol. 11, pp. 52–3.
202. This is our interpretation of the sentence that closes the anecdote. The sentence reads *fa-kāna hādhā wa-ashbāhuhu min awkad 'l-umūr fī ḍarbihi*: al-Khaṭīb al-Baghdādī, *Tārīkh Madīnat al-Salām*, vol. 13, p. 432; al-Dhahabī, *Siyar A*ᶜ*lām al-Nubalā*ᵓ, vol. 11, p. 53. In addition to the adjective *awkad* (see al-Zabīdī, *Tāj al-*ᶜ*Arūs*, vol. 5, p. 324), which is quite rare, the sentence is rather obscure. We concluded that this sentence refers to Ibn al-Madini and not Ibn Hanbal; therefore *ḍarbihi* here refers to Ibn al-Madini's humiliation and downfall and not to Ibn Hanbal's flogging by his interrogators.
203. Al-Khaṭīb al-Baghdādī, *Tārīkh Madīnat al-Salām*, vol. 13, pp. 433–4; Ibn al-Jawzī, *Manāqib*, p. 528; al-Dhahabī, *Siyar A*ᶜ*lām al-Nubalā*ᵓ, vol. 11, p. 54.
204. Al-Khaṭīb al-Baghdādī, *Tārīkh Madīnat al-Salām*, vol. 13, p. 432; al-Dhahabī, *Siyar A*ᶜ*lām al-Nubalā*ᵓ, vol. 11, p. 54.
205. Al-Dhahabī, *Siyar A*ᶜ*lām al-Nubalā*ᵓ, vol. 11, p. 53. On Yahya al-Qattan, see Lucas, *Constructive Critics*, pp. 149–51.
206. The *ḥadīth* in question, on the basis of which Yahya al-Qattan tagged Qays as *munkar al-ḥadīth*, recounts the story of the dogs of Hawᵓab, which was a well on the road to Basra. The dogs barked at ᶜAᵓisha and her escorts, so she decided to return because of a comment the Prophet told her about 'the dogs of Hawᵓab' (*kilāb al-ḥaw*ᵓ*ab*): al-Dhahabī, *Tārīkh al-Islām*, vol. 6, p. 459 (the biography of Qays ibn Abi Hazim).
207. Al-Dhahabī, *Siyar A*ᶜ*lām al-Nubalā*ᵓ, vol. 11, p. 54.
208. Ibn al-Madīnī, ᶜ*Ilal*, pp. 49–50. Al-Khaṭīb al-Baghdādī quoted this passage in *Tārīkh Madīnat al-Salām*, vol. 13, p. 433.
209. The shift in public opinion regarding Ibn al-Madini is best reflected in the biographical entry written by al-Khatib al-Baghdadi: *Tārīkh Madīnat al-Salām*, vol. 13, pp. 421–41. The praising anecdotes appear mostly on pp. 422–30, and the shameful ones on pp. 431–41; however, on p. 428, for example, Ibn al-Madini is described as a faithful Sunnite when he resided in Baghdad and a faithful Shiᶜite when he resided in Basra.
210. Al-Dhahabī, *Siyar A*ᶜ*lām al-Nubalā*ᵓ, vol. 11, pp. 54–9.
211. This claim that was first articulated in the *miḥna* by the qadi Ibn Abi Duwad became the crux of the rationalistic argumentation. It is interesting to see that this argument is articulated forcefully in the writings of nineteenth-century Ibadites. According to Valerie Hoffman, 'The Ibādīs, like the Muᶜtazila before them, see ocular vision of God as an impossibility, because the eye sees only

bodies, or parts of bodies, which have finite dimensions, occupy space, are composed of parts, and have substance and accidents, all of which are impossible for God, who does not have a body': Hoffman, 'Refuting the Vision of God', p. 248.

212. Ibn Kathīr, *Al-Bidāya wa'l-Nihāya*, vol. 14, p. 313 (the events of Hijri year 231). See also a detailed account based on several sources in Turner, *Inquisition in Early Islam*, pp. 104–14. On Ahmad ibn Nasr, see Cook, *Commanding Right and Forbidding Wrong*, pp. 51–2.

3

Gestures and *Aḥādīth al-Ṣifāt*

Introduction

In 1886, Ignaz Goldziher (d. 1921), the illustrious Jewish Hungarian scholar, published a relatively short article entitled 'Gestures and Sign Language among the Arabs'.[1] In the article's opening paragraph, Goldziher declared that what inspired him to write about this topic was the substantial amount of contemporary researches about gestures and sign language among 'natural peoples' (*Naturvölker*).[2] Apparently, Goldziher was fascinated by the work of the American ethnologist Garrick Mallery (d. 1894) on sign language among the Native American tribes of North America.[3] Goldziher was also familiar with the works of German cultural historical anthropologists such as Wilhelm Wundt (d. 1920).[4]

Although Goldziher's article was based on philological inquiries in classical Arabic sources in general, and Hadith literature in particular, the author chose to contribute his article to the *Zeitschrift für Völkerpsychologie und Sprachwissenschaft* instead of sending it to the more conventional platforms for philologists. The *Zeitschrift für Völkerpsychologie und Sprachwissenschaft* was founded in 1860 by the philologist and philosopher H. Steinthal (d. 1899) and his brother-in-law, the psychologist Moritz Lazarus (d. 1903). The journal was meant to provide an alternative for research that did not correspond with the dominant trend of German anthropology, which was, as these two scholars believed, 'too biological'. Steinthal and Lazarus sought to publish a journal that would investigate 'mental ethnology' (*Völkerpsychologie*), a phrase which they coined. This phrase expressed their hope that their new journal would host articles that investigated the cultures of ancient and newly discovered tribes and peoples from different perspectives such as language, mythology, religion and oral literature. For this purpose, they were required to attract humanists, and especially linguists, and persuade them to publish in their journal.[5] Goldziher was one of Steinthal's long-time acquaintances. Well-read in Steinthal's scientific work, Goldziher praised him considerably in his 1876 monograph on the myths among the Hebrew people.[6] Goldziher also shared Steinthal and Lazarus's views against the pseudo-scientific racism of the extremely influential philologist Ernest Renan (d. 1892).[7]

Goldziher's attraction to the topic of gestures and sign language, combined with his extremely erudite reading of the Arabic sources, produced a unique article. However, the *Zeitschrift für Völkerpsychologie und Sprachwissenschaft* never made a significant impact among the scholarly communities in German-speaking countries.[8] The journal's low visibility and the fact that Goldziher's article was 'planted' outside its natural habitat, help explain why the article sank into oblivion. The article was somewhat rescued by Georges-Henri Bousquet (d. 1978). Bousquet published a French summary of the article in 1961 in the widely accessible journal *Arabica*. Bousquet's summary is accurate, although he chose to omit several examples that appear in the original article.[9] Goldziher continued the line of investigation that he presented in his 1886 article in two later publications, where he concentrated on the Prophet's ritual, ceremonial and even magical gestures. These publications received some attention among his contemporaries.[10]

Only a small portion of 'Gestures and Sign Language among the Arabs' discussed the phenomenon of hand gestures accompanying speech as reflected in Hadith literature.[11] Goldizher's observation that Hadith literature is abundant in descriptions of gestures (*ishārāt*, sing. *ishāra*) allegedly performed by the Prophet while speaking in various settings, spotlighted a central finding in Hadith studies that no one seemed to notice. Unfortunately, Goldziher's line of investigation was never followed by later researchers. In fact, even research which focused on the orality of Hadith literature failed to recognise gestures as a significant feature in the process of Hadith transmission.[12]

In this chapter, we pick up the thread of Goldziher's unique inquiry and expand it on new trajectories: the vocabulary which is relevant to the phenomenon of gestures in Hadith literature and the way these gestures are depicted; how the gestures in *aḥādīth al-ṣifāt* reflect the relationships between the narrator and his audience; how these gestures were preserved throughout the ages; and, finally, how the *muḥaddithūn* perceived the role of gestures in *aḥādīth al-ṣifāt*. These trajectories were never pursued by Goldziher (he did not discuss gestures in *aḥādīth al-ṣifāt* at all), so we consider this chapter a continuance of his 1886 article, as were two of our previous publications which inaugurated a small scale research of this topic.[13] The present chapter systematises the references to gestures in *aḥādīth al-ṣifāt*, and offers a contextualised reading in Hadith material and the historical sources. Nourished by the approach of literary analysis that was applied in the previous chapters on the one hand, and by the terminology used in contemporary linguistic research on the other, the discussion here illuminates the role of gestures in the process of Hadith transmission.

The chapter comprises five sections. Section I presents typical gestures in Hadith material and defines the relevant terminology based on recent theoretical literature on gestures. Section II examines the performance of gestures in *aḥādīth al-ṣifāt* by presenting an in-depth inquiry into two case studies. Section III focuses on a third case study which reveals the inner dispute within one of the traditionalistic study circles regarding the gestural *aḥādīth al-ṣifāt*. This case study leads to Section IV, which presents the activity of the *muḥaddith* who actually promoted the trend of transmitting *aḥādīth al-ṣifāt*, with or without gestures. Section V reconsiders the place of gestures in the transmission process of *aḥādīth al-ṣifāt* and the hermeneutical solutions that the Hadith scholars offered to these gestures. In this closing segment, we argue that although these scholars were aware of the theological implications that these gestures might entail, they provided partial and undeveloped solutions to alleviate this problem.

I. The Prophet's Gestures: Iconic, Metaphoric and Deictic

Adam Kendon, an experimental psychologist and a leading authority on the study of gestures, explains that the term 'gestures'

> refers to that range of bodily actions that are, more or less, generally regarded as part of a person's willing expression . . . it includes hand wav-

ings or gesticulations that accompany talk and various kinds of more or less conventionalized actions which have a symbolic or semiotic function.[14]

Similar observations about gestures which accompany speech are found in a lengthy passage that the philologist al-Jahiz (d. 869) dedicated in his *Kitāb al-Bayān wa'l-Tabyīn*. Al-Jahiz, following the tradition of Classical Antiquity, claimed that although 'the gesture and the speech are partners', the gesture reveals more about a person's thoughts than his words. Al-Jahiz depicts a wide range of gestures: 'by a hand, head, eye, eyebrows, knees . . . a garment and a sword'.[15]

Both Kendon and al-Jahiz assume that deliberate gestures bear conventional meanings that the immediate environment easily deciphers. Although not all the Prophetic gestures were faithfully recorded and transmitted by the *muḥaddithūn*, we may assume that these gestures were considered part of the Prophetic conduct that needed to be preserved. The narrators of Hadith material shared one fundamental albeit implicit assumption: that the Prophet's gestures either displayed the verbal message or added information to it. The narrators, the audience and the later commentators of the Hadith material perceived the gestures of the Prophet as meaningful. This attitude is similar to the attitude of the Greeks and the Romans who recognised gestures as powerful devices of human self-expression.[16] We find that gestures were rarely ever explained in the narrative of a specific *ḥadīth*. This finding indicates that the audience shared the same view as the narrators; namely, the meaning enfolded in the gesture was specific, clear and translucent. However, as Goldziher correctly indicates, there were gestures which were unclear to the audience, and unless a later commentator deciphered them, they would have remained unclear.[17]

This gesture-meaning bond is called 'iconicity'. A key term in semiotics, 'iconicity' means that the gestural sign is not arbitrary and that 'the icon, the sign vehicle "resembles" its object'.[18] According to the widely accepted terminology suggested by the psychologist and theoretician David McNeill, gestures can be divided into four types: iconic, metaphoric, deictic and beat.[19] The categorisation of gestures is actually indefinite, because one may detect the 'dimensions' of each type in one gesture.[20] Iconic, metaphoric and deictic gestures are easily detectable in Hadith material. Beat, the least elaborate gesture according to McNeill's analysis, is not easy to detect in Hadith material.

'Beats' are flicks of the hand or hands along with the rhythm of speech in order to highlight parts of the speech.[21] The closest example in Hadith material that we were able to find is the following: ᶜAli ibn Abi Talib once recounted that one day at the break of dawn, the Prophet entered his and Fatima's house. He found the couple asleep, and expressed his irritation and amazement by asking them: 'Oh, you are not praying?' To that reproach ᶜAli responded: 'Our souls are in the hand of God. When he wants us to wake up, He wakes us up.' The Prophet withdrew from the door, and while beating his thigh with his hand, said: 'But man is exceedingly contentious' (*wa-kāna 'l-insānu akthara shayʾin jadalan*; Q. 18:54).[22] With the absence of a more accurate description of the 'beating', we assume that the gesture was meant to convey either the Prophet's frustration with ᶜAli's impertinence or his amazement at ᶜAli's cleverness. Similarly, we have no idea whether the gesture preceded the speech (and then conveyed either frustration or amazement), or accompanied the speech to highlight one of the words of the Quranic verse. We also do not know whether the Prophet beat his thigh once or several times. If, for example, the Prophet beat his thigh once while uttering the word *jadalan*, his intention would have been to emphasise the argumentative nature of ᶜAli's response by highlighting the word *jadal* (argument, dispute).

'Iconic gestures' (or 'iconic gesticulations') 'display in the form and manner of their execution similar aspects of the concrete scene that is presented in speech'.[23] The gesture, emphasises McNeill, expresses something analogous to the event being described.[24] As a referential symbol, the gesture 'functions via its resemblance to this event, iconically'.[25] While iconic gestures represent something concrete, the 'metaphoric gesture' represents 'images of the abstract' or abstract concepts.[26] 'Deictic gestures' are gestures that are mostly performed by pointing the index finger, and are performed sometimes with other body parts.[27]

Examples of iconic, metaphoric and deictic gestures that the Prophet performed are abundant in the Hadith literature. Sometimes their meanings are plain, even though they convey an abstract concept. For example, ᶜAbd Allah ibn ᶜUmar narrated: 'The Prophet said: "God will not torment [the deceased in their graves] because of shedding tears or feeling sad, but He will torment them because of this" and he pointed on his tongue (*fa-ashāra ilā lisānihi*).'[28] The meaning of the gesture was self-understood by the recipients of this text. They understood that the tongue symbolised the wailing and lamentation of the deceased's relatives. Through the combination of the Prophet's words and gestures, he conveyed the message that wailing on the deceased's grave represented unacceptable behaviour. If the mourners did not understand the message from the Prophet's tongue, then they certainly understood it from ᶜUmar ibn al-Khattab's behaviour at funerals. Whenever people started to lament, ᶜUmar used to beat them with his stick. If they did not stop, he used to throw pebbles at them and smear their faces with mud.[29]

The gestures were subjected to some speculation by scholars in later generations. These scholars raised several possibilities for the meaning of these gestures. In addition, with the increasing number of *muḥaddithūn*, the repertoire of gestures connected to one single *ḥadīth* widened. This phenomenon is best demonstrated by the *ḥadīth* on the advent of the Prophet and the Hour.[30] According to this *ḥadīth*, the Prophet declared that his advent and the coming of the Hour of Resurrection were very close, 'like this one to this one' (*ka-hādhihi min hādhihi*), or in a different wording, 'like these two' (*ka-hātayni*). Following his statement, the Prophet performed the following gesture: he extended his index finger and middle finger and kept them closely together (*wa-qarana bayna al-sabbāba wa'l-wusṭā*),[31] or according to a different description, he separated his index finger from the middle finger (*faraqa bayna al-sabbāba wa'l-wusṭā*).[32]

Ibn Hajar al-ᶜAsqalani (d. 1449), who meticulously studied two-dozen versions of this *ḥadīth* as they appear in Hadith compilations and works of Quran exegesis,[33] marked each version by the name of its *rāwī* (pl. *ruwāt*), the professional *muḥaddith* who transmitted the *ḥadīth* to his disciples. He also mentioned a few cases in which the *ruwāt* like Sufyan al-Thawri (d. 778) and Shuᶜba (d. 776) performed these gestures while transmitting this *ḥadīth*.[34] As previously mentioned, these gestures were meant to signal the coming of the Hour, or more precisely, that the coming of the Hour is near, like the proximity of the two fingers. One of the commentators of *Ṣaḥīḥ al-Bukhārī*, Shams al-Din al-Kirmani (d. 1384), wondered: 'Almost seven hundred and eighty years passed from the Prophet's advent to our days. So how can one claim that there was close proximity in time [between the Prophet's advent and the coming of the Hour]?' Al-Kirmani's answer was that the Prophet's gesture was misinterpreted. It was not the close proximity between the two fingers that represented the time left between the Prophet's advent and the coming of the Hour, but the difference in length between the Prophet's index finger and his middle finger.[35] Other scholars, like Ibn al-ᶜArabi (d. 1240), delved into rather complex calculations in which each finger was divided into seven in order to date the precise coming of the Hour.[36] Less complicated calculations preceded by dozens of variants of this narrative appear in the opening chapter of *Tārīkh al-Rusul wa'l-Mulūk* by the polymath Abu Jaᶜfar al-Tabari (d. 923).[37]

Hadith literature is inconsistent in its description of the gestures. Usually, the existence of the gesture in the text is signalled by the word *hākadhā* ('thusly' or 'like this'), which concludes the *matn*. The word *hākadhā* is a deixis, namely a word which can be interpreted by taking into account the position of the body of the speaker and his gestures. *Hākadhā* is compounded from the particle *hā*, which has a demonstrative force, the undeveloped noun *ka*, which means 'like', and the demonstrative pronoun *dhā*.[38] The emphasis of the speaker is always on the *hā,* which is distinctly aspirated.[39]

The combination of performing a gesture and uttering the emphasised *hākadhā* was a rhetorical device which made its mark on the captivated audience. The audience could see the gesture and hear the narrator utter the word *hākadhā*. However, in the written versions of the traditions *hākadhā* was usually followed by complimentary phrases which helped the readers complete the lacuna in the narrative. In other words, the reader could not 'see' the performed gesture, while *hākadhā* indicated that a gesture existed in the narrative. The reader was charged with the task of determining what the gesture was. For example, when the Prophet prayed in Umm Salama's house and one of her sons entered the room '[the Prophet] signalled with his hand like this (*fa-qāla bi-yadihi hākadhā*)'. Umm Salama, who narrated this anecdote, added: 'and he returned', meaning that the Prophet signalled to the boy that he was invited to join him in his prayer. However, when one of Umm Salama's daughters entered the room, the Prophet again signalled with his hand *hākadhā*, but this time the girl immediately left the room, therefore this time *hākadhā* accompanied a gesture of rejection.[40]

Sometimes *hākadhā* was followed by an explanatory description of the gesture. 'Do not wear silk – ᶜUmar ibn al-Khattab (d. 644) quoted the Prophet – unless it is *hākadhā*.' ᶜUmar added: 'And the Prophet signalled with two of his fingers.'[41] In this case, we can safely assume that ᶜUmar pinched the thumb and the index finger together. By this iconic gesture, he demonstrated the very small quantity of silk in a fabric which one was allowed to wear.

In some cases, a more detailed description appears after *hākadhā*. This is the case in Bilal ibn Rabah's (death date unknown, between 638 and 642) call for the morning prayer in the nights of Ramadan, just before dawn. In this *ḥadīth* attributed to ᶜAbd Allah ibn Masᶜud, the Prophet ordered the Muslims fasting in Ramadan to continue eating the *saḥūr*, the last meal before daybreak, even when they heard Bilal's call. The Prophet explained that the purpose of Bilal's call for prayer was to urge those who were already awake praying all night to return home, and those who were still asleep to awaken and eat their meal before the break of dawn. To illustrate the break of dawn, the Prophet performed two gestures combined with speech. The Prophet said the word *hākadhā* two or three times: the first two *hākadhā* signalled an iconic hand gesture which symbolised 'the first dawn, which is false and vertical' (*al-fajr al-awwal al-kādhib al-mustaṭīl*) also known as 'the pillar of dawn' (*ᶜamūd al-ṣubḥ*), which was the incorrect time to stop eating. The third *hākadhā* signalled another iconic hand gesture which symbolised 'the second dawn, which is true and horizontal' (*al-fajr al-thānī al-ṣādiq al-mustaṭīr*).[42] None of the versions of this *ḥadīth* describe the gestures as performed by the Prophet. All of them, however, describe the earliest transmitters as performing the gestures, thus supposedly reconstructing the gestures that the Prophet performed.[43]

In the case of this *ḥadīth*, the compilers and interpreters attributed the performance of the gestures to early Hadith authorities such as the *ṣaḥābī* ᶜAbd Allah ibn Masᶜud or the *ṣaḥābī* Samura ibn Jundub (d. sometime between 677 and 679). The *ḥadīth* has several versions and the gestures vary accordingly.[44] In one version, which appears in *Ṣaḥīḥ Muslim*, Muslim the compiler emphasised that the performer of the gestures was the later Hadith authority Hammad ibn Zayd (d. 784) from Basra. Hammad was one of the four most prominent *muḥaddithūn* of his era (the other three were Sufyan al-Thawri from Kufa, Malik ibn Anas from Medina and al-Awzaᶜi from Syria).[45]

Muslim first quotes the text: 'The Prophet said: "Be not misled by Bilal's call for prayer and quit your *saḥūr*. Be not misled by the whiteness of the horizon which is vertical like this, until it spreads horizontally like this".' After quoting the text, Muslim, the compiler, adds: 'Hammad used to narrate this *ḥadīth* using his hands, and then he said: "that is, horizontally".'[46] The gesture, as performed by Hammad and others, had several variations, all of which comprised two parts: in the first part, the narrator raised his hand in an upright position illustrating what the *ḥadīth* describes as 'the pillar of dawn' (*ᶜamūd al-ṣubḥ*), which is the false dawn. Alternatively, he clenched his fist and banged his hand on the ground. In the second part of the gesture, the narrator either stretched his hands, thus illustrating the spread of light of the true dawn, or he joined his two index fingers and then stretched his hands.[47] Qadi ᶜIyad (d. 1150), the author of one of the commentaries of *Ṣaḥīḥ Muslim*, emphasised that the meaning of the abovementioned *ḥadīth* was clarified by virtue of Hammad's gestures, and added that 'clarification through gesture' (*al-bayān bi'l-ishāra*) can indeed replace speech.[48] The point of 'clarification through gesture' is also relevant to the theological implications of gestures in *aḥādīth al-ṣifāt*.

II. 'The Instance of Narrating': The Narrator and his Audience

In his 1996 article, Daniel Beaumont coined the phrase 'the instance of narrating'.[49] 'The instance of narrating' comprises three elements: the narrator, the setting and the audience. The narrator is of course the centre of our attention. Sometimes we are fortunate to receive details about the narrator's posture, voice and gestures. These details enable us to recreate the instance of narrating as a lively performance of the narrator.

The gesture is the non-verbal message that the narrator sends to his audience. As powerful devices that were meant to accentuate the message of the *ḥadīth*, the iconic and metaphoric gestures were an inseparable part of the instance of narrating. The complex type of *aḥādīth al-ṣifāt* (that contains both a framing and an embedded narrative) record several features that the *muḥaddithūn* performed during the transmission process. These features were meant, among other things, to illustrate the Prophet's conduct in front of an audience. In both ᶜAlqama and ᶜAbida's versions of the *ḥadīth* of the divine fingers the Prophet laughed until his molars were revealed. In Abu

Razin's *ḥadīth* of allegiance the Prophet laughed in one part of the narrative, and opened his clenched fist in another part. The narrator, then, was describing the Prophet's gesticulations and not merely the Prophet's words.

In *aḥādīth al-ṣifāt*, the gestures were meant to highlight the anthropomorphic description of God. The *muḥaddithūn* carefully preserved these gestures that were supposedly performed by the Prophet. The process of preservation was triple-layered and included an actual demonstration, a claim for authenticity and a verbal description. First, the *muḥaddith* performed the gesture. Then, he claimed to have witnessed the Prophet or a *ṣaḥābī* perform it. Finally, the gesture was verbally described by the *muḥaddith* himself or his disciples. For example, the *muḥaddith* Harmala ibn ʿImran (d. 777) testified that Abu Yunus Sulaym ibn Jubayr (d. 740–1), who was the *mawlā* of Abu Hurayra, told him the following story:

> I once heard Abu Hurayra recite the following Quranic verse: 'God commands you to hand back your trusts to their rightful owners' (Q. 4:58). He continued reciting, but when he reached [the part of the verse] that states 'Surely God hears all and observes all', he put his thumb on his ear and his forefinger on his eye, and said: 'This is precisely (*hākadhā*) the way in which I heard [and saw] the Messenger of God recite this verse: [He] was putting his fingers [on his ear and his eye].'[50]

This dual-constructed narrative frames what Abu Yunus ṣaw and embeds what Abu Hurayra recounted. However, the actual narrator of this dual-constructed narrative is Harmala: he tells us that this is a story that he heard from Abu Yunus (*ḥaddathanī Abū Yūnus);* he further tells us that Abu Yunus (the protagonist of the framing narrative) saw Abu Hurayra; and that Abu Hurayara related Q. 4:58 to Abu Yunus while accompanying his recitation with a gesture. Harmala reconstructs the gesture that Abu Yunus performed, which is a reconstruction of the original gesture performed by Abu Hurayra. Abu Hurayra's gesture is in fact a reconstruction of a gesture performed by the Prophet. Moreover, Abu Hurayra (the protagonist of the embedded narrative) performs a gesture and then elaborates on the origin of the gesture and its meaning.

This reconstruction is the most fascinating point in this narrative: Haramla mirrors the words and gestures of two protagonist-narrators (Abu

Yunus and Abu Hurayra), while these protagonist-narrators mirror the words and the gesture of the Prophet. The reader does not 'see' the Prophet perform the gesture accompanying this specific Quranic verse; does not 'see' Abu Hurayra; does not 'see' Abu Yunus, who was Abu Hurayra's *mawlā*; but, the reader does 'see' Harmala, whose testimony is actually the complete narrative. From this respect, therefore, Harmala is the narrator who was responsible for the final original version of the narrative, namely he was the *rāwī* of the Abu Hurayra *ḥadīth*.

In Harmala's narrative (the embedded narrative), Abu Hurayra plays the role of a teacher and commentator, who demonstrated to his *mawlā* the precise meaning of 'God hears all and observes all', although the words *samīᶜ* and *baṣīr* are plain and need no explanation. The gesture in the narrative is accompanied by the deixis *hākadhā*. The combination of the gesture and the deixis is powerful. The gesture itself explains the Quranic verse and also emphasises the words *samīᶜ* ('hears all') and *baṣīr* ('observes all') in the verse. The deixis draws the attention to the gesture on the one hand, thus amplifying the conveyed message, and vouches for the authenticity of the gesture on the other hand. But what was the message? Was it that God literally sees and hears, or was it that God metaphorically sees and hears? In other words, is the gesture iconic or metaphoric? Surely, the gesture was meant to provide an unequivocal interpretation of the relevant Quranic text. But what was this interpretation? The interpretation depended entirely on the recipient of the *ḥadīth* and his theological stance.

The way the early traditionalists perceived this text and other similar texts, left no room for doubt. According to them, by performing the gesture of placing his thumb on his ear and his forefinger on his eye, Abu Hurayara (or Abu Hurayra's literary representation) tacitly conveyed a literal understanding of the anthropomorphic expression. Such a straightforward understanding of the Quranic text was the declared stance of the ultra-traditionalists, mostly Hanbalites. For this group, the gesture in this *ḥadīth* as well as the gestures in other *aḥādīth al-ṣifāt*, were iconic and not metaphoric. In the context of the traditionalistic curriculum, these gestures represent a concrete reality in which God actually sees and hears, laughs and descends, sits and stands.

The traditionalistic stance, however, was not entirely homogenous: not all the *muḥaddithūn* interpreted the gesture as iconic; and, accordingly, not all of them understood the words *samīᶜ* and *baṣīr* literally. In the eighth century, the Abu Hurayra *ḥadīth* spread among the *muḥaddithūn* of Egypt (see Appendix IV, chart 1). Abu Hurayra's *mawlā*, Abu Yunus, lived in Egypt, and so did Harmala, the narrator.[51] The Abu Hurayra *ḥadīth* was marginal and did not exceed the boundaries of Egypt. Sometime during the eighth century, this *ḥadīth* gained momentum due to the teachings of a prolific *muḥaddith* by the name of ᶜAbd Allah ibn Yazid al-Muqriᵓ (d. c. 828).[52] Al-Muqriᵓ ('the Reciter of the Quran'), a Persian who was a *mawlā* of the clan of ᶜUmar ibn al-Khattab, studied Hadith from luminaries like Abu Hanifa and Malik ibn Anas. Harmala ibn ᶜImran is listed in the biographical sources as one of his many teachers. Al-Muqriᵓ taught in Basra for more than thirty years, and afterwards held an official post in Mecca as *shaykh al-ḥaram* for an additional thirty-year period. Among his students were Ahmad ibn Hanbal and al-Bukhari.[53] Scholars from Iraq and Khurasan heard this *ḥadīth* from him, although it is unclear whether they heard it in Basra or in Mecca. Al-Muqriᵓ also added his original contribution to the narrative, as we learn from the testimony of two of Abu Dawud al-Sijistani's (d. 889) sources. According to these two anonymous scholars,[54] when al-Muqriᵓ cited this tradition, he added: 'It (i.e. the gesture) means that God hears all and observes all. In other words, God has the attributes of hearing and seeing.'[55] Al-Muqriᵓ's addition suggested that he saw the gesture as metaphoric rather than iconic. The stance attributed to him here represents another nuance in the overall traditionalistic stance, and is closer to the Ashᶜarite position. In this respect, it seems that al-Muqriᵓ was ahead of his time.

Another scholar who studied Hadith from al-Muqriᵓ was the prominent scholar from Nishapur, Muhammad ibn Yahya al-Dhuhli (d. 872). Al-Dhuhli was the teacher of many scholars, among them the authors of the canonical Hadith compilations. Muslim ibn al-Hajjaj (d. 875), the compiler of the *Ṣaḥīḥ* quoted him often, but after a bitter quarrel with al-Dhuhli, he refrained from using al-Dhuhli's material. According to al-Dhahabi, al-Dhuhli studied from al-Muqriᵓ while the latter resided in Mecca.[56] Due to al-Dhuhli's teachings, the Abu Hurayra *ḥadīth* and its accompanying gesture became part of the traditionalistic curriculum in Nishapur (see Appendix IV, chart 1). Ibn Khuzayma (d. 924; a prominent spokesman of Nishapuri traditionalism, see more about him in Chapter 5), who was al-Dhuhli's disciple, quoted al-Dhuhli's two versions of this *ḥadīth* in his influential *Kitāb al-Tawḥīd*.[57] Ibn Khuzayma also described a session of dictation in which he participated, where the Abu Hurayra *ḥadīth* was dictated by another teacher, Abu Musa Ishaq ibn Musa al-Khatmi (d. 858–9). According to Ibn Khuzayma, he himself was present in the session with a group of his friends and wrote the *ḥadīth* as al-Khatmi dictated it. Apparently, the session was crowded, because Ibn Khuzayma could not hear al-Khatmi properly. His only recourse was to write the *ḥadīth* as it was repeated by one of al-Khatmi's clerks (*al-mustamlī*). Ibn Khuzayma therefore admitted that some of the words in his version of the *ḥadīth* were taken from the clerk and not directly from al-Khatmi.[58]

A valuable testimony about al-Muqriʾ's performance during the transmission of this specific *ḥadīth* is presented by the illustrious Hadith scholar Ibn Abi Hatim al-Razi (d. 938, famous for being the author of *al-Jarḥ wa'l-Taʿdīl*). Ibn Abi Hatim travelled often 'in search for knowledge' and participated in the sessions of Hadith dictation conducted by Abu Zakariyya Yahya ibn ʿAbdak (d. 884–5), an important scholar from Qazwin, who was al-Muqriʾ's disciple.[59] According to Ibn Abi Hatim, Abu Zakariyya described to his students how al-Muqriʾ recited the above-mentioned *ḥadīth* with the accompanying gesture that was supposedly performed by Abu Hurayra. Abu Zakariyya, however, was not satisfied with describing the gesture and decided to actually perform the gesture while transmitting this *ḥadīth* (see Appendix IV, chart 2). This is how Ibn Abi Hatim described the event that he witnessed:

> Abu Zakariyya said: 'Al-Muqriʾ described this (i.e. the gesture) to us.' Abu Zakariyya then put his right thumb on his right eye, and his [right] forefinger on his right ear. He showed us [the gesture] and said: 'In this manner' (*hākadhā*).[60]

Abu Zakariyya's gesture differs from al-Muqriʾ's: while al-Muqriʾ put his right thumb on his right ear and his right forefinger on his right eye, Abu Zakariyya inverted the position of the hand. His gesture (which is quite awkward and difficult to perform) places the thumb on the eye and the forefinger on the ear. However, it is possible that Ibn Abi Hatim erroneously described the gesture, and that it was in fact similar to al-Muqriʾs. Thus, Abu Zakariyya from Qazwin reconstructed the gesture that al-Muqriʾ, who taught in Basra and Mecca, took from his teacher, the Egyptian Harmala. At least three generations of students of Hadith, then, learned the narrative of Abu Hurayra as a combination of speech and gesture. In all likelihood, Ibn Abi Hatim taught his students in al-Rayy this particular *ḥadīth* as a combination of speech and gesture.

When the instance of narrating comprised iconic gestures, the audience often responded in various ways. This interaction between the narrator and his audience was sometimes recorded, especially when the narrative described an energetic and colourful *ṣaḥābi* like ᶜAbd Allah ibn Masᶜud (d. 652–3).[61] One of Ibn Masᶜud's exchange of words with his disciples occurred when Ibn Masᶜud transmitted an extremely lengthy Prophetic *ḥadīth* on the Day of Resurrection.[62] The last part of the *ḥadīth* describes a dialogue between a sinner and God. The sinner would be the last person to leave Hell and therefore pleads with God to permit him to enter Heaven. The humorous dialogue between God and the sinner is concluded by a laconic sentence indicating that the sinner's words will amuse God to such a degree that He laughs. Ibn Masᶜud's disciples testified that they had heard Ibn Masᶜud recount this lengthy *ḥadīth* several times. Each time that he reached the point in which God laughed, Ibn Masᶜud demonstrated the laughter by laughing. Qays ibn al-Sakan (death date unknown), one of Ibn Masᶜud's prominent disciples, and Ibn Masᶜud's son, Abu ᶜUbayda (d. 700) recounted:

> We realized that each time ᶜAbd Allah ibn Masᶜud reached that point, he laughed until his last molar was revealed. We asked him: 'Oh, Abu ᶜAbd al-Rahman, you have recounted this *ḥadīth* to us time and again, and each time you reached this point you laughed until your last molar was revealed!' Ibn Masᶜud responded: 'I have seen the Messenger of God recounting this *ḥadīth* to us many times, and each time he reached this point he laughed until his last molar was revealed!'[63]

This version is a bit cryptic, because Ibn Masᶜud's laughter is presented as mere mimicry of the Prophet's laughter. However, there is a shorter version of the same *ḥadīth* in which Anas ibn Malik, one of Ibn Masᶜud's peers, described the first time that Ibn Masᶜud transmitted this *ḥadīth*. Ibn Masᶜud clarified to his disciples that his laughter indeed imitated the Prophet's laughter. From this text, we clearly see that the Prophet's laughter was in fact an iconic gesture meant to symbolise God's real or actual laughter:

> Ibn Masᶜud laughed, and then said: 'You have no intention of asking me what made me laugh?' The [disciples] answered: 'What made you laugh?' He answered: 'This is exactly what the Messenger of God did. [He recounted this *ḥadīth*] and then he laughed, and then he asked: 'You have no intention of asking me what made me laugh?' [Without waiting for our reply], he (i.e. the Prophet) continued: 'I am laughing because God, to Him belong might and glory, laughed …'[64]

The brief passage that described the alleged 'instance of narrating' of this *ḥadīth* conveyed one clear message: the gesture performed by the narrator should be preserved by later narrators, mainly because the gesture reverted to the Prophet himself. The *ḥadīth* was allegedly first transmitted in Kufa by ᶜAbd Allah ibn Masᶜud's disciples, like Masruq ibn al-Ajdaᶜ (d. 683) and Abu ᶜUbayda (d. 700), and in Basra by Ibn Masᶜud's peer Anas ibn Malik (d. 711). The widely cited version of the *ḥadīth* was transmitted in Basra by the eighth-century *muḥaddithūn* Thabit al-Bunani (d. 740) and his disciple Hammad ibn Salama (d. 784). Due to Hammad and his disciples' efforts, the *ḥadīth* gradually gained popularity and eventually reached the circles of the *muḥaddithūn* of Baghdad and Marw.[65] The longest version of this *ḥadīth* attributed to ᶜAbd Allah ibn Masᶜud was categorised by Hadith scholars as 'weak' (*ḍaᶜīf*), and was therefore preserved only in the ultra-traditionalistic thematic Hadith compilations (see Appendix IV, chart 3).[66] We have only one record of a study session in tenth-century Kufa in which this *ḥadīth* was dictated, and unfortunately there is no trace in the sources of the way the later *muḥaddithūn* actually transmitted this *ḥadīth*.[67] The question whether they indeed laughed in order to demonstrate Ibn Masᶜud's iconic laughter or not, remains open.

III. The Performing Trend

The message that a gesture performed by the 'original' narrator should be preserved by later narrators was also conveyed in the following tradition, in which Hammad ibn Salama, a leading and widely cited *muḥaddith*, reminisced about a study session conducted by the *muḥaddith* Abu Muhammad Thabit al-Bunani. As a long-time disciple of Anas ibn Malik,[68] Thabit recreated for his disciples a study session in which he participated as a student. In that historic study session, Thabit witnessed his teacher Anas, while Anas described the Prophet reciting Q. 7:143 ('And when his Lord revealed Himself to the Mountain, He levelled it to dust'). The Quranic verse refers to the wish that Moses expressed that God would reveal Himself to him; however, God clarified that Moses would never see Him, 'But look upon to the Mountain; if it remains firm upon its base, then only shall you see Me.' Thereafter, God indeed revealed Himself to the Mountain and it crumbled. Afterwards, God spoke to Moses (Q. 7:142–4). In the following narrative, Hammad ibn Salama testified what his teacher, Thabit, told him about Anas's study session. As the narrative progresses, it becomes evident that Hammad in fact adds to the description of Anas's study session: Hammad describes the session that Thabit as a teacher conducted. In the first part of the narrative, Hammad describes how Anas cited the Prophetic tradition and the iconic gesture that accompanied this *ḥadīth*:

> Hammad ibn Salama recounted to us on the authority of Thabit, [who recounted] on the authority of Anas ibn Malik, who transmitted the *ḥadīth* on the authority of the Prophet regarding the verse 'And when his Lord revealed Himself to the Mountain, He levelled it to dust'. [Anas] said: '[The Prophet gestured] with his finger like this.' [Anas] gesticulated by bringing together the tip of the little finger with the tip of the thumb.[69]

Thabit was the one who heard this Prophetic *ḥadīth* from Anas, and delivered this narrative to his disciples, and among them was Hammad. In the second part of Hammad's narrative, Hammad describes an unusual exchange of words that occurred immediately after Thabit transmitted Anas's *ḥadīth* to his students:

> [Hammad said]: Humayd said to Thabit: 'Stop doing this (*da*ᶜ *hādhā*), Abu Muhammad! What do you mean by doing this (*mā turīdu bi-hādhā*)?' Thabit struck Humayd's flank and said: 'Who are you and what are you, Humayd [to say this to me]? It was Anas ibn Malik who transmitted this *ḥadīth* to me on the authority of the Messenger of God, and you say: "Stop doing this"?'[70]

In another version of this narrative, also recounted by Hammad, Thabit performed a different gesture: he lifted slightly the tip of his little finger (presumably the other fingers were folded down). In this version, Thabit struck Humayd hard on the chest while emotionally responding to Humayd's remark: 'Who are you and what are you, Humayd [to say this to me]? It was Anas ibn Malik who transmitted this *ḥadīth* to me on the authority of the Messenger of God, and you say: "What do you mean by doing this"?'[71]

The event in Thabit al-Bunani's study session presents Thabit, Humayd and Hammad, three prominent *muḥaddithūn* from Basra.[72] Thabit ibn Aslam al-Bunani was one of Anas ibn Malik's most loyal disciples (the other one was Qatada ibn Diᶜama, d. 735), and a prominent authority on the material that was attributed to Anas. Humayd ibn Abi Humayd al-Tawil (d. 758) was Thabit's disciple. Hammad ibn Salama, who was Humayd's maternal nephew, was also Thabit's disciple. Hammad was in fact an expert on Thabit's material and held him in high esteem.[73] The anecdote about Humayd and Thabit highlights the various problematic aspects of the gestural *aḥādīth al-ṣifāt*. Specifically, these aspects begin with the meaning of the gesture and end with questions on the identity of the narrator, and the reaction of the audience; in sum, what was defined earlier in this chapter as 'the instance of narrating'.

As indicated earlier, the definition of the gesture as iconic or metaphoric presents two different approaches: the iconic gesture symbolises a concrete reality; the metaphoric gesture symbolises an abstract concept. In the eighth and ninth centuries, the gestures used by the *muḥaddithūn* during the transmission of *aḥādīth al-ṣifāt* were strictly iconic, because they were meant to illustrate a spatial position of God, a concrete attribute, a concrete action and, in extreme cases, a concrete limb. However, even in the early stages of Hadith transmission, the concreteness of the gestures was not entirely successful. First, the gestures of one *ḥadīth* were not always consistent. In the case of the Abu Hurayra *ḥadīth*, the basic thumb-forefinger gesture appears in the two existing versions of the *ḥadīth*. In the case of the Anas ibn Malik *ḥadīth*, there are several versions connected to the recitation of Q. 7:143. Thus, Anas ibn Malik made the following optional gestures to demonstrate God revealing Himself to the mountain: Anas pointed his little finger, placed his left thumb on the first knuckle next to the tip of the left little finger, lifted his little finger and seized its tip, or joined his thumb and little finger together.[74] Second, the meaning of the gesture was not entirely comprehensible in some cases. Thus, the thumb-forefinger gesture in the Abu Hurayra *ḥadīth* was supposedly more comprehensible than the variants of the little-finger gesture in the Anas ibn Malik *ḥadīth*. Pointing to one's eye and ear equally produces an immediate connection to body organs as it produces reasonable connection to the attributes of seeing and hearing. So, what did the narrator mean? That God has an eye and an ear, or that He sees and hears? Perhaps the gesture was meant to illustrate the divine attributes of seeing and hearing?

The eye-ear gesture is the easier case, while the variable gestures featuring the tip of one's little finger are not instantly decipherable. The most common interpretation of Anas's gesture is that it referred to the first part of the verse ('And when his Lord revealed Himself to the Mountain') rather than the second part ('He levelled it to dust'). This explanation becomes apparent when reading the following version of the *ḥadīth* which is attributed to the *muḥaddith* Muᶜadh ibn Muᶜadh al-ᶜAnbari (d. 811), Hammad's closeset disciple who would later become the qadi of Basra:

> Hammad ibn Salama recounted to us [the following *ḥadīth*] on the authority of Thabit al-Bunani. Thabit recounted it on the authority of Anas ibn Malik, who transmitted the *ḥadīth* on the authority of the Prophet regarding the verse 'And when his Lord revealed Himself to the Mountain'. [Anas] said: '[The Prophet gestured] like this', which means that he (i.e. Anas) stuck the tip of the little finger out.[75]

In this version, Anas supposedly stopped the recitation of the verse after the mention of God revealing Himself, thereby creating an immediate linkage between this part of the verse and the following gesture; that is, the gesture illustrates God revealing Himself to the Mountain. Two interpretative traditions quoted by Ibn Abi Hatim al-Razi explain that God revealed Himself only slightly 'like the extent of the little finger' or 'He threw open some of the veils'.[76] Although only a particle of God's essence was revealed to the Mountain, it was enough to crush the Mountain to dust. But was it Anas who stopped the recitation of the verse and performed the gesture? And who was the narrator who actually described the gesture that Anas performed?

Like the Abu Hurayra *ḥadīth*, the gesture in the Anas ibn Malik *ḥadīth* is attributed to the Prophet, although the narrative does not mention that the Prophet indeed performed the gesture. The gesture was performed by a *ṣaḥābī* (Abu Hurayra, Anas ibn Malik) who recreated the gesture that the Prophet supposedly performed. The gesture was performed also by a *tābiᶜī* (Abu Yunus, Thabit) who in turn recreated the gesture performed by the *ṣaḥābī*. As demonstrated in the case of the Abu Hurayra *ḥadīth*, the ritual of gesticulating while transmitting the *ḥadīth* did not stop with the *tābiᶜī*. Later *muḥaddithūn*, for example, al-Muqri' and Abu Zakariyya, were recorded performing the gesture that Abu Hurayra supposedly performed. In the case of the Anas ibn Malik *ḥadīth*, the gesture was performed by the *tābiᶜī* Thabit, but apparently he was not considered the narrator of the *ḥadīth*. The Hadith scholar Abu ᶜIsa Muhammad ibn ᶜIsa al-Tirmidhi (d. 892), who quoted one of the dozen versions of this *ḥadīth* in his canonical Hadith compilation, remarked: 'This *ḥadīth* is fair (*ḥasan*) with an uninterrupted chain of transmission (*ṣaḥīḥ*). However, [this *ḥadīth*] is strange (*gharīb*). We received it only through the narration of Hammad ibn Salama.'[77] According to al-Tirmidhi, Hammad was in fact the narrator responsible for the Anas ibn Malik *ḥadīth*, and he brought to light the story about the dispute between Thabit and Humayd.

Al-Tirmidhi's remark deserves our attention, as it reveals several additional possibilities for reconstructing the instance of narrating. The first possibility is that Thabit taught this *ḥadīth* to an undisclosed number of disciples, among them Humayd and Hammad; however, only Hammad regarded the *ḥadīth* worthy of transmitting. The second possibility is that only Thabit and Humayd were present in the room when the dispute between them occurred. Hammad would not have necessarily been present in the room with them; he could have heard about the incident later from Thabit or even from Humayd. The third possibility is that Hammad concocted the tale of the dispute for didactic purposes, and claimed to have heard it from Thabit. This does not mean that he deliberately fabricated or lied; he could have relied on an actual event or several actual events that indeed occurred. Hammad's motive in telling this story is discussed in the following section of this chapter. For now, we need to investigate the convoluted relationships between Thabit and Humayd, because they are the key to a full appreciation of the incident in Thabit's classroom.

If we take the argument between Thabit and Humayd as a historical event that indeed occurred, the incident raises several possibilities. Perhaps this incident reflected ill will between the two scholars, although there is no straightforward evidence in the biographical sources that such a relationship indeed existed. After all, Humayd enthusiastically studied Thabit's entire repertoire, as his nephew Hammad testified.[78] On the other hand, Humayd did not follow the binding rules of the master-disciple relationship. Apparently, most of the *aḥādīth* that Humayd taught came from Thabit, but he often failed to give Thabit credit for being the source of these traditions. Humayd's credibility as a *muḥaddith* was tainted in the eyes of some of his colleagues because he claimed to have heard his material directly from Anas. This accusation against Humayd was raised by Humayd's rival, the *muḥaddith* Shuᶜba (d. 776); it was corroborated by several embarrassing anecdotes recounted by Humayd's contemporaries and duplicated by later *muḥaddithūn*, among them Ahmad ibn Hanbal.[79] Still, Ahmad ibn Hanbal's *Musnad* contains numerous *aḥādīth* in which Humayd quoted Anas directly, so it seems that his claim to be a direct disciple of Anas was accepted, at least by the Hanbalites.[80]

Thabit was still an active *muḥaddith* when Humayd's career gained momentum. The narrative suggests that Hammad witnessed the event, which means that it occurred in the twilight of Thabit's career. Perhaps the old teacher was an easy target for the dynamic Humayd who built his entire career by helping himself freely to his teacher's curriculum. Perhaps challenging the old teacher in public was another useful device for Humayd to build his own reputation as a teacher. However, the rivalry between Humayd and Thabit as presented in the narrative of this *ḥadīth* was not personal, but doctrinal/ideological. After all, the narrative tells us that Humayd heard the Anas ibn Malik *ḥadīth* from Thabit. A thorough search in the entire corpus of Hadith compilations, a task easily performed in the era of the Internet and *al-Maktaba al-Shamela*,[81] reveals that Humayd himself never transmitted this *ḥadīth*; he never included it in his curriculum. This means that he indeed objected vehemently to this *ḥadīth*, although there was no room to doubt Thabit's credibility as a transmitter and an expert on Hadith material attributed to Anas. Since the Hanbalite theologian and historian Ibn al-Jawzi (d. 1201) cited this *ḥadīth* in his compilation of fabricated *aḥādīth* (*Kitāb al-Mawḍūᶜāt*),[82] Daniel Gimaret concluded that Humayd contested this *ḥadīth*'s authenticity, namely the narrative or the *matn* itself.[83] Apart from the fact that Humayd never referred to this issue, the sources point in a totally different direction. In our opinion, the dialogue between the two scholars reflects a fundamental dispute – whether or not one was permitted to use an iconic gesture alongside the recitation of one of *aḥādīth al-ṣifāt*.

Humayd's objection to Thabit's performance indicates that he understood the gesture performed by Thabit as illustrating something related to God. As demonstrated earlier, in the terminology typical of the 'performed' *aḥādīth* the deixis *hākadhā* refers to the way a gesture is performed in the instance of narrating. In our case, we gave a slightly different deixis: *hādhā* which refers to the gesture itself, not necessarily to the way it is performed. Thus, Humayd referred to the gesture performed by Thabit when he said: 'Stop doing this (*da*ᶜ *hādhā*), Abu Muhammad! What do you mean by doing this (*mā turīdu bi-hādhā*)?'[84] Humayd's question expresses uneasiness about using iconic gestures that were meant to illustrate something (attribute, action, spatial position) related to God during the process of Hadith transmission. More than uneasiness, Humayd's reaction is interpreted as a warning to Thabit not to transmit Hadith about the divine attributes while using accompanying gestures. Thabit's response, on the other hand, is interpreted as a rebuke to Humayd not to censure *aḥādīth al-ṣifāt*, text and gesture alike.[85] Humayd's objection could have relied on pure logic: one should not compare God to His creation by using either word or gesture. Although Humayd never expressed this rationalised argumentation, his need to silence Thabit indicates that this was indeed his intention.

The crux of the Thabit-Humayd dispute was therefore Thabit's style as a *muḥaddith*. Apart from being a *muḥaddith*, Thabit was a storyteller (*qāṣṣ*) and a preacher (*wā*ᶜ*iẓ*). In fact, Ibn al-Jawzi included his name in the list of Basra's most popular preachers. As Hammad ibn Salama recounted, storytellers were at best lax in their attitude about the exact wording of the *aḥādīth* they transmitted, and at worst they fabricated *aḥādīth*. Therefore, Hammad decided to test Thabit. Hammad recited distorted *aḥādīth* in front of Thabit, and Thabit in turn corrected his recitation.[86] Hammad recounted this anecdote with the intention of substantiating Thabit's impeccable reputation as a *muḥaddith*. In other words, Hammad conveyed the message that Thabit's involvement with amusing stories in his capacity as a storyteller should not have discredited him as a *muḥaddith*. On the other hand, storytellers were the ultimate performers in early Islamic civilisations. The storytellers used all the devices and tools at their disposal – mimicry, change of intonation, different costumes and gestures – in order to engage their audience.[87]

While Thabit used hand gestures, as did the storytellers, and claimed that these hand gestures were part of the narrative of the Prophetic Hadith, Humayd represented a more rigid approach to Hadith transmission, the one that rejected embellishments such as gestures.[88] He did not reject gestures entirely, because he is recorded as having gestured with his hand when imitating Anas ibn Malik. For example, Humayd reported that Anas was asked whether the Prophet used to dye his beard. Anas responded that God did not 'disfigure' the Prophet's beard with white hair, apart from several hairs. 'And Humayd pointed with his hand on the forepart of his beard.'[89] That Humayd knew how to use gestures in his classes is no surprise, because he was indeed attracted to storytelling. Again, Hammad is our source. As Hammad recounted, when Hammad was a young man, the qadi of Basra, Iyas ibn Mu^cawiya (d. 739) came to him one day, held his hand and asked him to promise that he would become a storyteller. 'Do not die until you tell a story!' – were the qadi's exact words to Hammad – 'At the time, I asked your maternal uncle Humayd exactly the same thing.' Hammad then added that both Humayd and he told stories occasionally, according to their promise to the qadi.[90]

Humayd's attack on Thabit expressed the anxiety that the fine line between Hadith transmission and storytelling would be crossed with the use of body and hand gestures, and perhaps facial expressions like laughter. Thabit's counterattack, on the other hand, was nourished by the traditionalistic total reliance on the teachings of the Salaf, the pious and worthy ancestors of Sunnite Islam. If Anas performed the gesture, so should Thabit. In the case of Q. 7:143, both trends were reflected in respective *aḥādīth*: the 'performing' trend was reflected in the Anas ibn Malik *ḥadīth*, while the 'rigid' trend was reflected in a parallel *ḥadīth* attributed to Ibn ^cAbbas (d. between 686 and 688) that appears in two versions:

> On the authority of Ibn ^cAbbas, [who addressed] the Quranic verse 'And when his Lord revealed Himself to the Mountain'. [Ibn ^cAbbas] said: Only

> the extent of the little finger was revealed from Him. 'He levelled it to dust.' [Ibn Abbas] said: To dirt. 'Moses fell down senseless.' [Ibn Abbas] said: He lost conscience.

> Al-Suddi (d. 745) claimed on the authority of ᶜIkrima (d. 623), [who transmitted] on the authority of Ibn ᶜAbbas that [Ibn ᶜAbbas] said: Only the extent of the little finger was revealed from Him, and thereafter He levelled the Mountain to dust. Moses fell down senseless, and remained so for a very long time.[91]

The Ibn ᶜAbbas version circulated among the *muḥaddithūn* of Kufa. These *muḥaddithūn* studied the exegetical material that was attributed to Ibn ᶜAbbas from al-Suddi's disciple, Asbat ibn Nasr (d. c. 787), who lived and taught only in Kufa.[92] This version never gained much popularity, and is found mainly in ᶜAbd Allah ibn Ahmad ibn Hanbal's *Kitāb al-Sunna*, al-Tabari's *Jāmiᶜ al-Bayān* and a handful of later works of *tafsīr* which cite al-Tabari.[93] There is a fascinating anecdote about this *ḥadīth* that appears in ᶜAbd Allah ibn Ahmad ibn Hanbal's *Kitāb al-Sunna*. ᶜAbd Allah first testified that he received this *ḥadīth* from the Baghdadian *muḥaddith* Abu Maᶜmar al-Hudhali (d. 850). Abu Maᶜmar 'imported' the text to Baghdad after he heard it from the Kufan *muḥaddith* ᶜAmr ibn Muhammad al-ᶜAnqazi (d. 815). ᶜAmr was the one who heard the text from al-Suddi's disciple, Asbat. Apparently, when this *ḥadīth* arrived from Kufa to the *muḥaddithūn* in Baghdad, Abu Maᶜmar al-Hudhali (d. 850) added a gesture to the text (see Appendix IV, chart 4):

> Asbat ibn Nasr transmitted [the following] to us on the authority of al-Suddi. Al-Suddi cited ᶜIkrima who in turn cited Ibn ᶜAbbas. Ibn ᶜAbbas said: 'He revealed [Himself] like the little finger.' Abu Maᶜmar then gestured with his finger to represent the Quranic verse 'And when his Lord revealed Himself to the Mountain' (Q. 7:143).[94]

Abu Maᶜmar could have picked up the gesture from the Kufan *muḥaddith* al-ᶜAnqazi, from whom he had heard the Ibn ᶜAbbas version. However, since al-Tabari quoted the same *ḥadīth* from al-ᶜAnqazi without the gesture, and since ᶜAbd Allah ibn Ahmad ibn Hanbal in fact described Abu Maᶜmar in action, it is more likely that it was Abu Maᶜmar's initiative to add the gesture to his performance. Abu Maᶜmar was one of the two Baghdadian *muḥaddithūn* who during the *miḥna* confessed that the Quran was created. After he admitted 'I blasphemed [God] and was released [from the *miḥna*]', he became a vociferous spokesman of the Baghdadian form of traditionalism. He made frequent professions of faith, some of which were utterly ridiculous ('were my mule able to speak, she would have declared that she was a Sunnite'). He succeeded in his endeavours, no doubt, because all the great *muḥaddithūn* of the ninth century (al-Bukhari, Muslim, Abu Dawud and others) cited his material.[95] Adding a gesture that was meant to accentuate the magnitude and omnipotence of God seems to be in accordance with Abu Maᶜmar's desperate efforts to be exonerated from his grave past mistakes. The gesture can be, therefore, interpreted as an external expression of devout traditionalism.

Returning to the Anas ibn Malik *ḥadīth*, Thabit's position prevailed in the circles of the later *muḥaddithūn*. These scholars never doubted the genuineness of the gesture performed by Thabit and its being an inseparable part of the text. In fact, when hearing about the dispute between Thabit and Humayd several decades after it occurred, one of the *muḥaddithūn* expressed his anger that Thabit did not respond more severely to Humayd. This *muḥaddith* claimed that Thabit could have sent Humayd to prison for two months![96]

Hammad's many disciples who became prominent *muḥaddithūn* distributed his version of the Anas ibn Malik *ḥadīth* – narrative and gesture – in Basra and Baghdad. Among these disciples, the most prominent were ᶜAffan ibn Muslim (d. 835)[97] and Sulayman ibn Harb (d. 838–9; see Appendix IV, chart 5).[98] These two disciples were rivals and represented two different styles of transmission: while Sulayman was flexible and even lax in his approach to the exact wording of the Hadith he transmitted,[99] ᶜAffan was fastidious and strict. 'I wrote ten thousand *aḥādīth* from the mouth of Hammad ibn Salama; – he once bragged – however I transmitted only two thousand of them.'[100] ᶜAffan was forced to sift through the material he had collected from Hammad and eliminate dubious texts because of Hammad's casual approach to Hadith transmission. In fact, ᶜAffan recounted that once he and another fellow student forced Hammad to dictate Hadith to them. This event occurred after the two studied with Hammad for a year and still found themselves struggling to take notes in Hammad's sessions. Hammad was not keen on dictating; he was a performer, and as such he preferred to speak freely and even extemporise. He was also quick to get bored and tired. At the end of one of Hammad's study sessions, ᶜAffan and his colleague discovered that each of them recorded Hammad's material with a different wording. This was bound to happen even if Hammad had bothered himself with strict dictation; however, the puzzled students hurried to Hammad at the end of the study session and asked him to re-dictate the material. Hammad was tired, so he invited the two eager disciples to his home. 'You will make people chase me like dogs chase their prey' – he complained. He meant that students would start knocking on his door, asking him to dictate Hadith to them. ᶜAffan and his friend insisted: 'We write only from dictation' – they declared, and the scholar obliged and started dictating.[101]

Both ᶜAffan and Sulayman quoted Hammad's version of the Anas ibn Malik *ḥadīth* as a combination of narrative and gesture, and contributed to its circulation. Both Sulayman and ᶜAffan are described in the texts as actually performing the gesture that they had witnessed Hammad perform. But while ᶜAffan 'demonstrated [Hammad's gesture] by pointing the tip of his little finger', Sulayman inserted Hammad into the narrative and described how Hammad performed the gesture:

> Sulayman ibn Harb told us: Hammad ibn Salama told us the following *ḥadīth* on the authority of Thabit, [and Thabit transmitted it] on the authority of Anas: The Prophet recited the following verse: 'And when his Lord revealed Himself to the Mountain'. Hammad said: 'Like this.' Sulayman pinched by pressing the tip of his thumb to the tip of his right forefinger, and said: 'He levelled it to dust. Moses fell down senseless' (Q. 7:143).[102]

There were other disciples of Hammad who circulated this *ḥadīth*. As mentioned earlier, the *muḥaddith* Muᶜadh ibn Muᶜadh al-ᶜAnbari (d. 811–2) from Basra, who was Hammad's closest disciple, demonstrated to his students, among them Ahmad ibn Hanbal, the gesture of sticking out the tip of his little finger.[103]

The Anas ibn Malik (or rather, the Hammad) *ḥadīth* was included in the prominent works of Islamic traditionalism like Ahmad ibn Hanbal's *Musnad*, ᶜAbd Allah ibn Ahmad ibn Hanbal's *Kitāb al-Sunna* and Ibn Khuzayma's

Kitāb al-Tawḥīd.[104] These works expanded the distribution range of this *ḥadīth* and thus it was assimilated into the traditionalistic curriculum. Other Hadith centres also produced their own versions which referred to *muḥaddithūn* other than Hammad as their source. For example, the *muḥaddith* Abu Ismaᶜil Qurra ibn ᶜIsa (d. 807–8) from al-Wasit presented a version that he himself had heard from the *muḥaddith* Sulayman ibn Mihran al-Aᶜmash from Kufa (d. 765). As one of his students testified, after quoting the relevant Quranic verse, Abu Ismaᶜil explained to his students that Anas made a gesture with his finger. 'Abu Ismaᶜil showed us the gesture by using his forefinger' – testified the student.[105] This anecdote clarifies that the use of gestures during the transmission of *aḥādīth al-ṣifāt* was not restricted to Basra and Baghdad; this practice was also accepted in Kufa.

There existed versions of the Anas ibn Malik *ḥadīth* with humorous errors. The Isfahani *muḥaddith* Abu ᶜAbd Allah ibn Manda (d. 1005) heard the Anas ibn Malik *ḥadīth* from the great scholar-traveller from Tripoli, Lebanon, Khaythama ibn Sulayman (d. 954). Khaythama was considered one of the luminaries of his era, but when Ibn Manda came to Tripoli as an eager student to study Hadith from him, Khaythama was more than a hundred years old (according to one of the reports, Khaythama died at the age of 116).[106] Ibn Manda spent a considerable period of time with Khaythama, because according to Ibn Manda's avowal, he recorded one thousand folios (*juzᵓ*) from Khaythama's curriculum.[107]. Khaythama's old age probably affected his memory, because his version of the Anas ibn Malik *ḥadīth,* as quoted by Ibn Manda in his polemical treatise *al-Radd ᶜalā al-Jahmiyya,* is quite odd. In Khaythama's version, Hammad ibn Salama is the narrator – but he also plays the role of the defiant student who tells Thabit that he should not transmit this *ḥadith* while using the iconic gesture.[108] Khaythama declared that the source of this version was Haytham ibn al-Jamil (d. 828–9), a *muḥaddith* from Basra who was Hammad's disciple. Khaythama also quoted another chain of transmission for this odd version,[109] but this chain was even more problematic. The first transmitter in this chain, who claimed to have heard this *ḥadīth* from Hammad ibn Salama himself, was ᶜUmar ibn Musa al-Wajihi (death date unknown, *fl.* in the second half of the eighth century). ᶜUmar was a dubious *muḥaddith* from Syria known for his numerous lies (see Appendix IV, chart 6).[110]

IV. The Ultimate Performer of *Aḥādīth al-Ṣifāt*

The two traditions that interpret Q. 7:143, namely the Anas ibn Malik *ḥadīth* and the Ibn ᶜAbbas *ḥadīth*, present two contrasting styles of narration. All the variants of the Anas ibn Malik *ḥadīth* present an interpretation of a Quranic verse while combining narrative and gesture. This interpretation is applicable to both the dominant Basran-Baghdadian versions and the marginal versions from al-Wasit and Tripoli. As opposed to the various versions of the Anas ibn Malik *ḥadīth*, the two versions of the Ibn ᶜAbbas *ḥadīth* present a more straightforward approach. Lacking the complex structure of a 'framing narrative' and an 'embedded narrative', these two versions that circulated first in Kufa, and later in Baghdad, merely present the Quranic verse and a strictly verbal explanation of the text. If gestures were performed by the *muḥaddith* they were not recorded by his disciples. 'The instance of narrating' in these *aḥādīth* is almost nonexistent. We only know the name of the *muḥaddith* who transmitted the material with barely any additional detail that sheds light on the instance of narrating.

The comparison between these two approaches of Hadith transmission clarifies Hammad's motives in transmitting the story about the dispute between Thabit and Humayd. Hammad used the story to make a statement that making gestures during Hadith transmission was desirable. Hammad was a performer, as the following example clarifies:

> ᶜAffan related to us that Hammad ibn Salama related the following [story] on the authority of Thabit [who related it] on the authority of Anas ibn Malik: 'A Persian man who was the Prophet's neighbour used to cook the most fragrant delicious soup. One day, he came to the Prophet and gestured with his hand like this.' Hammad demonstrated the gesture that signalled 'come!' with his hand [and continued]: 'The Prophet signalled in response: "ᶜAᵓisha is with me." The man responded by gesturing like this with his hand.' Hammad demonstrated the gesture that signalled: 'No' [and continued]: 'And then the Prophet responded like this, meaning 'No'. Afterwards, the Persian came back and [again asked the Prophet]: 'Come!' [by using a hand gesture]. This went on two or three more times. This one gesticulating 'like this', while the other one gesticulating 'like this'. Hammad demon-

> strated [the gesture that represented] 'like this' [and continued]: It actually meant 'no'. Finally, [the Persian] gestured 'like this', which meant 'You two should come'. So both [the Prophet and ᶜAᵓisha] went [to his house to have some delicious soup].[111]

The rhythmic 'dialogue' between the Prophet and the Persian comprised gestures only. Hammad, the narrator, 'translates' the hand gestures into words. The fact that the narrator succeeded in building a rhythmic dialogue from gestures is an excellent indicator of his professionalism both as a performer and as a storyteller.

Hammad was an exceptionally pious *muḥaddith* and grammarian from a family of *muḥaddithūn* in Basra.[112] He in fact belonged to the earliest generation of professional *muḥaddithūn*. Most of his professional activity was typical of this group: firstly, his Arabic was impeccable.[113] In addition, he was deeply involved in checking the biographies of the *ṣaḥāba* and the *tābiᶜun* to substantiate their merits and verify the reports attributed to them.[114] Hammad gained prominence among his contemporaries as one of the first *muḥaddithūn* to record the Hadith in writing.[115] Furthermore, his stature was enhanced as a pioneer in his generation: he was the first *muḥaddith* who composed a Hadith collection arranged by topics (*muṣannaf*). Unfortunately, his *muṣannaf* did not survive.[116] Most of the Hadith material attributed to him focused on eschatology, including dozens of versions of *aḥādīth al-ṣifāt*.[117]

Hammad's attraction to *aḥādīth al-ṣifāt* was described by his contemporaries as odd and perhaps embarrassing. For example, a marginal and dubious *muḥaddith* from Basra by the name of Ibrahim ibn ᶜAbd al-Rahman ibn Mahdi (death date unknown) claimed that Hammad never specialised in *aḥādīth al-ṣifāt* until he took a boat trip from Basra to ᶜAbbadan (an island in the Arvand Rud river in Iran). When Hammad returned from his trip, he started collecting this material and transmitting it. Ibrahim added: 'In my opinion, a devil went out of the sea and threw this material at him.'[118] Whether or not Hammad brought his material from ᶜAbbadan, Ibrahim's remark probably reflected the perception that Hammad's new area of interest was exotic and of foreign origin. Rationalising Hammad's occupation with *aḥādīth al-ṣifāt* as a demonic obsession was a concept embedded in the local belief system. According to this belief system, a sea-voyage was deemed dangerous and bound to harm one's core beliefs. The myth that Iblis (Satan) had his throne on the sea surface and that he sent his troops to tempt the Muslims, was even recorded in the Hadith as a Prophetic dictum.[119] In sum, Ibrahim's remark reflects the awe and wonder in which Hammad's *aḥādīth al-ṣifāt* were first received in Basra.

Hammad's skilful performances combined with his exciting repertoire attracted fervent listeners to his Hadith sessions, in which he recited and performed *aḥādīth al-ṣifāt*. The following anecdote, recounted by one of Hammad's disciples, clarifies that Hammad's popularity and the material that he taught threatened the stature of other *muḥaddithūn* in Basra:

> I was at Hammad ibn Salama's house when a letter from Abu Hurra arrived. In the letter, Abu Hurra reproached Hammad for transmitting these *aḥādīth* that Hammad used to transmit, namely about the beatific vision. Abu Hurra ordered Hammad to withdraw from transmitting his material on the *ruʾya*.[120]

Abu Hurra was a *muḥaddith* from Basra whose full name was Wasil ibn ᶜAbd al-Rahman (d. 769). Although later generations were not unanimous in their judgement regarding Abu Hurra's reliability as a *muḥaddith*, his stature among his contemporaries was unshakeable. He even was one of Hammad's Hadith teachers.[121] In his letter to Hammad, Abu Hurra was probably expressing the views of other Basran *muḥaddithūn*. According to Hammad's disciple, Hammad was furious: 'I will not do that!' – he declared – 'I heard them (i.e. *aḥādīth al-ruʾya*) from reliable people, and I transmit them exactly as I heard them!'[122] It is noteworthy that Hammad's declaration is identical to Thabit al-Bunani's position in his argument with Humayd.

Hammad's obsession to add more *aḥādīth al-ṣifāt* to his repertoire drove him to disregard the unwritten protocol of cautious transmission, and he made careless moves that astonished his disciples. For example, several lengthy versions of a *ḥadīth* attributed to Anas ibn Malik circulated among the *muḥaddithūn* of Basra. In these versions, the Prophet reported on an encounter he had with the archangel Gabriel. Gabriel appeared in front of the Prophet, while holding in his hand a beautiful white-coloured pearl mirror that was tainted by a black spot. Gabriel explained that the mirror symbolised Friday, and that the spot symbolised 'the Hour of Resurrection' that would occur on a Friday. Then Gabriel described to the Prophet the encounter between God and the believers on the Day of Resurrection.[123] One day, Hammad introduced to his students a man by the name of Hamza ibn Wasil al-Minqari. Hammad asked the students to listen to a *ḥadīth* Hamza wished to convey to them. Hamza was no stranger to the students; they had already known him as the timid man who had attended the classes that Hammad regularly taught in one of the Basra mosques.[124] Hamza started reciting the longest known version of the Friday *ḥadīth*, not before he claimed to have heard this version from the *muḥaddith* Qatada ibn Diᶜama, who was one of Anas's favoured disciples. In Hamza's version, God would descend from His throne into the valley in which the believers gathered. Hamza elaborated on the setting of the encounter between God and the believers: pulpits of light encircling the throne and horsemen dressed in silk and brocade, wearing bracelets of silver and gold would descend from Heaven. Suddenly, fountains of musk and perfume would sprinkle on the faces of the believers. The believers would hear God order the keeper of Heaven to draw the curtains, and when the curtains were drawn, God with all His glory and light would reveal Himself. Hamza continued his story, adding more and more colourful details.[125] Although Hammad gave him the tremendous opportunity to transmit Hadith to his disciples, Hamza's career as a *muḥaddith* started and ended with this tradition: his version fell into oblivion, and he was regarded as an unreliable *muḥaddith* who attributed to himself the material of others.[126] Hammad's decision to enable Hamza to transmit this *ḥadīth* was definitely ill-advised. In addition, the milieu of *muḥaddithūn* in Basra was teeming with stories about Hammad's tendency to bend the truth; other stories described his misconduct and poor judgement, especially when he reached an advanced age. Hadith scholars were consistently concerned about the veracity of Hammad's work when they encountered a *ḥadīth* of which Hammad was the sole source.[127]

Even later traditionalistic sources interpreted Hammad's attraction to *aḥādīth al-ṣifāt* as an obsession, although they recognised the importance of Hammad's mission in collecting this material. Furthermore, they saw his mission as a major part in shaping the traditionalistic credo. The Hanbalite theologian, Abu Yaᶜla ibn al-Farra (d. 1066), meticulously collected all *aḥādīth al-ṣifāt* that were attributed to Hammad, and included them in his controversial *Ibṭāl a-Taʾwīlāt.* Abu Yaʿla copied the following passage from a book which no longer exists:

> Sahl ibn Harun (a *muḥaddith* from Basra, d. 830) once recounted: Hammad ibn Salama was the first among the people of Basra to collect *aḥādīth al-ruʾya* in a book. One of his colleagues remarked: 'Abu Salama, you beat all your colleagues in collecting these *aḥādīth* about the description [of God].' [Sahl continued]: I heard Hammad ibn Salama respond: 'By God, my soul urged me to collect this [material] until I was satisfied that all the knowledge was recorded.' He said this sentence thrice while shaking his hand. I was very fond of his shyness, and the fact that he disseminated [his knowledge] among the common people, so the 'people of whimsical opinions' (*ahl al-ahwāʾ*, i.e. the rationalists) would not confuse them.[128]

This passage sketches in a nutshell Hammad and his pioneering intellectual endeavours. Apart from emphasising Hammad's modesty (note the gesture of dismissal that accompanies Hammad's words when he talks about his life project), the passage clarifies why Hammad encountered criticism within the circles of the Basran *muḥaddithūn*. He both distributed 'forbidden' material and disseminated it among *al-ʿāmma*, the commoners. His *majlis* was packed (we can assume that the *majlis* of Abu Hurra was deserted), and his vivid performances probably posed a challenge to his colleagues. However, this criticism was also ideological. Hammad's dedication to transmitting this material was shaped against the backdrop of the on-going controversy between the traditionalists and the rationalists, namely the Qadarites and the early Muʿtazilites. Hammad identified *aḥādīth al-ṣifāt* as the ultimate weapon that would help the traditionalists win theological debates, and he identified *aḥādīth al-ṣifāt* also as a 'litmus test'. Hammad believed that *aḥādīth al-ṣifāt* would distinguish the believers (the traditionalists) from the heretics (the rationalists). In other words, Hammad was the forerunner of the established form of traditionalism that Ahmad ibn Hanbal's disciples promoted a century after Hammad's death. Thus, later traditionalists perceived Hammad's material as one of the major traits of traditionalism. Two sayings attributed to Ahmad ibn Hanbal reflect Hammad's image as one of the forefathers of Islamic traditionalism. According to the Hanbalite Ibn Qayyim al-Jawziyya (d. 1350): 'The imam Ahmad [ibn Hanbal] used to say: "The *aḥādīth* transmitted by Hammad ibn Salama are a real pain in the neck for the innovators."'[129] The Hanbalite Sufi and theologian al-Ansari al-Harawi (d. 1089) quoted another saying: 'Ahmad ibn Hanbal used to say: "when you hear someone making fun of Hammad ibn Salama, accuse him of not being a Muslim, because [his words indicate] that he is a fervent innovator."'[130]

Although these sayings are nowhere to be found in Ibn Hanbal's writings, they were part of the traditionalistic curriculum. Moreover, these sayings indicate that Hammad was the backbone of the traditionalistic ethos and remained so for many generations. Ibn Taymiyya (d. 1328) remarked that the polymath al-Jahiz, who was a sworn Muᶜtazilite, defamed (in an unprecedented way) both Hammad ibn Salama and his closest disciple Muᶜadh ibn Muᶜadh. Al-Jahiz hated Muᶜadh because as a qadi of Basra he mistreated the Qadarites and the Muᶜtazilites.[131] Hammad was the target of al-Jahiz's mockery because 'he collected *aḥādīth al-ṣifāt* and taught them'.[132] Indeed, as a *muḥaddith*, Hammad promoted *aḥādīth al-ṣifāt* through all the available channels: he collected them, arranged them in a special book, taught them to the educated and laymen classes, argued about them with the rationalists, answered the questions posed by disciples and laymen, and dictated them in packed assemblies.[133] The *muḥaddith* and historian Shams al-Din al-Dhahabi, who was Ibn Qayyim al-Jawziyya's contemporary, determined that 'Hammad was the vehicle through which *aḥādīth al-ṣifāt* spread'.[134] Taking into consideration al-Dhahabi's comprehensive reading in the Hadith and the adjacent literature, we may assume that al-Dhahabi's view of Hammad's role in disseminating *aḥādīth al-ṣifāt* was well-balanced and reflected the overall estimation of Hammad in the traditionalistic circles.

Several of the more conspicuous *aḥādīth al-ṣifāt* that Hammad transmitted were subtle versions of *ḥadīth al-ruʾya* that do not describe God in explicitly anthropomorphic terms. These traditions, however, were constructed as compelling stories with an elaborate framing narrative. We included these stories in Chapters 1 and 2, without indicating that Hammad was the *muḥaddith* who disseminated them: the delightful scene of the *ṣaḥāba* asking the Prophet about the Day of Resurrection. The *ṣaḥāba* received a response that they will see God as they see the full moon (attributed to Abu Razin al-ᶜUqayli). Another story depicts Abu Burda's encounter with ᶜUmar ibn ᶜAbd al-ᶜAziz. This tale contains the *ḥadīth al-ruʾya* attributed to his father Abu Musa al-Ashᶜari (see Appendix IV, chart 7).[135]

However, Hammad also transmitted traditions which included an explicitly anthropomorphic language: these traditions included the brief *ḥadīth* about God's laughter (again, attributed to Abu Razin al-ᶜUqayli and Abu Musa al-Ashᶜari);[136] a version of the *ḥadīth* of the divine fingers attributed to ᶜAbd Allah ibn ᶜUmar, which included a description of ᶜAbd Allah ibn ᶜUmar using an iconic gesture which symbolises God's fingers;[137] the lengthy *ḥadīth* about God's laughter attributed to ᶜAbd Allah ibn Masᶜud;[138] several of the many versions of *ḥadīth al-nuzūl*;[139] and one of the several versions of the *ḥadīth* about God holding the believers' hearts between two of His fingers.[140]

Hammad's tendency to use iconic gestures in the anthropomorphic material is reflected in *ḥadīth aṭīṭ al-raḥl*, 'the *ḥadīth* on the moaning of the saddle'. The rationalists used to quote this *ḥadīth* in their polemics with the traditionalists, as one of the *aḥādīth maḥshūwa*, the *aḥādīth* of the riffraff, which provoked much laughter among the sophisticated rationalistic elite.[141] However, the traditionalists did their best to conceal this *ḥadīth*, and we find this particular version only in polemical treatises. This *ḥadīth* is also omitted from the *Musnad* of Ibn Hanbal and the traditionalistic thematic Hadith compilations. In this version, Hammad ibn Salama quotes the Kufan *tābiᶜī* al-Shaᶜbi (d. after 718):

> God, exalted and lofty is He, filled the throne until it made a sound like the moan of a new saddle. [Hammad] said: 'Just like this sound', and he put his right shank on his left knee [and produced the moaning sound].[142]

Finally, Hammad's name is connected to a group of *aḥādīth* (all attributed to Ibn ᶜAbbas) in which the Prophet is quoted as saying: 'I saw my Lord, exalted and lofty is He!' and: 'I saw my Lord in most beautiful form' (*fī aḥsan ṣūra*).[143] These *aḥādīth* appear only in the Hadith compilations of hardcore traditionalism such as Ibn Hanbal's *Musnad*, al-Ajurri's *Kitāb al-Sharīᶜa* and in thematic compilations on *aḥādīth al-ṣifāt* such as Abu 'l-Hasan al-Daraqutni's *Kitāb al-Ruʾya*.[144] The longer variants of this *ḥadīth* attributed to Hammad quote the Prophet as saying: 'I saw my Lord in the form of a curly beardless young man, wearing a green garb.'[145] This *ḥadīth* sometimes added a red garb, golden sandals and a veil of gold to the description of the youthful

God. Sometimes this *ḥadīth* placed that figure in luscious greenery or behind curtains draped with pearls. At any rate, this description caused much embarrassment to the traditionalists.[146]

Hammad's anthropomorphic material was one of the topics of heated discussions between the traditionalists and the rationalists in ninth-century Baghdad. One of the great opponents of the traditionalists, Muhammad ibn Shujja[c] al-Thalji (d. 266/880), harnessed the anecdotes about Hammad to discredit his material.[147] The hardcore Hanbalite traditionalists for their part held onto Hammad's anthropomorphic material.[148] Other Hadith scholars, however, were cautious with Hammad's material. Al-Bukhari did not include Hammad's material in his *Ṣaḥīḥ*. Muslim, on the other hand, was happy to use Hammad's *aḥādīth* on a variety of topics, but never on the divine attributes. In an attempt to exonerate Hammad from the accusations of fabricating *aḥādīth*, the scholars pointed the finger at others: Hammad's adopted son[149] and an unscrupulous forger by the name of Shaykh ibn Abi Khalid, a Sufi from Basra. According to Sulayman al-Harb, who himself was one of Hammad's disciples, Shaykh admitted that he had fabricated 400 *aḥādīth*, and after teaching them he realised that he had made them part of 'the people's curriculum' (*barnāmij al-nās*).[150] An unspecified number of those fabricated *aḥādīth* were *aḥadīth al-ṣifāt* that Shaykh claimed to have heard from Hammad.[151] Shaykh, by the way, was the disciple who recounted the story of Abu Hurra's letter to Hammad. In both cases, his testimonies sound perfectly reliable and honest.

V. The Predicament of the Traditionalists

As demonstrated in the previous sections of this chapter, the gestures that accompanied *aḥādīth al-ṣifāt* were quickly assimilated in the transmission process. When the first narrator used an iconic gesture for the first time, he created a pattern of narrating that his disciples, and later their disciples, duplicated. This pattern combined text and gesture, and it was recorded – whether in the memory of the students who attended the *muḥaddith*'s sessions, or in their notes. Some of these notes were later assimilated in the text of the single *ḥadīth* as 'performance instructions'. The several cases of *aḥādīth al-ṣifāt* to which performance instructions of gestures were connected reflect uneasiness and sometimes controversies among the *muḥaddithūn*. The question remains whether the scholars of Hadith discussed the issue of gestures in *aḥādīth al-ṣifāt*, and if they did, how did they define these gestures? Before we address this question, we would like to emphasise two important points that have emerged from this chapter: the perception of gestures as natural components of the spoken language and the place of gestures in the process of narrating.

Although the sources rarely mention these two points, it is possible to recreate the basic approach of the Hadith scholars from textual evidence scattered in the interpretations of the Hadith compilations and the theoretical Hadith literature (especially the manuals for *muḥaddithūn*). A fixed rule about the place of gestures in human speech is found in the teachings of Abu 'l-Hasan al-Ashᶜari (d. 935), the eponymous founder of the Ashᶜarite school. According to al-Ashᶜari, 'the gestures are the signifiers that point on the meanings (*maᶜānī*) that exist in the mind'. Al-Ashᶜari mentioned two gestures that the Prophet performed to indicate a 'complete' month of thirty days and a 'defective' month of twenty-nine days. These gestures were performed by the original narrator of this Prophetic *ḥadīth*; in the later phases of transmission, the word *hākadhā* signified the performed gesture.[152]

The first systematic attempt to discuss the place of gestures in the Hadith was probably established in the ninth century by al-Bukhari. In his *Ṣaḥīḥ*, he dedicated a chapter entitled 'gestures connected to divorce and other matters' to a cluster of *aḥādīth* in which the Prophet performed iconic, metaphoric and deictic gestures.[153] Al-Bukhari recorded these anecdotes in response to a specific legal matter which is connected to an oath of condemnation (*liᶜān*): in this case, a profoundly deaf husband divorced his allegedly adulteress wife by using hand gestures or a nod of his head instead of uttering the words of the divorce oath. According to al-Bukhari, these gestures were admissible in a court because their message was immediately perceived by the audience.[154] As al-Bukhari remarked in his succinct preface to this chapter:

> If a deaf man accuses his wife [of adultery] by writing [his accusation], by gesturing or by pointing [in a way which is] customary, [these actions are considered] as if he uttered [the oath of condemnation]. This is the opinion of some of the *muḥaddithūn* of the Hijaz and elsewhere.[155]

Al-Bukhari, then, believed that gestures were equivalent to speech, and to this end he presented the anecdotes of the Prophet gesticulating on several occasions. In the following chapter, al-Bukhari quotes five *aḥādīth* in which the Prophet performed gestures which his audience immediately understood. These *aḥādīth* do not revolve around the theme of divorce. In two *aḥādīth*, the Prophet performed iconic gestures that convey the numbers twenty-nine, thirty and two.[156] The other three *aḥādīth* describe metaphoric gestures that communicate abstract expressions: who was the best family among the Prophet's supporters (*al-anṣār*) in Medina, when was the coming of the Hour expected, and the high stature of the supporters of orphans in Heaven.[157] In the introduction to his chapter, al-Bukhari quotes a cluster of *aḥādīth* with distorted *isnāds* whose links are missing. Most of the gestures that he describes are functional: when seeing two *ṣaḥāba* argue over a debt, the Prophet made a gesture (which is not described in the text) which the creditor understood to mean that the Prophet ordered him to forgive half the debt.[158]

Al-Bukhari's discussion was limited, but it ignited the enthusiasm of his successors. From the later works interpreting al-Bukhari's *Ṣaḥīḥ*, like Ibn Battal's (d. 1057) *Sharḥ Ṣaḥīḥ al-Bukhārī* and Ibn Hajar al-ᶜAsqalani's (d. 1449) *Fatḥ al-Bārī*, it is apparent that the jurisprudents who discussed the case of the profoundly deaf man and his nonverbal *liᶜān* examined gestures and their use from different angles. They asked, for example, if the meaning of the gesture was coherent. In addition, they asked for whom was the gesture intended, and whether or not this individual understood the gesture's meaning. Finally, they considered the possibility that the person who performed the gesture was able to speak, and asked whether in this case his gesture was interpreted as a verbal *liᶜān*.

Ibn Battal was a Malikite judge in Cordoba and Valencia,[159] while Ibn Hajar was a Shafiᶜite judge in Mamluk Cairo. However, in this case their denominational beliefs and religious affiliations were irrelevant: Ibn Hajar cited Ibn Battal extensively and accepted his position. Ibn Battal, for his part, relied on the position of his contemporary, the Andalusian Malikite judge Abu 'l-Qasim al-Muhallab (d. 1044).[160] Ibn Battal further claimed that al-Muhallab's position reflected the original view of Malik ibn Anas, although Ibn Battal did not provide any textual evidence for this claim.[161] According to Ibn Battal and Ibn Hajar, al-Bukhari collected these *aḥādīth* to demonstrate the validity of gestures in legal rulings, and in particular in divorce cases. The Malikites assumed that the gestures performed in court were equivalent to an oral testimony.[162] Al-Bukhari who never adhered to any of the four schools of law,[163] needed the *aḥādīth* on gestures as textual proof in his ongoing controversy with the Hanafites. The Hanafites apparently rejected gestures as equivalent to speech.[164] The approach of al-Bukhari, and later the approach of al-Muhallab, Ibn Battal and Ibn Hajar, was that gestures were natural components of the spoken language. However, a gesture was admissible in a court of law provided that the public widely accepted its meaning as comprehensible. The example of the Prophet using gestures instead of words (*al-ishāra qāʾima maqām al-nuṭq*) was the only proof that al-Bukhari needed.[165] Another proof was the *ḥadīth* of the black slave-girl:

> [It was transmitted on behalf of] Abu Hurayra, who said: a man brought his slave-girl, who was a foreigner, to the Messenger of God, and asked: 'Should I free this slave? Is she a believer?' The Messenger of God asked her: 'Where is God?', and she pointed at the sky. The Messenger of God asked her: 'And who am I?', and she pointed at the Messenger of God and at the sky. She meant to say 'You are the Messenger of God'. Then the Messenger of God said: 'Set her free, for she is a believer.'[166]

This *ḥadīth* is an example of the explicit nature of the gesture. According to al-Muhallab:

> He (i.e. the Prophet) therefore confirmed [the girl's] Islam by using the proof of the gesture. [Confirming one's Islam] is one of the fundamentals of this religion. It spares one's life and guarantees that one's person and property are inviolate. It makes one entitled to Heaven and saves him from Hell. The Prophet determined that she was a believer exactly as he would have determined that one was a believer based on one's speech. Therefore, the gesture should be taken as valid in all other areas of religion. This is what the majority of the jurisprudents say.[167]

Ibn Hajar added that a clarifying gesture replaces speech (*al-ishāra idhā kānat mufhimatan tatanazzalu manzilata 'l-nuṭq*).[168] In addition, Ibn Hajar clarified that gestures regarding God (*fī ḥuqūq Allāh*) were widely acceptable among scholars even in cases where the performer of the gesture was able to speak. However, in the complex affairs of human beings (*fī ḥuqūq al-ādamiyyīn*) such as contracts, affirmations and wills, the scholars did not accept gestures instead of speech, except when a person was too depressed to speak (a view attributed to Abu Hanifa) or when a person was on his deathbed (a view attributed to several anonymous Hanbalites).[169]

As for the place of gestures in the process of narrating, it seems that gestures were clearly perceived as part of the 'show' of the *muḥaddithūn*. A saying attributed to ᶜAbd Allah ibn Masᶜud (a great performer in his own right) states: 'Transmit Hadith to the people as long as they fix their glance at you, but when they stop paying attention, stop talking!'[170] This saying presupposes that a Hadith session involves both watching and listening. In other words, the *muḥaddithūn* recognised gestures as a means to attract the audience's attention. In his manual for future *muḥaddithūn*, the Shafiᶜite (formerly Hanbalite) *muḥaddith* al-Khatib al-Baghdadi (d. 1071) dedicated an entire chapter to discussing the dangers of causing boredom among the students during Hadith sessions. All the citations in this chapter warn the *muḥaddith* not to prolong his dictation for fear of boring his audience. Furthermore, the *muḥaddith* was encouraged to dictate less text of Hadith than the amount that he initially planned to deliver, and not to tire his students with endless citations that 'force the student to passively listen to the teacher without any desire to do so'.[171] The sayings in this chapter guide the *muḥaddith* to manage his sessions by encouraging his students to actively participate in the session. To this end, al-Khatib al-Baghdadi quoted personas from outside the milieu of the *muḥaddithīn*, such as the philologist and man of letters al-Jahiz, and the poet and prince ᶜAbd Allah ibn al-Muᶜtazz (d. 908; Ibn al-Muᶜtazz was the son of the thirteenth ᶜAbbasid caliph). Al-Jahiz said: 'Better a preacher who says little while his listeners are brisk and animated, than a preacher who speaks a lot causing his listeners to be remote in their thoughts by casting tedium in their hearts.'[172] Ibn al-Muᶜtazz emphasised the performance qualifications of the *muḥaddithūn*:

> Among the *muḥaddithūn*, there are those whose voices are easily heard, and who at the same time listen to their students. They avoid tediousness by dictating a smaller amount of texts. They dictate additional material only if they detect such a request in their students' eyes. They know when to make a pause and to proceed. They speak and gesticulate. They adorn the profession as they are adorned by it.[173]

Ibn al-Muᶜtazz portrayed a teacher sensitive to perceive his audience's state of mind during a session of Hadith transmission. This teacher, no doubt, would dictate intriguing material using the arsenal of rhetorical devices in his possession (the flow of speech, the tone of voice, the pauses and the gestures) to captivate his students' attention. Thus, we learn that the professional *muḥaddith* was expected to be a performer.

Our difficulties in articulating a fixed rule about the place of gestures in the Hadith originate from lack of systematic discussions among the scholars about the use of gestures as rhetorical devices. The case of the deaf husband and his *liᶜān* had legal implications and therefore it drew the attention of the scholars who were required to issue their ruling on this case. However, the gestures in *aḥādīth al-ṣifāt* had no legal implications. The consideration of the Hadith scholars in these cases was not immediately required. In addition, the case of the deaf husband – as well as the cases of the black slave-girl and the Prophet's Persian neighbour – reflected the use of gestures as a result of objective obstacles (deafness and difficulties to communicate among the speakers of different languages). The gestures in the other cases that were presented in this chapter were different. It was not a pressing need or an objective obstacle that generated them, but a cluster of motives and reasons. The gestures in *aḥādīth al-ṣifāt* were rhetorical devices which were meant to adorn the narrative, attract the audience's attention and accentuate the theological message. The interest of the Hadith scholars in them was therefore rather limited, although they were well aware that the accompanying gestures in fact demonstrated the uttered words.

Nevertheless, for the Hadith scholars the gestures transmitted valuable messages just as the uttered words of the narrator did, and as such these gestures were an inherent part of the narrative. This perception is reflected in the remark that the Hadith scholar Abu Dawud al-Sijistani (d. 889) attached to the Abu Hurayra *ḥadīth*. After citing this *ḥadīth* with its accompanying iconic gesture that represented the divine attributes of seeing and hearing, Abu Dawud remarked: 'This [*ḥadīth*] is the ultimate answer to the [attacks] of the Jahmiyya', namely the Muᶜtazilites.[174] This short remark indicates that Abu Dawud perceived this specific *ḥadīth* as effective ammunition in the struggle with the Muᶜtazilites. The Muᶜtazilites negated the existence of the divine attributes of hearing and seeing, but this *ḥadīth* affirmed their existence, both by words and by a gesture that amplified the message.

The Hadith scholars wanted to make sure that when a certain *ḥadīth* recorded a gesture, this gesture would be performed by the *muḥaddith*, as any part of the text would. Their way of securing the place of the gestures in *aḥādīth al-ṣifāt* was by issuing corroborative declarations. These declarations were part of a set of argumentations that was mainly destined to build the *muḥaddith*'s self esteem as a professional and to amplify his self image as a custodian of the Prophetic heritage. Abu Bakr al-Ajurri's thematic Hadith compilation, *Kitāb al-Sharīᶜa*, listed the traditionalistic arguments as reflected in the declarations that were attributed to the leading *muḥaddithūn*. Usually, the argumentation was built as follows. The disciple would ask the traditionalistic scholar: 'People here reject the *ḥadīth* according to which God descends every night to the lowest heaven, and other *aḥādīth* in the same vein. What is your opinion?' The scholar would have answered:

> The scholars who brought us the *sunan* of the Messenger of God, namely the *aḥādīth* regarding the prayer, the fasting, the alms, and the pilgrimage, are the same people who brought us *aḥādīth al-ṣifāt*. God is the one who presented these *aḥādīth* to us.[175]

When the prominent disciple of Ahmad ibn Hanbal, Abu Bakr al-Marrudhi (d. 888), presented the same issue to his master, Ibn Hanbal produced a declaration which at first glance seemed to convey the usual traditionalistic message. This declaration, however, attached an additional nuance to the well-known traditionalistic argumentation. Al-Marrudhi focused his questions on 'those *aḥādīth* about the divine attributes and names, the beatific vision, and the summit of the heavenly throne', namely *aḥādīth al-ṣifāt* that the Muᶜtazilites (here, Jahmiyya) rejected.[176] The *ḥadīth* of 'the summit of the heavenly throne' (*qimmat al-ᶜarsh*) to which al-Marrudhi referred, is a unique version of *ḥadīth aṭīṭ al-raḥl*, 'the *ḥadīth* on the moaning of the saddle', which is attributed to Hammad ibn Salama. In the closing statement of this *ḥadīth*, the Prophet describes God on His throne with an accompanying gesture:

> [The Prophet said]: 'He is above His heavens, He is on His throne, and He is like this (*hākadhā*), like a dome.' [The Prophet] gestured with his hand [the form of a dome, and continued]: 'and [the throne] moans like the moan of a saddle under [the weight] of the rider.'[177]

Ahmad ibn Hanbal's response to al-Marrudhi varied slightly from the familiar formula that was used by his fellow traditionalists. First, he confirmed the authenticity of the entire corpus of these *aḥādīth*, that is, he did not discuss each and every one of them, but declared all to be authentic. Then he said: 'The scholars embraced these *aḥādīth* wholeheartedly. These *aḥādīth* should be further transmitted exactly as we received them' (*tusallamu al-akhbār ka-mā jā*ᵓ*at*).[178] Usually, a saying like this is interpreted as 'transmit the text as is, without interpretation'.[179] However, as the *aḥādīth* transmitted in the closed circle of Ibn Hanbal and his disciples were sometimes accompanied by body gestures, we suspect that Ibn Hanbal meant 'transmit the *aḥādīth* exactly as we received them', namely text and form or text accompanied by gestures.

Another concern of the Hadith scholars was the performance of spontaneous gestures (gestures that were not specifically mentioned in the text) while transmitting *aḥādīth al-ṣifāt* and reciting *āyāt al-ṣifāt*. The Shafiᶜite Hadith scholar Abu 'l-Qasim Hibat Allah al-Lalakaᵓi (d. 1027), who was active mostly in Baghdad, quoted an anecdote on this topic in his massive compilation of theological *aḥādīth*. According to this anecdote, a man once recited Q. 39:67 ('They underrate the might of God. But on the Day of Resurrection He will hold the entire earth in His grasp and fold up the heavens in His right hand') to Ahmad ibn Hanbal. The man accompanied his recitation by a hand gesture that was meant to illustrate the divine handgrasp. Ahmad cursed the man and wished that God would cut off his hand. Thereafter, Ahmad angrily left the place.[180] Ahmad's conduct in this anecdote suggests that he forbade the use of spontaneous gestures. Since there was no *ḥadīth* that prescribed an accompanying gesture to the recitation of Q. 39:67, the anonymous man's performance was unacceptable in Ahmad's eyes. This anecdote in fact sheds more light on Ahmad's saying: 'Transmit the *aḥādīth* exactly as we received them.'

The same concern is reflected in a more comprehensive overview on the subject penned by the Shafiᶜite historian and philosopher Abu 'l-Fath Muhammad ibn ᶜAbd al-Karim al-Shahrastani (d. 1153), who conducted his scholarly career in Nishapur. In his important work on heresiography entitled *al-Milal wa'l-Niḥal*, al-Shahrastani determines that the prominent ultra-traditionalists of the ninth century like Ahmad ibn Hanbal and Dawud ibn ᶜAli [ibn Khalaf] al-Isfahani (d. 884; founder of the scripturalist school of Zahirism)[181] followed 'the People of Hadith' (*aṣḥāb al-ḥadīth*) like Malik ibn Anas and Muqatil ibn Sulayman (d. 767),[182] and took 'the safe path' (*ṭarīq al-salāma*). By this term, al-Shahrastani refers to the approach that combines a devout adherence to the exact wording of the Quran and the Hadith, and an avoidance of figurative interpretation (*taʾwīl*) of the anthropomorphic accounts that appear in these texts. Al-Shahrastani then describes the ban on gestures as part of this ultra-traditionalistic approach:

> They were so cautious not to compare [God to His creation] to such a degree that they used to say: 'Whoever moves his hand while reciting "My own hands have made" (Q. 38:75) or points with his finger while transmitting [the Prophetic *ḥadīth*] "Every heart is held between two of the All-Merciful's fingers" his hand must be cut off and his finger must be pulled out (*wajaba qaṭᶜu yadihi wa-qalᶜu iṣbaᶜihi*).'[183]

Both al-Shahrastani and al-Lalakaʾi were Ashᶜarites: al-Shahrastani practised *kalām* and al-Lalakaʾi, who did not publicly profess his Ashᶜarism, was in fact affiliated to Ashᶜarite circles.[184] Their use of Ahmad ibn Hanbal's personality in this case seems instrumental. From the entire context, it seems that al-Shahrastani and al-Lalakaʾi wished to warn the unrestrained *muḥaddithūn* of their hometowns (the Hashwiyya or Mushabbiha who were, among others, Hanbalites; for the Hashwiyya see Chapters 4 and 5)[185] not to perform spontaneous gestures while reciting *āyāt al-ṣifāt* and transmitting *aḥādīth al-ṣifāt*. In al-Lalakaʾi's version, Ahmad ibn Hanbal only cursed the performer of the forbidden gesture, while in al-Shahrastani's description, Ahmad ibn Hanbal, Malik ibn Anas and the other respectable scholars saw the performance of the gesture as an offense to the Islamic law, and therefore they ruled that the gesticulating organ in the case of performing non-prescribed gestures should be cut off. This 'minor' difference between al-Lalakaʾi's version and al-Shahrastani's version may suggest that al-Shahrastani perceived the use of spontaneous gestures more severely than al-Lalakaʾi did. At any rate, we are not aware of any cases of cutting the hands and fingers of *muḥaddithūn* who recited *aḥādīth al-ṣifāt* while gesticulating spontaneously. Al-Shahrastani's text remains here as a mere curiosity. Furthermore, neither the anecdote about Ahmad ibn Hanbal nor the position attributed to him by al-Shahrastani is traceable in the Hanbalite sources. This fact in itself reinforces the assumption that these two Ashᶜarite scholars used the historical figure of Ahmad ibn Hanbal (whom they venerated)[186] to rebuke the behaviour of their contemporaries, who used the gestures to emphasise their literal understanding of the anthropomorphic descriptions of God in the Quran and the Hadith. Ahmad ibn Hanbal in the anecdote expresses a view that stands in stark contrast to the common practice of the Hanbalites of the tenth, eleventh and twelfth centuries, who used gestures in their recitations of the texts and promoted the literal understanding of the anthropomorphic texts (this point is further elaborated in Chapters 4 and 5). In sum, both al-Lalakaʾi and al-Shahrastani's views are part of Ashᶜarite propaganda, if we borrow George Makdisi's view on Ashᶜarite writings.[187]

Nevertheless, the absence of the Ahmad ibn Hanbal anecdote from the Hanbalite sources does not mean that the position it expresses was entirely farfetched or that it was invented by al-Lalakaʾi and al-Shahrastani. Al-Shahrastani also mentions that Malik ibn Anas, the eponymous founder of the Malikite school, articulated his firm stance against spontaneous gestures. Indeed, Malikite sources preserved an anecdote about Malik which is almost identical to the one recounted on Ahmad ibn Hanbal. One of these sources is the Hadith manual *al-Tamhīd* which was written by Ibn ᶜAbd al-Barr (d. 1070), the important Malikite scholar from Cordoba. In one of the chapters of *al-Tamhīd*, Ibn ᶜAbd al-Barr thoroughly discusses *aḥādīth al-ṣifāt*. His aim in this discussion is to prove that there was a consensus among the great scholars of Islam about the approach that should be taken regarding these anthropomorphic texts. In the beginning of his discussion on *aḥādīth al-ṣifāt*, Ibn ᶜAbd al-Barr declares that 'the intelligent people' (*dhawū al-ᶜuqūl*) describe God only by citing His own description of Himself as was conveyed in the Quran, and by citing the description of God as His Prophet provided in the Hadith. 'We never trespass this [limitation] by comparing [Him], depicting [Him], or drawing parallels [on Him]' – declares Ibn ᶜAbd al-Barr.[188] Elsewhere he adds that the Sunnites take the divine attributes in the Quran and the Hadith as an actual reality (*ḥaqīqa*) and not as a metaphor (*majāz*). He adds that the Sunnites do not inquire about the modality of these attributes and that they do not limit any of the divine attributes by using a 'restricted attribute' (*ṣifa maḥṣūra*) when referring to it.[189] In other words, any device that would draw parallels between God and His creation is undesirable. Thereafter, Ibn ᶜAbd al-Barr quotes an anecdote about Malik, and by doing so he clarifies that the 'restricted attribute' is in fact the spontaneous gesture.

The narrator of this anecdote, the Cairene Harmala ibn Yahya (d. 858), was the great-grandson of the Egyptian *muḥaddith* Harmala ibn ᶜImran (see this chapter, Section III).[190] In the following anecdote, Harmala cited the testimony of Malik's disciple, the famous Egyptian *muḥaddith* ᶜAbd Allah ibn Wahb (d. 813):[191]

> I heard that ᶜAbd Allah ibn Wahb said: Malik ibn Anas used to say: Whoever describes a detail of God's essence by gesticulating with his hand on his neck [when citing] the verse 'The Jews say: God's hand is chained' (Q. 5:64), his hand should be cut off. Another example is that when citing 'Surely God hears all and observes all' (Q. 4:58), [this man would] point on his eyes or his ears or any other part of his body. [Also in this case], this part of his body should be cut off [or pulled out], because he compared God to himself.[192]

The reason that Malik gave to this ruling is interesting. According to Malik, the *ṣaḥābī* al-Baraᵓ ibn ᶜAzib (d. between 690 and 692) once transmitted a saying by the Prophet about the four defective animals which are not accepted as sacrifice: the one-eyed, the sick, the lame and the one with the broken leg. The Prophet accompanied his words by counting the animals with his fingers. Al-Baraᵓ, who quoted him, said: 'My hand is shorter than the Prophet's.'[193] Malik remarked that al-Baraᵓ was uncomfortable with describing the Prophet by gesticulating and therefore he refrained from doing so. 'And this is regarding the Prophet, who was one of the created beings – added Malik – Just imagine how it is inconceivable to [describe] God who is incomparable [by gesticulating]!'[194]

In Section II, we discussed the *ḥadīth* that Harmala ibn ᶜImran transmitted (the Abu Hurayra *ḥadīth*), according to which the Prophet used to put his thumb on his ear and his forefinger on his eye when reciting 'Surely God hears all and observes all'. The above-quoted anecdote, which mentions this *ḥadīth*, is quite odd because the narrator, Harmala ibn Yahya, indirectly refutes here a *ḥadīth* transmitted by one of his ancestors, a *ḥadīth* which prescribes the use of an accompanying gesture along with the recitation of Q. 4:58. The attitude of this narrator in itself raises questions about the authenticity of the anecdote. In addition, it seems that this anecdote ascribes to Malik the strictest position against the use of gestures in general. The Malikite Quran exegete Abu ᶜAbd Allah al-Qurtubi (d. 1272), who also quoted this anecdote, clarifies that the point of this anecdote is to emphasise that a spontaneous origination (*ibtidāʾ*) of gestures and verbal descriptions of God that do not appear in the Quran and the Hadith are undesirable.[195] As far as our inquiries went, there is no record in the sources that Malik's position, as described in this anecdote, was indeed ever effective in Malikite law; however, this matter indeed requires further investigation which goes beyond the scope of this chapter.

The declarations that the Hadith scholars articulated for and against the use of gestures did not emerge out of thin air. The declarations for the use of gestures were crystallised against the backdrop of the constant attacks of the Muᶜtazila and other rationalistic trends on the anthropomorphic material in the Hadith. The declarations against the use of gestures emerged as a reaction to the conduct of the Hashwiyya or the Mushabbiha, the over-enthusiastic *muḥaddithūn* who transmitted dodgy Hadith material and accompanied their recitation of this material with exaggerated gestures. The Ashᶜarite theologian Abu Bakr Ibn Furak (d. 1015), who was active in Rayy, Baghdad and Nishapur, claimed that the Mushabbiha saw the Abu Hurayra *ḥadīth* as proof that 'God has an eye and an ear, and [claimed that] this is why [the Prophet] placed his hand on his eye and his ear'.[196]

It is noteworthy, that the rationalists of the eighth and ninth centuries did not present a coherent systematised rejection of the gestures of *aḥādīth al-ṣifāt*. Perhaps they did not see the point in referring specifically to the gestures when they rejected the entire corpus of *aḥādīth al-ṣifāt*. Only scholars who were well-versed in the Hadith material, like the Ashᶜarites, could be sensitive to the potential danger that the performance of the gestures entailed and could address this danger systematically. These scholars did not negate the use of gestures when these were specifically mentioned in the text; however, they did shed light on the theological consequences of the practice of gesticulating. The illustrious *muḥaddith* and Shafiᶜite lawyer from Nishapur, Abu Bakr Ahmad ibn al-Husayn al-Bayhaqi (d. 1066), discussed the gesture of placing the thumb on the ear and placing the forefinger on the eye that accompanied the recitation of 'Surely God hears all and observes all' (Q. 4:58). As a *muḥaddith*, al-Bayhaqi accepted the veracity of the Abu Hurayra *ḥadīth* and included it in his voluminous compilation of traditions about the divine attributes. As an Ashᶜarite theologian, he was appalled by the possibility that the gesture implicated that God had organs that were similar to the human organs. While pointing out the fact that the Prophet was the actual performer of this gesture, Al-Bayhaqi explained:

> The gesture which is described in this *khabar* (i.e. *ḥadīth*) is meant to affirm that God has the attributes of hearing and seeing. [The Prophet] pointed at the loci of hearing and seeing that all of us have because he wanted to substantiate the existence of the divine attributes of hearing and seeing in God. It is as if we say: 'So-and-so seized the property of another person', and we gesticulate with our hand to [accentuate] the meaning of this seizing. This *khabar* conveys the message that God [actually] hears-all and sees-all. Furthermore, the meaning of 'hears-all' and 'sees-all' is not 'omniscient', otherwise [the Prophet] would have pointed to his heart. The heart, as we all know, is the locus of knowledge in our body. At any rate, nothing in this *khabar* affirms the [the existence] of organs [in God], because God is extremely exalted upon the creatures.[197]

The nonconformist *muḥaddith* from Sijistan, Abu Hatim ibn Hibban (d. 965), a student of the ultra-traditionalist Ibn Khuzayma, provided a somewhat different explanation to the same *ḥadīth*:

> By placing his finger[s] on his ear and eye, the Prophet meant to inform the people that God does not hear through a [physical] ear with its canal and curves, and that God does not see through an eye which has an eyelid, a pupil and a white area around the iris. God, who is sublime and exalted upon His creation, does not at all resemble what He created. On the contrary, He hears and sees as He pleases, and not through any organ.[198]

Both these scholars, however, did not prohibit the use of gestures, but wanted to make sure that the gestures in *aḥādīth al-ṣifāt* would not be perceived as illustrating God in physical terms but as an extra-affirmation to the existence of the divine attributes. A similar position was expressed by the Ashᶜarite

Ibn Furak, who added: 'The gesture in this case returns to the hearing and seeing that are deduced from [indicating on] the eye and the ear; [the gesture] does not return to an actual eye and an actual ear.'[199] This position was fully adopted by Ibn Taymiyya. When referring to the Abu Hurayra *ḥadīth*, Ibn Taymiyya remarked: '[The Prophet] put his thumb on his ear and his forefinger on his eye. There is no doubt that by doing so he meant to affirm the actual existence of the [divine] attribute and not to compare the Creator to His creation.'[200]

The highly creative Hanbalite *muḥaddith*, theologian and historian, ᶜAbd al-Rahman Ibn al-Jawzi provided a psycho-pseudo historical explanation of the role of the gestures in *aḥādīth al-ṣifāt*. Ibn al-Jawzi's explanation is strikingly original and indeed deserves some elaboration. Ibn al-Jawzi himself used to interpret the anthropomorphic texts figuratively, although he stated that the scholars did not need the technique of *taʾwīl* (figurative interpretation) simply because they already knew that the anthropomorphic descriptions were metaphors denoting the divine attributes. This knowledge should not have been disseminated. Furthermore, the technique of *taʾwīl* certainly should not have been disclosed to the laymen, who were anyhow incapable of understanding it.[201] As we will see in the following passages, Ibn al-Jawzi recommended that the Hadith scholars lead the masses to a literal understanding of the texts, as part of their education.

According to Ibn al-Jawzi, the gestures formed an important part of the prophets' titanic endeavours to lead the masses to the monotheistic faith. Part of this belief was the concept that '[n]othing can be compared with Him' (Q. 42:11). This concept required a high degree of abstract thinking which the laymen and the children did not possess. Ibn al-Jawzi explains in his analysis how the prophets gradually led the masses to grasp this abstract concept: first, they depicted the image of God using anthropomorphic descriptions that the laymen could grasp. These descriptions (*awṣāf*) of God helped establish the belief in God and the affirmation of the divine attributes in the hearts of the laymen. The second stage was to introduce to the laymen the transcendentalism of Q. 42:11.

This process of educating the masses did not occur in a void: the concept of *ithbāt*, the affirmation of the divine attributes, was constantly attacked by the speculative theologians, 'those who understood the divine attributes figuratively (*al-muta*ʾ*awwilūn*) and those who negated the divine attributes (*nufāt al-ṣifāt*)'. These two terms usually refer to the Muʿtazilites and the Ashʿarites, but Ibn al-Jawzi 'plants' them in ancient times when the Biblical prophets operated as the educators of the masses. He claims that in their battle against these speculative theologians and their wrong concept of *nafy*, namely the negation of the existence of the divine attributes, the prophets had to use all the devices at their disposal to dispel the harmful sophistic notions and prevent them from taking hold of the souls of the laymen and the young people. One of the most powerful devices that the prophets used was to describe God and His attributes in a language that the masses would understand. According to Ibn al-Jawzi, '[the prophets] exaggerated (*bālaghū*) in affirming [the attributes] because they wanted to secure the concept of the existence of the Creator in the souls of the laymen'.[202]

After this introduction, which is all but historically tenable, Ibn al-Jawzi describes a timeless on-going cognitive process in the human soul that would never be completed. Ibn al-Jawzi's analysis here is taken from the realm of the classical discussions on the soul and he demonstrates an understanding of the human soul. According to Ibn al-Jawzi, the task of the prophets (and later, the task of other spiritual leaders who remain obscure in his analysis) was to guide the soul gradually and slowly to grasp the subtle combination between *ithbāt*, namely affirming the divine attributes, and *tanzīh*, namely transcendentalism. In the process, the prophets needed to use the most powerful rhetorical devices so that the misconception of *nafy* which was promoted by the sophists would not prevail in the souls of the laymen and the easily influenced young people.[203]

The first phase of the process was to establish the concept of *ithbāt*. This concept is reflected in the relevant Quranic verses such as 'the face of your Lord will abide forever' (Q. 55:27), 'His hands are both outstretched' (Q. 5:64; this is the Quranic answer to the claims of the Jews that God's hand is chained), 'God is angry with them' (Q. 48:6), and 'God is pleased with them' (Q. 5:119). Thereafter, the Prophet described God in his teachings which were recorded in *aḥādīth al-ṣifāt*. The Prophet described God as descending to the lowest heaven, holding the hearts of the believers between two of His fingers, writing the Torah in His own hand, and so on.[204] The Prophet recited all this to the masses; however the process of establishing the concept of *ithbāt* is timeless. Ibn al-Jawzi describes this process, the completion of the first phase and the occurrence of the second phase, in the present tense:

> And when the [soul of] the layman or the young boy are filled with *ithbāt*, and they almost get acquainted with these descriptions (*awṣāf*, of God) that the human senses are capable of perceiving, then it is time to present to him [the Quranic verse] 'Nothing can be compared with Him' (Q. 42:11). [By hearing this verse], he erases from his heart the images that his imagination engraved there, and only the expressions of the *ithbāt* remain steady [in his heart].[205]

This, in a nutshell, is Ibn al-Jawzi's view of the way to acquire the delicate combination of *ithbāt* and *tanzīh*: first, to collect as many 'physical' descriptions of God as possible; secondly, to assimilate these descriptions in order to guarantee that the concept of God is secured in the heart of the believer; thirdly, to expose the believer to the concept of a transcendent god. The gestures play an important part in the second phase. Here Ibn al-Jawzi quotes the last sentence of the *ḥadīth* of the summit of the heavenly throne (*qimmat al-ᶜarsh*): 'He is on His throne, and He is like this (*hākadhā*).' The *hākadhā* here indicates that the Prophet gestured with his fingers, creating with them the form of a dome. Ibn al-Jawzi here explains:

> All this (namely, the combination of verbal description and the gesture) was meant to establish the concept of *ithbāt* in the souls. Most people learn about *ithbāt* only through what they see with their own eyes. They become convinced by this [combination] until they are ready to understand *tanzīh*. However, if in the beginning we approach the layman who is devoid of any understanding of *ithbāt*, and say to him: '[God] is not in the heavens and not on the throne. He should not be described as having a hand. His word is an attribute that exists in His essence. We have no knowledge of Him. You cannot imagine His descent [to the lowest heavens]' – then the veneration of the Quran will be erased from this layman's heart, and he will never achieve the *ithbāt* of God in his heart.[206]

Ibn al-Jawzi, therefore, recognises the role of the gesture in forming an image of God in the hearts of the laymen, thus leading them to the secure path of *ithbāt*. Furthermore, in the conclusion of his discussion, Ibn al-Jawzi recommended the Hadith scholars:

> It is best that we advise the laymen: 'Transmit these things (*hādhihi 'l-ashyāʾ*) exactly as we received them (*amirrūhā ka-mā jāʾat*). Do not run the risk of interpreting them figuratively, because the purpose of these [texts and gestures] is to secure *ithbāt*. This was the original meaning of the *Salaf* (the pious and worthy ancestors of Sunnite Islam).'[207]

It is unavoidable to notice that Ibn al-Jawzi's advice to the Hadith scholars echoes Ibn Hanbal's advice to his disciple al-Marrudhi, namely to transmit the anthropomorphic texts as they were transmitted throughout the ages, with the problematic gestures that some of these texts included.

Ibn al-Jawzi's discussion of the gestures in *aḥādīth al-ṣifāt* was limited and undeveloped, and so were the discussions of al-Bayhaqi and Ibn Hibban. The absence of a systematic and thorough analysis of this phenomenon in the theological literature is perplexing, because the gestures, more than any other feature in the process of Hadith transmission, highlighted the different shades of traditionalism: while the Hanbalites faithfully performed the gestures, the Malikites forbade the performance of them. Both groups perceived the gestures in *aḥādīth al-ṣifāt* as iconic gestures that describe a concrete and even physical reality. The forerunners of Ashᶜarism in the ninth century and the Ashᶜarites of the tenth and eleventh centuries perceived these gestures as metaphoric gestures, just as they perceived the attributes of God figuratively. The Ashᶜarites, most of who were Hadith experts and taught Hadith, possibly transmitted *aḥādīth al-ṣifāt* with accompanying gestures. One may assume that, like ᶜAbd Allah al-Muqriʾ, these Ashᶜarite Hadith experts conveyed the idea that the divine attributes in *aḥādīth al-ṣifāt* were metaphoric and therefore the gestures illustrating these attributes were metaphoric as well. The Ashᶜarite worldview on *aḥādīth al-ṣifāt* and the techniques that the Ashᶜarite Hadith experts used in order to reconcile their rationalistic worldview and the anthropomorphic descriptions in *aḥādīth al-ṣifāt* are elaborated in Chapter 4.

In the fourteenth century, one gesture ignited the animosity between the ultra-traditionalists (the later Hanbalites) and the rationalists (the later Ashᶜarites). This gesture was inspired by the Prophet's conduct during his famous sermon in *ḥijjat al-wadāʾ* ('the Farewell Pilgrimage'). In this formidable event, the Prophet pointed his forefinger to the sky, then pointed at the convening crowd and said three times: 'Oh God, bear witness!'[208] This gesture was understood by generations of Hadith scholars as illustrating the whereabouts of God. For several centuries this gesture did not draw any attention. In the fourteenth century, a shift in the realm of Islamic theology occurred and all of a sudden this gesture stood amid a heated controversy. A Damascene source from the fourteenth century describes how the ultra-traditionalists, who pointed their finger to the sky to illustrate that God resided above the heavens on His throne, encountered harsh criticism from their fellow-townspeople, the Ashᶜarites. With a clear echo of the Malikite prohibition on the performance of gestures during the transmission of *aḥādīth al-ṣifāt*, these Ashᶜarites said that whoever pointed his finger to the sky when speaking about God, his finger should be cut off. The ideological roots of the clash between the later Hanbalites and the later Ashᶜarites of Damascus in the fourteenth century are examined in Chapter 5.

Notes

1. Goldziher, 'Ueber Gebärden', pp. 369–86.
2. Goldziher, 'Ueber Gebärden', p. 369. For the use of the dichotomy *Kulturvölker* (cultural peoples)/*Naturvölker* (natural or primitive peoples) and the exclusion of non-Europeans from the history of mankind in German anthropology and German history writing in the late eighteenth and nineteenth centuries, see Zimmerman, *Anthropology and Antihumanism*, pp. 38–44. It is clear that Goldziher did not refer to Muslims as *Naturvölker*. The prevailing viewpoint among German scholars during this time period credited Islam with bringing civilisation to some of the 'uncivilised' regions it conquered. In addition, the 'Orient' was perceived as civilised but at the same time as operating according to cultural norms, conventions, behaviour and values different than the comparable European attitudes and behaviour: Bailey, 'Germany: Redrawing of Civilizational Trajectories', pp. 87–90; for references to Goldziher's views on the Orient, see ibid. p. 93. Goldziher was Hungarian by birth and nationality, but aligned himself with the German academia.
3. Goldziher ('Ueber Gebärden', p. 369) named two of Mallery's works: Garrick Mallery, *Introduction to the Study of Sign Language among the North American Indians, Smithsonian Institution - Bureau of Ethnology* (Washington: Government Printing Office, 1880); 'Sign Language', *Internationale Zeitschrift für Allgemeine Sprachwissenschaft*, 1 (1884), pp. 193–210.

4. Wundt cited Goldziher's observations about sign language among the Arabs: Holtzman, 'Does God Really Laugh?', p. 177, footnote 37.
5. Kalmar, 'The Völkerpsychologie', pp. 673–4. Kalmar's article accentuates Lazarus and Stienthal's pluralistic worldview, surveys their stance against anti-Semitism, and evaluates their (long-forgotten) contribution to the field of modern anthropology: ibid. pp. 686–90.
6. Kalmar, 'Steinthal', pp. 136, 152. Goldziher's monograph entitled *Der Mythos bei den Hebräern und seine geschichtliche Entwicklung* (Leipzig: F. A. Brockhaus, 1876) was translated into English and published in 1877. The translation was approved by Goldziher himself. Goldziher testified that Steinthal's two essays on the legends of Prometheus and Samson inspired him in his work on Hebrew mythology: Goldziher, *Mythology*, pp. xxix–xxx. In addition, Goldziher quoted Steinthal extensively in this book.
7. On the critique of Steinthal, Lazarus and Goldziher of Ernest Renan, see Smith, 'Judeophobia', pp. 139–40.
8. Kalmar, 'The Völkerpsychologie', p. 686.
9. Bousquet, 'Études Islamologiques (IV)', pp. 269–72 (part XXX). Bousquet summarised a considerable number of Goldziher's scientific works in a five-part series of 'Études Islamologiques d'Ignaz Goldziher: Traduction Analytique', that was published in *Arabica* between 1960 and 1962.
10. Ed., 'Ishāra', *EI2*, vol. 4, p. 114; Goldziher, 'Neue Materialien', pp. 495–7; Goldziher, *Abhandlungen zur Arabischen Philologie*, vol. 1, pp. 55–7, vol. 2, civ–cvi (summarised by Bousquet, 'Études Islamologiques (I)', pp. 22–3); Goldziher, 'Zauberelemente', pp. 303–29 (summarised by Bousquet, 'Études Islamologiques (I)', pp. 18–22, 23–6); Holtzman, 'Does God Really Laugh?', pp. 176–7, footnote 37.
11. Goldziher, 'Ueber Gebärden', pp. 373–7; Bousquet, 'Études Islamologiques (IV), pp. 270–1.
12. Marston Speight offered the most systematic analysis of rhetorical features in Hadith literature. However, in his 1989 article, Speight enumerated the marks of oral composition that appear in Hadith literature, such as 'frequent repetition of expressions, expression upon action rather than description . . . conversational tone', but failed to mention gestures: Speight, 'Oral Traditions', p. 27. In his 2000 article, he emphasised that 'transmitters of *ḥadīth* were motivated by a concern to clothe the prophetic dicta in effective rhetorical dress', but again did not mention gestures: Speight, 'A Look', p. 175.

13. Holtzman, 'Does God Really Laugh?', pp. 165–84, and 'Anthropomorphism', *EI3*, pp. 47–9.
14. Kendon, 'Language and Gesture', p. 49.
15. Goldziher, 'Ueber Gebärden', p. 369; Bousquet, 'Études Islamologiques (IV)', p. 269 (part XXX). For further references, see Holtzman, 'Does God Really Laugh?', p. 175.
16. On the discussion of gesture in Classical Antiquity, see Kendon, *Gesture*, pp. 17–19.
17. Goldziher, 'Ueber Gebärden', p. 375; Bousquet, 'Études Islamologiques (IV)', p. 270 (part XXX).
18. Nöth, 'Semiotic Foundations', p. 18. Nöth is quoting Charles Sanders Peirce (d. 1914), 'the father of pragmatism'.
19. We chose McNeill's categorisation because it is comprehensible to non-linguists and straightforward in its approach. However, there are other sets of terminology and classification, as Kendon elaborates in his book: Kendon, *Gesture*, pp. 84–107.
20. McNeill, *Gesture and Thought*, p. 38.
21. McNeill, *Gesture and Thought*, pp. 40–1.
22. Ibn Ḥanbal, *Musnad*, vol. 2, pp. 13–14 (the *Musnad* of ᶜAli ibn Abi Talib).
23. Kendon, *Gesture*, p. 100.
24. McNeill, *Gesture and Thought*, p. 24.
25. McNeill, *Gesture and Thought*, p. 39.
26. McNeill, *Gesture and Thought*, p. 39; Kendon, *Gesture*, p. 100.
27. McNeill, *Gesture and Thought*, pp. 39–40; Kendon, *Gesture*, p. 101.
28. Al-Bukhārī, *Ṣaḥīḥ*, vol. 3, p. 411, introduction to the chapter (*Kitāb al-Ṭalāq, bāb al-ishāra fī 'l-ṭalāq wa'l-umūr*). A complete version of the *ḥadīth* appears in al-Bukhārī, *Ṣaḥīḥ*, vol. 1, p. 402, *ḥadīth* 1304 (*Kitāb al-Janāʾiz, bāb al-bukāʾ ᶜinda 'l-marīḍ*); Ibn Ḥajar, *Fatḥ al-Bārī*, vol. 3, pp. 209–10.
29. Al-Bukhārī, *Ṣaḥīḥ*, vol. 1, p. 402, *ḥadīth* 1304 (*Kitāb al-Janāʾiz, bāb al-bukāʾ ᶜinda 'l-marīḍ*).
30. Goldziher, 'Ueber Gebärden', p. 375; Bousquet, 'Études Islamologiques (IV)', p. 270 (part XXX).
31. Al-Bukhārī, *Ṣaḥīḥ*, vol. 3, pp. 412–13, *ḥadīth* 5301.
32. Al-ᶜAynī, *ᶜUmdat al-Qārī*, vol. 20, p. 417 (*Kitāb al-Ṭalāq, bāb al-liᶜān*).
33. Ibn Ḥajar, *Fatḥ al-Bārī*, vol. 9, p. 351 (*Kitāb al-Ṭalāq, bāb al-liᶜān*); ibid, vol. 11, pp. 357–8.
34. Ibn Ḥajar, *Fatḥ al-Bārī*, vol. 9, p. 351; vol. 11, pp. 357–8.

35. Ibn Ḥajar, *Fatḥ al-Bārī*, vol. 9, p. 351 (*Kitāb al-Ṭalāq, bāb al-liᶜān*); vol. 11, pp. 357–8 (*Kitāb al-Riqāq, bāb qawl al-nabī buᶜithtu anā wa'l-sāᶜa ka-hātayni*); al-ᶜAynī, *ᶜUmdat al-Qārī*, vol. 20, p. 417 (*Kitāb al-Ṭalāq, bāb al-liᶜān*).
36. Ibn Ḥajar, *Fatḥ al-Bārī*, vol. 11, pp. 358–9.
37. Al-Ṭabarī, *Tārīkh*, vol. 1, pp. 10–19.
38. Wright, *Grammar*, pp. i 266, 268, 287; Holes, *Modern Arabic*, pp. 192–3; Dat, 'Deixis', *Encyclopedia of Arabic Language*.
39. Wright, *Grammar*, p. i 7.
40. Ibn Ḥanbal, *Musnad*, vol. 44, p. 143, *ḥadīth* 26523 (*ḥadīth Umm Salama*).
41. Ibn Ḥanbal, *Musnad*, vol. 1, p. 394, *ḥadīth* 301 (*musnad ᶜUmar ibn al-Khaṭṭāb*); Goldziher, 'Ueber Gebärden', pp. 375–6; Bousquet, 'Études Islamologiques (IV)', p. 270 (part XXX).
42. Al-Nawawī, *Ṣaḥīḥ Muslim*, vol. 7, pp. 178–9 (*Kitāb al-Ṣiyām, bāb bayān anna al-dukhūl fī 'l-ṣawm yuḥṣal bi-ṭulūᶜ al-fajr, ḥadīth* 42/1094). Cf. the Hebrew Mishnaic phrase *ᶜamūd ha-shaḥar*: 'From what time may they recite the Shema in the evening? . . . Rabban Gamliel says, until the rise of dawn (*ᶜad she-yaᶜale ᶜamūd ha-shaḥar*)': Neusner, *Mishnah*, p. 3 (*Mishnah, Seder Zeraᶜim, Masekhet Berachot* A: a).
43. Al-Bukhārī, *Ṣaḥīḥ*, vol. 1, p. 210 (*Kitāb al-Ādhān, bāb al-ādhān qabla 'l-fajr, ḥadīth* 621; Muslim, *Ṣaḥīḥ*, pp. 423–4 (*Kitāb al-Ṣiyām, bāb bayān anna al-dukhūl fī 'l-ṣawm yuḥṣal bi-ṭulūᶜ al-fajr, ḥadīth* 39/1093, 40/1093, 41–4/1094); Ibn Ḥanbal, *Musnad*, vol. 6, pp. 166–7, footnote 2.
44. See references to several Hadith compilations in Ibn Ḥanbal, *Musnad*, vol. 6, p. 166–7, footnote 2.
45. Al-Dhahabī, *Siyar Aᶜlām al-Nubalāʾ*, vol. 7, p. 458 (The biography of Hammad ibn Zayd).
46. Al-Nawawī, *Ṣaḥīḥ Muslim*, vol. 7, pp. 178–9 (*Kitāb al-Ṣiyām, bāb bayān anna al-dukhūl fī 'l-ṣawm yuḥṣal bi-ṭulūᶜ al-fajr, ḥadīth* 43/1093).
47. Al-Nawawī, *Ṣaḥīḥ Muslim*, vol. 7, pp. 178–9 (*Kitāb al-Ṣiyām, bāb bayān anna al-dukhūl fī 'l-ṣawm yuḥṣal bi-ṭulūᶜ al-fajr, ḥadīth* 42/1093).
48. Qādī ᶜIyāḍ, *Ikmāl*, vol. 4, p. 31 (*Kitāb al-Ṣiyām, bāb bayān anna al-dukhūl fī 'l-ṣawm yuḥṣal bi-ṭulūᶜ al-fajr, ḥadīth* 43).
49. Beaumont, 'Hard-Boiled', p. 25.
50. Ibn Khuzayma, *Kitāb al-Tawḥīd*, p. 98, *ḥadīth* 2-47. In a slightly different version, Abu Hurayra declared: 'I have seen the Messenger of God do precisely this': ibid. p. 97, *ḥadīth* 2-46. The *ḥadīth* also appears in Abū Dāwud, *Sunan*, vol. 7, p. 110, *ḥadīth* 4728 (*Kitāb al-Sunna, bāb fī 'l-jahmiyya*). Ibn

Hibban quotes this *ḥadīth* from Ibn Khuzayma: Ibn Ḥibbān, *al-Iḥsān*, vol. 1, pp. 498–9, *ḥadīth* 265 (*Kitāb al-Īmān, bā mā jāʾa fī ʾl-ṣifāt*). The Hadith scholar Abu ʾl-Qasim al-Tabarani identifies Harmala as the sole narrator of this *ḥadīth*: al-Ṭabarānī, *al-Muʿjam al-Awsaṭ*, vol. 9, pp. 132–3, *ḥadīth* 9334.

51. Ibn Khuzayma, *Kitāb al-Tawḥīd*, p. 98, *ḥadīth* 2-47. For the biographies of these two scholars, see al-Bukhārī, *Tārīkh*, vol. 4, p. 122; vol. 3, p. 68; Ibn Abī Ḥātim, *al-Jarḥ waʾl-Taʿdīl*, vol. 3, p. 273. Ibn Qayyim al-Jawziyya (or rather his adaptor, Muhammad ibn al-Mawsili) cited this *ḥadīth* on the authority of Saʿid ibn Jubayr (instead of Sulaym b. Jubayr, namely Abu Yunus), but this seems to be a slip of the pen: Ibn Qayyim al-Jawziyya and Ibn al-Mawṣilī, *Mukhtaṣar al-Ṣawāʿiq*, p. 1420.
52. A sign of al-Muqriʾ's prominence as a scholar is the honorific title *shaykh al-islām* that al-Dhahabi bestowed upon him in his *Tadhkirat al-Ḥuffāẓ*: Lucas, *Constructive Critics*, pp. 57–9.
53. Ibn Abī Ḥātim, *al-Jarḥ waʾl-Taʿdīl*, vol. 5, p. 201; al-Dhahabī, *Siyar Aʿlām al-Nubalāʾ*, vol. 10, pp. 166–9 (the biography of al-Muqriʾ).
54. We were unable to detect any informative detail about these two scholars, ʿAli ibn Nasr and Muhammad ibn Yunus al-Nasaʾi. Both appear regularly in the *Sunan* of Abu Dawud. Apart from confirming their credibility, the scholars of Hadith knew nothing about them. Ibn Ḥajar, *Fatḥ al-Bārī*, vol. 13, p. 385 (*Kitāb al-Tawḥīd, bāb wa-kāna Allāh samīʿan baṣīran*).
55. Abū Dāwud, *Sunan*, p. 515, *ḥadīth* 4728 (*Kitāb al-Sunna, bāb fī al-ruʾya*).
56. Al-Dhahabī, *Siyar Aʿlām al-Nubalāʾ*, vol. 12, pp. 274–5.
57. Ibn Khuzayma, *Kitāb al-Tawḥīd*, pp. 97–8.
58. Ibn Khuzayma, *Kitāb al-Tawḥīd*, p. 98. For the position of the *muḥaddith*'s clerk, see Juynboll, 'Mustamlī', *EI2*, vol. 7, pp. 725–6.
59. Ibn Abī Ḥātim, *al-Jarḥ waʾl-Taʿdīl*, vol. 9, p. 173.
60. Ibn Abī Ḥātim, *Tafsīr*, vol. 3, p. 987 (interpretation of Q. 4:58). Also quoted by Ibn Kathīr, *Tafsīr*, vol. 2, pp. 341–2.
61. ʿAbd Allah ibn Masʿud is described in the sources as an extremely energetic person who demonstrated his words by using body gestures. These gestures were described in detail by his disciples. See, for example, Muslim, *Ṣaḥīḥ*, pp. 215–16, *aḥādīth* 534–5 (*Kitāb al-Masājid, bāb al-nadb ilā waḍʿ ʾl-aydī*).
62. Holtzman, 'Does God Really Laugh?', pp. 179–82.
63. Al-Ṭabarānī, *al-Muʿjam al-Kabīr*, vol. 9, p. 419, *ḥadīth* 9763.
64. Al-Ājurrī, *Kitāb al-Sharīʿa*, p. 298, *ḥadīth* 647.
65. A shorter version of the *ḥadīth* with the dialogue between ʿAbd Allah ibn

Masʿud and his disciples was included in Muslim, *Ṣaḥīḥ Muslim*, p. 104, *ḥadīth* 310/187 (*Kitāb al-Īmān, bāb adnā ahl al-janna manzilatan fīhā*). The Shafiʿite *muḥaddith* from Marw, al-Husayn ibn Masʿud al-Baghawi (d. 1122 or 1117), included the *ḥadīth* in his *Sharḥ al-Sunna*, vol. 15, pp. 186–8, *ḥadīth* 4355 (*bāb ākhir man yakhruju min al-nār*). Al-Baghawi emphasised that the *ḥadīth* is *ṣaḥīḥ*.

66. The longest version appears in al-Ṭabarānī, *al-Muʿjam al-Kabīr*, vol. 9, pp. 416–21, *ḥadīth* 9763. Ibn Qayyim al-Jawziyya, again heavily relying on al-Daraqutni, included the *ḥadīth* in the traditionalistic curriculum by tagging the *ḥadīth* as 'fair' (*ḥasan*): Ibn Qayyim al-Jawziyya, *Hādī al-Arwāḥ*, p. 643.
67. Most of the various versions of this *ḥadīth* revert to ʿAbd Allah ibn Masʿud. One of the versions is attributed to Abu Hurayra: Ibn Khuzayma, *Kitāb al-Tawḥīd*, pp. 564–5, 583–4, 754–6; al-Dāraquṭnī, *Kitāb al-Ruʾya*, pp. 258–70. The versions that al-Daraqutni cited were dictated to him in a dictation session (*imlāʾ*) conducted by the Kufi *muḥaddith* Yahya ibn Muhammad ibn Saʿid (d. 930). Ibn Saʿid received this version from the Meccan *muḥaddith* Muhammad ibn Abi ʿAbd al-Rahman al-Muqriʾ (d. 870).
68. Anas lived in Basra from 639 until his death at the age of 103: Juynboll, *Encyclopedia of Canonical Ḥadīth*, p. 131.
69. Ibn Khuzayma, *Kitāb al-Tawḥīd*, pp. 258–9 (*ḥadīth* 1-162).
70. Ibn Khuzayma, *Kitāb al-Tawḥīd*, pp. 258–9 (*ḥadīth* 1-162); Ibn Ḥanbal, *Musnad*, vol. 19, p. 281 (*ḥadīth* 12260).
71. Ibn Khuzayma, *Kitāb al-Tawḥīd*, p. 260 (*ḥadīth* 2-163). A less developed version with the same chain of transmission appears in Ibn Ḥanbal, *Musnad*, vol. 19, p. 281 (*ḥadīth* 12260).
72. According to the Basran Hadith expert, Abu Bakr al-Bazzar (d. 904–5), this *ḥadīth* was known only as a transmission of Hammad on the authority of Thabit: al-Bazzār, *al-Baḥr al-Zakhkhār*, vol. 13, p. 273, *ḥadīth* 6825 (*musnad* Anas).
73. Al-Dāraquṭnī, *Kitāb al-Ruʾya*, pp. 155–6; Lucas, *Constructive Critics*, pp. 338, 343, 357.
74. Ibn Ḥanbal, *Musnad*, vol. 20, p. 411, *ḥadīth* 13178 (*musnad* Anas); Ibn Khuzayma, *Kitāb al-Tawḥīd*, p. 260, *ḥadīth* 2-163; Ibn Khuzayma, *Kitāb al-Tawḥīd*, pp. 260–1, *ḥadīth* 2-164, p. 262, *ḥadīth* 6-166; al-Ṭabarī, *Jāmiʿ al-Bayān*, vol. 10, p. 429 (interpretation of Q. 7:143).
75. Ibn Ḥanbal, *Musnad*, vol. 19, p. 281 (*ḥadīth* 12260).
76. Ibn Abī Ḥātim, *Tafsir*, p. 1560, *ḥadīth* 8937–8. The first *ḥadīth* is attributed

to Ibn ᶜAbbas, whereas the second is attributed to Mujahid ibn Jabr (d. 720).

77. Al-Tirmidhī, *Sunan*, vol. 5, p. 265, *ḥadīth* 3074 (*kitāb al-Tafsīr, bāb wa-min sūrat al-aᶜrāf*).
78. Al-Dhahabī, *Siyar Aᶜlām al-Nubalāʾ*, vol. 6, p. 165 (the biographical entry of Humayd).
79. Al-Dhahabī, *Siyar Aᶜlām al-Nubalāʾ*, vol. 7, p. 213 (the biographical entry of Shuᶜba ibn Hajjaj); ibid. vol. 6, pp. 164–6 (the biographical entry of Humayd); al-Khaṭīb al-Baghdādī, *al-Jāmiᶜ li-Akhlāq al-Rāwī*, p. 260, anecdote 1147.
80. See the footnote of the editors of the *Musnad*, in Ibn Ḥanbal, *Musnad*, vol. 19, p. 9 (*musnad Anas ibn Mālik*).
81. *Al-Maktaba al-Shamela* (http://shamela.ws/) is software containing thousands of books of Arab heritage, which enables researchers and students to conduct advanced searches in the relevant texts.
82. Ibn al-Jawzī, *Kitāb al-Mawḍūᶜāt*, vol. 1, p. 175 (*Kitāb al-Tawḥīd, bāb fī tajallī Allāh ᶜazz wa-jalla li'l-ṭūr*).
83. Gimaret, *Dieu à l'image de l'homme*, pp. 227–8.
84. Ibn Khuzayma, *Kitāb al-Tawḥīd*, pp. 258–9 (*ḥadīth* 1-162); Ibn Ḥanbal, *Musnad*, vol. 19, p. 281 (*ḥadīth* 12260).
85. See the distorted version that appears in the heresiographical treatise of the Shafiᶜite scholar, Abu'l-Husayn al-Malati (d. 987). Although al-Malati confused Humayd and Thabit, presenting Humayd as the devout *muḥaddith* and Thabit as his disciple, al-Malati's addition to the text is enlightening: 'Thabit said to Humayd: "Do not transmit this *ḥadīth* while using this gesture (*lā tuḥaddith bi-hādhā*), oh Abu Muhammad!" Humayd rebuked him severely and said: "This is how Anas transmitted this *ḥadīth*, and Anas claimed that this is how the Messenger of God transmitted this *ḥadīth*, and you expect me to conceal it?": al-Malaṭī, *Tanbīh*, pp. 105–6.
86. Ibn al-Jawzī, *al-Quṣṣāṣ*, pp. 259-60; Swartz, *Ibn al-Jawzī's Kitāb al-Quṣṣāṣ*, p. 153; al-Dhahabī, *Siyar Aᶜlām al-Nubalāʾ*, vol. 5, p. 222 (the biographical entry of Thabit).
87. See Abu Hamid al-Ghazali's (d. 1111) description of the performance of young preachers and storytellers as quoted by Ibn al-Jawzi: Ibn al-Jawzī, *al-Quṣṣāṣ*, p. 298; Swartz, *Ibn al-Jawzī's Kitāb al-Quṣṣāṣ*, p. 174. Jonathan A. C. Brown discussed the fine line between storytelling and Hadith transmission in his illuminating 'Scholars and Charlatans', pp. 88–94. For Thabit al-Bunanai's dual capacity as storyteller and *muḥaddith*, see ibid. p. 89.

88. In Ahmad ibn Hanbal's *Musnad*, there are several examples of Thabit performing gestural *aḥādīth* that he heard from Anas, as opposed to only one example of Humayd. See the representative examples in Ibn Ḥanbal, *Musnad*, vol. 19, p. 420, *ḥadīth* 12431; vol. 20, p. 48, *ḥadīth* 12593; vol. 20, pp. 282–3, *ḥadīth* 12959; vol. 21, pp. 350–1, *ḥadīth* 13869 (the *Musnad* of Anas).
89. Ibn Saᶜd, *Ṭabaqāt*, vol. 1, p. 371 (*dhikr shayb Rasūl Allāh*).
90. Al-Dhahabī, *Siyar Aᶜlām al-Nubalāᵓ*, vol. 6, p. 167 (the biography of Humayd).
91. Al-Ṭabarī, *Jāmiᶜ al-Bayān*, vol. 10, p. 427 (interpretation of Q. 7:143).
92. Asbat had a dubious reputation as a *muḥaddith* who transmitted *aḥādīth* with distorted chains of transmission: al-Mizzī, *Tahdhīb al-Kamāl*, vol. 2, pp. 357–8 (the biographical entry of Asbat ibn Nasr).
93. ᶜAbd Allāh ibn Aḥmad ibn Ḥanbal, *Kitāb al-Sunna*, p. 527, *ḥadīth* 1211; al-Ṭabarī, *Jāmiᶜ al-Bayān*, vol. 10, p. 427 (interpretation of Q. 7:143); al-Suyūṭī, *al-Durr al-Manthūr*, vol. 6, pp. 558–9 (interpretation of Q. 7:143). A partial version appears in Ibn Abī Ḥātim, *Tafsīr*, p. 1560. For further references, consult al-Ṭabarī, *Jāmiᶜ al-Bayān*, vol. 10, p. 427, footnote 3.
94. ᶜAbd Allāh ibn Aḥmad ibn Ḥanbal, *al-Sunna*, vol. 1, pp. 270–1 (*ḥadīth* 504); vol. 2, p. 498 (*ḥadīth* 1149).
95. Al-Dhahabī, *Siyar Aᶜlām al-Nubalāᵓ*, vol. 11, pp. 69–71.
96. ᶜAbd Allāh ibn Aḥmad ibn Ḥanbal, *al-Sunna*, vol. 1, p. 269 (*ḥadīth* 500).
97. ᶜAffan ibn Muslim was a respectable *muḥaddith*, although as a gourmand who had a sweet tooth he was a source of ridicule to his contemporaries. He was one of the *muḥaddithūn* who were summoned to the *miḥna* and refused to declare that the Quran was created. He was not tortured or imprisoned; he was merely denied the generous stipend of one thousand dirham per month he received from the state. ᶜAffan's professional reputation was impeccable. His material was included in the six canonical Hadith compilations (*al-kutub al-sitta*): al-Dhahabī, *Siyar Aᶜlām al-Nubalāᵓ*, vol. 10, pp. 242–55 (the biography of ᶜAffan).
98. Sulayman ibn Harb was a Hadith expert from Basra; however, his main professional activity occurred in Baghdad. He was also nominated as a qadi in Mecca, but was dismissed from his post after five years. His relationships with the caliph al-Maᵓmun were excellent: Sulayman's *majlis* was attached to the palace, and al-Maᵓmun sat in his chambers, hidden behind gauze curtains and wrote the *aḥādīth* that Sulayman dictated. Sulyman's *majlis* were immense and it was claimed that forty thousand people participated in it. This means that there were several clerks who dictated the material on his behalf. Apparently,

Ahmad ibn Hanbal participated in Sulayman's *majlis*: al-Dhahabī, *Siyar A*ᶜ*lām al-Nubalā*ᵓ, vol. 10, pp. 330–4 (the biography of Sulayman).

99. Al-Dhahabī, *Siyar A*ᶜ*lām al-Nubalā*ᵓ, vol. 10, p. 334.
100. Al-Dhahabī, *Siyar A*ᶜ*lām al-Nubalā*ᵓ, vol. 10, p. 250.
101. Al-Dhahabī, *Siyar A*ᶜ*lām al-Nubalā*ᵓ, vol. 10, p. 246.
102. Ibn Khuzayma, *Kitāb al-Tawḥīd*, p. 261, *ḥadīth* 4-165; al-Tirmidhī, *Sunan*, vol. 5, p. 265, *ḥadīth* 3074 (*Kitāb al-Tafsīr, bāb wa-min sūrat al-a*ᶜ*rāf*).
103. Ibn Ḥanbal, *Musnad*, vol. 19, p. 281, *ḥadīth* 12260 (*musnad* Anas); Ibn Khuzayma, *Kitāb al-Tawḥīd*, p. 260, *ḥadīth* 2-163.
104. For full references, see Ibn Ḥanbal, *Musnad*, vol. 19, pp. 281–2 (footnote to *ḥadīth* 12260).
105. Al-Ṭabarī, *Jāmi*ᶜ *al-Bayān*, vol. 10, p. 429 (interpretation of Q. 7:143).
106. Ibn ᶜAsākir, *Tārīkh Dimashq*, vol. 17, p. 72 (the biography of Khaythama ibn Sulayman).
107. Al-Ṣafadī, *al-Wāfī*, vol. 17, p. 72 (the biography of Ibn Manda). For the definition of *juz*ᶜ, see Brown, *Canonization*, p. 61, n. 39.
108. Ibn Manda, *al-Radd* ᶜ*alā al-Jahmiyya*, p. 88, *ḥadīth* 26 (70).
109. Ibn Manda, *al-Radd* ᶜ*alā al-Jahmiyya*, p. 88, *ḥadīth* 26 (70).
110. Ibn ᶜAsākir, *Tārīkh Dimashq*, vol. 45, p. 349 (the biography of ᶜUmar ibn Musa).
111. Ibn Ḥanbal, *Musnad*, vol. 21, pp. 350–1, *ḥadīth* 13869 (*Musnad Anas*).
112. For an extensive biography of Hammad and an example of his material (mainly in law), see Juynboll, *Encyclopedia of Canonical Ḥadīth*, pp. 156–65. Hammad was one of 'the Substitutes' (*al-abdāl*), a group of seventy righteous men who belonged to the *tābi*ᶜ*ūn* and the following generations. As the saying goes, when one of the *abdāl* dies, God sends a substitute in his place. According to al-Dhahabi, 'the Substitutes' were characterised by never producing children. Thus, Hammad married seventy women and never had children: al-Dhahabī, *Mīzān al-I*ᶜ*tidāl*, vol. 1, p. 591 (the biography of Hammad ibn Salama). Hammad's piety is also demonstrated by his refusal to laugh: al-Dhahabī, *Mīzān al-I*ᶜ*tidāl*, vol. 1, p. 591; Ibn Ḥajar, *Tahdhīb*, vol. 1, p. 482; al-Iṣfahānī, *Ḥilyat al-Awliyā*ᵓ, vol. 6, p. 250. Seriousness was one of the key characteristics of the *muḥaddithūn*: Melchert, 'The Piety of the Hadith Folk', pp. 427–8. See also van Ess, *TG*, vol. 2, pp. 376–9.
113. Al-Jazāᵓirī, *Tawjīh*, pp. 303–4. As a grammarian, Hammad was meticulous about the language that the *muḥaddithūn* used. This was reflected in the following saying: 'Whoever transmits the Hadith from me using grammatically

incorrect Arabic, is falsely attributing material to me': Ibn al-Anbārī, *Nuzhat al-Alibbā*ʾ, p. 42. According to Ibn al-Anbari (d. 1181), at the beginning of his career the illustrious grammarian Sibawayhi (d. c. 796) served as Hammad's clerk. One day, Sibawayhi dictated a *ḥadīth* to Hammad's students. Hammad, who heard the dictation, corrected him although Sibawayhi's version was grammatically correct (the *ḥadīth* was *gharīb* anyhow). Sibawayhi, who in fact correctly dictated his version, was so offended that he left his position and started his career as a grammarian with al-Khalil ibn Ahmad (d. 791, 786 or 776). The various distorted versions of this anecdote appear in Ibn ᶜAsākir, *Tārīkh Dimashq*, vol. 25. p. 473.

114. Al-Jazāʾirī, *Tawjīh*, p. 114.
115. Al-Jazāʾirī, *Tawjīh*, pp. 17–18.
116. Al-Jazāʾirī, *Tawjīh*, p. 144; Lucas, *Constructive Critics*, p. 86, footnote 16.
117. Al-Iṣfahānī, *Ḥilyat al-awliyā*ʾ, vol. 6, pp. 252–7.
118. Al-Bayhaqī, *al-Asmā*ʾ *wa'l-Ṣifāt*, vol. 2, pp. 365–6; al-Dhahabī, *Mīzān al-I*ᶜ*tidāl*, vol. 1, p. 593; Ibn Fūrak, *Mushkil al-ḥadīth*, p. 202. See also van Ess, *TG*, vol. 2, p. 379; Williams, *Tajallī*, p. 175; Ritter, *The Ocean of the Soul*, p. 459. Ritter maintains that Hammad ibn Salama visited a Sufi settlement in ᶜAbbadan without substantiating his claim.
119. 'Jabir ibn ᶜAbd Allah said: I heard the Messenger of God say: The throne of Iblis is set upon the sea. He sends his troops and they tempt people. The greatest among them in his view is the one who causes the greatest dissension': Muslim, *Ṣaḥīḥ*, p. 1131, *ḥadīth* 2813 (*Kitāb Ṣifat al-Qiyāma wa'l-Janna wa'l-Nār, bāb taḥrīsh al-shayṭān wa-ba*ᶜ*thihi sarāyāhu li-fitnat 'l-nās*); Ibn Ḥanbal, *Musnad*, vol. 22, pp. 274–5, *ḥadīth* 14377 (*Musnad Jābir ibn* ᶜ*Abd Allāh*). A similar view is found in the Jewish sources: 'Rabbi Levi said, Satan harms people in three places: when one sets off for a journey alone, when one sleeps in a dark house alone, and when one sets sails on the ocean alone' (*Talmud Yerushalmi*, Tractate Shabbat, chapter six). This is our translation which differs from Guggenheimer's, *The Jerusalem Talmud*, vol. 2, part 1, p. 118.
120. Al-Marzubānī, *Nūr al-Qabas*, p. 48 (the biographical entry of Hammad).
121. On the diversified views about Abu Hurra, see Ibn Saᶜd, *Ṭabaqāt*, vol. 9, p. 275; Ibn Abī Ḥātim, *al-Jarḥ wa'l-Ta*ᶜ*dīl*, vol. 9, p. 31; Ibn Ḥajar, *Tahdhīb*, vol. 4, p. 302 (the biographical entry of Wasil ibn ᶜAbd al-Rahman). Abu Hurra's brother, Saᶜid, was a more prolific *muḥaddith* than his brother: Ibn ᶜAsākir, *Tārīkh Dimashq*, vol. 21, pp. 184–90 (the biographical entry of Saᶜid ibn ᶜAbd al-Rahman).

122. Al-Marzubānī, *Nūr al-Qabas*, p. 48 (the biographical entry of Hammad).
123. Al-Ājurrī, *Kitāb al-Sharīʿa*, pp. 280–2; al-Dāraquṭnī, *Kitāb al-Ruʾya*, pp. 172–89.
124. Al-Dhahabī, *Mīzān al-Iʿtidāl*, vol. 1, pp. 608–9 (biographical entry 2312).
125. Al-Dāraquṭnī, *Kitāb al-Ruʾya*, pp. 179–82, *ḥadīth* 64.
126. Al-Dhahabī, *Mīzān al-Iʿtidāl*, vol. 1, pp. 608–9 (biographical entry 2312).
127. Dickinson, *The Development*, pp. 87–90.
128. Abū Yaʿlā, *Ibṭāl al-Taʾwīlāt*, p. 50.
129. Ibn Qayyim al-Jawziyya, *Shifāʾ al-ʿAlīl*, p. 554.
130. Al-Dhahabī, *Siyar Aʿlām al-Nubalāʾ*, vol. 7, p. 450 (the biography of Hammad ibn Salama).
131. For Muʿadh's biography, see van Ess, *TG*, vol. 2, pp. 380–1.
132. Ibn Taymiyya, 'Al-Radd ʿalā al-Ṭawāʾif', *al-Fatāwā al-Kubrā*, vol. 6, p. 403.
133. Ibn Taymiyya, 'Al-Radd ʿalā al-Ṭawāʾif', *al-Fatāwā al-Kubrā*, vol. 6, p. 336.
134. Al-Dhahabī, *al-ʿUlūw*, p. 141.
135. Al-Ājurrī, *Kitāb al-Sharīʿa*, pp. 277–9 (*aḥādīth* 605–8).
136. Al-Ājurrī, *Kitāb al-Sharīʿa*, pp. 294–5 (*aḥādīth* 238–9, 241).
137. Ibn Ḥanbal, *Musnad*, vol. 9, p. 304, *ḥadīth* 5414 (*Musnad ʿAbd Allāh ibn ʿUmar*); Ibn Khuzayma, *Kitāb al-Tawḥīd*, pp. 170–1 (*ḥadīth* 1-95); pp. 564–5 (*ḥadīth* 1-329).
138. Ibn Khuzayma, *Kitāb al-Tawḥīd*, pp. 564–5 (*ḥadīth* 329-1).
139. Al-Ājurrī, *Kitāb al-Sharīʿa*, p. 326 (*aḥādīth* 715–16); Ibn Khuayma, *Kitāb al-Tawḥīd*, p. 316 (*ḥadīth* 39), pp. 322–4 (*ḥadīth* 46).
140. Al-Ājurrī, *Kitāb al-Sharīʿa*, p. 332 (*ḥadīth* 733).
141. The Baghdadian traditionalistic theologian and *muḥaddith* Abu Saʿid ʿUthman ibn Saʿid al-Darimi (d. between 892 and 895) quoted *ḥadīth aṭīṭ al-raḥl* in his polemical treatise against the rationalists: al-Dārimī, *Radd*, p. 74. For an excellent analysis on al-Darimi's discussion and the rationalistic argumentation as articulated by Bishr al-Marisi (d. 833), the archenemy of traditionalist Islam, see Shah, 'Al-Ṭabarī and the Dynamics of tafsīr', pp. 111–12.
142. Ibn Fūrak, *Mushkil al-Ḥadīth*, p. 196; Abū Shaykh al-Iṣbahānī, *al-ʿAẓama*, p. 593.
143. Al-Dāraquṭnī, *Kitāb al-Ruʾya*, pp. 345–7 (*aḥādīth* 264–7).
144. Ibn Ḥanbal, *Musnad*, vol. 4, pp. 350–54, *ḥadīth* 2580, p. 386, *ḥadīth* 2634; al-Ājurrī, *Kitāb al-Sharīʿa*, p. 492, *ḥadīth* 1033; al-Dāraquṭnī, *Kitāb al-Ruʾya*, pp. 345–7.

145. Al-Bayhaqī, *al-Asmāʾ waʾl-Ṣifāt*, vol. 2, pp. 363–4.
146. Williams, 'Aspects of the Creed', pp. 445–7, and *Tajalli*, pp. 172–6.
147. Al-Dhahabī, *Mīzān al-Iʿtidāl*, vol. 1, p. 593. For an exhaustive biography of al-Thalji, which investigates his position against anthropomorphism, see van Ess, *TG*, vol. 4, pp. 220–3.
148. See the thorough discussion in Williams, 'Aspects of the Creed', pp. 445–7.
149. Ibn al-Jawzī, *Mawḍūʿ*āt, p. 12.
150. See *barnāmij* in Dozy, *Supplément*, vol. 1, pp. 78–9.
151. Ibn Ḥajar, *Lisān al-Mīzān*, vol. 4, p. 271. Four fabricated *aḥādīth* that Shaykh transmitted in Hammad's name are recorded in the compilations of *al-mawḍūʿāt*: one of these texts describes the inscription on King Solomon's ring; two texts sketch the Day of Resurrection, and another text highlights the connection between nose hair and leprosy: al-Jurjānī, *al-Kāmil fī Ḍuʿafāʾ al-Rijāl*, vol. 5, p. 1368.
152. Ibn Fūrak, *Mujarrad Maqālāt*, p. 192.
153. Al-Bukhārī, *Ṣaḥīḥ*, vol. 3, pp. 411–13, *aḥādith* 5293–304 (*Kitāb al-Ṭalāq, bāb al-ishāra fī ʾl-ṭalāq waʾl-umūr*).
154. The chapter is entitled 'About sworn allegation of adultery': al-Bukhārī, *Ṣaḥīḥ*, vol. 3, pp. 412–13, *aḥādith* 5300–4 (*Kitāb al-Ṭalāq, bāb al-liʿān*).
155. Al-Bukhārī, *Ṣaḥīḥ*, vol. 3, p. 412.
156. Al-Bukhārī, *Ṣaḥīḥ*, vol. 3, p. 413, *aḥādith* 5302–3.
157. Al-Bukhārī, *Ṣaḥīḥ*, vol. 3, pp. 412–13, *aḥādith* 5300–1, 5304.
158. Al-Bukhārī, *Ṣaḥīḥ*, vol. 3, p. 411, introduction to the chapter (*Kitāb al-ṭalāq, bāb al-ishāra fī ʾl-ṭalāq waʾl-umūr*). A complete version of the *ḥadīth* appears in al-Bukhārī, *Ṣaḥīḥ*, vol. 2, p. 183 (*Kitāb al-Khuṣūmāt, bāb fī al-mulāzama*).
159. Al-Dhahabī, *Siyar Aʿlām al-Nubalāʾ*, vol. 18, pp. 47–8.
160. Al-Dhahabī, *Siyar Aʿlām al-Nubalāʾ*, vol. 17, p. 579. On al-Muhallab's commentary on *Ṣaḥīḥ al-Bukhārī*, see Brown, *Canonization*, p. 376.
161. Al-Muhallab's view was summarised by the Malikite Quran exegete Abu ʿAbd Allah al-Qurtubi (d. 1272) in his commentary to Quran 19:29. The verse refers to Mary, who returned to her people carrying baby-Jesus: 'She made a sign to them, pointing to the child' (*fa-ashārat ilayhim*). Al-Qurtubi used this verse to prove that gestures are part of the spoken language, and then he cited al-Muhallab's view in the case of the deaf man and his *liʿān*: al-Qurṭubī, *Jāmiʿ*, vol. 11, p. 71 (commentary on Q. 19:29–32).
162. Ibn Baṭṭāl, *Sharḥ*, vol. 7, p. 455; Ibn Ḥajar, *Fatḥ al-Bārī*, vol. 9, p. 347 (*Kitāb al-Ṭalāq, bāb al-ishāra fī ʾl-ṭalāq waʾl-umūr*).

163. Brown, *Canonization*, pp. 71–4.
164. Ibn Baṭṭāl, *Sharḥ*, vol. 7, p. 455; Ibn Ḥajar, *Fatḥ al-Bārī*, vol. 9, p. 347.
165. Ibn Ḥajar, *Fatḥ al-Bārī*, vol. 9, p. 347.
166. Ibn Khuzayma, *Kitāb al-Tawḥīd*, pp. 284–5. For references to other Hadith compilations, see ibid. p. 280. For various versions of this *ḥadīth*, see ibid. pp. 278–89.
167. Ibn Baṭṭāl, *Sharḥ*, vol. 7, p. 455.
168. Ibn Ḥajar, *Fatḥ al-Bārī*, vol. 9, p. 347.
169. Ibn Ḥajar, *Fatḥ al-Bārī*, vol. 9, pp. 347–8.
170. Rāmhurmuzī, *al-Muḥaddith al-Fāṣil*, p. 591.
171. Al-Khaṭīb al-Baghdādī, *al-Jāmiʿ li-Akhlāq al-Rāwī*, p. 314, anecdote 1389.
172. *Qalīl al-mawʿiẓa maʿa nashāṭ al-mawʿūẓ khayr min kathīr wāfaqa min al-asmāʿ nabwa wa-min al-qulūb malāla*: al-Khaṭīb al-Baghdādī, *al-Jāmiʿ li-Akhlāq al-Rāwī*, p. 315, anecdote 1392. Al-Jahiz speaks about preachers, but al-Khatib al-Baghdadi saw his words fit for his book – a manual for *muḥaddithūn*.
173. Al-Khaṭīb al-Baghdādī, *al-Jāmiʿ li-Akhlāq al-Rāwī*, pp. 315–16, anecdote 1398.
174. Abū Dāwud, *Sunan*, p. 515, ḥadīth 4728 (*Kitāb al-Sunna, bāb fī 'l-ruʾya*).
175. Al-Ājurrī, *Kitāb al-Sharīʿa*, pp. 319–20, ḥadīth 695; p. 268, ḥadīth 576. The scholars who were questioned in these two cases are Sharik ibn ʿAbd Allah (d. 793) and Sufyan ibn ʿUyayna (d. 813).
176. Al-Ājurrī, *Kitāb al-Sharīʿa*, p. 329, anecdote 726.
177. Al-Ājurrī, *Kitāb al-Sharīʿa*, p. 306, ḥadīth 667. Cf. Swartz, *A Medieval Critique of Anthropomorphism*, p. 271; Gimaret, *Dieu à l'image de l'homme*, p. 76.
178. Al-Ājurrī, *Kitāb al-Sharīʿa*, p. 329, anecdote 726. This saying does not appear in the *Musnad*.
179. Cf. the sayings attributed to the *muḥaddithūn* al-Awzaʿi, Sufyan al-Thawri, Malik ibn Anas and al-Layth ibn Saʿd: al-Ājurrī, *Kitāb al-Sharīʿa*, p. 327, anecdote 720.
180. Al-Lālakāʾī, *Sharḥ Uṣūl*, vol. 2, p. 432, anecdote 739.
181. Abrahamov, 'Scripturalist and Traditionalist Theology', pp. 265–6.
182. Muqatil ibn Sulayman (d. 767) had a reputation of being an extreme anthropomorphist. However, his *Tafsīr* of the Quran indicates that he struggled to find allegorical interpretations to the anthropomorphic expressions in the Quran. In this respect, he can be considered a forerunner of Ashʿarism: Abrahamov, *Anthropomorphism*, pp. 4–5.
183. Al-Shahrastānī, *al-Milal wa'l-Niḥal*, p. 92.

184. Al-Lalakaʾi was most probably an Ashʿarite: he studied Ashʿarite *kalām* with the illustrious *mutakallim* Abu Ishaq al-Isfaraʾini (d. 1027) and his most famous disciple was al-Khatib al-Baghdadi (d. 1071) who was uncompromising in his Ashʿarism: al-Lālakāʾī, *Sharḥ Uṣūl*, vol. 1, p. 86; Sellheim, 'Al-Khaṭīb al-Baghdādī', *EI2*.
185. Al-Shahrastani calls the Hanbalites 'the riffraff among the People of Hadith' (*aṣḥāb al-ḥadīth al-ḥashwiyya*), but also mentions the Mushabbiha among the Shiʿites: al-Shahrastānī, *al-Milal wa'l-Niḥal*, p. 93.
186. Al-Ashʿari himself claimed to be a follower of Ahmad ibn Hanbal: Watt, *The Formative Period*, p. 142; Makdisi, 'Ṭabaqāt', p. 380.
187. Makdisi, 'Ashʿari and Ashʿarites' (1962), pp. 48–52.
188. Ibn ʿAbd al-Barr, *Tamhīd*, vol. 7, p. 145.
189. Ibn ʿAbd al-Barr, *Tamhīd*, vol. 7, p. 145.
190. Al-Dhahabī, *Siyar Aʿlām al-Nubalāʾ*, vol. 11, pp. 389–91 (the biography of Harmala ibn Yahya).
191. Al-Dhahabī, *Siyar Aʿlām al-Nubalāʾ*, vol. 9, pp. 223–34 (the biography of ʿAbd Allah ibn Wahb).
192. Ibn ʿAbd al-Barr, *Tamhīd*, vol. 7, p. 145; al-Qurṭubī, *Jāmiʿ*, vol. 11, pp. 169–70 (commentary on Q. 20:121).
193. Ibn ʿAbd al-Barr, *Tamhīd*, vol. 7, p. 145; Ibn Ḥibbān, *Ṣaḥīḥ*, vol. 13, pp. 240–2, *ḥadīth* 5919 (*Kitāb al-Uḍḥiyya, bāb dhikr al-zajr ʿan an yuḍaḥḥiya 'l-marʾ*).
194. Ibn ʿAbd al-Barr, *Tamhīd*, vol. 7, p. 145.
195. Al-Qurṭubī, *Jāmiʿ*, vol. 11, p. 169 (interpretation of Q. 20:120–2).
196. Ibn Fūrak, *Mushkil al-Ḥadīth*, p. 126.
197. Al-Bayhaqī, *al-Asmāʾ wa'l-Ṣifāt*, vol. 1, pp. 462–3.
198. Ibn Ḥibbān, *al-Iḥsān*, vol. 1, pp. 498–9.
199. Ibn Fūrak, *Mushkil al-Ḥadīth*, pp. 127–8.
200. Ibn Taymiyya, *Sharḥ al-ʿAqīda al-Iṣfahāniyya*, p. 136.
201. Ibn al-Jawzī, *Ṣayd al-Khāṭir*, p. 103.
202. Ibn al-Jawzī, *Ṣayd al-Khāṭir*, p. 101.
203. Ibn al-Jawzī, *Ṣayd al-Khāṭir*, pp. 101–2.
204. Ibn al-Jawzī, *Ṣayd al-Khāṭir*, p. 102.
205. Ibn al-Jawzī, *Ṣayd al-Khāṭir*, p. 102.
206. Ibn al-Jawzī, *Ṣayd al-Khāṭir*, p. 102.
207. Ibn al-Jawzī, *Ṣayd al-Khāṭir*, p. 103.
208. Muslim, *Ṣaḥīḥ*, p. 484, *ḥadīth* 1218-147 (*Kitāb al-Ḥajj, bāb ḥajjat al-nabī*);

Abū Dāwūd, *Sunan*, p. 220, *ḥadīth* 1905 (*Kitāb al-Manāsik, bāb ṣifat ḥijjat al-nabī*). This part of *ḥijjat al-wadā*ᶜ does not appear in *Sīrat Abī Hishām*, but later authors of the *Sīra* included it in their texts. Cf. Ibn Kathīr, *al-Bidāya wa'l-Nihāya*, vol. 7, p. 564.

4

The Diversified Solution to the Challenge of Islamic Traditionalism: *Aḥādīth al-Ṣifāt* and *Bi-Lā Kayfa*

Introduction

As we learned in the previous chapters, *aḥādīth al-ṣifāt* which were discussed in scholarly circles, were also used as textual evidence in various theological controversies. In addition, these texts sometimes played a key role in several dramatic events that occurred in the public sphere. One such event was the *miḥna*, which was among the most prominent milestones in the development of Islamic thought. When Ahmad ibn Hanbal was required by his Muᶜtazilite interrogators in the *miḥna* to present evidence that corroborated his belief in the beatific vision, he presented *ḥadīth al-ruʾya* that featured a Prophetic promise that the believers would see God on the Day of Resurrection. For Ahmad ibn Hanbal, this *ḥadīth* was solid textual evidence, because it was attributed to the notable *ṣaḥābī* Jarir al-Bajali and transmitted by at least two reliable transmitters.

The interrogators of the *miḥna* were not impressed by Ahmad ibn Hanbal's response. For them, a *ḥadīth* should not have been used as textual evidence in the first place, unlike Quranic verses which they accepted as valid textual evidence. They considered *ḥadīth al-ruʾya* as a popular fable and not as an authentic religious text. In their fervent desire to discredit the authenticity of *ḥadīth al-ruʾya*, the interrogators no doubt attempted to disparage Ahmad ibn Hanbal as unprofessional, humiliate him and ruin his reputation in the eyes of his adherents and supporters. Moreover, Ahmad ibn Hanbal was not versed in the rationalistic vocabulary. Consequently, he failed to rebut his interrogators' argument which doubted the ability of the human eye to see God because – so the interrogator claimed – the human eye could only grasp physical objects.[1] The interrogators assumed that attacking Ahmad ibn Hanbal on his home base, namely in the field of Hadith, would expedite his capitulation. However, the interrogators' efforts to discredit the authenticity of this *ḥadīth*'s transmitters failed: the allegations against one of the transmitters were immediately proven fabricated. In the long run, Jarir's *ḥadīth al-ruʾya* was included in the Hadith compilations that were created in the ninth century;[2] this text was extensively taught in traditionalistic circles in the following centuries. Through the inclusion of Jarir's *ḥadīth al-ruʾya* in the venerated *al-Ṣaḥīḥān* of al-Bukhari and Muslim, this *ḥadīth* was accepted as a standard text in the Islamic canon. No one but the rationalists doubted its authenticity.

The efforts that the interrogators of the *miḥna* dedicated to discrediting the transmitter of *ḥadīth al-ruʾya* were typical of the rationalistic or Muᶜtazilite approach towards the Hadith material in general.[3] Were other *aḥādīth al-ṣifāt* presented by Ahmad ibn Hanbal during his interrogations, they would have been rejected as well because the rationalists in general did not consider the Hadith material as valid textual evidence (unlike the Quran) and did not use this material in theological controversies.[4] One cannot say that they categorically denied the veracity of the entire corpus of *aḥādīth al-ṣifāt*. However, they even rejected texts that were labelled as *ṣaḥīḥ* by Hadith experts. In the centuries following the *miḥna*, the rationalistic approach towards *aḥadīth al-ṣifāt* was not affected by the fact that some of these texts were canonised through their inclusion in *al-Ṣaḥīḥān*.[5] In fact, the rationalists saw almost no difference between *aḥādīth* which contained subtle innuendos to God's spatiality (like, for instance *ḥadīth al-nuzūl*) or corporeality (like, for instance, *ḥadīth al-ruʾya*) and *aḥādīth* with bold anthropomorphic language. For the rationalists, the fact that *ḥadīth al-ruʾya* did not claim that God had physical features and attributes was irrelevant. The rationalists considered this *ḥadīth* as problematic as the bold *ḥadīth aṭīṭ al-raḥl*, 'the *ḥadīth* on the moaning of the saddle', in which the *muḥaddith* actually demonstrated the moaning sound that was supposedly produced by the heavenly throne while God sat in it; or, *ḥadīth al-shābb al-qaṭaṭ*, 'the *ḥadīth* of the curly young man' which described God as a young curly man wearing a green garb and golden sandals.

After the *miḥna*, *aḥādīth al-ṣifāt* became one of the most powerful icons of Islamic traditionalism. As such, they were constantly attacked by the rationalists (mostly the Muᶜtazilites).[6] Each side of the theological controversy had its fixed set of argumentations for and against *aḥādīth al-ṣifāt*, and these argumentations were recycled and reused from the ninth century onward in debates and polemical treatises. The basic traditionalistic stance was the early *bi-lā kayfa* formula ('without asking how' or 'without further comment'), which presented complete adherence to the anthropomorphic texts in the Quran (*āyāt al-ṣifāt*) and the Hadith (*aḥādīth al-ṣifāt*). The traditionalists' major concern was to defend *aḥādīth al-ṣifāt* and affirm their veracity. Another concern of the traditionalists focused on the elimination of fabricated texts disguised as perfect versions of *aḥādīth al-ṣifāt*. These fabricated texts, which were promoted by unscrupulous charlatans, caused much embarrassment to the conservative traditionalists. The fabricated texts which were conspicuous in the public sphere led the rationalists to defame the traditionalists and call them *ḥashwiyya*, that is, vulgar anthropomorphists (henceforth, the Hashwiyya). *Aḥādīth al-ṣifāt*, then, were threatened from outside the traditionalistic circles (by the rationalists) and from within (by the extreme anthropomorphists, most of whom were identified with the traditionalists).

We note that there was no single unified traditionalistic approach towards *aḥādīth al-ṣifāt*, but several traditionalistic approaches. Between the rationalistic total rejection of *aḥādīth al-ṣifāt* and the ultra-traditionalistic complete adherence to these texts extended a wide spectrum of views, some of which were surprisingly nuanced and sophisticated. In the case of *aḥādīth al-ṣifāt*, as in other theological issues, the dichotomy between 'traditionalism' and 'rationalism' was not rigid and fixed.[7] Thus we read the critique on *aḥādīth al-ṣifāt* that was articulated by certain *muḥaddithūn* who were the backbone of Islamic traditionalism. These *muḥaddithūn* neither affiliated themselves with any rationalistic trend nor were they accused of rationalism by their colleagues. However, the caution that they demonstrated in handling *aḥādīth al-ṣifāt* and their nuanced approach to these texts situated these *muḥaddithūn* among the forerunners of the Ashᶜarite *bi-lā kayfa*.

With the emergence of Ashᶜarism in the tenth century, the imaginary dividing line between traditionalism and rationalism was even more blurred. On the basis of the original *bi-lā kayfa* formula, which was a rather limited device that prevented any possibility for an intellectual dialogue or a speculative theological contemplation, the Ashᶜarites developed a hermeneutical device which corroborated their more advanced and pensive version of the *bi-lā kayfa* formula.[8] Their version of the *bi-lā kayfa* formula meant 'without attributing physical characteristics' to God; however, this formula covered much more than a mere prohibition to attribute a hand, a leg or a face to God. The Ashᶜarite readings of *aḥādīth al-ṣifāt* and the set of the rationalistic argumentations that they developed in order to read these texts, affected the traditionalistic discourse. On one hand, the Ashᶜarite readings enriched the hermeneutical discourse that accompanied *aḥādīth al-ṣifāt* but, on the other hand, these readings threatened the traditionalistic curriculum.

This chapter examines the challenges that *aḥādīth al-ṣifāt* posed to the traditionalists and the way these challenges were met through the implementation of the *bi-lā kayfa* formula. A major decision in constructing this chapter involved the selection of the sources for discussion. The traditionalistic and Ashᶜarite writings offer an overwhelming variety of argumentations for and against *aḥādīth al-ṣifāt*, suggestions to read the texts, and discussions on the authenticity of these texts' respective transmitters. The scope of this chapter is too limited to cover them all. In addition, the diversity in the traditionalistic approaches was reflected mostly in the inner debates that occurred during the sessions of Hadith transmissions. These debates were recorded almost exclusively in the exegeses of the Hadith and not in the theological literature. It seems that a sufficient coverage of the inner debates on *aḥādīth al-ṣifāt* demands a combined reading in a limited number of sources of different genres. This demand entailed a strict selection of topics for discussion, and more so, it entailed the exclusion of topics that are generally deemed connected to anthropomorphism, but not necessarily to *aḥādīth al-ṣifāt*.

This chapter, therefore, focuses on five of the most prominent aspects of *aḥādīth al-ṣifāt* and discusses these aspects based on a combined reading in the historical sources, the compilations of Hadith exegesis and a limited number of theological treatises. The leitmotif of the chapter is the traditionalistic *bi-lā kayfa* formula; it is examined throughout this chapter vis-à-vis the Ashᶜarite formula. Section I presents the defining lines of the traditionalistic discourse about *aḥādīth al-ṣifāt* mainly as reflected in the work of the ninth-century polymath Ibn Qutayba (d. 889). Ibn Qutayba's well-articulated presentation demonstrates the complexity of the traditionalistic stance. Sections II, III and IV present the problematic aspects of *aḥādīth al-ṣifāt* in the traditionalistic discourse through the case study of what is undoubtedly the most extreme text in the repertoire of *aḥādīth al-ṣifāt*. Although extreme, this text serves as an excellent representative of the other anthropomorphic texts. Section II presents this problematic *ḥadīth*, analyses the earliest recorded debate which is connected to the text, and considers the implications of this debate on the way in which the later generations viewed this *ḥadīth*. Section III examines the transmission process of the text and focuses on several techniques that enabled the acceptance of this text in the Islamic canon. Section IV continues the discussion of the third section by investigating the different traditionalistic and Ashᶜarite solutions to the problematic *ḥadīth* in question. Section V argues that although the Ashᶜarite *bi-lā kayfa* formula expanded the border of the traditionalistic discourse and enabled the inclusion of *aḥādīth al-ṣifāt* in the Islamic canon, the Ashᶜarites were not too keen on spreading these texts and making them accessible to the lay public.

I. Drawing the Borderlines of the Traditionalistic Discourse

The four major components of the traditionalistic approach towards *aḥādīth al-ṣifāt* as identified in Chapters 2 and 3 are: (1) *aḥādīth al-ṣifāt*, and especially those that were labelled as genuine texts transmitted by reliable personas, are part of the Islamic canon; (2) *aḥādīth al-ṣifāt* should be treated by the same criteria that are applied to *aḥādīth al-aḥkām*; (3) the transmission process of *aḥādīth al-ṣifāt* should be as faithful as possible, including the performance of accompanying gestures (in case such gestures were recorded in the memory of the early *muḥaddithūn*); and (4) the content of these *aḥādīth* and the accompanying gestures by no means reflect undesirable, inappropriate and even forbidden comparison with God. The appropriateness of the discourse was a major concern for the Hadith scholars, as elaborated in this chapter.

As a rhetorical device, the early traditionalistic *bi-lā kayfa* served two purposes: first, it rejected any metaphorical interpretation of the anthropomorphic passages of the Quran and the Hadith; and, second, *bi-lā kayfa* rejected any literal reading of these texts because this type of reading led to *tajsīm* or *tashbīh*.[9] Although simplistic, the *bi-lā kayfa* formula had additional facets. It was a declaration on the part of the *muḥaddith* that he never engaged in interpreting anthropomorphic texts. Therefore, *bi-lā kayfa* should also be rendered 'without interpreting the text' or 'without adding one's personal interpretation to the text', in addition to the statements 'transmit the text verbatim' and 'transmit the text with the exact accompanying gestures' that were mentioned in Chapter 3.

The basic traditionalistic approach is presented here through the words of the renowned philologist and *muḥaddith*, Abu ᶜUbayd al-Qasim ibn Sallam (d. 838) from Baghdad. Abu ᶜUbayd recited to his students a cluster of *aḥādīth al-ṣifāt* on the beatific vision. He also recited *aḥādīth* on the heavenly throne and the heavenly pedestal (*al-kursī*) on which God's two feet rest, and *aḥādīth* that mentioned God's laughter. After the recitation, Abu ᶜUbayd added:

> These *aḥādīth* are authentic and valid (*ṣiḥāḥ*). The *muḥaddithūn* and jurisprudents transmitted them from generation to generation. For us, they reflect undeniable truth. But when we are asked: 'How does He laugh? How does He place His feet?' We should answer: 'We do not interpret them. We never heard anyone interpret them.'[10]

Elsewhere, Abu ᶜUbayd is quoted as saying: 'We did not reach the time of anyone who interpreted these *aḥādīth*. We anyhow do not interpret them.'[11] Although this statement of Abu ᶜUbayd suggests that the scholars of previous generations in fact interpreted *aḥādīth al-ṣifāt*, he obviously attested to the fact that none of his teachers and contemporaries was ever involved in interpreting these problematic texts. Abu ᶜUbayd's words were directed at the *muḥaddithūn* in their role as the educators of the masses. Abu ᶜUbayd's interpretation of the *bi-lā kayfa* formula makes three demands on the *muḥaddithūn*: first, to faithfully transmit *aḥādīth al-ṣifāt* to their students; second, to prohibit their students from asking clarifying questions about the anthropomorphic descriptions that appear in these texts; and, third, to express unequivocal disapproval of any attempt to interpret these texts. These three demands, that are also applicable to the study of the anthropomorphic verses in the Quran, marked the borders of the traditionalistic discourse about *aḥādīth al-ṣifāt* and established the early *bi-lā kayfa* formula.

In his 1958 research, Henri Laoust suggested that this basic traditionalistic approach originated in the Hanbalite circles in Baghdad of the ninth century;[12] however, the sources indicate otherwise.[13] Ahmad ibn Hanbal (d. 855) and his disciples systematised the scattered and random sayings that were attributed to their predecessors, namely the eighth-century traditionalists, into one coherent doctrine; nonetheless, the Hanbalites were not the exclusive source of the early formula of *bi-lā kayfa*. Abu ᶜUbayd, for example, was not a Hanbalite (although his biography is included in *Ṭabaqāt al-Ḥanābila*),[14] while his way of expressing the *bi-lā kayfa* formula corresponds with similar sayings by Ahmad ibn Hanbal and his successors.[15] The leading *muḥaddithūn* al-Awzaᶜi (d. 774), Sufyan al-Thawri (d. 778), al-Layth ibn Saᶜd (d. 791) and Malik ibn Anas (d. 796) made similar pronouncements that *aḥādīth al-ṣifāt* should be transmitted without interpretation, and they preceded Ahmad ibn Hanbal by several decades.[16] Similarly, the *muḥaddith* Sufyan ibn ᶜUyayna (d. 813), who was not a Hanbalite, declared: 'The only possible way to interpret the Quranic verses in which God describes Himself is by reciting these verses and then by uttering nothing additional about them.'[17]

In its earliest phase, the traditionalistic *bi-lā kayfa* formula was first and foremost a prohibition to ask questions about the anthropomorphic descriptions of *aḥādīth al-ṣifāt*. As such, the formula was embedded in the overall traditionalistic reservation of asking questions, as discussed in Chapter 2. In other words, this early version of the *bi-lā kayfa* formula thrived against the backdrop of sayings like 'I have never seen more virtuous people than the Companions of Muhammad; they asked him only twelve (in a different version, thirteen) questions until the day he died, all of which appeared in the Quran'.[18] Sayings in a similar vein that supported the traditionalistic *bi-lā kayfa* formula reinforced the image of the traditionalists as an unquestioning community, a community whose thirst for knowing the divine was self-suppressed. However, this image was a myth. We find frequent mention in the historical sources of *muḥaddithūn* who forbade their disciples to ask questions by using the *bi-lā kayfa* formula. This finding indicates that both students of Hadith and lay people were accustomed to ask questions about the divine and that *aḥādīth al-ṣifāt* provoked such questions. The reaction of the *muḥaddithūn* to these forbidden questions – as recorded in the sources – was intense and highly dramatic. For example, a man once asked Malik ibn Anas (d. 796) how exactly God sat on the throne. Malik did not respond. He bowed his head in silence and perspired profusely – a sign of his dissatisfaction and fury. After providing his formulaic answer ('the sitting [on the Throne] is undeniably known. The way it is actually done is incomprehensible. Believing it is obligatory, and questioning it is an undesirable innovation'), he accused the inquirer of heresy and had him expelled from his study session.[19] In another version of this anecdote, a man from Iraq asked Malik the same question. Malik was furious: he called the man vicious, and ordered his disciples to remove the man from his presence. The disciples grabbed the man by his arms and legs and threw him out.[20] A less dramatic reaction – albeit equally disapproving – was the reaction of Sufyan ibn ᶜUyayna from Mecca. He was asked to explain how God carries the sky on one finger and holds the hearts of the believers between two of His fingers. Sufyan evaded the question, but the disciple who asked him was persistent. 'Leave me be!' cried Sufyan, however the disciple continued to ask more and more questions. Finally, Sufyan provided the disciple with the traditionalistic *bi-lā kayfa* formula. This formula, apparently, put an end to the flow of questions from the disciple.[21]

The traditionalists toiled to emphasise that the *bi-lā kayfa* formula was the approach that all the great luminaries of the eighth century shared. However, in the literary and historical sources, we find evidence which contradicts this opinion. For instance, the Malikite scholar from Cordoba, Yahya ibn Ibrahim ibn Muzayn (d. 873; his grandfather was a *mawlā* of Ramla, the daughter of the caliph ᶜUthman ibn ᶜAffan), claimed that 'Malik hated transmitting these *aḥādīth*', namely *aḥādīth al-ṣifāt*, because their elaborate descriptions of God conceptualized an anthropomorphic and restricted image of God'. Yahya claimed that Malik advised the scholars to restrict themselves to the recitation of the relevant Quranic verses and refrain from transmitting *aḥādīth al-ṣifāt*. This view was not accepted by the majority of the Malikites. The Malikite Ibn ᶜAbd al-Barr (d. 1070) traced a saying by another great Malikite scholar, ᶜAbd al-Rahman ibn al-Qasim (d. between 807 and 816), who claimed that 'Malik did not object to the transmission of the *ḥadīth* about God's laughter, because God's laughter . . . is not the same as the laughter of His servants'.[22] Ibn ᶜAbd al-Barr therefore ruled that Malik's position was that *aḥādīth al-ṣifāt* should be transmitted 'exactly as they arrived to us, without inquiring about their modality (*kayfiyya*; namely without asking how)'.[23]

The early or traditionalistic *bi-lā kayfa* formula was apparently effective only in the inner circles of Islamic traditionalism: the formula repressed every inner doubt and question that a scholar might have had, it silenced every intrusion from the audience and, more importantly, it safeguarded the position of the teacher, the *muḥaddith*. Without admitting his ignorance about the mysteries of the divine (the answer 'I do not know' – *lā adrī* – was reserved for legal questions and not for theological ones),[24] the *muḥaddith* could simply fire off 'Do not ask about the meaning of this!' Asking about the meaning of the anthropomorphic texts or their origins was comparable to professing heretical views. These questions, no doubt, were considered dangerous in the eyes of the *muḥaddithūn*, because they could lead the inquirer to either one of two undesirable outcomes: the blunt and vulgar anthropomorphism of the Hashwiyya or the strict transcendentalism of the rationalists.

The *bi-lā kayfa* formula was too simplistic and rather useless in the polemics with the sceptic rationalists. These rationalists mocked the traditionalistic naivety and willingness to accept every fantastic story as a genuine religious account, provided that it was attributed to the Prophet or one of his *ṣaḥāba*. Some of the ninth-century traditionalists were sensitive to use the *bi-lā kayfa* formula only in their inner circles of study. When addressing outsiders who had the finesse of a more sophisticated education, these traditionalists employed a different strategy: they avoided the use of the *bi-lā kayfa* formula with its exclamation mark that blocked any possibility of a discussion on *aḥādīth al-ṣifāt* and the divine attributes, and used more subtle ways of expression. The following anecdote about the prolific traditionalist Abu Yaᶜqub Ishaq ibn Ibrahim ibn Rahwayh (d. 853; the Persian pronunciation of his name is Ibn Rahoya) demonstrates this point.

One day, Ibn Rahwayh (who mainly taught in Nishapur) visited Tahir ibn ᶜAbd Allah (d. 859), the governor of Khurasan. The governor's nephew asked Ibn Rahwayh: 'Tell me, Abu Yaᶜqub, does God really descend every night [to the lower heaven]?' Ibn Rahwayh sharply responded: 'This is what we believe. Had you believed in the existence of God in heaven, you wouldn't have had to ask me about it.' The amused governor reproached his nephew: 'Didn't I warn you about this sheikh?'[25]

Ibn Rahwayh probably sensed that the *bi-lā kayfa* formula could not have been used as an effective answer to this man of nobility. Instead, Ibn Rahwayh responded with an answer that was both accurate (we believe in

God's descent) and reproachful (you should not have asked about God's descent). Apart from Ibn Rahwayh's sophisticated and indirect method of promoting the *bi-lā kayfa* while educating his listeners, this anecdote reflects an entertaining and humorous presentation of the *bi-lā kayfa* formula. This presentation would not have been welcome in the circles of professional traditionalism with its solemnity, self awareness and self importance.[26] However, the presentation served Ibn Rahwayh well in his conversation with someone outside the traditionalistic circle.

Although Abu ᶜUbayd and Ibn Rahwayh were contemporaries and members of the ultra-traditionalistic circles in Baghdad and Nishapur, they expressed the *bi-lā kayfa* formula in different and almost opposite ways. While Abu ᶜUbayd's answer reflected the 'classical' *bi-lā kayfa*, Ibn Rahwayh's answers reflected the 'sophisticated' *bi-lā kayfa*. It is little wonder, then, that the historian and Hadith expert, Shams al-Din al-Dhahabi, one of the leading advocates of Islamic traditionalism in his generation, connected Abu ᶜUbayd's response to the true path of the Salaf, the pious and worthy ancestors of Sunnite Islam.[27] According to al-Dhahabi, the Salaf were well-informed about the Quran and the Prophet's sayings and they enthusiastically interpreted every expression, those deemed important as well as those deemed unimportant, in the Quran and the Hadith. The Salaf left no room for uncertainty in their interpretation (*wa-mā abqaw mumkinan*). However, the Salaf never discussed the meaning of both *āyāt al-ṣifāt* and *aḥādīth al-ṣifāt*, although these texts represent 'the most important part of the religion' (*ahamm al-dīn*). Al-Dhahabi concludes:

> Were the interpretation of [the anthropomorphic expressions in the Quran and the Hadith] permissible or necessary, they (i.e. the Salaf) certainly would have pursued this line of interpretation. From this, one must conclude that the only true way is to merely recite these texts exactly as they were received. No other interpretation is applicable to these texts. This is what we believe in. We keep our silence because we follow the Salaf.[28]

Al-Dhahabi recommended his readers to remain silent about *aḥādīth al-ṣifāt* for both practical and ideological reasons. Scholars who were not trained in public debates (*munāẓara*) were urged to refrain from discussing *aḥādīth al-ṣifāt*, especially when they were questioned by a sceptic rationalist. Apart from the fact that the prohibition to discuss theological matters reverts to the Quran (Q. 3:7) and is corroborated by numerous *aḥādīth*, a scholar untrained in debating skills could have been placed in an awkward position causing embarrassment to the group that he represented. Al-Dhahabi's recommendation is embedded in the reality that he knew first-hand, in which public debates about theological issues were part of public life.[29]

Ibn Rahwayh's sophisticated and rather amusing response was strikingly similar to the Ashᶜarite approach of which al-Dhahabi disapproved. Commenting on the Ibn Rahwayh anecdote, al-Dhahabi declares:

> The texts confirm the veracity of the divine attribute of sitting [on the throne], the divine attribute of coming, and the divine attribute of descending. The Khalaf, the scholars of later generations, transmitted these texts on the authority of the Salaf. The Khalaf never felt the need to comment about these attributes or to interpret them. Furthermore, they rebuked those who interpreted them. In addition, they unanimously agreed that these attributes should not be compared to the attributes of the created beings, because 'nothing can be compared with Him' (Q. 42:11). There is no need to debate over these [texts] or to argue about them. Because this kind of debate necessarily entails arguing with God and His Prophet, or hovering over [two approaches], either asking how God does this and that (*takyīf*) or divesting God of His attributes altogether (*taᶜṭīl*).[30]

Al-Dhahabi expresses here his concern that debating *aḥādīth al-ṣifāt* may lead to superfluous contemplation in two opposing approaches. Both approaches must be rejected because they represent the forces against which Islamic traditionalism fights: the vulgar anthropomorphists and the sceptical rationalists. In this passage, al-Dhahabi does not specifically name these groups, but refers to them by using the terms *takyīf* and *taᶜṭīl*. The *takyīf*, asking 'How does God descend, come or sit', is the method taken by the Hashwiyya. By asking these questions, the vulgar anthropomorphists led to a literal understanding of the problematic expressions in the Quran and the Hadith, and accordingly they compared God to humans.[31] The *taᶜṭīl*, a word of opprobrium of the Muᶜtazilite *tanzīh* (that is, denying that God resembles any existing being), was the jewel in the crown of the Muᶜtazilite dialectics.[32] Al-Dhahabi uses *taᶜṭīl* here to denote the Muᶜtazilite perception of God as transcendent and abstract, a perception that entails a figurative understanding (*taʾwīl*) of the anthropomorphic expressions in the Quran, alongside an almost complete rejection of *aḥādīth al-ṣifāt*.

Abu ᶜUbayd and Ibn Rahwayh represent two facets of the traditionalistic *bi-lā kayfa*: rigid scripturalism on the one hand and rationalised pragmatism on the other. These two apparently opposing approaches were combined to make one synthesised approach in the thought of Ibn Qutayba (d. 889). Ibn Qutayba, a traditionalistic scholar, was no doubt inspired by Abu ᶜUbayd and Ibn Rahwayh (he systematically studied the writings of Abu ᶜUbayd, and was a disciple of Ibn Rahwayh).[33] By incorporating their versions of the *bi-lā kayfa* formula in his hermeneutical approach, Ibn Qutayba created a new methodology that both used the *bi-lā kayfa* formula and applied figurative interpretation on *aḥādīth al-ṣifāt*. As reflected in his two theological treatises, *Kitāb al-Ikhtilāf fī 'l-Lafẓ wa'l-Radd ᶜalā al-Jahmiyya* (On the Disagreement over the Pronunciation of the Quran and the Refutation of the Jahmites) and *Taʾwīl Mukhtalif al-Ḥadīth* (Interpreting Contradictory Hadith), Ibn Qutayba's methodology predated the Ashᶜarites by at least five decades.[34] Ibn Qutayba wrote both works to defend the *muḥaddithūn* from the mockery and belittlement of the rationalists. As Gérard Lecomte writes, Ibn Qutayba 'put his literary talents at the service of the enterprise of the restoration of Sunnism'.[35] In both works, Ibn Qutayba expressed his mature theological views while he revealed his dazzling knowledge of philology, classical poetry, Quran exegesis and Hadith. In addition, Ibn Qutayba did not shy from the masterpieces of the ancient world; he extensively cited excerpts from the Arabic translations of the scriptures of Judaism and Christianity, Aristotelian and pseudo-Aristotelian works, and the works of Persian and Hindu *belles lettres*.[36] As this vast knowledge of different cultures indicates, Ibn Qutyaba was not a typical member of the milieu of the *muḥaddithūn*. Although his diversified education included a thorough apprenticeship with Ibn Rahwayh, Ibn Qutayba did not mature into the field of Hadith transmission. Rather, he successfully conducted a twenty-year career as a judge in Dinawar (in western Iran). After retirement, Ibn Qutayba spent the last eighteen years of his life in Baghdad writing and teaching his works.[37]

In both *Kitāb al-Ikhtilāf fī 'l-Lafẓ* and *Taʾwīl Mukhtalif al-Ḥadīth*, Ibn Qutayba described *aḥādīth al-ṣifāt* as the dividing line between two opposing groups: the traditionalists, or *ahl al-ḥadīth* (whom we usually refer to as *muḥaddithūn*), and the rationalists. This dividing line is reflected in a short traditionalistic creed penned by Ibn Qutayba. This creed is located in *Kitāb al-Ikhtilāf fī 'l-Lafẓ*. The creed is constructed from references to the widely accepted *aḥādīth al-ṣifāt*. In the following passage, Ibn Qutayba refers to one of the authenticated versions of *ḥadīth al-ruʾya*, in which God's astonishment and laughter are featured, and to *ḥadīth al-nuzūl*:

> The most accurate profession of faith regarding these *akhbār* (namely, *aḥādīth al-ṣifāt*) is that we believe only in the authentic texts that were transmitted by the most reliable Hadith authorities. We believe in the beatific vision, and that He will reveal Himself. We believe that He will be astonished. We believe that He goes down to the lowest heaven. We believe that He sits enthroned on high. We believe that [He has a] mind (*nafs*) and two hands. However, our belief does not include modality (*kayfiyya*, namely, we do not ask how, *bi-lā kayfa*) and spatiality (*ḥadd*). We also never make inappropriate comparisons based on what is written in these texts. We express our hope that this creed will lead us some time in the future to the road of salvation, God willing.[38]

The confident tone of this creed is meant to silence the Hashwiyya who, as we will see, caused tremendous damage to *ahl al-ḥadīth*. Ibn Qutayba's creed claims to present the overall traditionalistic stance. However, with the existence of the Hashwiyya, a faction that was considered an inherent part of the Islamic traditionalism, his creed is merely wishful thinking, an aspiration that all trends in the Islamic traditionalism would operate in unison.

The approach of the rationalists as presented by Ibn Qutayba in *Kitāb al-Ikhtilāf fī 'l-Lafẓ* is not as unified as the voice of the traditionalists. Both the rationalists and traditionalists included several factions; yet, it served Ibn Qutayba's best interests to portray the rationalists as theologians who held opposing and contradictory views. The first faction in the rationalist front is the speculative theologians. Ibn Qutayba calls these theologians *ahl al-kalām* and *al-mutakallimūn*, and by these terms he refers primarily to the Muʿtazilites (who are not specifically identified in this treatise) and other groups of *mutakallimūn* such as the speculative theologians of the *rāfiḍa*, the Shiʿites. The second faction is *aṣḥāb al-raʾy* (the proponents of personal opinion, mostly the Hanafites), who are also identified as part of *ahl al-ḥadīth*.[39] In addition, Ibn Qutayba uses the epithet *ahl al-naẓar*, which literally means 'the people of contemplation (or reflection)'. *Naẓar* is the conventional term in the theological literature for speculative theology, namely *kalām*. *Ahl al-naẓar* do not represent a fixed group: they could be either speculative theologians or professional Hadith transmitters. In both treatises, so it seems, Ibn Qutayba uses the epithet *ahl al-naẓar* in a more positive context. In fact, in the case of *aḥādīth al-ṣifāt,* Ibn Qutayba accepts various solutions to the anthropomorphic texts that *ahl al-naẓar* and even one specific rationalist (*baᶜḍ ahl al-naẓar*, 'one of the people of contemplation') who remains anonymous, suggested. Ibn Qutayba adopts these solutions as an inherent part of his approach.[40] However, the degree of contemplation or the extent of the use of speculative theology can tip the scales: for Ibn Qutayba, too much contemplation and too little reliance on the scriptures is harmful and leads to erroneous convictions. In *Kitāb al-Ikhtilāf fī 'l-Lafẓ*, Ibn Qutayba mentions people who were absorbed in *naẓar* to such a degree that 'they wished to correct the concept of the divine unity (*tawḥīd*) by removing any hint of comparison (*tashbīh*) from the Creator. Therefore they cancelled the divine attributes.'[41] These were, of course, the Muᶜtazilites whom he disliked.

According to Ibn Qutayba's description, the rationalists invested their intellectual efforts in applying figurative interpretations on the anthropomorphic expressions in the Quran. For example, the rationalists claimed that the two hands of God that are mentioned in the Quran (Q. 5:64: 'His hands are both outstretched') are in fact God's favours.[42] Ibn Qutayba rejected this figurative interpretation by using a basic exercise in logic, namely to replace the word *yad* (hand) in the verse with the word *niᶜma* (favour). The result, 'His favours are both outstretched', is both inconceivable and incoherent. Therefore, *yad* cannot be interpreted as *niᶜma*.[43] This discussion of the Quranic verse led Ibn Qutayba to mention the *ḥadīth* attributed to the *Ṣaḥābī* ᶜAbd Allah ibn ᶜAmr ibn al-ᶜAs (d. 684). Ibn al-ᶜAs quoted the Prophet as saying: 'Both His hands are two right hands.'[44] According to Ibn Qutayba's description, even in this case, a figurative interpretation (namely, that the hands are favours) is incomprehensible. However, Ibn Qutayba himself provided two alternative solutions to the problem of God's two right hands. These solutions cannot be described as other than figurative interpretations.[45] His first solution is that the expression 'God's two right hands' refers to God's perfection (*kamāl*) and completeness. It would have been inconceivable to attribute a left hand to God, because the left side symbolises deficiency, imperfection and misfortune, while the right hand symbolises potency, perfection and good fortune.[46] His second solution is a linguistic one: he claims that in Arabic the word *al-yumnā* (the right hand) denotes *al-ᶜaṭāᵓ* (granting or giving). Therefore, the expression 'Both His hands are two right hands' actually denotes the figure of speech 'granting [generously] with both hands'.[47] This figurative interpretation which is shaped according to the Muᶜtazilite linguistic approach stands in striking contrast to Ibn Qutayba's declaration: 'When we are asked, we simply quote what the texts state, and refrain from stating what they do not state.'[48] Ibn Qutayba's dual approach to *aḥādīth al-ṣifāt* reflects both his attraction to the hermeneutical approach of the rationalists and his unequivocal loyalty to the authentic Hadith material.

Further in *Kitāb al-Ikhtilāf fī 'l-Lafẓ*, Ibn Qutayba briefly described the Muᶜtazilite approach towards *aḥādīth al-ṣifāt*, and his description corresponds with the description of his contemporary, the Baghdadian traditionalistic theologian and *muḥaddith* Abu Saᶜid ᶜUthman ibn Saᶜid al-Darimi. Both Ibn Qutayba and al-Darimi emphasised that the Muᶜtazilites accepted the texts which can be interpreted figuratively. Thus, the Muᶜtazilites accepted the *ḥadīth* about God holding the hearts of the believers between two of His fingers, but rejected the *aḥādīth* about God's laughter. In fact, the Muᶜtazilites rejected the majority of *aḥādīth al-ṣifāt*.[49] Ibn Qutayba explains that when the Muᶜtazilites came across a *ḥadīth* which lacked a feasible solution, 'they transmitted it, they sought cure for it (namely, tried to interpret it), and deemed the transmitters of this [*ḥadīth*] liars. They did not mind whether this *ḥadīth* was regarded sound or unsound.'[50] Thus, the Muᶜtazilites were not impressed by the fact that the *ḥadīth* 'Every heart is held between two of the All-Merciful's fingers' was attributed to a number of the Prophet's companions (among who was Umm Salama, the Prophet's wife, as quoted in Chapter 1). They were further not impressed by the fact that this *ḥadīth* was considered by the Hadith scholars as authentic (*ṣaḥīḥ*).[51] Ibn Qutayba explains that the Muᶜtazilites accepted this *ḥadīth* because they found several poems and proverbs in which *iṣbaᶜ* (finger) was used as a metaphoric expression of *niᶜma* (favour, grace).[52] Ibn Qutayba rejects their figurative interpretation in this case by presenting a combination of textual evidence and rhetorical questions that prove the improbability of this interpretation.[53] In response to the rationalists' question: 'So what, then, is your perception of the finger?', Ibn Qutayba explains: 'It is similar to the other *ḥadīth*, which states that He carries the earth on one finger etc. The same goes for [holding the hearts of the believers] between two fingers.'[54] Ibn Qutayba refers to the *ḥadīth* of the divine fingers which was attributed, among others, to ᶜAbd Allah ibn Masᶜud (see Chapter 1). Ibn Qutayba's position is: 'We do not say that the finger is like our fingers . . . because none of the things that are connected to Him (*shayᵓ minhu*) resembles any of the things that are connected to us (*shayᵓan minnā*).'[55]

In spite of Ibn Qutayba's systematic criticism of the rationalists, they were not his major concern; he deemed the Hashwiyya, who came from the ranks of Islamic traditionalism, as the main enemy of *ahl al-ḥadīth*. The Hashwiyya are thoroughly discussed in *Taᵓwīl Mukhtalif al-Ḥadīth*. This sophisticated theological treatise (in fact, much more sophisticated than *Kitāb al-Ikhtilāf fī 'l-Lafẓ*) is a guidebook for the 'middle of the road' traditionalists, whose moderate world-view is threatened from all directions. In the introduction of *Taᵓwīl Mukhtalif al-Ḥadīth*, Ibn Qutayba uses the literary device of a letter which he allegedly received from an anonymous admirer. This admirer read an earlier work by Ibn Qutayba and believed that Ibn Qutayba was the most suitable scholar to address this dangerous situation. Of course this anonymous writer does not disclose any details about himself and we are led to assume that he describes the social and political situation in Baghdad of the tenth century. The anonymous writer complains about two matters: that the rationalists ridicule the traditionalists (*ahl al-ḥadīth, al-muḥaddithūn*) by belittling their professional skills, and the rationalists accuse the traditionalists of proliferating both contradictory and fabricated *aḥādīth*.[56]

The lion's share of *Taᵓwīl Mukhtalif al-Ḥadīth* confronts the rationalistic argumentation on the apparent contradictions in the Hadith material. According to the rationalists, these contradictions encouraged the rise of sects within the Muslim community, because each heretic group could find *aḥādīth* to support and verify its false doctrines. Since this issue is not central to the issue of *aḥādīth al-ṣifāt*, and since it was systematically surveyed by

Binymain Abrahamov in his defining work about rationalism and traditionalism in Islamic thought,[57] this topic will not be discussed here. According to Ibn Qutayba, the kernel of the rationalistic critique of the traditionalists is that by transmitting 'anthropomorphic traditions' (*aḥādīth al-tashbīh*), the traditionalists in fact blaspheme God (*al-iftirāʾ ʿalā Allāh*). *Aḥādīth al-tashbīh* is the derogatory name that, again according to Ibn Qutayba, the rationalists gave to *aḥādīth al-ṣifāt*.[58]

Following this introduction in *Taʾwīl Mukhtalif al-Ḥadīth*, Ibn Qutayba presents ten different *aḥādīth* that the rationalists deem blasphemous. This introduction was written for an audience who knew precisely which stories stood behind cryptic catchwords such as 'the sweat of the horse' (*ʿaraq al-khayl*), 'the fluffy hair on the chest' (*zaghab al-ṣadr*) and 'the light of the two arms' (*nūr al-dhirāʿayn*). This audience was equally familiar with the *aḥādīth* that stood behind more elaborate expressions such as 'the young man with the curly hair and the golden mattress under his [feet]' (*al-shābb al-qaṭaṭ wa-dūnahu firāsh al-dhahab*) or 'the heart of the believer is held between two of God's fingers' (*qalb al-muʾmin bayna iṣbaʿayn min aṣābiʾ Allāh taʿālā*). The rationalists – says Ibn Qutayba – accuse the traditionalists of teaching and spreading these silly texts. By doing so, the traditionalists (so the rationalists claim) exposed the religion of Islam to the mockery of the heretics. As a result, people who may have considered embracing Islam, refused to have anything to do with Islam. In addition, the rationalists claimed that the ridiculous teachings of the traditionalists increased doubts in the hearts of the sceptics.[59]

Ibn Qutayba in fact joins the rationalists in their attack on the *muḥaddithūn*. He informs us that among other derogative names, the rationalists call the *muḥaddithūn* Hashwiyya (namely, 'vulgar anthropomorphists' or 'scholars of little worth').[60] In fact, it is difficult to identify the point at which the rationalists' attacks end and Ibn Qutayba's attacks begin. Naturally, he defends the traditionalists from the defamation of the rationalists. The rationalists described the traditionalists with epithets such as 'scum' (*ghuthāʾ*) and 'riffraff' (*ghuthr*).[61] Ibn Qutayba of course condemns this language, but his line of defence is quite weak. He claims that the Prophet did not mention the Hashwiyya as one of the heretical sects of Islam. In other words, there is no substantial textual evidence of Prophetic *ḥadīth* for the use of this name of opprobrium against *ahl al-ḥadīth*. In contrast, there are Prophetic *aḥādīth* (which the rationalists naturally do not accept) that condemn the forerunners of the Muᶜtazila, the Qadarites. In other words, these *aḥādīth* prove that Ibn Qutayba's contemporaries the Muᶜtazilites are heretics.[62]

But who were the Hashwiyya (and in *Kitāb al-Ikhtilāf*, the Mushabbiha) whom the rationalists attacked so fiercely? From Ibn Qutayba's point of view, they were the unscrupulous *muḥaddithūn* who fabricated outrageous *aḥādīth al-ṣifāt*, according to which God created Himself from the sweat of horses, created the angels from His fluffy chest hair, and descended to the Mount of ᶜArafat sitting in a golden cage set on the back of a grey camel.[63] The rationalists, on the other hand, labelled every *muḥaddith* who transmitted *aḥādīth al-ṣifāt* (even the authenticated ones) – that is, the entire class of *muḥaddithūn* – as Hashwiyya.[64]

While Ibn Qutayba does not bluntly call his fellow traditionalists Hashwiyya, he clarifies that the unscrupulous *muḥaddithūn* deserve this derogatory name because of their lower professional standards and deficient knowledge: 'Not everyone is blessed by the same merits, and certainly knowledge is not divided among all people equally. Every class of people includes "stuffing and hot wind" (*ḥashw wa-shawb*).'[65] The phrase 'stuffing and hot wind', which is a clear reference to the Hashwiyya, indicates that Ibn Qutayba ridiculed this group of *muḥaddithūn* more than he judged them harshly. He adds that there is no comparison between them and the professional and skilful *muḥaddithūn* of former generations. Among the well-versed *muḥaddithūn*, Ibn Qutayba names the greatest *muḥaddithūn* of the eighth century: al-Zuhri (d. 742), Malik ibn Anas, Sufyan al-Thawri, al-Awzaᶜi and Shuᶜba. The first name on this list of the most respected *muḥaddithūn* is surprisingly Hammad ibn Salama, whose contribution to the circulation (and perhaps the creation) of the most controversial *aḥādīth al-ṣifāt* was mentioned in Chapter 3.[66] We note that Ibn Qutayba does not include the *muḥaddithūn* of the next generation in the list of the most respected in the profession of Hadith transmission. The name of Ahmad ibn Hanbal, Ibn Qutayba's townsman, a legendary *muḥaddith* and the eponymous founder of the Hanbalite school, is omitted from this list.

Ibn Qutayba is dissatisfied with the lower standards of the traditionalists. Most of them (*aktharahum*) neglected the meticulous study of the

Hadith. Instead of reading and truly comprehending (*tafaqquh*) the material they collected, they chased after different versions (*wajh*, pl. *awjuh*) of the same *ḥadīth*, collecting ten and perhaps twenty versions 'when one or two reliable versions are sufficient for the scholar who wishes to [get closer] to God by studying [Hadith]'. These scholars 'waste their lives and produce books which only cast exhaustion and fatigue on students'. In sum – declares Ibn Qutayba – 'I never failed from condemning them in my writings'.[67] Ibn Qutayba's description of the *muḥaddithūn* as obsessive antiquarians is a voice in the wilderness: the compilers of Hadith material in the decades after him (especially in the tenth century) indeed specialised in gathering more versions of the same *ḥadīth*. Two notable representative examples of such collections were Ibn Khuzayma's *Kitāb al-Tawḥīd* and Abu Bakr al-Ajurri's *Kitāb al-Sharīᶜa*.

Concerning *aḥādīth al-ṣifāt*, Ibn Qutayba's approach to this material is both critical and cautious. Aside from the obvious fabricated *aḥādīth* which he forthrightly rejected, he defended the *aḥādīth* which were authenticated and admitted into the Islamic canon. He claimed that these authenticated *aḥādīth* posed difficulties because their content was misunderstood. However, he claimed that these texts had *makhārij* (sing. *makhraj*), 'ways out'. These ways out are products of Ibn Qutayba's original reading and they were not followed by later thinkers. The most striking examples of Ibn Qutayba's solutions to the difficulties posed by *aḥādīth al-ṣifāt* are his reading of the Judaeo-Christian sources to solve these difficulties. Thus, he sourced Genesis 1:26 ('Let us make humankind in our image, according to our likeness') and 2:7–8 ('Then Lord God formed man from the dust of the ground; and breathed into his nostrils the breath of life') as textual evidence for the validity of the literal reading of the Prophetic *ḥadīth* 'God created Adam in His Image'.[68] When discussing Jarir al-Bajali's *ḥadīth al-ruʾya* (see Chapter 2), Ibn Qutayba corroborated the veracity of the beatific vision by citing Matthew 5:8 ('Blessed are the pure in heart for they will see God').[69] God's nocturnal descent to the lowest heaven as articulated in *ḥadīth al-nuzūl* is corroborated by a cluster of Quranic verses which Ibn Qutayba brilliantly analysed, but also by the surprising assertion that 'all nations, whether Arabs or non-Arabs, as long as they stay in their natural dispositions and are not pulled away from this [belief] by studying, believe that God is in heaven'.[70]

There is, however, a group of *aḥādīth al-ṣifāt* which Ibn Qutayba experienced difficulty in defending; yet, at the same time he hesitated to reject this group outright: for example, the *ḥadīth* which presents God as a young man. This *ḥadīth*, attributed to Hammad ibn Salama, is the longer variant of the *ḥadīth* attributed to Ibn ᶜAbbas in which the Prophet stated that he saw God 'in most beautiful form (*fī aḥsan ṣūra*)' (see Chapter 3). Ibn Qutayba included the variant of 'the young man with curly hair' among the *aḥādīth* which the rationalists claimed were forged by the traditionalists.[71] Later in the text, when Ibn Qutayba listed the *aḥādīth* which in his opinion were forged by unscrupulous *muḥaddithūn* (he called them *zanādiqa*, heretics), he omitted this *ḥadīth*.[72] Similarly, he did not include the *ḥadīth* among the authenticated *aḥādīth al-ṣifāt*. In brief, he preferred not to discuss this *ḥadīth*, which was accepted and recorded by the Hanbalites and other ultra-traditionalists in their thematic Hadith compilations.[73]

Another *ḥadīth* which he did not wholeheartedly defend, but likewise did not completely reject, is one of the short *aḥādīth* from the Abu Razin al-ᶜUqayli corpus (see Chapter 2). In this *ḥadīth*, Abu Razin asked the Prophet: 'Where was our Lord before He created the heaven and the earth?' The Prophet answered: 'He was in lofty clouds (*ᶜamāᵓ*), beneath which was a vacuity (*hawāᵓ*), and above which was a vacuity.'[74] Ibn Qutayba explained that according to the rationalists, this *ḥadīth* fell under the category of *tashbīh* and *taḥdīd*, namely comparing God to His creation and claiming that God is finite and confined to one specific space.[75] Ibn Qutyaba admitted that this *ḥadīth* was indeed controversial (*mukhtalaf fīhi*). Ibn Qutyaba's main argument against the inclusion of this *ḥadīth* in the traditionalistic curriculum was divided into two parts: first, the transmitters of this *ḥadīth* were Bedouins; second, Wakiᶜ ibn ᶜUdus (Abu Razin's nephew), who was the source of this *ḥadīth* (which was later transmitted by Hammad ibn Salama), was never identified by the Hadith scholars, hence there is much doubt whether there was such a man. In other words, Ibn Qutayba subtly hinted that Hammad ibn Salama was naive enough to believe that a tale concocted by Bedouins was in fact a reliable *ḥadīth* recounted by Abu Razin's nephew. Without checking his sources, Hammad transmitted this *ḥadīth*.[76]

Still, although Ibn Qutayba found these faults about this *ḥadīth* of Abu Razin, he did not reject it completely, because it was already extremely popular in his days. This *ḥadīth*, which was labelled by some Hadith scholars as 'good' (*ḥasan*), while others labelled it as 'weak' (*ḍaᶜīf*),[77] appears in the Hadith compilations of Ibn Qutayba's contemporaries, Ibn Maja (d. 887) and al-Tirmidhi (d. 892). Its inclusion in these two Hadith compilations suggests that the Abu Razin *ḥadīth*, with Wakiᶜ ibn ᶜUdus as its exclusive source, widely circulated in Iraq, Kurasan and further east.[78] As such, a wide audience of traditionalists was exposed to this text and embraced it. Ibn Qutayba, however, directed his sharp criticism to another text: he mentioned that the Abu Razin *ḥadīth* appeared in 'several other reprehensible versions'. He did not explain which version he referred to, but it is evident that he meant 'the *ḥadīth* of allegiance' or 'the lengthy *ḥadīth*' that we discussed in Chapter 2. This text, as we remarked in Chapter 2, was exclusively studied by the Hanbalites. Ibn Qutayba's cautious reservation about this *ḥadīth* indicates that he preferred not to openly confront the Hanbalites about a text which they cherished.

In the course of Ibn Qutayba's brief discussion about the Abu Razin *ḥadīth*, we obtain a glimpse of the sincere efforts made by the moderate traditionalists of the ninth century in order to insert problematic texts into the Islamic canon. According to Ibn Qutayba, one of Ahmad ibn Hanbal's disciples, Ahmad ibn Saᶜid al-Lihyani,[79] quoted Abu ᶜUbayd who examined the possibility of reading this *ḥadīth* differently, thus avoiding any suggestion that God is confined to one specific space. Instead of reading that God 'was in lofty clouds (*ᶜamāᵓ*), beneath which was a vacuity (*hawāᵓ*), and above which was a vacuity', Abu ᶜUbayd suggested reading the word *ᶜamāᵓ* (with a prolonged vowel and a glottal stop) as *ᶜaman* (with a short vowel and a *tanwīn*). Thus, instead of stating that God was in lofty clouds (*ᶜamāᵓ*), the text would state that God was in obscurity, namely you cannot know Him nor point at His location. *ᶜAman* literally means blindness; Abu ᶜUbayd therefore directed his disciples to the understanding that regarding God, we are completely blind.[80] In other words, Abu ᶜUbayd used his linguistic skills both to read the text literally and to include this text in the Islamic canon. Unidentified scholars presented a second surprising solution to the text by adding the negative particle *mā*. Accordingly, they read the text: '[He was in lofty clouds (*ᶜamāᵓ*)], beneath which there was no (*mā*) vacuity (*hawāᵓ*), and above which there was no (*mā*) vacuity'. Ibn Qutayba explained that these anonymous scholars wished to dispel the picture of God as being between two layers of vacuity (or air). However, Ibn Qutayba determined that this solution was untenable: 'you cannot expel the anxiety [about this depicted scene] because the words "above" and "below" remain anyhow'. By adding the remark 'and God knows best',[81] Ibn Qutayba signalled to his readers that one should not waste his time on this *ḥadīth.* As we indicated earlier, Ibn Qutayba very much doubted the veracity of this text because of the obscurity regarding the existence of Wakiᶜ ibn ᶜUdus. As a fabricated text, this *ḥadīth* would not have qualified to serve as material for study and contemplation. Without rejecting this text forthwith, Ibn Qutayba's reluctance to explain the difficulties of this anthropomorphic text, or even to add the *bi-lā kayfa* formula to it, equals a complete rejection of this text.

As we have noted in Chapter 2, the entire corpus of Abu Razin was assimilated in the Hanbalite curriculum via Ahmad ibn Hanbal's *Musnad.* Later in the fourteenth century, the corpus was revived due to the rigorous efforts that Ibn Qayyim al-Jawziyya dedicated to promote Abu Razin's lengthy *ḥadīth* and stabilise its position in the traditionalistic canon. Ibn Qutayba's hesitation to reject this *ḥadīth* completely suggests that he considered the sensitivities of the traditionalistic milieu regarding *aḥādīth al-ṣifāt.* Although the historical sources do not provide any evidence of discord between Ibn Qutayba and the *muḥaddithūn* (especially the Hanbalites) of his time, one may assume that withholding his critique against *aḥādīth al-ṣifāt,* which was accepted only by the ultra-traditionalists, was part of Ibn Qutayba's pragmatism.

Ibn Qutayba was unique in many respects, but as a traditionalist he aligned himself with the middle-of-the-road *muḥaddithūn.* This group wished both to weed *aḥādīth al-ṣifāt* from the fabricated material and to provide a reading of the texts that would reconcile the anthropomorphic descriptions with human reason. Notwithstanding his prudence in handling this material, Ibn Qutayba was deeply concerned by the authenticity of *aḥādīth al-ṣifāt* and the professional standards of the traditionalists who transmitted this material. These concerns were shared by later generations, as the following sections of this chapter demonstrate.

II. The Earliest Debate

As we have demonstrated in Chapters 1 and 2, the more complicated form of *aḥādīth al-ṣifāt,* the one containing an elaborate embedded narrative, is the form more liable to include references to God's physicality and spatiality than the simpler narrative forms. Perhaps the most noteworthy point about these blunt anthropomorphic texts is that they were not obliterated, eliminated or concealed. We could have expected to find an abundance of *aḥādīth al-ṣifāt* depicting God in an anthropomorphic language in the several books that present the corpus of *al-mawḍuᶜāt* (the fabricated *aḥādīth*).[82] The relatively marginal genre of collections of *al-mawḍūᶜāt* flourished to a certain extent in the end of the eleventh century. Since the methodology of compiling the collections of *al-mawḍuᶜāt* relied mostly on the criticism of the content of the texts, and not on the criticism of the chains of transmission, very few scholars were willing to engage in such a critical analysis.[83] The surprisingly meagre amount of *aḥādīth al-ṣifāt* in these collections indicates that the problematic anthropomorphic texts were not regarded inauthentic, and therefore were not quarantined. In fact, the lion's share of *aḥādīth al-ṣifāt* was scattered in the canonical Hadith compilations that were composed in the ninth century. In addition, *aḥādīth al-ṣifāt* were compiled in other lesser valued works such as al-Tabarani's *al-Muᶜjam al-Kabīr*. In this state of affairs, the problematic anthropomorphic texts were accessible to both scholars and the lay public.

This accessibility posed no difficulty for the traditionalists, because their version of the earliest *bi-lā kayfa* formula enabled them to warmly embrace the anthropomorphic texts. More importantly, this formula enabled them to ignore any problematic aspect in the texts and to silence any unwelcome questions about God's corporeality. As we will see, the traditionalistic form of the *bi-lā kayfa* formula in fact produced a tolerant and receptive approach towards the blunt anthropomorphism that the more complicated form of *aḥādīth al-ṣifāt* conveyed. This approach explains the wide selection of *aḥādīth al-ṣifāt* in the compilations of canonical Hadith and the much wider selection of anthropomorphic texts preserved in the writings that were cherished by the ultra-traditionalistic Hanbalites. The Hanbalites, who demonstrated the greatest degree of openness towards these texts, could have easily found additional *aḥādīth al-ṣifāt* in Ahmad Ibn Hanbal's *Musnad* and in the thematic Hadith compilations such as Ibn Khuzayma's *Kitāb al-Tawḥīd*. These additional *aḥādīth* were not canonised, as we have seen in the case of 'the *ḥadīth* of allegiance' attributed to Abu Razin. Thus, we find scholars who accepted unconditionally all anthropomorphic descriptions of God's corporeality through to scholars who expressed their reservations about the more colourful *aḥādīth al-ṣifāt*. These traditionalists measured the anthropomorphic descriptions in *aḥādīth al-ṣifāt* by the scale of appropriateness. They tackled inappropriate descriptions of God and tried to find elegant solutions to settle textual problems by using a combination of hermeneutical devices and common sense.

The following case illustrates the activity of these traditionalists: the case of 'the *ḥadīth* about the loin of the Merciful' (*ḥadīth ḥaqw al-raḥmān*; in several sources it is called *ḥadīth al-raḥim*; on *raḥim*, see further below). Although this graphic *ḥadīth* is surprisingly well-secured in the prestigious *Ṣaḥīḥ al-Bukhārī*, this text has failed to draw significant attention from western scholarship. The first scholar to mention this *ḥadīth* was, as could be expected, Ignaz Goldziher. He shed light on an important aspect regarding the process of transmission of this *ḥadīth* in a brief paragraph in his 1883 monograph on the Zahirites.[84] Translations of this *ḥadīth* were provided by Daniel Gimaret and Merlin Swartz.[85] As far as we know, the *ḥadīth* and its theological implications were never thoroughly discussed. Goldziher's brief remark on this *ḥadīth* that will be presented below in fact ignited the following discussion.

The *ḥadīth ḥaqw al-raḥmān* is quoted in *Ṣaḥīḥ al-Bukhārī* as an introduction to Q. 47:22, a verse which warns Muslims who wished to leave the Islamic faith against leaving the Muslim community. According to this verse, their intention to leave the faith behind threatened to violate the relationships already established between the members of the Muslim community. The Quranic text compares these relationships to strong bonds of kinship: 'If you [the hypocrites] renounced the Faith you would surely do evil in the land and violate the ties of blood (*wa-tuqaṭṭiᶜū arḥāmakum*).' *Arḥām*, the Quranic word for 'ties of blood' or 'kinship', is the plural form of *raḥim* or *riḥm*, which also denotes 'womb'. Thereby, *arḥām* are close or maternal kin.[86] In providing background for the verse, the Quran exegete Abu Jaᶜfar ibn Jarir al-Tabari explained that the verse refers to a group of Muslims who reacted with cowardice to the divine edict that ordered them to go to war. Although these people received the divine edict in the form of an unambiguous and straightforward text (*sūra muḥkama*), they looked at the Prophet 'with the look of a man who lost consciousness', namely as if this edict was not their concern. Al-Tabari also explained that 'violating the ties of blood' meant reverting to the state of affairs that prevailed before the arrival of Islam, when the people were scattered in the land and disunited, while the Prophet 'brought you together and reconciled between you'.[87]

The *ḥadīth ḥaqw al-raḥmān* which is usually quoted as an interpretation of Q. 47:22, demonstrates the importance of 'ties of blood'. The *ḥadīth* presents an obscure scene in which the *raḥim* (womb) functions as a feminine entity. Like most words in Arabic which denote body parts, the gender of *raḥim* is feminine. The word *raḥim*, however, also denotes 'kinship'. It is quite difficult to decide whether the *raḥim* in this specific *ḥadīth* stands for 'womb' or 'kinship'. This word is therefore not translated here:

> Abu Hurayra narrated on the authority of the Prophet: When God had completed the creation the *raḥim* stood up and seized the loin of the Merciful (*akhadhat bi-ḥaqwi al-Raḥmān*). He said to her: 'Stop it!' And she said: 'This is the place where a person seeks Your protection from the enmity among relatives.' He replied: 'Will you be satisfied if I stay close with the person who makes you close to him, and be detached from the person who detaches himself from you?' She said: 'Of course, my Lord.' And He said: 'So, here then, this shall be granted to you.' Abu Hurayra added: 'If you want, you can recite [the Quranic verse]: "If you [the hypocrites] renounced the Faith you would surely do evil in the land and violate the ties of blood".'[88]

The axis of this extraordinary text is the dialogue between the *raḥim* (which we tend to interpret as 'womb', although all previous translations of this text except one referred to this word as 'kinship' or 'relationship')[89] and *al-Raḥmān*, the Merciful. As opposed to the Quranic verse which refers to the relationships between the members of the Muslim community as bonds of kinship, the *ḥadīth* emphasises the primordial nature of the familial–biological ties by a personification of the *raḥim*, the womb. The *ḥadīth* creates a parallel between the close relationships in a person's family and the closeness of this person to God. In similar traditions, the anthropomorphic description is either considerably attenuated or euphemised. In one of these traditions, the *raḥim* clings to the divine throne (and not to God) and says: 'Whoever makes me close to him, God will be close to him. Whoever detaches himself from me, God will be detached from him.' In another tradition, she clings to God's waist (*ḥujzat al-Raḥmān*). Moreover, a different tradition suggests that the *raḥim* clings to God's side or shoulders. In addition, other traditions suggest that she grows a tongue and pleads God to punish those who are detached from her.[90] There are also more 'sterilised' versions which merely emphasise the linguistic connection of the *raḥim* to *al-Raḥmān*, as these two words are derived from the same root (*r.ḥ.m.*).[91] The following Prophetic dictum is a representative example:

> ᶜAbd Allah ibn ᶜAmr narrated on the authority of the Prophet: The Merciful has mercy upon the compassionate people. If you have mercy (*raḥma*) upon the dwellers of this earth, then the dwellers of heaven will have mercy upon you. The *raḥim* (the womb) is derived from *al-Raḥmān*. Whoever makes himself close to her, [*al-Raḥmān*] will be close to him. Whoever detaches himself from her, [*al-Raḥmān*] will be detached from him.[92]

The *ḥadīth ḥaqw al-raḥmān* with its outspoken language is a unique case. In principle, as the influential Hanbalite scholar Ibn Taymiyya remarked in his *Bayān Talbīs al-Jahmiyya* (Clarifying the Deception of the Jahmiyya),[93] this *ḥadīth* is similar to other *aḥadīth* that describe God or attribute bodily organs to God. According to Ibn Taymiyya, whoever affirms the veracity of other *aḥādīth* which resemble this *ḥadīth* in their anthropomorphic descriptions, should affirm the description of God in this *ḥadīth*.[94] In this case (as in many others), Ibn Taymiyya was singular in his courageousness. The *ḥadīth ḥaqw al-raḥmān* was in fact extremely problematic; this is attested by the discussions about it among the traditionalists. It is not too surprising to discover that Ibn Qayyim al-Jawziyya, Ibn Taymiyya's most faithful disciple, remained silent about this *ḥadīth*. A succinct version without any follow-up discussion of one of the more 'sterilised' versions indeed appears in the abridgement of Ibn Qayyim al-Jawziyya's prominent work about the divine attributes.[95] Ibn Qayyim al-Jawziyya's silence sharply clarifies the question of appropriate and inappropriate descriptions of God. His silence perhaps suggests that some of the more problematic *aḥādīth al-ṣifāt* were censored or concealed even in the ultra-traditionalistic circles. Since the questions of censorship and concealment of *aḥādīth al-ṣifāt* in general are closely connected to the circulation of *ḥadīth ḥaqw al-raḥmān*, we will start the discussion with the identification of the narrator of this *ḥadīth*.

A closer look at *ḥadīth ḥaqw al-raḥmān* as quoted by al-Bukhari, and especially its chains of transmission, reveals several facts:

> Khalid ibn Makhlad reported to us the following: Sulayman [ibn Bilal] reported to us the following: Muᶜawiya ibn Abi Muzarrid told me the following *ḥadīth* on the authority of Saᶜid ibn Yasar [who recounted the *ḥadīth* to him] on the authority of Abu Hurayra ...[96]

The *ḥadīth* was attributed to Muᶜawiya ibn Abi Muzarrid (d. 767), a *mawlā* of the Banu Hashim who resided in Medina. Muᶜawiya was a marginal *tābiᶜī* who did not transmit Hadith systematically or in great numbers. He had, however, precious access to the Prophetic knowledge, because his maternal uncle, Abu 'l-Hubab Saᶜid ibn Yasar (d. 734–5) was a *mawlā* of Maymuna (d. 681), the last wife of the Prophet.[97] Muᶜawiya claimed to have heard *ḥadīth ḥaqw al-raḥmān* from this uncle, who in turn claimed to have heard it from Abu Hurayra.[98] Literally speaking, Muᶜawiya is the narrator of the *ḥadīth* and his testimony and point of view are presented in the narrative.

Muᶜawiya is also 'the common link', the narrator whose name is mentioned in at least three different chains of transmission (see Appendix V, chart 1). Al-Bukhari cites three versions of this *ḥadīth* (actually, he gives three different *isnāds* to one *matn* which he quotes only once). According to these versions, Muᶜawiya recited this *ḥadīth* to the following *muḥaddithūn*: the Medinese Sulayman ibn Bilal (d. either in 788–9 or 793–4), who claimed to have heard the *ḥadīth* personally from Muᶜawiya; the Medinese Hatim ibn Ismaᶜil (d. 803); and the Persian travelling merchant and *muḥaddith* ᶜAbd Allah ibn al-Mubarak (d. 797).[99] This *ḥadīth*, then, circulated primarily among the people of Medina. Al-Bukhari himself learned about this *ḥadīth* while staying in Medina: he received it directly from the prominent Medinese *muḥaddith*, Ibrahim ibn Hamza al-Zubayri (d. 845).[100]

In the ninth century, Ahmad ibn Hanbal taught this *ḥadīth* without any reservation whatsoever according to his *bi-lā kayfa* approach. Ahmad ibn Hanbal received this *ḥadīth* from Abu Bakr al-Hanafi (d. 819–20), a *muḥaddith* from Basra, who claimed to have received the *ḥadīth* personally from Muᶜawiya (see Appendix V, chart 2).[101] Ahmad ibn Hanbal's inclusion of *ḥadīth ḥaqw al-Raḥmān* verbatim in his *Musnad*,[102] and hence in his syllabus, contrasted the position of his contemporary, the leading *muḥaddith*, preacher and Quran reciter from Damascus, Hisham ibn ᶜAmmar (d. 859–60, at the age of eighty-seven).[103] Hisham expressed his reservations about this *ḥadīth* and Ahmad ibn Hanbal commented on Hisham's reservation. The disagreement between the two is crucial to understand the state of turmoil that accompanied *ḥadīth ḥaqw al-Raḥmān* from the ninth century onward.

Hisham ibn ᶜAmmar, who emerges in the story as Ahmad ibn Hanbal's rival, began his scholarly career as a young boy, when he travelled with his father to the Hijaz especially to study Hadith and *fiqh* from the illustrious Malik ibn Anas.[104] Among Hisham ibn ᶜAmmar's many students, five of the six authors of the great Hadith compilations (*aṣḥāb al-kutub*) are the most conspicuous.[105] However, there were numerous complaints about Hisham's dubious moral behaviour and his tendency to transmit material without providing the necessary chains of transmission. In addition, rumours circulated that Hisham was greedy and sly: opposed to the ethical norms, he used to charge money from people who wanted to participate in his sessions of Hadith transmission. Several disturbing rumours about his frivolous behaviour of jesting and indecently exposing himself in public also circulated among his contemporaries.[106] In spite of all this, Hisham was considered a prominent and influential scholar in Damascus.[107]

Hisham's eccentricities aside, when one of the participants in his study sessions recited *ḥadīth ḥaqw al-Raḥmān* to him, Hisham rejected the text. We derive Hisham's reaction from two anecdotes that were preserved in later sources: Abu Yaᶜla's *Ibṭāl al-Taʾwīlāt* and Ibn Taymiyya's *Bayān Talbīs al-Jahymiyya*. Although these two sources are biased toward Ahmad ibn Hanbal and the ultra-traditionalistic position, they are the only historical sources that report on the earliest transmission phase of *ḥadīth ḥaqw al-Raḥmān*. A critical reading of these sources extracts vital evidence about this *ḥadīth* in particular and *aḥādīth al-ṣifāt* in general.

The first anecdote is the testimony of Abu Bakr al-Marwazi (or al-Marrudhi), who was Ahmad ibn Hanbal's most distinguished disciple and his personal assistant. Al-Marwazi reported that a group of Damascenes sent him letters requesting him to refer their inquiries to Ibn Hanbal. The authors of these letters wished to know Ahmad ibn Hanbal's opinion on

Hisham's theological views. In one of these letters, the Damascene informants recounted the following incident: a man recited *ḥadīth ḥaqw al-Raḥmān* in front of a *muḥaddith* (identity unknown), after which that man wholeheartedly expressed his belief in the *ḥadīth*.[108] Thereafter, the *muḥaddith* raised his head and said: 'I am afraid that you have already become a heretic.' Al-Marwazi reported that he showed this letter to Ahmad ibn Hanbal and the latter responded: 'This one (namely, the *muḥaddith*) is a Jahmite (namely, a Muᶜtazilite).'[109]

The *muḥaddith* who rejected *ḥadīth ḥaqw al-Raḥmān* was, of course, Hisham ibn ᶜAmmar. We learn this information from the second anecdote, which is recounted by another close companion of Ahmad ibn Hanbal, Abu Talib al-Mushkani (d. 858–9). According to Abu Talib's own account, he was present when Ahmad ibn Hanbal was asked about Hisham's reaction to *ḥadīth ḥaqw al-Raḥmān*; that is to say, Hisham was the *muḥaddith* to whom this text was recited. Ahmad ibn Hanbal disregarded the whole story: 'Hisham is a Syrian. What has he got to do with this [*ḥadīth*]?' Abu Talib asked Ahmad his opinion and Ahmad explained: 'The text of this *ḥadīth* should be transmitted exactly as it was received.'[110]

Ahmad's response is divided into two parts: the first part addresses the distribution of *aḥādīth al-ṣifāt*, while the second part addresses the methodology that these texts require. Ahmad implied that Hisham, who heard *ḥadīth ḥaqw al-Raḥmān* from the anonymous man in the mosque, reacted as he did because he was not familiar with the text. Moreover, the reference to Hisham's origin implies that the Damascene *muḥaddithūn* in general were not as well versed in the type of material that *ḥadīth ḥaqw al-Raḥmān* represented as were their colleagues from Baghdad. Generally, the first part of Ahmad's response reflects the (justifiable) sense of supremacy that he, as Iraq's leading *muḥaddith*, claimed over his Damascene colleague. Iraq, after all, was the leading centre of Hadith transmission during the ninth century, and Ahmad ibn Hanbal was a prominent *muḥaddith* and a charismatic leader in his community.[111]

The second part of Ahmad's response conveys reproach: *ḥadīth ḥaqw al-Raḥmān* required a strict application of the *bi-lā kayfa* principle and Hisham failed to apply this principle. It is difficult to know whether Ahmad believed that the *muḥaddithūn* of Syria were more inclined to paraphrase or express their personal opinions on the *aḥādīth* that they transmitted, whereas the *muḥaddithūn* of Iraq were accurate and particular about the details of the transmitted texts. All in all, Ahmad's remark about Hisham leaves no room for doubt: Ahmad believed that Hisham was wrong for rejecting *ḥadīth ḥaqw al-Raḥmān* instead of transmitting it without further remarks, *bi-lā kayfa*.

Hisham was generally considered a reliable *muḥaddith* and the *aḥādīth* that he transmitted reflected hardcore traditionalism.[112] However, he was also tainted by expressing theological views that transgressed the traditionalistic borderlines. In one of the letters that Ahmad received from the anonymous Damascenes, the inquirers reported that Hisham declared (probably during his sermon at the Umayyad Mosque) that when the archangel Gabriel and the Prophet Muhammad recited the Quran, their recitation (*lafẓ*) was created (*makhlūq*). Since this declaration supported the doctrine of the createdness of the Quran (at least, the createdness of one of the temporal manifestations of the Quran, that of the human voice reciting it), Hisham's declaration placed him among the Muᶜtazilites and excluded him from the traditionalistic camp.[113] Al-Marwazi delivered the letter to Ahmad ibn Hanbal, and he responded that Hisham 'became a Muᶜtazilite' (*tajahhama*).[114] When Hisham heard that people attributed to him the Muᶜtazilite view about the created recitation of the Quran, he became angry and immediately declared that the Quran, as God's speech, is uncreated. Thereafter, he recited *sūrat al-ikhlāṣ* (Q. 112:1–4) and said: 'What I have just recited, is the Word of God.'[115] Hisham was actually explaining to the people that the Quranic text, when recited by him and uttered through his created voice, was not created. Although there is no way to set a sound chronology of this specific report about Hisham (was it before or after the *miḥna*?), clearly, he was part of the traditionalistic community.

Assuming that Hisham heard *ḥadīth ḥaqw al-Raḥmān* for the first time from a man in the mosque, why did he reject it so vehemently? One possible explanation is connected to his views regarding God's corporeality. According to another letter from Damascus, in one of his sermons, Hisham praised 'the Lord who revealed Himself to the creatures which He created through His [incarnation] in the creatures'. Having heard this, Ahmad ibn Hanbal condemned Hisham for his frivolity calling him 'light-headed and unsteady' (*ṭayyāsh wa-khafīf*).[116] Hisham's saying about God tainted him with the suspicion of his being an incarnationist (*ḥulūlī*).[117] Since he believed that God was incarnated, Hisham was as far from Mu^ctazilism as possible. Hisham could have imagined the incarnation of God: he could actually 'see' God sitting in the middle arch between Paradise and Hell on the Day of Resurrection, and he could picture 'the most beautiful form' in which God was revealed to the Prophet Muhammad. These are two examples of *aḥādīth al-ṣifāt* that Hisham transmitted.[118] In the same vein, we can safely assume that having heard *ḥadīth ḥaqw al-Raḥmān*, Hisham rejected it because of the reference to the loin; he probably regarded this reference to God as too bold and inappropriate, because his worldview enabled him to imagine a figure of God, he was able to imagine this figure as having a loin.

The second possible explanation of Hisham's rejection of *ḥadīth ḥaqw al-Raḥmān* is that he believed that this *ḥadīth* was fabricated. Hisham is recorded among the transmitters of an abridged version of this *ḥadīth*, which appears in both *Ṣaḥīḥ Muslim* and *Ṣaḥīḥ al-Bukhārī* (see Appendix V, chart 3):

> Abu Hurayra narrated on the authority of the Prophet: When God had completed the creation the *raḥim* stood up and said: 'This is the place where a person seeks Your protection from the enmity among relatives.' He replied: 'Yes. Will you be satisfied if I stay close with the person who makes you close to him, and be detached from the person who detaches himself from you?' She said: 'Of course, my Lord.' And He said: 'So, here then, this shall be granted to you.'[119]

The abridged version sterilises the meaning of the depicted scene in this *ḥadīth*. In the full version of *Ṣaḥīḥ al-Bukhārī*, the *raḥim* (womb), as a feminine entity, makes an appeal to God whose masculinity is insinuated in the text by the mention of His loin. The message of the appeal which refers to blood ties and their practical meaning is much accentuated by the symbol of femininity imploring the symbol of masculinity. This entire symbolism is absent from the abridged version because of the omission of three words (*fa-akhadhat bi-ḥaqwi al-Raḥmān*; and seized the loin of the Merciful).

III. Transmission, Censorship and Euphemisms

The case of Hisham ibn ᶜAmmar illustrates the existence of two competing versions of the same *ḥadīth*. In this case, these are the full version in *Ṣaḥīḥ al-Bukhārī* and the abridged or 'censored' version in *Ṣaḥīḥ Muslim* and *Ṣaḥīḥ al-Bukhārī*. Apart from the omission of the three words in the censored version, the two versions of this *ḥadīth* are almost identical. Both versions of the *ḥadīth* are attributed to Muᶜawiya ibn Abi Muzarrid, whom we identified in the previous section as the actual narrator of *ḥadīth ḥaqw al-raḥmān*. To complicate matters, the three transmitters who are connected to the full version of the *ḥadīth*, (which they presumably heard from Muᶜawiya) appear in the sources also as the transmitters of the censored version. These transmitters are Sulayman ibn Bilal, Hatim ibn Ismaᶜil and ᶜAbd Allah ibn al-Mubarak. Al-Dhahabi, however, opined that only Sulayman actually heard Muᶜawiya recount the story and that Ibn al-Mubarak and Hatim merely followed Sulayman by appropriating this *ḥadīth* and claiming that they also heard it from Muᶜawiya. This extraordinary view is available only in al-Dhahabi's *Mīzān al-Iᶜtidāl*; therefore, it is impossible to know on what grounds al-Dhahabi based his view.[120] Al-Dhahabi's remark notwithstanding, Table 4.1 summarises the findings from the two most important Hadith compilations of the Islamic canon.[121]

It is beyond the scope of this chapter to investigate when exactly the censored version evolved from the full version. However, Hisham's case that we described in the previous section (Section II) evidently proves that at least in the first decades of the ninth century, when both he and Ahmad ibn Hanbal were active *muḥaddithūn*, the two versions circulated in parallel.

Table 4.1

The transmitter	The full version	The censored version
Sulayman ibn Bilal	*Ṣaḥīḥ al-Bukhārī*, *ḥadīth* 4830	*Ṣaḥīḥ al-Bukhārī*, *ḥadīth* 7502
Hatim ibn Ismaᶜil	*Ṣaḥīḥ al-Bukhārī*, *ḥadīth* 4831	*Ṣaḥīḥ Muslim*, *ḥadīth* 16-2554
ᶜAbd Allah ibn al-Mubarak	*Ṣaḥīḥ al-Bukhārī*, *ḥadīth* 4832	*Ṣaḥīḥ al-Bukhārī*, *ḥadīth* 5987

Hisham heard from the man in the mosque a version of the *ḥadīth* he did not approve of. His version of the *ḥadīth*, quoted in another source, indicates that only the sentence 'and seized the loin of the Merciful' (*fa-akhadhat bi-ḥaqwi al-Raḥmān*) was in his view problematic, because his censored version of the *ḥadīth* was, after all, almost identical to the full version.

Additional proof for the existence of two parallel versions of this *ḥadīth* in the ninth century derives from the names of the *muḥaddithūn* who transmitted these versions to al-Bukhari and Muslim. We already mentioned Ibrahim ibn Hamza, the Medinese *muḥaddith* who transmitted the full version to al-Bukhari. In contrast, Muslim received the censored version from Qutayba ibn Saᶜid (d. 854) and Muhammad ibn ᶜAbbad (d. 849), two *muḥaddithūn* from Baghdad.[122] All in all, al-Bukhari records the names of four additional contemporary *muḥaddithūn* from whom he directly received either version of this *ḥadīth*, as Table 4.2 shows.[123]

All these *muḥaddithūn* were active between 780 and 845, and al-Bukhari records in his *Ṣaḥīḥ* several dozens of *aḥādīth* in various topics that he heard from each of them (an average of twenty-five traditions per *muḥaddith*). Ibrahim ibn Hamza and Ismaᶜil ibn ᶜAbd Allah were the most respectable personalities of this small group, basically due to their noble descent: Ibrahim was a lineal descendant of the anti-caliph ᶜAbd Allah ibn Zubayr (d. 692),[124] while Ismaᶜil was the maternal nephew of Malik ibn Anas (d. 796), the eponymous founder of the Malikite school. Ismaᶜil heard Hadith from Malik and Sulayman ibn Bilal,[125] and indeed his material in *Ṣaḥīḥ al-Bukhārī* comes mainly from these two Medinese personalities. Ismaᶜil was a traditionalist through and through: it is said that Ahmad ibn Hanbal praised him for his

Table 4.2

The *muḥaddith*	**Year of death**	**Main place of scholarly activity**	**The transmitted version**	**Reference in *Ṣaḥīḥ al-Bukhārī***
Khalid ibn Makhlad	828	Kufa	full	*ḥadīth* 4830
Ibrahim ibn Hamza	845	Medina	full	*ḥadīth* 4831
Bishr ibn Muhammad	838–9	Basra	full and censored	*ḥadīth* 4832, *ḥadīth* 5987
Ismaᶜil ibn ᶜAbd Allah	840–1	Medina	censored	*ḥadīth* 7502

'honourable position' (*maqāman maḥmūdan*) during the *miḥna* (one cannot of course ignore the *double entendre* in Ibn Hanbal's compliment).[126] Khalid ibn Makhlad and Bishr ibn Muhammad, the other two *muḥaddithūn* in this group, also made their way into the prestigious *Ṣaḥīḥ al-Bukhārī*. Khalid also heard Hadith from Malik and Sulayman ibn Bilal. He was a member of the Banu Bajila from Kufa, a tribe which had a long tradition of storytelling and Hadith transmission (as discussed in Chapter 2).[127] Apart from *ḥadīth ḥaqw al-raḥmān*, *Ṣaḥīḥ al-Bukhārī* includes two anthropomorphic texts that Khalid quoted from Sulayman.[128] Khalid's contemporaries, however, mentioned his Shiᶜite tendencies and the great amount of objectionable Hadith material (*manākīr*, pl. of *munkar*) that was attributed to him.[129] Bishr ibn Muhammad al-Marwazi al-Sakhtyani, who transmitted material mainly from Ibn al-Mubarak, was also tainted by accusations of transgressing mainstream traditionalism; apparently he was a Murjiᵓite.[130]

As mentioned in Section II, the only difference between the full version and the censored version is the absence of the sentence 'and seized the loin of the Merciful' (*fa-akhadhat bi-ḥaqwi al-Raḥmān*). The structure of the narrative allowed the narrator to omit these words during the process of narration without the audience noticing this omission. In the full version, the *raḥim* stands up, seizes their loin, and declares: 'This is the place where a person seeks Your protection from the enmity among relatives.' In the censored text, she merely stands up and delivers the same declaration. Unless a participant in the audience asked the narrator what is 'the place' that the *raḥim* referred to in this *ḥadīth*, the omission would have remained unnoticeable. Unfortunately, there is no record of anyone asking such a question. The two parts of the *ḥadīth* are stitched carefully and nobody, except someone who knew the 'full' version, could have noticed that a sentence was missing. The possibility that the full version was thus tampered with in order to create a censored version emerges from the later sources.

First, we must emphasise that it is highly unlikely that the full version evolved from the censored one. While only a scarce number of later Hadith scholars quote the full version of *ḥadīth ḥaqw al-raḥmān*, there are two points that all these scholars share: first, they do not refer to the censored version at all; second, they include *Ṣaḥīḥ Muslim* in which only the censored version appears, among the list of Hadith compilations which present the full version of this *ḥadīth*. For example, when Jalal al-Din al-Suyuti (d. 1505) who presented the most extensive collection of *aḥādīth* about *raḥim* and *raḥma* in the commentary of Q. 47:22 quoted the full version of *ḥadīth ḥaqw al-raḥmān*, he preceded this quotation with a list of eleven Hadith compilations and Quran exegeses. These works, according to al-Suyuti, contain *ḥadīth ḥaqw al-raḥmān*. Among these works, al-Suyuti mentioned *Ṣaḥīḥ al-Bukhārī* and al-Tabari's *Jāmi*ᶜ *al-Bayān*, which indeed quote the full version of this *ḥadīth* verbatim.[131] However, al-Suyuti also included *Ṣaḥīḥ Muslim* in this list.[132] Another example is the quotation of the illustrious *muḥaddith* and Shafiᶜite lawyer from Nishapur, Abu Bakr Ahmad ibn al-Husayn al-Bayhaqi (d. 1066). In his compilation of *aḥādīth al-ṣifāt*, al-Bayhaqi also quoted the full version adding: 'This *ḥadīth* was transmitted by al-Bukhari in his *Ṣaḥīḥ* . . . and by Muslim.'[133]

What could be the reason that al-Suyuti and al-Bayhaqi did not mention the censored version? Why did they include *Ṣaḥīḥ Muslim* among the works that presented the full version of this *ḥadīth*? One possible explanation involves human error. In his voluminous Hadith compilation, al-Suyuti did the exact opposite from what he did in his commentary to Q. 47:22; namely, he quoted the censored version and listed seven Hadith compilations that – as he claimed – had this version. Among these works he mentioned *Ṣaḥīḥ Muslim*, which indeed has the censored version, and Ahmad ibn Hanbal's *Musnad*, which does not contain this censored version.[134] So, perhaps this error can also be explained in the opposite direction. In other words, human error is an acceptable explanation for the inclusion of *Ṣaḥīḥ Muslim* among the works which quote the full version of this *ḥadīth*. The meaning of this so-called error is that scholars did not deem the omission of the sentence 'and seized the loin of the Merciful' (*fa-akhadhat bi-ḥaqwi al-Raḥmān*) from the version in *Ṣaḥīḥ Muslim* important enough to mention. Although this presumption does not correspond with the linguistic sensitivity that these scholars possessed, it cannot be overruled completely. Perhaps scholars did not see the difference between the full version and the censored one, and considered both versions identical.

A more plausible assumption is that *ḥadīth ḥaqw al-raḥmān* was censored in several works in which it was included: namely, there were copies of *Ṣaḥīḥ al-Bukhārī* in which the full version was censored. This assumption is corroborated by some textual evidence first located by Goldziher in the manuscripts of the commentaries of *Ṣaḥīh al-Bukharī* authored by Ibn Hajar al-ᶜAsqalani (d. 1449) and Shihab al-Din al-Qastallani (d. 1517). These findings led Goldziher to determine that 'attempts were not lacking from the part of the spiritual dogmatics to remove anthropomorphical expressions from the text of the collections of traditions'. Goldziher adds: 'For spiritualists the loin of God might have sounded objectionable so that attempts were made to remove the offensive words from the texts.'[135] It should be noted, however, that there is the possibility that the process of censorship of the full version emerges only in *Ṣaḥīḥ al-Bukhārī* and its commentaries. No such possibility exists for *Ṣaḥīḥ Muslim*; the commentators of this work, Qadi ᶜIyad (d. 1150) and Muhyi al-Din al-Nawawi (d. 1277), did not disclose their knowledge of the full version in their commentary of this *ḥadīth* and they did not mention the possibility that such a version was included in *Ṣaḥīḥ Muslim*.

Goldziher summarised his findings in Ibn Hajar and al-Qastallani's commentaries, leaving too many points obscure and inexplicable. One point in particular which Goldziher did not mention is the identity of a mysterious Abu Zayd 'who did not read the words *bi-ḥaqw al-raḥmān*'.[136] Abu Zayd's identity, however, is crucial for this discussion. The following is therefore a re-examination of Goldziher's findings while providing the necessary clarifications and deepening the analysis. To Goldziher's reading of the commentaries of Ibn Hajar and al-Qastallani, we added Badr al-Din al-ᶜAyni (d. 1451), the author of another commentary to *Ṣaḥīḥ al-Bukhārī*, which clarifies another crucial dimension of Goldziher's findings.[137]

In *Fatḥ al-Bārī*, Ibn Hajar claimed that 'in most cases' (*li'l-akthar*), the words 'the loin of the Merciful' (*bi-ḥaqwi al-Raḥmān*) were omitted, although the verb 'and seized' (*fa-akhadhat*) remained. Al-ᶜAyni, who was Ibn Hajar's contemporary, claimed that 'the majority of the [*muḥaddithūn*] preferred not to mention the object of the verbal clause (namely, the loin of the Merciful) in their transmission'.[138] The testimonies of these two scholars lead us to the conclusion that *muḥaddithūn* who held in their possessions copies of *Ṣaḥīḥ al-Bukhārī*[139] in which the full version of the *ḥadīth* appeared, nonetheless omitted the embarrassing wording in question during the process of oral transmission. Thus, their students would have heard from the *muḥaddith* only the sentence 'the *raḥim* stood up and seized' (*qāmat al-raḥim fa-akhad-*

hat). In practice, because these students were expected to write the entire text of the *ḥadīth*, they probably would have completed the sentence by copying it from the book that the *muḥaddith* held in his hands. Another possibility is that the *mustamlī*, the clerk working for the *muḥaddith*, dictated this sentence to them. The problem with both testimonies of Ibn Hajar and Ibn al-ᶜAyni is that they are satisfied with a general and almost identical description and do not identify the *muḥaddithūn* who practiced this method of transmission. They also do not indicate when and where these *muḥaddithūn* were active. The case of the mysterious Abu Zayd, however, gives a partial answer to these questions.

Ibn Hajar quotes a fascinating testimony by Abu 'l-Hasan al-Qabisi (d. 1012), an important Maghrebian scholar who was responsible for introducing *Ṣaḥīḥ al-Bukhārī* to the Maghreb. Al-Qabisi collected his copy of *Ṣaḥīḥ al-Bukhārī* during the dictation sessions that occurred in Mecca under the guidance of Abu Zayd al-Marwazi (d. 981–2). Al-Marwazi was an authorised transmitter (*rāwī*) of *Ṣaḥīḥ al-Bukhārī*; namely, he received the approval of one of al-Bukhari's students, Muhammad ibn Yusuf al-Firbari (d. 932), to transmit al-Fibari's version of this Hadith compilation.[140] According to al-Qabisi, in one of these dictation sessions Abu Zayd al-Marwazi refused to read the problematic sentence to his disciples 'because it was ambiguous and posed difficulties' (*li-ishkālihi*).[141] Al-Qabisi's description of Abu Zayd's behaviour implies that the copy of *Ṣaḥīḥ al-Bukhārī* that Abu Zayd al-Marwazi held in his hands – which he received directly from al-Firbari himself – indeed contained the words 'and seized the loin of the Merciful'. Ibn Hajar remarks that these words appeared in a version of *Ṣaḥīḥ al-Bukhārī* that was transmitted by Ibn Sakan (d. 964), who was another direct disciple of al-Firbari and an authorised *rāwī* of al-Fibari's version of *Ṣaḥīḥ al-Bukhārī*.[142] Therefore, al-Firbari indeed transmitted the full version of the *ḥadīth* to his disciples. It was Abu Zayd who chose not to utter the embarrassing words.

The testimony of al-Qabisi about Abu Zayd's refusal to utter the embarrassing expression is the only solid historical evidence about the technique of censoring this *ḥadīth* during the process of oral transmission. Ibn Hajar, al-Qastallani and al-ᶜAyni record several other techniques used by the *muḥaddithūn* in order to avoid the embarrassing expression. During the process of oral transmission, apart from omitting (*ḥadhf*) the problematic expression, the *muḥaddith* could have used euphemistic expressions. For instance, an anonymous interpreter used to say that the *raḥim* 'seized one of the legs of the throne' (*akhadat bi-qāʾima min qawāʾim al-ʿarsh*).[143] This expression comes from a well-known and widely cited *ḥadīth* in which the Prophet testified to having seen Moses seize one of the legs of the throne.[144] This creative solution of soldering two traditions is not recorded in any of the Hadith compilations. Therefore, 'seized one of the legs of the throne' was obviously taken by the *muḥaddith* and his disciples as a code for 'seized the loin of the Merciful' and not as the genuine text of the *ḥadīth*.

The simplest technique of censorship was to delete the undesirable or embarrassing words altogether. A more sophisticated technique, which sought to remain loyal to the original text, was to add a special mark to the written text that instructed the scholar to skip the embarrassing words during his sessions of oral transmission. These techniques of censorship in the written text were applied by both the original scribe of the text and the copyists of the manuscript. Al-Qastallani, who elaborated on these techniques, based his comprehensive interpretation of *Ṣaḥīḥ al-Bukhāri* on the exemplary text of the *Ṣaḥīḥ* that was assembled and edited by the Syrian Hanbalite scholar Sharaf al-Din Abu al-Husayn ʿAli al-Yunini (d. 1302).[145] Al-Yunini produced *al-Yūnīniyya*, a definitive text of *Ṣaḥīḥ al-Bukhārī* which was based on a meticulous philological study of comparative readings in the different copies of the *Ṣaḥīḥ al-Bukhārī* that were attributed to al-Firbari's disciples.[146] Therefore, al-Yunini's *Ṣaḥīḥ* recorded the textual changes and the different readings in some of the traditions of *Ṣaḥīḥ al-Bukhārī* that prevailed between the middle of the tenth and the beginning of the eleventh centuries. Heavily relying on al-Yunini, al-Qastallani provided some noteworthy details about the way in which *ḥadīth ḥaqw al-raḥmān* was presented in the writings of al-Firbari's disciples and their followers.[147]

Al-Qastallani remarked that in Abu Dharr al-Harawi's (d. 1038) version of *Ṣaḥīḥ al-Bukhārī*, the words 'the loin of the Merciful' were completely omitted.[148] Abu Dharr's reading of the text was recorded in a copy of *Ṣaḥīḥ al-Bukhārī* which was prepared by al-Firbari's disciple, Abu Haytham al-Kushmihani (d. 999). By comparing al-Kushmihani's copy to other copies that were at his disposal, al-Yunini probably arrived at the conclusion that the embarrassing words should remain in the text. However, as al-Qastallani described it, he added the sign of deletion (*kasht*) above the words.[149] Since al-Yunini also consulted the testimony of Abu Zayd al-Marwazi,[150] we propose that al-Yunini's solution was based on Abu Zayd's approach: holding a copy which contains the embarrassing words, but not uttering them.

Al-Yunini's sign of deletion above the words *bi-ḥaqwi al-raḥmān* appears in an edition of *Ṣaḥīḥ al-Bukhārī* that was prepared according to his surviving manuscript. This edition, which was called *al-Sulṭāniyya*, was printed in the Bulaq printing house (*Maṭbaᶜat Bulāq*) in Cairo in 1895–6 on the order of the Ottoman Sultan ᶜAbd al-Hamid the second (r. 1876–1909),[151] and then reprinted at least twice in two annotated editions.[152] The set of symbols (*rumūz*) that al-Yunini used in the manuscript are mentioned in the preface to *al-Sulṭāniyya*.[153] Above the words *bi-ḥaqwi al-raḥmān* there are two signs: *lā* that means the beginning of an omission and *ilā* that means the end of an omission.[154] Al-Qastallani testified that he checked the text in a copy of *al-Yūnīniyya* prepared by another *muḥaddith* and that copy also included the two signs of omission.[155]

A more recent example of editorial censorship appears in the Arabic-English edition of *Ṣaḥīḥ al-Bukhārī* which was published in Medina in 1997. The complete edition of the translation was prepared by the Pakistani medical doctor and translator, Dr Muhammad Muhsin Khan. The work was published in a complete version of nine volumes and an abridged version of one volume. In the Arabic text of the *ḥadīth* in the complete edition, the words *bi-ḥaqw al-raḥmān* are omitted, but the word *fa-akhadhat* appears. Likewise, the English translation of the entire sentence is: 'the womb got up and caught hold of Allah'.[156] In the abridged version, however, the Arabic text of the *ḥadīth* remains intact, namely the sentence *fa-akhadhat bi-ḥaqw al-raḥmān* appears. However, the translation of this sentence avoids the embarrassing word combination and therefore is similar to the translation in the complete edition.[157]

IV. The All-inclusive *Tanzīh*: The Ashᶜarite Solution

Several questions regarding *ḥadīth ḥaqw al-raḥmān* remained open: to what extent did the ultra-traditionalists – primarily the Hanbalites – tolerate this *ḥadīth* and its forthright descriptive scene? Did they use this *ḥadīth* freely in their discourse? Were there hidden reasons for Abu Zayd's refusal to read the embarrassing words aloud? What significance did the later scholars assign to Abu Zayd's position? The answers to these questions eventually lead us to evaluate the doctrine that the Ashᶜarites promoted, the doctrine of *tanzīh*. This doctrine enabled them to accept every anthropomorphic description of God that appeared in *aḥādīth al-ṣifāt*, even *ḥadīth ḥaqw al-raḥmān*.

As we have already seen in Ahmad ibn Hanbal's sullen response to Hisham ibn ᶜAmmar, the sole device that the traditionalists had at their disposal for handling texts such as *ḥadīth ḥaqw al-raḥmān* was the watertight *bi-lā kayfa* formula. A representative of tenth-century ultra-traditionalism in the Persian city of Rayy, the illustrious Hadith scholar Ibn Abi Hatim (d. 938) recorded a conversation about *ḥadīth ḥaqw al-raḥmān* that he had with his father Abu Hatim al-Razi (d. 890), a great Hadith scholar in his own right. From the son's question, the father responded by invoking the *bi-lā kayfa* formula:

> I asked my father about the interpretation of the Prophetic *ḥadīth*: 'The *raḥim* is derived from *al-Raḥmān* and she seized the loin of the Merciful.' My father answered: 'Al-Zuhri (d. 742) said: "The duty of the Prophet is to deliver the message, and our duty is to accept it." He used to say: "Transmit the Hadith of the Messenger of God exactly as you received it."'[158]

Following this brief dialogue, Ibn Abi Hatim quoted two additional anecdotes which corroborated his father's position. In the first anecdote, the *muḥaddith* from Basra Sulayman ibn Tarkhan al-Taymi (d. 761) recounted that the *ṣaḥāba* hated to interpret the Hadith of the Messenger of God by expressing their own personal opinion, just as they hated to interpret the Quran by expressing their own views.[159] Sulayman's anecdote reflected the traditionalistic paradigm and not a historical fact. More conceivable was the second anecdote that Ibn Abi Hatim quoted. In this anecdote, al-Walid ibn Muslim (d. 810), a well-known and highly respected scholar (he was nicknamed *ᶜālim ahl al-shām*, 'the Scholar of the People of Syria'), testified that he asked the great luminaries of his time about 'those *aḥādīth* about the divine attributes, the beatific vision, and the Quran'. According to al-Walid, all these scholars unanimously replied: 'Transmit them exactly as you received them, *bi-lā kayfa*.' In other words, these scholars rejected any possibility of interpreting or altering these texts. The scholars whose opinion al-Walid sought were al-Awzaᶜi from Damascus, Sufyan al-Thawri from Kufa, Malik ibn Anas from Medina and al-Layth ibn Saᶜd from Cairo.[160] Al-Walid's mention of these scholars was symbolic: he wished to demonstrate that the term *bi-lā kayfa* was coined by the scholars of the eighth century, unanimously accepted and, more importantly, that the formula rapidly spread far and wide. Following Walid's line of thought, we can say that the *bi-lā kayfa* formula exceeded the limits of the Medinese hardcore traditionalism from which it originated with the teachings of Malik ibn Anas. Moreover, the traditionalistic *bi-lā kayfa* formula endured for centuries in the sessions of Hadith transmission.

Bi-lā kayfa was a brilliant slogan that represented a brilliant idea. Its formula was used in the oral sessions of the *muḥaddithūn* and it appeared in theological treatises from the ninth century such as *Al-Radd ᶜalā al-Zanādiqa* (a polemical response to the Muᶜtazilites, attributed to Ahmad ibn Hanbal) and *Naqḍ al-Imām* (authored by Abu Saᶜid al-Darimi).[161] By the tenth century this phrase was well established in the Hanbalite discourse: the leader of the Hanbalites of Baghdad, al-Hasan ibn ᶜAli al-Barbahari (d. 941), used this term in his long creed entitled *Sharḥ al-Sunna*:

> Know, may God have mercy upon you, that the Sunna does not tolerate the use of analogy. The Sunna does not speak in parables. One cannot trace any false conviction in the Sunna. [The Sunna merely requires] belief in the traditions of the Prophet without asking how (*bi-lā kayfa*), without interpretation, and without asking 'why?' and 'how?'[162]

The strict *bi-lā* formula did not serve as the correct response for all the possibilities of using *aḥādīth al-ṣifāt* in religious discourse. As already mentioned in Section I, the *muḥaddith* was expected to transmit the text exactly as it was transmitted to him, word for word and gesture for gesture. However, pressing issues sometimes forced him to paraphrase text. For example, the *muḥaddith* was compelled both to respond to the rationalists' objections and to articulate the most important articles of faith in a coherent, succinct way that would appeal to the masses.[163] In fact, Ibn Abi Hatim's question to his father includes such a paraphrase: he did not cite the two different texts precisely but soldered them into one single, new *ḥadīth*, namely: 'The *raḥim* is derived from *al-Raḥmān* and she seized the loin of the Merciful.'

Paraphrasing text was a common occurrence in the oral transmissions of the *muḥaddithūn* and formed a part of the regular exchange between the scholar and his disciples. Thus, when the eponymous founder of the Shafiᶜite school, Muhammad ibn Idris al-Shafiᶜi (d. 820), was asked by his students about *aḥādīth al-ṣifāt*, he provided a description constructed with citations from the Quran and paraphrases of *aḥādīth al-ṣifāt*. According to al-Shafiᶜi's description, God has two hands and both are outstretched (Q. 5:64), He has one right hand (Q. 39:67), He will place His foot in Hell, and He will laugh.[164] The last two descriptions paraphrase two Prophetic *aḥādīth*. The first *ḥadīth* alludes to the Day of Resurrection and expounds on Q. 50:30 ('On that day, We shall ask Hell: "Are you full?" And Hell will answer: "Are there any more?"'). According to this *ḥadīth*, Hell will not feel complete – even after all the heretics were tossed into its fire – until God places His foot in Hell.[165] The second *ḥadīth* (or rather, a cluster of *aḥādīth*) describes the Prophet's promise to the martyr that he will meet God, and God will laugh at his presence.[166]

The need to paraphrase text also created a new genre, the *ᶜaqīda*, or creed (see Ibn Qutayba's creed in this chapter, Section 1). The earliest creeds were created in the circles of lenient Hanafism, but as a new genre they were warmly embraced by all the traditionalistic groups, including Hanbalism.[167] As a product of the process of gathering the textual sources, sifting through them and emphasising the importance of a select few texts, some of these creeds contained paraphrased descriptions of God, which were based on *aḥādīth al-ṣifāt*. However, even the Hanbalite scholars refrained from adapting *ḥadīth ḥaqw al-Raḥmān* in their creeds. One of the six creeds attributed to Ahmad ibn Hanbal contains the following description of God, as translated by Christopher Melchert:

> God (mighty and glorious is He) has a throne, while the Throne has bearers who bear it. God (mighty and glorious is He) is on His throne . . . He moves, speaks, observes, looks, laughs, joys, and loves . . . He descends every night to the lowest heaven however He will . . . The servants' hearts are between two of the Most-Merciful's fingers . . . He created Adam with His hand and in His image. The heavens and earth on the Day of Resurrection are in His hand. He will put His foot in the fire, causing it to recoil . . . 'And

God spoke to Moses directly' (Q. 4:164) by His mouth. He gave Him the *Tawrāh* from His hand to his hand.[168]

Clearly, this section of the creed was inspired by the bulk of *aḥādīth* that referred to God's laughter, the numerous versions of *ḥadīth al-nuzūl*, the various *aḥādīth* that mention the divine fingers, and related anthropomorphic descriptions. This section does not contain any reference to the loin of the Merciful. The six Hanbalite creeds that were attributed to Ahmad ibn Hanbal were actually written in the decades following his death.[169] However, they reflected the essential parts of the ultra-traditionalistic dogma, if not the actual theological thought of Ahmad ibn Hanbal. The absence of this *ḥadīth* from the schematic texts of the six Hanbalite creeds indicates that Ahmad ibn Hanbal and the other traditionalists treated *ḥadīth ḥaqw al-Raḥmān* cautiously. Understandably, any paraphrase of this *ḥadīth* (as opposed to other *aḥādīth al-ṣifāt*) would have enhanced the embarrassment that accompanied it.

Such embarrassment, apparently, was not the concern of other traditionalists. One of the most prominent Hanbalites of the tenth century, Abu ᶜAbd Allah al-Hasan ibn al-Hamid al-Warraq (d. 1013), also referred to as *shaykh al-ḥanābila*, cited this *ḥadīth* in one of his books which unfortunately no longer exists.[170] According to the prominent Hanbalite scholar Abu Yaᶜla, Abu ᶜAbd Allah adhered to the literal meaning of the text (*akhadha bi-ẓāhirihi*) in the case of *ḥadīth ḥaqw al-raḥmān*. Abu Yaᶜla ruled that Abu ᶜAbd Allah's approach was faithful to the teachings of Ahmad ibn Hanbal.[171] To corroborate his and Abu ᶜAbd Allah's position, Abu Yaᶜla recounted the story of the anonymous letter of complaint which arrived from Damascus to Ahmad ibn Hanbal. Abu Yaᶜla's strategy of connecting the two anecdotes, the one about Abu ᶜAbd Allah al-Warraq and the one about the letter of the Damascenes that was sent to Ahmad ibn Hanbal, led his readers to the conclusion that by understanding this *ḥadīth* literally, Abu ᶜAbd Allah followed Ahmad ibn Hanbal's directive regarding this *ḥadīth*. This directive was: 'The text of this *ḥadīth* should be transmitted exactly as it was received.'[172] Of course, the question as to the 'literal meaning' of *ḥadīth ḥaqw al-raḥmān* remained open, as Abu Yaᶜla did not elaborate on this point.

The Hanbalite theologian Ibn al-Jawzi added a noteworthy and rare remark to the narrative provided by Abu Yaʿla. In contrast to Abu Yaʿla, who was the cherished disciple of Abu ʿAbd Allah, Ibn al-Jawzi severely criticised Abu ʿAbd Allah and held him responsible for introducing anthropomorphic traditions into the Hanbalite discourse.[173] According to Ibn al-Jawzi, 'Ibn Hamid (i.e. Abu ʿAbd Allah) said: It is essential to affirm that God indeed has a loin and that the *raḥim* actually seizes it.'[174] This affirmation by Abu ʿAbd Allah is obviously a paraphrase of the *ḥadīth*. Nevertheless, since Ibn al-Jawzi's ultimate goal was to wage war against the use of anthropomorphisms in the Hanbalite discourse, his citation of Abu ʿAbd Allah should be taken with a grain of salt, unless some other impartial source is discovered. The absence of similar evidence of different scholars paraphrasing *ḥadīth ḥaqw al-raḥmān* indicates that it was not a *natural* part of the traditionalistic discourse; nonetheless, it formed a part of this discourse.

Abu ʿAbd Allah's readiness to recite the embarrassing expression and to literally insert the concept of 'the loin of the Merciful' into the traditionalistic discourse is explained by the traditionalistic *bi-lā kayfa*. But what was the theological or ideological justification for Abu Zayd's approach? We cannot claim that it was sheer embarrassment that led Abu Zayd to avoid reciting the problematic expression altogether, because embarrassment is a poor theological argumentation. Perhaps the appropriateness of discourse when describing God was a better explanation? In contrast to Abu ʿAbd Allah's controversial approach, which was limited to the circle of the ultra-traditionalistic Hanbalites, Abu Zayd's approach to *ḥadīth ḥaqw al-raḥmān* was much greater than a mere curiosity. Abu Zayd was a prominent *muḥaddith* who educated a broad-based generation of scholars in many places. Furthermore, we know that he was fond of travelling and teaching *Ṣaḥīḥ al-Bukhārī* wherever he went.[175] Therefore, we assume that his approach to this *ḥadīth* accompanied him and spread throughout the Islamic world. In fact, the anonymous interpreter who said that the *raḥim* 'seized one of the legs of the throne' (*akhadat bi-qāʾima min qawāʾim al-ʿarsh*), based his choice of words on Abu Zayd's approach.[176]

The reason Abu Zayd refused to recite the problematic expression is not specified in Ibn Hajar's text. Al-Qastallani, who recorded an extended version of al-Qabisi's testimony about Abu Zayd, solved the mystery of Abu Zayd's refusal. According to al-Qabisi in al-Qastallani's version, Abu Zayd said that the veracity of the expression 'the loin of the Merciful' was undeniable; however, when this expression was stated, the *muḥaddith* – any *muḥaddith* – must also have stated that God was above (*tanzīh*) this type of attribution. The concept of *tanzīh*, according to Abu Zayd, allowed the *muḥaddith* to omit the problematic expression.[177] Abu Zayd's systematic refusal to read the inappropriate attribute, his strict adherence to the exact text in *Ṣaḥīḥ al-Bukhāri* and his insistence that an expressed *tanzīh* should accompany the recitation of the text differentiated him from the strict traditionalistic line, the line expressed by Ahmad ibn Hanbal and others. In fact, Abu Zayd's *tanzīh* articulated the inappropriateness of attributing a loin to God.

The device by which Abu Zayd expressed this concept was to censor the text and to explain the reason for the censorship. While he accepted the text, he implicitly censured the traditionalists who cited *ḥadīth ḥaqw al-raḥmān* verbatim, without giving adequate thought to the problematic text. Abu Zayd's *tanzīh* reflects reconciliation with the problematic text by accepting the anthropomorphic expression without attributing physical qualities to God. This *tanzīh* is an embryonic version of the Ashᶜarite *bi-lā kayfa.* As R. M. Frank succinctly explains: 'For the Ašᶜarites . . . to understand the descriptions of God which occur in the revealed texts *bi-lā kayfa* is to read them with *tanzīh*, i.e., with the understanding that God's being transcends description by any expression as that expression is commonly used in talking about the world and the things of our normal experience – says Frank, and adds a citation from al-Tabari's *Taʾwīl al-Āyāt al-Mushkilāt* – "God may be described only by what is appropriate to Him".'[178] We are not surprised therefore to discover Abu Zayd's name among the list of the direct disciples of Abu 'l-Hasan al-Ashᶜari (d. 935–6), the eponymous founder of the Ashᶜarite school. The biographical sources also describe Abu Zayd, in the spirit of later Ashᶜarism, as a devoted Shafiᶜite (most educated Shafiᶜites affiliated themselves with the Ashᶜarite school), a skilful speculative theologian and a well-known ascetic.[179]

All three commentators of *Ṣaḥīḥ al-Bukhārī* promoted the same approach as Abu Zayd's in their commentaries to *ḥadīth ḥaqw al-raḥmān.* Under the wings of the all-inclusive *tanzīh*, these scholars presented a creative three-stage solution to the problem posed by *ḥadīth ḥaqw al-raḥmān.* Their solution is almost identical: al-ᶜAyni who was Ibn Hajar's nemesis, heavily relied on Ibn

Hajar's work with the expectation to produce a better one, and al-Qastallani freely used the texts of both Ibn Hajar and al-ᶜAyni.[180] The solution of Ibn Hajar, al-ᶜAyni and al-Qastallani comprised three stages, while each stage demonstrated a different level of finesse and subtlety. The first two stages were rigorous efforts to erase several aspects of the depicted scene in *ḥadīth ḥaqw al-raḥmān*. These stages were designed to blur the depicted scene and were directed to a wide audience of both scholars and laymen. The third and more sophisticated stage of the solution was designed for the professional theologians who were well-acquainted with the rhetorical devices that corroborated the Ashᶜarite terminology. Ibn Hajar, al-ᶜAyni and al-Qastallani mined only works of Quran and Hadith exegesis in their search for a solution. In other words, the highly controversial *kalām* manuals were utterly excluded from this discussion. Our three commentators were themselves representatives of traditionalistic Islam, but their proposed solution was inspired by the all-inclusive *tanzīh* and bore distinctive Ashᶜarite characteristics. However, to enable their solution to be widely accepted, they needed to disassociate it from the Ashᶜarite *kalām*.

The first and simplest stage of the solution was philological, and its aim was to point out that the original text suffered from an inherent misunderstanding. This stage proposed that *ḥaqw* did not mean 'loin' but rather 'a loincloth'. While Ibn Hajar and al-ᶜAyni vigorously and persuasively advanced this meaning, al-Qastallani was less decisive than his colleagues and permitted his readers to decide whether this solution was acceptable. Ibn Hajar and al-ᶜAyni based their ruling on a passage that they found in the work of the commentator of *Ṣaḥīḥ Muslim*, Qadi ᶜIyad.[181] As previously mentioned, *Ṣaḥīḥ Muslim* did not include the full version of *ḥadīth ḥaqw al-raḥmān*; therefore, Qadi ᶜIyad did not tackle the question of *ḥaqw al-raḥmān*. However, he provided an explanation of the word *ḥaqw* as it appeared in another *ḥadīth*. This *ḥadīth* mentioned that the Prophet gave his *ḥaqw* to the women who prepared his daughter's body for burial, and asked them to wrap her in it. Accordingly, Qadi ᶜIyad interpreted the word *ḥaqw* as a loincloth.[182] Elsewhere, and in a different context, he provided an extended euphemistic explanation for the word *ḥaqw*. According to Qadi ᶜIyad, *al-ḥaqw maᶜqid al-izār*, that is, the *ḥaqw* is the place on the waist on which the knot of the loincloth rests (*maᶜqid al-izār* or *mashadd al-izār*). He also added that the word *ḥaqw* was therefore interchangeable with the *izār*, and *ḥaqw* in itself denoted a loincloth.[183] These two meanings of *ḥaqw*, namely the *izār* and the *mashadd al-izār*, were mentioned by al-Qastallani, who did not reveal his source for the dual meaning of *ḥaqw*. However, al-Qastallani mentioned that *ḥaqw* is *ḥaṣr*, namely the human abdomen.[184]

According to the first stage of the solution, the picture depicted in *ḥadīth ḥaqw al-raḥmān* was of a *raḥim* (its precise definition was discussed in this chapter, Section II), seizing the side knot, the ties of the loincloth of the Merciful. However, the coarse anthropomorphism that this stage represented was unsatisfactory. Our three commentators then formed the second stage which was meant to deprive the depicted scene from any hint to the Merciful's physicality; after all, a loincloth indeed was meant to cover the loin! These commentators focused on the philological aspect of the text. Ibn Hajar and al-ᶜAyni again relied on Qadi ᶜIyad,[185] while al-Qastallani relied on the Shafiᶜite scholar and Quran exegete Nasir al-Din al-Baydawi (d. probably in 1286).[186] The technique was simple: to prove that the seizing of the *maᶜqid al-izār* was a figure of speech among the Arabs, and therefore no actual seizing of the Merciful's loincloth occurred. According to this approach, when a person seeks protection, refuge and help, he intensifies his appeal by grabbing the *izār* or the knot that ties the loincloth of his potential helper.[187] Qadi ᶜIyad added that this custom was held and respected among the Arabs, and was reflected in the figure of speech 'to seize one's loincloth'.[188] Ibn Hajar concluded: 'The correct meaning [of this expression] is according to this [explanation].' In addition, Ibn Hajar expressed the conviction that 'God is above having any body part (*tanzīh Allāh ᶜani 'l-jāriḥa*)'.[189] In other words, understating the anthropomorphic expression figuratively is the appropriate way to read this text, because this reading enables the reader to both accept the text and reject its literal understanding. This is the meaning of the all-inclusive *tanzīh*.

Al-Baydawi (whom al-Qastallani faithfully quoted) presented a more sceptical approach: he was uncertain whether grabbing the loincloth or grabbing the knot of the loincloth was indeed a familiar figure of speech in Arabic. Al-Baydawi accepted the concept that a person who begs for help would often grab the hems of the garment of the one from whom he seeks protection; however, grabbing another person's loincloth seemed unreasonable behaviour. Al-Baydawi raised the possibility that a person in need of protection might seize the side of the loincloth or the knot of the loincloth of another person, however not as a regular acceptable behaviour, but in rare and urgent cases. Al-Baydawi also explained that such behaviour was meant to exaggerate (*mubālagha*) the nature of the seeker's distress, and to pressure the potential provider of protection. Al-Baydawi suggested that this extreme gesture conveyed the message that the individual seeking protection wished that the other person 'would protect him and defend him from whichever might have befallen on him, just as he protected what was under his loincloth'.[190] Al-Baydawi's cautious language suggests that while he proposed this solution, he was not entirely convinced of its veracity and validity. In the closing sentence of his discussion, al-Baydawi also raised the possibility that this remarkable metaphor (*majāz*) was meant to demonstrate to the audience the meaning of the *raḥim*'s appeal to God 'in a way that was more easily understood to them and more likely to be firmly fixed in their souls'.[191] This closing sentence in itself indicates that al-Baydawi did not appreciate this line of argumentation and thought it was suitable for laymen.

The third stage of the solution was much more sophisticated than the first two stages. Once more, our three commentators copied the relevant passage discussing *ḥadīth ḥaqw al-raḥmān* almost verbatim from an earlier source; in this case it was *al-Kāshif ᶜan Ḥaqā᾿iq al-Sunan*, a Hadith commentary composed by the Persian scholar Sharaf al-Din al-Tibi (d. 1343) from the city of Tabriz in Azerbaijan.[192] Not much is known about al-Tibi, whose literary output is yet to be researched.[193] In addition, his theological affiliation is not specified in the biographical sources. As a Hadith expert, he probably affiliated himself with *ahl al-sunna wa'l-jamāᶜa*. Al-Tibi defended the fundamentals of Islamic traditionalism and attacked Muᶜtazilism in his commentary on *al-Kashshāf*, the Quran commentary of the Muᶜtazilite Jar Allah al-Zamakhsahri (d. 1144).[194]

Al-Tibi, however, was profoundly inspired by al-Zamakhshari's perception of divinity as completely abstract. In fact, al-Tibi credited al-Zamakhshari for leading him to the correct reading of *ḥadīth ḥaqw al-raḥmān*, although al-Zamakhshari did not discuss this *ḥadīth* but other anthropomorphic expressions in the Quran.[195] The combination of traditionalism (in al-Tibi's case, accepting *ḥadīth ḥaqw al-raḥmān*) and rationalism (applying the Muᶜtazilite protocol of figurative reading to the anthropomorphic expressions) is the essence of Ashᶜarism. There is no doubt that al-Tibi's approach to *ḥadīth ḥaqw al-raḥmān* followed the Ashᶜarite approach. Our three commentators, and primarily al-ᶜAyni, relied on al-Tibi's highly theoretical analysis to promote their figurative reading of *ḥadīth ḥaqw al-raḥmān* and in fact adopted his position. Al-Tibi directed his readers to avoid a literal reading of *ḥadīth ḥaqw al-raḥmān*; however, his discussion did not address the well-known theological implications of this literal reading. Rather, al-Tibi harnessed the vocabulary of rhetoric (*balāgha*) to promote his creative reading of the text.[196]

Al-Tibi starts his discussion with the assertion that the *raḥim* in this *ḥadīth* was an abstract concept (*maᶜnā min al-maᶜānī*) denoting kinship. This is the key to al-Tibi's reading of the *ḥadīth*. He perceives the entire scene of the dialogue between the *raḥim* and God as a double-layered parable comprising two types of metaphors: an analogy (*al-istiᶜāra al-tamthīliyya*) and an imaginary or a 'make-believe' metaphor (*al-istiᶜāra al-takhyīliyya*).[197] According to al-Tibi, the *raḥim* in the story (an abstract concept) was in distress; she complained that she lacked affection and protection. This grave situation was reflected through the seizing of *ḥaqw al-raḥmān*. According to Al-Tibi, the action of seizing did not occur; however, 'the seizing of *ḥaqw al-raḥmān*' was a figure of speech meant to emphasise the *raḥim*'s vigorous plea for help. The analogy was clear: the intensity of the *raḥim*'s pledge for help and protection was similar to the seizing of *ḥaqw al-raḥmān*. But since this was an analogy (*al-istiᶜāra al-tamthīliyya*), it was not a 'real' event in the narrative. This layer of the parable was clear and in fact resembled the reading of al-Baydawi. The second stage was more noteworthy: here, the 'make-believe' metaphor (*al-istiᶜāra al-takhyīliyya*) is identified as the *ḥadīth*'s inner logic, and points out that the entire narrative is imaginary. The pretence that the *raḥim* is a physical being dictates its depiction in the narrative as performing actions like any other physical being: she stands up, she talks and she seizes *ḥaqw al-raḥmān*; however, she does none of these actions, not even metaphorically. At this point, al-Tibi remarked that the *ḥaqw* is another metaphor; unfortunately, he did not specify its meaning.[198]

Al-Tibi's reading of the *ḥadīth ḥaqw al-raḥmān* as an imaginary tale was not unique. The reading offered by the Quran exegete Abu ᶜAbd Allah al-Qurtubi (d. 1272) during his discussion of Q. 47:22, preceded al-Tibi's reading. According to al-Qurtubi, there are two possibilities to read the sentence 'the *raḥim* stood up and said' (*qāmat al-raḥim wa-qālat*): the first possibility is that God appointed one of the angels to speak on the *raḥim*'s behalf; the second possibility is to read the entire text as a tale, namely 'had the *raḥim* been able to speak, she would have said these words'.[199] Al-Qurtubi, by the way, quoted the censored version of the *ḥadīth* from *Ṣaḥīḥ al-Bukhārī* and ignored the problematic uncensored version.

Al-Tibi's highly sophisticated discussion represents the third stage of the solution to *ḥadīth ḥaqw al-raḥmān*. In this stage, Al-Tibi illustrates the Ashᶜarites' major concern: to disassociate God from any physical characteristics (*tanzīh*). *Tanzīh* was the goal of the Ashᶜarites' intellectual efforts and the rationale behind the variety of techniques they developed in their discussions of *aḥādīth al-ṣifāt*. *Tanzīh*, which was the essence of the Ashᶜarite *bi-lā kayfa* formula,[200] enabled the inclusion of the most problematic texts in the Islamic canon. Indeed, in several later Ashᶜarite sources, *tanzīh* is mentioned as the second of the two major characteristics of the Ashᶜarite worldview. The first characteristic is *tawḥīd*, the belief in the unity of God. The Ashᶜarites in these later sources, therefore, referred to themselves as 'the People of Transcendence and Unity' (*ahl al-tanzīh wa'l-tawḥīd*). This sobriquet echoes the name 'The People of Justice and Unity' (*ahl al-ᶜadl wa'l-tawḥīd*) with which the Muᶜtazilites adorned themselves.[201]

V. Expanding the Borders of the Traditionalistic Discourse

Throughout this chapter, we mentioned several times the simplistic *bi-lā kayfa* formula that dominated the traditionalistic discourse and some of its more prominent manifestations. The simplistic *bi-lā kayfa* formula was a prohibition to ask questions. This prohibition, as we learned in earlier sections of this chapter, characterised the Hanbalite theological discourse. However, it was also embraced by al-Ashᶜari himself, and later became the first component of the more sophisticated *bi-lā kayfa* of the Ashᶜarites. Thus, we find the *bi-lā kayfa* formula in its simplistic form in *al-Ibāna*, a creed authored by al-Ashᶜari:

> [We confirm] that God sits enthroned on high, based on what He said: 'The Merciful who sits enthroned on high' [Q. 20:5]. [We confirm] that He has

> a face without asking how (*bi-lā kayfa*), based on what He said: 'But the face of your Lord will abide forever' [Q. 55:27]. [We confirm] without asking how that He has two hands, based on what He said 'My own hands have made' [Q. 38:75]. [We confirm] without asking how that He has an eye, according to what He said 'under Our watchful eyes' [Q. 11:37].[202]

The frequent mention of *bi-lā kayfa* (alongside other characteristics of this creed such as an attack on the Muᶜtazilites and the paraphrasing of *ḥadīth al-ruʾya*) makes this document a Hanbalite-type creed.[203] A similar passage appears in the creed of 'the People of the Hadith and the Sunna' (*aṣḥāb al-ḥadīth wa-ahl al-sunna*) that al-Ashᶜari included in his magnum opus *Maqālāt al-Islāmiyyīn*.[204] In this passage, al-Ashᶜari stated that the basic stance of 'the People of the Hadith and the Sunna' is a complete adherence to the authentic *aḥādīth* that were transmitted by the trustworthy *muḥaddithūn*. Al-Ashᶜari added that the *aḥādīth* should be accepted 'without asking how and why, because asking is an undesirable innovation' (*bidᶜa*).[205]

According to Hanbalite sources, al-Ashᶜari made these traditionalistic declarations out of pure pragmatism: he wanted to move his centre of activity from Basra to Baghdad and needed the approval of the powerful al-Hasan ibn Ali al-Barbahari. Al-Barbahari served at that time as *shaykh al-ṭāʾifa*, the leader of the Hanbalites of Baghdad.[206] Al-Barbahari was an important political figure who promoted a violent form of Hanbalite activism. He enjoyed an extremely wide support base: the masses in Baghdad were his fervent troops and the caliph himself was cautious not to aggravate this powerful man. Al-Barbahari led his followers to violent raids in his battle against wine, music, pretty girl singers, dancers and other 'abominations'.[207] Al-Ashᶜari (who was a former Muᶜtazilite) needed al-Barbahari's recognition that he, al-Ashᶜari, had become a loyal traditionalist (or perhaps, a Hanbalite) and that the citizens of Baghdad were permitted to participate in his lectures. Without this approval, al-Ashᶜari had no chance of gathering students to his classes.

Ibn Abi Yaᶜla (d. 1131), the Hanbalite author of the biographical dictionary of Hanbalite scholars, described the decisive meeting between al-Barbahari and al-Ashᶜari that drove al-Ashᶜari to compose the highly traditionalistic *al-Ibāna*. Al-Ashᶜari is depicted in the following passage in an unflattering light. He is portrayed as a former *mutakallim* boasting of his success in the theological debates with the Muᶜtazilites and the members of other religions. In this passage Al-Ashᶜari mentions refuting the views of his celebrated teacher Abu ᶜAli al-Jubbaᵓi (d. 915–16), the head of the Muᶜtazilites of Basra, and his son Abu Hashim al-Jubbaᵓi (d. 933). Abu Hashim, who later succeeded his father as head of the Muᶜtazilites of Basra, was al-Ashᶜari's study-mate and colleague. It is noteworthy that al-Barbahari remains indifferent to al-Ashᶜari's boasting and shows no interest in *kalām*:

> When al-Ashᶜari entered Baghdad, he came to al-Barbahari and said: 'I succeeded in refuting the views of al-Jubbaᵓi and Abu Hashim. I harshly refuted their claims. I also refuted the Jews, the Christians, and the Magians. I said this and that to them, and they answered this and that.' Al-Ashᶜari went on and on, and when he finally finished talking, al-Barbahari said: 'I have absolutely no idea about the things you talked about. We only know what Abu ᶜAbd Allah Ahmad Ibn Hanbal said.' Al-Ashᶜari hurried out and composed *al-Ibāna*, but al-Barbahari refused to accept it from him. Thereafter, al-Ashᶜari could enter Baghdad only whenever al-Barbahari was out of the city.[208]

The Damascene historian Ibn ᶜAsakir (d. 1176), who was a fervent Ashᶜarite, refuted this report about al-Ashᶜari and posed well-reasoned arguments against it. Ibn ᶜAsakir remarked that the idea that al-Ashᶜari could not have entered Baghdad as long as al-Barbahari was there was inconceivable. According to Ibn ᶜAsakir, there were reports that al-Ashᶜari participated in a study circle of Hadith every Friday in the west wing of the mosque named after the caliph al-Mansur in Baghdad. Ibn ᶜAsakir added that there was no doubt that al-Ashᶜari made Baghdad his home after he left Basra (his conversion occurred in 912–3; however, his emigration date to Baghdad is unknown).[209] Ibn ᶜAsakir also dismissed the possibility that *al-Ibāna* was a product of the cold calculations of its author and that al-Ashᶜari in fact did not believe in what that text stated. He remarked that it was inconceivable that a Muslim would compose a book the contents of which he does not believe, and that this book would survive after its author. In other words, if writing *al-Ibāna* was merely a ploy, al-Ashᶜari or his students would have destroyed the book. However – claimed Ibn ᶜAsakir – *al-Ibāna* indeed reflected the Ashᶜarite viewpoint. By using this text – continued Ibn ᶜAsakir – the Ashᶜarites defended the fundamentals of Islamic traditionalism.[210]

Ibn ᶜAsakir's enthusiastic defence of *al-Ibāna* aside, one cannot ignore that *al-Ibāna* represented only one of the two facets of Ashᶜarism, that of accepting the anthropomorphic Hadith material 'without asking how', *bi-lā kayfa*. The other facet, that of figurative reading (*taʾwīl*), was completely absent from this text. Given the strong traditionalistic flavour of *al-Ibāna*, the anecdote about the meeting between al-Ashᶜari and al-Barbahari probably holds more than a grain of truth. Being a former Muᶜtazilite, al-Ashᶜari should have taken a step that symbolised his 'conversion' to the Islamic traditionalism or his repentance (*tawba*) from his Muᶜtazilism: a written creed was an appropriate step. *Al-Ibāna* was not a ploy: it reflected the authentic concerns of al-Ashᶜari, but simultaneously, it emphasised the issues that appealed to the Hanbalites. One of the main concerns that al-Ashᶜari has in *al-Ibāna* is to expand the variety of the divine attributes so they include the anthropomorphic descriptions in the Quran and the Hadith.[211] This expansion corresponds with the Hanbalite position which sees the anthropomorphic descriptions as undeniable parts of the divine attributes.[212] According to one of the later Ashᶜarites who analysed al-Ashᶜari's position, al-Ashᶜari saw the inclusion of the hand, the face and the eye in the divine attributes as a middle way between the blunt anthropomorphism of the Hashwiyya and the figurative reading of the Muᶜtazilites.[213]

We find that the creed in *al-Ibāna* was therefore authored especially for the Hanbalite 'commissar'. This is evident especially in the sections in which al-Ashᶜari paraphrases *ḥadīth al-ruʾya* and systematically refutes the Muᶜtazilite claim against the beatific vision.[214] As discussed in Chapter 2, this *ḥadīth* was one of the topics on which Ahmad ibn Hanbal was interrogated during the *miḥna*. By emphasising his unequivocal belief in this *ḥadīth*, al-Ashᶜari signalled to al-Barbahari that he was now a fully fledged Hanbalite, and that he had left his Muᶜtazilite past behind him.[215] Other sections in *al-Ibāna* were also written for the Hanbalite taste: according to *al-Ibāna*, 'God sits enthroned on high' means that God is high above the heavens or that He is in the sky.[216] However, unlike the Hanbalite methodology, al-Ashᶜari provided several logical explanations for his position. According to one of these explanations, God sits on the throne and not on 'everything which is on this earth' (like the Muᶜtazilites and the other rationalists claimed) simply because the claim that He could be anywhere entails that He was even sitting in the latrines (*ḥushūsh*).[217] Al-Ashᶜari's argumentation combined both basic logic and his perception of the appropriateness of the discourse about God. Al-Ashᶜari did not name his approach – which sought to disassociate any improper description from God – *tanzīh*. On the contrary, al-Ashᶜari exclaimed: 'God save us from *tanzīh* that necessarily entails the negation of the attributes, namely *taᶜṭīl*!'[218] However, as demonstrated in Section IV of this chapter, his successors would follow al-Ashᶜari's approach to the appropriateness of the discourse about God while giving this approach the name *tanzīh*.[219]

As for *aḥādīth al-ṣifāt*, although al-Ashᶜari cites several of these texts in *al-Ibāna*, he does not provide any insightful reading of them. The richness of the discussion of *aḥādīth al-ṣifāt* which appears in Ibn Qutayba's *Taʾwīl Mukhtalif al-Ḥadīth*, and the creative solutions offered by the Hadith scholars from the ninth century onward which also appear in this chapter, are completely absent from *al-Ibāna*. For example, al-Ashᶜari mentions the *ḥadīth* of the black slave-girl (see Chapter 3) as textual evidence of God's aboveness, but does not discuss the text.[220] Likewise, concerning the *ḥadīth* about God holding the hearts of the believers between two of His fingers and the *ḥadīth* of the divine fingers: Al-Ashᶜari professes his acceptance of these texts and does not provide any insights into the difficulties that these texts pose.[221] The only exception is al-Ashᶜari's lengthy discussion on God's two hands, which relies on the relevant Quranic verses ('The hand of God is above their hands', Q. 48:10; 'My own hand have made', Q. 38:75; 'His hands are both outstretched', Q. 5:64; 'We would have seized him by the right hand', Q. 69:45; and 'We built the heaven with Our hands', Q. 51:47)[222] and the Prophetic *ḥadīth* 'Both His hands are two right hands' (see Chapter 4, Section I).[223] Al-Ashᶜari negates the figurative reading of these texts and dismisses the possibility of interpreting the divine hand as the divine power. He therefore negates the original Muᶜtazilite *taʾwīl*.[224] At the same time, he negates the *tashbīh* of the ultra-traditionalists and rules out the possibility of conceiving God's hand as a body organ.[225] In comparison to Ibn Qutayba's harsh criticism of the way in which the ultra-traditionalists read *aḥādīth al-ṣifāt*, al-Ashᶜari's reference to this subject is insinuated and virtually nonexistent.

The Mushabbiha, the vulgar anthropomorphists, do not appear in *al-Ibāna* at all. Their absence can be explained, of course, by the political atmosphere that prevailed in Baghdad in al-Barbahari's times: it would have been extremely unwise for al-Ashᶜari to dismiss the anthropomorphic Hadith material that the Hanbalites embraced and call for stricter criteria of Hadith transmission. This was the stance that Ibn Qutayba took, several decades before al-Ashᶜari composed *al-Ibāna*. The consequences of al-Ashᶜari adopting a similar stance could have been extremely severe for him and his disciples (see al-Tabari's case as described in the Introduction).

The creed in *al-Ibāna* did not reflect the reading strategies that al-Ashᶜari most probably applied to the anthropomorphic texts. A glimpse of these strategies is provided by the Ashᶜarite theologian Muhammad ibn al-Hasan ibn Furak (d. 1015) from Isfahan. In a bulky treatise entitled *Mujarrad Maqālāt al-Ashᶜarī*, Ibn Furak claimed to have summarised Abu 'l-Hasan al-Ashᶜari's views on a variety of theological issues.[226] On the issue of the divine attributes, the *Mujarrad* is one of the most important sources from which to learn al-Ashᶜari's views. Although this allegedly faithful recording of al-Ashᶜari's teachings by Ibn Furak includes several figurative readings of the anthropomorphic texts (al-Ashᶜari recommended reading the divine hands in Q. 51:47 as the divine power, the opposite of what he declared in *al-Ibāna*),[227] the technique of figurative reading is not the centre of discussion in the *Mujarrad*. Rather, in this text, al-Ashᶜari provides the theoretical reasoning for applying such a technique to the anthropomorphic texts in the Quran and the Hadith. He describes his reasoning in the form of four general rules.

These rules (according to the written testimony of Ibn Furak), which appear in the course of the discussion of the divine attributes, are applicable to both *āyāt al-ṣifāt* and *aḥādīth al-ṣifāt*. According to the first rule, God's perfection (*kamāl*) entails the existence of some of the divine attributes in Him. Among the eight attributes that describe God in the scriptures, there are four attributes that should be confirmed, because their absence implies imperfection of the divine essence (*al-naqṣ ᶜan dhātihi*). These four attributes (His hearing, His seeing, His speech and His endurance – *baqāʾ*) are added to the four attributes that represent His actions and His essence (His life, His knowledge, His power and His will). The second rule determines that the anthropomorphisms in the Quran that are attributed to God such as His two hands, face, side and eye should be confirmed in a way which befits God, who is described by these attributes (*ᶜalā ḥasab mā yalīq bi'l-mawṣūf bi-hā*). The proper discourse obligates seeing these words as descriptions and attributes (*nuᶜūt wa-ṣifāt*), and not as body organs, like the hands of humans. The third rule refers to other attributes such as sitting on the throne (*istiwāʾ*) and descending into the lower heavens (*nuzūl*). These attributes appear both in the Quran and the Hadith. According to Ibn Furak, al-Ashᶜari said that although our knowledge of these attributes comes from the texts, an intellectual effort is required in order to explain them. This rule, however, is relevant only to the Quran and the massively transmitted *aḥādīth* (*al-akhbār al-mutawātira*). According to al-Ashᶜari, the attributes of God that are mentioned in the *aḥādīth* with few transmitters (*akhbār al-āḥād*) may or may not exist. In other words, these *aḥādīth* provide information which is probable and not evident and conclusive.[228] As described by Ibn Furak, this approach explains why al-Ashᶜari did not include God's laughter among the divine attributes in his creed in *al-Ibāna*. Al-Ashᶜari's rejection of a corpus of *aḥādīth al-ṣifāt* which was proliferated by merely a handful of the Prophet's companions is in fact a critique addressed to the Hanbalites. The Hanbalites wholeheartedly embraced *aḥādīth al-ṣifāt* whose veracity was questioned by other Hadith scholars. The *ḥadīth* of allegiance, attributed to Abu Razin, is one of the conspicuous examples of this questionable material.

The most important rule that Ibn Furak attributes to al-Ashᶜari is derived from the theologian's perception that Arabic is double-layered. Here we must remark that al-Ashᶜari's perception of the language was profound and emenated from his long time interest in the philosophical question of the origins of languages. In his defining article from 1974, Bernard Weiss clarified that al-Ashᶜari, following his former teacher al-Jubbaʾi, was a proponent of the 'revelationist' theory (*tawqīf*). According to this theory, language was originially revealed to man by God. This theory stood amid heated discussions among the Muᶜtazilites of Basra and, prior to them, among the early *mutakallimūn*. In fact, al-Jubbaʾi's son, Abu Hashim (who was also al-Ashᶜari's fellow-student when al-Ashᶜari practiced Muᶜtazilite *kalām*), challenged his father and advanced the 'conventionalist' theory (*iṣṭilāḥ*) according to which language is a social convention.[229]

The divine origin of language notwithstanding, al-Ashᶜari saw no fundamental difference between the everyday Arabic discourse (*khiṭāb*) and the language of the Quran and the Hadith. As far as al-Ashᶜari was concerned, the Arabic language comprised both the proper sense of the word (*ḥaqīqa*) and the metaphor (*majāz*).[230] At the onset of the Arabic language, words carried only their proper sense. Gradually, a metaphor grew (*ṭāriʾ*; literally, occurred) as a branch (*farᶜ*) from the proper sense of quite a number of words.[231] According to al-Ashᶜari's description, some of the scholars decided to withhold their judgement regarding the *ḥaqīqa* and *majāz*; when a problematic expression occurred, they did not rule whether the reader should accept its literal or figurative meaning.[232] Al-Ashᶜari found this approach reprehensible. He believed that the metaphor can be deciphered, whether through investing intellectual efforts or through comparing the text with other relevant works.[233] In other words, al-Ashᶜari accepted the basic hermeneutical principle of the Muᶜtzilites, that of *majāz*. Al-Ashᶜari's *bi-lā kayfa* formula, therefore, was probably much more expanded than the formula that he presented in *al-Ibāna*: it comprised the simplistic *bi-lā kayfa* formula alongside the use of *taʾwīl*, the figurative reading that al-Ashᶜari borrowed from the Muᶜtazilites. However, while the Muᶜtazilites applied *taʾwīl* only to the anthropomorphic verses in the Quran, al-Ashᶜari was probably willing to apply *taʾwīl* to *aḥādīth al-ṣifāt*. Unfortunately, we do not have direct evidence for al-Ashᶜari's *bi-lā kayfa* formula except from the approach that Ibn Furak presented as al-Ashᶜari's. Ibn Furak embraced the expanded formula and applied it to a huge collection of *aḥādīth al-ṣifāt*. By doing so, Ibn Furak expanded the borders of the traditionalistic discourse and paved the way for the inclusion of blunt anthropomorphic traditions in the Islamic canon.

A few words about Ibn Furak are appropriate here.[234] Ibn Furak's name is usually connected to the names of Abu Ishaq al-Isfarayini (d. 1027) from Isfarayin in northeast Iran and Abu Bakr al-Baqillani (d. 1013) from Basra. Ibn Furak, who was originally from Isfahan, studied Ashᶜarite *kalām* with al-Baqillani and al-Isfarayini in Baghdad under the tutorage of Abu 'l-Hasan al-Bahili (d. 980). Al-Bahili, a direct disciple of al-Ashᶜari, was an eccentric (*wālih wa-majnūn*) devout scholar, who delivered his lectures while sitting behind a screen.[235] Al-Bahili left no written legacy; however, his students were considered three of the greatest luminaries of their times. Recognition of the trio's visibility as prominent theologians is reflected in the rhymed aphorism attributed to the Muᶜtazilite al-Sahib ibn ᶜAbbad (d. 995): 'Ibn al-Baqillani is a deep ocean (*baḥr mughriq*). Ibn Furak is a viper, spitting its poison (*ṣill muṭriq*). Al-Isfarayini is an all-consuming fire (*nār taḥriq*).' This obviously unflattering rhyme should be taken here with several grains of salt: only Ibn al-Baqillani's scholarship and vast knowledge are actually appreciated here, while Ibn Furak and al-Isfrayini are portrayed as a quiet agitator and an over-enthusiastic eccentric, respectively. Nevertheless, this aphorism – which is quoted in two important Ashᶜarite sources – attests to their prominence as public figures.[236]

Ibn Furak and his friend al-Isfarayini were invited by the rich bourgeoisie of Nishapur to teach in two madrasas that were built especially for them. Nishapur in East Iran was an important centre of commerce and intellectual activities. At least in the case of Ibn Furak, we know that the elite of Nishapur wanted to save the Ashᶜarite scholar from the ordeal (*miḥna)* that he was subjected to while he stayed in the city of Rayy in North Iran. Apparently, Ibn Furak suffered harassments from the Karramites, a rationalistic group who held extreme corporealistic (not anthropomorphic) views.[237] The Shafiᶜites of Nishapur, having heard about Ibn Furak's difficulties with the Karramites, made an appeal to the governor of Khurasan, and the governor built a madrasa for Ibn Furak. Ibn Furak's madrasa was a fine establishment; however, the madrasa that the emir built for al-Isfarayini was exceptionally grandiose.[238] The two Ashᶜarite scholars settled in Nishapur and married into the most prominent families in the city, thus establishing their social stature among the town's elite. They in fact introduced Ashᶜarite *kalām* to Nishapur, which in a few decades would become one of the most important centres of Ashᶜarism.[239]

In his haven in Nishapur, Ibn Furak comfortably developed a reading methodology of the anthropomorphic Hadith material. His *Mushkil al-Ḥadīth aw Taʾwīl al-Akhbār al-Mutashābiha* (The Figurative Interpretation of the Ambiguous Hadith Material), one of the most famous works of Ashᶜarite *taʾwīl*, is dedicated to a systematic reading of *aḥādīth al-ṣifāt* in the spirit of the hermeneutical rules that were established by al-Ashᶜari. Michel Allard remarks that *Mushkil al-Ḥadīth* (this title is but one of the many titles attributed to this work)[240] was written against the backdrop of the clash between

Ibn Furak and the Karramites of Rayy.[241] However, *Mushkil al-Ḥadīth* also reflects Ibn Furak's concerns about the literal reading of *aḥādīth al-ṣifāt* that prevailed among the ultra-traditionalists. Thus, for example, Ibn Furak dedicated a large portion of his book to the ultra-traditionalist Ibn Khuzayma and his *Kitāb al-Tawḥīd*, one of the most important collections of anthropomorphic traditions (see Chapter 3, Section II and Chapter 5, Section II). Ibn Furak systematically refuted Ibn Khuzayma's literal reading of the anthropomorphic traditions, while presenting the figurative reading as the most appropriate alternative for understanding these texts.[242] In addition, Ibn Furak was equally concerned about the Muᶜtazilite approach of negating the divine attributes, and more so, their rejection of the entire corpus of *aḥādīth al-ṣifāt*. *Mushkil al-Ḥadīth*, therefore, represents a firm defence of *aḥādīth al-ṣifāt* and a fierce attack against both the rationalists and the ultra-traditionalists.[243]

Ibn Furak believed that *aḥādīth al-ṣifāt* should be discussed for one purpose only: to enable scholars to completely accept and confirm (*taḥqīq wa-tathbīt*) their content. He rejected the possibility of refuting or rejecting a *ḥadīth* which was already widely accepted as authentic (as did the Muᶜtazilites with *ḥadīth al-ruʾya*, for example). Since Ibn Furak was sensitive to the problematic content of these texts, he believed that the goal of *taḥqīq wa-tathbīt* could be achieved only through the hermeneutical mechanism of *taʾwīl*. This mechanism secures the discourse about God: it eliminates any possible understanding of the anthropomorphic expressions as actual body organs of God, and it does not imply that God is less than perfect.[244] This approach can also be referred to as the all-inclusive *tanzīh*. Ibn Furak's approach defied the traditionalistic *bi-lā kayfa*: he believed that *aḥādīth al-ṣifāt* required reasonable explanations of their content and that an intelligent person could not be satisfied with the prohibition to ask questions about the divine attributes. The option of accepting these texts without deeply contemplating their content and investigating their problematic descriptions of God seemed inconceivable to Ibn Furak, especially in light of the attacks of the sophisticated rationalists (Khawarij, Muᶜtazilites, Shiᶜites and Karramites) on these texts. Ibn Furak believed that it was possible to find strong argumentations in favour of the content of these texts, although this task required a lot of effort.[245]

Ibn Furak's *taʾwīl* is a flexible approach to the anthropomorphic text and it is not restricted to the device of figurative reading. Naturally, Ibn Furak invested his intellectual efforts into identifying the metaphorical layer of the anthropomorphic descriptions. Thus, for instance, he toiled to prove that God's laughter was actually God's grace, and God's eye and ear were the divine attributes of hearing and seeing (which were among the eight attributes that al-Ashᶜari defined).[246] When the limited possibilities to provide a figurative interpretation of the anthropomorphic texts were exhausted, Ibn Furak turned to the recourse of creative interpretation. He offered a wide selection of argumentations to achieve the desirable *taḥqīq wa-tathbīt* while strictly maintaining *tanzīh*, namely describing God in an appropriate language. For example, let us consider the gesture of the black slave-girl who pointed with her finger to the sky, thus implying that God was actually in heaven. Ibn Furak explained that the girl meant that God's presence in heaven was a metaphor of His lofty and exalted status, in comparison to all creatures. Ibn Furak further suggested that the girl was probably deaf, and that by pointing with her finger she did not mean that God was actually in heaven.[247]

Another example of Ibn Furak's creative reading is his discussion of the variants of the *ḥadīth* 'I saw my Lord in the form of a curly beardless young man, wearing a green garb' (see Chapter 3, Section IV). This *ḥadīth* is undoubtedly the centrepiece of the anthropomorphic material and one cannot imagine how it is possible to read it figuratively. Ibn Furak's reading is therefore refreshing and surprising. He examined two possibilities that were completely detached from any literal understanding of the text: the first possibility was to interpret the young man in this *ḥadīth* as God, and the second possibility was to interpret him as the Prophet. As for the first possibility, Ibn Furak explained that this *ḥadīth* and its variants were meant to emphasise the Prophet's profound piety and submission to God, and the fact that the Prophet indeed was blessed by the beatific vision. Ibn Furak's reading here is quite creative, because he recruits the theological concept of Prophetic infallibility (*ᶜiṣma*) to read this problematic text.[248] Ibn Furak claimed that during the ascension to heaven (*al-miᶜrāj*) and the visit in Paradise, the Prophet witnessed beautiful sights like the young man wearing a green or red garb, sitting on a golden throne, his crown decorated with pearls, golden sandals on his feet and a golden veil on his face. However, the Prophet was not distracted by these sights and in every sight he had seen God. Thus, 'I had seen my Lord in the form of a beardless young man wearing a red garb', does not mean that God was in the form of a young man, but that the Prophet saw God, who is indescribable, through and even despite the presence of the beautiful form that was revealed to him. This was God's grace to the Prophet: he created the Prophet infallible (*ma^{c}ṣūm*) and immune from all desires. Therefore the Prophet's mind was not distracted. Extremely focused in his belief, he knew how to see God beyond the beautiful forms that God had created for him.[249]

The second possibility, of seeing the young man in the *ḥadīth* as the Prophet himself, offers another creative reading of the text. Here, Ibn Furak applied the grammatical rule of *ḥāl*, namely the state or condition of the subject or the object in a given sentence.[250] Ibn Furak read the *aḥādīth* in the spirit of the famous grammatical example 'I saw Zayd riding' (*ra$^{\circ}$aytu zaydan rākiban*). Thus, the *ḥadīth* 'I saw my Lord in the form of a curly beardless young man' should therefore be understood as 'I saw my Lord *when I was* in the form of a curly beardless young man'.[251]

Ibn Furak's creative reading enabled him to include even the *aḥādīth* of dubious origin in the Ash^{c}arite syllabus. His motives were not antiquarian – he was not interested in collecting as many *aḥādīth* as possible – but educational. Thus, he mentioned the spiritual and moral lessons (*fā$^{\circ}$ida*, lit. benefit) of the texts. In the case of the *ḥadīth* about God as a curly young man, Ibn Furak provided a description of the Prophet's mental state during the scene of the beatific vision:

> When he (i.e. the Prophet) saw God, he felt stable, empowered and confident, so this scene did not frighten, disturb or humiliate him . . . The lesson of this *ḥadīth* is to know that it was God who granted him these stability and reassurance.[252]

Ibn Furak's flexible approach to *aḥādīth al-ṣifāt*, however, did not mean that he was willing to lower his professional standards. During his discussion of the *ḥadīth* of God as a curly young man, Ibn Furak did not claim that the luscious descriptions in this *ḥadīth* and its variants are metaphors of divine attributes. Moreover, he refused to include these descriptions in the list of 'authorised' *ṣifāt*, like the divine hand, eye and face, because the variants of this *ḥadīth* were transmitted by only a few transmitters (*akhbār al-āḥād*). This fact – claimed Ibn Furak – does not allow the Hadith scholars to draw any conclusive information (*lam yuqṭaᶜ 'l-ᶜudhr*) about the divine attributes from this text.[253] Ibn Furak's approach in this matter corresponds with al-Ashᶜari's. As stated before, al-Ashᶜari did not take *akhbār al-āḥād* as a potential source of knowledge of the divine attributes.[254] In addition, Ibn Furak could not accept the anthropomorphic texts that were rejected by most of the Hadith scholars and labelled as dubious or fabricated. These texts were circulated by some *muḥaddithūn* with low professional standards. For example, Ibn Furak did not accept the *ḥadīth* according to which God had created Himself from the sweat of a horse. This *ḥadīth* was attributed to Abu Hurayra and transmitted by Hammad ibn Salama, whom Ibn Furak did not much appreciate as a *muḥaddith*.[255] In the case of the *ḥadīth* according to which God created the angels from the hair on His arms and chest, Ibn Furak remarked that its origin was quite dubious and that such blunt anthropomorphisms were mostly prevalent among the Jews. However, Ibn Furak did not completely reject the text, but preferred another variant of it, according to which God created the angels from 'the light of the two arms and the chest'. Ibn Furak draws our attention to the fact that the text does not refer to God's arms and chest.[256]

Ibn Furak believed that his work was the genuine representative of the traditionalists, *aṣḥāb al-ḥadīth*. The traditionalists – declared Ibn Furak – in fact comprised two groups: the first group was the *muḥaddithūn* who were occupied in transmitting the Hadith material, sifting through it and separating the authentic *aḥādīth* from the dubious ones; the second group was the speculative theologians who used rationalistic argumentations to defend the true convictions of *aṣḥāb al-ḥadīth*. Ibn Furak provided a beautiful parable to illustrate these two groups: 'To this religion, the first group is like the king's treasurers, while the second group is like the army commanders who defend the king's treasures from aggressors and assailants.'[257] Ibn Furak therefore perceived the Ashᶜarite *mutakallimūn* as the true defenders of Islamic traditionalism.

In sum, Ibn Furak embraced the lion's share of the corpus of *aḥādīth al-ṣifāt* because he believed that these texts contained moral lessons and concepts that Muslims need. However, he also emphasised that the texts were complicated and required the intensive investment of intellectual effort to decipher them. Ibn Furak's basic approach was that every anthropomorphic expression had a reasonable explanation. All one needed was a solid understanding of the Arabic language, the firm knowledge of the principles of the religion, and the ability to find the accurate meaning for every problematic phrase.[258] However, these skills were not accessible to everyone: Ibn Furak emphasised that the ability to decipher the true meanings of the anthropomorphic expressions was reserved for 'those who are well-grounded in knowledge' (*al-rāsikhūn fī 'l-ᶜilm*, a reference to Q. 3:7).[259] In other words, the true understanding of the anthropomorphic expressions in the Hadith material was esoteric and only the Ashᶜarite *mutakallimūn* were its custodians.

Ibn Furak's position was not unique: the Ashᶜarites perceived *aḥādīth al-ṣifāt* as highly sensitive material that can easily lead to the false convictions of *tashbīh*. As opposed to the Hanbalites, whose Hadith sessions were open to everybody, the Ashᶜarite scholars of the Hadith were reluctant to expose the laymen to this material. This view is reflected in al-Khatib al-Baghdadi's (d. 1071) manual for *muḥaddithūn*. Al-Khatib al-Baghdadi was a Hanbalite who became a Shafiᶜite and, as a result, an Ashᶜarite. His turbulent relationships with the Hanbalites (who harassed and afflicted him)[260] are also reflected in his writings. Al-Khatib al-Baghdadi was aware of the role of the *muḥaddith* as the educator of the masses.[261] He was also sensitive to the capabilities of his audience, and was concerned about exposing the uneducated masses to *aḥādīth al-ṣifāt*. His approach was therefore elitist:

> In his dictation-sessions, the *muḥaddith* should refrain from transmitting material that is beyond the grasp of the minds of the laymen, because when exposed to [this material] they are not immune from mistakes and false notions. They are not immune from comparing God to His creation, or attributing to Him absurd descriptions which correspond to the literal meaning of *aḥādīth al-ṣifāt*, and necessitate anthropomorphism and corporealism (*tashbīh wa-tajsīm*). The literal reading of these texts entail the affirmation of bodily organs to the Eternal. Although these texts are reliable and authentic, and there are many ways to interpret them, it is best that they are transmitted only to those who are competent [and able to understand them correctly], for fear they will lead the person who has no knowledge of their meanings, astray. This person might understand them literally or deny their

content, and accordingly he might reject the transmitters of these *aḥādīth* and regard them as liars.[262]

In this passage, al-Khatib al-Baghdadi conveys the idea that the transmission of *aḥādīth al-ṣifāt* should be minimised, or at least strictly transmitted to an exclusive audience of scholars. This view was dominant among the Ashᶜarites, but not only them. Other elitist traditionalistic scholars were concerned about the proliferation of anthropomorphic views among the uneducated masses. These scholars – whether Ashᶜarites or not – were disturbed by the turbulent events in which unscrupulous politicians and preachers used *aḥādīth al-ṣifāt* to incite the masses. The following chapter examines the approaches of the Hanbalites and the Ashᶜarites to *aḥādīth al-ṣifāt* by focusing on four important milestones in the theological discourse.

Notes

1. An elaborate refutation of the traditionalistic claim that the believers will see God using their own eyes is located in the writings of the Zaydite imam al-Qasim ibn Ibrahim al-Rassi (d. 860): Abrahamov, *Anthropomorphism*, pp. 109–45. Al-Qasim also mentioned the anthropomorphic Hadith material that the 'vulgar anthropomorphists', the Hashwiyya, used as evidence to corroborate their claim: ibid. p. 133. A thorough summary of the long-time scholarly debate concerning al-Qasim's affiliation to the Muᶜtazila appears in Ansari, Schmidtke and Thiele, 'Zaydī Theology', pp. 474–5.
2. Al-Bukhārī, *al-Jāmiᶜ*, vol. 1, p. 190, *ḥadīth* 554 (*Kitāb Mawāqīt al-Ṣalāt, bāb faḍl ṣalāt al-ᶜaṣr*), vol. 1, p. 96, *ḥadīth* 573 (*Kitāb Mawāqīt al-Ṣalāt, bāb faḍl ṣalāt al-fajr*), vol. 3, p. 296, *ḥadīth* 4851 (*Kitāb al-Tafsīr, bāb wa-sdbbiḥ bi-ḥamdi rabbika*); Muslim, *Ṣaḥīḥ*, p. 249, *ḥadīth* 211 (*Kitāb al-Masājid, bāb faḍl ṣalātay 'l-ṣubḥ wa'l-ᶜaṣr*); al-Tirmidhī, *Sunan*, vol. 4, p. 687, *ḥadīth* 2551 (*Kitāb Ṣifat al-Janna, bāb mā jāᵓa fī ruᵓyat al-rabb*); Ibn Māja, *Sunan*, p. 47, *ḥadīth* 177 (*bāb fīmā ankarat al-jahmiyya*); Ibn Ḥanbal, *Musnad*, vol. 31, pp. 526–30 (*Musnad Jarīr*).
3. Van Ess, 'Ein Unbekanntes Fragment des Naẓẓām', pp. 171–8.
4. Abrahamov, *Islamic Theology*, pp. 43–4.
5. On the canonisation of *al-Ṣaḥīḥān*, see Brown, *Canonization*, pp. 367–70.
6. Note that the Muᶜtazilite approach to the Hadith material was subtle and not monolithic. There were *aḥādīth al-ṣifāt* that the Muᶜtazilites regarded as

'less abominable' than others. Thus, for instance, they regarded 'I have seen my Lord in the most beautiful form' (*ra*ʾ*aytu rabbi fī aḥsan ṣūra*) as the most abominable text: Ibn Khuzayma, *Kitāb al-Tawḥīd*, p. 201. The Muᶜtazilite approach to Hadith material in general is discussed in Abrahamov, *Islamic Theology*, pp. 45–7; van Ess, *TG*, vol. 4, pp. 649–54. The most extensive analysis of the Muᶜtazilite approach to Hadith material, including *aḥādīth al-ṣifāt*, is El-Omari, 'Accommodation and Resistance', esp. pp. 248–9, ft 126.

7. Abrahamov, *Islamic Theology*, pp. ix–x.
8. Abrahamov, 'The *Bi-Lā Kayfa* Doctrine', pp. 368–9.
9. Goldziher, *The Ẓāhirīs*, p. 125
10. Al-Dhahabī, *Siyar Aᶜlām al-Nubalā*ʾ, vol. 10, p. 505 (the biography of Abu ᶜUbayd).
11. Al-Dhahabī, *Siyar Aᶜlām al-Nubalā*ʾ, vol. 8, p. 162 (the biography of al-Layth ibn Saᶜd).
12. Laoust, *Le profession de foi d'Ibn Baṭṭa*, p. 102.
13. Abrahamov, 'The *Bi-lā Kayfa* Doctrine', p. 366.
14. Ibn Abī Yaᶜlā, *Ṭabaqāt al-Fuqahā*ʾ *al-Ḥanābila*, vol. 1, pp. 360–4.
15. Al-Ājurrī, *Kitāb al-Sharīᶜa*, pp. 329–30, *ḥadīth* 726.
16. Al-Ājurrī, *Kitāb al-Sharīᶜa*, p. 327, *ḥadīth* 720.
17. Al-Bayhaqī, *al-Asmā*ʾ *wa'l-Ṣifāt*, vol. 2, p. 307, *ḥadīth* 869.
18. The first saying attributed to Ibn ᶜAbbas, appears in the early Hadith compilation of the *muḥaddith* ᶜAbd Allah al-Darimi from Samarqand (d. 869, not Abu Saᶜid al-Darimi, the Baghdadian *muḥaddith*): al-Dārimī, *Sunan*, vol. 1, p. 63, *ḥadīth* 125. Accordingly, this *ḥadīth* also appears in al-Ṭabarānī, *al-Muᶜjam al-Kabīr*, vol. 11, p. 454, *ḥadīth* 12288, and Ibn Rajab, *Rawa'iᶜ al-Tafsir*, vol. 1, p. 452 (interpretation of Q. 5:101).
19. Al-Bayhaqī, *al-Asmā' wa'l-Ṣifāt*, vol. 2, pp. 305–6, anecdote 867.
20. Ibn ᶜAbd al-Barr, *Tamhīd*, vol. 7, p. 151.
21. Al-Dhahabī, *Siyar Aᶜlāma al-Nubalā*ʾ, vol. 8, pp. 465–6 (the biography of Sufyan ibn ᶜUyayna).
22. Ibn ᶜAbd al-Barr, *Tamhīd*, vol. 7, pp. 151–2.
23. Ibn ᶜAbd al-Barr, *Tamhīd*, vol. 7, p. 149.
24. Dickinson, *The Development*, p. 8.
25. Al-Dhahabī, *Siyar Aᶜlām al-Nubalā*ʾ, vol. 11, p. 376 (the biography of Ibn Rahwayh).
26. The psychological profile of the traditionalists is skilfully depicted by Christopher Melchert in his 'The Piety of the Hadith Folk', pp. 427–8.

27. Al-Dhahabī, *Siyar Aᶜlām al-Nubalāʾ*, vol. 10, p. 506 (the biography of Abu ᶜUbayd).
28. Al-Dhahabī, *Siyar Aᶜlām al-Nubalāʾ*, vol. 10, p. 506.
29. The literature about the *munāẓara* (public debate) in Islam is vast. See the excellent survey of Belhaj, *Argumentation et dialeqtique*, pp. 5–15. For an example of a *munāẓara* in the Mamluk period, see Holtzman 'Debating the Doctrine of *Jabr*', 66–92.
30. Al-Dhahabī, *Siyar Aᶜlām al-Nubalāʾ*, vol. 11, p. 376.
31. That *takyīf* is the *modus operandi* of the Hashwiyya is best clarified in al-Dārimī, *Naqḍ al-Imām*, p. 689. Al-Darimi connects the term *takyīf* with the belief that 'God has organs, body parts and the like, which is vulgar anthropomorphism and fables' (*ḥashw wa-khurāfāt*).
32. Two good summaries of the various views of the Muᶜtazilites on this subject are Gilliot, 'Attributes of God', *EI3*, and Shah, 'Classical Islamic Discourse', pp. 316–17.
33. Lecomte, *Ibn Qutayba*, pp. 55–6, 62 (chap. 3); Lecomte, *Le Traité des divergences*, p. 274 (index).
34. For the approach of Abu 'l-Hasan al-Ashᶜari himself, see Abrahamov, 'The *Bi-lā Kayfa* Doctrine', p. 369.
35. Lecomte, 'Ibn Ḳutayba', *EI2*.
36. Lowry, 'Ibn Qutaybah', pp. 173–82. See the illuminating remark of G. Lecomte in the introduction of Ibn Qutayba's *Taʾwīl Mukhtalif al-Ḥadīth*: Lecomte, *Le Traité des divergences*, pp. 3–4, section 6 and p. 11, section 59 (Avant-propos).
37. Lecomte, *Le Traité des divergences*, p. 3, section 3 (Avant-propos).
38. Ibn Qutayba, *Ikhtilāf*, p. 53.
39. The rationalists in *Taʾwīl Mukhtalif al-Ḥadīth* are the speculative theologians (*aṣḥāb al-kalām, al-mutakallimūn*), the Hanafaites and the Shiᶜites whom he calls 'the People of Personal Reasoning' (*ahl al-raʾy* or *aṣḥāb al-raʾy*): Ibn Qutayba, *Taʾwīl Mukhtalif al-Ḥadīth*, pp. 61–126; Lecomte, *Le Traité des divergences*, pp. 38–74, sections 23–203 (chap. I).
40. Ibn Qutayba, *Taʾwīl Mukhtalif al-Ḥadīth*, pp. 309, 321.
41. Ibn Qutayba, *Ikhtilāf*, p. 36.
42. Ibn Qutayba, *Ikhtilāf*, p. 40.
43. Ibn Qutayba, *Ikhtilāf*, p. 40.
44. Muslim, *Ṣaḥīḥ*, p. 763, *ḥadīth* 1827 (*Kitāb al-Imāra, bāb faḍīlat al-imām al-fāḍil*). According to this *ḥadīth*, the Prophet said (probably in a sermon):

'Those who act justly will be with God [enthroned] on pulpits made of light. [They will be seated] at the right hand of the Merciful. Both His hands are right.'

45. Heinrichs, 'On the Genesis of the *Ḥaqīqa-Majāz* Dichotomy', p. 138; Shah, 'The Philological Endeavours (Part II)', p. 44.
46. Ibn Qutayba, *Ikhtilāf*, p. 42; Ibn Qutayba, *Taʾwīl Mukhtalif al-Ḥadīth*, p. 304. The argument about God's perfection was fully adopted by Ibn Taymiyya in his discussion on God's laughter: Holtzman, 'Does God Really Laugh?', pp. 194–9.
47. Ibn Qutayba, *Ikhtilāf*, pp. 42–3; Ibn Qutayba, *Taʾwīl Mukhtalif al-Ḥadīth*, p. 304.
48. Ibn Qutayba, *Ikhtilāf*, p. 42.
49. Ibn Qutayba, *Ikhtilāf*, p. 51; al-Dārimī, *Naqḍ al-Imām*, pp. 373, 769.
50. Ibn Qutayba, *Ikhtilāf*, p. 51.
51. Al-Ājurrī, *Kitāb al-Sharīʿa*, p. 331, *ḥadīth* 730.
52. Ibn Qutayba, *Ikhtilāf*, p. 51; Ibn Qutayba, *Taʾwīl Mukhtalif al-Ḥadīth*, pp. 302–3.
53. Abrahamov, 'The *Bi-lā Kayfa* Doctrine', p. 371.
54. Ibn Qutayba, *Taʾwīl Mukhtalif al-Ḥadīth*, p. 303.
55. Ibn Qutayba, *Taʾwīl Mukhtalif al-Ḥadīth*, p. 303. The last sentence (*kull shayʾ minhu lā yushbihu shayʾan minnā*) is a bit tricky. Lecomte translated *shayʾ* as 'a term designating a thing' and not a 'thing' *per se*: Lecomte, *Le Traité des divergences*, p. 149, section 486 (chap. III).
56. Ibn Qutayba, *Taʾwīl Mukhtalif al-Ḥadīth*, pp. 47–8. For useful summaries of the introduction, see Abrahamov, *Islamic Theology*, p. 42; Lowry, 'Ibn Qutayba', p. 181.
57. Abrahamov, *Islamic Theology*, pp. 42–4.
58. Ibn Qutayba, *Taʾwīl Mukhtalif al-Ḥadīth*, p. 53; Lecomte, *Le Traité des divergences*, p. 32, section 17 (Introduction); Abrahamov, *Islamic Theology*, p. 42.
59. Ibn Qutayba, *Taʾwīl Mukhtalif al-Ḥadīth*, p. 54; Lecomte, *Le Traité des divergences*, p. 32, section 18 (Introduction).
60. Ibn Qutayba, *Taʾwīl Mukhtalif al-Ḥadīth*, p. 136; Lecomte, *Le Traité des divergences*, p. 78, section 33 (chap. II).
61. Ibn Qutayba, *Taʾwīl Mukhtalif al-Ḥadīth*, p. 136. Lecomte translates these epithets as *l'Écume* (scum) and *la Lie* (scum): Lecomte, *Le Traité des divergences*, p. 78, section 33 (chap. II).

62. Ibn Qutayba, *Taʾwīl Mukhtalif al-Ḥadīth*, p. 136; Lecomte, *Le Traité des divergences*, p. 78, section 33 (chap. II).
63. Ibn Qutayba, *Taʾwīl Mukhtalif al-Ḥadīth*, pp. 53, 129; Lecomte, *Le Traité des divergences*, p. 32, section 17 (Introduction), p. 76, section 100 (chap. II).
64. Halkin, 'The Ḥashwiyya', pp. 12–28, esp. pp. 22–3.
65. Ibn Qutayba, *Taʾwīl Mukhtalif al-Ḥadīth*, p. 133.
66. Ibn Qutayba, *Taʾwīl Mukhtalif al-Ḥadīth*, p. 133.
67. Ibn Qutayba, *Taʾwīl Mukhtalif al-Ḥadīth*, p. 135.
68. Ibn Qutayba, *Taʾwīl Mukhtalif al-Ḥadīth*, p. 321.
69. Ibn Qutayba, *Taʾwīl Mukhtalif al-Ḥadīth*, p. 300.
70. Ibn Qutayba, *Taʾwīl Mukhtalif al-Ḥadīth*, p. 395. The natural dispositions (*fiṭar*) that Ibn Qutayba refers to are connected to the concept of *fiṭra*. This concept has its roots in the Quran and the Hadith, and was developed by early thinkers to denote the purity of the religion of Islam: Hoover, 'Fiṭra', *EI3*.
71. Ibn Qutayba, *Taʾwīl Mukhtalif al-Ḥadīth*, p. 53.
72. Ibn Qutayba, *Taʾwīl Mukhtalif al-Ḥadīth*, p. 129.
73. Ibn Ḥanbal, *Musnad*, vol. 4, pp. 350–4, *ḥadīth* 2580, p. 386, *ḥadīth* 2634; al-Ājurrī, *Kitāb al-Sharīʿa*, p. 492, *ḥadīth* 1033; al-Dāraquṭnī, *Kitāb al-Ruʾya*, pp. 345–7.
74. Ibn Qutayba, *Taʾwīl Mukhtalif al-Ḥadīth*, p. 323. The version that Ibn Qutayba cited was recorded in al-Ṭayālisī, *Musnad*, vol. 2, p. 418, *ḥadīth* 1189; Ibn Ḥanbal, *Musnad*, vol. 26, p. 108, *ḥadīth* 16188, pp. 117–18, *ḥadīth* 16200.
75. Ibn Qutayba, *Taʾwīl Mukhtalif al-Ḥadīth*, p. 323.
76. Ibn Qutayba, *Taʾwīl Mukhtalif al-Ḥadīth*, p. 323.
77. Al-Tirmidhī, *Sunan*, vol. 5, p. 288, *ḥadīth* 3109 (*Kitāb Tafsīr al-Qurʾān, bāb wa-min sūrat Hūd*).
78. Ibn Māja, *Sunan*, p. 48, *ḥadīth* 182 (*bāb ma ankarathu al-jahmiyya*). *Aḥādīth* 180 and 181 are also attributed to Wakiʿ ibn ʿUdus and record the questions that Abu Razin directed at the Prophet.
79. Ibn Abī Yaʿlā, *Ṭabaqāt al-Fuqahāʾ al-Ḥanābila*, vol. 1, p. 77.
80. Ibn Qutayba, *Taʾwīl Mukhtalif al-Ḥadīth*, p. 323.
81. Ibn Qutayba, *Taʾwīl Mukhtalif al-Ḥadīth*, p. 323.
82. The compilations of *al-mawḍūʿāt* present, first and foremost, the personal opinion of their composers and do not represent a consensus among the traditionalists: Ibn al-Jawzi's (d. 1201) *Kitāb al-Mawḍūʿāt*, for example, presents a fierce attack against the anthropomorphic trends of Ibn al-Jawzi's fellow-Hanbalites.

83. Brown, *Hadith*, pp. 99–100; Hilali, 'Compiler, exclure, cacher', pp. 163–74.
84. Goldziher, *The Ẓāhirīs*, pp. 154–5.
85. Gimaret, *Dieu à l'image de l'homme*, pp. 229–32; Swartz, *A Medieval Critique of Anthropomorphism*, pp. 241–2. The *ḥadīth* is also mentioned in Williams, 'Aspects of the Creed', p. 449.
86. See, Asad, 'Kinship', *EQ*. We note that Asad emphasises that the *arḥām* are not 'ties of blood' and that kinship in the Quran is not based on 'common blood', which he claims to be a western idiom.
87. Al-Ṭabarī, *Jāmiᶜ al-Bayān*, vol. 21, p. 213 (interpretation of Q. 47:22); al-Bukhārī, *al-Jāmiᶜ*, vol. 3, p. 292 (*Kitāb al-Tafsīr, bāb wa-tuqaṭṭiᶜū arḥāmakum)*.
88. Al-Bukhārī, *al-Jāmiᶜ*, vol. 3, p. 292 (*Kitāb al-Tafsīr, bāb wa-tuqaṭṭiᶜū arḥāmakum*). For the sentence 'I stay close with the person who makes you close to him, and be detached from the person who detaches himself from you', see Lane, *Arabic-English Lexicon*, vol. 3, p. 1056 (the entry *raḥim*).
89. Goldziher, *The Ẓāhirīs*, pp. 154–5; Gimaret, *Dieu à l'image de l'homme*, pp. 229–30; Swartz, *A Medieval Critique of Anthropomorphism*, pp. 241–2; Khan, *The Translation of the Meaning of Ṣaḥīḥ al-Bukhārī*, vol. 6, p. 307, *ḥadīth* 4830 (The Book of Commentary, chapter '... And sever your ties of kinship'). Qadi ᶜIyad, the interpreter of *Ṣaḥīḥ Muslim*, suggested that *raḥim* is 'kinship' or 'relationship': Qāḍī ᶜIyaḍ, *Ikmāl*, vol. 8, p. 19 (*Kitāb al-Birr wa'l-Ṣila wa'l-Ādāb, bāb ṣilat al-raḥim wa-taḥrīm qaṭīᶜatihā*); al-Nawawī, *Ṣaḥīḥ Muslim*, vol. 16, p. 91, *ḥadīth* 2554 (*Kitāb al-Birr wa'l-Ṣila wa'l-Ādāb, bāb ṣilat al-raḥim wa-taḥrīm qaṭīᶜatihā*).
90. The most comprehensive collection of *aḥādīth* on the same theme is recorded in al-Suyūṭī, *al-Durr al-Manthūr*, vol. 13, pp. 437–45 (commentary of Q. 47:22). See also a reference to the same material used by a twentieth-century village preacher in Jordan: Reichmuth, 'Religion and Language', *Encyclopedia of Arabic Language and Linguistics*.
91. The etymological connection between 'womb' and 'mercy' goes way back to the Biblical Hebrew: the Hebrew word for womb is *reḥem*. The verb *riḥem* ('to take pity on') belongs to a group of denominative verbs of body parts that bear a metaphorical meaning: Warren-Rothlin, 'Idioms: Biblical Hebrew', *Encyclopedia of Hebrew Language and Linguistics*. Both *reḥem* and *riḥem* come from the Proto-Semitic bi-phonetic root *ḥ.m.m.* ('to be warm'): Kirtchuk, 'Onomatopoeia', *Encyclopedia of Hebrew Language and Linguistics*. It seems that the Hebrew *raḥamīm* ('mercy') is a plural form of *reḥem* ('womb', and also

'maternal love'): Kaddari, *A Dictionary of Biblical Hebrew*, p. 1002. The symbolic connection between *reḥem* ('womb') and *raḥamīm* ('mercy') is reflected in the Biblical images of God as a paternal-creator and as a mother with breasts. The latter image is derived from the most controversial of all the divine names in the Hebrew Bible, *El-Shaddai*: Biale, 'The God with Breasts', p. 247; Umansky, 'God as Mother', p. 252; Stone, 'Justice, Mercy, and Gender', p. 166. The word *raḥmān* ('merciful') appears in the Hebrew Bible, but only in the plural form (*raḥmāniyōt*, 'compassionate women'; Lamentations 4:10). However, it appears in Talmudic texts and is used as an epithet for both man and God. An addendum to the Jewish Prayer for Food produced from five common grains (*birkat ha-mazōn*) contains a lengthy section in which each sentence opens with an appeal to *ha-Raḥmān*, God the Merciful: Even Shoshan, *Ha-Milon He-Chadash*, vol. 4, p. 1705; *The Academy of the Hebrew Language*, a private correspondence dated 9 June 2016.

92. Al-Suyūṭī, *al-Durr al-Manthūr*, vol. 13, p. 441 (commentary of Q. 47:22). For the sentence 'The *raḥim* is derived from *al-Raḥmān*', see Lane, *Arabic-English Lexicon*, vol. 4, p. 1509 (the entry *shijna*).
93. Ibn Taymiyya's *Bayān Talbīs al-Jahmiyya* is a systematic refutation of Fakhr al-Din al-Razi's *Asās al-Taqdīs*. See Chapter 5.
94. Ibn Taymiyya, *Bayān Talbīs al-Jahmiyya*, vol. 6, p. 206.
95. Ibn Qayyim al-Jawziyya and Ibn al-Mawṣilī, *Mukhtaṣar al-Ṣawāᶜiq*, pp. 883–4. The paraphrase that Ibn Qayyim al-Jawziyya offered goes as follows: 'When God created the *raḥim*, He gave her a name that was derived from His name [*al-Raḥmān*], and meant to send her down to earth. She clung to Him (*taᶜallaqat bi-hi*), and He said: 'Stop it!', and she replied: 'This is the place where a person seeks Your protection from the enmity among relatives.' He replied: 'Will you be satisfied if I stay close with the person who makes you close to him, and be detached from the person who detaches himself from you?'
96. Al-Bukhārī, *al-Jāmiᶜ*, vol. 3, p. 292, *ḥadīth* 4830 (*Kitāb al-Tafsīr, bāb wa-tuqaṭṭiᶜū arḥāmakum*).
97. Al-Dhahabī, *Siyar Aᶜlām al-Nubalāʾ*, vol. 5, pp. 93–4 (the biography of Saᶜid ibn Yasar).
98. Al-Bukhārī, *al-Jāmiᶜ*, vol. 3, p. 292, *ḥadīth* 4830 (*Kitāb al-Tafsīr, bāb wa-tuqaṭṭiᶜū arḥāmakum*).
99. Al-Bukhārī, *al-Jāmiᶜ*, vol. 3, p. 292, *aḥādīth* 4830–2 (*Kitāb al-Tafsīr, bāb wa-tuqaṭṭiᶜū arḥāmakum*); al-Bukhārī, *Tārīkh*, vol. 4, p. 335.

100. This is the analysis of the Hadith scholar Abu Bakr al-Bayhaqi (d. 1066): al-Bayhaqī, *al-Asmā' wa'l-Ṣifāt*, vol. 2, p. 223.
101. Ibn Ḥanbal, *Musnad*, vol. 14, p. 103, *ḥadīth* 8367 (the *Musnad* of Abu Hurayra): al-Dhahabī, *Siyar Aᶜlām al-Nubalāʾ*, vol. 9, pp. 489–90 (the biography of Abu Bakr al-Hanafi ᶜAbd al-Kabir ibn ᶜAbd al-Majid).
102. Ibn Ḥanbal, *Musnad*, vol. 14, p. 103, *ḥadīth* 8367 (the *Musnad* of Abu Hurayra).
103. Ahmad ibn Hanbal from Baghdad, Hisham ibn ᶜAmmar from Damascus and ᶜAbd Allah ibn Saᶜid al-Ashajj (d. 871) were considered the greatest luminaries of Hadith science in their times. In his *Tadhkirat al-Ḥuffāẓ*, al-Dhahabi granted only these three scholars from among their entire generation the honorific title *shaykh al-Islām*: Lucas, *Constructive Critics*, pp. 74–5. This title attests to a scholar's status in the traditionalistic community, his complete avoidance of speculative theology and his exceptional erudition: Lucas, *Constructive Critics*, pp. 57–61.
104. Al-Dhahabī, *Siyar Aᶜlām al-Nubalāʾ*, vol. 11, p. 429 (the biography of Hisham ibn ᶜAmmar). An evaluation about Hisham's theological affinity appears in van Ess, *TG*, vol. 1, pp. 139–40.
105. Muslim ibn al-Hajjaj, the compiler of *Ṣaḥīḥ Muslim*, was not included in the list because he never visited Damascus. Abu ᶜUbayd al-Qasim ibn Sallam, who was mentioned above in Section I, was also one of Hisham's many students: al-Dhahabī, *Siyar Aᶜlām al-Nubalāʾ*, vol. 11, p. 422.
106. Al-Dhahabī, *Siyar Aᶜlām al-Nubalāʾ*, vol. 11, pp. 427–8.
107. Al-Dhahabī, *Mīzān al-Iᶜtidāl*, vol. 4, pp. 302–4 (the biography of Hisham ibn ᶜAmmar).
108. Abū Yaᶜlā, *Ibṭāl al-Taʾwīlāt*, p. 421; Ibn Taymiyya, *Bayān Talbīs al-Jahmiyya*, vol. 6, p. 209. When joined with the verbal nouns *qabūl* and *taslīm*, *talaqqin* (the verbal noun of the fifth form) expresses a wholehearted submission or acceptance. The problem is that the text in both sources is distorted. The editor of *Bayān Talbīs al-Jahmiyya* suggested that indeed the man expressed his acceptance of the text by adding the verb *talaqqāhu* in square brackets. This suggestion seems reasonable.
109. Abū Yaᶜlā, *Ibṭāl al-Taʾwīlāt*, p. 421; Ibn Taymiyya, *Bayān Talbīs al-Jahmiyya*, vol. 6, pp. 209–10.
110. Abū Yaᶜlā, *Ibṭāl al-Taʾwīlāt*, p. 421; Ibn Taymiyya, *Bayān Talbīs al-Jahmiyya*, vol. 6, pp. 210–11.
111. Lucas, *Constructive Critics*, pp. 70–7.

112. See, for example, the anti-Murjiʾite material that he transmitted: al-Ājurri, *Kitāb al-Sharīʿa*, p. 132, *ḥadīth* 256; pp. 146–7, *ḥadīth* 296; p. 151, *ḥadīth* 306.
113. Shah, 'Classical Islamic Discourse', p. 317.
114. Al-Dhahabī, *Mīzān al-Iʿtidāl*, vol. 4, p. 303 (the biography of Hisham ibn ʿAmmar).
115. Al-Dhahabī, *al-ʿUlūw*, pp. 181–2, anecdote 493.
116. Al-Dhahaī, *Siyar Aʿlām al-Nubalāʾ*, vol. 11, p. 427 (the biography of Hisham ibn ʿAmmar).
117. Al-Dhahabī, *Siyar Aʿlām al-Nubalāʾ*, vol. 11, p. 431 (the biography of Hisham ibn ʿAmmar).
118. For the *ḥadīth* about God sitting in the middle arch between Paradise and Hell on the Day of Resurrection, see al-Dhahabī, *al-ʿUlūw*, p. 116, anecdote 310. The *ḥadīth* was regarded as objectionable (*munkar*). Ibn al-Jawzi, however, labelled it as fabricated (*mawḍūʿ*): Ibn al-Jawzī, *Kitab al-Mawḍūʿat*, p. 184, *ḥadīth* 268 (*Kitāb al-Tawḥīd, bāb mā ruwiya anna Allāh taʿālā yajlisu bayna al-janna wa'l-nār yawma 'l-qiyāma*). For the *ḥadīth* about God revealing Himself to Muhammad 'in most beautiful form' (*fī aḥsan ṣūra*), see Ibn Taymiyya, *Bayān Talbīs al-Jahmiyya*, vol. 7, p. 347.
119. Muslim, *Ṣaḥīḥ*, p. 1032, *ḥadīth* 16-2554 (*Kitāb al-Birr wa'l-Ṣila wa'l-Ādāb, bāb ṣilat al-raḥim wa-taḥrīm qaṭīʿatihā*); al-Bukhārī, *al-Jāmiʿ*, vol. 4, p. 89, *ḥadīth* 5987 (*Kitāb al-Adab, bāb man waṣala waṣalahu Allāh*); vol. 4, p. 404, *ḥadīth* 7502 (*Kitāb al-Tawḥīd, bāb yurīdūna an yubaddilū kalām Allāh*). Hisham is not mentioned in the *Ṣaḥīḥān*. However, in a biographical entry of one of his disciples, the disciple quotes Hisham as one of the later links in the chain of transmission of a similar (although not entirely identical) version: Ibn ʿAsākir, *Tārīkh Dimashq*, vol. 53, pp. 392–3 (the biography of Muhammad ibn ʿAbd Allah al-Ramli). This chain of transmission is obviously broken because it presents Hisham as receiving the *ḥadīth* personally from the Medinese *muḥaddith*, Hatim ibn Ismaʿil (d. 803). There is a gap of sixty years between Hatim's death date and Hisham's. All the other versions of this *ḥadīth* insert at least one more transmitter between Hatim and the transmitters of Hisham's generation. The chain of transmission in *Ṣaḥīḥ Muslim* is a representative example of this intermediary transmission. However, because there is a slim chance that Hisham met Hatim, this *ḥadīth* cannot be disregarded completely.
120. Al-Dhahabī, *Mīzān al-Iʿtidāl*, vol. 2, p. 573 (the biography of ʿAbd al-Rahman ibn ʿabd Allah ibn Dinar al-Madani). Al-Dhahabi used the technical

term *tābaʿa* to denote this process of imitation. For *tābaʿ* and *mutābaʿa*, see Juynboll, *Encyclopedia of Canonical Hadith*, pp. xxvi–xxviii. Following al-Dhahabi's view, al-Qastallani claims that Sulayman ibn Bilal heard this *ḥadīth* personally from Muʿawiya while the two were alone (*bi'l-ifrād*): al-Qasṭallānī, *Irshād al-Sārī*, vol. 7, p. 342 (*Kitāb Tafsīr al-Qurʾān, bāb sūrat Muḥammad*).

121. The full version appears in al-Bukhārī, *al-Jāmiʿ*, vol. 3, p. 292, *ḥadīth* 4830, 4831, 4832 (*Kitāb al-Tafsīr, bāb wa-tuqaṭṭiʿū arḥāmakum*). The censored version appears in Muslim, *Ṣaḥīḥ*, p. 1032, *ḥadīth* 16-2554 (*Kitāb al-Birr wa'l-Ṣila wa'l-Ādāb, bāb ṣilat al-raḥim wa-taḥrīm qaṭīʿatihā*); al-Bukhārī, *al-Jāmiʿ*, vol. 4, p. 89, *ḥadīth* 5987 (*Kitāb al-Adab, bāb man waṣala waṣalahu Allāh*); vol. 4, p. 404, *ḥadīth* 7502 (*Kitāb al-Tawḥīd, bāb yurīdūna an yubaddilū kalām Allāh*).
122. Al-Bayhaqī, *al-Asmā' wa'l-Ṣifāt*, vol. 2, p. 223; Muslim, *Ṣaḥīḥ*, p. 1032, *ḥadīth* 16-2554 (*Kitāb al-Birr wa'l-Ṣila wa'l-Ādāb, bāb ṣilat al-raḥim wa-taḥrīm qaṭīʿatihā*).
123. The data in this table is confirmed by the relevant biographical entries in the following sources. Al-Bukhārī, *Tārīkh*, vol. 4, p. 174, biographical entry 595 (Khalid ibn Makhlad); vol. 1, p. 283, biographical entry 912 (Ibrahim ibn Hamza); vol. 2, p. 84, biographical entry 1772 (Bishr ibn Muhammad); vol. 1, p. 364, biographical entry 1152 (Ismaʿil ibn ʿAbd Allah). Al-Dhahabī, *Tārīkh al-Islām*, vol. 15, pp. 137–8, biographical entry 113 (Khalid ibn Makhlad); vol. 16, pp. 61–2, biographical entry 33 (Ibrahim ibn Hamza); vol. 16, p. 114, biographical entry 81 (Bishr ibn Muhammad); vol. 16, pp. 91–4, biographical entry 68 (Ismaʿil ibn ʿAbd Allah). Al-Dhahabī, *Siyar Aʿlām al-Nubalā'*, vol. 10, p. 217, biographical entry 55 (Khalid ibn Makhlad); vol. 11, pp. 60–1, biographical entry 23 (Ibrahim ibn Hamza).
124. Al-Dhahabī, *Siyar Aʿlām al-Nubalāʾ*, vol. 11, pp. 60–1; al-Bukhārī, *Tārīkh*, vol. 1, p. 283.
125. Al-Bukhārī, *Tārīkh*, vol. 1, p. 364 (biographical entry no. 1152).
126. Al-Dhahabī, *Tārīkh al-Islām*, vol. 16, p. 93 (the biographical entry of Ismaʿil ibn ʿAbd Allah).
127. Al-Bukhārī, *Tārīkh*, vol. 3, p. 174 (biographical entry no. 595).
128. Al-Bukhārī, *al-Jāmiʿ*, vol. 4, p. 389, *ḥadīth* 7430 (*Kitāb al-Tawḥīd, bāb qawl Allāh taʿālā taʿruju 'l-malāʾika wa'l-rūḥ ilayhi*); vol. 4, p. 192, *ḥadīth* 6502 (*Kitāb al-Riqāq, bāb al-tawāḍuʿ*).
129. Al-Dhahabi, *Siyar Aʿlām al-Nubalā'*, vol. 10, p. 218 (the biographical entry of Khalid ibn Makhlad).

130. Al-Dhahabī, *Tārīkh al-Islām*, vol. 16, p. 114 (the biographical entry of Bishr ibn Muhammad).
131. Al-Tabari attributes this version to Sulayman ibn Bilal and to Ghundar Muhammad ibn Ja^cfar al-Hudhali (d. 809). Ghundar was quoted by Muslim and other luminaries of Hadith: al-Ṭabarī, *Jāmi^c al-Bayān*, vol. 21, p. 214 (interpretation of Q. 47:22).
132. Al-Suyūṭī, *al-Durr al-Manthūr*, vol. 13, p. 436.
133. Al-Bayhaqī, *al-Asmā' wa'l-Ṣifāt*, vol. 2, p. 223.
134. Al-Suyūṭī, *Jam^c al-Jawāmi^c*, vol. 2, p. 170, *ḥadīth* 336/4825.
135. Goldziher, *The Ẓāhirīs*, p. 154.
136. Goldziher, *The Ẓāhirīs*, p. 155.
137. On the controversy between Ibn Hajar and al-^cAyni regarding *Ṣaḥīḥ al-Bukhārī*, see Goldziher, *Abhandlungen*, vol. 2, p. xxiv, footnote 2.
138. Al-^cAynī, *^cUmdat al-Qārī*, vol. 19, p. 247, *ḥadīth* 352/4830 (*Kitāb Tafsīr al-Qur'ān, bāb wa-tuqaṭṭi^cū arhāmakum*).
139. Ibn Hajar merely indicates the word *li'l-akthar*, which is vague and not specific: Ibn Ḥajar, *Fatḥ al-Bārī*, vol. 8, p. 454 (*Kitāb Tafsīr al-Qur'ān, bāb sūrat Muḥammad*). Goldziher understood Ibn Hajar's description thus: '[I]n many editions the object of the verb *akhadhat* is missing': Goldziher, *The Ẓāhirīs*, p. 155. Al-^cAyni's reading certainly provides the correct way to read Ibn Hajar's wording.
140. Al-Dhahabī, *Siyar A^clām al-Nubalā'*, vol. 16, pp. 313–15 (the biography of Abu Zayd al-Marwazi); *idem*, vol. 17, pp. 158–61 (the biography of Abu 'l-Hasan al-Qabisi); Ibn ^cAsākir, *Tabyīn*, p. 188; Lucas, *Constructive Critics*, p. 232 footnote 69, pp. 375–6; Brown, *Canonization*, pp. 120–1.
141. Ibn Ḥajar, *Fatḥ al-Bārī*, vol. 8, p. 454 (*Kitāb Tafsīr al-Qur'ān, bāb sūrat Muḥammad*).
142. Ibn Ḥajar, *Fatḥ al-Bārī*, vol. 8, p. 454 (*Kitāb Tafsīr al-Qur'ān, bāb sūrat Muḥammad*). The same remark appears in al-^cAynī, *^cUmdat al-Qārī*, vol. 19, p. 65 (*Kitāb Tafsīr al-Qur'ān, bāb wa-tuqaṭṭi^cū arḥāmakum*). On Ibn Sakan's career, see Brown, *Canonization*, p. 120.
143. Ibn Ḥajar, *Fatḥ al-Bārī*, vol. 8, p. 454 (*Kitāb Tafsīr al-Qur'ān, bāb sūrat Muḥammad*); vol. 10, p. 431 (*Kitāb al-Adab, bāb man waṣala waṣalahu Allāh*).
144. Al-Bukhārī, *al-Jāmi^c*, vol. 2, pp. 179–80, *ḥadīth* 2412 (*Kitāb al-Khuṣūmāt, bāb ma yudhkaru fī 'l-ishkhāṣ wa'l-mulāzama wa'l-khuṣūma bayna 'l-muslim wa'l-yahūdī*).
145. Quiring-Zoches, 'How al-Bukhārī's Ṣaḥīḥ was edited', pp. 191–2, 205–6.

146. Quiring-Zoches, 'How al-Bukhārī's Ṣaḥīḥ was edited', pp. 200–5.
147. Al-Qasṭallānī, *Irshād al-Sārī*, vol. 7, pp, 342–3 (*Kitāb al-Tafsīr, bāb wa-tuqaṭṭiᶜū arḥāmakum*); vol. 9, p. 12 (*Kitāb al-Adab, bāb man waṣala waṣalahu Allāh*); vol. 10, p. 437 (*Kitāb al-Tawḥīd, bāb yurīdūna an yubaddilū kitāb Allāh*).
148. Al-Qasṭallānī, *Irshād al-Sārī*, vol. 7, p. 343.
149. Al-Qasṭallānī, *Irshād al-Sārī*, vol. 7, p. 342; Goldziher, *The Ẓāhirīs*, pp. 154–5.
150. Quiring-Zoches, 'How al-Bukhārī's Ṣaḥīḥ was edited', pp. 203–4.
151. On al-Yunini's copy of *Ṣaḥīḥ al-Bukhārī* and the preparation of *al-Sulṭāniyya* edition, see the informative article penned by the Egyptian Hadith scholar sheikh Ahmad Muhammad Shakir (d. 1958). This article is attached to the undated reprint of *al-Sulṭāniyya* prepared by Dar al-Jil publishing house in Beirut: Shākir, 'al-Nuskha al-Yūnīniyya', pp. 1–14. For additional information, see Quiring-Zoches, 'How al-Bukhārī's Ṣaḥīḥ was edited', p. 206; al-Bukhārī, *Ṣaḥīḥ*, vol. 1, p. 43 (Introduction).
152. The first edition is the undated reprint of *al-Sulṭāniyya* prepared by the publishing house Dar al-Jil in Beirut. The second edition was printed in 2001 in the publishing house Dar Tawq al-Najah in Beirut. This excellent, annotated edition contains footnotes which refer to the commentaries of the *Ṣaḥīḥ*.
153. Al-Bukhārī, *Ṣaḥīḥ*, vol. 1, p. 5 (the text).
154. Al-Bukhārī, *Ṣaḥīḥ*, vol. 6, p. 134 (the text).
155. Al-Qasṭallānī, *Irshād al-Sārī*, vol. 7, p. 342.
156. Khan, *The Translation of the Meaning of Ṣaḥīḥ al-Bukhārī*, vol. 6, p. 307, *ḥadīth* 4830 (The Book of Commentary, chapter '… And sever your ties of kinship').
157. Khan, *Summarized Sahîh al-Bukharî Arabic-English*, p. 865, *ḥadīth* 1778 (The Book of Commentary, chapter '… And sever your ties of kinship').
158. Ibn Abī Ḥatim, *Kitāb al-ᶜIlal*, vol. 5, pp. 465–7. On Ibn Abi Hatim and his father, see the extensive treatment in Dickinson, *The Development*, pp. 13–28; Lucas, *Constructive Critics*, pp. 134–7.
159. Ibn Abī Ḥatim, *Kitāb al-ᶜIlal*, vol. 5, pp. 465–7.
160. Ibn Abī Ḥatim, *Kitāb al-ᶜIlal*, vol. 5, pp. 465–7.
161. Aḥmad ibn Ḥanbal, *al-Radd ᶜalā al-Jahmiyya*, p. 160; al-Dārimī, *Naqḍ al-Imām*, p. 428. For the attribution of *al-Radd ᶜalā al-Jahmiyya* to Ahmad ibn Hanbal, see Holtzman, 'Aḥmad ibn Ḥanbal', *EI3*.
162. Al-Barbahārī, *Sharḥ al-Sunna*, p. 70; Ibn Abī Yaᶜlā, *Ṭabaqāt al-Fuqahāᵓ al-Ḥanābila*, vol. 2, pp. 28–9 (the biography of al-Barbahari). For the attribution of *Sharḥ al-Sunna* to al-Barbahari, see Melchert, 'The Ḥanābila and Early Sufis', pp. 361–2, and 'al-Barbahārī', *EI3*.

163. Al-Sarhan and Melchert, 'The Creeds of Aḥmad', p. 30.
164. Ibn Abī Yaᶜlā, *Ṭabaqāt al-Fuqahāᵓ al-Ḥanābila*, vol. 1, pp. 391–2 (the biography of Muhammad ibn Idris al-Shafiᶜi).
165. Al-Bukhārī, *al-Jāmiᶜ*, vol. 3, p. 296, *aḥādīth* 4848–50 (*Kitāb al-Tafsīr, bāb wa-taqūlu hal min mazīd*).
166. Al-Ājurrī, *Kitāb al-Sharīᶜa*, pp. 292–3, *aḥādīth* 629–34. This source includes references to al-Bukhari, Muslim and other Hadith compilations.
167. The fundamental literature on the Islamic creeds includes Wensinck, *The Muslim Creed* and Watt, *Islamic Creeds*. The most recent and comprehensive contribution to this subject is J. Hoover, 'Creed', *EI3*.
168. Melchert, 'Early Hanbalite Creeds', pp. 5–6. This creed is quoted in Ibn Abī Yaᶜlā, *Ṭabaqāt al-Fuqahāᵓ al-Ḥanābila*, vol. 1, pp. 56–7 (the biography of Ahmad ibn Jaᶜfar al-Istakhri). This creed was partially translated by W. Montgomery Watt. The quoted passage, apart from the sentence about God and Moses, appears in Watt, *Islamic Creeds*, p. 37.
169. In a recent article, Saud Al-Sarhan argues that none of the six creeds which were attributed to Ahmad ibn Hanbal was actually his, although they transmit the general spirit of his teachings. Creed I, for example, first appeared in Damascus in the tenth century and was actually composed by a disciple of Ahmad by the name of Harb al-Kirmani (d. 893): Al-Sarhan and Melchert, 'The Creeds of Aḥmad', pp. 33–7.
170. Al-Dhahabī, *Siyar Aᶜlām al-Nubalāᵓ*, vol. 17, pp. 203–4. See also the biographical note by Swartz, *A Medieval Critique*, p. 94, footnote 72.
171. Abū Yaᶜlā, *Ibṭāl al-Taᵓwīlāt*, p. 421, paragraph 393; Ibn Taymiyya, *Bayān Talbīs al-Jahmiyya*, vol. 6, p. 208. Abu Yaᶜla's assessment of Abu ᶜAbd Allah's approach is quite obscure. Abu Yaᶜla says: 'It is the literal meaning of Ahmad's words' (*wa-huwa ẓāhir kalām Aḥmad*): Abū Yaᶜlā, *Ibṭāl al-Taᵓwīlāt*, p. 421, paragraph 393. Abu Yaᶜla used the expression *ẓāhir kalām* several times in *Ibṭāl al-Taᵓwīlāt* to denote the true or genuine meaning of someone's words: Abū Yaᶜlā, *Ibṭāl al-Taᵓwīlāt*, pp. 123, 132, 223.
172. Abū Yaᶜlā, *Ibṭāl al-Taᵓwīlāt*, p. 421, paragraph 395; Ibn Taymiyya, *Bayān Talbīs al-Jahmiyya*, vol. 6, p. 211.
173. For Ibn al-Jawzi's criticism of Abu ᶜAbd Allah, see Swartz, *A Medieval Critique*, pp. 94–5, footnote 72.
174. Ibn al-Jawzī, *Kitāb Akhbār al-Ṣifāt*, p. 87; Swartz, *A Medieval Critique*, p. 243, passage 177.

175. Al-Dhahabī, *Siyar Aᶜlām al-Nubalāᵓ*, vol. 16, pp. 313–15 (the biography of Abu Zayd al-Marwazi).
176. Ibn Ḥajar, *Fatḥ al-Bārī*, vol. 8, p. 454 (*Kitāb Tafsīr al-Qurᵓān, bāb sūrat Muḥammad*); vol. 10, p. 431 (*Kitāb al-Adab, bāb man waṣala waṣalahu Allāh*).
177. Al-Qasṭallānī, *Irshād al-Sārī*, vol. 7, p. 342 (*Kitāb Tafsīr al-Qurᵓān, bāb sūrat Muḥammad*). The original text states *huwa thābit lākin maᶜa tanzīh Allāh taᶜālā*. Because the expressions *thābit* and *tanzīh* need elaboration, we saw no recourse but to combine the explanation with the translation.
178. Frank, 'Elements in the Development', p. 155.
179. The source that points emphatically to Abu Zayd's affiliation as an Ashᶜarite is Ibn ᶜAsakir's (d. 1176) *Tabyīn Kadhib al-Muftarī*. According to Ibn ᶜAsakir, '[Abu Zayd] was among the people of Khurasan who benefitted from Abu 'l-Hasan al-Ashᶜari': Ibn ᶜAsākir, *Tabyīn*, p. 147. The other biographers do not associate Abu Zayd with al-Ashᶜari, but merely depict Abu Zayd according to the Ashᶜarite ethos, as a highly skilful *mutakallim* by using the phrase *ḥasan al-naẓar* (literally, good in theological speculation): al-Subkī, *Ṭabaqāt al-Shāfiᶜiyya*, vol. 3, p. 73; al-Dhahabī, *Siyar Aᶜlām al-Nubalāᵓ*, vol. 16, p. 312.
180. Goldziher, *Abhandlungen*, vol. 2, p. xxiv, footnote 2. Al-Qastallani described the rivalry between Ibn Hajar and al-ᶜAyni in *Irshād al-Sārī*, vol. 9, p. 326 (*Kitāb al-Riqāq, bāb ṣifat al-janna wa'l-nār*).
181. Ibn Ḥajar, *Fatḥ al-Bārī*, vol. 8, p. 454 (*Kitāb Tafsīr al-Qurᵓān, bāb sūrat Muḥammad*); al-ᶜAynī, *ᶜUmdat al-Qārī*, vol. 19, p. 247, *ḥadīth* 352/4830 (*Kitāb Tafsīr al-Qurᵓān, bāb wa-tuqaṭṭiᶜū arhāmakum*).
182. Qāḍī ᶜIyāḍ, *Ikmāl*, vol. 3, p. 386, *ḥadīth* 36/939 (*Kitāb al-Janāᵓiz, bāb fī ghusl al-mayyit*). The daughter can be either Zaynab (d. 629) or Umm Kulthum (d. 630).
183. Qāḍī ᶜIyāḍ, *Ikmāl*, vol. 6, p. 70, *ḥadīth* 45/1754 (*Kitāb al-Jihād waᵓl-Siyar, bāb istiḥqāq al-qātil salab al-qatīl*).
184. Al-Qasṭallānī, *Irshād al-Sārī*, vol. 7, p. 342 (*Kitāb Tafsīr al-Qurᵓān, bāb sūrat Muḥammad*). For a list of the different meanings of the word *ḥaqw* in the classical dictionaries, see al-Zabīdī, *Tāj al-ᶜArūs*, vol. 19, p. 332; Lane, *Arabic-English Lexicon*, vol. 2, pp. 613–14.
185. Ibn Ḥajar, *Fatḥ al-Bārī*, vol. 8, p. 454; al-ᶜAynī, *ᶜUmdat al-Qārī*, vol. 19, pp. 247–8, *ḥadīth* 352/4830.
186. Al-Bayḍāwī, *Tuḥfat al-Abrār*, vol. 3, p. 250, *ḥadīth* 1250/3825 (*Kitāb al-Adab, bāb al-birr wa'l-ṣila*); al-Qasṭallānī, *Irshād al-Sārī*, vol. 7, p. 342.

187. Ibn Ḥajar, *Fatḥ al-Bārī*, vol. 8, p. 454; al-ᶜAynī, *ᶜUmdat al-Qārī*, vol. 19, pp. 247–8, *ḥadīth* 352/4830; al-Qasṭallānī, *Irshād al-Sārī*, vol. 7, p. 342.
188. Al-ᶜAynī, *ᶜUmdat al-Qārī*, vol. 19, p. 247, *ḥadīth* 352/4830.
189. Ibn Ḥajar, *Fatḥ al-Bārī*, vol. 8, p. 454.
190. Al-Bayḍāwī, *Tuḥfat al-Abrār*, vol. 3, p. 250, *ḥadīth* 1250/3825; al-Qasṭallānī, *Irshād al-Sārī*, vol. 7, p. 342. Also quoted by al-Ṭībī, *al-Kāshif*, p. 3161, *ḥadīth* 4919 (*Kitāb al-Ādāb, bāb al-birr wa'l-ṣilā*).
191. Al-Bayḍāwī, *Tuḥfat al-Abrār*, vol. 3, p. 250, *ḥadīth* 1250/3825. Al-Qastallani omitted this section from his citation.
192. Al-Tibi commented on the Hadith compilation entitled *Mishkāt al-Maṣābīḥ* which was authored by al-Tibi's colleague and disciple, Wali Allah al-Khatib al-Tabrizi (d. 1337). See ᶜAbd al-Hamid Hindawi's introduction in al-Tībī, *al-Kāshif*, pp. 26–7.
193. See the account of Walid Saleh's first encounter with al-Tibi's commentary to al-Zamakhshri's *al-Kashshāf*: Saleh, *The Formation of the Classical Tafsīr Tradition*, p. 205.
194. See ᶜAbd al-Hamid Hindawi's introduction in al-Tībī, *al-Kāshif*, pp. 5–46.
195. See al-Tibi's commentary on Q. 39:67 ('They underrate the might of God. But on the Day of Resurrection He will hold the entire earth in His grasp and fold up the heavens in His right hand'): al-Tībī, *al-Kāshif*, p. 3616, *ḥadīth* 4919 (*Kitāb al-Ādāb, bāb al-birr wa'l-ṣila*).
196. Al-Tibi authored a treatise on the vocabulary of rhetoric (*Laṭā'if al-Tibyān fi ᶜIlmay al-Maᶜānī wa'l- Bayān*) which is printed along with his commentary of *Mishkāt al-Maṣābīḥ*: al-Tībī, *al-Kāshif*, pp. 47–157.
197. For *al-istiᶜāra al-tamthīliyya* and *al-istiᶜāra al-tamthīliyya*, see Heinrichs, 'Metaphor', pp. 524–5.
198. Al-Tībī, *al-Kāshif*, p. 3616, *ḥadīth* 4919 (*Kitāb al-Ādāb, bāb al-birr wa'l-ṣila*); Ibn Ḥajar, *Fatḥ al-Bārī*, vol. 8, p. 454 (*Kitāb Tafsīr al-Qur'ān, bāb sūrat Muḥammad*); al-ᶜAynī, *ᶜUmdat al-Qārī*, vol. 19, p. 247, *ḥadīth* 352/4830 (*Kitāb Tafsīr al-Qur'ān, bāb wa-tuqaṭṭiᶜū arḥāmakum*); al-Qasṭallānī, *Irshād al-Sārī*, vol. 7, p. 342 (*Kitāb Tafsīr al-Qur'ān, bāb sūrat Muḥammad*).
199. Al-Qurṭubī, *Jāmiᶜ*, vol. 16, p. 164 (interpretation of Q. 47:22).
200. Frank, 'Elements in the Development', pp. 155–9.
201. See, for example, al-Rāzī, *Mafātīḥ al-Ghayb*, vol. 13, p. 126 (commentary of Q. 6:102). Fakhr al-Din al-Razi uses the term *al-tawḥīd wa'l-tanzīh* throughout his commentary of the Quran when he identifies Quranic verses that describe God and His rule in this world. According to al-Razi, all these verses prove the

concepts of *tawḥīd* and *tanzīh*. The Damascene historian Ibn ᶜAsakir (d. 1176) also expressed the Ashᶜarite acceptance of *tawḥīd* and *tanzīh* as the two pillars of Ashᶜarism; however, without using the term *ahl al-tawḥīd wa'l-tanzīh*: Ibn ᶜAsākir *Tabyīn*, p. 362; McCarthy, *The Theology of al-Ashᶜarī*, p. 186. This term was probably coined by al-Razi to describe the Ashᶜarites: al-Rāzī, *Asās al-Taqdīs*, p. 23. In his elaborate response to *Asās al-Taqdīs*, Ibn Taymiyya doubted whether the later Ashᶜarites were entitled to this epithet, because of their use of *taʾwīl* which Ibn Taymiyya perceived as a false methodology: Ibn Taymiyya, *Bayān Talbīs al-Jahmiyya*, vol. 1, p. 421. A later Ashᶜarite who used the epithet *ahl al-tawḥīd wa'l-tanzīh* to describe the Ashᶜarites was the Damascene Shafiᶜite scholar Ibn Jahbal (d. 1332–3). Ibn Jahbal wrote a long refutation of Ibn Taymiyya which is recorded in al-Subki's *Ṭabaqāt al-Shāfiᶜiyya*, vol. 9, pp. 34–91. The term *al-tawḥīd wa'l-tanzīh* describes the later Ashᶜarite worldview, and appears on p. 36 in Ibn Jahbal's refutation (see Chapter 5).

202. Al-Ashᶜarī, *al-Ibāna*, p. 9; Frank, 'Elements in the Development', pp. 175–6, 178.
203. Watt, *The Formative Period*, pp. 306–7.
204. Al-Ashᶜarī, *Maqālāt al-Islāmiyyīn*, vol. 1, p. 290. For a comparative translation of al-Ashᶜari's two creeds in *al-Ibāna* and *Maqālāt al-Islāmiyyīn*, see McCarthy, *The Theology of al-Ashᶜarī*, p. 237.
205. Al-Ashᶜarī, *Maqālāt al-Islāmiyyīn*, vol. 1, p. 294. Al-Ashᶜari mentions only *ḥadīth al-nuzūl* as a text that 'the People of the Hadith and the Sunna' accept with no reservation, and does not quote other *aḥādīth al-ṣifāt*. Alongside *ḥadīth al-nuzūl*, he quotes 'and your Lord comes down with the angels, in their ranks' (Q. 89:22) and '[We] are closer to him than his jugular vein' (Q. 50:16): al-Ashᶜarī, *Maqālāt al-Islāmiyyīn*, vol. 1, p. 295.
206. Allard, *Le problème des attributs divins*, pp. 52, 103–4; Melchert, *The Formation of the Sunni Schools*, pp. 150–3.
207. Cook, *Commanding Right*, pp. 116–17.
208. Ibn Abī Yaᶜlā, *Ṭabaqāt al-Fuqahāʾ al-Ḥanābila*, vol. 2, p. 27 (the biography of al-Hasan ibn ᶜAli al-Barbahari). This anecdote is also translated and analysed in: Frank, 'Elements in the Development', pp. 171–2.
209. Ibn ᶜAsākir, *Tabyīn*, pp. 288–9.
210. Ibn ᶜAsākir, *Tabyīn*, pp. 286–7; McCarthy, *The Theology of al-Ashᶜarī*, pp. 196–7.
211. Gilliot, 'Attributes of God', *EI3*.

212. El-Bizri, 'God: Essence and Attributes', pp. 124–31.
213. Allard, *Le problème des attributs divins*, pp. 80–1.
214. Al-Ash^{c}arī, *al-Ibāna*, pp. 10, 18–20. See also the remark by Gimaret, 'Un document majeur', p. 218.
215. Wensinck's estimation of the 'Hanbalism' in the creed of *al-Ibāna* hits the mark: Wensinck, *The Muslim Creed*, pp. 88–94. For a summary of the question whether al-Ash^{c}ari remained a *mutakallim* after he left Mu^{c}tazilism and became a traditionalist, see Thiele, 'Between Cordoba and Nīsābūr', p. 227, note 2.
216. Al-Ash^{c}arī, *al-Ibāna*, pp. 33, 35. Later Ash^{c}arites would refute this concept: Holtzman and Ovadia, 'On Divine Aboveness' (forthcoming).
217. Al-Ash^{c}arī, *al-Ibāna*, p. 34; Wensinck, *The Muslim Creed*, p. 90.
218. Al-Ash^{c}arī, *al-Ibāna*, p. 36; Wensinck, *The Muslim Creed*, p. 90.
219. See also Ibn ^{c}Asakir's declaration that the way of the Ash^{c}arites is a combination of *taʾwīl* and *tanzīh*: Ibn ^{c}Asākir, *Tabyīn*, p. 287.
220. Al-Ash^{c}arī, *al-Ibāna*, pp. 36–7.
221. Al-Ash^{c}arī, *al-Ibāna*, p. 10.
222. N. J. Dawood, whose interpretation of the Quran in English is used throughout this book, translated Q. 51:47: 'We built the heaven with Our might', thus applying the rule of *taʾwīl* (figurative reading). The Quranic text uses the plural form of *yad* (hand, *aydin*): Dawood, *The Koran*, p. 521.
223. Gimaret, *La doctrine d'al-Ash^{c}arī*, pp. 324–5.
224. See, especially, al-Ash^{c}arī, *al-Ibāna*, p. 41, and Allard's corresponding analysis: Allard, *Le problème des attributs divins*, pp. 281–2.
225. Al-Ash^{c}arī, *al-Ibāna*, pp. 37-41; Abrahamov, 'The *Bi-Lā Kayfa* Doctrine', p. 369.
226. Gimaret, *Les noms divins*, pp. 32–3; 'Un document majeur', pp. 194–6.
227. Ibn Fūrak, *Mujarrad Maqālāt*, p. 192.
228. Ibn Fūrak, *Mujarrad Maqālāt*, p. 41.
229. Weiss, 'Medieval Muslim Discussions', pp. 35–8; Shah, 'The Philological Endeavours (Part I)', p. 29. Weiss's debt to former scholarship, including the works of Ignaz Goldziher, Henri Loucel and Roger Arnaldez on the subject of the origins of language, is duly clarified in footnote 2 in his article.
230. Ibn Fūrak, *Mujarrad Maqālāt*, p. 191. The fundamental discussions of *ḥaqīqa* and *majāz* appear in Heinrichs, 'On the Genesis of the *Ḥaqīqa-Majāz* Dichotomy', pp. 111–17; Gilliot, 'Exegesis of the Qurʾan', pp. 108–9; Simon, 'Majāz', *Encyclopedia of Arabic Language and Lingustics*.

231. Ibn Fūrak, *Mujarrad Maqālāt*, pp. 27, 191. For the theory of *waḍ*ᶜ *al-lughgha*, see Versteegh, 'Linguistic Attitudes', p. 22.
232. Ibn Fūrak, *Mujarrad Maqālāt*, p. 192; Weiss, 'Medieval Muslim Discussions', p. 35.
233. Ibn Fūrak, *Mujarrad Maqālāt*, pp. 26–7.
234. An excellent survey on the Ashᶜarites of Nishapur is Nguyen, *Sufi Master and Qur*ᵓ*an Scholar*, pp. 220–5.
235. Ibn ᶜAsākir, *Tabyīn*, pp. 140–1; al-Subkī, *Ṭabaqāt al-Shāfi*ᶜ*iyya*, vol. 3, p. 369 (the biography of Abu 'l-Ḥasan al-Ashᶜarī).
236. Ibn ᶜAsākir, *Tabyīn*, p. 188 (the biography of Abū Isḥāq al-Isfarāyīnī); al-Subkī, *Ṭabaqāt al-Shāfi*ᶜ*iyya*, vol 4, p. 257 (the biography of Abū Isḥāq al-Isfarāyīnī).
237. On the corporealism of the Karramites, see Holtzman and Ovadia 'On Divine Aboveness' (forthcoming), and Zysow, 'Karrāmiyya', pp. 255–8.
238. Al-Subkī, *Ṭabaqāt al-Shāfi*ᶜ*iyya*, vol. 4, p. 256 (the biography of Abū Isḥāq al-Isfarāyīnī).
239. Ibn ᶜAsākir, *Tabyīn*, pp. 232–3; al-Subkī, *Ṭabaqāt al-Shāfi*ᶜ*iyya*, vol. 4, pp. 127–35 (the biography of Ibn Fūrak); Bulliet, *The Patricians of Nishapur*, pp. 160–1.
240. See Daniel Gimaret's introduction: Ibn Fūrak, *Mushkil al-Ḥadīth*, pp. 11m–14m (of the Introduction).
241. Allard, *Le problème des attributs divins*, pp. 326–7.
242. Ibn Fūrak, *Mushkil al-Ḥadīth*, pp. 217–52.
243. Nishapur of the eleventh century was divided between several hostile factions: the Hanafites, the Shafiᶜites, the Karramites and the Shiᶜites. The learned elite of the city was comprised mainly of Hanafites and Shafiᶜites, while the lower socio-economic strata of Nishapuri society were Karramites: Bulliet, *The Patricians of Nishapur*, pp. 76–7. See Chapter 5.
244. Ibn Fūrak, *Mushkil al-Ḥadīth*, pp. 1, 213.
245. Ibn Fūrak, *Mushkil al-Ḥadīth*, p. 2.
246. Ibn Fūrak, *Mushkil al-Ḥadīth*, pp. 65–72, 124–9.
247. Ibn Fūrak, *Mushkil al-Ḥadīth*, pp. 76–8. Cf. Gimaret, *La doctrine d'al-Ash*ᶜ*arī*, p. 342.
248. Zouggar, 'L'Impeccabilité du Prophète Muḥammad', pp. 73–7.
249. Ibn Fūrak, *Mushkil al-Ḥadīth*, pp. 210–14; Gimaret, *Dieu à l'image de l'homme*, p. 163.
250. Wright, *Grammar*, p. ii 113.

251. Ibn Fūrak, *Mushkil al-Ḥadīth*, p. 214; Gimaret, *Dieu à l'image de l'homme*, p. 163.
252. Ibn Fūrak, *Mushkil al-Ḥadīth*, p. 214; Gimaret, *Dieu à l'image de l'homme*, p. 164.
253. Ibn Fūrak, *Mushkil al-Ḥadīth*, pp. 214–15.
254. Ibn Fūrak, *Mushkil al-Ḥadīth*, pp. 9–10.
255. Ibn Fūrak, *Mushkil al-Ḥadīth*, pp. 17, 202. This *ḥadīth* was included in the compilation of fabricated *aḥādīth* by the Hanbalite scholar Ibn al-Jawzi: Ibn al-Jawzī, *al-Mawḍūʿāt*, p. 149, *ḥadīth* 231 (*Kitāb al-Tawḥīd, bāb fī anna Allāh ʿazza wa'jalla qadīm*).
256. Ibn Fūrak, *Mushkil al-Ḥadīth*, pp. 69–70.
257. Ibn Fūrak, *Mushkil al-Ḥadīth*, p. 2.
258. Ibn Fūrak, *Mushkil al-Ḥadīth*, pp. 253, 305. Q. 3:7 discusses the ambiguous verses (*mutashābihāt*) in the Quran, and states that their interpretation (*taʾwīl*, here as a synonym of *tafsīr*) is known only to God, while *al-rāsikhūn fī 'l-ʿilm* believe in these verses. This is the conventional Sunnite reading of the verse. The Shiʿites read the verse differently: both God and *al-rāsikhūn fī 'l-ʿilm* possess the knowledge of how to interpret the ambiguous verses: Bar-Asher, 'Hidden and the Hidden', *EQ*; Steigerwald, 'Twelver Shīʿī Taʾwīl', p. 377.
259. Ibn Fūrak, *Mushkil al-Ḥadīth*, p. 254. Ibn Furak's reading of Q. 3:7 follows the traditionalistic reading.
260. Sellheim, 'al-Khaṭīb al-Baghdādī', *EI2*; Brown, *Canonization*, p. 267.
261. Al-Khaṭīb al-Baghdādī, *al-Jāmiʿ li-Akhlāq al-Rāwī*, p. 302, passage 1337.
262. Al-Khaṭīb al-Baghdādī, *al-Jāmiʿ li-Akhlāq al-Rāwī*, p. 300, passage 1328.

5

Iconic Books and Gestures: *Aḥādīth al-Ṣifāt* in the Public Sphere

Introduction

The intensive use of the *bi-lā kayfa* formula among the traditionalists safeguarded them from a literal understanding of the anthropomorphic traditions. However, as we have seen in the previous chapter, the traditionalistic trend was in fact not entirely immune from a literal understanding of *aḥādīth al-ṣifāt*. Several members of the scholarly circles read the anthropomorphic descriptions in *aḥādīth al-ṣifāt* literally. The prevalent assumption in modern scholarship was that none of these scholars presented an overall systemised theory which argued in favour of such a reading.[1] One may argue that the literal reading did not require educated argumentations in its favour. Furthermore, the literal understanding of *aḥādīth al-ṣifāt* was more widespread among the lay public than among the scholarly circles. Anthropomorphism was identified with the ignorant masses and the popular preachers who incited them. Nonetheless, and as we further prove in this chapter, there was at least one successful attempt to articulate the rules for a literal reading of *aḥādith al-ṣifāt*. Apart from this scholarly attempt, the literal understanding of the anthropomorphic expressions was ubiquitous in the public sphere. This understanding was promoted by highbrow professional *muḥaddithūn* who openly articulated their literal reading of *aḥādīth al-ṣifāt*, mostly by gesticulating but also by expressing occasional remarks. The records of such gestures and remarks are scattered throughout the historical sources.

An example of a professional *muḥaddith* with clear anthropomorphic inclinations was the Zahirite Andalusian scholar Abu ᶜAmir al-ᶜAbdari

(d. 1130), who lived and taught in Baghdad.[2] According to the testimony of al-ᶜAbdari's former student, the illustrious historian of Damascus Ibn ᶜAsakir (d. 1176), al-ᶜAbdari was highly esteemed as a *muḥaddith* despite his known anthropomorphic tendencies. Ibn ᶜAsakir studied with al-ᶜAbdari in Baghdad, but at some point he withdrew from al-ᶜAbdari's classes because al-ᶜAbdari slandered the Hadith scholars who preceded him.[3] It is noteworthy that it was al-ᶜAbdari's 'lack of respect' (*sūʾ al-adab*) for the former generations and not his anthropomorphic views that prompted Ibn ᶜAsakir to break away from him. At any rate, Ibn ᶜAsakir remarked that al-ᶜAbdari held incorrect dogmatic views (*kāna sayīʾ 'l-iᶜtiqād*) because he understood *āyāt al-ṣifāt* and *aḥādīth al-ṣifāt* literally. Thus, al-ᶜAbdari was recorded as saying that he did not accept the interpretation of the Muᶜtazilites (to whom he referred as 'The People of Innovation', *ahl al-bidaᶜ*) to Q. 42:11 'Nothing can be compared with Him'. The Muᶜtazilites used this verse to prove that God was transcendent and different from all existing creations. To this Muᶜtazilite argumentation, al-ᶜAbdari offered the following explanation to the meaning of this Quranic verse: in terms of divinity (*ilāhiyya*), God is incomparable; namely, there is no other god but He. However, 'in terms of form (*ṣūra*), He is just like you and me'. To corroborate his unconventional and daring understanding of Q. 42:11, al-ᶜAbdari quoted Q. 33:32, 'Wives of the Prophet, you are not like other women,' and added: 'when it comes to sacredness (*fī al-ḥurma*)'. Al-ᶜAbdari meant, of course, that 'in terms of form' the wives of the Prophet were like any other women.[4]

More than two centuries later, the well-known sceptic Shams al-Din al-Dhahabi (d. 1348) critically read Ibn ᶜAsakir's report. Al-Dhahabi remarked that he did not believe that al-ᶜAbdari actually said 'these heretical words of the Mujassima, the corporealists', because the source of this anecdote was unknown.[5] Elsewhere, al-Dhahabi stated: 'The stories about [al-ᶜAbdari]'s *tashbīh* were never proven. If they turn out to be true, I will be the first to say: "Away with him!".'[6] However, Ibn ᶜAsakir obviously believed the veracity of what he was told, although he signalled to his readers that the source of these anecdotes was unreliable; instead of naming the person who reported them, Ibn ᶜAsakir merely wrote in the preface of the anecdote: *balaghanī*, which means 'I heard' or even 'rumour has it'.[7] Ibn ᶜAsakir in fact corroborated these stories that labelled al-ᶜAbdari as a blunt anthropomorphist with the following report. According to Ibn ᶜAsakir, he had a conversation with al-ᶜAbdari in which the latter admitted that he understood *aḥādīth al-ṣifāt* literally. Al-ᶜAbdari told Ibn ᶜAsakir:

> People have disagreed about [*aḥādīth al-ṣifāt*]. Some use the figurative interpretation (*taʾwīl*), some refrain from using it (*imsāk*), and some believe the literal meaning (*ẓāhir*) of these texts. My methodology is one of these three methodologies.[8]

The blunt anthropomorphism that al-ᶜAbdari represented was not at all characteristic of the Zahirites. Being extreme literalists, it is understandable that the Zahirites would adopt extreme anthropomorphic views. It is noteworthy, however, that the most famous Zahirite, the Andalusian theologian and jurist Ibn Hazm (d. 1064), rejected anthropomorphism; he developed independent and original views regarding this topic.[9] However, Ibn Hazm was a formidable exception and, more so, he was an elitist scholar. Al-ᶜAbdari, on the other hand, spread his anthropomorphic views to a wide audience, as a close look at the following anecdote indicates. This anecdote describes an incident that occurred in the marketplace of Bab al-Azaj in Baghdad sometime between 1126 and 1130.[10]

> Ibn ᶜAsakir testified:
> I heard that one day, when [al-ᶜAbdari] was in the market of Bab al-Azaj, he recited [Q. 68:42] 'Upon the day when the shank shall be bared' (*yawma yukshafu ᶜan sāqin*).[11] [While reciting] he stroke his shank and said: 'a shank like my shank that you see.'[12]

The Bab al-Azaj anecdote is a rich and vivid text which – despite its brevity – includes six different elements: a specific setting (the market of Bab al-Azaj in Baghdad), an audience (the people in the marketplace), a protagonist (al-ᶜAbdari), a recited text ('Upon the day when the shank shall be bared', Q. 68:42), a performed gesture (stroking the shank) and an interpretation ('a shank like my shank that you see'). The dramatic scene features al-ᶜAbdari, an eccentric *muḥaddith*, who was depicted in other anecdotes as deformed and dressed in rags.[13] Al-ᶜAbdari stands in the crowded marketplace and performs before an audience. The audience, which is not mentioned in the text, was probably divided between people who watched al-ᶜAbdari (at least one of the audience reported about this incident to Ibn ᶜAsakir) and others who proceeded with their daily business. Our point is that al-ᶜAbdari's bold anthropomorphic interpretation of the Quranic verse, which comprised both a gesture and a verbal explanation, did not stir any excitement or riot in the marketplace; otherwise, Ibn ᶜAsakir would have mentioned such an occurrence. The audience's indifference can be explained by the fact that Bab al-Azaj was a stronghold of the Hanbalites of Baghdad.[14] The Hanbalites were a convenient receptive audience for the message that al-ᶜAbdari brought because (as explained in Chapters 3 and 4) they were familiar with such an anthropomorphic discourse. This audience anticipated that the religious message brought by this eccentric scholar would be accompanied by a performance, and we can safely assume that the audience delighted in both the text and the performance. *Aḥādīth al-ṣifāt* (and in our case, *āyāt al-ṣifāt*) were the spiritual nourishment of the lay public and the accompanying performance was their entertainment. For an Ashᶜarite like Ibn ᶜAsakir and for a stern traditionalist like Shams al-Din al-Dhahabi, the combination of a recitation of an anthropomorphic text, an accompanying gesture and a verbal interpretation that led to a literal understanding of the text was both outrageous and inconceivable. Ibn ᶜAsakir and al-Dhahabi believed that the proper way to handle this text was to recite it and conclude it by adding the expression *bi-lā kayfa*. However, the people in the marketplace who surrounded al-ᶜAbdari accepted his performance as a natural part of their daily landscape.

The different elements in the Bab al-Azaj anecdote shed light on the presence of the anthropomorphic texts (in this case, a Quranic verse) in the public sphere, the role that they played in certain events, and their impact on the people who transmitted and received them. As William A. Graham indicated in his 1987 study on the oral use of scriptures, '[t]he significant "scriptural" characteristics of a text belong not only to the text itself but also to its role in a community and in individual lives'.[15] As the dozens of cases that were recorded in the historical sources demonstrate, the professional scholars were not the exclusive recipients of *aḥādīth al-ṣifāt*, and accordingly, these texts were not confined to the solitude of the scholar's study and the elitist madrasa. *Aḥādīth al-ṣifāt* were part of a rich oral literature that was performed in different venues and received by different audiences. They were not buried in the pages of holy codices or whispered by awed apprentices of great scholars. Rather, *aḥādīth al-ṣifāt* were shouted in the marketplace and recited in the mosque. In addition, they stood amid heated discussions that were open to the public. These features of *aḥādīth al-ṣifāt* reflect the interface between text and society, between theology and politics, between an abstract message and its physical manifestation.

The following chapter examines the ubiquitous presence of *aḥādīth al-ṣifāt* in the public sphere by focusing on milestones in the theological debates on the anthropomorphic texts in the Hadith. These milestones are roughly represented by four iconic texts: the caliphal Qadiri Creed, Ibn Khuzayma's *Kitāb al-Tawḥīd*, Fakhr al-Din al-Razi's *Asās al-Taqdīs* and Ibn Taymiyya's *al-Ḥamawiyya al-Kubrā*. The Qadiri Creed was an official document issued by the caliph. The other three texts are full-scale books which were written by political figures whose public persona was substantial and conspicuous in their home towns. These books stood at the centre of public attention and were discussed in the confrontations between the main trends of Islamic traditionalism, mainly the Hanbalites (the ultra-traditionalists) and the Ashᶜarites (the traditional-rationalists). Since the scope of this chapter does not allow a full-scale discussion on the content and line of argumentation of each of these three books, the following chapter focuses on aspects in these books' iconicity. According to James W. Watts, '[i]conic books are texts revered as objects of power rather than just as words of instruction, information, or insight'.[16] Watts's 2006 model of scriptures inspired the theoretical framework of this chapter. In addition, this chapter benefitted from William A. Graham's 2010 observations about iconic books. In Section I, we present Watts's and Graham's description of an iconic text and examine the Qadiri Creed in view of both these scholars' approaches to iconic texts and scriptures. Section II is dedicated to an examination of Ibn Khuzayma's *Kitāb al-Tawḥīd* in view of the three building-blocks of Watts's theory of iconic texts, namely *interpretation*, *performance* and *iconicity*. Section III focuses on Fakhr al-Din al-Razi's *Asās al-Taqdīs* which was authored as a direct response to *Kitāb al-Tawḥīd*. Section IV establishes the connection between Fakhr al-Din al-Razi's *Asās al-Taqdīs* and Ibn Taymiyya's iconic treatise *al-Ḥamawiyya al-Kubrā*. The iconicity of *Asās al-Taqdīs* and *al-Ḥamawiyya al-Kubrā* is (following Graham's observations) reflected by the visibility of these texts in the public sphere: both these texts ignited a public controversy about the performance of two iconic gestures that are linked to the recitations of *aḥādīth al-ṣifāṭ*. Section V highlights *al-Ḥamawiyya al-Kubrā*'s iconicity by addressing the derogative name *ḥashwiyya* (vulgar anthropomorphists) which was central to this public controversy. The connection between *ḥashwiyya* and the public debate on *aḥādīth al-ṣifāt* will be explained in Section V. The iconic books and gestures that are discussed here underscore the interface between theology and politics, and reflect on the controversies between the ultra-traditionalists and the traditional-rationalists.

I. The Iconicity of the Qadiri Creed

In a definitive article published in 2006, James W. Watts presented his three-dimensional model of scriptures. Placing the scriptures in their cultural context, this model explained the impact of scriptures on historical and contemporary affairs. Watts applied his model to several public debates and political events that occurred in recent years in the United States. In these events, the scriptures of the three monotheistic religions played definitive roles.[17] Although Watts's model seems to grow from his view of the Bible and its various manifestations in the public sphere, we found his model appropriate for discussing *aḥādīth al-ṣifāt* and their place in the public sphere. The following text briefly presents Watts's model.

According to Watts, religious communities 'ritualize scriptures along three different dimensions: a semantic dimension, a performative dimension, and an iconic dimension . . . all three forms of ritualization are intrinsic to scriptures and necessary to their nature and function.'[18] These dimensions reflect the prolonged attention given by the society to the iconic book. The book is constantly interpreted, publicly displayed and reproduced.[19] The semantic dimension of scriptures 'has always received most if not all of the attention of scholars . . . [it] includes all aspects of interpretation and commentary as well as appeals to the text's contents in preaching and other forms of persuasive rhetoric'.[20] The performative dimension of scriptures, according to Watts's model, is the dramatisation of the text. In this context, Watts mentions artistic displays of scriptural quotations, namely the ritualised forms of private and public reading, chanting and singing the sacred words.[21] The iconic dimension is 'the physical form, ritual manipulation, and artistic representation of scriptures'.[22] Thus, the book itself as a material object conveys religious significance. Watts's model easily befits the Quran.[23] The semantic dimension is manifested in the numerous commentaries of the Quran and in the presence of the Quran in religious texts like theological treatises and sermons. The performative dimension of the Quran is manifested, for example, in the various public events in which the Quran is recited. These events are videoed and uploaded to YouTube. Also available are Smartphone applications that provide recitations of the Quran by professional reciters. The iconic dimension of the Quran is manifested in the luxurious copies of the Quran that are made of expensive materials, with bindings decorated in gold, or the delicate calligraphies of Quranic verses like *āyat al-kursī* ('the verse of the throne', Q. 2:255) that are used for decorating houses and work spaces. However, Watts's theory is applicable to other texts, for example, the Qadiri Creed.

The Qadiri Creed (*al-iᶜtiqād al-qādiri*; also known as *al-risāla al-qādiriyya*) was a document issued by the caliph al-Qadir Bi-Allah (d. 1031) in approximately 1018. The brief text presented the various elements of the Sunnite creed and its purpose was to reaffirm the ᶜAbbassid caliph's commitment to the fundamentals of Islamic traditionalism. Politically, the issuance of al-Qadiri Creed was meant to pacify the traditionalists who enjoyed the unrestricted support of *al-ᶜāmma*, the masses, and to assure them that their beliefs were accepted as the state's dogma. In the background of publishing this document were the bitter memories of the ordeals that the traditionalists, and especially Ahmad ibn Hanbal (d. 855), experienced during the *miḥna* of the caliph al-Maᵓmun (d. 833). During the *miḥna*, which also occurred in the reign of the caliphs al-Muᶜtasim (d. 842) and al-Wathiq (d. 847), the state demanded that the traditionalists accept the Muᶜtazilite doctrine of the createdness of the Quran and other fundamentals of Muᶜtazilism. As we discussed in Chapter 2, the discussions in the *miḥna* also included references to the divine attributes and *aḥādīth al-ṣifāt*. A counter-declaration to the rationalistic policy of the *miḥna*, the Qadiri Creed, proclaimed that 'he who asserts that [the word of God] is created is a heretic and it is permitted to shed his blood after he is called to repent [and refuses to do so]'.[24] In other words, the Qadiri Creed was more than the official call for excommunication of the Muᶜtazilites; the Creed was a call for their execution.

The theme of the divine attributes was also briefly mentioned in the Qadiri Creed:

> [God] should be described only by the attributes that He used to describe Himself, or the attributes that His Prophet used to describe Him. And this should be known: every attribute by which He described Himself or by which His Prophet described Him is an attribute of actuality and not a metaphor (*ṣifa ḥaqīqiyya wa-lā majāziyya*).[25]

The Qadiri Creed introduced only the noncontroversial attributes that are mentioned in the Quran (hearing, seeing, knowing, etc.) and did not address the problematic attributes that appear in *aḥādīth al-ṣifāt* (descending, laughing, appearing, etc.). In 1018, the Qadiri Creed was read for the first time by state officials in the presence of the caliph in a public gathering. The Creed was re-read and reaffirmed several times during the reign of al-Qadir bi-Allah's successor, al-Qa᾿im Bi-Amr Allah (d. 1074), who ruled for 44 years. The reaffirmed text (*al-iʿtiqād al-qā᾿imī*, the Qa᾿imi Creed) probably expanded on the topics that appeared in the original text that was attributed to the caliph al-Qadir bi-Allah; therefore, the Qadiri Creed and the Qa᾿imi Creed were in fact two different texts that were considered as one.[26] The Hanbalite historian Ibn al-Jawzi (d. 1201), who copied the Qadiri – or rather, the Qa᾿imi – Creed into his magnificent work of history *Al-Muntaẓam fī Tārīkh al-Rusul wa'l-Mulūk*, received the text from a *muḥaddith* who received it from Abu al-Husayn Muhammad ibn Muhammad ibn al-Farra᾿ (murdered in 1131), also known as Ibn Abi Yaʿla.[27] Ibn Abi Yaʿla received the text from his father, the Hanbalite theologian Abu Yaʿla (d. 1066), who was present at an event in the caliphal palace in 1040 in which the Qadiri Creed was read in public. Abu Yaʿla probably made his copy of the text shortly after this event.[28]

The semantic dimension of the Qadiri Creed is reflected in the way that the recipients of this simplistic text perceived it. The traditionalists in general and the Hanbalites in particular highly regarded the Qadiri Creed as an official verification of their dominance in the public sphere. The document confirmed the veracity of the traditionalistic faith and excluded any possibility for any other dogma in Baghdad to exist. The performative dimension of this text is of course reflected in its ritualised public readings. This dimension, as well as the text's iconic dimension, is reflected in the following event that occurred fifty years after the first public reading of the Qadiri Creed. On Saturday the fifteenth of Jumada al-Ula in Hijri year 460 (22.03.1068), a group of traditionalistic scholars and notables of various religious trends, led by the leader of the Hanbalites of Baghdad, *sharīf* Abu Jaᶜfar (d. 1077–8), walked in procession through the streets of Baghdad, from the great mosque named after the caliph al-Mansur, near the Basra Gate, to the caliphal palace. The participants of the procession demanded that the Qadiri Creed be removed from storage, read in public and reaffirmed. The caliph, al-Qaᵓim Bi-Amr Allah, accompanied by his vizier Ibn Jahir (d. 1090–1) received the protesters (*al-jamāᶜa*) in the caliphal palace and assented to their demand: the Qadiri Creed was ceremoniously read in the palace in front of both the caliph and an audience comprised of the city's notables and traditionalistic scholars.[29]

The event was successful: the entire audience reaffirmed the Qadiri Creed. One of the most distinguished participants in the event, Ibn Furak,[30] jumped to his feet, cursed the innovators and heretics, and said: 'We have no creed but this creed and what it contains.' The participants congratulated Ibn Furak for his enthusiasm and religious zeal. The *sharīf* Abu Jaᶜfar then requested to receive a copy of the Creed. The vizier Ibn Jahir apologised that there was only one copy of the text, the one from which they read, but he promised the *sharīf*: 'We will prepare a copy for you, so you will read it in your assemblies.' Although the *sharīf* thanked the vizier, he could not avoid a word of criticism directed to the current caliph: 'This is what we used to do in the days of [the caliph] al-Qadir [bi-Allah] – said the *sharīf* – the text was read in the mosques, both private and public.' The vizier hurried to hush the bold *sharīf*: 'And so you shall – the vizier promised him – for we have no creed but this creed.' The protesters hurried to take their leave, while uttering words of gratitude to the vizier. The vizier kept his promise: three weeks later, on the seventh of Jumada al-Akhira (13.04.1068), the *sharīf* Abu Jaᶜfar stood in the great mosque near the Basra gate and read the Qadiri Creed in front of an audience of 'scholars and laymen', just as he claimed that he had done in the days of the caliph al-Qadir bi-Allah.[31] The event described here seems to highlight the two other dimensions in which the Qadiri Creed was ritualised. First, the performative dimension of this text is expressed through the ritual of public readings and the demand of the *sharīf* to renew them. Second, the iconic dimension of the text is reflected in the careful treatment of the sole copy of this text, and the demand of the *sharīf* to appropriate a copy for himself.

Watts's model is indeed applicable to the Qadiri Creed; however, the model does not provide a sufficient answer concerning the importance of this text. William Graham's 2010 article offers a different perspective on scriptures or 'iconic texts'. Graham's view of iconic texts is more comprehensive than Watts's because Graham includes in this category both scriptures and works of literature, poetry and philosophy. Graham sees these texts as

> texts that are truly *iconic* in the sense of being among the highest achievements of their particular linguistic, ethnic, regional, national, or cultural traditions, and thus emblematic of those traditions – and as such also influenced by, and important to, one or more religious traditions of their respective cultures as well.[32]

Elsewhere, he clarifies that icons are

> objects with symbolic, signifying capacity and observable power and/or authority in their respective contexts: objects that are culturally or religiously meaningful for anyone who sees them as emblematic of something larger . . . I use 'iconic' to designate a book (or anything else) that carries significant cultural and/or religious, and consequently intellectual and/or spiritual, meaning.[33]

Graham's observations helps clarify the major points regarding the *iconicity* of the Qadiri Creed. Adopting Graham's observations, we note that the Qadiri Creed was an iconic text both because of its content and because it was cherished by a highly motivated and activist community: the Hanbalites of Baghdad. This community took the Qadiri Creed as a symbol of its political power. The circumstances that led the other traditionalists to join the Hanbalites in their claim to re-establish this text's stature, explain why the Hanbalites and other traditionalists chose the Creed to make their demands on the caliph. The participants in the procession for the Qadiri Creed were motivated by their genuine concern for the fate of the true Islamic faith. Several months prior to the procession, on the thirteenth of Muharram 460 (23.11.1067), they lost the powerful patron of the Hanbalites of Baghdad, Abu Mansur ibn Yusuf. The Hanbalites and the other traditionalists benefitted significantly from Abu Mansur's generous sponsorship in their everyday life. This sponsorship compensated to a large degree for the financial incompetence of their other benefactor, the caliph of Baghdad. In addition to the generous stipends that Abu Mansur endowed on the dozens of holders of formal and informal religious positions in Baghdad, from the imams in the mosques to storytellers, Sufis and preachers, Abu Mansur was responsible for the gigantic endeavour of reconstructing the dysfunctional local hospital. He was instrumental in hiring its staff and donating the hospital *awqāf* properties that would guarantee its financial stability and independence.[34]

However, the protesters were not merely mourning the loss of their powerful benefactor for material reasons; they were worried because they remained without protection in their battle against the other political movement in Baghdad, the rationalists. The rationalists comprised two groups: the powerful Ashᶜarites and the rapidly dwindling Muᶜtazilites. The Ashᶜarites were supported by Nizam al-Mulk (assassinated in 1092), the vizier of the Seljuki sultan. Unlike the social base of the traditionalists which was wide and relied on *al-ᶜāmma* (the commoners), the rationalists were an elite group. Nizam al-Mulk's gift to this thin layer of Ashᶜarite scholars and their wealthy families of merchants was al-Madrasa al-Nizamiyya, an establishment of higher education that was opened in Baghdad in 1066, several months before the protest occurred. The sudden death of Abu Mansur (the word on the street was that his death was due to unnatural causes, and that perhaps Nizam al-Mulk was responsible for his death) and the spiritually intensified religious activities of the Ashᶜarites in al-Madrasa al-Nizamiyya were enough to stir the traditionalists. The straw that broke the camel's back, however, was the renewal of the teaching sessions of the Muᶜtazilite Abu ᶜAli ibn al-Walid (d. 1086). The Muᶜtazilites of Baghdad assured Ibn al-Walid that, with the death of Abu Mansur, the traditionalists had lost their benefactor and that he was free to recommence his teaching activities. Once Ibn al-Walid's classes of logic and *kalām* commenced, the *sharīf* Abu Jaᶜfar decided that the time was ripe for the caliph to reaffirm his commitment to the traditionalists. The *sharīf* Abu Jaᶜfar sat in daily protests in the great mosque at the Basra Gate, an infamous spot for the fights and riots that occurred there frequently. From his position in the great mosque, the *sharīf* Abu Jaᶜfar started to enlist the traditionalists to join the protest procession.[35] In view of the growth of the Ashᶜarite and Muᶜtazilite activities in the city, it was easy for the *sharīf* to entice all trends of Islamic traditionalism to participate in his protest procession.

The Hanbalites used the Qadiri Creed to put pressure on the caliph. Their move was wise in every respect. First, the Hanbalites placed an iconic text in the middle of their protest. This text supposedly did not undermine the authority of the caliph, because it symbolised the commitment of the caliphal state to Islamic traditionalism. Second, by demanding that the Qadiri Creed be restored to its rightful place, the Hanbalites in fact blamed the caliph himself for allowing the Ashᶜarties and the Muᶜtazilites to prosper in Baghdad and freely spread their teachings. Third, the Hanbalites hinted that al-Qaᵓim Bi-Amr Allah had failed to follow his father's legacy. More than its content, the Qadiri Creed drew its authority as an icon from the meaning that the Hanbalites attributed to it. In itself, the Qadiri Creed is an unnoteworthy text. It is therefore little wonder that the Creed did not inspire any theological debate and was not included in the traditionalistic syllabus. The Creed's iconicity emanated mainly from a rare coincidence of political events that accentuated the role of the Qadiri Creed as a symbol of the traditionalistic dominance in Baghdad.

II. The Three Dimensions of *Kitāb al-Tawḥīd*

There was a book that circulated in eleventh-century Baghdad that easily overshadowed the Qadiri Creed. It was Ibn Khuzayma's *Kitāb al-Tawḥīd.* This book, authored in the tenth century, seems at first glance to be a mere compilation of *aḥādīth al-ṣifāt.* In point of fact, it is a theological treatise that reflects Ibn Khuzayma's unique version of ultra-traditionalism. First, by housing *aḥādīth* that were rejected by other Hadith scholars on the grounds of these texts' dubious origin and questionable authenticity, Ibn Khuzayma expressed his unequivocal acceptance of the entire corpus of anthropomorphic *aḥādīth.* Second, Ibn Khuzayma paraphrased and sometimes discussed *aḥādīth al-ṣifāt,* thus disclosing his theological stance and his own understanding of the *bi-lā kayfa* formula. In addition to being an indispensable part of the ultra-traditionalistic curriculum, this book in fact played a role in two turbulent political affairs that we will describe shortly. The presence of this book in the public sphere was conspicuous and continued to be so decades after its author had died.

Kitāb al-Tawḥīd has not been fully studied in western research and its author, Ibn Khuzayma, failed to attract the attention of many western scholars. Nonetheless, the book is well-known to researchers who study Islamic traditionalism: for example, Daniel Gimaret translated portions of the book in his *Dieu à l'image de l'homme*, although he did not provide a systematic account of *Kitāb al-Tawḥīd* and its author. Joseph van Ess also illuminated a few points on *Kitāb al-Tawḥīd* in several footnotes in the fourth volume of his colossal *Theologie und Gesellschaft im 2. und 3. Jahrhundert Hidschra*. ᶜAbd al-ᶜAziz al-Shahwan, who published *Kitāb al-Tawḥīd* in a scientific edition, prefaced a full-scale study to the edited text. As far as we know, this is the only comprehensive existing study on *Kitāb al-Tawḥīd*. However, al-Shahwan's treatment of Ibn Khuzayma's biography is sketchy and lacks many important details. To learn about the stature of Ibn Khuzayma and his *Kitāb al-Tawḥid*, one needs to read the historical sources. The following discussion presents our understanding of these sources.

Western research's lack of interest in Ibn Khuzayma notwithstanding, the biographical sources depict him as a prominent scholar and a political activist. As we have already noted in Chapter 1, Shams al-Din al-Dhahabi's *Siyar Aᶜlām al-Nubalāʾ* is a reliable indicator to appreciate the stature of Hadith scholars among their contemporaries. The author dedicated an eighteen-page biographical entry to the ultra-traditionalistic Shafiᶜite scholar Abu Bakr Muhammad ibn Ishaq ibn Khuzayma al-Sulami al-Nisaburi (d. 924, at the age of eighty nine). The length of this entry is in itself sufficient proof that Ibn Khuzayma was regarded as one of the most important scholars of his generation. Al-Dhahabi grouped the biographies of Ibn Khuzayma's contemporaries under the title 'the seventeenth class [of notables]', (*al-ṭabaqa al-sābiᶜa ᶜashara*); Ibn Khuzayma's entry was one of the longest entries in this class.[36]

Ibn Khuzayma's political involvement was expressed through his good relationships with the ruling elite of emirs, town governors and army officers,[37] combined with his activities against heretical sects. Thus, in addition to the banal descriptions of Ibn Khuzayma as a pious and charitable *muḥaddith*, who was famous for his legendary memory,[38] we find noteworthy information about Ibn Khuzayma's stance against *kalām* in the entry that al-Dhahabi authored.[39] Nishapur, where Ibn Khuzayma worked and taught, was a stormy centre of political and theological controversies, with a salient presence of Muᶜtazilites, Shiᶜites (by that time the Shiᶜites fully adopted the Muᶜtazilite dogma) and Karramites (they were rationalists who promoted the idea of corporealism).[40] There were also Kharijites in the outskirts of Nishapur and a strong presence of Hanafites in the city proper. The Hanafites, who were part of Islamic traditionalism, were in fact the main rivals of the Shafiᶜites in the struggle on religious hegemony (which meant assuming the religious positions that the emirs funded) in Nishapur.[41] These groups often quarrelled with each other publicly on matters of dogma. The traditionalists, who were not trained to use sophistic argumentations, often reached poor results in those debates in comparison to the rationalists whose main training was in the art of debate (*ᶜilm al-munāẓara*). The traditionalists' deficient theological training notwithstanding, there were several outstanding traditionalists who participated in such debates and even excelled in them. Ibn Khuzayma's teacher, Ishaq ibn Rahwayh, is one such example (see Chapter 4). Probably, Ibn Khuzayma himself used sophistic argumentations in public debates: one can trace this kind of argumentation in his *Kitāb al-Tawḥid.* Ibn Khuzayma repeatedly warned his companions and disciples against practicing *kalām*, however they participated in theological debates and even sought their master's advice about the ways to win such debates.[42]

In his prime, Ibn Khuzayma stood out in public life in Nishapur as a zealous traditionalist with a growing circle of admirers. He flourished against the backdrop of the ongoing public debates and confrontations with the Muᶜtazilites, and as the record in *Kitāb al-Tawḥīd* shows, with other rationalistic groups as well (see below). In these confrontations, he voiced his strict adherence to the Quran and the Hadith. Ibn Khuzyama's circle of disciples was therefore more than a group of students and intellectuals learning texts together or discussing issues in Islamic law; his group was a political party. The Khuzaymiyya, or *aṣḥāb Ibn Khuzayma* ('the Companions of Ibn Khuzayma'), as Ibn Khuzayma's disciples called themselves, was the most prominent group among the traditionalists in Nishapur. One of its members even claimed that the Khuzaymiyya was a match for the Sunnite schools of law, namely it was a school of law (*madhhab*) in itself.[43] In spite of its centrality, the Khuzaymiyya did not develop into a separate school of law and was dismantled during the lifetime of Ibn Khuzayma (for the events leading to this group's dismantling, see below).

We possess scarce information about the oral teachings of Ibn Khuzayma. This information indicates that the Khuzaymiyya saw themselves as the fiercest defenders of traditionalist Islam, mainly against the Muᶜtazilites. We take note of one particular saying attributed to Ibn Khuzayma on this topic. One of the pious men of the traditionalistic community in Nishapur, a marginal *muḥaddith* by the name of Muhammad ibn Salih ibn Haniᵓ (d. 951) testified:

> I heard Abu Bakr Muhammad ibn Ishaq (namely, Ibn Khuzayma) say: 'Whoever does not affirm that God sits enthroned on high and is situated above His seven heavens, blasphemes his Creator. He should be encouraged to repent. If he repents, [he will be forgiven]. If he does not repent, he should be decapitated, and his body should be thrown to the dunghill, so that the devout Muslims who are committed to their faith will not suffer from the stench of his corpse. His property becomes booty. No Muslim is allowed to inherit him because it is unlawful for a Muslim to inherit the infidel, so said the Prophet.'[44]

In the context of his times and his environment, Ibn Khuzayma's view was unmistakably a call for his disciples and followers to demand the execution of their Muᶜtazilite and Shiᶜite neighbours. In *Kitāb al-Tawḥīd*, however, Ibn Khuzayma was more cautious in expressing his criticism of the Muᶜtazilites. After citing an abundance of *aḥādīth* about God's aboveness and God's sitting on the throne, Ibn Khuzayma concluded:

> These *akhbār* (namely, *aḥādīth*) are clear evidence that the Prophet was carried from this world to the seventh heaven. In that occasion and place, God had prescribed to him the performance of the prayers. All these *akhbār* indicate that the Creator is situated above His seven heavens. This is certainly not as the deniers of the attributes (the *muᶜaṭṭila*, namely the Muᶜtazilites) claim. They claim that their 'object of worship' (*maᶜbūd*, namely, God) is with them in their homes and in their bosoms. They deny that He is enthroned on high.[45]

It is quite understandable why Ibn Khuzayma did not call for the execution of the Muᶜtazilites in his book: he used two different sets of language when he wrote his academic treatise and when he preached to an audience. Given the turbulent atmosphere in tenth-century Nishapur, there is no doubt that Ibn Khuzayma often enticed his listeners against the Muᶜtazilites. The grand mufti of the Shafiᶜites in Khurasan, Abu 'l-Walid Hasan ibn Muhammad al-Faqih (d. 960–1) testified that he personally heard Ibn Khuzayma calling for the execution of whoever expressed the view that the Quran was created.[46] Since the concept of the createdness of the Quran was a cornerstone of the Muᶜtazilite dogma, the Muᶜtazilites were clearly the target of Ibn Khuzayma's attacks.

Ibn Khuzayma's 'formal' occupations were teaching Hadith and issuing legal opinions. However, he was both a *muḥaddith* and a *muṣannif*, that is, an author (it was claimed that Ibn Khuzayma composed more than 140 books).[47] His books, the most prominent of which was *Kitāb al-Tawḥīd*, formed the core curriculum in his study sessions: *Kitāb al-Tawḥīd*, one of the few of Ibn Khuzayma's works that survived, was dictated to his disciples. *Kitāb al-Tawḥīd* was also summarised and paraphrased by at least one of the disciples to produce the Khuzaymiyya's creed (see below). This book's iconicity can be understood with the help of Watt's three-dimension theory. First, the performative dimension existed in this book even before it was written. In the introduction of the book, Ibn Khuzayma recounts that he planned to compose a book that would play a leading role in the public debates in Nishapur. In other words, *Kitāb al-Tawḥīd* was written as a political manifesto and a manual for the traditionalistic debater; the book's content was intended to be heard in public venues. The semantic dimension of this book is traced in the reports about its prominent position in the traditionalistic curriculum both during Ibn Khuzayma's lifetime and centuries after his death. Finally, the book's prominence stimulated the composition of treatises that attacked the book and its author (see in Section III). None of these oppositional works would have been written if *Kitāb al-Tawḥīd* was marginal and unimportant.

Kitāb al-Tawḥīd was intended to summarise Ibn Khuzayma's knowledge about two topics: the divine attributes and divine predetermination. These topics were the bone of contention between the traditionalists and the rationalists. However, the lion's share of the book that we possess is a collection of *aḥādīth al-ṣifāṭ*. There is a handful of *aḥādīth* on various theological topics like the Prophetic intercession (*shafāᶜa*) and only several *aḥādīth* that fall under the title of predetermination. We therefore suggest that either the section on the divine predetermination in *Kitāb al-Tawḥīd* was lost or that it was never written. As previously indicated, *Kitāb al-Tawḥīd* was composed to provide the Khuzaymiyya with the most efficient weapon in defending the traditionalistic tenets. In the introduction to *Kitāb al-Tawḥīd*, Ibn Khuzayma explained that although he disliked the idea of writing a work 'that could be wrongly perceived as a work of *kalām*', he decided to neglect his favourite occupation of writing books on *fiqh* and composed *Kitāb al-Tawḥīd*. This decision was stimulated by the reports that he received from his disciples who participated in gatherings and debates (*majālis wa-munāẓara*) with the Muᶜtazilites of Nishapur. Fearing that some of his students would be caught in the snares of rationalism, Ibn Khuzayma decided to write a book that would prove the Muᶜtazilite convictions wrong by massively quoting from the Quran and the Hadith.[48]

The outcome of Ibn Khuzayma's efforts was a huge compilation of *aḥādīth al-ṣifāt* sprinkled with a handful of the author's valuable remarks. Ibn Khuzayma guided his readers in implementing the most convincing method to refute a Muᶜtazilite opponent, developed quasi-rationalistic argumentations and bestowed acrid remarks on his personal nemeses. Ibn Khuzayma attacked 'the deniers of the attributes' (the *muᶜaṭṭila*, namely the Muᶜtazilites) for their rejection of *aḥādīth al-ṣifāt*.[49] However, as befits the colourful and diversified public arena of Nishapur, the book addressed other rivals as well. Thus, Ibn Khuzayma mentioned frequently an unidentified group which he names 'the people of ignorance and stubbornness' (*ahl al-jahl wa'l-ᶜinād*). Towards the end of the book, he explained that the stubborn and the ignorant people are the Muᶜtazilites, the radical Kharijites and the lenient Hanafites.[50] The critique that Ibn Khuzayma directed to these groups is that they dared to read *aḥādith al-ṣifāt* and argued about them while their knowledge of the Hadith material was insufficient at best. According to Ibn Khuzayma, these ignorant sects misquoted the Hadith, misinterpreted it, and promoted ridiculous and even heretical ideas based on their lack of knowledge.[51] For example, their literal reading of the *ḥadīth al-ṣūra* (the *ḥadīth* that states that 'God created Adam in His image') led them to liken God to man, because they claimed that the *ṣūra*, image, that was mentioned in this *ḥadīth* was God's image (see our discussion in

Chapter 4). Ibn Khuzayma, however, provided a different approach to this *ḥadīth* (see below, in Section III).[52]

Ibn Khuzayma's accounts of his personal rivalries provide noteworthy details about the debates that were held in Nishapur in terms of content and participants. Thus, for example, Ibn Khuzayma recounted one of the stormiest discussions that evolved around the *ḥadīth* of the divine fingers (see Chapter 1). The debate began with a Muᶜtazilite (described by Ibn Khuzayma as 'a pretentious ignorant who never bothered to learn Hadith, and had no clue of our craft of combining the different Prophetic reports together and reconciling between them') who pointed out the contradictions in two different versions of the *ḥadīth*: the widely circulated version of the divine fingers *ḥadīth* attributed to Ibn Masᶜud and the version attributed to Ibn ᶜAbbas. The Muᶜtazilite asked: one version of this *ḥadīth* claims that God's fingers will grab (*amsaka*) the earth and sky, and the other version claims that God will place (*waḍaᶜa*) the earth, the heavens on His fingers. So, which of these versions is correct? – the Muᶜtazilite cunningly wondered. To answer this question, Ibn Khuzayma provided a rather convoluted explanation that all three options in fact describe the same situation.[53] Ibn Khuzayma based his answer on a technique which he calls *al-taʾlīf bayna al-akhbār.*[54] In this case, Ibn Khuzayma proved that the actual meaning of *amsaka* is 'to place', and certainly not 'to grab'. Therefore, *amsaka* and *waḍaʾa* have the same meaning and the apparent contradiction between the two traditions is resolved.[55] The same technique was widely applied by Ibn Qutayba in his *Kitāb Mukhtalif al-Ḥadīth* and is also mentioned by Ahmad ibn Hanbal, who said: 'It is impossible to understand a *ḥadīth* without compiling its various versions (*ṭuruq*), because the single text-unit in the Hadith literature is interpreted by another text-unit. A *ḥadīth* interprets a *ḥadīth.*'[56]

Here, Ibn Khuzayma proved the inferiority of the Muᶜtazilite in the Hadith. However, the Muᶜtazilite in fact started the debate with one sophisticated argument up his sleeve. As we have shown in Chapter 1, in all versions of the *ḥadīth* of the divine fingers, the Jewish rabbi conveyed the message that 'God will place the heavens on one finger, the earth on one finger, the mountains on one finger, the trees on one finger, and all the creatures on one finger'.[57] In some versions of the *ḥadīth*, the Prophet laughed as a sign of approval of the rabbi's words.[58] Addressing the content of the *ḥadīth*, the

Mu^c^tazilite rightfully mentioned that the description of the divine fingers holding the universe was in fact the words of the Jewish rabbi. He therefore claimed that this description was not part of the Prophetic discourse, and concluded that the Prophet's laughter did not signify his approval of this description of the divine fingers.[59] Representing the commonplace traditionalistic reading, Ibn Khuzyama protested. According to him, it was inconceivable to believe that the Prophet would laugh when he heard a supposedly inappropriate description of God (or, at least, inappropriate according to the Mu^c^tazilite reading). Ibn Khuzayma continued this line of argumentation and claimed that the Prophet's laughter signified his approval of the discourse of the Jewish rabbi. In other words, the description of the divine fingers was accurate. Had the Prophet thought that this description was wrong or blasphemous, he would have demonstrated his anger by condemning the person who thus blasphemed God, rather than laughing after listening to his words. God deemed His Prophet too valuable to act in such a hypocritical manner. Furthermore, no Muslim who believes in the Prophet's mission would dare describe him as a hypocrite.[60] The conclusion is therefore, that the divine fingers indeed hold the earth, the sky, etc., just as the Jewish rabbi described and the Prophet approved.

Another noteworthy topic that Ibn Khuzayma criticised in his book is the phenomenon of theologians who shifted their doctrinal loyalty from one theological trend to another. Ibn Khuzayma described an anonymous *muḥaddith* who came to Nishapur and settled there. This *muḥaddith* conducted extremely long Hadith sessions. He also composed books which Ibn Khuzayma claimed to have read. Ibn Khuzayma, who personally knew this man, noticed that in his sessions and books this *muḥaddith* showed no consistency in his approach towards *aḥādīth al-ṣifāt*: once he cited *aḥādīth* with sound chains of transmission, another time he cited *aḥādīth* with weak chains of transmission. He even was heard rejecting *aḥādīth al-ṣifāt* with the best chains of transmission while claiming that these texts expressed heresy.[61] Thus, Ibn Khuzayma described this scholar as wavering between traditionalism, ultra-traditionalism and rationalism. Identifying this *muḥaddith* as well as identifying any other of Ibn khuzayma's nemeses is nearly impossible, because Ibn Khuzayma wisely did not name any of his rivals.

The main point in *Kitāb al-Tawḥīd* is to strengthen one's belief in the description of God as it appears in *aḥādīth al-ṣifāt*. One might have expected therefore to find Ibn Khuzayma inserting the *bi-lā kayfa* formula after citing an anthropomorphic *ḥadīth*. However, Ibn Khuzayma does not use this formula even once in *Kitāb al-Tawḥīd*. Instead of promoting the traditionalistic *bi-lā kayfa* approach, namely to silence the urge to ask undesirable questions, Ibn Khuzayma leads his readers (or listeners) in a different direction: he encourages them to expand the narrow basis of their belief by explaining their own so-far silent acceptance of *aḥādīth al-ṣifāt*. In other words, he does not hesitate to describe to them in vivid and colourful language the anthropomorphic descriptions that they accepted, and encourages them to do likewise. For example, Ibn Khuzayma determines: 'Our Lord is far more sublime and exalted [upon His creatures] than to have a face which resembles the face of some of His creatures or not to have a face at all.'[62] Elsewhere, Ibn Khuzayma defines this approach as a middle way between the literalism of the Mushabbiha and the negation of the divine attributes of the Muᶜtazila: on the one hand, God is not compared to the creatures, as the Mushabbiha depict Him; on the other hand, He is not described as void (*ᶜadam*), as the *muᶜaṭṭila* or the Muᶜtazila depict Him.[63] This approach leads Ibn Khuzayma to compose passages like the following one, in which he addresses his disciples. Throughout *Kitāb al-Tawḥīd*, as well as in this passage, Ibn Khuzayma refers to his disciples as 'you witty people' (*yā dhawī al-ḥijā*) or 'you intelligent people' (*yā dhawī al-albāb*):

> Listen, you witty people, to what I have to say on this subject . . . We say: our Lord the Creator has two eyes which He uses to see what lies under the moist soil, and what lies beneath the seven earths. He uses His eyes to see what lies above the sky, and to see the big things and the small things that lie between the sky and the earth. Nothing in the seven heavens and the seven earths escapes His eyes. Nothing escapes His gaze. He sees what lies in the depth of the sea and the bottom of the sea, as He sees His throne on which He is enthroned on high.[64]

However, Ibn Khuzayma was prudent not to include details in his discourse that were irrelevant to the basic material. When discussing God's face, Ibn Khuzayma therefore declares: 'We cited the sufficient amount of the verses and *aḥādīth* that mention our Lord's face, and we added some explanation to it.'[65] Ibn Khuzayma's goal was to strengthen his readers' faith by explaining to them the precise nature of the discourse that they accepted as true. Thus, he confirms repeatedly that the anthropomorphic description indeed refers to a certain reality in which God has a form, a face and the ability to see and hear. This description perhaps does not sound so different from the *bi-lā kayfa* approach; however, Ibn Khuzayma's insistence on describing these attributes from different angles and affirming their existence makes him more of a literalist than any traditionalist we have encountered. Ibn Khuzayma's approach was severely criticised by the ultra-traditionalist al-Dhahabi (see Section III).

Ibn Khuzayma also used a polemical approach in preparing his disciples for a debate with a Muᶜtazilite. The following passage about the divine hands is typical of Ibn Khuzayma's matter-of-fact approach to *aḥādīth al-ṣifāt*. The conversational tone leaves no room for doubt; in this passage, we almost hear Ibn Khuzayma talking to his disciples who eagerly await his sage advice. The lecture begins with a citation of the *ḥadīth* which states that every heart is held between two of the All-Merciful's fingers (see Chapter 1).[66] Ibn Khuzayma begins his lecture by mentioning the names of two of the *muḥaddithūn* who transmitted this text:

> I am exempt from [elaborating on this *ḥadīth*] because here we have the sound testimony of Shurahbil ibn al-Hakam and ᶜAmir ibn Naᵓil.[67] God, whom we should praise again and again, provided us with so many texts about this subject that are similar to the *ḥadīth* of [the All-Merciful's two fingers] and serve as textual evidence. All you have to do, you bright people, is to realize that what we have to say in the subject of the divine two hands is similar to what we said about the divine face and the divine two eyes. If you realize that, you will know for certain the facts to which God guides you. You will know for certain that He widens you breast so you believe in the divine attributes as God has specified to you in the Quran and clarified for you through the words of His Prophet. With the help of God, you will know for certain that our way, the way of 'the People of Hadith' and their followers is the true, correct and just way. You will also realize that whoever calls these people Mushabbiha (anthropomorphists) is ignorant. The Jahmiyya who deny the divine attributes (i.e. the Muᶜtazila) know not what anthropomorphism is.[68]

In Ibn Khuzayma's discussion of the divine hands, we find attempts to explain the traditionalistic creed by using self-developed rationalistic and quasi-rationalistic argumentations which echo the *kalām* terminology and argumentations. Ibn Khuzayma's methodology somewhat resembles Ibn Qutayba's, although Ibn Khuzayma lacked Ibn Qutayba's finesse and eloquence. The lameness of Ibn Khuzayma's discourse is reflected in the first part of his argumentation: based on Q. 39:67 ('He will hold the entire earth in His grasp and fold up the heavens in His right hand'), Ibn Khuzayma determines that even the fittest and strongest person on earth could not hold one of the seven earths. The conclusion is, therefore, that God's hands are not similar to human hands. Following this line of argumentation, Ibn Khuzayma states that even if all humankind from Adam until today assembled in one place and assisted each other in this task, they could not have lifted one of the seven earths. Ibn Khuzayma triumphantly concludes: 'So, you intelligent people! How could a person be an anthropomorphist when he admits that the hand of God is mighty and that the hands of the human beings are incompetent?'[69]

In the second part of his argument, Ibn Khuzayma uses a mixture of *kalām* and traditionalistic terminology. He determines that God's hands (which are two right hands, as God does not have a left hand) are eternally pre-existent (*qadīma*) and everlasting (*bāqiya*); while the human hands are created (*makhlūqa muḥdatha*), are not eternal and everlasting, and will eventually be annihilated (*fāniya*). All these terms are *kalām*ic. The following description of the human hands as worn out, dead and rotten, waiting for God to resurrect them is on the other hand inspired by the descriptions of the Resurrection in the Quran and the eschatological traditions.[70] Again, Ibn Khuzayma wondered how could a person who merely affirms the description of God in the Quran and the Hadith be considered an anthropomorphist and a heretic. Ibn Khuzayma therefore concludes that the Muᶜtazila were the heretics because they rejected what was written in the scriptures.[71] In an attempt to refine this argumentation, Ibn Khuzayma proves that the use of the word *yad*, 'hand', in itself does not indicate that two different hands are equal. Thus, the hand of a strong man who is able to lift heavy weight is not identical to the hand of a weak man who is not able to lift a heavy weight. The hand of a human does not resemble the hand of an ape, a pig, a bear, a dog or any other beast of prey. Ibn Khuzayma concludes: 'A signifier can refer to two different things which have different qualities and different meanings.'[72] To summarise Ibn Khuzayma's approach: God has two right hands which do not resemble human hands in any respect. Although both the divine hand and the human hand are called *yad*, there is no basis for comparing them.

According to the ambitions of its author, *Kitāb al-Tawḥīd* was meant to become a guide for the traditionalists who participated in debates with the Mu^ctazilites; however, the work became much more than a guidebook. During Ibn Khuzayma's lifetime, the book was the definitive code of the Khuzaymiyya. When this code was broken, the Khuzaymiyya ceased to exist. The historical sources preserve an incredible story about the closing of the Khuzaymiyya, and they retain some details about the identity of the Khuzaymiyya. There were many visitors to Nishpaur who joined Ibn Khuzayma's classes for a limited period of time; among them were the illustrious al-Bukhari and Muslim. However, the backbone of the Khuzaymiyya was the permanent residents of Nishapur. The crown jewels among these were Ibn Khuzayma's four closest disciples. These disciples were local notables and respectable *muḥaddithūn*. The eldest of the four was the Shafi^cite mufti Abu ^cAli Muhammad ibn ^cAbd al-Wahhab al-Thaqafi (d. 940, at the age of ninety eight).[73] The youngest of the four, the fifty-year-old Abu Bakr Ahmad ibn Ishaq al-Sibghi (d. 954), was chosen by Ibn Khuzayma to issue *fatāwā* in the great mosque of Nishapur whenever Ibn Khuzayma was absent from the mosque due to his many travels. Al-Sibghi faithfully served as a replacement (*khalīfa*) for Ibn Khuzayma for more than ten years.[74] Al-Sibghi's great advantage over his colleagues was his ability to skilfully perform political manoeuvres; he was a frequent visitor to the courts of emirs and governors.[75]

Towards the end of Ibn Khuzayma's life a rupture occurred between him and his four disciples. This rupture (actually a scandal) was at the time the talk of Nishapur, because this split undermined the stability of the entire *muḥaddithūn* community. In Nishapur, which witnessed constant clashes between the traditionalists and the rationalists, this scandal was no less than a major political crisis. The scandal started when a Mu^ctazilite provocateur from Tus arrived in Nishapur with the ambition 'to cause alienation' (*īqā^c al-waḥsha*) among the city's distinguished *muḥaddithūn*. In order to build his reputation as a serious *mutakallim* who fiercely fought all kinds of heresies in defence of the true Islam, the Muᶜtazilite, whose name was Mansur ibn Yahya al-Tusi (death date unknown), needed to perform a spectacular event: debate a supposedly devout Muslim and expose his opponent as a heretic. With the help of a local preacher, this Muᶜtazilite chose the Khuzaymiyya, the most prominent study circle among the traditionalists of Nishapur, in which to invest his political efforts. The Muᶜtazilite first tried to lure Ibn Khuzayma's companions to delve into a theological controversy with him. His constant attempts failed, and the frustrated Muᶜtazilite complained to the local preacher: 'This imam (namely, Ibn Khuzayma) does not hasten to argue on theological issues, and he forbids his followers to be engaged with *kalām* and teach *kalām*. But what he does not know is that several Kullabites in the guise of "companions" participate in his study circle.'[76] The Kullabiyya (named after their eponymous father, ᶜAbd Allah ibn Kullab, d. 855) was a theological trend which presented a quasi-compromise between rationalism and traditionalism: this trend defended what it perceived as the fundamentals of Islamic traditionalism by using rationalistic argumentations. For instance, the Kullabites accepted the anthropomorphic descriptions of God because they were part of the revelation. However, unlike the traditionalists who accepted these attributes *bi-lā kayfa*, the Kullabites added the rationalistic assertion that 'His attributes are neither Himself nor other than Himself' (*wa-anna ṣifātihi lā hiya huwa wa-lā ghayruhu*).[77]

Since Ibn Khuzayma's companions did not take the bait by responding to Mansur ibn Yahya's provocations, his mission to 'expose' them as Kullabites nearly failed. Finally, an opportunity presented itself. One evening, Ibn Khuzayma threw a big party in his garden to celebrate the death of one of his ideological rivals.[78] After this unusual party ended, several participants who left Ibn Khuzayma's premises reconvened in the house of another scholar. The group started to argue about the topic of the eternity of the Quran. They debated whether the Quran was eternal from eternity to eternity, as the traditionalists claimed, or did God speak the Quran through a temporal speech, as the Muᶜtazilites claimed? Because the group did not reach a final conclusion, one of the participants, who was a *mutakallim*, came to the house of Ibn Khuzayma's most senior companion, the old Abu ᶜAli al-Thaqafi, and asked for his opinion. Unfortunately, al-Thahqafi was tempted to answer. Instead of saying 'the Quran is eternal and uncreated' (according to the traditionalistic formula that was shaped in the days after the events of the *miḥna*),[79] al-Thaqafi answered: 'Whoever denies that [the word of God] is eternal, believes that it is created.'[80] Al-Thaqafi's mistake was that he articulated a traditionalistic dogma by using a rationalistic syllogism and terminology, and not by using the traditionalistic wording.

Although the answer that al-Thaqafi provided did not, as far as we know, express a Kullabite dogma *per se* al-Thaqafi's response was sufficient for the Muᶜtazilite Mansur ibn Yahya to accuse al-Thaqafi of being a Kullabite.[81] By making frequent visits to Ibn Khuzayma and convincing the elderly scholar that his disciples turned against him, the Muᶜtazilite succeeded in isolating Ibn Khuzayma. As a result, Ibn Khuzayma detached himself from his former disciples, while the four disciples believed that they were compelled to establish their own study circle. In this new study circle, they continued studying the Hadith material that they learned from Ibn Khuzayma. The offended scholar reacted by condemning his former disciples. He claimed that they were Kullabites and accused them of being liars who cited forged Hadith material in his name, which they claimed to have studied from him. As the author of the thoroughly studied and well-accepted *Kitāb al-Tawḥīd*, Ibn Khuzayma issued the following written statement:

> The People of the East and the People of the West know that no one has ever composed a comprehensive book about the unity of God, predetermination and other theological issues like the book that I have composed. Since I verified beyond doubt that these [former disciples] are liars, it is forbidden to any student of Hadith to receive from them material that they claim to having transmitted on my authority and under my name.[82]

We may assume that this statement was read in the mosque where the Khuzaymiyya regularly met. The attack on Ibn Khuzayma's former companions was harsh and merciless. No wonder, then, that they did their best to reconcile with their teacher. Accompanied by an objective arbitrator, three of the four disciples came to Ibn Khuzayma, and the elderly scholar again accused them of being Kullabites. In response, Abu Bakr al-Sibghi, the former protégé of Ibn Khuzayma, presented a booklet in which he recorded the traditionalistic tenets to which he and his colleagues adhered. Ibn Khuzayma confirmed the veracity of these tenets with his signature, and added a creed at the bottom of this document. Sadly, only a part of the creed was preserved in al-Dhahabi's *Siyar Aᶜlām al-Nubalāᵓ* and al-Sibghi's booklet which summarised *Kitāb al-Tawḥīd* was never preserved. Based on the existing text, we note that this creed or rather, what remained of it, was a pale shadow of *Kitāb al-Tawḥīd*. Indeed, the creed reflected Ibn Khuzayma's traditionalism by refuting two Muᶜtazilite tenets (the createdness of the Quran and the negation of the divine attributes). However, while Ibn Khuzayma's *Kitāb al-Tawḥīd* offered a mild literalist reading of *aḥādīth al-ṣifāt*, al-Sibghi's creed merely accepted *āyāt al-ṣifāt* and *aḥādīth al-ṣifāt* 'without asking how', *bi-lā kayfa*.[83] Nevertheless, Ibn Khuzayma's immediate acceptance of this text suggests that he perceived his own reading methodology as identical to the *bi-lā kayfa* approach.

The signing of the creed did not put an end to the feud between the ultra-traditionalistic scholar and his former disciples; the Muᶜtazilite and his ally the local preacher persuaded Ibn Khuzayma that his former disciples played a trick on him: Ibn Khuzayma was informed that he did not notice that his former disciples changed the wording of the creed or gave him a different piece of paper to sign. Abu Khuzayma asked Abu ᶜAmr al-Hiri, the trustee who received the document for safekeeping, to see the creed again. The trustee refused because he probably knew about the harmful influence of the Muᶜtazilite on Ibn Khuzayma. Because the reputation of several scholars was at stake here, the trustee's decision was wise. The rupture between Ibn Khuzayma and his former disciples continued until the day of the scholar's death. Al-Sibghi, who was the companion most offended by the incident, requested that when he died, the creed would be buried with him. Al-Sibghi's good name was restored to him and he became one of the greatest scholars of the Shafiᶜites.[84] As for Ibn Khuzayma, ironically, towards the end of his life the fierce fighter against Muᶜtazilism was trapped in the snares of the politically ambitious Muᶜtazilite. This shameful friendship severely damaged Ibn Khuzayma's social and intellectual connections in Nishapur, and in fact left him, in his old age, isolated and frightened of his own disciples.

In addition to illustrating the elderly scholar's isolation and fear, the case of Ibn Khuzayma and his disciples illustrates the semantic and performative dimensions of *Kitāb al-Tawḥīd*. The existence of al-Sibghi's booklet which was based on *Kitāb al-Tawḥīd* is in itself an indication of the degree of seriousness and depth in which *Kitāb al-Tawḥīd* was studied among the members of the Khuzaymiyya. This is the semantic dimension. The performative dimension is reflected in the significant role which al-Sibghi's booklet and creed played in the ceremony of exonerating the names of Ibn Khuzayma's former disciples. Although the ceremony occurred in Ibn Khuzayma's house, the event was public and included many participants. Al-Sibghi's booklet, the summarised text of *Kitāb al-Tawḥīd*, was as important a key-player in the ceremony as were Ibn Khuzayma, al-Sibghi and Abu ᶜAmr al-Hiri who accepted the text for safekeeping. The text had several functions: both as a creed in which a complete adherence to *aḥādīth al-ṣifāt* was elaborated, and as a text that was meant to prove to a Hadith master that his disciples did not abandon him. As a creed, the summarised text of *Kitāb al-Tawḥīd* was designed to express the theological identity of its author (al-Sibghi) and the people who accepted it (the other three disciples of Ibn Khuzayma). With complete compatibility between theology and politics, and especially in tenth-century Nishapur, this creed also expressed one's political and social affinities.

Kitāb al-Tawḥīd was studied among the former members of the Khuzaymiyya. These members transmitted their versions of the book to other scholars, who in turn contributed to the proliferation of the book outside Nishapur. Ibn Khuzayma's grandson Abu Tahir Muhammad ibn al-Fadl (death date unknown)[85] owned a copy of *Kitāb al-Tawḥīd* which he assembled in Ibn Khuzayma's dictation sessions. Abu Tahir dictated his copy to other scholars in August 921, while his grandfather was still alive. In the next phases of transmission, this copy was dictated to scholars from Egypt and Syria. Thus, this copy was dictated to the great *muḥaddith* of Damascus, Abu'l-Ḥajjaj al-Mizzi (d. 1341), who in turn dictated it to others, until this version was dictated to the illustrious Hadith expert and the Shafiᶜite chief judge of Cairo, Ibn Hajar al-ᶜAsqalani (d. 1449). Additional names of the scholars who studied *Kitāb al-Tawḥīd* and in turn dictated the book to their disciples were preserved in the existing three manuscripts of the book, and require further investigation.[86]

In 1068, almost 150 years after Ibn Khuzayma's death, we encounter the name of *Kitāb al-Tawḥīd* in the description of the procession arranged by the Hanbalite *sharīf* Abu Jaᶜfar. In several sources we read that when the Hanbalites learned that the Muᶜtazilite Ibn al-Walid recommenced his classes, they gathered in the great mosque named after al-Mansur. Other traditionalists joined the session, in which the *sharīf* Abu Jaᶜfar announced that they would go in procession to the caliphal palace to present their demands to the caliph.[87] One of the participants in the gathering in the mosque was the squint-eyed *muḥaddith* Abu Muslim al-Laythi al-Bukhari (d. c. 1074–6). Al-Laythi was infamous for his greediness, impudent behaviour and his association with 'the innovators' (*ahl al-bidaᶜ*, namely the philosophers, the Muᶜtazilites and other heretics). However, he was also a prominent *muḥaddith* who composed books (none of them survived).[88] He was most welcome in the gathering of the Hanbalites, because he brought to the mosque a copy of Ibn Khuzayma's *Kitāb al-Tawḥīd* and read the entire book to the audience.[89] The reading of *Kitāb al-Tawḥīd* was intended to encourage the audience of ultra-traditionalists to take action against the Muᶜtazilites. This event illustrates the iconicity of *Kitāb al-Tawḥīd.* In addition to Baghdad of the eleventh century, we encounter the name of *Kitāb al-Tawḥīd* in 1134 in Herat in western Afghanistan. Apparently, an elderly *muḥaddith* by the name of Muhammad ibn Ismaᶜil ibn Husayn ibn Hamza al-ᶜAlawi al-Harawi dedicated that year, which was also the last year of his life, to teach *Kitāb al-Tawḥīd* to the people of Herat.[90]

In itself, *Kitāb al-Tawḥīd* was authored to achieve several goals: both to express the correct creed and to teach the traditionalists how to defend it; and both to cite the relevant *aḥādīth* and to present their correct reading. The fact that the outcome was a somewhat dull compilation of *aḥādīth al-ṣifāt* is almost irrelevant. The book symbolised traditionalism and filled a void in the traditionalistic public life. In addition, *Kitāb al-Tawḥīd* was studied by a high-profile group of *muḥaddithūn* who were responsible for its proliferation. However, the iconic dimension of *Kitāb al-Tawḥīd* is mostly reflected in the reactions that it generated.

III. Fakhr al-Din al-Razi's Response to *Kitāb al-Tawḥīd*

As the public reading of *Kitāb al-Tawḥīd* in Baghdad in 1068 indicates, the Hanbalites warmly embraced the book. Accordingly, the book is mentioned in a list of recommended works about the divine attributes which appears in Ibn Taymiyya's *al-Ḥamawiyya al-Kubrā*, an iconic book in its own right.[91]

Ibn Taymiyya's *Bayān Talbīs al-Jahmiyya fī Taʾsīs Bidaʿihim al-Kalāmiyya* (Clarifying the Deception of the Jahmiyya Who Established Their *Kalām*ic Innovations) mentioned Ibn Khuzayma several times as a Hadith expert whose judgement about the veracity of this *ḥadīth* or the other was decisive. According to Ibn Taymiyya, Ibn Khuzayma's rulings about the veracity of these texts were accepted by other scholars as obligating. Thus, for example, Ibn Taymiyya confirmed the veracity of *ḥadīth al-ruʾya* attributed to Abu Razin (see Chapter 2) by relying on Ibn Khuzayma's testimony that he only used the most reliable Hadith accounts as textual proof in his *Kitāb al-Tawḥīd*.[92] Ibn Qayyim al-Jawziyya provided an admiring description of Ibn Khuzayma in his long didactic poem on the divine attributes, *al-Kāfiya al-Shāfiya*. In a section which discusses the sayings that were attributed to the traditionalists of Khurasan, Ibn Qayyim al-Jawziyya described Ibn Khuzayma as a key player in the ongoing debate about God's sitting on the throne. According to Ibn Qayyim al-Jawziyya, Ibn Khuzayma was inspired by the Persian *muḥaddith* ʿAbd Allah ibn al-Mubarak (d. 797). A group of inquirers, whose identity is unknown to us, asked Ibn al-Mubarak: 'Tell us what is the actual reality of our Lord, so we become believers.' Ibn al-Mubarak replied: 'We describe Him by saying that He is above His heavens, separated from all beings.'[93] According to the poeticised description of Ibn Qayyim al-Jawziyya,

> These words empowered Ibn Khuzayma. He immediately drew the sword of truth and knowledge. He firmly determined that those who negated God's aboveness should be executed after they were called on to repent. He ruled that their bodies should be thrown to the dunghill, where the corpses of animals decayed and the stench was unbearable.[94]

The sceptic historian Shams al-Din al-Dhahabi, who was Ibn Taymiyya and Ibn Qayyim al-Jawziyya's contemporary, was less impressed by Ibn Khuzayma's militancy than was Ibn Qayyim al-Jawziyya. As we noted in Section II, al-Dhahabi eulogised Ibn Khuzayma and sang his praises in the biographical entry that he wrote about him in *Siyar Aʿlām al-Nubalāʾ*; however, al-Dhahabi was also appalled by Ibn Khuzayma's call to execute the Muʿtazilites for their disbelief in God's sitting on His throne above His seven heavens. In his matter-of-fact tone, al-Dhahabi remarked that although

Ibn Khuzayma expressed his true conviction, he was wrong in calling for the execution of the Muᶜtazilites. Al-Dhahabi concluded: 'Although Ibn Khuzayma's words were truthful, they were blunt and intolerable in the eyes of many of the scholars of the later generations.'[95]

Although Ibn Khuzayma's book was embraced by the Hanbalites, there was one particular passage in it that did not correspond with the Hanbalites' approach to *bi-lā kayfa.* Al-Dhahabi mentioned this passage in his argumentation against Ibn Khuzayma's unacceptable call to accuse Muslims who held non-traditionalistic views of infidelity (*takfīr*). Al-Dhahabi's unrelenting stance was that the execution of Muslims who expressed doctrinal opinions which negated the traditionalistic line was inconceivable. To prove his point, Al-Dhahabi referred to this passage from *Kitāb al-Tawḥīd* in which Ibn Khuzayma discussed *ḥadīth al-ṣūra.* The following text, based on the authority of Abu Hurayra, is one of several versions of this *ḥadīth*: 'The Messenger of God said: "When one of you fights [someone], he must avoid hitting [his rival's] face, because God created Adam in His image" (*fa-inna Allāha khalaqa Ādama ᶜalā ṣūratihi*).'[96]

As we noted in Section II, Ibn Khuzayma rejected the straightforward reading of *ḥadīth al-ṣūra.* Furthermore, Ibn Khuzayma accused the Muᶜtazilites, during their debates with the traditionalists, of providing a literal interpretation to the text in order to mock the traditionalists. This interpretation, at least according to Ibn Khuzayma, led the Muᶜtazilites to accuse the traditionalists of likening God to man – when in fact the traditionalists, as Ibn Khuzayma claimed, did not read the *ḥadīh* literally. The problem was, however, that Ibn Khuzayma's reading of the text was contrary to the traditionalistic *bi-lā kayfa.* According to Ibn Khuzayma, the correct reading of this text required the reader to consider Arabic grammar and the entire context in which the sentence 'God created Adam in His image' was embedded. First, Ibn Khuzayma read the bound pronoun *hi* (in the word *ṣūratihi*) as referring to Adam and not to God. According to this reading, the meaning of this text was 'God created Adam in his image' (*ᶜalā ṣūratihi),* namely the image of Adam and not the image of God. Secondly, Ibn Khuzayma clarified that this *ḥadīth* referred to a man who struck another man. The Prophet wanted to warn the attacker not to strike his rival in the face. Therefore, the Prophet explained to the attacker that both the attacker's and his rival's faces were alike, as both were created in the image of Adam.[97] To corroborate his stance, Ibn Khuzayma referred to another version of this *ḥadīth*, in which the phrase *ᶜalā ṣūratihi* (in His image) was replaced by the phrase *ᶜalā ṣūrat al-Raḥmān* (in the image of the All-Merciful). Ibn Khuzyama rejected this version on the basis of flaws in the chain of transmitters.[98] Thus, he ruled out any possibility to read this *ḥadīth* in its various versions as referring to God's image.

Al-Dhahabi, in his turn, utterly rejected Ibn Khuzayma's suggested reading of this *ḥadīth*. Al-Dhahabi used his rejection to demonstrate that Ibn Khuzayma's extremism was unacceptable. This was al-Dhahabi's view of Ibn Khuzayma:

> His book on *al-Tawḥīd* comprises a huge volume, and in it he provided a figurative interpretation (*taʾwīl*) to *ḥadīth al-ṣūra*. We must forgive those who provide figurative interpretations to some of the divine attributes. Even the Salaf, the pious and worthy ancestors, were not engaged in figurative interpretation: they merely believed [the texts] and said no more [after quoting them]. They merely said that only God and His Messenger knew [the meaning of the texts]. If we executed every scholar who made mistakes during the process of issuing his legal opinions – in spite of the fact that he was a true believer who only meant to follow the truth – the number of religious leaders in our nation would have drastically dropped off. God have mercy upon us all![99]

The rejection of Ibn Khuzayma's so-called *taʾwīl* is explained by al-Dhahabi's stature, both as an ultra-traditionalist and a Hadith expert. Al-Dhahabi was not a Hanbalite but a Shafiᶜite, who would not adhere to the Ashᶜarite school, as was customary in the Mamluk period. His ultra-traditionalistic rigidity in matters of dogma was well known among his contemporaries. 'He was inclined to Hanbalism' – his former disciple, the Ashᶜarite historian Taj al-Din al-Subki (d. 1368), testified.[100] Al-Dhahabi, as his criticism of Ibn Khuzayma's *ḥadīth al-ṣūra* proves, adopted the strictest (some would say, the Hanbalite) form of the *bi-lā kayfa* approach.[101] Ibn Khuzayma, as we have already seen, formally adhered to the *bi-lā kayfa* approach, although not in *Kitāb al-Tawḥīd*. He also examined other possibilities, like reading the text literally or searching for a different reading of a problematic text by using linguistic devices. His approach was therefore a mix of ultra-traditionalism and independent rationalism. In addition, one may assume that al-Dhahabi was critical of Ibn Khuzayma's skills as a *muḥaddith*, because Ibn Khuzayma included in *Kitāb al-Tawḥīd* controversial Hadith material that professional Hadith experts (like al-Dhahabi himself) rejected. It is noteworthy, that despite al-Dhahabi's criticism of Ibn Khuzayma, he also expressed his appreciation of Ibn Khuzayma's scholarship and cited him in his treatise on the divine throne.[102]

Kitāb al-Tawḥīd was extremely popular among the ultra-traditionalists in Nishapur and Baghdad between the tenth and the thirteenth centuries. As we have seen from Ibn Taymiyya and Ibn Qayyim al-Jawziyya's description of Ibn Khuzayma and his book, *Kitāb al-Tawḥīd* received much acclaim in fourteenth-century Damascus. The popularity of this work can be explained first by Ibn Khuzayma's deliberate intention to write a book that would appeal to a wide audience. In the introduction of *Kitāb al-Tawḥīd*, Ibn Khuzayma declared that he wrote the book with the intention of guiding his disciples through the labyrinth of theological debates. However, in the body of the text, we see clearly that Ibn Khuzayma aimed for a much wider audience. In a chapter that discusses the concept of God's aboveness, Ibn Khuzayma clarified that the Muslims who were born with the *fiṭra*, the natural, inherent and instinctive belief in God, had the firm knowledge that God was above in the sky; this firm knowledge required no proof.[103] These people, according to Ibn Khuzayma, were 'the Muslims, whether scholars or illiterates, freedmen or slaves, males or females, adults or children'.[104] Ibn Khuzayma, whose worldview encompassed the entire echelons of society, probably envisioned a book that would be read in public venues and reach the masses. The second reason for this book's popularity is the wide selection of *aḥādīth al-ṣifāt* that Ibn Khuzayma included, and the efforts that the author made in explaining why these *aḥādīth* should be accepted into the Islamic curriculum. This is a major issue, because Ibn Khuzayma, the Shafiᶜite *muḥaddith*, included Hadith material that only the Hanbalites accepted. To this wide selection of *aḥādīth*, Ibn Khuzayma added his clarifications and analyses written in a defiant and fanatical tone. In some of these passages, Ibn Khuzayma described God in anthropomorphic language, while claiming in the same breath that his discourse was not anthropomorphic in any way. In other words, Ibn

Khuzayma brewed a unique concoction that was to everyone's taste, provided that they were inclined to ultra-traditionalism and not rationalism.

Kitāb al-Tawḥīd was probably the first scholarly work which made room for ideas that were not elucidated in former theological treatises. The book was not entirely compatible with the official voice of the majority of the traditionalists, because it did not express the *bi-lā kayfa* approach. In addition, Ibn Khuzayma was more attentive to the lay audience. *Kitāb al-Tawḥīd* did not forbid its readers to ask difficult questions about problematic texts. On the contrary, the book provided paraphrases of the anthropomorphic texts that portrayed God in the form of a man, thus bypassing the strict *bi-lā kayfa* formula. *Kitāb al-Tawḥīd* recorded the discourse that prevailed in the public sphere. Similar to the case of al-ᶜAbdari, the eccentric *muḥaddith* who hit his shank, *Kitāb al-Tawḥīd* persisted that the anthropomorphic descriptions represented an actual reality. The voice of *Kitāb al-Tawḥīd*, however, did not express blunt anthropomorphic views like those of the Murjiᵓite *muḥaddith* and Quran exegete Muqatil ibn Sulayman (d. 767). In the heresiographical literature, Muqatil's followers were claimed to have believed that

> God is a body, with a mass of hair. He is shaped like a man, with flesh and blood, hair and bones. He has body organs like hand, leg, head and two eyes. He is massive, but nevertheless no one resembles Him and He resembles no one.[105]

Kitāb al-Tawḥīd is a celebration of the ethos of a naive faith, the faith of the innocent uneducated laymen. This ethos was marked by the phrase 'the religion of old women' (*dīn al-ᶜajāᵓiz*). The lay public, namely the old women, the innocent children and the Bedouins, were the holders of the natural firm belief in God, the *fiṭra*. Their naivety safeguarded them from the confusion that was the lot of the rationalists. When asked 'where is God?' the lay public naturally lifted their heads and pointed with their fingers to the sky to indicate God's direction.[106] Although we do not find the phrase 'the religion of old women' in *Kitāb al-Tawḥīd*, we do find this phrase in later texts. Without a doubt, *Kitāb al-Tawḥīd* was the forerunner of a trend in Islamic traditionalism which glorified the laymen and their naive beliefs. Several traditionalistic scholars who initially were rationalists and repented, used the phrase 'the religion of old women' to describe their adherence to the principles of Islamic traditionalism, including the belief in *aḥādīth al-ṣifāt*. The somewhat eccentric and controversial *muḥaddith* Abu 'l-Muzaffar al-Samᶜani (d. 1096), a Hanafite-Muᶜtazilite who converted to Shafiᶜism-Ashᶜarism,[107] was also a fierce fighter for the tenets of Islamic traditionalism. When his disciples asked him about *aḥādīth al-ṣifāt*, al-Samᶜani did not provide the standard response of *bi-lā kayfa;* instead, he demanded that his student accept 'the religion of the old women and the boys of the elementary school'.[108] Another famous repentant was Abu 'l-Maᶜali al-Juwayni (d. 1085), an Ashᶜarite theologian who abandoned his occupation in *kalām*. On his deathbed, he declared: 'I have withdrawn from any conviction that I previously held which contradicted the beliefs of the pious and worthy ancestors (*al-salaf al-ṣāliḥ*). I will die holding the same beliefs as the old women of Nishapur hold.'[109]

One may argue of course that the actual beliefs of the old women (or the illiterate or the laymen) were quite different from the idealistic concept of 'the religion of the old women' that the traditionalists promoted. While 'the old women' may have believed, for example, that God was revealed to the Prophet in the form of a young man wearing a green garb, the sophisticated scholars distanced themselves from the literal understanding of such a text. The old women could have imagined the young man, his curls and his garb. Unlike the old women, the scholars would reject the picture that could have appeared in their heads, and exclaimed: *Bi-lā kayfa*! It is more probable therefore that these scholars used the phrase 'the religion of the old women' in their address to their followers for political and even pragmatic reasons. By using this phrase, these scholars flattered their listeners for being genuine believers and tapped into their hostility against the elitist rationalists. In addition, the traditionalistic scholars also shielded themselves from any suspicion of being rationalists. For example, the sheikh of the Hanafites in Baghdad, Abu Bakr Muhammad ibn Musa ibn Muhammad al-Khwarizmi (d. 1013), used this phrase to enhance his followers' self-identity and sense of belonging to the traditionalistic camp: 'Our religion is the religion of the old women. We have absolutely nothing to do with the *kalām*.'[110] This saying was part of al-Khwarizmi's efforts to distance himself from Muᶜtazilism and befriend the Hanbalites of Baghdad. Like many Hanafites in eleventh-century Baghdad, al-Khwarizmi was probably tainted by the suspicions of being a Muᶜtazilite.[111] In addition, Hanafism was regarded as a rationalist school of law, because of the extensive use of *raʾy*, namely personal reasoning and common sense in the issuance of legal opinions. No wonder, then, that al-Khwarizmi, 'the sheikh of the People of Reasoning' (*shaykh ahl al-raʾy*) regularly prayed with a Hanbalite *imām* and professed his beliefs in the fundamentals of traditionalism.[112]

A more perplexing example of the use of 'the religion of old women' is that of Fakhr al-Din al-Razi (d. 1210), who was quoted as saying: 'Whoever adheres to the religion of the old women, wins his share in the afterlife.'[113] Fakhr al-Din al-Razi, the Ashᶜarite elitist intellectual who was the embodiment of Islamic rationalism,[114] certainly did not adhere to 'the religion of the old women'. In fact, in his great *Tafsīr* of the Quran, he explained that this phrase merely meant 'entrusting our affairs to God and relying on Him'.[115] This explanation which sterilises 'the religion of the old women' from its folkloristic essence is compatible with the rationalistic stance of al-Razi the Ashᶜarite theologian. However, al-Razi was also a Shafiᶜite jurisprudent and a traditionalistic preacher whose training as a scholar was largely formed by the study of Hadith. Therefore, when he promised a share in the afterlife to whomever held the beliefs of the old women, he did so in his capacity as a traditionalistic preacher in the mosque, that is, when addressing a wider audience.[116]

These two supposedly contradictory sides to al-Razi's scholarly personality are also fully reflected in his harsh attack on *Kitāb al-Tawḥīd* and its author. On the one hand, al-Razi called Ibn Khuzayma 'this poor ignoramus who fell headlong into these fables' (*khurāfāt*).[117] On the other hand, when mentioning the word *khurāfāt,* al-Razi did not necessarily refer to the lavishly detailed versions of *aḥādīth al-ṣifāt* that Ibn Khuzayma collected and included in his *Kitāb al-Tawḥīd.* Al-Razi referred to Ibn Khuzayma's literal understanding of these texts.[118] It is noteworthy that al-Razi never questioned Ibn Khuzayma's scholarship as a *muḥaddith*. In fact, he accepted Ibn Khuzayma's view about the dubious origins of one of the versions of *ḥadīth al-ṣūra.*[119] Furthermore, unlike the Muᶜtazilites, al-Razi never rejected the use of *aḥādīth al-ṣifāt* as textual evidence in theological debates. Throughout his attack on *Kitāb al-Tawḥīd*, al-Razi mentioned the teachings of the Shafiᶜite *muḥaddith* Muhyi al-Din Abu Muhammad al-Husayn ibn Masᶜud al-Farraʾ al-Baghawi (d. 1117 or 1122), and cited from al-Baghawi's *Sharḥ al-Sunna*, a Hadith compilation which also contains *aḥādīth al-ṣifāt* in some of its various sections.[120] So, what was the issue in Ibn Khuzayma's *Kitāb al-Tawḥīd* that ignited al-Razi's attack, if not the anthropomorphic Hadith material that formed the lion's share of the book?

Al-Razi, who conducted his scholarly career in Persia and in the Persian speaking areas in Central Asia, was a fierce fighter against what he perceived as deviations from the true path of Islam. Al-Razi conducted public debates against the corporealist Karramites, the rationalist Muᶜtazilites and (what he perceived as) the anthropomorphist Hanbalites.[121] His battle against *Kitāb al-Tawḥīd* corresponded with these debates. Al-Razi composed *Asās al-Taqdīs* (literally, The Foundation of Veneration; also entitled in various sources as *Taʾsīs al-Taqdīs*, namely Building the Foundations of Veneration) in direct response to *Kitāb al-Tawḥīd*. The circumstances accompanying the birth of *Asās al-Taqdīs* (approximately in the year 1193) are as follows: Al-Razi lived in Herat (in present-day west Afghanistan) when he received word that Muhammad ibn Ayyub (d. 1218), the brother of Salah al-Din al-Ayyubi (d. 1193; known in European sources as Saladin), assumed the position of the Ayyubid sultan. Al-Razi immediately mentioned the name of the new sultan (who was renamed al-Malik al-ᶜAdil) in his Friday sermon, although al-Razi was not a subordinate of the Ayyubid sultan. Thereafter, al-Razi composed *Asās al-Taqdīs* as a gift for the sultan and had the treatise dispatched to the sultan's Cairo residence.[122] In the introduction of *Asās al-Taqdīs*, al-Razi mentioned that he heard the news about al-Malik al-ᶜAdil's appointment. Al-Razi decided to dedicate this work to the sultan and send him the book, despite the distance between the Persian lands and Egypt. Al-Razi also expressed his hope that the book would benefit the people of both countries.[123] Al-Razi left the title of the work unexplained and obscure. We assume that al-Razi used the term *taqdīs* in the title of the book rather than the term *tawḥīd* to indicate that his book includes a presentation of the purest form of monotheism, distinct from the distorted form of monotheism that Ibn Khuzayma presented in *Kitāb al-Tawḥīd*. We note that the word *taqdīs* is mentioned in the book next to the term *tanzīh*, namely denying any corporeal attributes for the divine essence.[124] In other words, al-Razi used the word *taqdīs* to indicate that his book presents the Ashᶜarite concept of *tanzīh*. Al-Razi's decision to send the book to al-Malik al-ᶜAdil probably denotes a desire that 'The Foundation of

Veneration', which presented the principles of the Ashᶜarite (hence, true) form of Islamic faith, would bring together these two distant parts of the caliphate. Furthermore, 'The Foundation of Veneration' might serve as common ground for a future political framework under al-Malik al-ᶜAdil. The new sultan, who was by far the most powerful Muslim ruler at the time, was also attentive to religious scholars and their opinions. He paid al-Razi 1000 dinars (probably to cover the 'travel' expenses of the book; after all, al-Razi subtly mentioned in the introduction the distance between Egypt and the Persian lands), but also as a token of his appreciation.[125] In the Mamluk period, *Asās al-Taqdīs* was enthusiastically studied in Cairo and Damascus by the elitist Shafiᶜite-Ashᶜarites, like other works by al-Razi.

Asās al-Taqdīs provides a systematic refutation of more than 250 pages in print to *Kitāb al-Tawḥīd*. The purpose of *Asās al-Taqdīs* was to expose Ibn Khuzayma both as an anthropomorphist (*mushabbih*) and a corporealist (*mujassim*). At the end of his treatise, Fakhr al-Din al-Razi considered the possibility of condemning Ibn Khuzayma as a heretic. Ahmad Hijazi al-Saqa, the capable editor of *Asās al-Taqdīs*, claimed that al-Razi passed judgement that Ibn Khuzayma was a heretic.[126] We suggest otherwise, as demonstrated below. *Asās al-Taqdīs*, like al-Razi's other works, is complicated, rich with examples, and it is difficult to follow its line of argumentation. In addition, al-Razi used the platform of *Kitāb al-Tawḥīd* to refute the Karramites and the Hanbalites.[127] For these reasons, it is not simple to identify al-Razi's argumentations against Ibn Khuzayma in the overall entangled, albeit coherent discussion of *Asās al-Taqdīs*. Fortunately, al-Razi also dedicated a fairly coherent passage to Ibn Khuzayma in *Mafātīḥ al-Ghayb*, his great *Tafsīr* of the Quran. This passage appears in al-Razi's interpretation of the Quranic verse 'Nothing can be compared with Him' (*laysa ka-mithlihi shayʾun*, Q. 42:11).[128] Written some fifteen years after the completion of *Asās al-Taqdīs* (al-Razi completed his interpretation to *sūra* 42 in July 1207)[129] the passage in *Mafātīḥ al-Ghayb* is definitely based on *Asās al-Taqdīs*.[130] The following presentation of al-Razi's main arguments against Ibn Khuzayma and *Kitāb al-Tawḥīd* is therefore based on the relevant passage in *Mafātīḥ al-Ghayb*, with further clarifications from *Kitāb al-Tawḥīd* and *Asās al-Taqdīs*.

In the beginning of the discussion, al-Razi emphasised the important role of Q. 42:11 in the controversy about God's corporeality. According to al-Razi, the Ashᶜarites whom he called 'the scholars of unity' (*ᶜulamāʾ al-tawḥīd*) and 'our friends' (*aṣḥābunā*) used this verse as textual proof that God had no body consisting of organs; He had no spatiality, and was not able to be 'located' in any specific direction. Al-Razi explained that the Ashᶜarites proved that if God had a body, it would have necessarily entailed God's resemblance to others. The guiding rule of the Ashᶜarites was *tanzīh*, namely denying that God resembles any existing being (see Chapter 4). Al-Razi further clarified that according to 'our friends', Q. 42:11 referred to God's essence (*dhāt*) and not to His attributes (*ṣifāt*). In other words, on the ontological level there was no comparison between God and His creatures. However, on the semantic level, people and indeed other creatures can be compared to God. According to al-Razi, humans possess the attributes of 'knowing', 'potent', 'known' and 'remembered', while these attributes are applicable also to God.[131] Al-Razi presented this rationalistic proof against God's corporeality in order to expose the discourse that Ibn Khuzayma promoted as a corporealistic, hence heretical, discourse. Thus, while Ibn Khuzayma named his book *Kitāb al-Tawḥīd*, 'The Book of Monotheism (or unity)', al-Razi labelled it as *Kitāb al-Shirk*, 'The Book of Polytheism (or idolatry)'. Ibn Khuzayma tried to refute the rationalistic argumentation against God's corporeality and present his approach as a more appropriate solution to the problem of God's corporeality. However, as al-Razi claimed, Ibn Khuzayma failed in this attempt because he presented a deficient solution that ultimately led to corporealism. Al-Razi spiced his attack with an *ad hominem* argument: he claimed that he was forced to summarise Ibn Khuzayma's convoluted discussion, because Ibn Khuzayma was 'an inarticulate man with a meagre degree of understanding; a man who was not entirely sane'.[132] This is a clear reference to the last phase in Ibn Khuzayma's life and perhaps to other details of Ibn Khuzayma's biography which were accessible to al-Razi, but inaccessible to us.

As presented in the previous section, Ibn Khuzayma's basic claim was that the anthropomorphic descriptions in the Quran and the Hadith signified the actual existence of these attributes in God. Ibn Khuzayma added the reservation that the divine attributes existed in a different form of existence than in humans and other creatures. Hence, he understood the anthropomorphic descriptions literally, both on the ontological and semantic levels. In order to distance any charge of *tashbīh*, comparing God to His creations, Ibn

Khuzayma added that there was no comparison between the human hand, signified by the word *yad*, and the divine hand, also signified by the word *yad*.[133] He systematically repeated this same argument on every anthropomorphic description in the Quran and the Hadith. Thus, in the case of God's face, Ibn Khuzayma declared:

> We say, as say all the scholars of Islam throughout the world that God whom we worship has a face. We say this according to what God has taught us through the unambiguous verses in His book which He revealed. God has attributed majesty and glory to His face. God ruled that His face would abide forever. He denied that His face would ever perish. We say: Our Lord's face is so bright, luminous, and radiant, that had He unveiled His face, the dignified splendour of His face would have burnt everything that He saw. His face is veiled, hidden from the sight of the people of this world. No human being will see His face as long as he lives in this world which is also doomed to perish. We say: His face is everlasting. It was in constant duration of existence in the past. It will be in constant duration of existence in the future. It will never perish.[134]

This passage, which al-Razi faithfully paraphrased,[135] is noteworthy because it combines the Quranic vocabulary[136] with the vocabulary of *kalām*: Ibn Khuzayma described God's face as 'everlasting' (*qadīm*), a term he borrowed from the sophistic discourse of *kalām*. The peak of Ibn Khuzayma's rationalistic argument follows the literary description of God's face. This argument is identical to Ibn Khuzayma's argument about the total dissimilarity between the human hand and the divine hand. First, Ibn Khuzayma stated that the human face is created and is doomed to perish, unlike the divine face. Secondly, Ibn Khuzayma claimed that just as there was dissimilarity between the faces of different beasts (and he unfolded quite a lengthy list of what he perceived as 'ugly' animals: pigs, monkeys, dogs and scorpions) and the human face, so there was dissimilarity between the human face and the divine face.[137] Ibn Khuzayma concluded:

> Think about it, you intelligent people! Do the faces [of the beasts] that we mentioned resemble in any way the faces of human beings? Does the face of our Creator resemble in any way the faces of human beings? Since the Arabs

> do not compare the face of human beings to the faces of the beasts that we have mentioned, and the word *wajh*, 'face', might as well denote the faces of these beasts as well as the faces of human beings, how is it possible to call us Mushabbiha, anthropomorphists?[138]

Al-Razi saw Ibn Khuzayma's attempt to present his literalist understanding of the anthropomorphic descriptions in the Quran within the framework of a rationalistic argumentation as lame, ineffective and pretentious.[139] This is the place to clarify that the discussions in *Asās al-Taqdīs* and in *Mafātīḥ al-Ghayb* do not offer any insights to al-Razi's own theology. Both texts are targeted to refute the stance of a theological rival, whether Ibn Khuzayma, the Karramites or the Hanbalites. We rarely observe a glimpse of al-Razi's personal stance. Important questions like 'how did al-Razi perceive the anthropomorphic attributes on the ontological level?' leave us without answers in the present discussion. Al-Razi merely took upon himself to demonstrate Ibn Khuzayma's lack of understanding of the *kalām*ic discourse and the invalidity of Ibn Khuzayma's argumentations. However, al-Razi's attack on Ibn Khuzayma also yielded a coherent stance for the use of his followers, the later Ashᶜarites. In the course of his attack on Ibn Khuzayma, al-Razi clearly articulated the desirable understanding of *aḥādīth al-ṣifāt,* and provided his readers with a clear 'plan of action' that was meant to answer the challenge posed by these texts. First, al-Razi presented the rationale behind the figurative interpretation (*taʾwīl*) of the anthropomorphic descriptions in the Quran and the Hadith. Second, al-Razi provided a set of 'ready-made' answers to those who understood *aḥādīth al-ṣifāt* literally. Third, al-Razi's most important contribution to the discussion was his definition of anthropomorphism. We henceforth briefly examine these three points.

The first point is clarified during al-Razi's refutation of Ibn Khuzayma's insufficient argumentation. Adopting the argumentations of 'our friends', al-Razi clarified that one of the basic irrefutable principles of logic was the difference between essence (*dhāt*) and attributes (*ṣifāt*). This principle determines that essence is permanent (*bāqiya*), while attributes are interchangeable (*mukhtalifa*). The essence always remains permanent and is unaffected by the interchangeability of the attributes.[140] Therefore, the word *yad* as the divine 'hand' was interchangeable with the divine attribute of *qudra*, 'power'. In other words, the 'hand' of God does not represent an essence or a physical body in the shape of a hand, but simply signifies an attribute and as such it can be replaced by another attribute, for example, 'power'. Al-Razi condescendingly added:

> The laymen (*al-ᶜawāmm*) do not know the difference between the essences and the attributes, so it is understandable that they would claim that the face of a human being is different than the face of a donkey. Of course they are right that in terms of shape, colour, and other attributes there is no similarity between these two faces. However, physical bodies (*ajsām*) as such resemble each other and are equal to each other. It is thus proven that he (namely, Ibn Khuzayma) wrote what he wrote simply because he belonged to the laity, and because he did not know that in terms of similarity and difference the factor that counts was the essences of things and their quiddities (*ḥaqāʾiq al-ashyāʾ wa-māhiyātuhā*) and not the accidents and attributes (*al-aᶜrāḍ wa'l-ṣifāt*) that existed in these things.[141]

We note that al-Razi's explanation provided the rational reasoning for using figurative interpretation (*taʾwīl*). Instead of using the Ashᶜarite argumentation of the appropriateness of the discourse about God (see Chapter 4), al-Razi presented an argumentation based on what he determined was an irrefutable principle of logic. The principle as described by al-Razi is applicable to any divine attribute. Thus, for example, 'enthronement' (*istiwāʾ*), does not imply an actual 'enthronement' (*fī tamām al-ḥaqīqa*), otherwise God would have been considered a physical body.[142]

Aside from this philosophical justification of *taʾwīl*, al-Razi provided an arsenal of arguments for *taʾwīl* and against the literal understanding of the texts. Some of these 'ready-made' arguments were banal and belonged to the Ashᶜarite discourse of appropriateness and inappropriateness, while others were more sophisticated and drew from the *kalām*ic discourse.[143] The opening paragraph of the second part of *Asās al-Taqdīs* presents a banal argument while using a rather amused tone:

> The [divine] face is mentioned in the Quran, and so are the [divine] eyes, side,[144] hands, and the sole shank. Understanding these phrases literally would have inevitably led us to confirm the existence of one person who

> had one face, in which many eyes were set, one side on which many hands dangled, and a sole shank. We have never seen in this world such a person whose figure was as ugly as this imaginable figure. I find it hard to believe that any intelligent person would feel at ease to describe his Lord in such a manner.[145]

Another argument for *taʾwīl* that al-Razi presented was that the literal meaning contradicted both common sense and facts of life. Thus, referring to Q. 57:25 ('We have sent down iron') and Q. 39:6 ('He has sent down for you four different pairs of cattle'), al-Razi remarked: 'It is well-known that neither iron nor cattle goes down to earth from the sky.'[146] Another example is the *ḥadīth* of the All-Merciful's two fingers:

> The Prophet said: 'The heart of the believer is held between two of the All-Merciful's fingers.' There is no doubt that this *ḥadīth* should be interpreted figuratively because we know for sure that there are no two fingers in our chests that hold our hearts.[147]

Elsewhere al-Razi clarified:

> [The literal reading of this text] necessitates that two fingers on behalf of God would hold every heart. It also necessitates that God has only two fingers, and that these two fingers exist in the belly of every human being. This entails that the single body (namely, the finger) exists in many places. This whole reading is feeble and absurd.[148]

Al-Razi's technique was to use the banal and false argument as a platform to present more subtle and accurate arguments. In the case of the *ḥadīth* of the All-Merciful's two fingers, al-Razi presented a figurative reading which was embedded in his unique theory of the human action.[149] According to al-Razi's understanding of the human psyche, the heart is the abode in which the human motives (*dāʿī*, pl. *dawāʿin*) are created. However, unlike the Muʿtazilite perception of the motives, God is the creator of the motives; hence, God is the true agent and not the human being. Al-Razi claimed that the heart is the only free agent in the body, because the entire organs obey its commands and are operated by it. However, the heart is not really a free agent, because it is controlled by God. The heart is constantly wavering between two states (*ḥālatān*): the state in which a motive to perform (*fiʿl*) a certain action is created in the heart, and the state in which a motive not to perform (*tark*) this action is created in the heart. Al-Razi claimed that this *kalām*ic explanation stood behind the metaphor of the human heart and the two divine fingers in the *ḥadīth* of the All-Merciful's two fingers. Furthermore, he thus implied that his *kalām*ic interpretation of this *ḥadīth* reflected the Prophet's intention, thus attributing to the Prophet the knowledge of *kalām*. In the following paragraph, al-Razi presented the divine fingers as metaphors of the motives of action and non-action that God creates in the human heart:

> The free agent (*al-mutaṣarrif*) in the body is the heart. The heart is always attached to the state of performing (*fiʿl*) a certain action and to the state of not performing (*tark*) it. The action is dependent on the occurrence of the motives of action, while the opposite, namely not performing the action, is dependent on the occurrence of the motives of not performing the action. These two opposing states – the performing of an action and not performing it – are the only two options, and there is no escape from them, because it is impossible to escape [to a third option] when only two opposing ends are given. God, and not the human being, creates the motive of action. Otherwise the human being would have needed another motive in the process of causing the motive of action to occur. This would have entailed infinite regress (*tasalsul*) which is impossible.[150] Thus we have established that the heart wavers between these two states. If the motive of action occurs in the heart, then the heart will embark on performing the action. If the motive of not performing the action occurs in it, then it will remain in the position of not performing the action. The occurrence of these two states is represented [in the *ḥadīth*] by the two fingers that turn various objects over. The 'turning over' of the heart because of the two motives of performing the action and not performing it is represented [in the *ḥadīth*] by the turning over of an object which is held between two fingers. These fingers turn the object over from one state to the other. Just as the human being unrestrictedly inverts the object that his fingers hold by moving his fingers, so does God unrestrictedly invert the hearts of His servants by creating these motives. This is the greatest secret and the noblest code of predetermination. The Prophet expressed this subtle secret by using this concise and delicate figure of speech.[151]

Not all of al-Razi's figurative interpretations of other anthropomorphic expressions in *aḥādīth al-ṣifāt* are as complex as the above paragraph. It is, for example, disappointing to discover that *ḥadīth ḥaqw al-raḥmān* received only the laconic remark: 'This *ḥadīth* must be read figuratively',[152] without deciphering the meaning of the divine loin (see Chapter 4). In *Asās al-Taqdīs*, al-Razi obviously addressed a thin layer of educated readers, *al-khawāṣṣ*, the elite. The concluding sentence in the above paragraph attests to his readership: al-Razi shared with his readers a subtle secret that only people of refinement and finesse were able (so he believed) to grasp.

Only the audience of educated readers could have digested the most important contribution of *Asās al-Taqdīs* to the polemics on *aḥādīth al-ṣifāt*: providing a concrete definition of *tashbīh*. This definition, which appears in the two last chapters of *Asās al-Taqdīs*, was indeed unique, because it relied on logic and was thusly articulated in a straightforward manner. In *Asās al-Taqdīs*, as in the short passage of his interpretation of Q. 42:11, al-Razi clarified that the literal reading of *aḥādīth al-ṣifāt* inevitably resulted in perceiving God as a body confined to the physical dimensions of place, limitation and directionality. According to al-Razi, Ibn Khuzayma's literal reading of *aḥādīth al-ṣifāt* inevitably entailed perceiving God as a corporeal being; hence, Ibn Khuzayma's declarations against *tashbīh* were insignificant. Accordingly, al-Razi saw Ibn Khuzayma (and indeed any scholar who read *aḥādīth al-ṣifāt* literally) as a corporealist. In the two final chapters of *Asās al-Taqdīs*, al-Razi did not mention Ibn Khuzayma by name, but referred to him as 'the corporealist' (*al-mujassim*). In these chapters, al-Razi answered two questions: 'Did Ibn Khuzayma's corporealism necessarily mean that he was a *mushabbih* promoting *tashbīh* (here, not anthropomorphism, but comparing God to His creation)?' and 'Should Ibn Khuzayma have been condemned as a heretic for his views?'

There is no doubt that Ibn Khuzayma wholeheartedly believed that his repeated declarations that God was different in essence from any other being safeguarded him from the accusation of anthropomorphism. As al-Razi described the situation, the corporealist could have insisted that 'there are forms and attributes that exist in God and are equivalent to the forms and attributes in human beings', and at the same time declare that 'in essence, God is different than any other body'. The corporealist claimed that 'God

Himself declared in the Quran that there were many attributes [in Him] that were equivalent to the attributes of human beings. Furthermore, no one ever claimed that this equivalence entailed *tashbīh*.'[153] Al-Razi clarified that 'the corporealist' (actually, Ibn Khuzayma) was indeed a *mushabbih*:

> The kernel of what we say is as follows: in the first section of this book, we have proven that the physical bodies resemble each other in their essence and quiddity. Were God a physical body, He would have been comparable in essence to these physical bodies. This comparability necessarily entails *tashbīh*.[154]

Thus, according to al-Razi's definition, *tashbīh* was attributing a form to God. Any declaration that indicated that in essence the divine form was different from any existing form was irrelevant and substantially ineffective.

The question of whether or not to condemn Ibn Khuzayma as a heretic is discussed in the final chapter of *Asās al-Taqdīs* and in the brief passage of al-Razi's interpretation of Q. 42:11. Despite al-Razi's criticism of Ibn Khuzayma, at the end of the relevant passage of Q. 42:11, al-Razi demonstrated some compassion towards him:

> This man (namely, Ibn Khuzayma) said what he said because he was not versed in the science of the essences (ontology). He was carried away by the words of the laity. He was dazzled by these ideas that he mentioned and misled by them.[155]

The same forgiving approach is reflected in the concluding chapter of *Asās al-Taqdīs*. In this chapter, al-Razi examined the possibility to condemn 'those who believe that God is a physical body and has a direction' (*al-qāʾilūn bi'l-jismiyya wa'l-jiha*) as heretics; again, this was al-Razi's way to describe Ibn Khuzayma. Since he already had determined that Ibn Khuzayma was a corporealist, al-Razi examined two options in this chapter: either that 'the corporealist' was a heretic or that he was not. In the first option, the corporealists were heretics because they refused to recognise the existence of an existent that our senses could not perceive. According to al-Razi's understanding of the corporealists, they refused to recognise God's unique existence. God was not confined to the limitations of space and direction and was not perceived by the senses; however, they adhered to the concept of a divinity which was confined to the limitations of space and direction. Al-Razi, therefore, concluded that the corporealists were heretics.[156] The other option that al-Razi presented was to avoid declaring the corporealists heretics. Here al-Razi presented an interesting argument: perhaps belief in a divinity that was absolutely transcendent was not a prerequisite to faith. Obviously, al-Razi examined this notion because the laity in his immediate environment held 'the beliefs of the old women' – they understood *aḥādīth al-ṣifāt* literally. But in *Asās al-Taqdīs* he presented a different argument:

> Were understanding *tanzīh* prerequisite to the correct belief, it would have forced the Prophet not to accept a person's profession of faith until he first inquired whether this person described God by using only the attributes of *tanzīh* (namely, non-anthropomorphic attributes like existent, all-knowing, and all-mighty), or not. But since the Prophet accepted people's professions of faith without conducting this inquiry first, we conclude that understanding *tanzīh* is not a prerequisite of faith.[157]

Elsewhere in *Asās al-Taqdīs*, al-Razi clarified that the laymen (*al-ᶜawāmm*) were incapable of grasping the concept of *tanzīh* when this was presented to them in a *kalām*ic language (as he presented):

> When a layman hears that he should confirm the existence of an existent who is not a physical body, is not confined to the limitations of space, and you cannot point at his direction, he consequently thinks that this existent is mere void (*ᶜadam maḥḍ*). This can lead the layman to negate (*taᶜṭīl*) the divine attributes.[158]

Although *Asās al-Taqdīs* was not the first Ashᶜarite work to offer a systematic refutation of Ibn Khuzayma and his literal reading of *aḥādīth al-ṣifāt* (the first was Ibn Furak's *Mushkil al-Ḥadīth*),[159] it was certainly the most influential and its repercussions lasted for centuries. Al-Razi's eloquent writing style that combined banality and sophistication made *Asās al-Taqdīs* an accessible theological treatise with arguments that its readers could 'easily digest'. This treatise's accessibility explains its unprecedented popularity among the Ashᶜarites of Cairo and Damascus in the Mamluk era. The Ashᶜarites used the ready-made argumentations that *Asās al-Taqdīs* provided in their polemics with the ultra-traditionalists. The use of these argumentations in the public sphere will be elucidated in the following section.

IV. Ibn Taymiyya's *al-Ḥamawiyya al-Kubrā* and Two Iconic Gestures

Asās al-Taqdīs promoted a strict concept of *tanzīh* that was both theoretical and had practical implications in at least two daily applications. One application was the raising of both hands (*rafᶜ al-yadayn*) to the sky during the performance of the obligatory prayers (*ṣalāt*) and during the personal invocation (*duᶜāʾ*) to God. The second application was pointing the index finger (*al-ishāra bi'l-sabbāba*) to the *qibla* (the direction of prayer) and moving the finger (*taḥrīk al-sabbāba*) to indicate that God was one. This iconic gesture was performed during obligatory and non-obligatory prayers while uttering the profession of faith (*tashahhud*).[160] Both practices were linked to the laws of prayer, and were thoroughly discussed in Hadith compilations and manuals of Islamic law.

Rafᶜ al-yadayn, the raising of both hands, was a highly controversial topic for centuries because the relevant Hadith material provided two contradictory reports about this practice: one report claimed that the Prophet raised both his hands in prayer; the other report claimed that he did not raise his hands at all.[161] In fact, this topic is highly controversial even today, as indicated in numerous responsa, popular booklets and dedicated Internet websites.[162] Muhammad ibn Ismaᶜil al-Bukhari (d. 870) articulated the overall traditionalistic stance towards *rafᶜ al-yadayn*. He said: 'Whoever claims that the raising of hands was an undesired innovation (*bidᶜa*), defames the companions of the Prophet, the worthy ancestors and the scholars who were their successors.'[163] However, the vigorous and decisive tone in which al-Bukhari opined on this topic indicated that the controversy about this issue that raged in his days was at its peak.[164] *Rafᶜ al-yadayn* elicited numerous discussions about fundamental questions related to prayer. We find questions related to classification, definition and practical aspects. For instance, what is the legal status of these practices? Are they regarded obligatory, recommended or forbidden? In which section of the prayer should these practices be performed? In the obligatory prayer, should the hands be raised before exclaiming *Allāhu Akbar*, or simultaneously with the exclamation? Which non-obligatory prayers were connected to these practices?[165] We also find similar discussions which involved the practice of *al-ishāra bi'l-sabbāba*, pointing the index finger.[166] We find a detailed section of *aḥādīth* on this topic in Ibn Khuzayma's Hadith compilation.[167]

The practices of *rafᶜ al-yadayn* and *al-ishāra bi'l-sabbāba* were indirectly linked to the theological topics of God's aboveness, directionality and spatiality, as we learn from al-Razi's discussion in *Asās al-Taqdīs*. These were the topics that occupied the lion's share of *Asās al-Taqdīs*. Al-Razi did not address the legal and practical aspects of these two iconic gestures, but he concentrated on their implied meaning.[168] His discussion on these topics included a thorough examination of the common perceptions that God was in the sky, His throne was up in the seventh heaven (or rather, above the seventh heaven) and that He was enthroned on high. Al-Razi could not ignore the Quranic verses (for example, Q. 20:5) that indicated that God was enthroned on high. In addition, he could not ignore the relevant *aḥādīth al-ṣifāt*, for example, *ḥadīth al-bayᶜa* attributed to Abu Razin or the *ḥadīth* on the black slave-girl. However, by using the device of figurative interpretation and applying several *kalām*ic argumentations, al-Razi determined that God was not in the sky, sitting on a throne.[169] In *Mafātīḥ al-Ghayb*, al-Razi articulated this position. Accordingly, his interpretation to the Quranic phrase 'He who is in heaven' (*man fī 'l-samāᵓ*) was figurative. Al-Razi claimed that this phrase indicated God's power and sovereignty.[170] His conclusion was that although the Quran and the Hadith suggested that God was 'up above' (*fawq*), this phrase should be read metaphorically. The meaning of this description was that God ruled over creation.[171]

Al-Razi did not prohibit explicitly the performance of *rafᶜ al-yadayn* and *al-ishāra bi'l-sabbāba*; there is no doubt that as a pious Shafiᶜite, he performed both practices faithfully. However, he disapproved of their implied meaning in several well-articulated passages in *Asās al-Taqdīs*. The rationale of his disapproval was quite simple: God was not a body confined to the physical dimensions of place, limitation and directionality. Consequently, the practices of pointing with a finger and raising hands were not meant to indicate that God was in the sky.[172] Al-Razi emphasised that the claim that God was in the sky was in fact sheer absurdity. The phrase that al-Razi used in his discussion was *al-ishāra al-ḥissiyya*, that is, gesturing at something which is perceivable by at least one of the senses.[173] In the context of our discussion, *al-ishāra al-ḥissiyya* is pointing a finger upwards or raising the hands.[174] Al-Razi mentioned two groups that used the practice of pointing a finger upwards as proof that God was in the sky: the Hanbalites and the Karramites. Al-Razi admitted that the Hanbalites had every right – logically speaking – to claim that God was in the sky. After all, their literal reading of *aḥādīth al-ṣifāt* entailed a perception of God who had organs, was composite (*murakkab*), had dimensions and was limited to a certain space. Following their literal understanding of *aḥādīth al-ṣifāt*, it was logical that the Hanbalites believed that one could point to the estimated direction in the sky where God supposedly was located. However, the Karramites who perceived God as an endless body were logically incorrect to point to the sky in their claim that God was there, because an endless body has no defined direction.[175]

In addition, Al-Razi was well-aware of the fact that his views negated the common perception that prevailed in Khurasan where he lived, and in fact elsewhere. He directed his ideas to the Ashᶜarite elite and not to the masses. His goal was to expose the false intellectualism of scholars who were not Ashᶜarites: they could have been Hanbalites, traditionalists of other trends or Karramites. In *Asās al-Taqdīs*, al-Razi reported that his ideological rivals in this controversy claimed that raising one's hands to the sky 'was practiced by the authoritative leaders of all religions, which proved that the concept that God was above was established in the minds of all the people'.[176] Al-Razi was not impressed by this argument: 'This practice stands in contradiction to another common practice that was established in the minds of all the people, which is to place their forehead on the ground while worshipping God. Does it not?'[177] This rhetorical question implies, of course, that God was not on the ground. Thereafter, al-Razi determined that the purpose of raising the hands above while mentioning God, was not to point to God's alleged direction, but to point to all the blessings that come from above: light, air and rain. The angels who were the agents that brought benefits to the world came from above. Upwards was therefore the direction that was the most respectable direction in the minds of the people. Al-Razi concluded: 'God determined that we perform our invocations and supplications (*duᶜāʾ*) in the direction of the throne, just as He determined that we perform the official ritualistic prayer (*ṣalāt*) in the direction of the Kaᶜba.'[178] Al-Razi concluded that these practices did not indicate or prove that God was upwards.

Al-Razi's interpretation of the two gestures of pointing a finger to the sky while referring to God and raising both hands during personal supplications had some impact in Cairo and Damascus, a century after al-Razi's death. Al-Razi's version of Ashᶜarite *kalām* was the most dominant trend in these two important cities of the Mamluk sultanate, where being an Ashᶜarite was a symbol of status and prestige.[179] Ashᶜarite *kalām* was a favourite pastime of the rich and the powerful by which they differentiated themselves from the 'ignorant' traditionalists. These Ashaᶜrites came mainly from the Shafiᶜite school of law, where the majority of the Shafiᶜites were traditionalists. While the prominent representatives of Shafiᶜite traditionalism (like the Hadith expert Jamal al-Din al-Mizzi, and the Hadith expert and historian Shams al-Din al-Dhahabi) were preoccupied with the study of Hadith, the Shafiᶜite-Ashᶜarite elite demonstrated interest in al-Razi's convoluted *kalām*ic discourse. Although there were tensions between the traditionalists and the Ashᶜarites, the tranquil status quo between these two groups was apparently maintained.[180]

Since most of the occupants of important positions in the religious establishment in Cairo and Damascus were identified as Ashᶜarites, they set the tone for a pro-Raziyyan rationalistic discourse. This tone prevailed in the public debates on theology. However, when the activist Hanbalite Taqi al-Din Ahmad ibn ᶜAbd al-Halim ibn Taymiyya (d. 1328) made his appearance on the public scene, the controversy between the traditionalists (Ibn Taymiyya's followers were both Hanbalites and Shafiᶜites) and the Ashᶜarites reached a new level and became stormy.[181] Ibn Taymiyya vigorously targeted the newest form of Ashᶜarite *kalām* which Fakhr al-Din al-Razi shaped and the *ᶜulamāᵓ* of Mamluk Damascus and Cairo promoted.[182] Ibn Taymiyya was undoubtedly a true expert in al-Razi's writings, more than most of the Ashᶜarites who claimed to be fervent fans of al-Razi.[183] Ibn Taymiyya wrote several works which directly responded to al-Razi. Thus, for example, his voluminous *Bayān Talbīs al-Jahmiyya* was a response to *Asās al-Taqdīs*.[184] Likewise, his *al-Ḥamawiyya al-Kubrā* (the Grand [Response Written] for the People of Hamat) referred to ideas inspired by al-Razi's thought. However, while *Bayān Talbīs al-Jahmiyya* (like *Asās al-Taqdīs*) was an inaccessible text written for scholars, *al-Ḥamawiyya al-Kubrā* was a *fatwā*, a legal response that was issued for a wide audience of educated and lay traditionalists. Thus, ideas that are discussed in length in *Bayān Talbīs al-Jahmiyya* appear in a digestible form in *al-Ḥamawiyya al-Kubrā*. This text's iconicity is explained by the role it played in a chain of events that directly led to Ibn Taymiyya's hardships and persecutions by the Shafiᶜite-Ashᶜarite establishment.

The initiative for composing *al-Ḥamawiyya al-Kubrā* came from the people of Hamat, a town in northern Syria. At the beginning of December 1298 (Rabiᶜ al-Awwal of Hijri year 698),[185] Ibn Taymiyya received the following question from a representative of the people of Hamat (most probably, the local sheikhs and community leaders):

> What do you, the most prominent scholar, the leader of religion, think of *āyāt al-ṣifāt* such as 'The Merciful who sits enthroned on high' (Q. 20:5), 'and then ascended on the throne' (Q. 7:54, 10:3), 'Then, turning to the sky, which was but a cloud of vapour' (Q. 41:11) and so forth? [What do you think of] *aḥādīth al-ṣifāt* such as 'The hearts of the human beings are [held] between two of the All-Merciful's fingers', and 'The Almighty placed His foot in hellfire' and so on? What did other scholars say about these [texts]? Please clarify the matter, may you be rewarded by God, if God wills.[186]

Ibn Taymiyya initially refused to answer the question and referred the inquirer to other Damascene scholars. However, the man insisted that the group he represented sought only Ibn Taymiyya's opinion.[187] On the tenth of December 1298 (the fifth of Rabiᶜ al-Awwal 698), Ibn Taymiyya dictated his lengthy response (seventy printed pages) to the people of Hamat during 'one sitting'. This 'one sitting' lasted approximately four hours, 'between the noon prayer and the afternoon prayer'. Ibn Rajab, who wrote an admiring biography of Ibn Taymiyya, remarked that judging from *al-Ḥamawiyya al-Kubrā*'s magnitude, its writing should have taken much more time than four hours. However, Ibn Taymiyya was known for his extraordinary writing ability. There were days in which Ibn Taymiyya single-handedly wrote an entire volume on theology or law.[188]

Al-Ḥamawiyya al-Kubrā was not a theoretical discussion on *taʾwīl* and *aḥādīth al-ṣifāt* but rather a political manifesto. This work contained a coherent creed that expressed Ibn Taymiyya's uncompromising novel form of radical traditionalism. His creed was shaped in opposition to the so-called rationalistic positions that his political rivals adopted. In the context of *al-Ḥamawiyya al-Kubrā*, Ibn Taymiyya warned the people of Hamat not to listen to the rationalists and not to adhere to their heretical views. He implied that these rationalists were part of the religious establishment in every major city of Islam. *Al-Ḥamawiyya al-Kubrā* accused the muftis and qadis from Hamat and elsewhere of being adherents of the Raziyyan form of the Ashᶜarite *kalām*, namely of rationalism.

In the opening paragraphs of *al-Ḥamawiyya al-Kubrā*, Ibn Taymiyya briefly presented his distinctive approach towards the anthropomorphic attributes. His approach was neither the traditionalistic *bi-lā kayfa* nor the Ashᶜarite *bi-lā kayfa*, but a unique combination of *bi-lā kayfa* that merged four elements. The first element was the traditionalistic method of reading the anthropomorphic descriptions without asking how God performed any act. The second element was unique to Ibn Taymiyya: while rejecting the device of *taʾwīl*, Ibn Taymiyya insisted that the divine attributes and anthropomorphic descriptions deserved linguistic inquiry which would lead to an understanding compatible with the appropriate discourse about God. Thus, he investigated the meaning of the attributes. The third element was developed by Ibn Taymiyya's predecessors, for example Ibn Khuzayma (see Section III): Ibn Taymiyya recognised that the divine attributes in general and the anthropomorphic descriptions in particular referred to an actual reality in God. The fourth element was borrowed from the traditionalistic scholars with rationalistic tendencies like Ibn Qutayba, and it appeared also in the thought of Ibn Furak (see Chapter 4): Ibn Taymiyya defined the divine attributes and the anthropomorphic descriptions as representations of God's perfection (*kamāl*).[189] The following key passage from *al-Ḥamawiyya al-Kubrā* presents these four elements. We have added numbers to the translated text to help identify the elements in Ibn Taymiyya's unique *bi-lā kayfa* formula:

> The general approach in this matter [of the divine attributes] is as follows: God should be described by using [the same words] that He used to describe Himself, or by using [the same words] that His Prophet used to describe God, or by using [the same words] that the previous and worthiest generations used to describe Him, provided that these words did not go beyond the Quran and the Hadith. This is what Ahmad ibn Hanbal

> said. The approach of the worthy ancestors was to describe God by using the exact words that He used to describe Himself and the words that the Prophet used to describe Him. [1] They (i.e. the worthy ancestors) did not distort the text; they did not negate the divine attributes; they did not ask how God did this or that; and they did not compare God to created beings (*min ghayr taḥrīf wa-lā taᶜṭīl wa-min ghayr takyīf wa-lā tamthīl*). [2] We know that God's description of Himself is true; it contains neither riddles nor puzzles. The meaning of this description is comprehended inasmuch as the intention of a speaker is comprehended by his words, especially because this speaker (namely, the Prophet) knew best what he meant to say, and he knew it more than any human being. He knew how to say what he wanted to say, and was the most eloquent human being. [3] In spite of what we said so far, 'nothing can be compared with Him' (*laysa ka-mithlihi shayᵓun*; Q. 42:11). Nothing can be compared to His sacred essence, which is described by the divine names and attributes. Nothing can be compared to His actions. We know through certain knowledge that He has an entity in reality (*lahu dhāt ḥaqīqatan*), and that He has actions in reality (*lahu afᶜāl ḥaqīqatan*), and also His attributes exist in reality (*lahu ṣifāt ḥaqīqatan*). We also know through certain knowledge that 'nothing can be compared with Him', with His essence, attributes or actions. [4] God is above anything which implies or necessitates deficiency. He is above anything that implies creation. God is above these things in reality. He deserves the highest degree of perfection (*kamāl*).[190]

This paragraph was exceptional in the framework of *al-Ḥamawiyya al-Kubrā*: the response for the citizens of Hamat was not a highbrow discussion on the divine attributes, but a popular text with a definite political agenda. The nub of *al-Ḥamawiyya al-Kubrā* was refuting the rationalists' critique of the literal understanding of *āyāt al-ṣifāt* and *aḥādīth al-ṣifāt* and their approach to these anthropomorphic texts. As Ibn Taymiyya described in his response, the rationalists 'were constantly wavering' between accepting the words without investigating their meanings (*tafwīḍ*) and deploying a figurative interpretation (*taᵓwīl*). *Tafwīḍ*, which the Ashᶜarites claimed to be 'the way of the worthy ancestors' (*ṭarīqat al-salaf*), was the equivalent of the ultra-traditionalistic *bi-lā kayfa*. *Taᵓwīl*, which the Ashᶜarites claimed to be 'the way of later generations' (*ṭarīqat al-khalaf*) combined, according to Ibn Taymiyya, 'false rationalistic methods' (*fasād al-ᶜaql*) with 'unbelief in the Hadith material' (*al-kufr bi'l-samᶜ*).[191] The rationalists applied this method to *āyāt al-ṣifāt*, while they rejected the lion's share of *aḥādīth al-ṣifāt*. On the minute amount of *aḥādīth al-ṣifāt* that they did accept, the rationalists deployed *taᵓwīl*. Apologising for the limited scope of his *fatwā* which prevented him from discussing this issue thoroughly, Ibn Taymiyya advised his inquirers to be aware of the dangers of foreign theories that penetrated Islamic scholarship through the writings of the Greek philosophers and the Muᶜtazilites. In *al-Ḥamawiyya al-Kubrā* and elsewhere, Ibn Taymiyya (later followed by his disciple Ibn Qayyim al-Jawziyya) identified the Raziyyan theology as an Islamised form of Greek philosophy or as a new form of Muᶜtazilism; either way, al-Razi's theology was the major target of Ibn Taymiyya's constant attacks.[192] Ibn Taymiyya advised his readers to find their recourse in the writings that reflected the true spirit of Islam, the writings that faithfully recorded the 'sayings of the worthy ancestors' (*kalām al-salaf*).[193]

Ibn Taymiyya took a risk in identifying Raziyyan Ashᶜarism as a new form of Muᶜtazilism. His subtle insults of the Ashᶜarites and their adherents as found in *al-Ḥamawiyya al-Kubrā* did not escape the notice of Ibn Taymiyya's enemies. For example, in *al-Ḥamawiyya al-Kubrā*, Ibn Taymiyya warned Hamat's citizens of two categories of dangerous books: the first category refers to books written by respectable Sunnite scholars who were, according to Ibn Taymiyya's perception, Muᶜtazilites in disguise. Ibn Taymiyya claimed that although some of these scholars declared that they rejected the figurative interpretation, 'and they have agreeable opinions in several other matters', their figurative interpretations (*taᵓwīlāt*) were identical to the methods of the Muᶜtazilites.[194] The second category refers to books which contain figurative interpretations of the anthropomorphic texts. The only two books that Ibn Taymiyya mentioned in this category were Ibn Furak's *Mushkil al-Ḥadīth* (here entitled *Kitāb al-Taᵓwīlāt*) and Fakhr al-Din al-Razi's *Asās al-Taqdīs* (here entitled *Taᵓsīs al-Taqdīs*). These two books formed the essential reading material for Ibn Taymiyya's contemporaries. According to Ibn Taymiyya, 'these are the *taᵓwīlāt* that circulate among people these days . . . The essence of their figurative interpretations is identical to the essence of the figurative interpretations of Bishr al-Marisi.'[195]

Bishr al-Marisi (d. 833), whom Ibn Taymiyya mentioned numerous times in his writings, was the archenemy of traditionalist Islam. In his capacity as the most prolific *mutakallim* of his generation, he participated in public debates against the traditionalists.[196] The analogy that Ibn Taymiyya made between the ninth-century *mutakallim* Bishr al-Marisi and the Ashᶜarites Ibn Furak and Fakhr al-Din al-Razi was deliberate: the rationalistic views that Bishr expressed, and especially his approach to the anthropomorphic verses and *aḥādīth*, directly connected him – in Ibn Taymiyya's worldview – to Ibn Furak and al-Razi. In addition, Bishr was part of the traditionalistic milieu, as were Ibn Furak and Fakhr al-Din al-Razi. In fact, Bishr studied Hadith with Hammad ibn Salama and Sufyan ibn ᶜUyayna, and was regarded as one of the senior jurisprudents of his times.[197] Also, al-Marisi wrote a book entitled *Kufr al-Mushabbiha* (The Unbelief of the Anthropomorphists), which provided figurative interpretations of some *aḥādīth al-ṣifāt* while he rejected the content of other *aḥādīth al-ṣifāt*. This book, like the lion's share of Bishr's scholarly output, did not survive.[198]

By describing the later Ashᶜarites (*al-mutaᵓakhkhirūn*) as the successors of Bishr, Ibn Taymiyya disclosed his worldview in a nutshell. He in fact told Hamat's citizenry that their religious and political leaders held views that did not correspond with the worldview of the worthy ancestors. Although Ibn Taymiyya did not explicitly condemn Ibn Furak and al-Razi as heretics, he implied that they deserved to be labelled as heretics:

> A man who asks for God's guidance must realize that the Leaders of the Right Path (*aᵓimmat al-hudā*)[199] unanimously agreed that the followers of al-Marisi were to be condemned. He must realize that most of [the leaders] declared them heretics or misguided. When he suddenly realizes that the belief that was deeply rooted among the scholars of later generations (i.e. the later Ashᶜarites) was indeed the teachings of al-Marisi, the right path will be revealed to him.[200]

After identifying the 'enemies', namely the books by Ibn Furak and Fakhr al-Din al-Razi, Ibn Taymiyya listed the most effective weapons to attack them: these were twenty-four books written by traditionalistic scholars between the ninth and eleventh centuries. Among these works the name of Ibn Kuhzayma's *Kitāb al-Tawḥīd* is conspicuous.[201] As we have mentioned in

Section III, Ibn Khuzayma ruled that the denier of God's aboveness was a heretic who should be executed. Ibn Taymiyya accurately cited Ibn Khuzayma's ruling in *al-Ḥamawiyya al-Kubrā*.[202] We know that Ibn Taymiyya sided with Ibn Khuzayma, because he did not add any remark or reservation to his accurate quotation of Ibn Khuzayma. This was another bold step on the part of Ibn Taymiyya. By quoting Ibn Khuzayma in *al-Ḥamawiyya al-Kubrā*, Ibn Taymiyya signalled that the Ashᶜarites of his time (in fact, the entire religious establishment) were heretics. In Section III, we noted that Shams al-Din al-Dhahabi, a contemporary of Ibn Taymiyya, did not accept Ibn Khuzayma's view. Given the pro-Raziyyan atmosphere in Damascus, al-Dhahabi was politically prudent and inherently critical and sceptical when he discussed Ibn Khuzayma's ruling. Ibn Taymiyya, on the other hand, was anything but prudent in his declarations against the Ashᶜarites.

Among the many debates on *āyāt al-ṣifāt* and *aḥādīth al-ṣifāt* that *al-Ḥamawiyya al-Kubrā* contained was the confrontation between the Ashᶜarites and the traditionalists about the theological implications of *rafᶜ al-yadayn* and *al-ishāra bi'l-sabbāba*. After quoting several *aḥādīth* in which the believer raised his hands to the sky while invoking God's name, Ibn Taymiyya determined:

> There are 'massively transmitted *aḥādīth*' with identical wording; there are 'massively transmitted *aḥādīth*' with different wording but identical meaning (*al-mutawātirāt al-lafẓiyya wa'l-maᶜnawiyya*). Both kinds of texts convey to us the most undisputable and certain knowledge (*ᶜilm yaqīn*). This knowledge is the highest degree of all the branches of necessary knowledge (*al-ᶜulūm al-ḍarūriyya*).[203] [According to this certain knowledge], the Prophet who brought the message delivered [his great sermon] to the Muslims whom he summoned. [In this great sermon], he confirmed that God was enthroned on high, and that He was above in heaven. This is the *fiṭra*, the inherent belief that God had granted to all the nations, whether Arabs or foreigners, in the times prior and after the rise of Islam. [All the people] believe in it, apart from those whom the devils caused to deviate from their *fiṭra*.[204]

Ibn Taymiyya thereafter explained to the citizens of Hamat that ideas that they probably heard from the Ashᶜarites of their hometown were innovations. These ideas were alien to the spirit of the genuine Islam of the Prophet and the initial generations of Islam. There is no doubt that the Ashᶜarite ideas as Ibn Taymiyya described them were articulated by al-Razi's adherents:

> There are numerous sayings attributed to the Salaf, the worthy ancestors. Had we collected them, we would have gathered hundreds and thousands of them. No textual proof from the Quran, Hadith or the sayings of the worthy ancestors contradicts the assertion that God was above in heaven.[205] None of the worthy ancestors ever said that God was not above in heaven, that He was not enthroned on high. None of them ever said that He, in His essence, was everywhere, and that all the places were equal as far as He was concerned. None of them ever said that He was not in this world, or that He was not outside this world.[206]

Ibn Taymiyya concluded:

> None of them ever said that it was impossible to point a finger at His direction (*al-ishāra al-ḥissiyya ilayhi bi'l-aṣābiᶜ*). On the contrary, in a reliable *ḥadīth* that appears in *Ṣaḥīḥ Muslim*, the *ṣaḥābī* Jabir ibn ᶜAbd Allah (d. 697) was quoted as saying: 'The Prophet gave his great sermon in the Day of ᶜArafat which was the largest gathering in which the Prophet had participated. In this gathering, the Prophet said: "Have I not told you?" The people responded: "O yes!" Thereafter he pointed his finger to the sky, and then turned his finger to the audience and said: "O God, bear witness."'[207]

The textual proof that Ibn Taymiyya quoted here was part of the extremely lengthy *ḥadīth* that described the Prophet's sermon during *ḥijjat al-wadāᶜ* ('the Farewell Pilgrimage'). According to the numerous historical accounts of this event, the Prophet delivered his sermon (one of several) on the ninth of *Dhu al-Hijja*, Hijri year 10 (March 632) near Mount ᶜArafat, east of Mecca. The series of sermons that the Prophet delivered during the Farewell Pilgrimage is regarded as his testament.[208] In the sermon in ᶜArafat (actually, in a dry creek at the bottom of the mount), the Prophet mentioned that a person's blood and property are sacred. Thereafter, the Prophet abolished the pre-Islamic laws.[209] In the Farewell Pilgrimage, the Prophet also specified the laws regarding a person's wives, and concluded:

> 'I have left for you the Book of God; if you adhere to it, you will never go astray. [After I am gone], you will be asked about me. What will you say?' The audience replied: 'We will testify that you conveyed the message, you fulfilled [your task], and gave us sincere advice.' Thereafter, he lifted his index finger to the sky, then turned it to the people [and said]: 'O God, bear witness!' That he said three times.[210]

Ibn Taymiyya saw this text as the strongest response to al-Razi's claim against the two gestures. We note that Ibn Taymiyya emphasised that the Prophet's message to the audience was that God was in the sky, although the Prophet did not say so. For Ibn Taymiyya, the Prophet's gestures were equivalent to his words. Although Ibn Taymiyya saw this text as valid evidence to justify using the gesture of pointing the index finger to the sky, he moved on to quote dozens of scholars, including al-Ashᶜari himself. In fact, one of the largest sections of *al-Ḥamawiyya al-Kubrā* includes a detailed account of Abu 'l-Hasan al-Ashᶜari's traditionalistic views as he clarified them in *Maqālāt al-Islāmiyyīn* and *al-Ibāna fī Uṣūl al-Diyāna*. Ibn Taymiyya in particular emphasised al-Ashᶜari's assertion that God was not everywhere but sitting on His throne. In addition, Ibn Taymiyya referred to al-Ashᶜari's traditionalistic reading of the anthropomorphic expressions by using the *bi-lā kayfa* formula.[211] By extensively quoting al-Ashᶜari, Ibn Taymiyya demonstrated the unbridgeable gap and even contradictions between the approach of al-Ashᶜari and his early followers, and the novel approach of the later Ashᶜarites, Ibn Taymiyya's contemporaries who followed al-Razi.

Al-Ḥamawiyya al-Kubrā instantly became a political symbol.[212] Years before its issuance, Ibn Taymiyya antagonised the established scholars of Cairo and Damascus because of his genius, unconventional legal and theological opinions, and the blunt approach of belittlement which he displayed towards the holders of religious positions. Most of all, Ibn Taymiyya antagonised these scholars because of his growing popularity among the masses. It is noteworthy that the enemies of Ibn Taymiyya included both Shafiᶜite jurists and judges who were engaged with Ashᶜarite *kalām*' (*jamāᶜa min al-shāfiᶜiyya al-mutakallimīn*), and their fervent followers (*adhnāb al-fuqahā*ʾ) who were scholars of little worth or no scholars at all.[213] Immediately after the issuance of *al-Ḥamawiyya al-Kubrā*, the Shafiᶜite-Ashᶜarite scholars wrote a lengthy response to this provocative text that would prove the supremacy of the Raziyyan form of Ashᶜarite *kalām* over Ibn Taymiyya's theological thought. These scholars and their enthusiastic followers also conducted a massive well-organised campaign against Ibn Taymiyya. During the heavy December 1298 rain and hailstorms which continued for days, they scurried through the muddy streets of Damascus to lobby all of the city's judges and jurisprudents. They accused Ibn Taymiyya of anthropomorphism and corporealism. They used *al-Ḥamawiyya al-Kubrā* as proof that Ibn Taymiyya corrupted the minds of the masses.[214]

The efforts of these lobbyists finally came to fruition when the Chief Hanafite judge in Damascus, Jalal al-Din Abu al-Mafakhir Ahmad ibn Husam al-Din al-Hanafi (d. 1344), was persuaded to prosecute Ibn Taymiyya for expressing and disseminating his unconventional doctrine among the masses. Jalal al-Din and the lobbyists hurried to Dar al-Hadith al-Ashrafiyya, the notable establishment of traditionalistic studies situated near the Damascus citadel, where Ibn Taymiyya spent his days. The Hanafite judge and the lobbyists entered the institution and the judge demanded that Ibn Taymiyya appear in his court to explain the creed that he articulated in *al-Ḥamawiyya al-Kubrā*. Ibn Taymiyya refused. Thereafter, the Hanafite judge sent messengers to Ibn Taymiyya, again demanding his attendance at his court. Ibn Taymiyya sent the following message to the judge: 'Matters of belief are of no concern of yours. The sultan appointed you to rule between people. Denouncing reprehensible beliefs is none of the qadi's concern.' The messenger delivered this answer to the judge. The lobbyists, who were present at his court, seized the opportunity to incite the Hanafite judge against Ibn Taymiyya: how dare Ibn Taymiyya demonstrate yet again his disrespect towards the representatives of the religious establishment! The offended judge therefore declared publicly that *al-Ḥamawiyya al-Kubrā* was banned.[215]

The procedure of banning this work included an impaling of *al-Ḥamawiyya al-Kubrā* on a cane. The lobbyists carried the text through the streets of Damascus, while one of the group, who assumed the position of herald (*al-munādī*), pronounced that no one should consult Ibn Taymiyya on juridical matters, neither orally nor in writing. Due to the interference of one of the governors of Damascus,[216] the Mamluk emir Sayf al-Din Jaghan (d. 1299–1300), the procession was halted before the herald could walk through all of the quarters in Damascus. The emir then ordered his men to capture the lobbyists. While many of them evaded capture, several were caught, including the herald. The prisoners were flogged and severely humiliated, until the issue – and Jaghan's anger – subsided.[217]

On Friday, the nineteenth of December 1298, Ibn Taymiyya held his regular study session. Afterwards, he invited the Shafiᶜite chief judge of Damascus, Imam al-Din ᶜUmar ibn ᶜAbd al-Rahman al-Shafiᶜi (d. 1299–1300) to read *al-Ḥamawiyya al-Kubrā* with him. Ibn Taymiyya certainly knew that the Shafiᶜite judge was also among the lobbyists who strove to refute *al-Ḥamawiyya la-Kubrā*. The judge came the next day to Ibn Taymiyya's study session accompanied by his brother Jalal al-Din Muhammad ibn ᶜAbd al-Rahman al-Shafiᶜi (d. 1338–9).[218] The session, packed with notables, lasted from Saturday morning until the wee hours of Sunday. Not a word of objection to Ibn Taymiyya's creed was heard during the session. When the session ended, the excited Imam al-Din exclaimed: 'I will prosecute whoever dares to talk against the sheikh (Ibn Taymiyya).' His brother, Jalal al-Din, declared: 'We will rebuke whoever dares to talk against the sheikh.' The two Shafiᶜite brothers departed cordially from Ibn Taymiyya.[219]

Although this episode ended well, this was not the end of the story. Seven years after its issuance, *al-Ḥamawiyya al-Kubrā* stood as the backdrop to Ibn Taymiyya's ordeals (*miḥan*). 'The ordeals' were a series of events in which Ibn Taymiyya was prosecuted and harassed by his enemies.[220] The beginning of the ordeals occurred in January 1306 (Rajab of Hijri year 705). The sultan issued Ibn Taymiyya a summons to appear in court before the emir Jamal al-Din al-Afram (d. 1319), the viceroy of Damascus. Ibn Taymiyya was ordered to explain his approach to the divine attributes and *aḥādīth al-ṣifāt*. Unlike Ibn Taymiyya's appearance before the Hanafite judge, this summons to appear in court was due to the efforts of the Cairene Ashᶜarites. Like in 1298, Ibn Taymiyya was accused by the Ashᶜarites of anthropomorphism and corporealism, and he was ordered to explain his creed in several court sessions (or trials) that were held in Damascus and Cairo.[221]

The details of Ibn Taymiyya's trials are fascinating, especially the discussions on his creed regarding the divine attributes. Although this topic falls outside the scope of this chapter, we will, however, focus on one aspect of the ordeals which was overlooked by the previous scholarship.[222] This aspect involves the controversy between Ibn Taymiyya and his interrogators about the iconic gestures of *rafᶜ al-yadayn* and *al-ishāra bi'l-sabbāba.* In Cairo's Citadel Court in April 1306 (Ramadan of Hijri year 705), the Malikite chief judge Zayn al-Din ᶜAli ibn Makhluf (d. 1318) interrogated Ibn Taymiyya about a statement in *al-Ḥamawiyya al-Kubrā.* The statement mentioned that it was possible to point a finger at God's direction. The historical sources have a record of this part of the interrogation, which occurred one day after Ibn Taymiyya arrived in Cairo by the orders of the sultan:

> On the second day after [Ibn Taymiyya]'s arrival [in Cairo], the judges and the jurists were gathered in the Citadel of Cairo. Ibn ᶜAdlan (a Shafiᶜite-Ashᶜarite jurist, d. 1349) was appointed as the prosecutor, while the Malikite Chief Judge Ibn Makhluf presented the charges against him. [Ibn Makhluf thus presented the charges]: 'This man claims that God uttered the Quran through syllables and sounds; that God in His essence is enthroned on high, and that it is possible to point a finger at God's direction' (*anna Allāh yushāru ilayhi al-ishāra al-ḥissiyya*).[223]

Ibn Taymiyya, who started his reply, was cut short by Ibn Makhluf; thereafter, Ibn Taymiyya refused to answer these accusations.[224] However, his stance was elucidated both in *al-Ḥamawaiyya al-Kubrā* and in the more elaborate *Bayān Talbīs al-Jahmiyya*:

> Gesturing upwards in God's [direction] whether with a finger, a hand, the eye, or the head during the personal invocation or at any other occasion is substantiated by *aḥādīth* with multiple chains of transmission on the authority of the Prophet himself (*qad tawātarat bihi 'l-sunan ᶜan 'l-nabī*). The gesturing is accepted by Muslims and non-Muslims alike.[225]

After corroborating this statement by numerous pieces of textual evidence from the Hadith literature,[226] Ibn Taymiyya determined: 'There are innumerable descriptions of the Prophet raising his hands during the personal invocation.'[227] One may conclude therefore that Ibn Taymiyya approved of gesturing with the finger upwards to indicate God's spatiality and raising both hands during the supplications, and that for this stance – among others – he was put to trial.

Apart from Ibn Taymiyya's imprisonment, the 1306 trial in Cairo had one important consequence: the sultan al-Malik al-Nasir (r. 1293–1341) issued a royal decree denouncing Ibn Taymiyya and his views as vulgar corporealism. The sultan's decree, issued on the thirteenth of April 1306 (twenty-eighth of Ramadan Hijri year 705), duplicated the allegations of Ibn Taymiyya's enemies that he corrupted the masses. The sultan's decree was sent to Damascus and to other cities in Syria so it would be read publicly in the Friday mosques. The decree prohibited the sultan's subjects to adopt Ibn Taymiyya's corporealistic views. Among these views, the decree specified the concept of God's directionality and spatiality. 'As far as we are concerned, whoever declares that God is confined to a certain direction (*yuḥayyiz Allāh fī jiha*), or delves in questions like the whereabouts [of God] and the modality [of His attributes] (*yataᶜarraḍ ilā ḥaythu wa-kayfa*), has only the sword reserved for him' – determined the sultan.[228] In spite of the uncompromising tone of the decree, Ibn Taymiyya was not executed; he was merely placed in detention. The historian Shihab al-Din al-Nuwayri (d. 1333), a Shafiᶜte-Ashᶜarite who participated in the sultan's administration in Cairo, provided a detailed description of Ibn Taymiyya's repudiation of his doctrines that occurred in the Cairene court on the twenty-fourth of September 1307 (twenty-fifth of Rabiᶜ al-Awwal Hijri year 707). According to al-Nuwayri's description, in front of witnesses Ibn Taymiyya declared: 'I am an Ashᶜarite' while raising the books of the Ashᶜarites above his head.[229] Whether these were Fakhr al-Din al-Razi's books or not, we do not know. We have only al-Nuwayri's testimony as a witness to this event, while other sources remain suspiciously silent. The result of this event (if it indeed occurred) was Ibn Taymiyya's release from prison. Ibn Taymiyya, however, was not allowed to return to Syria. His ordeals continued until his death in 1328. The narrative of his remaining life story will wait for another opportunity.[230]

V. Iconic Gestures and the Hashwiyya

Ibn Taymiyya's approval of gesturing with the finger upwards to indicate God's spatiality and raising both hands during supplications was perceived by the Shafiᶜite-Ashᶜarites as vulgar corporealism; likewise, were his readings of the anthropomorphic traditions. Accordingly, Ibn Taymiyya was labelled as a *ḥashwī*, *mushabbih* or *mujassim*.[231] While the terms *mushabbih* (anthropomorphist) and *mujassim* (corporealist) refer to the views that were supposedly expressed by the holder of this derogative name, *ḥashwī* also referred to the lack of sophistication and finesse of the anthropomorphist. *Ḥashwiyya* (henceforth, Hashwiyya), the plural form of *ḥashwī*, was an emotionally charged term; the term expressed contempt for a certain group of people who were regarded as lower-class, culturally inferior, uneducated and uncultivated. Between the ninth and the thirteenth centuries, the Hashwiyya were mostly identified with the Hanbalites of Baghdad.[232] In the fourteenth century, the Shafiᶜite-Ashᶜarites of Damascus used this long-lived pejorative name to describe their own sense of superiority over the illiterate masses whose naive perception of divinity was anthropomorphic. The Hashwiyya were also immediately identified with Hanbalism, although the Hanbalites of Damascus were economically prosperous and well-educated. The Shafiᶜite-Ashᶜarites perceived Ibn Taymiyya as encouraging the naive beliefs of the masses, thus they referred to him as *ḥashwī*. From a sociological point of view, Ibn Taymiyya did not belong to the Hashwiyya, because he came from a family of scholars and belonged to the elite of Damascus. His Hanbalism, his popularity among the masses and his refusal to align himself with the religious establishment were the main reasons the Shafiᶜite-Ashᶜarites called him a *ḥashwī*.

In one of the Damascene trials (held from the end of January until the end of February 1306), Ibn Taymiyya was confronted with allegations that many Hanbalites were indeed anthropomorphists; in fact, one of the interrogators in the trial posed these accusations. Ibn Taymiyya responded to this interrogator that there were more anthropomorphists who were not Hanbalites than there were anthropomorphists who were Hanbalites:

> One can find more anthropomorphists among the different Kurd tribes that are affiliated to the Shafiᶜite school than among any other group. Among the people of Gilan (a region in Iran that lies along the Caspian Sea) there are Shafiᶜites and Hanbalites. The pure Hanbalites (*al-ḥanbaliyya al-maḥḍa*) do not have anthropomorphists among them like the anthropomorphists whom you can find among other trends. The Karramiyya, who are corporealists, are all Hanafites.[233]

In this response, Ibn Taymiyya wanted to distance the derogative name of Hashwiyya from the Hanbalites and to nullify the image of the Hanbalites as an ignorant mob. A closer look in the above-quoted passage reveals that Ibn Taymiyya presented anthropomorphism both as a phenomenon that went beyond the boundaries of sectorial affiliation (he was very cautious not to completely deny the existence of Hanbalites who were anthropomorphists) and a phenomenon which was geographically remote from the familiar and perhaps cultural (or more cultivated) surroundings of Damascus, Cairo, and even the destroyed city of Baghdad. Anthropomorphists, according to Ibn Taymiyya, resided in the Iranian wilderness and in the Iraqi and Syrian deserts. On the other hand, one cannot ignore the elitist tone in the second part of Ibn Taymiyya's response in which he vehemently defended the Hanbalite scholars from any suspicion of anthropomorphism: 'I said to him (i.e. to the interrogator in the trial): Who among our people [the Hanbalites] was a *ḥashwī* as you claim?' Subsequent to asking this rhetorical question, Ibn Taymiyya named a list of scholars, among whom were several disciples of Ahmad ibn Hanbal, and the Hanbalites of later generations like the qadi Abu Yaᶜla ibn al-Farraᵓ (d. 1066) and the controversial Ibn ᶜAqil (d. 1119).[234] Ibn Taymiyya's claim that neither the traditionalistic Abu Yaᶜla nor the rationalistic Ibn ᶜAqil expressed anthropomorphic views in their oral and written teachings was only partially true; apparently, Abu Yaᶜla compiled *aḥādīth al-ṣifāt* of dubious origin that expressed blatant anthropomorphism. Abu Yaᶜla's compilation was harshly attacked by the Hanbalite Ibn al-Jawzi (d. 1201). Ibn al-Jawzi, whose form of strict Hanbalism was refined by rationalistic views (see Chapters 3 and 4), criticised Abu Yaᶜla for contributing to the proliferation of these inferior texts among the masses, thereby encouraging their tendency to accept anthropomorphism.[235] Nevertheless, Ibn Taymiyya's acknowledgement that the general public indeed held anthropomorphic convictions was truthful.

The Shafiᶜite-Ashᶜarites fuelled their animosity towards Ibn Taymiyya with juicy tales. Two of these tales survived in pro-Ashᶜarite sources. The more famous of these two tales was recounted by the illustrious traveller Ibn Battuta (d. 1377). Ibn Battuta, who visited in Damascus in 1326, claimed to have witnessed Ibn Taymiyya accompanying his recitation of *ḥadīth al-nuzūl* with an iconic gesture and a statement. This is Ibn Battuta's testimony:

> I happened to participate in the Friday prayer in Damascus, when he (namely, Ibn Taymiyya) was preaching from the pulpit to the crowd,

> encouraging them to invoke God's name. One of his declarations was the following: 'God descends to the lowest heaven exactly as I am descending now (*ka-nuzūlī hādhā*).' Thereafter, he stepped one step down from the pulpit. A Malikite scholar by the name of Ibn Zahraᵓ attacked him and contradicted his theological claim. In response, the mob attacked the Malikite scholar and beat him severely until his turban fell and a silk skull-cap was revealed. This was enough for them to condemn him for wearing silk, so they carried the Malikite scholar to the court of the chief judge of the Hanbalites, and the judge ordered to put this man in jail and rebuke him.[236]

The less famous tale appears in an anti-Taymiyyan treatise authored by the Sufi scholar, Taqi al-Din al-Hisni (d. 1426), who was a fervent Ashᶜarite.[237] This is al-Hisni's report:

> The person who told us this story, while we were sitting in the open arcaded courtyard (*ṣaḥn*) of the Umayyad Mosque, was Abu 'l-Hasan ᶜAli al-Dimashqi.[238] He heard this story from his father who recounted: We were sitting in one of Ibn Taymiyya's sessions. Ibn Taymiyya invoked God's name, preached, and quoted *āyāt al-istiwāᵓ* (the verses that mention God's sitting on the throne). At a certain point, he declared: 'God sat on His throne exactly as I am sitting now (*ka-ʿstiwāᵓī hādhā*).' All the participants in the session jumped on their feet, dragged him down from his chair, and started striking him with their fists, shoes and whatever they had. Thereafter they took him to one of the judges. The religious scholars assembled in the court session, while he (namely, Ibn Taymiyya) started debating with them. They asked: 'What is the proof that you have [to justify] your behaviour?' He replied: 'The Lord had said "The Merciful who sits enthroned on high" (Q. 20:5).' They laughed having realized that he was an ignoramus who had no knowledge in the basic principles of religious knowledge. Thereafter they transported him [to Cairo] to investigate his case. They asked him: 'What say you about the words of the Lord: "Whichever way you turn there is the face of God" (Q. 2:115)?' He gave them such answers that made them realize he was definitely an ignoramus who knew not what he was saying. He was deluded about himself because of the admiration of the masses and the admiration of the rigid scholars among the jurisprudents, those who had no

> knowledge whatsoever in the science in which all the textual and rational evidence are assembled in the most optimal way (namely, *kalām*).[239]

The narrators of these anecdotes skilfully wove details that were historically accurate to add to their credibility; however, the narrators also presented detailed statements that were inaccurate. Al-Hisni's anecdote contains a contradiction: Al-Hisni describes Ibn Taymiyya as severely beaten by the crowd in the mosque, and at the same time al-Hisni emphasises the people's admiration of Ibn Taymiyya. On the other hand, the anecdote persuasively connects the link between Ibn Taymiyya's scandalous conduct and the 1306 Damascene trials in which he was accused of anthropomorphism. A reader who is unfamiliar with the massive literature on Ibn Taymiyya's trials may easily believe this account which provides a plausible explanation as to why Ibn Taymiyya was initially put on trial.

Previous researchers already observed that Ibn Battuta's account was unreliable, based on a chronology of events. Ibn Battuta arrived in Damascus on the ninth of Ramadan Hijri year 726 (9.8.1326), whereas Ibn Taymiyya was arrested on the sixth of Sha^cban (7.7.1326) and was kept in the Damascus Citadel until his death two years later (twentieth of Dhu al-Qa^cda 728; 25.9.1328).[240] We find a similar report in Ibn Hajar al-^cAsqalani's (d. 1449) biographical dictionary, *al-Durar al-Kāmina*. Ibn Hajar relied on an early source who was one of Ibn Taymiyya's disciples. According to this disciple, the incident occurred in Ramadan Hijri year 705 (March 1306).[241] At that time, Ibn Taymiyya was put on trial in Damascus. Therefore, we assume that it is highly unlikely that Ibn Taymiyya provoked his interrogators by publicly performing iconic gestures alongside the recitation of anthropomorphic texts.

Donald Little, who investigated both Ibn Battuta's and Ibn Hajar's reports, tended to accept the core of the story as reflecting an incident that indeed occurred.[242] However, we believe that both anecdotes are works of fiction. Ibn Taymiyya's conduct as presented in these anecdotes is identical to the conduct of the Zahirite al-^cAbdari in the Bab al-Azaj anecdote. This anecdote circulated in Shafi^cite-Ash^carite circles more than 100 years before Ibn Taymiyya was born. There is no doubt that the anecdotes of Ibn Battuta and al-Hisni duplicate the Bab al-Azaj anecdote for didactic purposes: Ibn Battuta and al-Hisni wanted to present Ibn Taymiyya's approach towards *āyāt al-ṣifāt* and *aḥādīth al-ṣifāt* in a memorable descriptive way. Khaled El-Rouayheb discussed Ibn Battuta's anecdote correctly. El-Rouayheb observed that the dramatic performance of the literary Ibn Taymiyya clarified Ibn Taymiyya's rejection of the traditionalistic *bi-lā kayfa* (or *tafwīḍ*) and the Ashᶜarite *taʾwīl.*[243] Both anecdotes indeed dramatise Ibn Taymiyya's declarations that the anthropomorphic descriptions depicted an actual reality of God. Finally, the anecdotes presented Ibn Taymiyya as a *ḥashwī*, a vulgar anthropomorphist.

Ibn Taymiyya probably did not perform the controversial iconic gestures as claimed by the narrators of the two anecdotes. However, he and his disciples were involved in a heated controversy about the two iconic gestures of pointing with the finger upwards to indicate God's spatiality and raising both hands during supplications. Our main source of information regarding the controversy about the iconic gestures is Ibn Qayyim al-Jawziyya's influential theological treatise in verse, *al-Kāfiya al-Shāfiya fī 'l-Intiṣār li'l-Firqa al-Nājiya* (The Sufficient and Healing [Poem] on the Vindication of the Saved Sect).[244] This text directly addressed the Shafiᶜite-Ashᶜarites, attacking them on their perception of the divine attributes. In one of the passages in *al-Kāfiya al-Shāfiya*, Ibn Qayyim al-Jawziyya (who naturally followed Ibn Taymiyya's opinion) declared that God's direction was upwards, because the Prophet pointed his finger upwards in *ḥijjat al-wadāᶜ*.[245] Elsewhere, Ibn Qayyim al-Jawziyya described a dispute between a Shafiᶜite-Ashᶜarite and a traditionalist. While the traditionalist cited the Prophet's concluding statement in *ḥijjat al-wadāᶜ* and described (or performed) the gesture of pointing the finger to the sky, the Shafiᶜite-Ashᶜarite declared: 'We do not point a finger at God's direction, but we allude to him in our minds.' These words are a clear reference to Fakhr al-Din al-Razi's discussion on *al-ishāra al-ḥissiyya.*[246] In another passage, Ibn Qayyim al-Jawziyya directly addressed the Shafiᶜite-Ashᶜarites of his times:

> God is the greatest! In the gathering of the great Hajj, in the place of atonement which lies at the base of Mount ᶜArafat His Messenger pointed at Him, in actual reality (*ḥaqqan*), with his forefinger and fingertip. Those of you [who declare]: 'Whoever points with his finger [at God's direction], his finger should be cut off!' will [receive their punishment] when they are assembled before God [in the Day of Judgement].[247]

Ibn Qayyim al-Jawziyya's fragmentary description suggests that the controversy between the followers of Ibn Taymiyya (Hanbalites and others) and the Shafiᶜite-Ashᶜarites about the iconic gestures was not confined to the courtroom in which Ibn Taymiyya was tried, but was present also in the public sphere. The description implies that some Ashᶜarites attacked Ibn Taymiyya's followers for performing this gesture and cursed them that their fingers would be cut off (see the Ashᶜarite sources mentioned in Chapter 3). The Cairene judge and Ashᶜarite *mutakallim* Taqi al-Din al-Subki (d. 1355),[248] who refuted Ibn Qayyim al-Jawziyya's *al-Kāfiya al-Shāfiya*, described Ibn Qayyim al-Jawziyya's accusations as 'sheer stupidity', 'false accusations and bubbles of air'.[249] He did not accept Ibn Qayyim al-Jawziyya's literal reading that the Prophet pointed to God 'in actual reality' (*ḥaqqan*). Furthermore, al-Subki explained that raising the hands in supplication was meant to symbolise submission to God's sovereignty,[250] so the gesture was metaphoric and not iconic.

We are not certain about the extent of this controversy and its impact because, unfortunately, the historical sources are silent about this specific debate. However, this controversy was ignited by the dissemination of Ibn Taymiyya's *al-Ḥamawiyya al-Kubrā*. Soon after the issuance of *al-Ḥamawiyya al-Kubrā*, the Damascene *muḥaddith* and jurist Shihab al-Din Ahmad ibn Yahya ibn Ismaᶜil ibn Jahbal (d. 1333) responded to this text by writing a bulky leaflet (*nubdha*), in which he presented himself as a fervent Ashᶜarite.[251] In the beginning of his response, Ibn Jahbal declared: 'What made me compose this *nubdha*, is something that happened recently, namely that one of them wrote a piece in which he asserted that God has a direction.'[252] Taj al-Din al-Subki (d. 1368), the Cairene judge (and Taqi al-Din al-Subki's son) who copied the entire response of Ibn Jahbal into his magnum opus *Ṭabaqāt al-Shāfiᶜiyya*, identified the person to whom Ibn Jahbal responded as Ibn Taymiyya.[253] However, even without this identification there is no doubt that Ibn Jahbal referred to Ibn Taymiyya because his *nubdha* is abundant in citations from *al-Ḥamawiyya al-Kubrā*, which he vehemently refuted. Thus, for example, Ibn Taymiyya quoted several Quranic verses that proved that God was in heaven.[254] One of these verses presented Pharaoh's speech when he asked his vizier 'Oh, Haman! Build me a tower that I may reach the highways – the very highways – of heaven, and look upon the god of Moses'

(Q. 40:36–7). Ibn Jahbal mocked Ibn Taymiyya's decision to use this verse as proof that God was above the heavens:

> I wish I knew how he (namely, Ibn Taymiyya) deduced from Pharaoh's speech that God was above the heavens and above the throne so that it was possible to look upon the God of Moses. The Quran did not mention that the God of Moses was in the heavens. [Ibn Taymiyya] deduced this from Pharaoh's speech. I wonder how it is possible to use Pharaoh's opinion and misconception as evidence, when the Quran specifically states: 'Thus was Pharaoh seduced by his foul deeds and was turned away from the right path. Pharaoh's cunning led only to perdition' (Q. 40:37). Moreover, when Pharaoh asked Moses: 'And who is the Lord of the heavens?',[255] Moses did not point in God's direction (*jiha*) but merely mentioned a very specific divine attribute which is the ability to create. If the direction definitely existed then it would have been more reasonable to introduce it, because pointing a finger (*al-ishāra al-ḥissiyya*) is one of the most powerful means of transmitting information (*al-muᶜarrifāt*) in terms of [the human] senses and common practice.[256]

Elsewhere, Ibn Jahbal wonders how was it possible to conclude from the description of the Prophet in *ḥijjat al-wadāᶜ* that gesturing with a finger upwards to indicate God's place was permissible – as Ibn Taymiyya argued in *al-Ḥamawiyya al-Kubrā*[257] – and exclaims:

> How does this prove that it was permissible to point a finger at Him? The Prophet was merely described as raising his finger and then pointing at them. Does this prove that when he raised his finger he was pointing at God's direction?[258]

Ibn Jahbal's overall attack on Ibn Taymiyya as reflected in *al-Ḥamawiyya al-Kubrā* covered the four elements of Ibn Taymiyya's doctrine of the divine attributes that we specified previously in Section IV. Ibn Jahbal focused primarily on Ibn Taymiyya's understanding of the divine attributes as denoting an actual reality. In fact, this was the main pretext for charging Ibn Taymiyya with anthropomorphism and corporealism and putting him on trial. Ibn Jahbal accused Ibn Taymiyya of distorting the words of the worthy ancestors when he claimed that the anthropomorphic descriptions existed 'in actual reality' (*ḥaqīqatan*). Ibn Jahbal also accused Ibn Taymiyya of deviating from the road of the worthy ancestors when he insisted on inquiring about the meaning of the anthropomorphic descriptions in the problematic texts. According to Ibn Jahbal, Ibn Taymiyya should have read these descriptions 'without inquiring about the modality of the attributes' (*bi-lā kayfa*). In other words, Ibn Jahbal argued that although Ibn Taymiyya claimed to have attentively followed the traditionalistic *bi-lā kayfa*, he was in fact reading the texts literally.[259] Judging from Ibn Jahbal's frequent mention of the need to read the anthropomorphic texts without inquiring about their literal or figurative meanings, the traditionalistic *bi-lā kayfa* was a prominent component in the Shafiᶜite-Ashᶜarite approach to these texts. Ibn Jahbal's response to one passage in *al-Ḥamawiyya al-Kubrā* illustrates this point. Let us first examine the passage in *al-Ḥamawiyya al-Kubrā*.

According to this passage, Ibn Taymiyya's conclusion that God's direction was upwards was based on a series of sayings attributed to the prominent traditionalists of the eighth century, like al-Awzaᶜi and Malik ibn Anas. Al-Awzaᶜi said that 'at the time when the successors (*al-tābiᶜūn*) were alive and available [for us], we used to say: God is above His throne',[260] while Malik's widely quoted saying was: 'The sitting [on the Throne] is undeniably known. The way it is actually done is incomprehensible. Believing it is obligatory.'[261] Based on these two sayings and other similar sayings, Ibn Taymiyya concluded that:

> These sayings are compatible with the sayings of the rest of [the worthy ancestors]: 'Transmit them as they arrived to us, without inquiring about their modality.' They (namely, the worthy ancestors) merely opposed to inquiring [these attributes'] modality. They did not deny the actuality of the attributes (*ḥaqīqat al-ṣifa*).[262]

Ibn Jahbal's mocking reply to Ibn Taymiyya's argument focuses on Ibn Taymiyya's insistence that God's direction was upwards:

> You decided that the only meaning of the throne and the heaven is that their direction is upward. Even if we tolerate this saying coming from you, al-Awzaᶜi never said that God was above the throne in actual reality. Where did you find this addition to al-Awzaᶜi's words? You quoted what Malik

> ibn Anas and others were saying about *aḥādīth al-ṣifāt*: 'transmit them as they arrived to us'. One should tell you: why did you not adhere to the instructions of the religious leaders? Moreover, you described God as being upwards. But there is no *ḥadīth* stating that. You would never be satisfied with my words even if you paid the earth's weight in gold to hear the same words from a scholar who possessed a unique knowledge of God (*ᶜālim rabbānī*). You anyhow would have done whatever you wanted. You would have taught whatever came to your mind. You would have transmitted the sayings of the religious leaders without properly adhering to their exact wording, without affirming what needed to be affirmed and without taking the path of the worthy ancestors.[263]

Elsewhere, Ibn Jahbal repeated his accusation that Ibn Taymiyya paraphrased text as befits his convoluted argumentation on God's aboveness. Accordingly, Ibn Jahbal presents the Shafiᶜite-Ashᶜarites as the true custodians of the Hadith material:

> He (namely, Ibn Taymiyya) quoted Abu ᶜUbayd al-Qasim ibn Sallam (d. 838) as saying: 'When we are asked about the meaning of [the anthropomorphic texts], we never explain them.' He also said: 'We never heard anyone interpret them.'[264] Our response to what he himself (namely, Ibn Taymiyya) quotes here is: Praise the Lord! Our goal is achieved! However, I wish I knew who was the one who explained [to him] that the meaning of the heaven and the throne was that their direction was upwards? And who was the one who refrained from explaining their meaning and transmitted the texts as they arrived to us?[265]

Ibn Jahbal's response to Ibn Taymiyya's *al-Ḥamawiyya al-Kubrā* was more than a scholarly discussion on God's aboveness. He responded with a vicious attack on a new form of traditionalism that threatened the hegemony of Ashᶜarite theology in the Mamluk sultanate. Ibn Jahbal excelled in transmitting the feeling of an intellectual elite perplexed by Ibn Taymiyya's bold new reading of *aḥādīth al-ṣifāt*. Ibn Taymiyya's reading dared to challenge the traditionalistic and the Ashᶜarite formulas of *bi-lā kayfa*. In addition, his reading encouraged the undesirable questions of laymen and encouraged public performances of the problematic texts, accompanied by unrestrained gestures. Because of Ibn Taymiyya's undesirable behaviour, the Shafiᶜite-Ashᶜarite scholars derisively endowed upon him the title *ḥashwī*, an anthropomorphist:

> The doctrine of the Hashwiyya according to which they affirm a direction to God, is a feeble and corrupting doctrine. Its corruption immediately becomes evident whenever one tries to imagine what it says. Consequently, the religious leaders said that they would have not given much thought or spent one drop of ink in refuting the Hashwiyya had the masses were not so attracted to them.[266]

According to Ibn Jahbal, while there were anthropomorphists who did not hide their tendencies, Ibn Taymiyya was dangerous in the eyes of the Shafiᶜite-Ashᶜarites. Ibn Taymiyya was particularly dangerous because he belonged to a group of anthropomorphists under the guise of traditionalism; or rather anthropomorphists who pretended to belong to 'the School of worthy ancestors' (*madhhab al-salaf*). The following encoded passage, reveals Ibn Jahbal's profound disdain of the commoners combined with a demonisation of Ibn Taymiyya as their leader. The emphasis in this passage is the unhealthy ideas which emanated from Ibn Taymiyya's literal reading of *aḥādīth al-ṣifāt* with which he fed the commoners. These unhealthy ideas are presented in a series of metaphors:

> The other group [of Hashwiyya] pretended to belong to 'the School of worthy ancestors' while they were eating the forbidden fruit (*suḥt*), taking broken reed of a staff (*ḥuṭām*), and gathering the insignificant commoners and the riffraff by spreading their far-fetched ideas. This group knew that Satan only toils to destroy the religion of Muhammad's nation. Therefore, he (namely, Satan) brings the hearts of the commoners together by spreading innovations and heresies which he uses to destroy the religion.[267]

From a brief passage in Ibn Jahbal's response, we learn about the role of Ibn Taymiyya in stirring the anthropomorphic viewpoints of the commoners. In this passage, Ibn Jahbal takes an indirect approach to describe Ibn Taymiyya's political power. Ibn Jahbal describes what the worthy ancestors did not do, thus emphasising what Ibn Taymiyya was accustomed to do:

> Whoever inquires, investigates and searches in the sources will discover that the Prophet's companions, their successors and all the first generations of Islam were persistent not to engage with these matters (namely, delving in the meaning of the divine attributes). They neither mentioned these topics openly in public assemblies nor did they administer them to the masses [like poisonous drug]. They neither talked about these topics while standing on the pulpits, nor did they awaken foolish ideas that lay dormant in people's hearts and inflame them like bonfires. These are well-known facts reflected from the biographies of these people. Upon their ways we established our doctrine and founded our belief. You, the reader, will find out how we resemble the worthy ancestors and how this person who claims to follow them in fact violates their ways. This person takes the path of innovation.[268]

Ibn Jahbal protested against discussing *aḥādīth al-ṣifāt* with the commoners, thereby exposing the masses to ideas beyond their mental capacity.[269] This protest echoes the elitist intellectualism of the rationalists. 'Keeping silent is obligatory for the commoners' – declares Ibn Jahbal, and explains – 'because when a commoner asks a question, he becomes exposed to ideas beyond his capacity. If a commoner asks an ignoramus, his ignorance increases. If he asks a scholar, the scholar cannot make this man grasp these ideas.'[270] It is evident that Ibn Taymiyya focused on *aḥādīth al-ṣifāt* in his public performances to the masses thus giving the anthropomorphic texts a political context. In view of the Hanbalite riots that occurred after Ibn Taymiyya's arrest,[271] the Shafiᶜite-Ashᶜarites were indeed justified in expressing their concerns about discussing or performing *aḥādīth al-ṣifāt* in the public sphere.

Notes

1. Abrahamov, 'Scripturalist and Traditionalist Theology', p. 268.
2. Muhammad ibn Saᶜdun ibn Murajja ibn Saᶜdun Abu ᶜAmir al-Qurashi al-ᶜAbdari al-Mayurqi al-Andalusi came from Cordoba, Majorca or Cyrenaica: al-Dhahabī, *Siyar Aᶜlām al-Nubalāʾ*, vol. 19, p. 579 (the biographical entry of al-ᶜAbdari); Ibn al-Jawzī, *Al-Muntaẓam*, vol. 17, pp. 261–2 (the biographical entry of al-ᶜAbdari). See a brief mention of him in Goldziher, *The Ẓāhirīs*, p. 171, footnote 178. Al-ᶜAbdari was the last known Zahirite of Baghdad: Ephrat, *A Learned Society*, p. 48.
3. Ibn ᶜAsakir elaborates about his confrontation with al-ᶜAbdari due to the

Andalusian scholar's defamations of his predecessors: Ibn ᶜAsākir, *Tārīkh Dimashq*, vol. 53, p. 59.

4. Ibn ᶜAsākir, *Tārīkh Dimashq*, vol. 53, p. 60. A more comprehensible version is found in al-Dhahabī, *Siyar Aᶜlām al-Nubalā*ᵓ, vol. 19, p. 582. Al-Dhahabi quotes Ibn ᶜAsakir, of course, but either he corrected the version or (more likely) the editor of *Siyar Aᶜlām al-Nubalā*ᵓ made the correction. Similar versions appear in al-Dhahabi's *Tadhkirat al-Ḥuffāẓ*, vol. 4, pp. 1272–5 and *Tārīkh al-Islām*, vol. 36, pp. 103–6. We used each of these versions to achieve the optimal accurate understanding of the text.
5. Al-Dhahabi used the phrase *ḥikāya munqaṭiᶜa*, which literally means 'a version with an interrupted *isnād* or a lacuna in the *isnād*'. This usage is noteworthy because here al-Dhahabi applied the rules of Hadith criticism to an anecdote: al-Dhahabī, *Tadhkirat al-Ḥuffāẓ*, vol. 4, p. 1274.
6. Al-Dhahabī, *Siyar Aᶜlām al-Nubalā*ᵓ, vol. 19, p. 583.
7. Ibn ᶜAsākir, *Tārīkh Dimashq*, vol. 53, p. 60. The anonymous editor of *Tadhkirat al-Ḥuffāẓ* adds that because Ibn ᶜAsakir respected al-ᶜAbdari, it is unlikely that he believed that this anecdote was accurate. This editor also adds that the anecdote is farfetched (he describes it as 'a weak riding-animal', *maṭiyya mahzūla*) and that Ibn ᶜAsakir was probably forced to include it in his book because of some unknown urgent need: al-Dhahabī, *Tadhkirat al-Ḥuffāẓ*, vol. 4, p. 1274.
8. Al-ᶜAbdari said: *wa-madhhabī aḥadu hādhihi 'l-thalāthati madhāhiba*, that is, 'my methodology is one of these three methodologies': Ibn ᶜAsākir, *Tārīkh Dimashq*, vol. 53, p. 60; al-Dhahabī, *Siyar Aᶜlām al-Nubalā*ᵓ, vol. 19, p. 582. According to a slightly different version, al-ᶜAbdari either said: *ākharu hādhihi 'l-thalāthati madhāhiba* or *ākhiru hādhihi 'l-thalāthati madhāhiba*, that is, 'my methodology is different than the other three' or 'my methodology is the last of the three': al-Dhahabī, *Tārīkh al-Islām*, vol. 36, p. 105.
9. Goldziher, *The Ẓāhirīs*, pp. 151–4; Makin, 'The Influence of Ẓāhirī Theory', pp. 115–17; Arnaldez, *Grammaire et théologie*, pp. 288–94; Abrahamov, 'Scripturalist and Traditionalist Theology', p. 269.
10. Ibn ᶜAsakir arrived in Baghdad in 1126 to study at the Ashᶜarite elite university, al-Madrasa al-Nizamiyya. He stayed in Baghdad for five years, although during this period of time he also made the pilgrimage to Mecca and Medina: al-Dhahabī, *Siyar Aᶜlām al-Nubalā*ᵓ, vol. 20, p. 555 (the biography of Ibn ᶜAsakir). The rift between Ibn ᶜAsakir and al-ᶜAbadri continued until the latter's death. According to Ibn ᶜAsakir, he did not attend al-ᶜAbdari's funeral: Ibn ᶜAsākir, *Tārīkh Dimashq*, vol. 53, p. 61.

11. Throughout this book, we systematically use N. J. Dawood's translation of the Quran, which is a personal favourite. However, in the case of Q. 68:42, Dawood provided a translation which obliterated the literal phrasing of the verse. Dawood translated: 'On the day when the dread event unfolds and they are told to prostrate themselves, they will not be able': Dawood, *The Koran*, p. 564. We happily embraced his translation to Q. 68:42 in Chapter 1, when the literal reading of the verse could not have contributed to the discussion. However, here we relied on Arthur Arberry's translation and altered it to make the literal reading more precise. Arberry translated the word *sāq* as leg: Arberry, *The Koran Interpreted*, p. 601. 'Shank' is more precise lexically, given the use of the idiom of the *sāq* in classical poetry: Holtzman, 'Accused of Anthropomorphism', pp. 572–3, footnote 56.
12. Ibn ᶜAsākir, *Tārīkh Dimashq*, vol. 53, p. 60. This anecdote also appears in Goldziher, *Introduction to Islamic Theology and Law*, p. 93.
13. Ibn ᶜAsākir, *Tārīkh Dimashq*, vol. 53, p. 61.
14. Ephrat, *A Learned Society*, p. 27.
15. Graham, *Beyond the Written Word*, pp. 5–6.
16. Watts, the motto of his blog: http://iconicbooks.blogspot.co.il (last accessed: 15 December 2016).
17. Watts, 'The Three Dimensions', pp. 135–6.
18. Watts, 'The Three Dimensions', p. 140.
19. Watts, 'The Three Dimensions', pp. 145–6.
20. Watts, 'The Three Dimensions', p. 141.
21. Watts, 'The Three Dimensions', p. 141.
22. Watts, 'The Three Dimensions', p. 142.
23. Watts, 'The Three Dimensions', p. 147.
24. Ibn al-Jawzī, *Al-Muntaẓam*, vol. 15, p. 128 (the events of Hijri year 409); vol. 16, p. 280 (the events of Hijri year 433). For a full text of the Creed, see Ibn al-Jawzī, *Al-Muntaẓam*, vol. 15, pp. 279–82 (the events of Hijri year 433). For a full translation of the Qadiri Creed, see Mez, *The Renaissance of Islam*, pp. 207–9.
25. Ibn al-Jawzī, *Al-Muntaẓam*, vol. 15, p. 280.
26. Ibn al-Jawzī, *Al-Muntaẓam*, vol. 16, p. 106.
27. Ibn al-Jawzī, *Al-Muntaẓam*, vol. 16, p. 279. For Abu al-Husayn's biography, see Ibn Rajab, *Dhayl Ṭabaqāt al-Ḥanābila*, vol. 1, pp. 391–5.
28. Ibn Abī Yaᶜlā, *Ṭabaqāt al-Ḥanābila*, vol. 2, p. 263 (the biography of Abu Yaᶜla).

29. The event is briefly described by Ibn al-Jawzī, *Al-Muntaẓam*, vol. 16, pp. 105–6; Ibn Kathīr (d. 1373), *al-Bidāya wa'l-Nihāya*, vol. 16, pp. 14–15 (the events of Hijri year 460); and Ibn Rajab (d. 1392), *Dhayl Ṭabaqāt al-Ḥanābila*, vol. 1, pp. 37–8 (the biography of *sharīf* Abu Jaᶜfar). Ibn Kathir claimed that the audience consisted of traditionalist and rationalist notables (*al-aᶜyān min al-fuqahāᵓ wa-ahl al-kalām*): Ibn Kathīr, *al-Bidāya wa'l-Nihāya*, vol. 16, p. 15. However, given the low status of the rationalists in Baghdad at the time, it is unlikely that any Muᶜtazilite was invited to the palace for the public reading. It is more probable that Ashᶜarites were present at this event, although this particular point needs further investigation.
30. This was not the Ashᶜarite theologian Ibn Furak, but Abu Bakr Ahmad ibn Muhammad ibn Ayyub, who in Hijri year 450 served as the representative of Toghril Beg (d. 1064) in Baghdad: Ibn al-Athīr, *al-Kāmil*, vol. 8, p. 345. It is unclear what position Ibn Furak assumed in 1068.
31. Ibn al-Jawzī, *Al-Muntaẓam*, vol. 16, p. 106; Ibn Kathīr, *al-Bidāya wa'l-Nihāya*, vol. 16, p. 15. See also the description of the event in Makdisi, *Ibn ᶜAqīl et la résurgence de l'Islam traditionaliste*, pp. 337–40; van Renterghem, 'Structure et fonctionnement', pp. 212–13.
32. Graham, 'Winged Words', p. 8.
33. Graham, 'Winged Words', p. 9.
34. Makdisi, 'Abū Manṣūr b. Yūsuf', *EI2*; Ibn al-Jawzī, *Al-Muntaẓam*, vol. 16, pp. 107–10.
35. Ibn al-Jawzī, *Al-Muntaẓam*, vol. 16, pp. 105–6; Ibn Kathīr, *al-Bidāya wa'l-Nihāya*, vol. 16, pp. 14–15; Ibn Rajab, *Dhayl Ṭabaqāt al-Ḥanābila*, vol. 1, pp. 37–8.
36. Al-Dhahabī, *Siyar Aᶜlām al-Nubalāᵓ*, vol. 14, pp. 365–82 (the biography of Ibn Khuzayma; an almost identical entry appears in al-Dhahabī, *Tadhkirat al-Ḥuffāẓ*, vol. 2, pp. 720–31). Al-Dhahabi relies heavily on the biography of Ibn Khuzayma that was authored by al-Hakim al-Nisaburi (d. 1014) in *Tārīkh Nīsābūr*, which is now lost. According to al-Dhahabi, the biography of Ibn Khuzayma in this nonextant work comprised more than twenty pages that included Ibn Khuzayma's spiritual will (*waṣiyya*) and two poems of lamentation written after Ibn Khuzayma's death: al-Dhahabī, *Siyar Aᶜlām al-Nubalāᵓ*, vol. 14, p.382. There is a brief biographical entry of Ibn Khuzayma in al-Hakim al-Nisaburi's *Maᶜrifat ᶜUlūm al-Ḥadīth*, pp. 283–7. Most entries of the seventeenth class in *Siyar Aᶜlām al-Nubalāᵓ* average half a page each, meaning that the scholars of the seventeenth class were not considered prominent by

al-Dhahabi and his predecessors. Only the massive entry on the controversial mystic al-Ḥallaj (d. 922) surpasses Ibn Khuzayma's entry: al-Dhahabī, *Siyar Aᶜlām al-Nubalāᵓ*, vol. 14, pp. 313–54 (the biography of al-Hallaj).

37. On Ibn Khuzayma's visit to Cairo in 923 with several companions and the charity they received from the emir Ahmad ibn Tulun (d. 884), see Ibn al-Jawzī, *Al-Muntaẓam*, vol. 13, pp. 234–6.
38. Ibn Khuzayma's disciples testified that he cited *aḥādīth* to them as if he was reading from a book: al-Dhahabī, *Siyar Aᶜlām al-Nubalāᵓ*, vol. 14, p. 372.
39. Al-Dhahabī, *Siyar Aᶜlām al-Nubalāᵓ*, vol. 14, pp. 377–82.
40. Madelung, *Religious Trends*, p. 188; Holtzman and Ovadia, 'On Divine Aboveness' (forthcoming).
41. Madelung, *Religious Trends*, p. 31.
42. Al-Dhahabī, *Siyar Aᶜlām al-Nubalāᵓ*, vol. 14, p. 379.
43. Abu Zakariyya Yahya ibn Muahmmad al-ᶜAnbari (d. 979), one of the members of the Khuzaymiyya, said that there were only five classes of traditionalists and each class was named after its most prominent scholar. The first three classes, the Malikiyya, the Shafiᶜiyya and the Hanbaliyya, are named after the eponymous founders of the three most traditionalistic schools of law (Malik ibn Anas, Muhammad ibn Idris al-Shafiᶜi and Ahmad ibn Hanbal). The other two classes are the Rahawiyya, named after Ishaq ibn Rahwayh, and the Khuzaymiyya: Ibn Qayyim al-Jawziyya, *Iᶜlām al-Muwaqqiᶜīn*, vol. 4, p. 41.
44. Al-Ḥākim al-Nīsābūrī, *Maᶜrifat ᶜUlūm al-Ḥadīth*, pp. 285–6. Al-Dhahabi summarised this harsh saying and censored the part about the decapitation and the disposal of the body: al-Dhahabī, *Siyar Aᶜlām al-Nubalāᵓ*, vol. 14, p. 373. Al-Dhahabi probably felt that such a view as the one that was attributed to Ibn Khuzayma should not be highlighted.
45. Ibn Khuzayma, *Kitāb al-Tawḥīd*, p. 273. The last sentence, as the editor indicated, is distorted. Our translation of this sentence is therefore approximate.
46. Al-Dhahabī, *Siyar Aᶜlām al-Nubalāᵓ*, vol. 14, p. 374.
47. Al-Dhahabī, *Siyar Aᶜlām al-Nubalāᵓ*, vol. 14, p. 376.
48. Ibn Khuzayma, *Kitāb al-Tawḥīd*, pp. 9–11.
49. See, for example, Ibn Khuzayma, *Kitāb al-Tawḥīd*, pp. 202ff.
50. Ibn Khuzayma, *Kitāb al-Tawḥīd*, pp. 769–70.
51. Ibn Khuzayma, *Kitāb al-Tawḥīd*, pp. 19, 187, 769, 816, 905.
52. Ibn Khuzayma, *Kitāb al-Tawḥīd*, pp. 81, 84.
53. Ibn Khuzayma, *Kitāb al-Tawḥīd*, pp. 184–6.
54. Ibn Khuzayma, *Kitāb al-Tawḥīd*, p. 185. Possibly this technique was called

al-jam^{c} *bayna al-akhbār al-mutaḍādda* (reconciling contradicting versions), as a title of a non-extant book indicates: al-Khaṭīb al-Baghdādī, *al-Jāmi*^{c} *li-Akhlāq al-Rāwī*, p. 432.

55. Ibn Khuzayma, *Kitāb al-Tawḥīd*, p. 185.
56. Al-Khaṭīb al-Baghdādī, *al-Jāmi*^{c} *li-Akhlāq al-Rāwī*, p. 370.
57. Ibn Khuzayma, *Kitāb al-Tawḥīd*, pp. 180–1, *ḥadīth* 2-103.
58. Ibn Khuzayma, *Kitāb al-Tawḥīd*, p. 182 (unnumbered *ḥadīth*).
59. Ibn Khuzayma, *Kitāb al-Tawḥīd*, p. 187. Ibn Khuzayma did not specify the Mu^{c}tazilite's claim about the meaning of the Prophet's laughter in this case. However, Qadi ^{c}Iyad (d. 1150) who also discussed this *ḥadīth* remarked that the Mu^{c}tazilites interpreted the Prophet's laughter as a sign of his rejection of the Jewish rabbi's discourse: Qāḍī ^{c}Iyāḍ, *Ikmāl*, vol. 8, pp. 315–16 (*Kitāb Ṣifat al-Qiyāma wa'l-Janna wa'l-Nār*, *ḥadīth* 2786).
60. Ibn Khuzayma, *Kitāb al-Tawḥīd*, p. 178.
61. Ibn Khuzayma, *Kitāb al-Tawḥīd*, pp. 200–1.
62. Ibn Khuzayma, *Kitāb al-Tawḥīd*, p. 45.
63. Ibn Khuzayma, *Kitāb al-Tawḥīd*, p. 26.
64. Ibn Khuzayma, *Kitāb al-Tawḥīd*, p. 114.
65. Ibn Khuzayma, *Kitāb al-Tawḥīd*, p. 53.
66. Ibn Khuzayma, *Kitāb al-Tawḥīd*, pp. 191–2.
67. As the editor of *Kitāb al-Tawḥīd* remarked, these two individuals are not mentioned in the biographical dictionaries, therefore there is no information about their identity: Ibn Khuzayma, *Kitāb al-Tawḥīd*, pp. 191–2, footnote 9.
68. Ibn Khuzayma, *Kitāb al-Tawḥīd*, p. 193.
69. Ibn Khuzayma, *Kitāb al-Tawḥīd*, pp. 194–5.
70. Ibn Khuzayma, *Kitāb al-Tawḥīd*, p. 195. See Q. 36:77–8, 'Who will give life to rotten bones? Say: He who first brought them into being will give them life again.'
71. Ibn Khuzayma, *Kitāb al-Tawḥīd*, pp. 195–6.
72. Ibn Khuzayma, *Kitāb al-Tawḥīd*, p. 196.
73. The common perception among the traditionalists and Ash^{c}arites was that Abu ^{c}Ali Muhammad ibn ^{c}Abd al-Wahhab al-Thaqafi was one of the scholars who introduced the teachings of al-Shafi^{c}i in Khurasan: al-Dhahabī, *Siyar A*^{c}*lām al-Nubalā*ʾ, vol. 14, p. 377; al-Subkī, *Ṭabaqāt al-Shāfi*^{c}*iyya*, vol. 3, pp. 192–4.
74. Al-Dhahabī, *Siyar A*^{c}*lām al-Nubalā'*, vol. 25, pp. 256–8 (al-Sibghi's biography).
75. Al-Dhahabī, *Siyar A*^{c}*lām al-Nubalā*ʾ, vol. 14, p. 377.
76. Al-Dhahabī, *Siyar A*^{c}*lām al-Nubalā*ʾ, vol. 14, pp. 377–8.

77. Al-Ashᶜarī, *Maqālāt al-Islāmiyyīn*, p. 546. On the possibility that al-Ashᶜari was influenced by Ibn Kullab, see Frank, 'Elements in the Development', pp. 183–7.
78. The deceased person whom Ibn Khuzayma gloated over was probably a Muᶜtazilite. He is mentioned in al-Dhahabi's account as al-Hakim Abu Saᶜid. This individual could be al-Hasan ibn ᶜAbd al-Hamid ibn ᶜAbd al-Rahman ibn al-Husayn Abu Saᶜid al-Nisaburi, who is mentioned among al-Hakim al-Nisaburi's many teachers. Al-Hakim al-Nisaburi also remarked that al-Hakim Abu Saᶜid was an imam and a *mutakallim* (*baᶜḍ ahl al-naẓar*): al-Khalīfa al-Nīsābūrī, *Talkhīṣ Tārīkh Nīsābūr*, p. 85. Despite our efforts, we could not locate any more details about al-Hakim Abu Saᶜid. The party to celebrate his death is described in so many details as an exceptionally festive event that the only reasonable explanation for it is that the deceased was a Muᶜtazilite: al-Dhahabī, *Siyar Aᶜlām al-Nubalāʾ*, vol. 14, p. 378.
79. Madelung, 'The Origins of the Controversy', pp. 512–15.
80. Al-Dhahabī, *Siyar Aᶜlām al-Nubalāʾ*, vol. 14, p. 379 (the biographical entry of al-Thaqafi).
81. ᶜAbd Allah ibn Kullab (d. 854), a contemporary of Ahmad ibn Hanbal was most probably the chief architect of the concept of the eternity of the Quran: van Ess, *TG*, vol. 4, pp. 411–12. Madelung believed that Ahmad ibn Hanbal was responsible for this concept; however, he based his argument on Ahmad ibn Hanbal's *al-Radd ᶜalā al-Zanādiqa*, a work whose attribution to Ahmad ibn Hanbal was refuted even by Shams al-Din al-Dhahabi: Holtzman, 'Aḥmad b. Ḥanbal', *EI3*; Madelung, 'The Origins of the Controversy', p. 523. Ibn Kullab basically argued that the Quran is uncreated and is an attribute subsisting in God. '[I]t is created only in so far as God said to it "be! (*kun*)" (Q. 16:40–2)': Daiber, 'The Quran as a "Shibboleth"', p. 275.
82. Al-Dhahabī, *Siyar Aᶜlām al-Nubalāʾ*, vol. 14, pp. 377–8.
83. Al-Dhahabī, *Siyar Aᶜlām al-Nubalāʾ*, vol. 14, pp. 380–1. The Ashᶜarite theologian Ibn Furak (d. 1015) systematically refuted a book by al-Sibghi entitled *Kitāb al-Asmāʾ wa'l-Ṣifāt*. Ibn Furak's refutation of al-Sibghi's book allows us to obtain a glimpse of the content of the non-extant *Kitāb al-Asmāʾ wa'l-Ṣifāt*: Ibn Fūrak, *Mushkil al-Ḥadīth*, pp. 253–308.
84. Al-Dhahabī, *Siyar Aᶜlām al-Nubalāʾ*, vol. 14, pp. 381–2.
85. The grandson recounted several touching anecdotes about Ibn Khuzayma: al-Dhahabī, *Siyar Aᶜlām al-Nubalā'*, vol. 14, pp. 370–2.
86. ᶜAbd al-ᶜAziz al-Shahwan copied the relevant *ijāza* (license to transmit a

book) from the three existing manuscripts, but did not study the *ijāza*: Ibn Khuzayma, *Kitāb al-Tawḥīd*, pp. 52–4.

87. Ibn al-Jawzī, *Al-Muntaẓam*, vol. 16, p. 105 (the events of Hijri year 460).
88. Al-Dhahabī, *Tārīkh al-Islām*, vol. 31, pp. 208–11 (the biography of Abu Muslim al-Laythi).
89. Ibn al-Jawzī, *Al-Muntaẓam*, vol. 16, p. 105 (the events of Hijri year 460); Ibn Rajab, *Dhayl Ṭabaqāt al-Ḥanābila*, vol. 1, p. 38 (the biography of *sharīf* Abu Ja^{c}far); Ibn Kathīr, *al-Bidāya wa'l-Nihāya*, vol. 16, p. 14 (the events of Hijri year 460). The event is also recorded in one of the three surviving manuscripts of *Kitāb al-Tawḥīd*.
90. Al-Dhahabī, *Tārīkh al-Islām* (the Bashar edition), vol. 11, p. 478 (the biography of al-^{c}Alawi al-Harawi).
91. Ibn Taymiyya, '[Al-Ḥamawiyya al-Kubrā]', *Majmū^{c}at al-Fatāwā*, vol. 5, p. 19.
92. Ibn Taymiyya, *Bayān Talbīs al-Jahmiyya*, vol. 7, p. 46.
93. Ibn Qayyim al-Jawziyya, *al-Kāfiya al-Shāfiya*, p. 122 (verses 1378–9).
94. Ibn Qayyim al-Jawziyya, *al-Kāfiya al-Shāfiya*, p. 122 (verses 1381–4).
95. Al-Dhahabī, *Siyar A^{c}lām al-Nubalā'*, vol. 14, p. 374 (the biographical entry of Ibn Khuzayma).
96. Ibn Khuzayma, *Kitāb al-Tawḥīd*, p. 84, *ḥadīth* 6-40. For other versions of this *ḥadīth*, see Ibn Khuzayma, *Kitāb al-Tawḥīd*, pp. 81–94.
97. Ibn Khuzayma, *Kitāb al-Tawḥīd*, p. 84.
98. Ibn Khuzayma, *Kitāb al-Tawḥīd*, p. 85.
99. Al-Dhahabī, *Siyar A^{c}lām al-Nubalā'*, vol. 14, pp. 374–6.
100. Al-Subkī, *Ṭabaqāt al-Shāfi^{c}iyya*, vol. 9, p. 103 (the biographical entry of al-Dhahabi). Elsewhere, al-Subki harshly criticised al-Dhahabi's *Tārīkh al-Islām* for using scornful language to describe the Ash^{c}arites and overly sympathetic language to describe the 'corporealists' (*al-mujassima*), namely the ultra-traditionalists: ibid. vol. 2, p. 22.
101. Cf. al-Dhahabi's approach to Ahmad ibn Hanbal's position to *ḥadīth al-ṣūra*: Melchert, 'God Created Adam', pp. 118, 123, note 28.
102. Al-Dhahabī, *Kitāb al-^{c}Arsh*, p. 111.
103. On *fiṭra*, see Hoover, 'Fiṭra', *EI3*.
104. Ibn Khuzayma, *Kitāb al-Tawḥīd*, p. 254.
105. Al-Ash^{c}ari, *Maqālāt al-Islāmiyyīn*, p. 153.
106. Ibn Khuzayma, *Kitāb al-Tawḥīd*, p. 254; Ibn Taymiyya, 'Suʾāl ^{c}an rajulayn ikhtalafā fi 'l-i^{c}tiqād', *Majmū^{c}at al-Fatāwā*, vol. 5, p. 160.
107. Abu 'l-Muzaffar al-Sam^{c}ani was the grandfather of the illustrious biographer

Abu Sa[c]d al-Sam[c]ani (d. 562/1166). On Abu 'l-Muzaffar, see Lange, 'Sins, expiation and non-rationality', pp. 154–5.

108. Ibn Kathīr, *al-Bidāya wa'l-Nihāya*, vol. 16, p. 159 (the notables who passed away in Hijri year 489).
109. Al-Dhahabī, *al-[c]Ulūw*, p. 258. Cf. al-Juwayni's view of the belief of the masses in his theological writings: Frank, 'Knowledge and *Taqlīd*', pp. 41–2, note 15.
110. Ibn Kathīr, *al-Bidāya wa'l-Nihāya*, vol. 15, p. 550 (the notables who passed away in Hijri year 403).
111. Many Hanafites in eleventh-century Baghdad were connected to Mu[c]tazilism. On the efflorescence of Hanafism in Iran and Central Asia, see Madelung, 'The Westwards Migration of Ḥanafī Scholars', pp. 42–5. On the emigration of Iranian Hanafites to Baghdad, see ibid. pp. 46–7. The close relations between Hanafism and Mu[c]tazilism are described in Ansari amd Schmidtke, 'The Mu[c]tazilī and Zaydī Reception', pp. 90ff.
112. Ibn al-Jawzī, *Al-Muntaẓam*, vol. 15, p. 97 (the biography of Abu Bakr al-Khwarizmi).
113. Ibn Kathīr, *al-Bidāya wa'l-Nihāya*, vol. 17, p. 12 (the notables who passed away in Hijri year 606).
114. Shihadeh, *The Teleological Ethics*, pp. 4–5; Anawati, 'Fakhr al-Dīn al-Rāzī', *EI2*.
115. Al-Rāzī, *Tafsīr*, vol. 1, part 2, p. 106 (Q. 2:21–2, the fifth position).
116. Shihadeh, *The Teleological Ethics*, pp. 4-5; Anawati, 'Fakhr al-Dīn al-Rāzī', *EI2*.
117. Al-Rāzī, *Mafātīḥ al-Ghayb*, vol. 27, p. 152 (interpretation of Q. 42: 11).
118. As part of the rationalistic lexicon, the word *khurāfāt* was used to denote *aḥādīth al-ṣifāt* which the rationalists rejected: Holtzman, 'Anthropomorphism', *EI3*.
119. Al-Rāzī, *Asās al-Taqdīs*, p. 116.
120. See, for example, al-Rāzī, *Asās al-Taqdīs*, p. 116. For *aḥādīth al-ṣifāt* in al-Baghawi's Hadith compilation, see al-Baghawī, *Sharḥ al-Sunna*, vol. 1, pp. 163–80.
121. Shihadeh, *The Teleological Ethics*, p. 5.
122. Griffel, 'On Fakhr al-Dīn al-Rāzī's Life', p. 339. The year of the composition of *Asās al-Taqdīs* is indicated by Ahmad Hijazi al-Saqa, the editor of the text: al-Saqā, 'Qaḍiyyat al-Kitāb', in al-Rāzī, *Asās al-Taqdīs*, p. 259.
123. Al-Rāzī, *Asās al-Taqdīs*, pp. 10–11.
124. Al-Rāzī, *Asās al-Taqdīs*, pp. 35–6.
125. According to Khalil ibn Aybak al-Safadi (d. 1363), a most informed Mamluk biographer and historian, al-Malik al-[c]Adil appreciated the company of

religious scholars: al-Ṣafadī, *al-Wāfī*, vol. 2, pp. 168–9 (the biography of al-ᶜAdil al-Kabir). Cf. al-Dhahabī, *Tārīkh al-Islām*, vol. 44, p. 270 (the biography of al-ᶜAdil al-Kabir).

126. See the illuminating essay authored by al-Saqa, 'Qaḍiyyat al-Kitāb', in al-Rāzī, *Asās al-Taqdīs*, p. 260.
127. Al-Razi defined the Hanbalites and the Karramites as 'our rivals in this matter' (namely, in the literal understanding of the anthropomorphic descriptions in the Quran and the Hadith) in the beginning of *Asās al-Taqdīs*: al-Rāzī, *Asās al-Taqdīs*, p. 19. According to al-Razi, the anthropomorphic ideas of the Hanbalites were more preferable than the corporealistic ideas of the Karramites: al-Rāzī, *Asās al-Taqdīs*, pp. 19–21, 64.
128. See the introduction of ᶜAbd al-ᶜAziz al-Shahwan to *Kitāb al-Tawḥīd*: Ibn Khuzayma, *Kitāb al-Tawḥīd*, pp. 39–40.
129. Lagard, *Index*, p. 56.
130. Al-Razi mentioned *Ta'sīs al-Taqdīs* twice in his *Mafātīḥ al-Ghayb*. Al-Razi recommended that his readers who wanted to expand their knowledge about God's transcendence and the proper way to understand *āyāt al-ṣifāt* and *aḥādīth al-ṣifāt*, study *Ta'sīs al-Taqdīs*: al-Rāzī, *Mafātīḥ al-Ghayb*, vol. 22, p. 7 (commentary to Q. 20:1–8); vol. 27, p. 17 (commentary to Q. 39:67–70).
131. Al-Rāzī, *Mafātīḥ al-Ghayb*, vol. 27, p. 151 (interpretation of Q. 42:11). Cf. al-Rāzī, *Asās al-Taqdīs*, p. 198.
132. Al-Rāzī, *Mafātīḥ al-Ghayb*, vol. 27, p. 151.
133. Ibn Khuzayma, *Kitāb al-Tawḥīd*, p. 196.
134. Ibn Khuzayma, *Kitāb al-Tawḥīd*, p. 53.
135. Al-Rāzī, *Mafātīḥ al-Ghayb*, vol. 27, p. 151 (interpretation of Q. 42:11).
136. Ibn Khuzayma's concept of God's face basically emanates from two Quranic verses: 'No mortal eyes can see Him, though He sees all eyes' (Q. 6:103) and 'All that lives on earth is doomed to die. But the face of your Lord will abide forever, in all its majesty and glory' (Q. 55:26–7): Ibn Khuzayma, *Kitāb al-Tawḥīd*, pp. 51–2.
137. Ibn Khuzayma, *Kitāb al-Tawḥīd*, pp. 54–5; al-Rāzī, *Mafātīḥ al-Ghayb*, vol. 27, p. 151.
138. Ibn Khuzayma, *Kitāb al-Tawḥīd*, p. 55; al-Rāzī, *Mafātīḥ al-Ghayb*, vol. 27, p. 151.
139. Al-Rāzī, *Mafātīḥ al-Ghayb*, vol. 27, p. 152 (interpretation of Q. 42:11). In *Asās al-Taqdīs*, al-Razi explained that the problem with the corporealists is their understanding of the anthropomorphic descriptions. There was no problem

or dispute regarding their understanding of a set of other attributes like 'existent' (*mawjūd*), 'knowing' (*ʿālim*), 'potent' (*qādir*), etc.: al-Rāzī, *Asās al-Taqdīs*, p. 256.

140. Al-Rāzī, *Mafātīḥ al-Ghayb*, vol. 27, p. 152.
141. Al-Rāzī, *Mafātīḥ al-Ghayb*, vol. 27, pp. 152–3. Cf. al-Rāzī, *Asās al-Taqdīs*, p. 37.
142. Al-Rāzī, *Mafātīḥ al-Ghayb*, vol. 27, p. 153. Cf. al-Rāzī, *Asās al-Taqdīs*, p. 256.
143. Al-Rāzī, *Asās al-Taqdīs*, pp. 105–9.
144. The divine side is mentioned in Quran 39:56 in the idiomatic phrase *fī janb Allāh* (literally, by the side of God) that means obedience. In Dawood's translation: 'Lest any man should say: "Alas! I have disobeyed God and scoffed at His revelations."' In Arberry's translation: 'Lest any soul should say, "Alas for me, in that I neglected my duty to God, and was a scoffer."'
145. Al-Rāzī, *Asās al-Taqdīs*, p. 105.
146. Al-Rāzī, *Asās al-Taqdīs*, p. 106.
147. Al-Rāzī, *Asās al-Taqdīs*, p. 108.
148. Al-Rāzī, *Asās al-Taqdīs*, p. 177.
149. Al-Razi's theory of the human action is thoroughly discussed in Shihadeh, *The Teleological Ethics*, pp. 17–29.
150. The impossibility of infinite regress is central to the *kalām*ic argumentation. For al-Razi's use of *tasalsul*, see Holtzman 'Debating the Doctrine of *Jabr*', pp. 82–5.
151. Al-Rāzī, *Asās al-Taqdīs*, p. 178.
152. Al-Rāzī, *Asās al-Taqdīs*, p. 108.
153. Al-Rāzī, *Asās al-Taqdīs*, p. 251.
154. Al-Rāzī, *Asās al-Taqdīs*, p. 256.
155. Al-Rāzī, *Mafātīḥ al-Ghayb*, vol. 27, p. 153.
156. Al-Rāzī, *Asās al-Taqdīs*, p. 257.
157. Al-Rāzī, *Asās al-Taqdīs*, p. 258.
158. Al-Rāzī, *Asās al-Taqdīs*, p. 249.
159. At the request of his disciples, the Ashʿarite theologian Abu Bakr Muhammad ibn al-Hasan ibn Furak (d. 1015) dedicated a large portion of his *Mushkil al-Ḥadīth* to figurative interpretations of *aḥādīth al-ṣifāt* from *Kitāb al-Tawḥīd*: Ibn Fūrak, *Mushkil al-Ḥadīth*, pp. 215–52. The Hanbalite Abu Yaʿla Ibn al-Farraʾ (d. 1066) authored *Ibṭāl al-Taʾwīlāt* as a response to Ibn Furak's *Mushkil al-Ḥadīth*: Abū Yaʿlā, *Ibṭāl al-Taʾwīlāt*, pp. 41–2.
160. Goldziher, 'Zauberelemente', pp. 320–1; Bousquet, 'Études Islamologiques

d'Ignaz Goldziher (I)', pp. 22–1; G. Monnot, 'ṣalāt', *EI2*; L. Gardet, 'duʿāʾ', *EI2*.

161. The first scholar to address this topic was Ignaz Goldziher, who observed that the opposition to the practice of raising one's hands in prayer was motivated by this practice's supposedly pagan origins: Goldziher, 'Zauberelemente', pp. 320–9; Bousquet, 'Études Islamologiques d'Ignaz Goldziher (I)', pp. 22–6. See the comprehensive survey of the relevant literature in Fierro, 'La polémique', pp. 69–72, esp. pp. 70–1, footnote 6.

162. See, for example, a *fatwā* issued by the Saʿudi sheikh Muhammad ibn Salih al-ʿUthaymin (d. 2001). In this *fatwā*, al-ʿUthaymin elaborates on the non-obligatory prayers in which the gesture of raising the hands is intrinsic, and the prayers in which it is forbidden: Muḥammad ibn Ṣāliḥ al-ʿUthaymin, '*ḥukm rafʿ al-aydī fī 'l-duʿāʾ*' on the salafi website *Ṭarīq al-Islām* (Islamway.net), http://ar.islamway.net/fatwa/18089 (last accessed 26 October 2016).

163. Al-Bukhārī, *Rafʿ al-Yadayn*, p. 127.

164. Ibn Hajar al-ʿAsqalani quoted al-Bukhari extensively on this issue. The controversy about the raising of hands was relevant in al-Bukhari's days. According to al-Bukhari, the people of Kufa, the Malikites and the Hanafites, did not accept the practice of raising hands during the obligatory prayers: Ibn Ḥajar, *Fatḥ al-Bārī*, vol. 2, p. 257, *ḥadīth* 257 (*Kitāb al-Adhān, bāb rafʿ alyadayn fī al-takbīra*). Al-Bukhari also dedicated a brief treatise on the topic of *rafʿ al-aydī*. In this treatise, al-Bukhari tried to reconcile the contradictory *aḥādīth* about the practice of raising both hands during personal invocations: al-Bukhārī, *Rafʿ al-Yadayn*, p. 148. Another comprehensive source on the subject is Abu Jaʿfar al-Tahawi's (d. 933) compendium of the legal disputes between scholars: al-Ṭaḥāwī, *Mukhtaṣar Ikhtilāf al-ʿUlamāʾ*, vol. 1, pp. 199, 373, 391; vol. 2, pp. 131–2, 162. The controversy in ninth-century Cordoba is thoroughly analysed and discussed in Fierro, 'La polémique', pp. 73–80.

165. See, for example, al-Bukhārī, *al-Jāmiʿ*, vol. 1, pp. 241–2 (*Kitāb al-Ādhān, bāb rafʿ al-yadayan fī 'l-takbīra al-ūlā, bāb ilā ayna yurfaʿ yadayhi, bāb rafʿ al-yadayn idhā qāma min al-rakʿatayn*); vol. 1, p. 324 (*Kitāb al-Istisqāʾ, bāb rafʿ al-imām yadahu fī 'l-istisqāʾ*); vol. 4, p. 161 (*Kitāb al-Daʿawāt, bāb rafʿ al-aydī*).

166. Al-Qaḥṭānī, *Ṣalāt al-Muʾmin*, pp. 220–4.

167. Ibn Khuzayma collected *aḥādīth* on the minutiae of the practice of *al-ishāra bi'l-sabbāba* that do not appear in earlier compilations like al-Bukhari and Muslim's *al-Ṣaḥīḥān*. His compilation holds a rich selection of texts depicting

the Prophet moving his index finger during the *tashahhud*: Ibn Khuzayma, *Ṣaḥīḥ*, vol. 1, pp. 352–6 (*Kitāb al-ṣalāt*). More interesting are two texts about the Prophet during the Friday sermon in which he gestured with his index finger: Ibn Khuzayma, *Ṣaḥīḥ*, vol. 3, pp. 147–8 (*Kitāb al-Jumuᶜa*).

168. Holtzman and Ovadia, 'On Divine Aboveness' (forthcoming).
169. Al-Rāzī, *Asās al-Taqdīs*, pp. 41–3, 194–203.
170. Al-Rāzī, *Mafātīḥ al-Ghayb*, vol. 30, pp. 69–70 (interpretation of Q. 67:16–17: 'Are you confident that He who is in heaven will not cause the earth to cave beneath you, so that it will shake to pieces and overwhelm you? Are you confident that He who is in heaven will not let loose a sandy whirlwind?').
171. Al-Rāzī, *Asās al-Taqdīs*, p. 204.
172. A similar discussion appears in al-Razi's interpretation of Q. 7:54 ('Your Lord is God, who created the heavens and the earth in six days and then ascended the throne …'): al-Rāzī, *Mafātīḥ al-Ghayb*, vol. 14, pp. 112–13.
173. Al-Razi's discussions on *al-ishāra al-ḥissiyya* mirror to some extent the discussions that prevailed among the Basran school of grammarians in the ninth and tenth centuries. However, al-Razi discussed man gesticulating towards God, while the grammarians' debates were about God gesticulating towards man (or any other existent). The most thorough analyses of these discussions are in Shah, 'Classical Islamic Discourse', pp. 314, 321–2, and 'The Philological Endeavours (Part I)', pp. 31–2. As we pointed out in Chapter 4, Abu 'l-Hasan al-Ashᶜari also took part in these discussions. A key concept in these debates was the *muwāḍaᶜa*, namely, the idea that language was established via common convention and agreement. The proponents of this concept (followers of Abu Hashim's 'conventionalist' theory of the origins of language, *iṣṭilāḥ*) wished to prove that language was a human creation, and not the creation of God (the 'revelationist' theory, *tawqīf al-lughgha*). The argument that these scholars used was as follows: prior to the process of *muwāḍaᶜa* (namely, assigning words to objects, actions etc.), people used observable acts of gesticulation (*al-īmā wa'l-ishāra*) when they wanted to convey their thoughts. Since a gesticulation is performed by a gesticulating organ (*jāriḥa*), it is inconceivable that God gesticulated, because He has no organs. Hence, the language is human creation and not God's. This argument is defied by the Muᶜtazilite grammarian Ibn Jinni (d. 1002), who promoted the idea that God created language: Ibn Jinnī, *Al-Khṣāʾiṣ*, pp. 44–6.
174. Al-Rāzī, *Asās al-Taqdīs*, pp. 64–7.
175. Al-Rāzī, *Asās al-Taqdīs*, pp. 64, 71.

176. Al-Rāzī, *Asās al-Taqdīs*, p. 97.
177. Al-Rāzī, *Asās al-Taqdīs*, p. 97.
178. Al-Rāzī, *Asās al-Taqdīs*, p. 98.
179. Bori, 'Theology, Politics, Society', p. 65.
180. Makdisi's lucid assessment of the relationships between the Ashʿarites and the traditionalists within the Shafiʿite school remains accurate to date: Makdisi, 'Ashʿari and the Ashʿarites', 1963, pp. 34–9; Jackson, 'Ibn Taymiyyah on Trial in Damascus', p. 48, footnote 48. For a literary and hence fictional debate between a traditionalist and an Ashʿarite, see Holtzman, 'Debating the Doctrine of *Jabr*'. For a stylish debate between Ashʿarites and Ibn Taymiyya, see Holtzman, 'The Dhimmi's Question'.
181. The most comprehensive description of the Ashʿarite-Hanbalite polemics in fourteenth-century Cairo and Damascus is Bori, 'Theology, Politics, Society', pp. 64ff. The literature about Ibn Taymiyya is extremely vast. In recent years, Ibn Taymiyya has become the centre of scholarly attention. A good guide to Ibn Taymiyya and the research conducted on his life and oeuvre is Hoover, 'Ibn Taymiyya'.
182. On the centrality of al-Razi's theology among scholars of the Mamluk period, see Bori, 'Theology, Politics, Society', pp. 62–5.
183. Ibn Taymiyya's expertise in *kalām* was evident in the course of the 1306 Damascene trials, where he was interrogated by Ashʿarites and succeeded in crushing the Ashʿarite *kalām*: Jackson, 'Ibn Taymiyyah on Trial', p. 53.
184. Hoover, 'Ḥanbalī Theology', p. 634.
185. Ibn Taymiyya, *Al-Fatwā al-Ḥamawiyya al-Kubrā* (al-Tuwayjiri's edition), p. 193. The year is not indicated in any of the manuscripts that formed the basis for the preparation of al-Tuwajiri's edition; nonetheless, the year was added by al-Tuwayjiri based on an indication in several historical and biographical sources. See, for example, Ibn ʿAbd al-Ḥādī, *al-ʿUqūd al-Durriyya*, p. 148.
186. Ibn Taymiyya, '[Al-Ḥamawiyya al-Kubrā]', *Majmūʿat al-Fatāwā*, vol. 5, p. 7. The authors of the *fatwā* did not cite the *aḥādīth* verbatim. For the most complete version of the first *ḥadīth*, see Muslim, *Ṣaḥīḥ*, p. 1065 (*Kitāb al-Qadar, bāb taṣrīf Allāh taʿālā al-qulūb*), *ḥadīth* 2654; for the second *ḥadīth*, see Muslim, *Ṣaḥīḥ*, pp. 1142–3 (*Kitāb al-Janna, bāb al-nār yadkhuluhā al-jabbārūn*, *ḥadīth* 2846).
187. Ibn Taymiyya, *Bayān Talbīs al-Jahmiyya*, vol. 1, p. 4.
188. Ibn Rajab, *Dhayl Ṭabaqāt al-Ḥanābila*, vol. 4, p. 501 (the biography of Ibn Taymiyya); Ibn ʿAbd al-Ḥādī, *al-ʿUqūd al-Durriyya*, p. 91.

189. Hoover, 'Ḥanbalī Theology', pp. 637–9.
190. Ibn Taymiyya, '[Al-Ḥamawiyya al-Kubrā]', *Majmūᶜat al-Fatāwā*, vol. 5, p. 20.
191. Ibn Taymiyya, '[Al-Ḥamawiyya al-Kubrā]', *Majmūᶜat al-Fatāwā*, vol. 5, p. 10. *Tafwīḍ* means to avoid any attempt to explain problematic passages: Makdisi, 'Ashᶜari and the Ashᶜarites', 1962, p. 51. For the most comprehensive discussion of this term in the writings of anti-Taymiyyan Ashᶜarites, see El-Rouayheb, 'From Ibn Ḥajar al-Haytamī', pp. 275–87, 301–2.
192. On al-Razi's impact on Islamic thought, see Shihadeh, 'From al-Ghazālī to al-Rāzī', pp. 178–9. On al-Razi's place in the thought of Ibn Taymiyya and Ibn Qayyim al-Jawziyya, see Holtzman, 'Debating the Doctrine of *jabr*', pp. 61ff; Langermann, 'The Naturalization of Science', pp. 220–8.
193. Ibn Taymiyya, '[Al-Ḥamawiyya al-Kubrā]', *Majmūᶜat al-Fatāwā*, vol. 5, pp. 17–18.
194. Ibn Taymiyya, '[Al-Ḥamawiyya al-Kubrā]', *Majmūᶜat al-Fatāwā*, vol. 5, p. 18. Among these scholars, Ibn Taymiyya mentioned the names of the Hanbalite theologian Ibn ᶜAqil (d. 1119) and the Ashᶜarite theologian Abu Hamid al-Ghazali (d. 1111).
195. Ibn Taymiyya, '[Al-Ḥamawiyya al-Kubrā]', *Majmūᶜat al-Fatāwā*, vol. 5, p. 18.
196. Watt, *The Formative Period*, pp. 196–9.
197. See the evaluation of al-Dhahabī, *Siyar Aᶜlām al-Nubalāᵓ*, vol. 10, pp. 199–200 (the biography of al-Marisi).
198. The systematic polemical treatise that the prolific traditionalistic theologian Abu Saᶜid al-Darimi (d. between 893 and 895) wrote in response to Bishr's views helps us reconstruct the content of *Kufr al-Mushabbiha*. See the introduction of Rashid al-Almaᶜi to al-Dārimī, *Naqḍ al-Imām*, vol. 1, p. 71.
199. In the Taymiyyan terminology, *aᵓimmat al-hudā* are the scholars who are the authentic followers of all the Quranic prophets and the Prophet throughout the ages. These scholars are the traditionalists. *Aᵓimma al-ḍalāl* are the Muᶜtazilites, and their successors are the Ashᶜarites: Ibn Qayyim al-Jawziyya and Muḥammad ibn al-Mawṣilī, *Mukhtaṣar al-Ṣawāᶜiq*, p. 1408.
200. Ibn Taymiyya, '[Al-Ḥamawiyya al-Kubrā]', *Majmūᶜat al-Fatāwā*, vol. 5, p. 19.
201. Ibn Taymiyya, '[Al-Ḥamawiyya al-Kubrā]', *Majmūᶜat al-Fatāwā*, vol. 5, p. 19.
202. Ibn Taymiyya, '[Al-Ḥamawiyya al-Kubrā]', *Majmūᶜat al-Fatāwā*, vol. 5, p. 36.
203. Ibn Taymiyya's assertion that 'the massively transmitted *aḥādīth*' (*al-aḥādīth al-mutawātira*) yielded 'necessary and certain knowledge' was the view of the majority of the scholars (traditionalists, ultra-traditionalists and rationalist-traditionalists). All of these scholars used the rationalistic vocabulary of *yaqīn* and

ḍarūrī in this context. In fact, al-Razi himself discussed this topic in his manual of Islamic jurisprudence: Al-Rāzī, *al-Maḥṣūl*, vol. 4, pp. 227–70 (*fī 'l-tawātur*).

204. Ibn Taymiyya, '[Al-Ḥamawiyya al-Kubrā]', *Majmūʿat al-Fatāwā*, vol. 5, pp. 13–14.

205. Here Ibn Taymiyya elaborated on the pious ancestors: the Prophet's companions (*al-ṣaḥāba*), their righteous followers (*al-tābiʿūn*) and the religious leaders (*aʾimma*) who led the traditionalists during the periods when the false convictions of the Muʿtazilites and other rationalists prevailed, causing huge theological disputes: Ibn Taymiyya, '[Al-Ḥamawiyya al-Kubrā]', *Majmūʿat al-Fatāwā*, vol. 5, p. 14.

206. Ibn Taymiyya, '[Al-Ḥamawiyya al-Kubrā]', *Majmūʿat al-Fatāwā*, vol. 5, p. 14. Cf. Ibn Taymiyya, *Bayān Talbīs al-Jahmiyya*, vol. 3, pp. 423–4.

207. Ibn Taymiyya, '[Al-Ḥamawiyya al-Kubrā]', *Majmūʿat al-Fatāwā*, vol. 5, p. 14.

208. Adang, 'The Prophet's Farewell Pilgrimage', p. 113.

209. Adang, 'The Prophet's Farewell Pilgrimage', p. 123.

210. Muslim, *Ṣaḥīḥ*, p. 484, *ḥadīth* 1218-147 (*Kitāb al-Ḥajj, bāb ḥijjat al-nabī*); Abū Dāwūd, *Sunan*, p. 220, *ḥadīth* 1905 (*Kitāb al-Manāsik, bāb ṣifat ḥijjat al-nabī*).

211. Ibn Taymiyya, '[Al-Ḥamawiyya al-Kubrā]', *Majmūʿat al-Fatāwā*, vol. 5, pp. 60–7.

212. The most elaborate description of the events that occurred after the issuance of *al-Ḥamawiyya al-Kubrā* appears in Ibn Taymiyya's biography which was authored by Ibn ʿAbd al-Hadi (d. 1343). Ibn ʿAbd al-Hadi was Ibn Taymiyya's disciple: Ibn ʿAbd al-Hādī, *al-ʿUqūd al-Durriyya*, pp. 148–50. Ibn ʿAbd al-Hadi also summarised *al-Ḥamawiyya al-Kubrā*: ibid. pp. 91–104. The story of *al-Ḥamawiyya al-Kubrā* is briefly mentioned in several sources, like al-Dhahabī, *Tārīkh al-Islām*, vol. 52, pp. 61–2 (the biography of Ibn Taymiyya); al-Ṣafadī, *al-Wāfī* , vol. 7, pp. 15–16 (the biography of Ibn Taymiyya); Ibn Kathīr, *al-Bidāya wa'l-Nihāya*, vol. 17, pp. 711–12 (the events of Hijri year 698); Ibn Rajab, *Dhayl Ṭabaqāt al-Ḥanābila*, vol. 4, p. 511 (the biography of Ibn Taymiyya). Al-Dhahabi and al-Safadi knew Ibn Taymiyya personally. Ibn Kathir and Ibn Rajab were affiliated with the circle of Ibn Qayyim al-Jawziyya's disciples; therefore, these two scholars were fervent adherents of Ibn Taymiyya. Another description of the events following the issuance of *al-Ḥamawiyya al-Kubrā* appears in a rare biography of Ibn Taymiyya which was authored by al-Dhahabi. The text was critically edited and translated by Caterina Bori; the text also appeared in an anthology of Ibn Taymiyya's responses: Bori, 'A New

Source'; al-Dhahabī, 'Tarjamat shaykh al-islām Ibn Taymiyya', in Ibn ᶜUkāsha (ed.), *al-Masāʾil wa'l-Ajwiba*, pp. 244–5. An excellent integration of several historical and biographical sources about these events appears in Murad, 'Ibn Taymiya on Trial', p. 3. A similar description of the events, albeit without providing references to the historical sources, appears in the introduction to the scientific edition of Ibn Taymiyya's epistles, authored by Muhammad ᶜUzayr Shams: Ibn Taymiyya, *Jawāb al-Iᶜtirāḍāt al-Miṣriyya*, vol. 1, pp. 5–9. See also Laoust, *La profession de foi d'Ibn Taymiyya*, pp. 13–14.

213. This is how Shams al-Din al-Dhahabi characterised Ibn Taymiyya's enemies: al-Dhahabī, *Tārīkh al-Islām*, vol. 52, pp. 61–2 (the biography of Ibn Taymiyya).
214. Ibn ᶜAbd al-Hādī, *al-ᶜUqūd al-Durriyya*, p. 149; al-Dhahabī, *Tārīkh al-Islām*, vol. 52, p. 61.
215. Ibn ᶜAbd al-Hādī, *al-ᶜUqūd al-Durriyya*, p. 149.
216. Ibn Rajab remarked that there was no viceroy (*nāʾib*) in Damascus at the time of the incident; therefore, 'one of the governors' (*baᶜḍ al-wulāt*) came to Ibn Taymiyya's rescue: Ibn Rajab, *Dhayl Ṭabaqāt al-Ḥanābila*, vol. 4, p. 511.
217. Ibn ᶜAbd al-Hādī, *al-ᶜUqūd al-Durriyya*, p. 149; Bori, 'A New Source', pp. 335, 345; Ibn ᶜUkāsha (ed.), *al-Masāʾil wa'l-Ajwiba*, p. 244. ; al-Dhahabī, *Tārīkh al-Islām*, vol. 52, pp. 61–2; Ibn Kathīr, *al-Bidāya wa'l-Nihāya*, vol. 17, p. 711.
218. According to the historian Ibn Kathir, the two brothers fled their hometown Qazwin (Qazvin, today a province northwest to Tehran) with the advent of the Mongol army. Ibn Kathir indicates that they arrived in Damascus sometime after 1291. Immediately upon their arrival in Damascus, both were appointed to several positions in the religious establishment. The position of the Shafiᶜite chief judge, which both of them assumed at different periods, was the highest position in the religious establishment. For Imam al-Din's biography, see Ibn Kathīr, *al-Bidāya wa'l-Nihāya*, vol. 17, p. 732 (the deceased of Hijri year 699). For Jalal al-Din's biography, see ibid. vol. 18, p. 411 (the deceased of Hijri year 739).
219. Ibn ᶜAbd al-Hādī, *al-ᶜUqūd al-Durriyya*, p. 149; al-Dhahabī, *Tārīkh al-Islām*, vol. 52, p. 61; Ibn Kathīr, *al-Bidāya wa'l-Nihāya*, vol. 17, p. 711; al-Ṣafadī, *al-Wāfī*, vol. 7, pp. 15–16. Al-Dhahabi remarked that Jalal al-Din promised to support Ibn Taymiyya, but later he retracted his promise.
220. During 'the ordeals', Ibn Taymiyya was ordered to stand trial several times in Damascus and Cairo, was sent to detention in Egypt and was forced to stay in exile in Egypt for seven years. The ordeals began in January 1306 and

ended in February 1313, when Ibn Taymiyya returned to Damascus from his Egyptian exile. For the literature on Ibn Taymiyya's ordeals, see Hoover, 'Ibn Taymiyya'; Holtzman, 'Accused of Anthropomorphism', p. 567, footnote 30. For *al-Ḥamawiyya al-Kubrā* and the ordeals, see Bori, 'Theology, Politics, Society', pp. 72–9.

221. Little, 'The Historical and Historiographical Significance', pp. 324–5.
222. The prominent secondary literature on Ibn Taymiyya's trials is Michot, *Ibn Taymiyya,* pp. 156–60; Murad, 'Ibn Taymiya on Trial', pp. 1–32; Laoust, *Essai sur les doctrines sociales et politiques,* pp. 125-39; Jackson, 'Ibn Taymiyyah on Trial', pp. 41–85; Laoust, *La profession de foi d'Ibn Taymiyya*, pp. 20–31; Little, 'The Historical and Historiographical Significance', pp. 311–27.
223. Ibn ᶜAbd al-Hādī, *al-ᶜUqūd al-Durriyya,* p. 147; Bori, 'A New Source', pp. 344–5; al-Dhahabī, 'Tarjamat shaykh al-islām Ibn Taymiyya', in Ibn ᶜUkāsha (ed.), *al-Masāʾil wa'l-Ajwiba*, pp. 244–5.
224. Murad, 'Ibn Taymiya on Trial', p. 13.
225. Ibn Taymiyya, *Bayān Talbīs al-Jahmiyya*, vol. 4, p. 497.
226. Ibn Taymiyya, *Bayān Talbīs al-Jahmiyya*, vol. 4, pp. 497–514.
227. Ibn Taymiyya, *Bayān Talbīs al-Jahmiyya*, vol. 4, p. 514.
228. Al-Nuwayrī, *Nihāyat al-Arab*, vol. 32, p. 83; Little, 'The Historical and Historiographical Significance', pp. 320–1; Murad, 'Ibn Taymiya on Trial', pp. 13–14.
229. Al-Nuwayrī, *Nihāyat al-Arab*, vol. 32, pp. 84–5. The repudiation is also described by Ibn Hajar al-ᶜAsqalani in his biography of Ibn Taymiyya. The text is fully quoted by Shams and al-ᶜImrān, *al-Jāmiᶜ li-Sīrat Shaykh al-Islām*, pp. 470–2.
230. The most comprehensive biography of Ibn Taymiyya which contains a critical reading of the biographical and historical sources is Caterina Bori's *Ibn Taymiyya: una vita essemplare Analisi delle fonti classiche della sua biografia*, which unfortunately has not yet been translated into English. For Ibn Taymiyya's repudiation, see Bori, *Ibn Taymiyya,* p. 44, footnote 75; p. 115, footnote 13.
231. Holtzman, 'Accused of Anthropomorphism', pp. 566 footnote 28, 568.
232. Halkin, 'The Ḥashwiyya', pp. 12–20; Hurvitz, 'Miḥna as Self-Defense', pp. 98–9.
233. Ibn Taymiyya, 'Ḥikāyat al-Shaykh ᶜAlam al-Dīn', *Majmūᶜat al-Fatāwā*, vol. 3, p. 127. This text is a brief account given by the traditionalist-Shafiᶜite historian ᶜAlam al-Din al-Birzali (d. 1339). For an evaluation of this account, see Jackson, 'Ibn Taymiyyah on Trial', pp. 42–5.

234. Ibn Taymiyya, 'Ḥikāyat al-Shaykh ʿAlam al-Dīn', *Majmūʿat al-Fatāwā*, vol. 3, p. 127.
235. Abu Yaʿla's compilation of anthropomorphic traditions entitled *Ibṭāl al-Taʾwīlāt li-Akhbār al-Ṣifāt* was the target of Ibn al-Jawzi's attacks in his treatise *Kitāb Akhbār al-Ṣifāt*. See the analysis of Merlin Swartz in the introduction of *Kitāb Akhbār al-Ṣifāt*: Swartz, *A Medieval Critique of Anthropomorphism*, pp. 56–62.
236. Ibn Battuta's text is quoted in full by Shams and al-ʿImrān, *al-Jāmiʿ li-Sīrat Shaykh al-Islām*, p. 398. This anecdote also appears in Goldziher, *Introduction to Islamic Theology and Law*, p. 93.
237. For Taqi al-Din al-Hisni's biography, see Ibn al-ʿImād, *Shadharāt al-Dhahab*, vol. 9, pp. 273–5 (the notables who died in Hijri year 829). According to his lineage, al-Hisni was a descendent of the first eleven Shiʿite imams.
238. We could not identify Abu 'l-Hasan ʿAli al-Dimashqi in the biographical sources. Neither Muhammad al-Kawthari nor ʿAbd al-Wahid Mustafa, who were in charge of the publication of this manuscript in two separate editions, identified this scholar. This scholar could be Abu 'l-Hasan ʿAli ibn Ahmad ibn Muhammad ibn Salih al-ʿUrdi al-Dimashqi (d. 1363), a marginal *muḥaddith* who was also a tradesman. For his biography, see the appendix (*dhayl*) to al-Dhahabī's *al-ʿIbar fī Khabar Man Ghabar*, vol. 4, p. 204. The appendix was authored by Abu 'l-Mahasin al-Dimashqi (d. 1364).
239. Al-Ḥiṣnī, *Dafʿ Shubah Man Shabbaha* (2003), pp. 258–9; (2010), p. 65.
240. Shams and al-ʿImrān, *al-Jāmiʿ li-Sīrat Shaykh al-Islām*, p. 398, footnote 1.
241. Shams and al-ʿImrān, *al-Jāmiʿ li-Sīrat Shaykh al-Islām*, p. 477.
242. Little, 'Did Ibn Taymiyya Have a Screw Loose?', pp. 96–9.
243. El-Rouayheb, 'From Ibn Ḥajar al-Haytamī', p. 279.
244. *Al-Kāfiya al-Shāfiya* was discussed and analysed in Holtzman, 'Insult, Fury, and Frustration' and 'Accused of Anthropomorphism'.
245. Ibn Qayyim al-Jawziyya, *al-Kāfiya al-Shāfiya*, pp. 338–9, verses 1252–8, p. 451, verses 1698–700.
246. Ibn Qayyim al-Jawziyya, *al-Kāfiya al-Shāfiya*, p. 566, verses 2248–9.
247. Ibn Qayyim al-Jawziyya, *al-Kāfiya al-Shāfiya*, p. 892, verses 4738–40.
248. Taqi al-Din al-Subki was the father of the great historian Taj al-Din al-Subki's (d. 1368). For Taqi al-Din's biography, see al-Subkī, *Ṭabaqāt al-Shāfiʿiyya*, vol. 10, pp. 139–338. For al-Subki's confrontations with Ibn Qayyim al-Jawziyya, see Bori and Holtzman, 'A scholar in the shadow', pp. 22–6. In 1348, al-Subki wrote a response to Ibn Qayyim al-Jawziyya's *al-Kāfiya al-Shāfiya*

entitled *al-Sayf al-Ṣaqīl fī al-Radd ᶜalā Ibn Zafīl* (The Burnished Sword in Refuting Ibn Zafil). Al-Subki invented the derogative name Ibn Zafil for Ibn Qayyim al-Jawziyya. The meaning of this name of opprobrium has never been clarified and remains an enigma to this day. In fact, none of the biographical sources attribute the name Ibn Zafil to Ibn Qayyim al-Jawziyya. The illustrious Saudi scholar Bakr Abu Zayd (d. 2008), who edited the lion's share of Ibn Qayyim al-Jawziyya's literary output, believed that the editor of *al-Sayf al-Ṣaqīl*, the Hanafite scholar Muhammad Zahid ibn al-Hasan ibn ᶜAli al-Kawthari (d. 1952), fabricated the text. However, after he found a quotation from the text in al-Zabidi's (d. 1791) *Itḥāf al-Sāda*, Abu Zayd was forced to agree that *al-Sayf al-Ṣaqīl* was authentic. Al-Kawthari claimed that Zafil was Ibn Qayyim al-Jawziyya's maternal grandfather, and that the name Ibn Zafil was therefore a name of opprobrium. Bakr Abu Zayd, however, did not accept al-Kawthari's explanation: Abū Zayd, *Ibn Qayyim al-Jawziyya*, pp. 32–6. Al-Murtada al-Zabidi explained that *al-Sayf al-Ṣaqīl* was written as a response to a 6000-verse *qaṣīda* authored by 'Ibn Zafil, one of the Hanbalites'. He also did not identify Ibn Zafil with Ibn Qayyim al-Jawziyya: al-Zabīdī, *Itḥāf al-Sāda*, vol. 2, p. 14.

249. Al-Subkī, *al-Sayf al-Ṣaqīl*, pp. 112–13.
250. Al-Subkī, *al-Sayf al-Ṣaqīl*, p. 81.
251. For Ibn Jahbal's biography, see Ibn al-ᶜImād, *Shadharāt al-Dhahab*, vol. 8, pp. 183–4 (the notables who died in Hijri year 733); al-Subkī, *Ṭabaqāt al-Shāfiᶜiyya*, vol. 9, p. 34. The *nubdha* was copied in its entirety by al-Subki: ibid. vol. 9, pp. 35–91. The text was skilfully translated by Gibril Fouad Haddad and published as Ibn Jahbal al-Kilābī, *The Refutation of Him [Ibn Taymiyya] Who Attributes Direction to Allāh* (Birmingham, UK: Aqsa Publications, 2008). However, in the several excerpts we cited here, we preferred to translate the text. Ibn Jahbal was involved in the arrest of Ibn Taymiyya and Ibn Qayyim al-Jawziyya in 1326. The details of this affair appear in the account of Shams al-Din al-Jazari (d. 1339). The text is quoted in Shams and al-ᶜImrān, *al-Jāmiᶜ li-Sīrat Shaykh al-Islām*, pp. 137–46.
252. Al-Subkī, *Ṭabaqāt al-Shāfiᶜiyya*, vol. 9, p. 34.
253. Al-Subkī, *Ṭabaqāt al-Shāfiᶜiyya*, vol. 9, p. 35.
254. Ibn Taymiyya, '[Al-Ḥamawiyya al-Kubrā]', *Majmūᶜat al-Fatāwā*, vol. 5, p. 12.
255. This is a paraphrase of Q. 26:23 'Who is the Lord of the Universe?'
256. Al-Subkī, *Ṭabaqāt al-Shāfiᶜiyya*, vol. 9, p. 50.
257. Ibn Taymiyya, '[Al-Ḥamawiyya al-Kubrā]', *Majmūᶜat al-Fatāwā*, vol. 5, p. 14.
258. Al-Subkī, *Ṭabaqāt al-Shāfiᶜiyya*, vol. 9, p. 64.

259. Al-Subkī, *Ṭabaqāt al-Shāfiᶜiyya*, vol. 9, p. 64.
260. Ibn Taymiyya, '[Al-Ḥamawiyya al-Kubrā]', *Majmūᶜat al-Fatāwā*, vol. 5, pp. 27–8.
261. Ibn Taymiyya, '[Al-Ḥamawiyya al-Kubrā]', *Majmūᶜat al-Fatāwā*, vol. 5, p. 29.
262. Ibn Taymiyya, '[Al-Ḥamawiyya al-Kubrā]', *Majmūᶜat al-Fatāwā*, vol. 5, p. 29.
263. Al-Subkī, *Ṭabaqāt al-Shāfiᶜiyya*, vol. 9, p. 73. Ibn Jahbal's repetitive and incoherent style requires a massive paraphrasing of text. Gibril Fouad Haddad's excellent translation is literally more faithful to the text than the translation we offer here. Our translation, however, reflects our understanding of Ibn Jahbal's mocking style: Haddad [Ibn Jahbal], *The Refutation of Him*, pp. 238–9.
264. Ibn Taymiyya, '[Al-Ḥamawiyya al-Kubrā]', *Majmūᶜat al-Fatāwā*, vol. 5, p. 35.
265. Al-Subkī, *Ṭabaqāt al-Shāfiᶜiyya*, vol. 9, p. 76.
266. Al-Subkī, *Ṭabaqāt al-Shāfiᶜiyya*, vol. 9, p. 36.
267. Al-Subkī, *Ṭabaqāt al-Shāfiᶜiyya*, vol. 9, p. 36. For the meaning of *suḥt* and *ḥuṭām*, see Lane, *Arabic-English Lexicon*, vol. 4, pp. 1314–15; vol. 2, pp. 594–5. Here, too, the translation we offer differs from Gibril Fouad Haddad's [Ibn Jahbal], *The Refutation of Him*, p. 153.
268. Al-Subkī, *Ṭabaqāt al-Shāfiᶜiyya*, vol. 9, p. 40; Haddad [Ibn Jahbal], *The Refutation of Him*, p. 162.
269. Al-Subkī, *Ṭabaqāt al-Shāfiᶜiyya*, vol. 9, pp. 40–41, 44, 54, 72, 74. Cf. the views of the Ashᶜarite theologian al-Juwayni (d. 1085): Frank, 'Knowledge and *Taqlīd*', p. 55.
270. Al-Subkī, *Ṭabaqāt al-Shāfiᶜiyya*, vol. 9, p. 82.
271. Holtzman, 'Accused of Anthropomorphism', pp. 570–1.

Final Remarks and Conclusions

The Hadith scholar Abu 'l-Hasan al-Daraqutni (d. 995) composed a brief didactic poem in which he declared:

> We attribute the *ḥadīth* of the intercession in the honourable [station] to [our Prophet], the chosen and most laudable. There is another *ḥadith* reporting that [God] will make [Muhammad] sit on the throne. We do not reject this *ḥadīth* either. You should transmit this *ḥadīth* (about Muhammad sitting next to God) verbatim, and never insert any word which might corrupt its exact wording. Never deny that [Muhammad] will sit [on the throne]. Never deny that [God] will make him sit.[1]

In this poem (which is translated here without any regard to rhythm and rhyme), al-Daraqutni referred to the two known versions of the *ḥadīth* which interprets the phrase 'an honourable station' (*maqāman maḥmūdan*, see Q. 17:79), namely the anthropomorphic version attributed to Mujahid and the mild version attributed to several of Muhammad's companions. According to the anthropomorphic version, 'an honourable station' is Muhammad's sitting on the throne with God. In contrast, according to the mild version, 'an honourable place' refers to Muhammad's intercession on behalf of the Muslims on the Day of Resurrection (see Introduction). Although al-Daraqutni declared that he accepted both versions, by attributing the mild version to the Prophet himself, al-Daraqutni signalled to his readers that the mild version was his version of choice. Al-Daraqutni therefore perceived 'an honourable station' as intercession (*shafāʿa*). In comparison, al-Daraqutni's acceptance of the anthropomorphic version as reflected in the poem was much more reserved. Al-Daraqutni, a Shafiᶜite resident of Baghdad, would have likely dismissed the anthropomorphic version as unreliable, if Baghdad's public atmosphere was more favourable to middle-of-the-road traditionalism. However, Baghdad was dominated by the Hanbalite zealots, which made the rejection of the anthropomorphic version almost impossible.

Aside from the implicit choice of the mild version over the anthropomorphic version, the poem contains specific instructions to the *muḥaddithūn* who were bewildered when they encountered these two different, if not contradictory, texts. In this brief poem, al-Daraqutni forthrightly expressed the most important component of the Ashᶜarite approach to *aḥādīth al-ṣifāt*: a systematic insistence on a rigid transmission process in which the text was transmitted verbatim without any verbal or gestural decorations.

No doubt, al-Daraqutni saw this strict process as a safeguard against anthropomorphism. In other words, the middle-of-the-road traditionalists of Baghdad in the tenth century were more or less coerced into accepting the anthropomorphic version because of Hanbalite violence. The only recourse of these middle-of-the-road traditionalists, who were intimidated by the Hanbalites, was to promote the mild version as their preferred one. This situation completely changed several centuries later in the learning centres of the Mamluk sultanate. In these centres, the dispute over this *ḥadīth* still continued; nonetheless, due to the Ashᶜarite dominance in the public sphere it appeared that selecting one version over the other was more a matter of personal preference rather than a solution dictated by the religious establishment or the environment in the streets. Accordingly, the Quran exegete Jalal al-Din al-Suyuti (d. 1505) mentioned only 'the station of intercession' (*maqām al-shafāᶜa*) as an interpretation of 'an honourable station' in his early work of Quran exegesis, namely, his part of *Tafsīr al-Jalālayn*.[2] Al-Suyuti composed the first half of this work when he was twenty-one years old. At that time, he inclined to middle-of-the-road traditionalism, and perhaps was influenced by Ashᶜarism. At the age of forty-seven, al-Suyuti included all the variants of the anthropomorphic version and the mild version in his Hadith-based exegesis of the Quran, his magnum opus, *al-Durr al-Manthūr*.[3] More than an indication to al-Suyuti's antiquarianism, the inclusion of all the possible variants of the anthropomorphic version in *al-Durr al-Manthūr* signalled the ultra-traditionalistic stance that al-Suyuti embraced as a mature and established scholar.

In the fourteenth century, approximately 400 years after the forced entry of the anthropomorphic version into the traditionalistic canon (see Introduction), the idea of Muhammad sitting on the throne was securely established in the traditionalistic discourse. The fully fledged Ashᶜarites, such as the Quran exegete Abu 'l-Hasan ᶜAli ibn Ahmad al-Wahidi (d. 1076) from Nishapur and Fakhr al-Din al-Razi (d. 1209) from Herat, were the only theologians who dared to harshly criticise this problematic dogma. Unlike the usual practice among Hadith scholars, namely to meticulously examine the names in the chains of transmission and refrain from addressing the content of the Hadith material, both al-Wahidi and al-Razi addressed the anthropomorphic content of this *ḥadīth*. Al-Wahidi labelled this *ḥadīth* as 'an ugly saying that causes much uneasiness',[4] while al-Razi explained that God's actual sitting on the throne was inconceivable because it entailed the perception of God as a limited physical body (*mutaḥaddidan mutanāhiyan*).[5]

The radical ultra-traditionalists Ibn Taymiyya (d. 1328) and Ibn Qayyim al-Jawziyya (d. 1350) responded to this Ashᶜarite rejection of the anthropomorphic version by reaffirming the unique status of this *ḥadīth* in their two works that were dedicated to a refutation of the rationalistic arguments against *aḥādith al-ṣifāṭ*. These works are the bulky theological treatise *Bayān Talbīs al-Jahmiyya* by Ibn Taymiyya and the lengthy didactic poem *al-Kāfiya al-Shāfiya* by Ibn Qayyim al-Jawziyya. In his brief discussion of the anthropomorphic version, Ibn Taymiyya relied on the views of his Hanbalite predecessors. In particular, Ibn Taymiyya quoted the verdict of one of the most prominent Hanbalites of the tenth century, Abu ᶜAbd Allah al-Hasan ibn Hamid al-Warraq (d. 1013). Ibn Hamid claimed that Ahmad ibn Hanbal taught this *ḥadīth*. Ibn Hamid further determined that 'one must believe and confirm that the Prophet will be physically close to God (*al-mumāssa wa'l-qurb min 'l-ḥaqq li-nabiyyihi*), because our friends (the Hanbalites) relied on the response of Ahmad ibn Hanbal in this matter'. Finally, Ibn Hamid explained that 'an honourable station' possibly meant 'a station allotted for the Prophet to sit in'.[6] Ibn Hamid's opinion that Ahmad ibn Hanbal himself taught this *ḥadīth* was exaggerated, to say the least, because there was no textual evidence that Ahmad ibn Hanbal ever knew the anthropomorphic *ḥadīth* let alone transmitted it. However, this exaggeration served well Ibn

Taymiyya's purpose to reaffirm the status of this *ḥadīth*, therefore he unhesitatingly adopted Ibn Hamid's view.

Ibn Qayyim al-Jawziyya went even further than Ibn Taymiyya. First, he determined that this *ḥadīth* referred to the Prophet himself,[7] which we disproved in the Introduction. Then, Ibn Qayyim al-Jawziyya went on the offensive against both al-Razi and al-Wahidi. As both al-Razi and al-Wahidi were Quran exegetes, Ibn Qayyim al-Jawziyya wondered how they claimed that this *ḥadīth* conveyed a corporealistic message. According to Ibn Qayyim al-Jawziyya's argumentation, this *ḥadīth* was attributed to Mujahid, and therefore indirectly to Mujahid's master Ibn ᶜAbbas, the founder of the science of Quran exegesis. Ibn Qayyim al-Jawziyya sarcastically remarked: 'Isn't Mujahid their sheikh? Isn't his sheikh (Ibn ᶜAbbas) their sheikh as well?'[8] This *argumentum ad hominem* implicitly conveyed Ibn Qayyim al-Jawziyya's view that both al-Wahidi and al-Razi did not merit the title of Quran exegetes if they refuted Mujahid's opinion as articulated in the anthropomorphic version. We note that Ibn Qayyim al-Jawziyya did not claim here that the anthropomorphic version was directly quoted from the mouth of Ibn ᶜAbbas, because such a text was never found. Ibn Qayyim al-Jawziyya simply expressed here a view prevalent among the Hanbalites that Ahmad ibn Hanbal believed that the anthropomorphic text should have been attributed to Ibn ᶜAbbas (see Introduction).

Thereafter, Ibn Qayyim al-Jawziyya mentioned more evidence to corroborate the anthropomorphic version. His evidence is rather peculiar and not entirely convincing. According to Ibn Qayyim al-Jawziyya, the Prophet's cousin, the *ṣaḥābī* Jaᶜfar ibn Abi Talib (d. 629), also referred to Muhammad's sitting on the divine throne. This reference appears in an anecdote that Jaᶜfar recounted to the Prophet himself when he returned from Abyssinia.[9] The anecdote is not thematically identical to the anthropomorphic version, but rather reflects the prophecy of an old Christian woman from Abyssinia. While being in Abyssinia, Jaᶜfar witnessed the following event: an old woman carrying a large basket on her head was pushed away from the road by a young man riding his horse. The basket fell on the ground, and the angry woman cried: 'Woe unto you [young man]! Just wait for the day in which the king will sit on his throne and return like for like to the oppressors for harassing the oppressed.' Upon hearing Jaᶜfar's story, the Prophet's eyes were filled with pearly tears. Thereafter he said: 'May God curse the nation whose oppressors will be forced to return to the oppressed what was rightfully theirs.'[10] This anecdote supposedly conveyed the idea of the Prophet's sitting on the throne, but in fact the story provided flimsy evidence of the antiquity of this idea. Clearly the old woman referred to 'the Future Second Return' of Christ and not to the Prophet Muhammad whom she probably did not know. However, Ibn Qayyim al-Jawziyya enthusiastically added that this text recounted by the Prophet's cousin and other parallel texts 'form the clearest demonstration of the truth'. Specifically, these texts formed the best available evidence that Muhammad would sit on the divine throne.[11] Finally, Ibn Qayyim al-Jawziyya praised al-Daraqutni 'who fiercely and courageously confirmed the veracity of the texts in this matter'. Obviously, Ibn Qayyim al-Jawziyya did not read al-Daraqutni's poem as a reticent approval of the anthropomorphic version, because he complimented al-Daraqutni's courageous support of the anthropomorphic version during the riots in Baghdad. Ibn Qayyim al-Jawziyya perhaps referred to riots other than those which erupted in the year 929 in Baghdad. In 929, al-Daraqutni was merely eleven years old, so it was unlikely that he participated in any theological debate on the anthropomorphic version.[12]

As reflected in the passages from *al-Kāfiya al-Shāfiya*, it is evident that Ibn Qayyim al-Jawziyya expanded the search for textual evidence of Muhammad's sitting on the throne. His efforts are a clear indication that, centuries after the crushing victory of the Hanbalites over the middle-of-the-road traditionalists in the tenth century, the dispute between the ultra-traditionalists (the Hanbalites) and the traditional-rationalists (the Ashᶜarites) refused to die. In fact, the ultra-traditionalists toiled to rekindle the dispute on the anthropomorphic version, just as they rekindled other disputes on different texts of *aḥādīth al-ṣifāt*. The literal reading and understanding of *aḥādīth al-ṣifāt* was the most prominent component in the ultra-traditionalistic identity, a battle which the ultra-traditionalists waged fiercely. Ibn Taymiyya and Ibn Qayyim al-Jawziyya lived in a challenging time, when the ultra-traditionalistic identity was at risk constantly. As ultra-traditionalists, they were intimidated and harassed by the Ashᶜarite *ᶜulamā'* of the Mamluk period. Both Ibn Tayimyya and Ibn Qayyim al-Jawziyya provoked the Ashᶜarites by promoting an outspoken literal reading of the anthropomorphic texts, unearthing additional problematic texts and paraphrasing these texts. These ultra-traditionalists further provoked their Ash^carite opponents by reciting these texts in front of the masses. Unlike the claims of their ideological rivals the Ash^carites, Ibn Taymiyya and Ibn Qayyim al-Jawziyya probably did not use spontaneous body gestures in their public performances to emphasise their literal understanding of the anthropomorphic descriptions in the Hadith material. However, their fervent support in the two iconic gestures of raising one's finger to the sky and raising both hands in prayer suggests that they indeed performed these two iconic gestures that were attributed to the Prophet and the *ṣaḥāba*. A deeper understanding of Ibn Taymiyya's and Ibn Qayyim al-Jawziyya's ultra-traditionalistic activism and their approach to the anthropomorphic texts could have been achieved only by contextualising *aḥādīth al-ṣifāt* and their place in the traditionalistic discourse. This contextualisation was the core of our endeavours in the present monograph. In fact, our long-term ambition to fully grasp the meaning of Ibn Qayyim al-Jawziyya's *al-Kāfiya al-Shāfiya* was one of the sparks that ignited the idea to write this book. With the progress of our project, *al-Kāfiya al-Shāfiya* was set aside, and *aḥādīth al-ṣifāṭ*, the men and women who transmitted them throughout the ages, their disputes and performances, occupied centre stage and became the *raison d'etre* of the project.

This monograph presented a range of issues that encompassed the problematics of *aḥādīth al-ṣifāṭ*. We focused here on the following three prominent issues: *aḥādīth al-ṣifāt* as popular oral literature; the use of *aḥādīth al-ṣifāṭ* in the traditionalistic discourse; and *aḥādīth al-ṣifāt* as iconic texts in the public sphere. We saw these issues form the demarcation lines between ultra-traditionalism, middle-of-the-road traditionalism and traditional-rationalism. We first demonstrated the popularity of *aḥādīth al-ṣifāt* by highlighting 'the tribal connection'. The more critical Hadith scholars, like Ibn Qutayba (d. 889) and Shams al-Din al-Dhahabi (d. 1348), explicitly stated their opinion that the most problematic among *aḥādīth al-ṣifāṭ* were part of the cultural legacy of secluded tribes in Iraq like the Banu al-Muntafiq and urbanised tribes like the Banu Bajila of Kufa. While in other cultures the tribal stories were considered myths and legends, in the Islamic world these stories were sacralised as they were connected to the Prophet. The traces of the systematic efforts of these two tribes to possess portions of the magnificent past by claiming that their founding fathers were close to the Prophet, were never completely obliterated from the historical sources. The more prominent the tribe's founding father, the more likely his legacy would enter the canon. This is the case of Jarir al-Bajali (d. 671 or 674). The case of Abu Razin (death date unknown) proves this hypothesis from the opposite direction: apparently, when the founding father of a tribe was a marginal figure, his material albeit unique and compelling, would not be admitted into the canon. The efforts of tribesmen to proliferate their tribe's legacy were recorded in the *isnād* of a given *ḥadīth* and in the literature that emerged with the great intellectual efforts of the study of Hadith. In the eighth century, with the intensive efforts of *muḥaddithū*n like Isma^cil ibn Abi Khalid (d. 762–3) and Hammad ibn Salama (d. 784), the texts were already in the 'blood stream' of the religious discourse, and widely accepted as true. As time passed, the Promethean efforts of scholars to expel these texts were doomed to fail. Varied devices were used in the scholarly circles to expel such traditions from the traditionalistic discourse. Nevertheless, the texts gained such popularity that even labelling them as inauthentic did not prevent their proliferation.

Thus, *aḥādīth al-ṣifāṭ* proliferated due to the intensive efforts of individuals who were venerated by later generations as reliable *muḥaddithūn*. At the same time, the relevant literature of *^cilm al-rijāl* (the science dedicated to the *muḥaddithūn* and their biographies) and the biographical dictionaries consistently revealed the entanglement of personal motivations that drove these people to spread the anthropomorphic Hadith material. Abu Burda (d. *c*. 721–3), ^cAbida (d. between 691 and 693), ^cAlqama (d. between 681 and 692), Thabit al-Bunani (d. 740) and Humayd al-Tawil (d. 758) are cases in point. The literature of *^cilm al-rijāl* and the biographical dictionaries became crucial through this study. At an early stage of the research, we discovered that only a combined reading of the Hadith material, the historical sources and the theological treatises could have yielded substantial insights regarding the place of *aḥādīth al-ṣifāt* in the traditionalistic discourse. Another strategy of crucial importance was implementing literary analysis on *aḥādīth al-ṣifāt*. Apart from the fact that this endeavour had never been performed in western scholarship before, literary analysis led us to identify the major building blocks in the self-perception of the ultra-traditionalists as *muḥaddithūn*. These building blocks (specified in Chapters

4 and 5) are the major findings of this monograph. Here is a short summary of these findings.

First, we note that the ultra-traditionalists (the predecessors of the Hanbalites in the eighth century, the Hanbalites themselves from the middle of the ninth century onward, and other individual *muḥaddithūn*) were **more receptive** to *aḥādīth al-ṣifāt* than other middle-of-the-road *muḥaddithūn.* This material was regarded by other traditionalists as mere curiosities at best and blunt fabrication at worst. As a community of scholars and laymen, the Hanbalites were more open to stories that came from secluded areas and were recounted by members of secluded tribes, stories that featured marginal figures in the Islamic discourse. Second, the ultra-traditionalists and later the Hanbalites were **more attentive** to the social function that *aḥādīth al-ṣifāt* served in offering the masses an Islamic religiosity which provided a direct way to perceive God without the interference of mediators. To enable the masses to comfortably connect to this religiosity, and probably because there was a growing demand from the masses to hear these texts, the ultra-traditionalistic *muḥaddithūn* brought *aḥādīth al-ṣifāt* into the public sphere: to the street, the mosque and the marketplace. These *muḥaddithūn* transformed these literary works into a popular icon of devotion. This icon at times, as we observed in Chapter 5, became the core of a radical political ideology. Third, and this is our most important conclusion, the ultra-traditionalists **structured the iconicity** of *aḥādīth al-ṣifāt* by perfecting their skills as performers. This is why we focused on the use of gestures during the process of Hadith transmission in this book. A feature previously neglected by researchers on Hadith, apart from the illustrious Ignaz Goldziher (see Chapter 3), was thoroughly examined here. This is the first time that such a large-scale examination of gestures has been applied to *aḥādīth al-ṣifāt.*

The three insights that we specified here enabled us to fully grasp the difference between an ultra-traditionalistic (Hanbalite) *muḥaddith* and a middle-of-the-road one: the ultra-traditionalist enthusiastically and systematically performed gestures; the middle-of-the-road *muḥaddith* performed the gestures while adding his reservations, or he did not perform gestures at all. We assume that many of these gestures disappeared over the years; we are entirely dependent on the written records, that in spite of their generous display of gestures by the *muḥaddithūn* who transmitted *aḥādīth al-ṣifāt*, they rarely refer to the 'unofficial' presentation of *aḥādīth al-ṣifāt* in the public sphere. We regret that we have only a handful of stories like the story about Abu ᶜAmir al-ᶜAbdari (d. 1130) and his colourful display of iconic (not metaphoric) gestures in connection with anthropomorphic descriptions of God. This is the place to emphasise that even middle-of-the-road *muḥaddithūn* had to sometimes perform gestures. This happened when a *muḥaddith* had to repeat the gesture that he saw his teacher perform, or when gestures appeared in the written sources as part of the performance directions issued by the *muḥaddithūn*. In such a case, the middle-of-the-road *muḥaddith* would perform the gesture reticently; that is, he would clarify that the gesture he performed was metaphoric and not iconic. This issue was thoroughly discussed in Chapter 3.

The most challenging period for the traditionalistic discourse in general, and *aḥādīth al-ṣifāt* in particular, was the end of the tenth and the beginning of the eleventh century. This period was characterised by the strengthening of rationalistic features in the traditionalistic discourse. The rationalistic features affected the transmission and reception of *aḥādīth al-ṣifāt*. Here, we offered a different understanding of the *bi-lā kayfa* formula which seemed to unite and at the same time separate the ultra-traditionalists (the Hanbalites) and the traditional-rationalists (the Ashᶜarites). The Hanbalite understanding of the *bi-lā kayfa* formula enabled the Hanbalite *muḥaddithūn* to add gestures to their transmission, to embellish the narrative with pictorial scenes, and to paraphrase text. The Hanbalites used *aḥādīth al-ṣifāt* as their raw material, to shape as they wished in several religious genres: the *ᶜaqīda*, or creed, was the most conspicuous of these genres. Unlike the Hanbalites, the Ashᶜarites tended to stick to scholarly discussions on *aḥādīth al-ṣifāt*. Their understanding of the *bi-lā kayfa* formula included both hermeneutical efforts to divest these anthropomorphic descriptions from any depiction of God, and to rigidly follow a fixed protocol of transmitting this material. This rigid approach to Hadith transmission, as opposed to the creative and flexible approach of the Hanbalites, came from the Ashᶜarite perception that *aḥādīth al-ṣifāt* were highly sensitive material that could have easily led to the false convictions of *tashbīh*. As opposed to the Hanbalites, whose Hadith sessions were open to everybody, the Ashᶜarite scholars of the Hadith were reluctant to expose this material to the masses. Chapter 4 presented all the possible aspects of the Hanbalite and Ash^carite *bi-lā kayfa* approaches, especially regarding the problematic *ḥadīth* of 'the loin of God'.

Finally, it seems that only Fakhr al-Din al-Razi, the proponent of an intellectualised form of extreme *tanzīh* – transcendence or deanthropomorphism (which he named *taqdīs*) – examined the actual meaning and definition of anthropomorphism (*tashbīh*). His approach instigated a belated chain reaction in the Mamluk period. First, the Ashᶜarites of Mamluk Cairo and Damascus zealously embraced al-Razi's ideas about *tanzīh* and adopted them as the state religion. The sophisticated ultra-traditionalists (Ibn Taymiyya and Ibn Qayyim al-Jawziyya) refuted al-Razi's ideas, thus clashing with the religious establishment. The Ashᶜarites responded by prosecuting the ultra-traditionalists. Here, again, the gesture of pointing the finger to the sky to indicate God's location and direction encapsulated the lengthy history of *aḥādīth al-ṣifāt* in the traditionalistic discourse. This gesture was metaphoric, according to the Ashᶜarites. In contrast, the Hanbalites viewed this gesture as iconic. This gesture symbolised both the possible or actual whereabouts of God, and the main features of the long-term debate on *aḥādīth al-sifāt*: **Hanbalite flexibility versus Ashᶜarite rigidity; anthropomorphism versus transcendentalism; metaphors versus iconicity**. The major point in this debate focused on the texts that the *muḥaddithūn* were willing to accept into the canon and the degree of tolerance that these professional Hadith transmitters practised towards the views of their peers. The traditionalistic scholars were tolerant, but the traditionalistic politicians were not. The texts were exploited for political purposes and *aḥādīth al-ṣifāt* became the most controversial material in the religious discourse. These circumstances did not arise because *aḥādīth al-ṣifāt* compared God to humans or used anthropomorphic language to describe God and by doing so compared Him to His creatures. These texts were considered dangerous because they motivated people (the masses) to action (see the 929 riots in Baghdad). The danger of *aḥādīth al-ṣifāt* lay in the environment that encouraged the constant use of these texts through the entry of these texts into the political discourse.

When examining a singular text unit of *aḥādīth al-ṣifāt* and its history, we see that in different periods in the history of Islamic thought, specific text units of *aḥādīth al-ṣifāt* earned an iconic status and accordingly played a political role. *Aḥādīth al-ṣifāt* were among the most powerful icons of Islamic traditionalism, whether articulated by the ultra-traditionalistic Hanbalites or the traditional-rationalistic Ash^{c}arites. The role of *aḥādīth al-ṣifāt* extends the boundaries of the religious discourse: they often represent the dividing line between traditionalism and rationalism. In certain periods, *aḥādīth al-ṣifāt* served as a litmus test between belief and disbelief, between Islam and heresy. But most of all, *aḥādīth al-ṣifāt* were fascinating stories with a potential to entertain, stimulate, provoke or frighten a captive audience. As such, *aḥādīth al-ṣifāt* were precious in the eyes of the masses who found in them comfort, elation and enjoyment. These aspects regarding the history of *aḥādīth al-ṣifāt* can and will be further pursued.

Notes

1. Ibn Qayyim al-Jawziyya, *Badā$^{\circ}$i^{c} al-Fawā$^{\circ}$id*, vol. 4, p. 1380.
2. Al-Maḥallī and al-Suyūṭī, *Tafsīr al-Jalālayn*, p. 375. Al-Suyuti describes the circumstances of composing his part of *Tafsīr al-Jalālayn*, including the exact dates in *Tafsīr al-Jalālayn*, pp. 379–80.
3. Al-Suyūṭī, *al-Durr al-Manthūr*, vol. 9, pp. 419–27.
4. Al-Wāḥidī, *al-Tafsīr al-Basīṭ*, vol. 23, p. 445 (the interpretation of Q. 17:79).
5. Al-Rāzī, *Mafātīḥ al-Ghayb*, vol. 21, p. 33 (the interpretation of Q. 17:79).
6. Ibn Taymiyya, *Bayān Talbīs al-Jahmiyya*, vol. 6, pp. 214–16.
7. Ibn Qayyim al-Jawziyya, *al-Kāfiya al-Shāfiya*, p. 474, verse 1758.
8. Ibn Qayyim al-Jawziyya, *al-Kāfiya al-Shāfiya*, p. 478, verse 1759.
9. Ibn Qayyim al-Jawziyya, *al-Kāfiya al-Shāfiya*, p. 478, verse 1760.
10. The text of this rare anecdote was located and fully quoted by the editors of *al-Kāfiya al-Shāfiya*: Ibn Qayyim al-Jawziyya, *al-Kāfiya al-Shāfiya*, p. 478, footnote to verse 1760.
11. Ibn Qayyim al-Jawziyya, *al-Kāfiya al-Shāfiya*, p. 480, verse 1761.
12. Ibn Qayyim al-Jawziyya, *al-Kāfiya al-Shāfiya*, pp. 482–4, verses 1762–8.

Appendix I
Full Translations of Lengthy Traditions

This appendix presents full translations of the lengthy traditions that are analysed in Chapter 1.

1. A Marginal Version of *Ḥadīth al-Nuzūl*

Ibn Khuzayma wrote this *ḥadīth* in a dictation session of the *muḥaddith* Muhammad ibn ᶜAbd Allah ibn Maymun (d. 875). The session took place in Alexandria. Ibn Maymun received the text from the *muḥaddith* al-Walid ibn Muslim (d. 810), who in turn received the text from the *muḥaddith* al-Awzaᶜi (d. 774). These three scholars agreed that this *ḥadīth* was recounted by Hilal ibn Abi Maymuna (d. c. 737). Ibn Abi Maymuna heard the *ḥadīth* from ᶜAtaᵓ ibn Yasar (d. 721). ᶜAtaᵓ claimed that the *ṣaḥābī* Rifaᶜa ibn ᶜAraba al-Juhani told him the following story in person:

We left Mecca with the Messenger of God. The people asked the Prophet for permission to return to their families, and he granted their request. Suddenly, the Prophet said: 'Why do you detest the side of this tree, which is adjacent to the Messenger of God, and not the other side of the tree?' All the people started to cry. Abu Bakr the righteous said: 'Whoever asks for a permission to leave after hearing your words is a fool.' The Prophet stood up, praised the Lord, said the *shahāda*, and pronounced the following oath:

> By God who grasps my soul in His hand, I hereby swear before God that each one of you who believes in God and in the Final Day, will be guided by God and led to Heaven. My Lord has promised me that He will let

> seventy thousand members of my *Umma* to Paradise without judging their deeds or punishing them for their deeds. I do hope that you will enter Paradise and live there. I do hope that your wives, children, and the other dwellers of your residence will enter Paradise.

Then he said:

> Each night, at the last third of the night, our Lord the Blessed and Sublime descends to the lower heaven and says: 'No one but Me can fulfil the wishes of My servants. Who calls for Me [in his prayer] that I may answer? Who is in need of something that I may grant? Who is asking for My forgiveness, so I forgive him?'[1]

2. The Lengthy *Ḥadīth al-Ruʾya*

Abu 'l-Qasim ᶜAbd Allah ibn Muhammad ibn ᶜAbd al-ᶜAziz al-Baghawi (d. 929) told us that he heard the following *ḥadīth* from Hudba ibn Khalid (d. sometime between 849 and 851): Hammad ibn Salama (d. 784) told us the following story on the authority of ᶜAli ibn Zayd (d. 748) who quoted ᶜUmara al-Qurashi (death date unknown) who in turn quoted Abu Burda (d. *c.* 721–3), the son of Abu Musa al-Ashᶜari. Abu Burda testified:

I was sent [as head of the Kufan delegation] to al-Walid ibn ᶜAbd al-Malik. ᶜUmar ibn ᶜAbd al-ᶜAziz was in charge of providing for all my needs. When I accomplished my mission, I came to ᶜUmar and bade him farewell. I then went on my way, when suddenly I recalled a *ḥadīth* my father had once told me, a *ḥadīth* he had heard from the Messenger of God. I wanted to recount it to ᶜUmar who kindly took care of my needs. So I returned to him. When he saw me, he said: 'The sheikh remembered that he needs something else, and that is why he returned.' I approached him, and he said: 'What made you return? Have you not accomplished your mission?' I said: 'Yes, of course. However, there is a *ḥadīth* that I heard from my father, who in turn heard it from the Prophet, and I wished to recount it to you, because you were so kind to me.' He said: 'What is it?' And I said: 'My father told me that he heard the Messenger of God say:

> When the Day of Resurrection arrives, [the idols] that each nation used to worship in this world will be presented before them. Each nation will

> approach [the idol] that they used to worship in this world, and only the monotheists (*ahl al-tawḥīd*) will remain. Someone will then say to them: 'What are you waiting for, when everyone else has already gone?' And they will answer: 'We have a lord whom we used to worship in the material world, but we have never seen him.' They will be asked: 'Will you know him when you see him?' They will say: 'Yes.' They will be asked: 'So, how will you recognize him, when you have never seen him?' They will answer: 'Because there is nothing similar to him.' Suddenly, the curtain will be drawn in front of them, and they will see God, the mighty and powerful. Immediately they will prostrate themselves on the ground – all, but a group of people who will want to prostrate themselves but will be unable to do so, because their backs will be stuck and erect like cattle's horns. This [scene] will be exactly as described in the Quranic verse (Q. 68:42): 'On the day when the dread event unfolds and they are told to prostrate themselves, they will be unable.' So God will say to them: 'Raise your heads up, because for each and every one of you I marked a substitute who is either a Jew or a Christian, to be sent instead of you to Hell.'

ᶜUmar ibn ᶜAbd al-ᶜAziz said: 'Allah, there is no god but Him! Did your father tell you this *ḥadīth*? Did he hear it from the Prophet?' [Abu Burda said]: At his request, I made an oath in his presence three times, and then ᶜUmar ibn ᶜAbd al-ᶜAziz said: 'I have never heard a *ḥadīth* about the monotheists that I loved better than this one.'[2]

3. The Lengthy *Ḥadīth Fidāʾ al-Muʾmin* from Ibn ᶜAsakir's *Tārīkh Dimashq*

i. Saᶜid ibn Abi Burda

The source of this story is the man of letters al-Hasan ibn ᶜAbd al-Malik Abu ᶜAbd Allah al-Khallal (d. 1138). How this story came to the attention of Ibn ᶜAsakir is unknown. The narrator is Abu Burda's grandson, ᶜAbd al-Rahman ibn Saᶜid ibn Abi Burda, whose father, Saᶜid, told him that Abu Burda was sent to ᶜUmar [ibn ᶜAbd al-ᶜAziz] or Sulayman [ibn al-Walid]. The story presents Saᶜid's point of view:

> After his needs were taken care of, [Abu Burda] said to me in the middle of the night: 'Wake up!' I woke up. [Abu Burda] went to the house of

the governor and knocked on his gate. The gatekeeper said: 'Who is it?' And he replied: 'Abu Burda, ask [the governor's] permission that I enter.' The gatekeeper replied: '[The governor] already retired to bed.' Abu Burda replied: 'Let him know that I am waiting at his gate.' The gatekeeper let [the governor] know, and the latter went out to meet Abu Burda. Abu Burda asked for permission to enter. The governor asked: 'Is something wrong, Abu Burda?' Abu Burda replied: 'Everything is fine.' The governor asked: 'What is it that you want?' Abu Burda replied: 'I finished my business, but I remembered a *ḥadīth* that my father had told me. And here it is: The Messenger of God said: When the people will be gathered for Judgement Day, a Jew or a Christian will be brought, and [a voice] will say: Oh believer! This is the sacrifice that will redeem you from Hell.' The governor asked: 'Did you hear it from your father?' Abu Burda said: 'I heard it from my father.'[3]

ii. A Family Member of Talha ibn ᶜUbayd Allah

One of Ibn ᶜAsakir's sources in *Tārīkh Dimashq* is the Sufi and *muḥaddith* Abu Sahl Muhammad ibn Ibrahim ibn Saᶜdawayh al-Muzakki (d. c. 1136) from Isfahan. Abu Sahl transmitted the following story to Ibn ᶜAsakir. The narrator is an anonymous family member of the prominent *ṣaḥābī* Talha ibn ᶜUbayd Allah (d. 656):

I was at ᶜUmar ᶜAbd al-ᶜAziz's humble home when Abu Burda the son of Abu Musa al-Ashᶜari entered. ᶜUmar said: 'Tell us a few *aḥādīth* that you heard concerning the sayings of the Messenger of God.' Abu Burda replied: 'I heard my father say: The Messenger of God said: My nation is a nation blessed by the compassion of God: God allowed them to inflict punishment on themselves in this world. However, on the Day of Resurrection, when the members of all religions will be assembled, each man will be given another man which will be his sacrifice in Hell.' ᶜUmar ordered that the inkwell and paper be brought to him, and he made sure this *ḥadīth* was written down.[4]

iii. Qudama ibn Hamata al-Dabbi from Kufa

Another prominent source of Ibn ᶜAsakir in *Tārīkh Dimashq* is the *muḥaddith* Abu ᶜAli al-Hasan ibn Ahmad ibn al-Hasan al-Haddad al-Muqriᵓ (d. 1122) from Isfahan. He transmitted the following story to Ibn ^{c}Asakir, with the Kufan Qudama ibn Hamata al-Dabbi as a narrator:

> I was sitting at ^{c}Umar ^{c}Abd al-^{c}Aziz's humble home when suddenly Abu Burda, the son of Abu Musa entered, and told ^{c}Umar ibn ^{c}Abd al-^{c}Aziz that he once heard his father tell the following *ḥadīth* on the authority of the Prophet, who said: 'In the Day of Resurrection, the Jew and the Christian will be brought, and a voice will say: "Oh Muslim, this is the sacrifice that will redeem you from Hell."' ^{c}Umar ibn ^{c}Abd al-^{c}Aziz said to Abu Burda: 'Allah, there is no god but Him! Did you hear your father tell this *ḥadīth* on the authority of the Messenger of God?' [Abu Burda] said: 'Allah, there is no god but Him! My father indeed told me this *ḥadīth*, and he in his turn heard it from the Messenger of God.' [Qudama said]: I then saw ^{c}Umar ibn ^{c}Abd al-^{c}Aziz prostrate himself in adoration three times.[5]

Notes

1. Ibn Khuzayma, *Kitāb al-Tawḥīd*, pp. 312–15, *ḥadīth* 39. Three distorted versions appear in al-Ṭabarānī, *al-Mu^{c}jam al-Kabīr*, vol. 5, pp. 49–51, *aḥādīth* 4556–9.
2. Al-Ājurrī, *Kitāb al-Sharī^{c}a*, p. 278, *ḥadīth* 607. For a different version, see al-Ājurrī, *Kitāb al-taṣdīq*, p. 80; al-Ṭabarānī, *Al-Mu^{c}jam al-Kabīr*, vol. 9, p. 418.
3. Ibn ^{c}Asakir, *Tārīkh Dimashq*, vol. 26, p. 47.
4. Ibn ^{c}Asākir, *Tārīkh Dimashq*, vol. 25, pp. 134–5.
5. Ibn ^{c}Asākir, *Tārīkh Dimashq*, vol. 49, pp. 301–2.

Appendix II
Full Translation of 'the *Ḥadīth* of Allegiance' of Abu Razin

Abu Razin's '*ḥadīth* of allegiance' is located in Ahmad ibn Hanbal's (d. 855) *Musnad*. The *Musnad* is a voluminous Hadith compilation that was in fact edited by Ahmad ibn Hanbal's son, ᶜAbd Allah (d. 903). ᶜAbd Allah included in this compilation a letter that he received from the Medinese *muḥaddith* Ibrahim ibn Hamza al-Zubayri (d. 845). The letter opens with a statement about the *muḥaddithūn* who transmitted this *ḥadīth*. The following is a translation of the text:

ᶜAbd Allah ibn Ahmad said: Ibrahim ibn Hamza ibn Muhammad ibn Hamza ibn Musᶜab ibn al-Zubayr al-Zubayri wrote to me the following words: 'I am writing this *ḥadīth* to you. I rigorously recorded this work in the exact wording that I heard it. I ask you to transmit this *ḥadīth* in my name. The *muḥaddith* who taught me this *ḥadīth* was ᶜAbd al-Rahman ibn al-Mughira al-Hizami (a Medinese *muḥaddith*, died between 816 and 826). Al-Hizami heard this *ḥadīth* from ᶜAbd al-Rahman ibn ᶜAyyash al-Samaᶜi al-Ansari al-Qubaᵓi (a Medinese *muḥaddith*, death date unknown) from the clan of ᶜAmr ibn ᶜAwf. ᶜAbd al-Rahman ibn ᶜAyyash heard this *ḥadīth* from Dalham ibn al-Aswad ibn ᶜAbd Allah ibn ᶜAmir ibn al-Muntafiq al-ᶜUqayli (death date unknown). Dalham heard the *ḥadīth* from his father, al-Aswad. The father heard the *ḥadīth* from his uncle, Abu Razin Laqit ibn ᶜAmir. This is what Dalham recounted: My father, al-Aswad, told me the following *ḥadīth* which he heard from Abu Razin's son, ᶜAsim. He told me that Laqit was sent by his tribe as a delegate to the Messenger of God. His friend, Nahik ibn ᶜAsim ibn al-Muntafiq, accompanied him on his journey. This is what Laqit recounted:

> My friend and I were travelling. By the end of the month of Rajab we arrived in the city of the Messenger of God. We entered the Prophet's mosque and approached him shortly after he completed the morning prayer. The Prophet stood in front of the people and preached to them. He said: 'O people, hear me well! I refrained from talking to you in the last four days. But hear me well! I am now going to speak to you. Hear me well! Is there someone whose tribe sent him [to me], saying: "Tell us what the Messenger of God says?" Is there among you a person whose mind is diverted by his own thoughts or by what his friends say? Is there among you someone whose mind is diverted by misguidance? Hear me well! You can ask me [anything], have I not told you? Hear me well! Hear me well, so you will live. Hear me well! Sit down! Sit down!'

Laqit continued his story:

> The people sat down, and I and my friend stood there, until the Prophet's mind opened to us and his eyes fell on us. I asked: 'Oh Messenger of God, what have you from the knowledge of the invisible?' By the Eternal God! The Prophet laughed and shook his head, because he already knew that I wished to trick him. Finally, the Prophet said: 'God used keys to lock five secrets that only He knows,' and he gestured with his hand the number five. I asked: 'What are these five secrets?' The Prophet answered: 'He knows the destiny of each and every one of you, and you do not. He knows when the sperm enters the womb, and you do not. He knows what will happen tomorrow, and what you will eat tomorrow, and you do not. He knows when the rain will fall. He watches you when you are wretched, afraid and long for compassion. And all this time He keeps on laughing, because He knows that the time for the change in your situation is near.'

Laqit said:

> I responded: 'A Lord who laughs benevolently will never deprive us of His bounty'. To the five secrets known only to God, the Prophet added a sixth: 'He knows when the Day of Resurrection comes.'

Laqit said:

> I asked: 'Oh Messenger of God, please teach us some of the things that you teach your people, things that they have no knowledge of. Because we belong to a clan whose rights no one acknowledges: neither the tribesmen of Madhhij who consider themselves above us, nor the tribesmen of Khathᶜam who patronize us. Not even our own tribesmen acknowledge our rights.' The Prophet responded: 'You will remain in the same situation for a long time. Thereafter, your Prophet will die. However, you will continue to remain in the same situation for a long time. Thereafter, the Cry will come.[1] By the everlasting existence of your Eternal God! The Cry will reach every living soul on earth and kill it. The angels will accompany your Lord while He will move about the earth, and the earth will be devoid of life. Thereafter, your Lord the Almighty will order the heaven that surrounds the throne to pour rain. By the everlasting existence of your Eternal God! This rain will reach every patch of land which is the resting place of every slaughtered person. This rain will reach every grave in which a dead person lies. And each and every patch of land and grave will cleave and push out the dead person who lies in it. The dead person will sit erect. Your Lord will ask: "How do you feel? Do you feel any different?" And the newly resurrected person will answer: "Today seems just like yesterday", because he will feel that he departed his people only recently.'

Laqit said:

> So I asked the Prophet: 'Oh Messenger of God! How will He be able to assemble us when our decaying corpses will be torn out by the winds and the wild beasts?' The Prophet answered: 'I will tell you by using a similar example from God's blessings. Sometimes you look at the face of the earth that was worn out and shabby with its dry clods, and say: "This earth will never live again." Thereafter your Lord sends rain to this earth. Within a few days you will look at the face of the earth again, and suddenly you will see it soft and moist, covered with greenery. By God! Is He not the most capable to summon the dead from the water like He summoned the plants of the earth to appear? And so they will come out from beneath the stones and from their resting places, they will look at Him, and He will look at them.'

Laqit continued:

> I said: 'Oh Messenger of God, how is it possible that in the Day of Resurrection we will look at Him and He will look at us, and there will be so many of us in the land while He is but one person?' The Prophet answered: 'I will tell you by using a similar example from God's blessings. The sun and the moon are both signs from Him, and they are small. You see both of them and they see all of you at the same time, and you do not differ one from the other in seeing them. By your Eternal God! There is no doubt that He has more power to make you all see Him and see all of you than the sun and the moon have, and all the same, you see both of them and they see all of you at the same time, and you do not differ one from the other in seeing them.'
>
> I said: 'Oh Messenger of God, what is our Lord going to do to us when we meet Him?' The Prophet answered: 'You will be presented to Him with your heads uncovered; no secret will be hidden from Him. He will then take a handful of water in His hand and moisten your faces. By God! Not a drop will miss your faces: the drops will make the Muslim's face as white as a piece of cotton, but it will leave the heretic's nose as black as a lump of coal. Then your Prophet will start walking, and the righteous will follow him. They will cross a bridge of fire. One of them will step on the live coal and cry out in pain. God will then say: 'This man's time has come.' Hear me well! Upon reaching Paradise, you will see the Prophet's basin. You will be dying of thirst, desperate to gulp its water. By God! When you reach out your hand, you will all of a sudden find a tumbler in it to help you cleanse yourselves from your excrements, urine, and dirt. The sun and the moon will vanish, you will see neither of them, so there will be no light while you cleanse yourselves.' I said: 'And with what will we see?' The Prophet answered: 'With the same organ you use today in order to see, just before the sun rises and shines on the earth and mountains.'

Laqit continued:

> I said: 'Oh Messenger of God, how are we going to be rewarded for our good deeds and punished for our bad deeds?' He answered: 'You will be rewarded ten times for a good deed. You will receive ten times its equal. For

> the bad deed you will be punished one time its equal unless God forgives you.'

Laqit continued:

> I said: 'Oh Messenger of God, tell me about Paradise and Hell.' He said: 'By God! Hell has seven gates. The distance between one hemistich of the gate to the other hemistich takes seventy years when one is mounted on a horse. Paradise has eight gates. The distance between one hemistich of the gate to the other hemistich takes seventy years when one is mounted on a horse.'

Laqit continued:

> I said: 'Oh Messenger of God, what is the view that we will see in Paradise?' He said: 'You will see rivers of clarified honey, and rivers of wine that do not inflict headache or intoxication on its drinker, and rivers of milk forever fresh, and rivers of water undefiled. You will have fruit that – By God! – you have never tasted before. These fruits will come in pairs.[2] There you will see chaste spouses.'[3] So I said: 'Will we be entitled to take these spouses? Will there be righteous women among these spouses?' He answered: 'The righteous women will be given to the righteous men. You will take pleasure in them like you do in this life, and they will take pleasure in you but will never bear children.'

Laqit continued:

> I said: 'What will be our ultimate goal?' The Prophet did not respond. So I said: 'What am I committed to when I pledge allegiance to you?' The Prophet extended his hand and said: 'You are committed to perform the prayers, to give the alms, to distance yourself from the idolater, and to never be an idolater.' I said: 'What land will be given to us between the east and the west?' The Prophet clenched his fist because he thought I was trying to demand that he promise me a patch of land which he did not want to give me. So I clarified: 'We need a piece of land so we are able to inhabit whichever territory we desire, and dwell in solitude, so each man will conduct his life and harm no one but himself.' Upon hearing my words, the Prophet spread his clenched fist and said: 'This land is yours. You will inhabit which-

ever territory you desire, and dwell in solitude, so if any harm is inflicted on you, it will come from your own hands.'

Laqit continued:

We pledged our allegiance to him. We were preparing to take our leave when all of a sudden the Prophet said: 'By God! These two (namely, Laqit and his friend) are the most pious of all people of this world and the hereafter.' Ka^{c}b ibn al-Khudariyya from the clan of Abu Bakr ibn Kilab asked: 'Who are the most devout people, oh Messenger of God?' The Prophet responded: 'The most deserving of all people for this title are the Banu al-Muntafiq.'

Laqit continued:

So, as I said, we took our leave, but then I approached him again and said: 'Is there any good in the afterlife that is promised to those who died in the days of the *Jāhiliyya*, namely prior to the advent of the Prophet, while they were still infidels?' One of the people of Quraysh exclaimed: 'By God! Your ancestor, al-Muntafiq, is in Hell!'

Laqit described:

I felt as if my skin, my face, and my entire body burnt because of what he said about my father in front of all these people. I almost cried: 'And what about your father, Oh Messenger of God?', but I thought about this matter for a while, and asked in a more polite manner: 'And what about your family, oh Messenger of God?' He answered: 'My family is also included in this miserable fate. By God! When you stumble upon a grave of an infidel from the tribe of ^{c}Amir or Quraysh, you must say: "Muhammad sent me to tell you about the wretched fate that awaits you: You will be dragged to the fire with your face and belly down."'

Laqit continued:

I said: 'Oh Messenger of God, why did they deserve this lot when their deeds were all good and they were regarded as benevolent people?' He answered: 'This is because God sent a prophet to the last of seven nations. Whoever disobeyed his prophet was considered among the misguided people; whoever obeyed his prophet was considered one of those people who was shown the true path.'[4]

Notes

1. 'The Cry' (*al-ṣayḥa*), which is one of the events that will occur in the Last Day is mentioned in Q. 11:67, 11:94, 15:73,15:83 and 23:41.
2. Cf. Q. 47:15.
3. Cf. Q. 2:25.
4. Ibn Ḥanbal, *Musnad*, vol. 26, pp. 121–35, *ḥadīth* 16206; Ibn Khuzayma, *Kitāb al-Tawḥīd*, pp. 460–76.

Appendix III
Chains of Transmission

Chart 1a

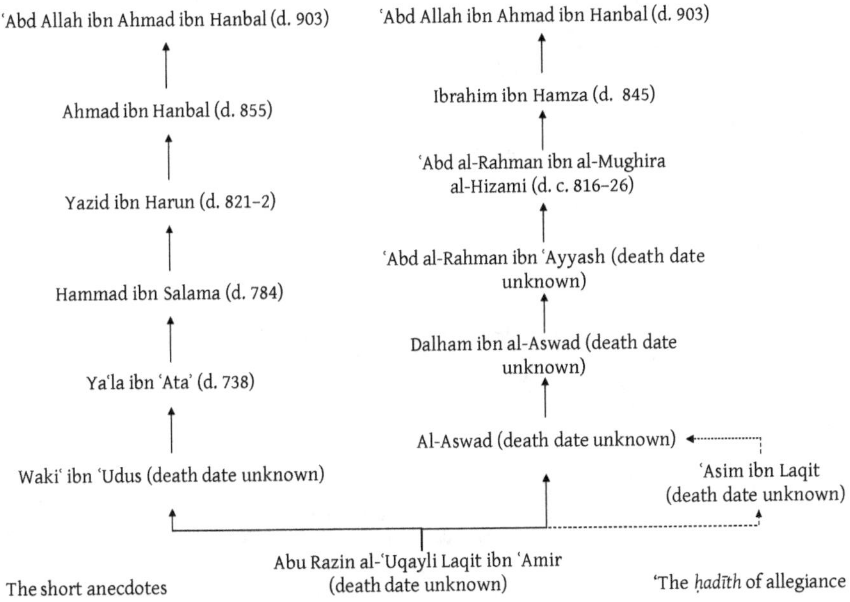

The Abu Razin Corpus
Al-Ṭayālisī, *Musnad*, vol. 2, pp. 414–19; Ibn Ḥanbal, *Musnad*, vol. 26, pp. 100–20

Chart 1b

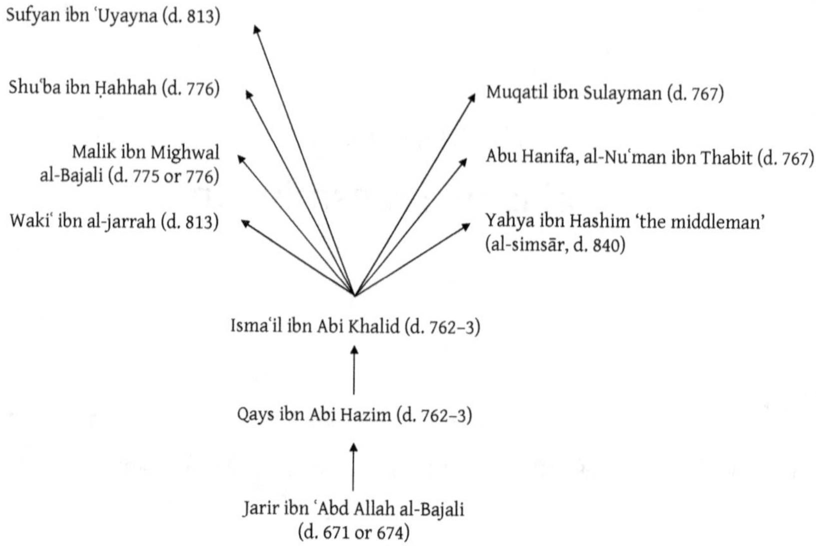

Jarir's *ḥadīth al-ru'ya*
Al-Ājurrī, *Kitāb al-Sharīʿa*, pp. 272–3 (*ḥadīth* 592–4)

Chart 2a

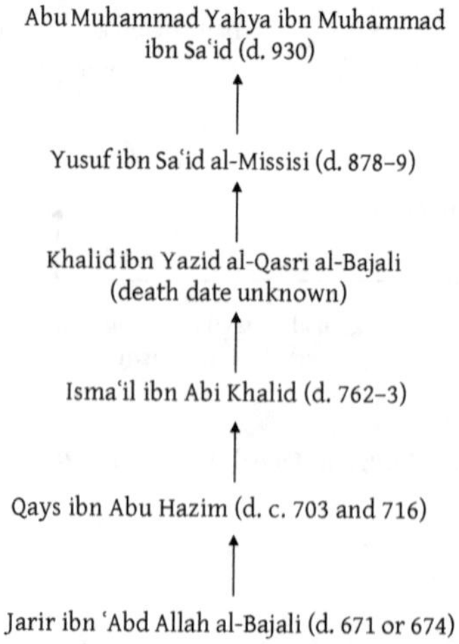

The dialogue between Muhammad and the archangel Gabriel – Jarir's version
Al-Ajurri, *Kitab al-Sharia*, p. 196, *hadith* 380

Chart 2b

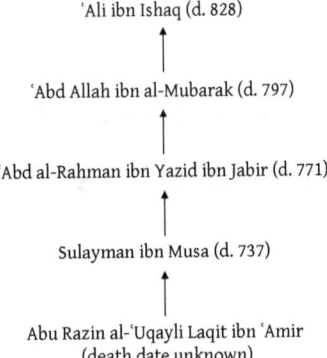

ʿAli ibn Ishaq (d. 828)

↑

ʿAbd Allah ibn al-Mubarak (d. 797)

↑

ʿAbd al-Rahman ibn Yazid ibn Jabir (d. 771)

↑

Sulayman ibn Musa (d. 737)

↑

Abu Razin al-ʿUqayli Laqit ibn ʿAmir
(death date unknown)

The dialogue between Muhammad and the archangel Gabriel – Abu Razin's version
Ibn Ḥanbal, *Musnad*, vol. 26 pp. 113–14, *ḥadīth* 16194

Appendix IV
Chains of Transmission

Chart 1

Muhammad ibn Yahya al-Dhuhli (d. 872)

↑

ʿAbd Allah ibn Yazid al-Muqriʾ (d. c. 828)

↑

Yazid, al-Muqriʾ's father

↑

Harmala ibn ʿImran (d. 776)

↑

Abu Yunus Sulaym ibn Jubayr (d. 740–1)

↑

Abu Hurayra (d. 678)

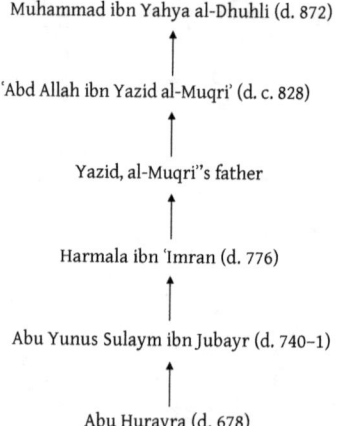

The Abu Hurayra *ḥadīth*
Ibn Khuzayma, *Kitāb al-Tawḥīd*, pp. 97–8

Chart 2

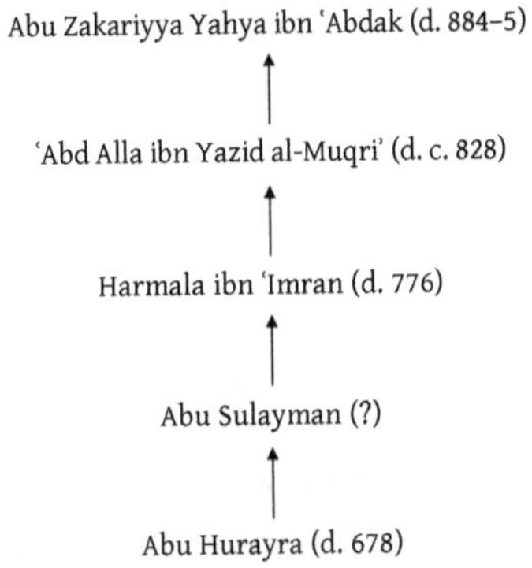

The Abu Hurayra *ḥadīth*
Ibn Abī *Ḥātim*, *Tafsīr*, vol. 3, p. 987 (interpretation of Q 4: 58).
Also quoted by Ibn Kathīr, *Tafsīr*, vol. 2, pp. 341–2

Chart 3

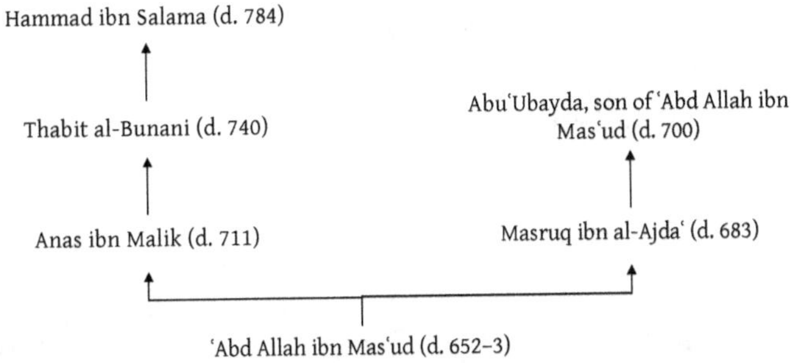

The Laughter *ḥadīth* attributed to ʿAbd Allah ibn Masʿud
Al-Ājurrī, *Kitāb al-Sharīʿa*, p. 298, *ḥadīth* 647; *Ṣaḥīḥ Muslim*, p. 104, *ḥadīth* 310/187 (*Kitāb al-īmān, bāb adnā ahl al-janna manzilatan fīhā*)
Al-Ṭabarānī, *al-Muʿjam al-Kabīr*, vol. 9, pp. 416–21, *ḥadīth* 9763; Ibn Qayyim al-Jawziyya, *Ḥādī al-Arwāḥ*, p. 643

Chart 4

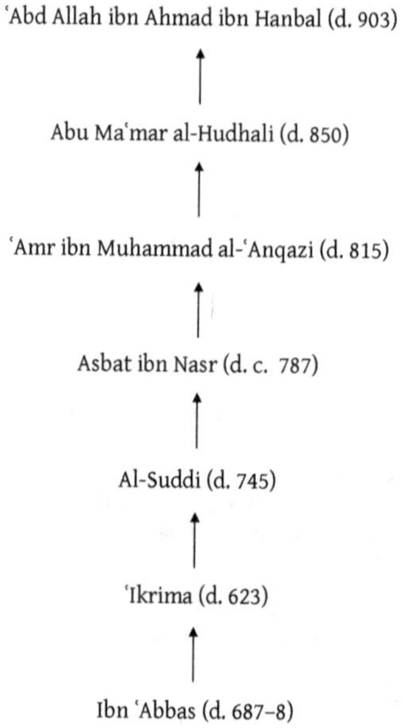

The ibn ʿAbbas version
ʿAbd Allāh ibn Aḥmad ibn Ḥanbal, *al-Sunna*, vol. 1, pp. 270–1 (*ḥadīth* 504); vol. 2, p. 498 (*ḥadīth* 1149)

Chart 5

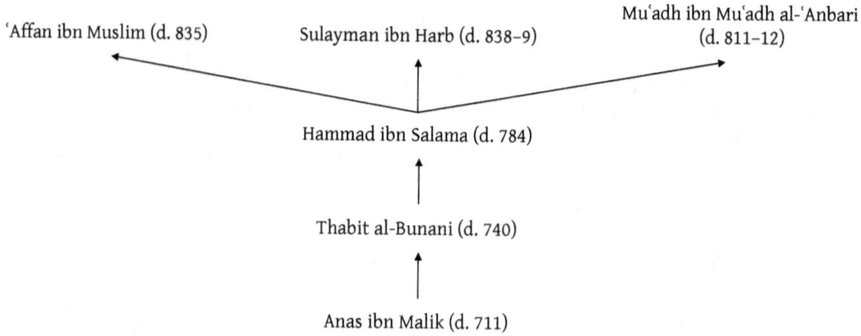

The Anas ibn Malik *ḥadīth*
Ibn Khuzayma, *Kitāb al-Tawḥīd*, p. 261, *ḥadīth* 4–165; Al-Tirmidhī, *Sunan*, vol. 5, p. 261, *ḥadīth* 3074 (*kitāb al-tafsīr, bāb wa-min sūrat al-aʿraf*); Ibn Ḥanbal , *Musnad*, vol. 19, p. 281, *ḥadīth* 12260 (*musnad Anas*); Ibn Khuzayma, *Kitāb al-Tawḥīd*, p. 260, *ḥadīth* 2–163

Chart 6

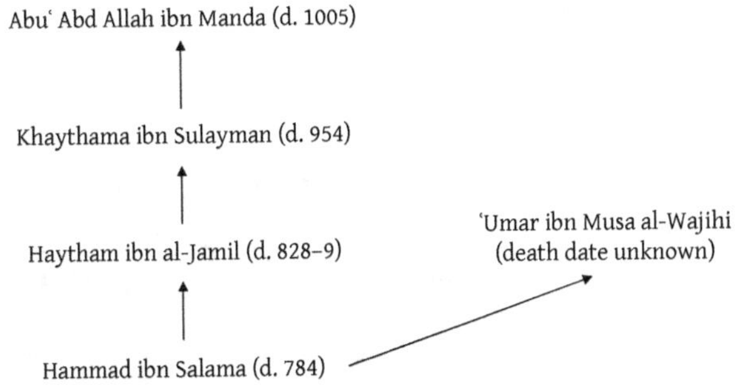

The Anas ibn Malik *ḥadīth*
Ibn 'Asākir, *Tārikh Dimashq*, vol. 45, p. 349 (the biography of 'Umar ibn Musa)

Chart 7

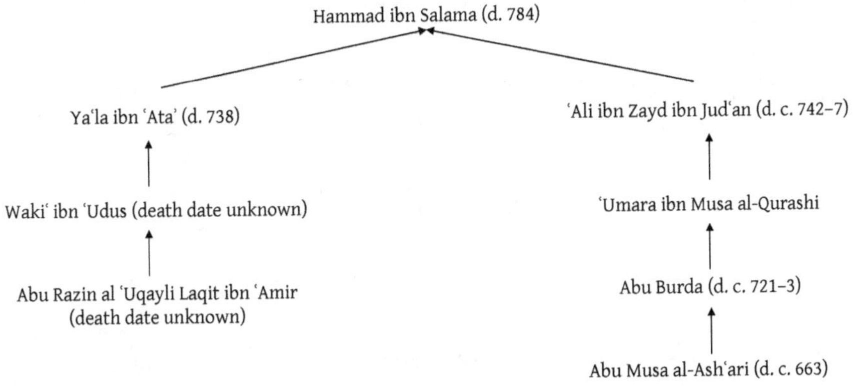

Two versions of *ḥadīth* al-ru'ya
Al-Ajurri, *Kitāb al-Sharī'a*, pp. 277–8 (*ḥadīth* 605–6)
Al-Ajurri, *Kitāb al-Sharī'a*, pp. 278–9 (*ḥadīth* 607–8)

Appendix V
Chains of Transmission

Chart 1

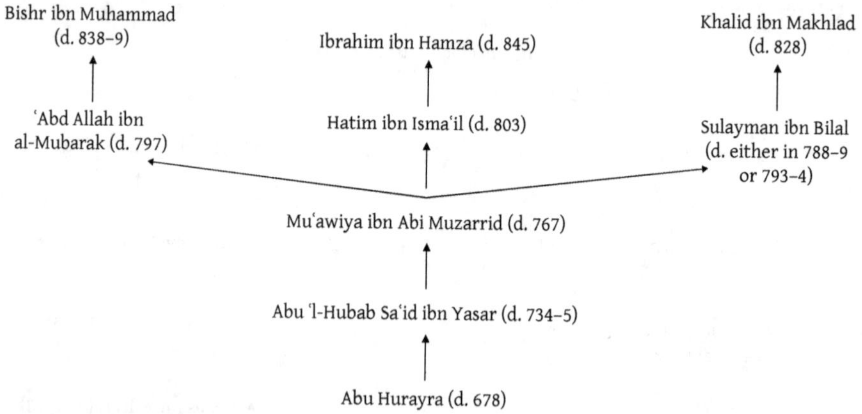

Ḥadīth ḥaqw al-raḥmān **– full version**
Al-Bukhārī, *al-Jāmiʿ al-Ṣaḥīḥ*, vol. 3, p. 292, *ḥādīth* 4830–2 (*Kitāb al-tafsīr, bāb wa-tuqaṭṭiʿū arḥāmakum*); al-Bukhārī, *al-Tārīkh al-Kabīr*, vol. 4, p. 335

Chart 2

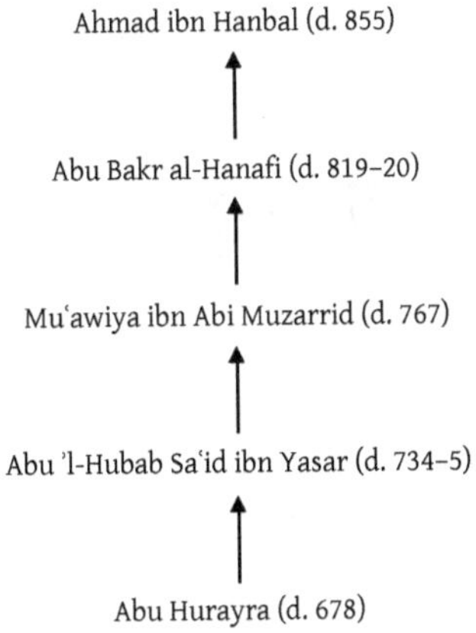

Ḥadīth ḥaqw al-raḥmān – full version
Ibn Ḥanbal, *Musnad*, vol. 14, p. 103, *ḥadīth* 8367 (the *Musnad* of Abu Hurayra)

Chart 3

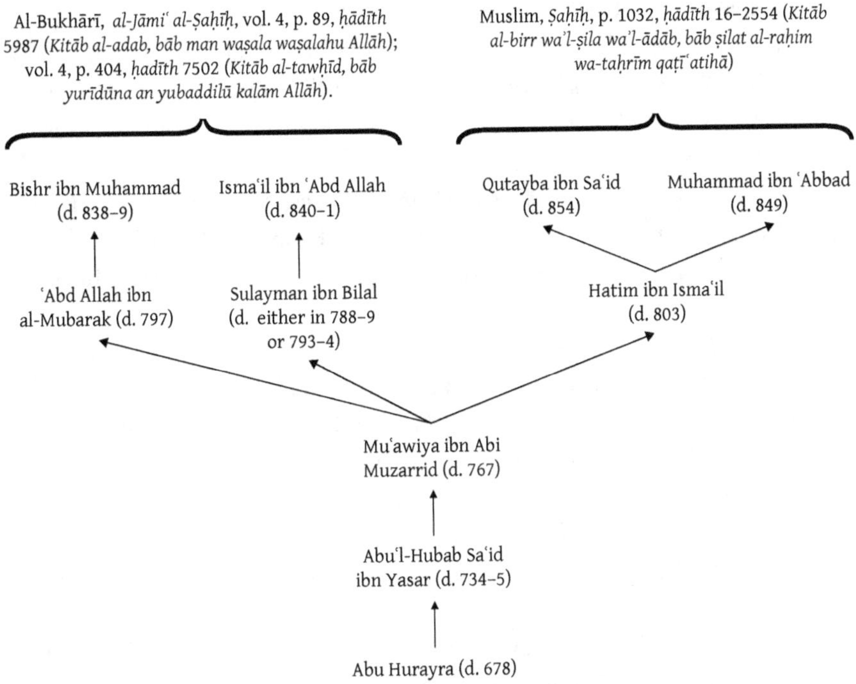

Ḥadīth ḥaqw al-raḥmān **– censored version**

Bibliography

I. Primary Sources

Abū Dāwūd, Sulaymān ibn al-Ash^c^ath al-Sijistānī, *Sunan Abī Dāwud*, ed. Muḥammad al-Rājiḥī (Riyadh: Bayt al-Afkār al-Dawliyya, 1420/1999).

Abū 'l-Shaykh al-Iṣbahānī, Abū Muḥammad ^c^Abd Allāh ibn Muḥammad ibn Ja^c^far ibn al-Ḥayyān, *Kitāb al-^c^Aẓama*, ed. Riḍā^o^ Allāh ibn Muḥammad Idrīs al-Mubārakfūrī (Riyadh: Dār al-^c^Āṣima, 1408/[1987]).

Abū Ya^c^lā, Muḥammad ibn al-Ḥusayn ibn Muḥammad ibn al-Farrā^o^, *Ibṭāl al-Ta^o^wīlāt li-Akhbār al-Ṣifāt*, ed. Abū ^c^Abd Allāh Muḥammad ibn Muḥammad al-Ḥamūd al-Najdī (Kuwait: Dār Īlāf al-Duwaliyya li'l-Nashr wa'l-Tawzī^c^, [1410/1989]).

Aḥmad ibn Muḥammad ibn Ḥanbal, *Kitāb al-^c^Ilal wa-Ma^c^rifat al-Rijāl*, ed. Waṣī Allāh ibn Muḥammad ^c^Abbās (Riyadh: Dār al-Khānī, 1422/2001).

———, *Musnad al-Imām Aḥmad*, eds. Shu^c^ayb al-Arnā^o^ūṭ *et al.* (Beirut: Mu^o^assasat al-Risāla, 1416/1995).

———, *Al-Radd ^c^alā 'l-Jahmiyya wa'l-Zanādiqa*, ed. Ṣabrī ibn Salāma Shāhīn (Riyadh: Dār al-Thabāt li'l-Nashr wa'l-Tawzī^c^, 1424/2003).

Al-Ājurrī, Abū Bakr Muḥammad ibn al-Ḥusayn ibn ^c^Abd Allāh, *Kitāb al-Sharī^c^a*, eds Editorial Board of Mu^o^assasat al-Rayyān (Beirut: Mu^o^assast al-Rayyān, 1421/2000).

———, *Kitāb al-Taṣdīq bi'l-Naẓar ilā Allāh Ta^c^ālā fī al-Ākhira*, ed. Muḥammad Ghayyāth al-Junbāz (Riyadh: Dār ^c^Ālam al-Kutub li'l-Nashr wa'l-Tawzī^c^, 1406/1986).

Al-Ash^c^arī, Abu 'l-Ḥasan ^c^Alī ibn Ismā^c^īl, *Al-Ibāna ^c^an Uṣūl al-Diyāna*, no editor mentioned (Beirut: Dār Ibn Zaydūn, n.d.).

———, *Kitāb Maqālāt al-Islāmiyyīn wa-'khtilāf 'l-Muṣallīn*, ed. Hellmut Ritter (Wiesbaden: Franz Steiner Verlag, 1963).

Al-ᶜAynī, Badr al-Dīn Abū Muḥammad Maḥmūd ibn Aḥmad, *ᶜUmdat al-Qārī Sharḥ Ṣaḥīḥ al-Bukhārī*, ed. ᶜAbd Allāh Maḥmūd Muḥammad ᶜUmar (Beirut: Dār al-Kutub al-ᶜIlmiyya, 1421/2001).

Al-Baghawī, Abu 'l-Qāsim ᶜAbd Allāh ibn Muḥammad ibn ᶜAbd al-ᶜAzīz, *Muᶜjam al-Ṣaḥāba*, ed. Muḥammad al-Amīn Muḥammad Maḥmūd (Kuwait: Maktabat Dār al-Bayān, 1420/2000).

Al-Baghawī, al-Ḥusayn ibn Masᶜūd, *Sharḥ al-Sunna*, ed. Shuᶜayb al-Arnāᵓūṭ (Damascus-Beirut: al-Maktab al-Islāmī, 1403/1983, 2nd edn).

Al-Balādhurī, Abu 'l-ᶜAbbās Aḥmad ibn Yaḥyā ibn Jābir, *Futūḥ al-Buldān*, eds ᶜAbd Allāh Anīs al-Ṭabbāᶜ and ᶜUmar Anīs al-Ṭabbāᶜ (Beirut: Muᵓassasat al-Maᶜārif, 1407/1987).

Al-Barbahārī, Abū Muḥammad al-Ḥasan ibn ᶜAlī ibn Khalaf, *Sharḥ al-Sunna*, ed. Abū Yāsir Khālid ibn Qāsim al-Radādī (Medina: Maktabat al-Ghurabāᵓ al-Athriyya, 1414/1993).

Al-Bayḍāwī, Nāṣir al-Dīn ᶜAbd Allāh ibn ᶜUmar, *Tuḥfat al-Abrār Sharḥ Maṣābīḥ al-Sunna*, eds special committee under the supervision of Nūr al-Dīn Ṭālib (Kuwait: Wizārat al-Awqāf wa'l-Shu'ūn al-Islāmiyya, 1433/2012).

Al-Bayhaqī, Abū Bakr Aḥmad ibn al-Ḥusayn, *Al-Jāmiᶜ li-Shuᶜab al-Īmān*, ed. ᶜAbd al-ᶜAlī ᶜAbd al-Ḥamīd Ḥāmid (Riyadh: Maktabat al-Rushd, 1423/2003).

———, *Kitāb al-Asmāᵓ wa'l-Ṣifāt*, ed. ᶜAbd Allāh ibn Muḥammad al-Ḥāshidī (Jedda: Maktabat al-Sawādī lil-Tawzīᶜ, 1993).

———, *Al-Sunan al-Kabīr*, ed. Markaz Hagar li'l-Buḥūth wa'l-Dirāsāt al-ᶜArabiyya wa'l-Islāmiyya (Cairo: Hagar, 1432/2011).

Al-Bazzār, Abu Bakr Aḥmad ibn ᶜAmr ibn ᶜAbd al-Khāliq al-ᶜAtakī, *Al-Baḥr al-Zakhkhār al-Maᶜrūf bi-Musnad al-Bazzār*, ed. ᶜĀdil ibn Saᶜd (Medina: Maktabat al-ᶜUlūm wa'l-Ḥikam, 1426/2005).

Al-Bukhārī, Abū ᶜAbd Allāh Muḥammad ibn Ismāᶜīl, *Al-Jāmiᶜ al-Ṣaḥīḥ*, eds Muḥibb al-Dīn al-Khaṭīb, Muḥammad Fuᵓād ᶜAbd al-Bāqī and Quṣayy Muḥibb al-Dīn al-Khaṭīb (Cairo: al-Maktaba al-Salafiyya, 1400/[1980]).

———, *Kitāb Rafᶜ al-Yadayn fī al-Ṣalāt*, ed. Badr ibn ᶜAbd Allāh al-Badr (Beirut: Dār Ibn Ḥazm, 1416/1996).

———, *Kitāb al-Tārīkh al-Kabīr*, ed. Muḥammad ᶜAbd al-Muᶜīd Khān (Hyderabad-Deccan: The Dairatu'l-Maᶜarif-I Osmania, 1375/1955).

———, *Ṣaḥīḥ al-Imām al-Bukhārī al-Musammā bi'l-Jāmiᶜ al-Musnad al-Mukhtaṣar min Umūr Rasūl Allāh wa-Sunanihi wa-Ayyāmihi*, ed. Muḥammad Zuhayr ibn Nāṣir al-Nāṣir (Beirut: Dār Ṭawq al-Najā, 1422/[2001]).

Al-Dāraquṭnī, Abu 'l-Ḥasan ᶜAli ibn ᶜUmar, *Al-ᶜIlal al-Wārida fī al-Aḥādīth al-Nabawiyya*, vols 1–11, ed. Maḥfūẓ al-Raḥmān Zayn Allāh al-Salafī (Riyadh: Dār Ṭayba, 1405/1985).

———, *Al-ᶜIlal*, vols 12–16, ed. Muḥammad ibn Ṣāliḥ ibn Muḥammad al-Dabāsī (Dammam: Dār Ibn al-Jawzī, 1427/[2006]).

———, *Kitāb al-Nuzūl- Kitāb al-Ṣifāt*, ed. ᶜAlī ibn Muḥammad ibn Nāṣir al-Faqīhī ([Medina: al-Jāmiᶜa al-Islāmiyya], 1403/1983). Published as part of the series *Silsilat ᶜAqāʾid al-Salaf.*

———, *Kitāb al-Ruʾya*, eds Ibrāhīm Muḥammad al-ᶜAlī and Aḥmad Fakhrī al-Rifāᶜī (Zarqa: Maktabat al-Manār, 1411/1990).

Al-Dārimī, ᶜAbd Allāh ibn ᶜAbd al-Raḥmān al-Samarqandī, *Sunan al-Dārimī*, eds Fawāz Aḥmad Zimrlī and Khālid al-Sabᶜ al-ᶜAlamī (Karachi: Qadīmī Kutubkhāne, 1407/[1986]).

Al-Dārimī, ᶜUthmān ibn Saᶜīd, *Naqḍ al-Imām Abī Saᶜīd ᶜUthmān ibn Saᶜīd ᶜalā al-Marīsī al-Jahmī al-ᶜAnīd*, ed. Rashīd ibn Ḥasan al-Almaᶜī (Riyadh: Maktabat al-Rushd and Sharikat al-Riyāḍ li'l-Nashr wa'l-Tawzīᶜ, 1418/1998).

———, *Al-Radd ᶜalā al-Jahmiyya*, ed. Badr al-Badr (Huli, Kuwait: al-Dār al-Salafiyya, 1405/1985).

———, *Radd al-Imām al-Dārimī ᶜUthmān ibn Saᶜīd ᶜalā Bishr al-Marīsī al-ᶜAnīd*, ed. Muḥammad Ḥāmid al-Fiqqī (Beirut: Dār al-Kutub al-ᶜIlmiyyah; a reproduction of Cairo: Maṭbaᶜat Nuṣṣār al-Sunna al-Muḥammadiyya, 1358/1939).

Al-Dhahabī, Shams al-Dīn Abū ᶜAbd Allāh Muḥammad ibn Aḥmad ibn ᶜUthmān, *Al-ᶜIbar fī Khabar Man Ghabar*, ed. Abū Hājir Muḥammad al-Saᶜīd ibn Basyūnī (Beirut: Dār al-Kutub al-ᶜIlmiyya, 1403/1985).

———, *Kitāb al-ᶜArsh wa-Yalīhi Tashabbuh al-Khasīs bi-Ahl al-Khamīs*, ed. Muḥammad Ḥasan Muḥammad Ḥasan Ismāᶜīl (Beirut: Dār al-Kutub al-ᶜIlmiyya, 1424/2003).

———, *Mīzān al-Iᶜtidāl fī Naqd al-Rijāl*, ed. ᶜAlī Muḥammad al-Bijāwī (Beirut: Dār al-Maᶜrifa, 1382/1963).

———, *Siyar Aᶜlām al-Nubalāʾ*, eds Shuᶜayb al-Arnaʾūṭ and Ḥusayn al-Asad (Beirut: Muʾassasat al-Risāla, 1405/1985, 3rd edn).

———, *Tadhkirat al-Ḥuffāẓ*, [ed. ᶜAbd al-Raḥmān ibn Yaḥyā al-Muᶜallimī] (Beirut: Dār al-Kutub al-ᶜIlmiyya, n.d.); a reprint of the Indian edition: Abu ᶜAbdillah Shamsu'd Dīn Adh-Dhahabī, *Kitab Tadhkiratu'l-Huffāz*, ed. Bureau from the Meccan Library Ms. under the Auspices of the Ministry of Education Government of India, ed. in chief M. Nizāmu'd Dīn (Hyderabad-Deccan: The Dairatu'l-Maᶜarif-I Osmania, 1375/1955).

———, *Tārīkh al-Islām*, ed. ᶜUmar ᶜAbd al-Salām Tadmurī (Beirut: Dār al-Kitāb al-ᶜArabī, 1411/1991).

———, *Tārīkh al-Islām*, ed. Bashār ᶜAwwād Maᶜrūf (Beirut: Dār al-Gharb al-Islāmī, 1424/2003).

———, *Al-ᶜUlūw li'l-ᶜAlī al-Ghaffār fī Iḍāḥ Ṣaḥīḥ al-Akhbār wa-Saqīmihā*, ed. Abū Muḥammad Ashraf ibn ᶜAbd al-Maqṣūd (Riyadh: Maktabat Aḍwāᵓ al-Salaf, 1416/1995).

Al-Fīrūzābādī, Majd al-Dīn Muḥammad ibn Yaᶜqūb, *al-Qāmūs al-Muḥīṭ*, ed. Muḥammad Naᶜīm al-ᶜArqasūsī (Beirut: Muᵓassasat al-Risāla, 1426/2005).

Al-Ḥākim al-Nīsabūrī, Abū ᶜAbd Allāh Muḥammad ibn ᶜAbd Allāh, *Maᶜrifat ᶜUlūm al-Ḥadīth wa-Kamiyyat Ajnāsihi*, ed. Aḥmad ibn Fāris al-Salūm (Beirut: Dār Ibn Ḥazm, 1464/2003).

Al-Ḥiṣnī, Taqī al-Dīn Abū Bakr al-Shāfiᶜī al-Dimashqī, *Dafᶜ Shubah Man Shabbaha wa-Tamarrada wa-Nasaba Dhālika ilā al-Sayyid al-Jalīl al-Imām Aḥmad*, ed. ᶜAbd al-Wāḥid Muṣṭafā (Leiden: Dār al-Muṣṭafā, 1424/2003).

———, *Dafᶜ Shubah Man Shabbaha wa-Tamarrada wa-Nasaba Dhālika ilā al-Sayyid al-Jalīl al-Imām Aḥmad*, ed. Muḥammad Zāhid ibn al-Ḥasan al-Kawtharī (Cairo: al-Maktaba al-Azhariyya li'l-Turāth, 2010).

Ibn ᶜAbd al-Barr, Abū ᶜUmar Yūsuf ibn ᶜAbd Allāh ibn Muḥammad al-Namarī al-Andalūsī, *Al-Tamhīd li-mā fī 'l-Muwaṭṭaᵓ mina 'l-Maᶜānī wa'l-Asānīd*, eds Muṣṭafā ibn Aḥmad al-ᶜAlawī and Muḥammad ᶜAbd al-Kabīr al-Bakrī (Morocco: Wizārat ᶜUmūm al-Awqāf wa'l-Shuᵓūn al-Islāmiyya, 1387/1967).

Ibn ᶜAbd al-Hādī, Abū ᶜAbd Allāh Muḥammad ibn Aḥmad ibn ᶜAbd al-Wahhāb, *Al-ᶜUqūd al-Durriyya* (as part of an anthology of biographies entitled *al-Qawl al-Jalī*), ed. Yaḥyā Murād (Beirut: Dār al-Kutub al-ᶜIlmiyya, 1426/2005).

Ibn ᶜAbd Rabbihi, Aḥmad ibn Muḥammad, *Al-ᶜIqd al-Farīd*, ed. ᶜAbd al-Majīd al-Tarḥīnī (Beirut: Dār al-Kutub al-ᶜIlmiyya, 1404/1983).

Ibn Abī Ḥātim, Abū Muḥammad ᶜAbd al-Raḥmān al-Tamīmī al-Ḥanẓalī al-Rāzī, *Kitāb al-ᶜIlal*, eds Saᶜd ibn ᶜAbd Allāh al-Ḥumayyid and Khālid ibn ᶜAbd al-Raḥmān al-Juraysī (Riyadh: Khālid ibn ᶜAbd al-Raḥmān al-Juraysī, 1427/2006).

———, *Kitāb al-Jarḥ wa'l-Taᶜdīl*, [ed. ᶜAbd al-Raḥmān ibn Yaḥyā al-Muᶜallimī al-Yamānī] (Beirut: Dār al-Kutub al-ᶜImiyya, 1372/1953).

———, *Tafsīr al-Qurᵓān al-ᶜAẓīm*, ed. Asᶜad Muḥammad al-Ṭayyib (Mecca-Riyadh: Maktabat Nazār Muṣṭfā al-Bāz, 1417/1997).

Ibn Abī Yaᶜlā, Abu 'l-Ḥusayn Muḥammad, *Ṭabaqāt al-Fuqahāᵓ al-Ḥanābila*, ed. ᶜAlī Muḥammad ᶜUmar (Cairo: Maktabat al-Thaqāfa al-Dīniyya, 1419/1998).

Ibn al-Anbārī, Abu 'l-Barakāt Kamāl al-Dīn ᶜAbd al-Raḥmān ibn Muḥammad, *Nuzhat al-Alibbāᵓ fī Ṭabaqāt al-Udabāᵓ* (Al-Zarqāᵓ: Maktabat al-Manār, 1405/1985).

Ibn ᶜAsākir, Abu 'l-Qāsim ᶜAlī ibn al-Ḥasan ibn Hibat Allāh ibn ᶜAbd Allāh, *Tabyīn Kadhib al-Muftarī fīmā Nusiba ilā al-Imām Abī 'l-Ḥasan al-Ashᶜarī* (Cairo: al-Maktaba al-Azhariyya li'l-Turāth and al-Jazīra li'l-Nashr wa'l-Tawzīᶜ, 2010).

———, *Tārīkh Madīnat Dimashq*, ed. ᶜUmar ibn Gharāma al-ᶜUmrawī *et al.* (Beirut: Dār al-Fikr, 1995–2001).

Ibn al-Athīr, ᶜIzz al-Dīn Abu 'l-Ḥasan ᶜAlī ibn Muḥammad al-Jazarī, *Al-Kāmil fī 'l-Tārīkh*, ed. Muḥammad Yūsuf al-Daqqāq (Beirut: Dār al-Kutub al-ᶜIlmiyya, 1407/1987).

———, *Usd al-Ghāba fī Maᶜrifat al-Ṣaḥāba*, ed. ᶜAlī Muḥammad Muᶜawwaḍ and ᶜĀdil Aḥmad ᶜAbd al-Mawjūd (Beirut: Dār al-Kutub al-ᶜIlmiyya, 1417/1996).

Ibn Baṭṭāl, Abu 'l-Ḥasan ᶜAlī ibn Khalaf al-Qurṭubī, *Sharḥ Ṣaḥīḥ al-Bukhārī*, ed. Abū Tamīm Yāsir ibn Ibrāhīm (Riyadh: Maktabat al-Rushd, 1420/2000).

Ibn Fūrak, Abū Bakr Muḥammad ibn al-Ḥasan al-Iṣbahānī al-Ašᶜarī, *Kitāb Muškil al-Ḥadīṯ aw Taᵓwīl al-Aḫbār al-Mutašābiha* [here *Kitāb Mushkil al-Ḥadīth*], ed. Daniel Gimaret (Damascus: Institut Français d'Études Arabes de Damas, 2003).

———, *Mujarrad Maqālāt al-Shaykh Abī 'l-Ḥasan al-Ashᶜarī*, ed. Daniel Gimaret (Beirut: Dār al-Mashriq, 1987).

Ibn Ḥajar al-ᶜAsqalānī, Abu 'l-Faḍl Aḥmad ibn ᶜAlī Shihāb al-Dīn, *Fatḥ al-Bārī bi-Sharḥ Ṣaḥīḥ al-Imām Abī ᶜAbd Allāh Muḥammad ibn Ismāᶜīl-Bukhārī*, ed. ᶜAbd al-Qādir Shaybat al-Ḥamd (Riyadh: Maktabat al-Malik Fahd al-Waṭaniyya, 1421/2001).

———, *Hady al-Sārī: Muqaddimat Fatḥ al-Bārī*, ed. ᶜAbd al-Qādir Shaybat al-Ḥamd (Riyadh: Maktabat al-Malik Fahd al-Waṭaniyya, 1421/2001).

———, *Līsān al-Mīzān*, ed. ᶜAbd al-Fattāḥ Abū Ghudda (Beirut: Maktabat al-Maṭbūᶜāt al-Islāmiyya, 1423/2002).

———, *Tahdhīb al-Tahdhīb*, eds Ibrāhīm al-Zaybak and ᶜĀdil Murshid (Beirut: Muᵓassasat al-Risāla, 1416/1995).

Ibn Ḥanbal, ᶜAbd Allāh ibn Aḥmad, *Kitāb al-Sunna*, ed. Muḥammad ibn Saᶜīd ibn Sālim al-Qaḥṭānī (Dammam: Dār Ibn al-Qayyim, 1406/1986).

Ibn Ḥanbal, Ḥanbal ibn Isḥāq, *Dhikr Miḥnat al-Imām Aḥmad ibn Ḥanbal*, ed. Muḥammad Naghsh ([Cairo: Maṭbaᶜat Saᶜdī wa-Shandī], 1403/1983).

Ibn Ḥibbān, Abū Ḥātim Muḥammad al-Tamīmī al-Bustī, *al-Iḥsān fī Taqrīb Ṣaḥīḥ ibn Ḥibbān*, ed. Shuᶜayb al-Arnāᵓūṭ (Beirut: Muᵓassasat al-Risāla, 1408/1988).

———, *Kitāb al-Majrūḥīn min al-Muḥaddithīn*, ed. Ḥamdī ibn ᶜAbd al-Majīd ibn Ismāᶜīl al-Salafī (Riyadh: Dār al-Ṣamīᶜī li'l-Nashr wa'l-Tawzīᶜ, 1420/2000).

———, *Kitāb al-Thiqāt*, ed. Muḥammad ᶜAbd al-Muᶜīd Khān (Hyderabad: Maṭbaᶜat Majlis Dāᵓirat al-Maᶜārif al-ᶜUthmāniyya, 1393/1973).

Ibn Hishām, Abū Muḥammad ᶜAbd al-Malik, *Al-Sīra al-Nabawiyya*, ed. ᶜUmar ᶜAbd al-Salām Tadmurī (Beirut: Dār al-Kitāb al-ᶜArabī, 1410/1990).

Ibn al-ᶜImād, Shihāb al-Dīn Abu 'l-Falāḥ ᶜAbd al-Ḥayy ibn Aḥmad ibn Muḥammad al-ᶜAkarrī al-Ḥanbalī al-Dimashqī, *Shadharāt al-Dhahab fī Akhbār Man Dhahab*, eds ᶜAbd al-Qādir al-Arnāᵓūṭ and Maḥmūd al-Arnāᵓūṭ (Damascus-Beirut: Dār Ibn Kathīr, 1412/1991).

Ibn al-Jawzī, Abu 'l-Faraj ᶜAbd al-Raḥmān ibn ᶜAlī ibn Muḥammad, *Kitāb Akhbār al-Ṣifāt*, ed. Merlin Swartz (Leiden: Brill, 2002) [English title: Merlin L. Swartz, *A Medieval Critique of Anthropomorphism: Ibn al-Jawzī's* Kitāb Akhbār aṣ-Ṣifāt (Leiden: Brill, 2002)].

———, *Kitāb al-mawḍūᶜāt min al-aḥādīth al-marfūᶜāt*, ed. Nūr al-Dīn ibn Shukrī ibn ᶜAlī Būyā Jīlār (Riyadh: Aḍwāᵓ al-Salaf, 1418/1997).

———, *Kitāb al-Quṣṣāṣ wa'l-Mudhakkirīn*, ed. Muḥammad ibn Luṭfī al-Ṣabbāgh (Beirut: al-Maktab al-Islāmī, 1403/1983).

———, *Manāqib al-Imām Aḥmad ibn Ḥanbal*, ed. ᶜAbd Allāh ibn ᶜAbd al-Ḥasan al-Turkī (Cairo: Hagar, 1409/1988).

———, *Al-Muntaẓam fī Tārīkh al-Rusul wa'l-Mulūk*, ed. Muḥammad ᶜAbd al-Qādir ᶜAṭā and Muṣṭafā ᶜAbd al-Qādir ᶜAṭā (Beirut: Dār al-Kutub al-ᶜIlmiyya, 1412/1992).

———, *Ṣayd al-Khāṭir*, ed. ᶜAbd al-Qādir Aḥmad ᶜAṭā (Beirut: Dār al-Kutub al-ᶜIlmiyya, 1412/1992).

Ibn Jinnī, Abu 'l-Fatḥ ᶜUthmān, *Al-Khaṣāᵓiṣ*, ed. Muḥammad ᶜAlī al-Najjār (Cairo: Dār al-Kutub al-Miṣriyya, 1952).

Ibn Kathīr, ᶜImād al-Dīn Abu 'l-Fidāᵓ Ismaᶜīl ibn ᶜUmar, *Al-Bidāya wa'l-Nihāya fī al-Tārīkh*. ed. ᶜAbd Allah ibn ᶜAbd al-Muḥsin al-Turkī ([Cairo]: Dār Hagar li'l-Ṭibāᶜa wa'l-Nashr wa'l-Tawzīᶜ wa'l-Iᶜlān, 1424/2003).

———, *Tafsīr al-Qurᵓān al-ᶜAẓīm*, ed. Sāmī ibn Muḥammad al-Salāma (Riyadh: Dār Ṭayyiba li'l-Nashr wa'l-Tawzīᶜ, 1420/1999, 2nd edn).

Ibn Khallikān, Abu'l al-ᶜAbbās Shams al-Dīn Aḥmad, *Wafayāt al-Aᶜyān wa-Anbāᵓ Abnāᵓ al-Zamān*, ed. Iḥsān ᶜAbbās (Beirut: Dār Ṣādir, 1970).

Ibn Khuzayma, Abū Bakr Muḥammad ibn Isḥāq, *Kitāb al-Tawḥīd wa-Ithbāt Ṣifāt al-Rabb ᶜAzza wa-Jalla*, ed. ᶜAbd al-ᶜAzīz ibn Ibrāhīm al-Shahwān (Riyadh: Dār al-Rushd, 1408/1988).

———, *Ṣaḥīḥ Ibn Khuzayma*, ed. Muḥammad Muṣṭafā al-Aᶜẓamī (Beirut-Damascus: al-Maktab al-Islāmī, 1400/[1980]).

Ibn al-Madīnī, ᶜAlī ibn ᶜAbd Allāh ibn Jaᶜfar al-Saᶜdī, *al-ᶜIlal*, ed. Muḥammad Muṣṭafā al-Aᶜẓamī (Beirut-Damascus: al-Maktab al-Islāmī, 1980).

Ibn Māja, Abū ᶜAbd Allāh Muḥammad ibn Yazīd al-Qazwīnī, *Sunan Ibn Māja*, ed. Muḥammad Nāṣir al-Dīn al-Albānī (Riyadh: Maktabat al-Maᶜārif li'l-Nashr wa'l-Tawzīᶜ, 1417/[1996]).

Ibn Manda, Abū ᶜAbd Allāh Muḥammad ibn Isḥāq ibn Muḥammad ibn Yaḥyā, Al-*Radd ᶜalā al-Jahmiyya*, ed. ᶜAlī ibn Muḥammad Nāṣir al-Faqīhī (Medina: Maktabat al-Ghurabāᵓ al-Athariyya, 1402/1982).

Ibn Manjuwayh, Aḥmad ibn ᶜAlī al-Iṣbahānī, *Rijāl Ṣaḥīḥ Muslim*, ed. ᶜAbd Allāh al-Laythī (Beirut: Dār al-Maᶜrifa, 1407/1987).

Ibn Manẓūr, Muḥammad ibn Mukarram, *Lisān al-ᶜArab*, eds ᶜAbd Allāh ᶜAlī al-Kabīr *et al.* (Cairo: Dār al-Maᶜārif, n.d.).

Ibn Qayyim al-Jawziyya, Abū ᶜAbd Allāh Muḥammad ibn Abī Bakr ibn Ayyūb, *Badāᵓiᶜ al-Fawāᵓid*, ed. ᶜAlī ibn Muḥammad al-ᶜImrān (Mecca, Dār ᶜĀlim al-Fawāᵓid, [1424/2003]).

———, *Ḥādī al-Arwāḥ ilā Bilād al-Afrāḥ*, ed. Zāᵓid ibn Aḥmad al-Nushayrī (Mecca: Dār ᶜĀlim al-Fawāᵓid, 1428/[2007]).

———, *Iᶜlām al-Muwaqqiᶜīn ᶜan Rabb al-ᶜĀlamīn*, ed. Abū ᶜUbayda Mashhūr ibn Ḥasan Āl Salmān (Dammam: Dār Ibn al-Jawzī, 1423/[2002–3]).

———, *Al-Kāfiya al-Shāfiya fī al-Intiṣār li'l-Firqa al-Nājiya*, eds Muḥammad ibn ᶜAbd al-Raḥmān al-ᶜArīfī *et al.* (Mecca: Dār ᶜĀlim al-Fawāᵓid li'l-Nashr wa'l-Tawzīᶜ, 1428/[2007]).

———, *Miftāḥ Dār al-Saᶜāda wa-Manshūr Wilāyat al-ᶜIlm wa'l-Irāda*, eds Sayyid Ibrāhīm and ᶜAlī Muḥammad (Cairo: Dār al-Ḥadīth 1418/1997).

———, *Shifāᵓ al-ᶜAlīl fī Masāᵓil al-Qaḍāᵓ wa'l-Qadar wa'l-Ḥikma wa'l-Taᶜlīl*, eds al-Sayyid Muḥammad al-Sayyid and Saᶜīd Maḥmūd (Cairo: Dār al-Ḥadīth, 1414/1994).

———, *Zād al-Maᶜād fī Hady Khayr al-ᶜIbād*, no editor mentioned (Cairo: Dār al-Fajr li'l-Turāth, 1425/2004).

Ibn Qayyim al-Jawziyya and Muḥammad ibn al-Mawṣilī, *Mukhtaṣar al-Ṣawāᶜiq al-Mursala*, ed. al-Ḥasan ibn ᶜAbd al-Raḥmān al-ᶜAlawī (Riyadh: Maktabat Aḍwāᵓ al-Salaf, 1425/2004).

Ibn Qutayba, Abū Muḥammad ᶜAbd Allāh ibn Muslim, *al-Ikhtilāf fī al-Lafẓ wa'l-Radd ᶜalā al-Jahmiyya wa'l-Mushabbiha*, ed. ᶜUmar ibn Maḥmūd Abū ᶜUmar (Riyadh: Dār al-Rāya li'l-Nashr wa'l-Tawziᶜ, 1412/1991).

———, *Taʾwīl Mukhtalif al-Ḥadīth*, ed. Muḥammad Muḥyī al-Dīn al-Aṣfar (Beirut and Doha: al-Maktab al-Islāmī and Muʾassasat al-Ishrāq, 1419/1999).

Ibn Rajab, ᶜAbd al-Raḥmān ibn Aḥmad, *Al-Dhayl ᶜalā Ṭabaqāt al-Ḥanābila*, ed. ᶜAbd al-Raḥmān ibn Sulaymān al-ᶜUthaymin (Mecca: Maktabat al-ᶜAbīkān 1425/2005).

———, *Rawāʾiᶜ al-Tafsīr: Tafsīr Ibn Rajab al-Ḥanbalī*, ed. Abū Muᶜādh Ṭāriq ibn ᶜAwḍ Allāh ibn Muḥammad (Riyadh: Dār al-ᶜĀṣima li'l-Nashr wa'l-Tawzīᶜ, 1422/2001).

Ibn Saᶜd, Muḥammad al-Zuhrī, *Kitāb al-Ṭabaqāt al-Kabīr*, ed. ᶜAlī Muḥammad ᶜUmar (Cairo: Maktabat al-Khāngī, 1421/2001).

Ibn Taymiyya, Taqī al-Dīn Aḥmad ibn ᶜAbd al-Ḥalīm, *Bayān Talbīs al-Jahmiyya fī Ta'sīs Bidaᶜihim al-Kalāmiyya*, eds team under the supervision of sheikh ᶜAbd al-ᶜAzīz al-Rājiḥī (Medina: Majmaᶜ al-Malik Fahd li-Ṭibāᶜat al-Muṣḥaf al-Sharīf, 1426/2005).

———, *al-Fatwā al-Ḥamawiyya al-Kubrā*, ed. Ḥamd ibn ᶜAbd al-Muḥsin al-Tuwayjirī (Riyadh: Dār al-Ṣumayᶜī li'l-Nashr wa'l-Tawzīᶜ, 1419/1998).

———, 'Ḥikāyat al-Shaykh ᶜAlam al-Dīn', in *Majmūᶜat al-Fatāwā*, eds ᶜĀmir al-Jazzār and Anwar al-Bāz (Al-Mansura and Riyadh: Dār al-Wafāʾ li'l-Ṭibāᶜa wa'l-Nashr wa'l-Tawzīᶜ and Maktabat al-ᶜAbīkān, 1419/1998), vol. 3, pp. 125–9.

———, *Jawāb al-Iᶜtirāḍāt al-Miṣriyya ᶜalā al-Futyā al-Ḥamawiyya*, ed. Muḥammad ᶜUzayr Shams (Mecca: Dār ᶜĀlim al-Fawāʾid, 1429/[2008]).

———, 'Kitāb al-Radd ᶜalā al-Ṭawāʾif al-Mulḥida', in *al-Fatāwā al-Kubrā*, eds Muḥammad ᶜAbd al-Qādir ᶜAṭā and Muṣṭafā ᶜAbd al-Qādir ᶜAṭā (Beirut: Dār al-Kutub al-ᶜIlmiyya, 1408/1987), vol. 6, pp. 321–664.

———, '[Al-Ḥamawiyya al-Kubrā]', in *Majmūᶜat al-Fatāwā*, eds ᶜĀmir al-Jazzār and Anwar al-Bāz (Al-Mansura and Riyadh: Dār al-Wafāʾ li'l-Ṭibāᶜa wa'l-Nashr wa'l-Tawzīᶜ and Maktabat al-ᶜAbīkān, 1419/1998), vol. 5, pp. 7–78.

———, *Sharḥ al-ᶜAqīda al-Iṣfahāniyya*, ed. Saᶜīd ibn Naṣr ibn Muḥammad (Riyadh: Maktabat al-Rushd, 1422/2001).

———, 'Suʾāl ᶜan rajulayn ikhtalafā fī 'l-iᶜtiqād', in *Majmūᶜat al-Fatāwā*, eds ᶜĀmir al-Jazzār and Anwar al-Bāz (Al-Mansura and Riyadh: Dār al-Wafāʾ li'l-Ṭibāᶜa wa'l-Nashr wa'l-Tawzīᶜ and Maktabat al-ᶜAbīkān, 1419/1998), vol. 5, pp. 158–61.

Al-Iṣfahānī, Abū Nuʿaym Aḥmad ibn ʿAbd Allāh ibn Aḥmad ibn Isḥāq ibn Mihrān, *Ḥilyat al-awliyāʾ wa-ṭabaqāt al-aṣfiyāʾ*, no editor mentioned (Beirut: Dār al-Kutub al-ʿIlmiyya, 1409/1988).

———, (spelled: al-Iṣbahānī), *Maʿrifat al-Ṣaḥāba*, ed. ʿĀdil ibn Yūsuf al-ʿAzāzī (Riyadh: Dār al-Waṭan li'l-Nashr, 1419/1998).

ʿIyāḍ ibn Mūsā, al-Qāḍī Abu 'l-Faḍl al-Yaḥṣūbī, *Ikmāl al-Muʿlim bi-Fawāʾid Muslim*, ed. Yaḥyā Ismāʿīl (Mansoura: Dār al-Wafāʾ li'l-Ṭibāʿa wa'l-Nashr wa'l-Tawzīʿ, 1419/1998).

Al-Jazāʾirī, Ṭāhir ibn Ṣāliḥ ibn Aḥmad, *Kitāb Tawjīh al-Naẓar ilā Uṣūl al-Athar*, eds Aḥmad Nājī al-Jamālī, Muḥammad Amīn al-Khānjī and his brother (Cairo: al-Maṭbaʿa al-Jamāliyya, 1328/1901).

Al-Jurjānī, Abū Aḥmad ʿAbd Allāh ibn ʿAdī, *Al-Kāmil fī Ḍuʿafāʾ al-Rijāl*, ed. editorial board on behalf of the publisher (Beirut: Dār al-Fikr, 1404/1984).

Al-Khalīfa al-Nīsābūrī, Aḥmad ibn Muḥammad ibn al-Ḥasan ibn Aḥmad, *Talkhīṣ Tārīkh Nīsābūr*, ed. Bahman Karimi (Tehran: Ketabkhane Ibn Sina, n.d.).

Al-Khallāl, Abū Bakr Aḥmad ibn Muḥammad, *Al-Sunna*, ed. ʿAṭiyya al-Zahrānī (Riyadh: Dār al-Rāya li'l-Nashr wa'l-Tawzīʿ, 1410/1989).

Al-Khaṭīb al-Baghdādī, Abū Aḥmad ibn ʿAlī ibn Thābit, *al-Jāmiʿ li-Akhlāq al-Rāwī wa-Ādāb al-Sāmiʿ*, ed. Abū ʿAbd al-Raḥmān Ṣalāḥ ibn Muḥammad ibn ʿAwīḍa (Beirut: Dār al-Kutub al-ʿIlmiyya, 1417/1996).

———, *Ṣaḥīḥ al-Faqīh wa'l-Mutafaqqih*, ed. Abū ʿAbd al-Raḥmān ʿĀdil ibn Yūsuf al-ʿAzāzī (Riyadh: Dār al-Waṭan, 1418/1997).

———, *Tārīkh Madīnat al-Salām wa-Akhbār Muḥaddithīhā wa-Dhikr Quṭṭānihā al-ʿUlamāʾ min Ghayr Ahlihā wa-Wāridīhā* (*Tārīkh Baghdād*), ed. Bashār ʿAwwād Maʿrūf (Beirut: Dār al-Gharb al-Islāmī, 1422/2001).

Al-Lālakāʾī, Abu 'l-Qāsim Hibat Allāh ibn Ḥasan ibn Manṣūr al-Ṭabarī, *Sharḥ Uṣūl Iʿtiqād Ahl al-Sunna wa'l-Jamāʿa*, ed. Aḥmad Saʿd Ḥamdān (Mecca: no editing house mentioned, 1411/[1991]).

Al-Maḥallī, Jalāl al-Dīn Muḥammad ibn Aḥmad and ʿAbd al-Raḥmān ibn Abī Bakr Jalāl al-Dīn al-Suyūṭī, *al-Qurʾān al-Karīm bi'l-Rasm al-ʿUthmānī wa-bi-Hāmishih Tafsīr al-Imāmayn al-Jalālayn*, no editor mentioned (Beirut: Dār al-Maʿrifa, 1403/1983).

Al-Malaṭī, Abu'l-Ḥusayn Muḥammad ibn Aḥmad ibn ʿAbd al-Raḥmān, *al-Tanbīh wa'l-Radd ʿalā Ahl al-Ahwā' wa'l-Bidaʿ*, ed. Muḥammad Zāhid ibn al-Ḥasan al-Kawtharī (Cairo: al-Maktaba al-Azhariyya li'l-Turāth, 1428/2007).

Al-Marzubānī, Abū ʿUbayd Allāh Muḥammad ibn ʿImrān, *Kitāb Nūr al-Qabas al-Mukhtaṣar min al-Muqtabas bi-Ikhtiṣār Abī al-Maḥāsin Yūsuf ibn Aḥmad ibn Maḥmūd al-Ḥāfiẓ al-Yaghmūri*, ed. Rudolph Sellheim [published under the title: *Die Gelehrtenbiographien des Abū ᶜUbaidallāh al-Marzubānī in der Rezension des Ḥāfiẓ al-Yaġmūrī*] (Wiesbaden: Franz Steiner Verlag, 1964).

Al-Mizzī, Jamāl al-Dīn ibn al-Ḥajjāj Yūsuf, *Tahdhīb al-Kamāl fī Asmāʾ al-Rijāl*, ed. Bashār ᶜAwwād Maᶜrūf (Beirut: Muʾssasat 'l-Risāla 1413/1992).

———, *Tuḥfat al-Ashrāf wa-Maᶜrifat al-Aṭrāf*, ed. Bashār ᶜAwwād Maᶜrūf (Beirut: Dār al-Gharb al-Islāmī, 1999).

Muslim ibn Ḥajjāj, Abu 'l-Ḥusayn al-Qushayrī al-Nīsābūrī, *Ṣaḥiḥ Muslim*, ed. Abū Ṣuhayb al-Karmī (Riyadh: Bayt al-Afkār al-Duwaliyya, 1419/1998).

Naṣr ibn Muzāḥim al-Minqarī, *Waqᶜat Ṣiffīn*, ed. ᶜAbd al-Salām Muḥammad Hārūn (Cairo: al-Muʾassasa al-ᶜArabiyya al-Ḥadītha li'l-Ṭabᶜ wa'l-Nashr wa'l-Tawzīᶜ, 1382/1962).

Al-Nawawī, Muḥyī al-Dīn Abū Zakariyyāʾ Yaḥyā ibn Sharaf, *Ṣaḥīḥ Muslim bi-Sharḥ al-Nawawī*, ed. Muḥammad Fuʾād ᶜAbd al-Bāqī (Beirut: Dār al-Kutub al-ᶜIlmiyya, 1421/2000; reprint of Cairo: Idārat al-Ṭibāᶜa al-Munīriyya, 1972 edn).

———, *Tahdhīb al-Asmāʾ wa'l-Lughāt*, no editor mentioned (Beirut: Dār al-Kutub al-ᶜIlmiyya, n.d.; reprint of Cairo: Idārat al-Ṭibāᶜa al-Munīriyya, 1927 edn).

Al-Nuwayrī, Shihāb al-Dīn Aḥmad ibn ᶜAbd al-Wahhāb, *Nihāyat al-Arab fī Funūn al-Adab* (Beirut: Dār al-Kutub al-ᶜIlmiyya, 1424/2004).

Al-Qalqashandī, Abu 'l-ᶜAbbās Aḥmad, *Nihāyat al-Arab fī Maᶜrifat Ansāb al-ᶜArab*, ed. Ibrāhīm al-Abyārī (Beirut: Dār al-Kitāb al-Lubnānī, 1400/1980).

Al-Qārī, Nūr al-Dīn ᶜAlī ibn Muḥammad ibn Sulṭān al-Mullā ᶜAlī, *Al-Asrār al-Marfūᶜa fī al-Akhbār al-Mawḍūᶜa*, ed. Muḥammad ibn Luṭfī al-Sabbāgh (Beirut-Damascus: al-Maktab al-Islāmī, 2nd edn 1406/1986; 1st edn 1391/1971).

Al-Qasṭallānī, Shihāb al-Dīn Aḥmad ibn Muḥammad ibn Abī Bakr, *Irshād al-Sārī li-Sharḥ Ṣaḥīḥ al-Bukhārī*, no editor mentioned (Cairo: al-Maṭbaᶜa al-Kubrā al-Amīriyya Būlāq, 1323/1905).

Al-Qurṭubī, Abū ᶜAbd Allāh Muḥammad ibn Aḥmad al-Anṣārī, *Al-Jāmiᶜ li-Aḥkām al-Qurʾān*, ed. Sālim Muṣṭafā al-Badrī (Beirut: Dār al-Kutub al-ᶜIlmiyya, 1420/2000).

Al-Rāmhurmuzī, al-Ḥasan ibn ᶜAbd al-Raḥmān, *Al-Muḥaddith al-Fāṣil bayna al-Rāwī wa'l-Wāᶜī*, ed. Muḥammad ᶜAjāj al-Khaṭīb (Beirut: Dār al-Fikr, 1391/1971).

Al-Rāzī, Fakhr al-Dīn Muḥammad Ḍiyaāʾ al-Dīn ᶜUmar ibn al-Khaṭīb, *Asās al-Taqdīs*, ed. Aḥmad Ḥijāzī al-Saqā (Cairo: Maktaba Kulliyyāt al-Azhariyya, 1406/1989).

———, *Al-Maḥṣūl fī ᶜIlm Uṣūl al-Fiqh*, ed. Jābir Fayyāḍ al-ᶜAlwānī (Beirut: Muᵓassasat al-Risāla, 1412/1992).

———, *Tafsīr al-Fakhr al-Rāzī al-Mushtahar bi'l-Tafsīr al-Kabīr wa-Mafātīḥ al-Ghayb*, no editor mentioned (Beirut: Dār al-Fikr, 1414/1993; 1st edn 1401/1981).

Al-Ṣafadī, Ṣalāḥ al-Dīn Khalīl Aybak, *Kitāb al-Wāfī bi'l-Wafayāt*, eds Aḥmad al-Arnāᵓūṭ and Turkī Muṣṭafā (Beirut: Dār Iḥyāᵓ al-Turāth al-ᶜArabī, 1420/2000).

Al-Samᶜānī, Abū Saᶜd ᶜAbd al-Karīm ibn Muḥammad ibn Manṣūr al-Tamīmī, *Al-Ansāb*, ed. ᶜAbd Allāh ᶜUmar al-Bārūdī (Beirut: Dār al-Jinān, 1408/1988).

Al-Shahrastānī, Abu 'l-Fatḥ Muḥammad ibn ᶜAbd al-Karīm, *Al-Milal wa'l-Niḥal* (Beirut: Dār al-Kutub al-ᶜIlmiyya, 1413/1992).

Al-Subkī, Tāj al-Dīn Abū Naṣr ᶜAbd al-Wahhāb ibn ᶜAlī, *Ṭabaqāt al-Shāfiᶜiyya al-Kubrā*, eds Maḥmūd Muḥammad al-Ṭināḥī and ᶜAbd al-Fattāḥ Muḥammad al-Ḥilw (Cairo: Dār Iḥyāᵓ al-Kutub al-ᶜArabiyya, [1992]).

Al-Subkī, Taqī al-Dīn ᶜAlī ibn ᶜAbd al-Kāfī, *Al-Sayf al-Ṣaqīl fī al-Radd ᶜalā Ibn Zafīl*, ed. Muḥammad Zāhid ibn al-Ḥasan al-Kawtharī (Cairo: al-Maktaba al-Azhariyya li'l-Turāth, n.d.).

Al-Suyūṭī, Jalāl al-Dīn ᶜAbd al-Raḥmān, *Al-Durr al-Manthūr fī al-Tafsīr bi'l-Maᵓthūr*, ed. ᶜAbd Allāh ibn ᶜAbd al-Muḥsin al-Turkī (Cairo: Markaz Hagar li'l-Buḥūth wa'l-Dirāsāt 'l-ᶜArabiyya wa'l-Islāmiyya, 1424/2003).

———, *Jamᶜ al-Jawāmiᶜ al-Maᶜrūf bi'l-Jāmiᶜ al-Kabīr*, no editor mentioned (Cairo: Dār al-Saᶜāda li'l-Ṭibāᶜa, 1426/2005).

———, *Al-Lāᵓālī al-Maṣnūᶜa fī al-Aḥādīth al-Mawḍūᶜa*, no editor mentioned (Beirut, n.d.).

Al-Ṭabarī, Abū Jaᶜfar Muḥammad ibn Jarīr, *Tafsīr al-Ṭabarī: Jāmiᶜ al-Bayān ᶜan Taᵓwīl Āy al-Qurᵓān*, ed. ᶜAbd Allāh ibn ᶜAbd al-Muḥsin al-Turkī (Cairo: Dār Hagar, 1422/2001).

———, *Tārīkh al-Ṭabarī: Tārīkh al-Rusul wa'l-Muluk*, ed. Muḥammad Abu 'l-Faḍl Ibrāhīm (Cairo: Dār al-Maᶜārif, 1960–9).

Al-Ṭabarānī, Abū al-Qāsim Sulaymān ibn Aḥmad, *al-Aḥādīth al-Ṭiwāl*, ed. Ḥamdī ᶜAbd al-Majīd al-Salafī (Beirut: al-Muktab al-Islāmī, 1419/1990).

———, *Al-Muᶜjam al-Awsaṭ*, eds Abū Muᶜādh Ṭāriq ibn ᶜAwḍ Allāh ibn Muḥammad and Abu 'l-Faḍl ᶜAbd al-Muḥsin ibn Ibrāhīm al-Ḥusaynī (Cairo: Dār al-Ḥaramayn, 1416/1995).

———, *Al-Muᶜjam al-Kabīr*, ed. Ḥamdī ᶜAbd al-Majīd al-Salafī (Cairo: Maktabat Ibn Taymiyya, 1984).

Al-Ṭaḥāwī, Abū Ja^cfar Aḥmad ibn Muḥammad ibn Salāma, *Mukhtaṣar Ikhtilāf al-^cUlamā^ɔ* [the abridgement by Abū Bakr Aḥmad ibn ^cAlī al-Jaṣṣāṣ al-Rāzī], ed. ^cAbd Allāh Nadhīr Aḥmad (Beirut: Dār al-Bashā^ɔir al-Islāmiyya, 1416/1995).

Al-Ṭayālisī, Sulaymān ibn Dāwūd ibn al-Jārūd, *Musnad Abī Dāwūd al-Ṭayālisī*, ed. Muḥammad ibn ^cAbd al-Muḥsin al-Turkī (Giza: Dār Hagar, 1419/1999).

Al-Ṭībī, Sharaf al-Dīn al-Ḥusayn ibn ^cAbd Allāh ibn Muḥammad, *Sarḥ al-Ṭībī ^calā Mishkāt al-Maṣābīḥ al-Musammā bi'l-Kāshif ^can Ḥaqā'iq al-Sunan*, ed. ^cAbd al-Ḥamīd Hindāwī (Mecca-Riyadh: Maktabat Nizār Muṣṭafā al-Bāz, 1417/1997).

Al-Tirmidhī, Muḥammad ibn ^cĪsā ibn Sawra, *Sunan al-Tirmidhī*, ed. Muḥammad Nāṣir al-Albānī (Riyadh: Maktabat al-Ma^cārif li'l-Nashr wa'l-Tawzī^c, 1417/[1996–7]).

Al-Wāḥidī, Abu 'l-Ḥasan ^cAlī ibn Aḥmad ibn Muḥammad, *Al-Tafsīr al-Basīṭ*, eds ^cAbd al-^cAzīz ibn Siṭām Āl Sa^cūd and al-Turkī ibn Sahw al-^cAtībī (Riyadh: Jāmi^cat al-Imām Muḥammad ibn Sa^cūd al-Islāmiyya, 1430/2009).

Yāqūt al-Ḥamawī al-Rūmī, *Mu^cjam al-Udabā': Irshād al-Arīb ilā Ma^crifat al-Adīb* (Beirut: Dār al-Gharb al-Islāmī, 1993).

Al-Zabīdī, Muḥammad Murtaḍā, *Itḥāf al-Sāda al-Muttaqīn bi-Sharḥ Iḥyā^ɔ ^cUlūm al-Dīn*, no editor mentioned (Beirut: Dār al-Kutub al-^cIlmiyya, 1426/2005).

———, *Tāj al-^cArūs min Jawāhir al-Qāmūs*, ed. ^cAlī Shīrī (Beirut: Dār al-Fikr li'l-Ṭibā^ca wa'l-Nashr wa'l-Tawzī^c, 1414/1994).

II. Secondary Sources

Abbott, H. Porter, *The Cambridge Introduction to Narrative*, 2nd edn (Cambridge: Cambridge University Press, 2008).

Abrahamov, Binyamin, *Anthropomorphism and Interpretation of the Qur^ɔān in the Theology of al-Qāsim ibn Ibrāhīm* (Leiden: Brill, 1996).

———, 'The *Bi-lā Kayfa* Doctrine and its Foundations in Islamic Theology', *Arabica* 42 (1995), pp. 365–79.

———, *Islamic Theology: Traditionalism and Rationalism* (Edinburgh: Edinburgh University Press, 1998).

———, 'Scripturalist and Traditionalist Theology', in Sabine Schmidtke (ed.), *The Oxford Handbook of Islamic Theology* (New York: Oxford University Press, 2016), pp. 263–79.

Abū Zayd, Bakr ibn ^cAbd Allāh, *Ibn Qayyim al-Jawziyya: Ḥayyātuhu, Āthāruhu, Mawāriduhu*, 2nd edn (Riyadh: Dār al-^cĀṣima li'l-Nashr wa'l-Tawzī^c, 1423/[2002]).

Adang, Camilla, 'The Prophet's Farewell Pilgrimage (*Ḥijjat al-Wadā^c*): The True

Story According to Ibn Ḥazm', *Jerusalem Studies of Arabic and Islam* 30 (2005), pp. 112–53.

Allard, Michel, *Le problème des attributs divins* (Beyrouth: Éditions de l'Imprimerie Catholique, 1965).

Anawati, George C., 'Fakhr al-Dīn al-Rāzī', in P. Bearman, T. Bianquis, C. E. Bosworth, E. van Donzel and W. P. Heinrichs (eds), *The Encyclopaedia of Islam, 2nd edn (EI2)* (Leiden: Brill, 1965), vol. 2, pp. 751–5; available at Brillonline.com.

Ansari, Hassan and Sabine Schmidtke, 'The Muᶜtazilī and Zaydī Reception of Abū l-Ḥusayn al-Baṣrī's *Kitāb al-Muᶜtamad fī Uṣūl al-Fiqh*: A Bibliographical Note', *Islamic Law and Society* 20, 1–2 (2013), pp. 90–109.

Ansari, Hassan, Sabine Schmidtke and Jan Thiele, 'Zaydī Theology in Yemen', in S. Schmidtke (ed.), *The Oxford Handbook of Islamic Theology* (New York: Oxford University Press, 2016), pp. 473–93.

Arberry, Arthur J., *The Koran Interpreted* (New York: Oxford University Press, 1964, 1982).

Arnaldez, Roger, *Grammaire et théologie chez Ibn Ḥazm de Cordoue* (Paris: Libraire philosophique J. Vrin, 1956).

Asad, Talal, 'Kinship', in Jane Dammen McAuliffe (ed.), *Encyclopaedia of the Qur'ān* (Leiden: Brill, 2001), vol. 3, pp. 95–100; available at Brillonline.com.

Bar-Asher, Meir M., 'Hidden and the Hidden', in Jane Dammen McAuliffe (ed.), *Encyclopaedia of the Qur'ān* (Leiden: Brill, 2001), vol. 2, pp. 423–6; available at Brillonline.com.

Bailey, Christian, 'Germany: Redrawing of Civilizational Trajectories', in Margrit Pernau *et al.* (eds), *Civilizing Emotions: Concepts in Nineteenth Century Asia and Europe* (Oxford: Oxford University Press, 2015), pp. 83–103.

Bal, Mieke, *Narratology: Introduction to the Theory of Narrative*, 2nd edn (Toronto: University of Toronto Press, 2007).

Baron de Slane, William MacGuckin (trans.), *Ibn Khallikān's Biographical Dictionary* (Paris: Printed for the Oriental Translation Fund of Great Britain and Ireland, 1842–71).

Beaumont, Daniel, 'Hard-Boiled: Narrative Discourse in Early Muslim Traditions', *Studia Islamica* 83 (1996), pp. 5–31.

Belhaj, Abdessamad, *Argumentation et dialectique en islam: Formes et séquences de la* munāẓara (Louvain: UCL Presses universitaires de Louvain, 2010).

Berg, Herbert, 'The *Isnād* and the Production of Cultural Memory: Ibn ᶜAbbās as a Case Study', *Numen* 58 (2011), pp. 259–83.

Biale, David, 'The God with Breasts: El Shaddai in the Bible', *History of Religions* 21, 3 (1982), pp. 240–56.

Bori, Caterina, 'A New Source for the Biography of Ibn Taymiyya', *Bulletin of SOAS* 67, 3 (2004), pp. 321–48.

———, *Ibn Taymiyya: una vita essemplare – Analisi delle fonti classiche della sua biografia* (Pisa: Istituti Editoriali e Poligrafici Internazionali, 2003).

———, 'Theology, Politics, Society: The Missing Link. Studying Religion in the Mamluk Period', in Stephan Conermann (ed.), *Ubi Sumus? Quo Vademus? Mamluk Studies – State of the Art* (Bonn: Bonn University Press, 2013), pp. 57–94.

Bori, Caterina and Livnat Holtzman, 'A scholar in the shadow', in Caterina Bori and Livnat Holtzman (eds), *A Scholar in the Shadow – Essays in the Legal and Theological Thought of Ibn Qayyim al- Ğawziyyah, Oriente Moderno* 90, 1 (2010), pp. 13–44.

Bousquet, Georges-Henri, 'Études Islamologiques d'Ignaz Goldziher: Traduction Analytique (I)', *Arabica* 7, 1 (1960), pp. 1–29.

———, 'Études Islamologiques d'Ignaz Goldziher. Traduction Analytique (IV)', *Arabica* 8, 3 (1961), pp. 238–72.

Brown, Jonathan A. C., *The Canonization of al-Bukhārī and Muslim: The Formation and Function of the Sunnī Ḥadīth Canon* (Leiden: Brill, 2007).

———, 'Critical Rigor vs. Juridical Pragmatism: How Legal Theorists and Ḥadīth Scholars Approached the Backgrowth of *Isnāds* in the Genre of *ʿIlal al-Ḥadīth*', *Islamic Law and Society* 14, 1 (2007), pp. 1–41.

———, *Hadith: Muhammad's Legacy in the Medieval and Modern World* (Oxford: Oneworld, 2009).

———, 'Scholars and Charlatans on the Baghdad-Khurasan Circuit from the Ninth to the Eleventh Centuries', in Paul M. Cobb (ed.), *The Lineaments of Islam: Studies in Honor of Fred McGraw Donner* (Leiden: Brill, 2012), pp. 85–95.

Bulliet, Richard, *The Patricians of Nishapur: A Study in Medieval Islamic Social History* (Cambridge, MA: Harvard University Press, 1972).

Chapman, Seymour, *Story and Discourse: Narrative Structure in Fiction and Film* (Ithaca: Cornell University Press, 1978).

Coogan, Michael D., *The New Oxford Annotated Bible: The Fully Revised Fourth Edition* (Oxford: Oxford University Press, 2010).

Cook, Michael, *Commanding Right and Forbidding Wrong in Islamic Thought* (Cambridge: Cambridge University Press, 2000).

———, 'The Opponents of the Writing of Tradition in Early Islam', *Arabica* 44, 4, *Voix et Calame en Islam Médiéval* (October 1997), pp. 437–530.

Cooperson, Michael, *Classical Arabic Biography: The Heirs of the Prophets in the Age of al-Ma'mūn* (Cambridge: Cambridge University Press 2000).

Cribiore, Raffaella, 'School Structures, Apparatus, and Material', in W. Martin Bloomer (ed.), *A Companion to Ancient Education* (Chichester: Wiley, 2015), pp. 149–59.

Crone, Patricia, *Roman, Provincial and Islamic Law: The Origins of the Islamic Patronate* (Cambridge: Cambridge University Press, 1987).

Cuddon, J. A., *The Penguin Dictionary of Literary Terms and Literary Theory*, 3rd edn (London: Penguin Books, 1992).

Daiber, Hans, 'The Quran as a "Shibboleth" of Varying Conceptions of the Godhead', in Ilai Alon *et al.*, *Israel Oriental Studies: Concepts of the Other in Near Eastern Religions* (Leiden: Brill, 1994), pp. 249–5.

Dat, Mihai, 'Deixis', in Lutz Edzard and Rudolf de Jong (eds), *Encyclopedia of Arabic Language and Linguistics* (Brill Online, 2011).

Dawood, N. J. (trans.), *The Koran with a Parallel Arabic Text* (London: Penguin Classics, 2000 [1st edn 1956]).

Dickinson, Eerik, *The Development of Early Sunnite* Ḥadīth *Criticism: The* Taqdima *of Ibn Abī Ḥātim al-Rāzī (240/854–327/938)* (Leiden: Brill, 2001).

Djaït, Hicem, 'al-Kūfa', in P. Bearman, T. Bianquis, C. E. Bosworth, E. van Donzel and W. P. Heinrichs (eds), *The Encyclopaedia of Islam, 2nd edn (EI2)* (Leiden: Brill, 1978), vol. 5, pp. 345–51; available at Brillonline.com.

Donner, Fred M., *The Early Islamic Conquests* (Princeton, NJ: Princeton University Press, 1981).

Dozy, Reinhart, *Supplément aux Dictionnaires Arabes* (Leiden/Paris: Brill/ Maisonneuve Frères, 1927).

Dupriez, Bernard, *A Dictionary of Literary Devices: Graduz, A-Z*, trans. and ed. Albert W. Halsall (Toronto: University of Toronto Press, 1991).

Ed., 'Ishāra', in P. Bearman, T. Bianquis, C. E. Bosworth, E. van Donzel and W. P. Heinrichs (eds), *The Encyclopaedia of Islam, 2nd edn (EI2)* (Leiden: Brill, 1978), vol. 4, pp. 113–14; available at Brillonline.com.

El-Bizri, Nader, 'God: Essence and Attributes', in Tim Winter (ed.), *The Cambridge Companion to Classical Islamic Theology* (New York: Cambridge Univerity Press, 2008), pp. 121–40.

El Calamawy, Sahair, 'Narrative Elements in the *Ḥadīth* Literature', in A. F. L. Beeston *et al.* (eds), *The Cambridge History of Arabic Literature: Arabic Literature to the End of the Umayyad Period* (Cambridge: Cambridge University Press, 1983), pp. 308–16.

El-Omari, Racha, 'Accommodation and Resistance: Classical Muᶜtazilites on Ḥadīth', *Journal of Near Eastern Studies* 17, 2 (2012), pp. 231–56.

El-Rouayheb, Khaled, 'From Ibn Ḥajar al-Haytamī (d. 1566) to Khayr al-Dīn al-Ālūsī (d. 1899): Changing Views of Ibn Taymiyya among Non-Ḥanbalī Sunni Scholars', in Yossef Rapoport and Shahab Ahmed (eds), *Ibn Taymiyya and His Times* (Karachi: Oxford University Press, 2010), pp. 269–318.

Ephrat, Daphna, *A Learned Society in a Period of Transition: The Sunni ᶜUlamaᵓ of Eleventh-Century Baghdad* (Albany: State University of New York, 2000).

———, 'Religious Leadership and Associations in the Public Sphere of Seljuk Baghdad', in Miriam Hoexter, Shmuel N. Eisenstadt and Nehemia Levtzion (eds), *The Public Sphere in Muslim Societies* (Albany: State University of New York Press, 2002), pp. 31–48.

Even Shoshan, Avraham, *Ha-Milon He-Chadash* ([Tel-Aviv]: Ha-Milon He-Chadash, 2000) (in Hebrew).

Fahd, T., 'Dhu 'l-Khalaṣa', in P. Bearman, T. Bianquis, C. E. Bosworth, E. van Donzel and W. P. Heinrichs (eds), *The Encyclopaedia of Islam, 2nd edn (EI2)* (Leiden: Brill, 1965), vol. 2, pp. 241–2; available at Brillonline.com.

Fierro, Maribel, 'La polémique à propos de *rafᶜ al-yadayn fī al-ṣalāt* dans al-Andalus', *Studia Islamica* 65 (1987), pp. 69–90.

Fludernik, Monika, 'Narratology and Literary Linguistics', in Robert I. Binnick (ed.), *The Oxford Handbook of Tense and Aspect* (Oxford: Oxford University Press, 2012), pp. 75–101.

Frank, Richard M., 'Elements in the Development of the Teaching of al-Ashᶜari', in Dimitri Gutas (ed.), *Early Islamic Theology: The Muᶜtazilites and al-Ashᶜarī* (Aldershot: Ashgate Variorum, 2007), part VI, pp. 141–90 [originally published in *Le Museon: Revue d'Etudes Orientales*, Tome 104, 1991].

———, 'Knowledge and *Taqlīd*: The Foundations of Religious Belief in Classical Ashᶜarism', *Journal of the American Oriental Society* 109 (1989), pp. 37–62.

Gardet, Louis, 'duᶜāᵓ', in P. Bearman, T. Bianquis, C. E. Bosworth, E. van Donzel and W. P. Heinrichs (eds), *The Encyclopaedia of Islam, 2nd edn (EI2)* (Leiden: Brill, 1965), vol. 2, pp. 617–18; available at Brillonline.com.

Genette, Gérard, *Fiction and Diction*, trans. Catherine Porter (Ithaca: Cornell University Press, 1993).

Gilliot, Claude, 'Attributes of God', in Kate Fleet, Gudrun Krämer, Denis Matringe,

John Nawas and Everett Rowson (eds), *Encyclopaedia of Islam, 3rd edn (EI3)* (Leiden: Brill, 2007), fasc. 2, pp. 176–82; available at Brillonline.com.

———, *Exégèse, langue, et théologie en islam. L'exégèse coranique de Tabari* (Paris: Libr. J. Vrin, 1990).

———, 'Exegesis of the Qur'ān: Classical and Medieval', in Jane Dammen McAuliffe (ed.), *Encyclopaedia of the Qur'ān* (Leiden: Brill, 2001), vol. 2, pp. 99–124; available at Brillonline.com.

Gimaret, Daniel, *Dieu à l'image de l'homme* (Paris: Cerf, 1997).

———, *La doctrine d'al-Ashᶜarī* (Paris: Cerf, 1990).

———, 'Un document majeur pour l'histoire du kalām: Le Muǧarrad Maqālāt al-Ašᶜarī d'ibn Fūrak', *Arabica* 32, 2 (1985), pp. 185–218.

———, *Les noms divins en Islam: Exégèse lexicographique et théologique* (Paris: Cerf, 1988).

———, 'Ruʾyat Allāh', in P. Bearman, T. Bianquis, C. E. Bosworth, E. van Donzel and W. P. Heinrichs (eds), *The Encyclopaedia of Islam, 2nd edn (EI2)* (Leiden: Brill, 1995), vol. 8, p. 649; available at Brillonline.com.

Goldziher, Ignaz, *Abhandlungen zur Arabischen Philologie* (Leiden: Brill, 1896–9).

———, *Introduction to Islamic Theology and Law,* trans. Andras and Ruth Hamori (Princeton, NJ: Princeton University Press, 1981 [translation of *Vorlesungen über den Islam*, Heidelberg, 1910]).

———, *Mythology among the Hebrews and Its Historical Development*, trans. Russell Martineau (London: Longmans, Green and Co., 1877).

———, 'Neue Materialien zur Litteratur des Ueberlieferungswesens bei den Muhammendanern', *Zeitschrift der Deutschen Morgenländischen Gesellschaft* 50 (1896), pp. 465–506.

———, *Die Richtungen der islamischen Koranauslegung* (Leiden: Brill, 1920).

———, 'Ueber Gebärden – und Zeichensprache bei den Arabern', *Zeitschrift für Völkerpsychologie und Sprachwissenschaft* 16 (1886), pp. 369–86.

———, *The Ẓāhirīs: Their Doctrine and Their History, A Contribution to the History of Islamic Theology*, trans. and ed. Wolfgang Behn (Leiden: Brill, 2008).

———, 'Zauberelemente im islamischen Gebet', in Carl Bezold (ed.), *Orientalische Studien Theodor Nöldeke* (Gieszen: Verlag von Alfred Töpelmann, 1906), vol. 1, pp. 303–29.

Görke, Andreas, 'The Historical Tradition about al-Ḥudaybiya: A Study of ᶜUrwa b. al-Zubayr's Account', in Harald Motzki (ed.), *The Biography of Muḥammad: The Issue of the Sources* (Leiden: Brill, 2000), pp. 240–75.

Graham, William A., *Beyond the Written Word: Oral Aspects of Scripture in the History of Religion* (Cambridge: Cambridge University Press, 1987).

———, '"Winged Words": Scriptures and Classics as Iconic Texts', *Postscripts* 6, 1–3 (2010), pp. 7–22.

Griffel, Frank, 'On Fakhr al-Dīn al-Rāzī's Life and the Patronage He received', *Journal of Islamic Studies* 18, 3 (2007), pp. 313–44.

Grohmann [van Donzel], 'al-Sarāt', in P. Bearman, T. Bianquis, C. E. Bosworth, E. van Donzel and W. P. Heinrichs (eds), *The Encyclopaedia of Islam, 2nd edn (EI2)* (Leiden: Brill, 1997), vol. 9, p. 40; available at Brillonline.com.

Guggenheimer, Heinrich W., *The Jerusalem Talmud* (Berlin: de Gruyter, 1999).

Günther, Sebastian, 'Fictional Narration and Imagination within an Authoritative Framework: Towards a New Understanding of Ḥadīth', in Stefan Leder (ed.), *Story-telling in the Framework of Non-Fictional Arabic Literature* (Wiesbaden: Harrassowitz Verlag, 1998), pp. 433–71.

———, 'Modern Literary Theory Applied to Classical Arabic Texts: Ḥadīth Revisited', in Beatrice Gruendler and Verena Klemm (eds), *Understanding Near Eastern Literatures: A Spectrum of Interdisciplinary Approaches* (Literaturen im Kontext: Arabisch – Persisch – Türkisch, vol. 1) (Wiesbaden: Reichert, 2000), pp. 171–6.

Haddad, Gibril Fouad (trans.), Ibn Jahbal al-Kilābī, *The Refutation of Him [Ibn Taymiyya] Who Attributes Direction to Allāh* (Birmingham: Aqsa Publications, 2008).

Halkin, A. S., 'The Ḥashwiyya', *Journal of the American Oriental Society* 54 (1934), pp. 1–28.

Hawting, G. R., 'Khālid b. ᶜAbd Allāh al-Ḳasrī', in P. Bearman, T. Bianquis, C. E. Bosworth, E. van Donzel and W. P. Heinrichs (eds), *The Encyclopaedia of Islam, 2nd edn (EI2)* (Leiden: Brill, 1978), vol. 4, pp. 925–7; available at Brillonline.com.

Heck, Paul L., 'The Epistemological Problem of Writing in Islamic Civilization: al-Ḫaṭīb al-Baġdādī's (d. 463/1071) *Taqyīd al-ᶜIlm*', *Studia Islamica* 94 (2002), pp. 85–114.

Heinrichs, Wolfhart P., 'Metaphor', in Julie Scott Meisami and Paul Starky (eds), *Encyclopedia of Arabic Literature* (London: Routledge, 1998), vol. 2, pp. 522–4.

———, 'On the Genesis of the *Ḥaqīqa-Majāz* Dichotomy', *Studia Islamica* 59 (1984), pp. 111–40.

Hilali, Asma, 'Compiler, exclure, cacher. Les traditions dites "forgées" dans l'Islam sunnite (VIe /XIIe siècle)', *Revue de l'histoire des religions* 228, 2 (2011), pp. 163–74.

Hinds, Martin, 'Kūfan politics alignments and their background in the mid-seventh century AD', *International Journal of Middle East Studies* 2 (1971), 346–67.

Hoffman, Valerie J., 'Refuting the Vision of God in Ibāḍī Theology', in Ersilia Francesca (ed.), *Ibadi Theology: Reading Sources and Scholarly Works* (Hildesheim: Georg Olms Verlag, 2015), pp. 245–55.

Holes, Clive, *Modern Arabic: Structures, Functions, and Varieties*, rev. edn (Washington, DC: Georgetown University Press, 2004).

Holtzman, Livnat, 'Accused of Anthropomorphism: Ibn Taymiyya's *Miḥan* as Reflected in Ibn Qayyim al-Jawziyya's *al-Kāfiya al-Shāfiya*', *The Muslim World* 106, 3 (2016), pp. 561–87.

———, 'Aḥmad b. Ḥanbal', in Kate Fleet, Gudrun Krämer, Denis Matringe, John Nawas and Everett Rowson (eds), *Encyclopaedia of Islam 3* (*EI3*) (Leiden: Brill, 2009), fasc. 4, pp. 15–23; available at Brillonline.com.

———, 'Anthropomorphism', in Kate Fleet, Gudrun Krämer, Denis Matringe, John Nawas and Everett Rowson (eds), *Encyclopaedia of Islam 3 (EI3)* (Leiden: Brill, 2011), fasc. 4, pp. 46–55; available at Brillonline.com.

———, 'Debating the Doctrine of *Jabr* (Compulsion): Ibn Qayyim al-Jawziyya Reads Fakhr al-Dīn al-Rāzī', in Birgit Krawietz and Georges Tamer (eds), *Islamic Theology, Philosophy and Law: Debating Ibn Taymiyya and Ibn Qayyim al-Jawziyya* (Berlin: Walter de Gruyter, 2013), pp. 61–93.

———, 'The Dhimmi's Question on Predetermination and the Ulama's Six Responses: the Dynamics of Composing Polemical Didactic Poems in Mamluk Cairo and Damascus', *Mamluk Studies Review* 16 (2012), pp. 1–54.

———, 'Does God Really Laugh? Appropriate and Inappropriate Descriptions of God in Islamic Traditionalist Theology', in Albrecht Classen (ed.), *Laughter in the Middle Ages and Early Modern Times* (Berlin: de Gruyter, 2010), pp. 165–200.

———, 'Ḥanbalis', in Andrew Rippin (ed.), *Oxford Bibliographies Online* (2015), doi: 10.1093/OBO/9780195390155-0210.

———, 'Insult, Fury, and Frustration: the Martyrological Narrative of Ibn Qayyim al-Jawziyah's al-Kafiyah al-Shafiyah', *Mamluk Studies Review* 17 (2013), pp. 155–98.

Holtzman, Livnat and Haggai Ben-Shammai, 'kalām', in Michael Berenbaum and Fred Skolnik (eds), *Encyclopedia Judaica*, 2nd edn (New York: Macmillan, 2006), vol. 11, pp. 729–31; available at Gale Virtual Reference Library.

Holtzman, Livnat and Miriam Ovadia, 'On Divine Aboveness (*al-Fawqiyya*): the Development of Rationalized Ḥadīth-Based Argumentations in

Islamic Theology', in Yohanan Friedmann and Christoph Markschies (eds), *Rationalization in Religions* (Berlin: De Gruyter, forthcoming).

Hoover, Jon, 'Fiṭra', in Kate Fleet, Gudrun Krämer, Denis Matringe, John Nawas and Everett Rowson (eds), *Encyclopaedia of Islam 3 (EI3)* (Leiden: Brill, 2016), fasc. 2, pp. 104–6; available on Brillonline.com.

———, 'Ibn Taymiyya', in Andrew Rippin (ed.) *Oxford Bibliographies Online* (2014), doi: 10.1093/OBO/9780195390155-0150.

———, 'Ḥanbalī Theology', in S. Schmidtke (ed.), *The Oxford Handbook of Islamic Theology* (New York: Oxford University Press, 2016), pp. 625–46.

———, *Ibn Taymiyya's Theodicy of Perpetual Optimism* (Leiden: Brill, 2007).

Hurvitz, Nimrod, *The Formation of Ḥanbalism: Piety into Power*, (London: Routledge Curzon, 2002).

———, 'Miḥna as Self-Defence', *Studia Islamica* 92 (2001), pp. 93–111.

Ibn ᶜUkāsha, Abū ᶜAbd Allāh Ḥusayn (ed.), *Al-Masāʾil wa'l-Ajwiba* (Cairo: Maṭbaᶜat al-Fārūq al-Ḥadīth li'l-Ṭibāᶜa wa'l-Nashr, 1423/2004).

Jackson, Sherman A., 'Ibn Taymiyyah on Trial in Damascus', *Journal of Semitic Studies* 39, 1 (Spring 1994), pp. 41–85.

Jordan, William, *Ancient Concepts of Philosophy* (London: Routledge, 1992).

Judd, Steven C., *Religious Scholars and the Umayyads* (London: Routledge, 2014).

Juynboll, G. H. A., *Encyclopedia of Canonical Ḥadīth* (Leiden: Brill, 2007).

———, 'Munkar' in P. Bearman, T. Bianquis, C. E. Bosworth, E. van Donzel and W. P. Heinrichs (eds), *The Encyclopaedia of Islam, 2nd edn (EI2)* (Leiden: Brill, 1993), vol. 7, p. 576; available at Brillonline.com.

———, *Muslim Tradition: Studies in Chronology, Provenance and Authorship of Early Ḥadīth* (Cambridge: Cambridge University Press, 1983).

———, 'Mustamlī', *EI2*, vol. 7, pp. 725–6.

———, 'The Role of *Muᶜammarūn* in the Early Development of the *Isnād*', *Wiener Zeitschrift für die Kunde des Morgenlandes* 81 (1991), pp. 155–75.

Kaddari, Menahem Zevi, A *Dictionary of Biblical Hebrew (Alef-Taw)* (Ramat-Gan: Bar Ilan, 2007) (in Hebrew).

Kalmar, Ivan, 'Steinthal, the Jewish Orientalist', in Hartwig Wiedebach and Annette Winkelmann (eds), *Chajim H. Steinthal: Linguist and Philosopher in the 19th Century* (Leiden: Brill, 2002), pp. 132–52.

———, 'The Völkerpsychologie of Lazarus and Steinthal and the Modern Concept of Culture', *Journal of the History of Ideas* 48, 4 (1987), pp. 671–90.

Kendon, Adam, *Gesture: Visible Action as Utterance* (Cambridge: Cambridge University Press, 2004).

———, 'Language and Gesture: Unity or Duality?', in David McNeill (ed.), *Language and Gesture* (Cambridge: Cambridge University Press, 2000), pp. 47–63.

Khan, Muhammad Muhsin (trans.), *Summarized Sahîh al-Bukharî Arabic-English* (Riyadh: Darrusalam Publishers and Distributors, 1994).

———, *The Translation of the Meaning of Sahîh al-Bukharî Arabic-English* (Riyadh: Darrusalam Publishers and Distributors, 1997).

Kirtchuk, Pablo, 'Onomatopoeia', in Geoffrey Khan (ed.), *Encyclopedia of Hebrew Language and Linguistics* (Brill Online, 2016; first appeared online 2013).

Kraemer, Joel L., *Humanism in the Renaissance of Islam: The Cultural Revival during the Buyid Age*, 2nd edn (Leiden: Brill, 1992).

Lagard, Michel, *Index du Grand Commentaire de Fakhr al-Dīn al-Rāzī* (Leiden: Brill, 1996).

Lane, Edward William, *An Arabic-English Lexicon* (Beirut: Librairie du Liban 1968; reprint of London: Williams and Norgate, 1863 edn).

Lange, Christian, 'Sins, Expiation and Non-Rationality in Ḥanafī and Shāfiᶜī Fiqh', in Kevin Reinhart and Robert Gleave (eds), *Islamic Law in Theory: Studies on Jurisprudence in Honor of Bernard Weiss* (Leiden: Brill, 2014), pp. 143–75.

Langermann, Tzvi Y., 'The Naturalization of Science in Ibn Qayyim al-Ǧawziyyah's *Kitāb al-Rūḥ*', in Caterina Bori and Livnat Holtzman (eds), *A Scholar in the Shadow: Essays in the Legal and Theological Thought of Ibn Qayyim al-Ǧawziyyah*, *Oriente Moderno* 15 (2010), pp. 211–28.

Laoust, Henri, *Essai sur les doctrines sociales et politiques de Taḳī-d-Dīn Aḥmad b. Taimīya, canoniste ḥanbalite né à Ḥarrān en 661/1262, mort à Damas en 728/1328* (Cairo: Imprimerie de l'institut français d'archéologie orientale, 1939).

———, *La profession de foi d'Ibn Baṭṭa* (Damas: Institut français de Damas, 1958).

———, *La profession de foi d'Ibn Taymiyya: Textes, traduction et commentaire de la Wāsiṭiyya* (Paris: Librairie orientaliste Paul Geuthner, 1986).

Lecker, Michael, 'Ṣiffīn', in P. Bearman, T. Bianquis, C. E. Bosworth, E. van Donzel and W. P. Heinrichs (eds), *The Encyclopaedia of Islam, 2nd edn (EI2)* (Leiden: Brill, 1997), vol. 9, pp. 552–6; available at Brillonline.com.

Lecomte, Gérard, *Ibn Qutayba: (mort en 276/889); l'homme, son oeuvre, ses idées* (Damas: [s.n.]; Impr. Catholique, 1965) (e-book).

——— (ed.), *Le Traité des divergences du ḥadīṯ d'Ibn Qutayba (mort en 276/889): Traduction annotée du Kitāb ta'wīl muḫtalif al-ḥadīṯ* (Damas: Publications de l'Institut français du Proche-Orient, 1962) (e-book).

Leder, Stefan, 'The Literary Use of the Khabar: A Basic Form of Historical Writing', in Averil Cameron and Lawrence I. Conrad (eds), *The Byzantine and Early*

Islamic Near East vol 1: Problems in the Literary Source Material (Princeton, NJ: Darwin Press, 1992), pp. 277–315.

Levi Della Vida, G., 'al-Muntafiḳ', in P. Bearman, T. Bianquis, C. E. Bosworth, E. van Donzel and W. P. Heinrichs (eds), *The Encyclopaedia of Islam, 2nd edn (EI2)* (Leiden: Brill, 1993), vol. 7, pp. 582–3; available at Brillonline.com.

Little, Donald P., 'The Historical and Historiographical Significance of the Detention of Ibn Taymiyya', *International Journal of Middle East Studies* 4, 3 (1973), pp. 311–27.

———, 'Did Ibn Taymiyya Have a Screw Loose?' *Studia Islamica* 41 (1975), pp. 93–111.

Lowry, Joseph E., 'Ibn Qutaybah', in Michael Cooperson and Shawkat M. Toorawa (eds), *Dictionary of Literary Biography, vol. 311: Arabic Literary Culture* (Detroit: Gale Research Company, 2005), pp. 172–83.

Lucas, Scott C., *Constructive Critics, Ḥadīth Literature, and the Articulation of Sunnī Islam* (Leiden: Brill, 2004).

Madelung, Wilfred, 'The Origins of the Controversy concerning the Creation of the Koran', in J. M. Barral (ed.), *Orientalia Hispanica* (Leiden: Brill, 1974), vol. 1, pp. 504–25.

———, *Religious Schools and Sects in Medieval Islam* (London: Variorum Reprints, 1985).

———, *Religious Trends in Early Islamic Iran* (Columbia Lectures on Iranian Studies, no. 4) (Albany: State University of New York Press and Bibliotheca Persica, 1988).

———, 'The Spread of Māturīdism and the Turks', *Actas de IV Congresso de Estudos Árabes e Islâmicos, Coimbra-Lisba 1968* (Leiden: Brill, 1971), pp. 109–68a.

———, 'The Westwards Migration of Hanafī Scholars from Central Asia in the 11th to 13th Centuries', *Ankara Ūniversitesi Ilāhiyat Fakültesi Dergisi* 43, 2 (2002), pp. 42–55.

Makdisi, George, 'Ashᶜarī and the Ashᶜarites in Islamic Religious History I', *Studia Islamica* 17 (1962), pp. 37–80.

———, 'Ashᶜarī and the Ashᶜarites in Islamic Religious History II', *Studia Islamica* 18 (1963), pp. 19–39.

———, *Ibn ᶜAqīl et la résurgence de l'Islam traditionaliste au XIe siècle (Ve siècle de l'Hégire)* (Damas: Institut français de Damas, 1963).

———, 'Ṭabaqāt-Biography: Law and Orthodoxy in Classical Islam', *Islamic Studies* 32, 4 (Winter 1993), pp. 371–96.

Makin, Al, 'The Influence of Ẓāhirī Theory on Ibn Ḥazm's Theology: The Case of

His Interpretation of the Anthropomorphic Text "The Hand of God"', *Medieval Encounters* 5, 1 (1999), pp. 112–20.

McCarthy, Richard J., *The Theology of al-Ashʿarī* (Beyrouth: Imprimerie Catholique, 1953).

McNeill, David, *Gesture and Thought* (Chicago: University of Chicago Press, 2005).

Meisami, J. S. and Paul Starkey (eds), *The Routledge Encyclopedia of Arabic Literature* (London: Routledge, 2010; first published 1998).

Melchert, Christopher, *Ahmad Ibn Hanbal* (Oxford: Oneworld, 2006).

———, 'al-Barbahārī', in Kate Fleet, Gudrun Krämer, Denis Matringe, John Nawas and Everett Rowson (eds), *Encyclopaedia of Islam 3 (EI3)* (Leiden: Brill, 2009), fasc. 3, pp. 160–1; available at Brillonline.com.

———, 'The Early Controversy over Whether the Prophet Saw God', *Arabica* 62, 4 (2015), pp. 459–76.

———, 'Early Ḥanbali Creed', provided by the author as part of a private correspondence and available only online at https://www.academia.edu/16133657/Early_Hanbali_creeds.

———, *The Formation of the Sunni Schools of Law, 9th–10th Centuries C.E.* (Leiden: Brill, 1997).

———, 'God Created Adam in His Image', *Journal of Qurʾanic Studies* 13, 1 (2011), pp. 113–24.

———, 'The Ḥanābila and Early Sufis', *Arabica* 48, 3 (2001), pp. 352–67.

———, 'The Piety of the Hadith Folk', *International Journal of Middle East Studies* 34, 3 (August 2002), pp. 425–39.

Mez, Adam, *The Renaissance of Islam*, English trans. by Salahuddin Khuda Bukhsh and D. S. Margoliouth (London: Luzac and Co., 1937).

Michot, Yahya, *Muslim under Non-Muslim Rule: Ibn Taymiyya* (Oxford: Interface Publications, 2006).

Monnot, G., 'ṣalāt', in P. Bearman, T. Bianquis, C. E. Bosworth, E. van Donzel and W. P. Heinrichs (eds), *The Encyclopaedia of Islam, 2nd edn (EI2)* (Leiden: Brill, 1995), vol. 8, pp. 925–34; available at Brillonline.com.

Morony, Michael G., *Iraq after the Muslim Conquest* (Princeton: Princeton University Press, 1984).

Motzki, Harald, 'Dating Muslim Traditions: A Survey', *Arabica* 52, 2 (2005), pp. 204–53.

———, 'Introduction', in Harald Motzki (ed.), *Ḥadīth: Origins and Developments* (Aldershot: Ashgate Variorum, 2004), pp. xiii–lxiii.

Murad, Hasan Qasim, 'Ibn Taymiya on Trial: A Narrative Account of His Miḥan', *Islamic Studies* 18 (1979), pp. 1–32.

Neusner, Jacob, *The Mishnah: A New Translation* (New Haven: Yale University Press, 1988).

Nguyen, Martin, *Sufi Master and Qur'an Scholar: Abū'l-Qāsim al-Qushayrī and the Laṭā'if al-Ishārāt* (London: Oxford University Press in association with the Institue of Ismaili Studies, 2012).

Nöth, Winfried, 'Semiotic Foundations of Iconicity in Language and Literature', in Olga Fischer and Max Nänny (eds), *The Motivated Sign: Iconicity in Language and Literature 2* (Amsterdam: John Benjamins, 2000), pp. 17–28.

Postman, Neil, *The End of Education: Redefining the Value of School* (New York: Alfred Knopf, 1996).

Al-Qaḥṭānī, Saᶜīd ibn ᶜAlī, *Ṣalāt al-Mu'min: Mafhūm wa-Faḍā'il wa-Ādāb wa-Anwāᶜ wa-Aḥkām wa-Kayfiyya fī Ḍaw' al-Kitāb wa'l-Sunna* (Riyadh: Mu'assasat al-Juraysī li'l-Tawzīᶜ wa'l-Iᶜlān, 1423/[2002]).

Quiring-Zoches, Rosemarie, 'How al-Bukhārī's *Ṣaḥīḥ* was Edited in the Middle Ages: ᶜAlī al-Yūnīnī and His *Rumūz*', *Bulletin d'Ètudes Orientales* 50 (1998), pp. 191–222.

Ramadān, Ṭāhā Muḥammad Najjār, *Uṣūl al-Dīn ᶜinda 'l-Imām al-Ṭabarī* (Riyadh: Dār al-Kiyān, 1426/2005).

Rapoport, Yossef, *Marriage, Money and Divorce in Medieval Islamic Society* (Cambridge: Cambridge University Press, 2005).

Reichmuth, Stefan, 'Religion and Language', in Lutz Edzard and Rudolf de Jong (eds), *Encyclopedia of Arabic Language and Linguistics* (Brill Online, 2011).

Ritter, Hellmut, *The Ocean of the Soul: Man, the World and God in the Stories of Farīd al-Dīn ᶜAṭṭār*, trans. John O'kane, ed. Bernd Radtke (Leiden: Brill, 2003).

Rosenthal, Franz, 'General Introduction', in Franz Rosenthal (trans.), *The History of al-Ṭabarī* (Albany: State University of New York Press, 1989).

Saleh, Walid, *The Formation of the Classical Tafsīr Tradition: The Qur'an Commentary of al-Thaᶜlabi (d. 427/1035)* (Leiden: Brill, 2004).

Al-Saqā, Aḥmad Ḥijāzī, 'Qaḍiyyat al-Kitāb', in Fakhr al-Dīn al-Rāzī, *Asās al-Taqdīs*, ed. Aḥmad Ḥijāzī al-Saqā (Cairo: Maktaba Kulliyyāt al-Azhariyya, 1406/1989), pp. 259–78.

Al-Sarhan, Saud and Christopher Melchert, 'The Creeds of Aḥmad ibn Ḥanbal', in Robert Gleave (ed.), *Books and Bibliophiles: Studies in Honour of Paul Auchterlonie on the Bio-Bibliography of the Muslim World* (Oxford: Gibb Memorial Trust, 2014), pp. 29–44.

Schacht, Joseph, 'Al-Ashᶜarī, Abū Burda', in P. Bearman, T. Bianquis, C. E. Bosworth, E. van Donzel and W. P. Heinrichs (eds), *The Encyclopaedia of Islam, 2nd edn (EI2)* (Leiden: Brill, 1960), vol. 1, pp. 693–4; available at Brillonline.com.

———, *The Origins of Muhammadan Jurisprudence* (Oxford: Clarendon Press, 1967; 1st edn 1950).

Sellheim, R., 'al-Khaṭīb al-Baghdādī', in P. Bearman, T. Bianquis, C. E. Bosworth, E. van Donzel and W. P. Heinrichs (eds), *The Encyclopaedia of Islam, 2nd edn (EI2)* (Leiden: Brill, 1978), vol. 4, pp. 1111–12; available at Brillonline.com.

Senturk, Recep, *Narrative Social Structure: Anatomy of the Hadith Transmission Network, 610–1505* (Stanford: Stanford University Press, 2005).

Shah, Mustafa, 'Classical Islamic Discourse on the Origins of Language: Cultural Memory and the Defense of Orthodoxy', *Numen* 58 (2011), pp. 314–43.

———, 'Ḥadīṯ, Language of', in Lutz Edzard and Rudolf de Jong (eds), *Encyclopedia of Arabic Language and Linguistics* (Brill Online, 2011).

———, 'The Philological Endeavours of the Early Arabic Linguists: Theological Implications of the *tawqīf-iṣṭilāḥ* Antithesis and the Majāz Controversy (Part I), *Journal of Qurᵓanic Studies* 1, 1 (1999), pp. 27–46.

———, 'The Philological Endeavours of the Early Arabic Linguists: Theological Implications of the *tawqīf-iṣṭilāḥ* Antithesis and the Majāz Controversy (Part II), *Journal of Qurᵓanic Studies* 2, 1 (2000), pp. 44–66.

———, 'Al-Ṭabarī and the Dynamics of *tafsīr*: Theological Dimensions of a Legacy', *Journal of Qurᵓanic Studies* 15, 2 (2003), pp. 83–139.

———, 'Trajectories in the Development of Islamic Theological Thought: The Synthesis of *Kalām*', *Religion Compass* 1, 4 (2007), pp. 430–54.

Shākir, Muḥammad Aḥmad, 'Al-Nuskha al-Yūnīniyya min Ṣaḥīḥ al-Bukhārī', in al-Muhammad ibn Ismāᶜīl al-Bukhārī, *al-Jāmiᶜ al-Ṣaḥīḥ* (Beirut: Dār al-Jīl, n.d.).

Shams, Muḥammad ᶜUzayr and ᶜAlī ibn Muḥammad al-ᶜImrān (eds), *Al-Jāmiᶜ li-Sīrat Shaykh al-Islām Ibn Taymiyya (661–728) khilāl Sabᶜati Qurūn* (Mecca: Dār ᶜĀlim al-Fawāᵓid, 1420/[2000]).

Shihadeh, Ayman, 'From al-Ghazālī to al-Rāzī: 6th/12th Century Developments in Muslim Philosophical Theology', *Arabic Sciences and Philosophy* 15 (2005), pp. 141–79.

———, *The Teleological Ethics of Fakhr al-Dīn al-Rāzī* (Leiden: Brill, 2006).

Simon, Udo, 'Majāz', in Lutz Edzard and Rudolf de Jong (eds), *Encyclopedia of Arabic Language and Lingustics* (Brill Online, 2011).

Smith, David Norman, 'Judeophobia, Myth, and Critique', in S. Daniel Breslauer (ed.), *The Seductiveness of Jewish Myth* (Albany: State University of New York Press, 1997), pp. 123–54.

Speight, Marston, R., 'A Look at Variant Readings in the Ḥadīth', *Der Islam* 77 (2000), pp. 169–79.

———, 'Narrative structures in the Ḥadīth', *Journal of Near Eastern Studies* 59,4 (2000), pp. 265–71.

———, 'Oral Traditions of the Prophet Muḥammad: A Formulaic Approach', *Oral Tradition* 4, 1–2 (1989), pp. 27–37.

Sperl, Stefan, 'Man's "Hollow Core": Ethics and Aesthetics in Ḥadīth Literature and Classical Arabic Adab', *Bulletin of the School of Oriental and African Studies* 70, 3 (2007), pp. 459–86.

Steigerwald, Diana, 'Twelver Shīʿī Taʾwīl', in Andrew Rippin (ed.), *The Blackwell Companion to the Qurʾān* (Malden, MA: Blackwell Publishing, 2006), pp. 373–85.

Stone, Suzanne Last, 'Justice, Mercy, and Gender in Rabbinic Thought', *Cardozo Studies in Law and Literature* (A Commemorative Volume for Robert M. Cover) 8, 1 (Spring–Summer 1996), pp. 139–77.

Swartz, Merlin L., *A Medieval Critique of Anthropomorphism: Ibn al-Jawzī's* Kitāb Akhbār aṣ-Ṣifāt (Leiden: Brill, 2002).

———, *Ibn al-Jawzī's* Kitāb al-Quṣṣaṣ wa'l-Mudhakkirīn (Beirut: Dār al-Mashriq, 1971).

Thiele, Jan, 'Between Cordoba and Nīsābūr: The Emergence and Consolidation of Ashʿarism (Fourth–Fifth/Tenth–Eleventh Century)', in S. Schmidtke (ed.), *The Oxford Handbook of Islamic Theology* (New York: Oxford University Press, 2016), pp. 225–41.

Turner, John P., *Inquisition in Early Islam: The Competition for Political and Religious Authority in the Abbasid Empire* (London: I. B. Tauris, 2013).

Umansky, Ellen M., 'God as Mother', in Judith Kornberg Greenberg (ed.), *Encyclopedia of Love in World Religions* (Santa Barbara: ABC Clio, 2008), vol. 1, pp. 252–3.

van Ess, Josef, 'Ein Unbekanntes Fragment des Naẓẓām', in Wilhelm Hoenerbach (ed.), *Der Orient in der Forschung: Festschrift für Otto Spies* (Wiesbaden: Otto Harrassowitz, 1967), pp. 170–201.

———, *Theologie und Gesellschaft im 2. und 3. Jahrhundert Hidschra* [*TG*] (Berlin-New York: Walter de Gruyter, 1997).

van Renterghem, Vanessa, 'Structure et fonctionnement du réseau hanbalite bagdadien dans les premiers temps de la domination seldjoukide (milieu du ve/xie siècle)', in Damien Coulon, Christophe Picard et Dominique Valérian (eds), *Espaces et réseau en Méditerranée, II. La formation des réseaux* (Paris: Editions Bouchene, 2010), pp. 207–32.

Versteegh, Kees, 'Linguistic Attitudes and the Origin of Speech in the Arab World', in Petr Zemánek (ed.), *Studies in Near Eastern Languages and Literatures: Memorial Volume of Karel Petráček* (Prague: Academy of Sciences of the Czech Republic, 1996), pp. 589–603.

Warren-Rothlin, Andy, 'Idioms: Biblical Hebrew', in Geoffrey Khan (ed.), *Encyclopedia of Hebrew Language and Linguistics* (Brill Online, 2016).

Watt, Montegomery W., 'Badjīla', in P. Bearman, T. Bianquis, C. E. Bosworth, E. van Donzel and W. P. Heinrichs (eds), *The Encyclopaedia of Islam, 2nd edn (EI2)* (Leiden: Brill, 1960), vol. 1, p. 865; available at Brillonline.com.

———, *The Formative Period of Islamic Thought* (Edinburgh: Edinburgh University Press, 1973).

———, *Islamic Creeds: A Selection* (Edinburgh: Edinburgh University Press, 1994).

Watts, James, 'The Three Dimensions of Scriptures', *Postscripts* 2, 2–3 (2006), pp. 135–59.

Weiss, Bernard, 'Medieval Muslim Discussions of the Origins of Language', *Zeitschrift der Deutschen Morgenlandischen Gesellschaft* 124, 1 (1974), pp. 33–41.

Wensinck, Arent Jan, *The Muslim Creed: Its Genesis and Historical Development* (London: Frank Cass, 1932).

Williams, W. Wesley, 'Aspects of the Creed of Imam Ahmad ibn Hanbal: A Study of Anthropomorphism in Early Islamic Discourse', *International Journal of Middle East Studies* 34, 3 (August 2002), pp. 441–63.

———, *Tajallī wa-Ruʾya: A Study of Anthropomorphic Theophany and Visio Dei in the Hebrew Bible, the Qurʾān and Early Sunnī Islam*, unpublished doctoral dissertation, University of Michigan, 2008.

Wright, Benjamin (trans.), 'Sirach', in Albert Pietersma and Benjamin Wright (eds), *A New English Translation of the Septuagint (NETS)* (Oxford: Oxford University Press 2007); available online at http://ccat.sas.upenn.edu/nets/edition/30-sirach-nets.pdf and at Oxford Biblical Studies Online http://www.oxfordbiblicalstudies.com/article/book/obso-9780195288803/obso-9780195288803-miscMatter-7.

Wright, William, *A Grammar of the Arabic Language* (Cambridge: Cambridge University Press, 1997 [1st edn: vol. 1, 1859; vol. 2, 1862]).

Zimmerman, Andrew, *Anthropology and Antihumanism in Imperial Germany* (Chicago: University of Chicago Press, 2001).

Zouggar, Nadjet, 'L'impeccabilité du Prophète Muḥammad dans le credo Sunnite d'al-Ašʿarī (m. 324/935) à Ibn Taymiyya (m. 728/1328)', *Bulletin d'études orientales* 60 (2011), pp. 73–89.

Zysow, Aron, 'Karrāmiyya', in Sabine Schmidtke (ed.), *The Oxford Handbook of Islamic Theology* (New York: Oxford University Press, 2016), pp. 252–62.

Index

Note: n indicates an endnote and t a table

Abbott, H. Porter: *The Cambridge Introduction to Narrative*, 25

^{c}Abd al-Hamid the second, sultan, 223

^{c}Abd al-Wahid Mustafa, 357n238

al-abdāl ('The Substitutes'), 178n112

al-^{c}Abdari, Abu ^{c}Amir Muhammad ibn Sa^{c}dun ibn Murajja ibn Sa^{c}dun al-Qurashi al-Mayurqi al-Andalusi, 267–70, 332, 368

al-^{c}Abid al-Da^{cc}aʾ, Muhammad ibn Mus^{c}ab, 7–8

Abrahamov, Binyamin, 201

Abu ^{c}Amr al-Hiri, 292, 293

Abu Bakr, caliph, 26, 31

Abu Bakr, Yahya, 7, 10

Abu Burda al-Ash^{c}ari, 56, 366

  ḥādīth al-ruʾya, 38–43, 44, 45, 46–7, 48, 151–2

Abu Dharr al-Harawi: *Ṣaḥīḥ al-Bukhārī*, 222

Abu Hanifa, al-Nu^{c}man ibn Thabit, 97–8, 157

Abu Hurayra, 6, 27, 28, 31, 94, 97, 106n18, 129, 130, 131, 136, 137, 138, 156, 164, 165, 209, 211, 215, 246

Abu Hurra, Wasil ibn ^{c}Abd al-Rahman, 148

Abu Ja^{c}far, *sharif*, 275, 277, 293–4

Abu Mansur ibn Yusuf, 276–7

Abu Muslim al-Agharr, 31, 75

Abu Razin al-^{c}Uqayli, 68, 72, 128–9, 151, 152, 240, 366

  ḥādīth al-ruʾya, 73, 75–87, 89–90, 104, 204, 205, 295

  meeting with the Prophet, 78–9, 80–2, 84, 93–4

Abu Sa^{c}id al-A^{c}rabi, 87

Abu Talib al-Mushkani, 213–14, 216

Abu Tayba, 64n110

Abu ^{c}Ubayd al-Qasim ibn Sallam, 190, 191, 194, 196, 205, 249n10, 250n27, 255n105, 337

Abu ^{c}Ubayda, ibn ^{c}Abd Allah ibn Mas^{c}ud, 133, 134

Abu Ya^{c}la ibn al-Farraʾ, 227, 228, 274

  Ibṭāl al-taʾwīlāt, 12, 149–50, 212

Abu Yunus Sulaym ibn Jubayr, 129–30, 131, 138

Abu Zakariyya Yahya ibn ^{c}Abdak, 132, 138

Abu Zayd, Bakr, 358n248

Abyssinia, 363

ahl al-ḥadīth, 197, 200, 202; *see also muḥaddithūn*

ahl al-kalām, 197; *see also mutakallimūn*

ahl al-naẓar, 198

ahl al-sunna, 232

al-Ahmas clan, 96, 98

al-Ahmasi al-Bajali, Tariq ibn ^{c}Abd al-Rahman, 115n177

^{c}Aʾisha (the Prophet's wife), 9, 29, 53, 103, 108nn55, 206, 146–7

al-Ajurri, Abu Bakr: *Kitāb al-Sharī^{c}a*, 6–7, 33, 58n21, 90, 152, 159, 203

al-^{c}Alawi al-Harawi, Muhammad ibn Isma^{c}il ibn Husayn ibn Hamza, 294

^{c}Ali ibn Abi Talib, caliph, 92, 94, 95, 124

Allard, Michel, 242–3

al-A^{c}mash, Sulayman ibn Mihran, 145

al-Anbari, Abu Zakariyya Yahya ibn Muhammad, 343n43

al-ᶜAnbari, Muᶜadh ibn Muᶜadh, 137, 144
angels, 89, 91, 202, 234, 246, 315; *see also* Gabriel, Archangel
al-ᶜAnqazi, ᶜAmr ibn Muhammad, 142
al-Ansari al-Harawi, 151
anthropology, 170n2
anthropomorphism (*tashbīh*), 14–15, 329
 in Hadiths, 33–4, 129, 246, 267, 364
 in the Quran, 14, 100, 190, 192–3, 196, 198
 see also God: anthropomorphic descriptions of; *tashbīh*
anthropomorphists, 187, 338
anti-Semitism, 171n5
Arabic, 179n113, 241, 296
Arabica (journal), 121
Arberry, Arthur, 341n11, 349n144
al-Arnaᵓut, Shuᶜayb, 64n112
al-Asad, Husayn, 64n112
asceticism, 2
aṣḥāb al-raᵓy, 197–8, 250n39; *see also ahl al-ḥadīth*
al-Ashajj, ᶜAbd Allah ibn Saᶜid, 255n103
al-Ashᶜari, Abu 'l-Hasan, 12, 154, 229, 240, 241
 al-Ibāna, 234–6, 238–9, 324
 Maqālāt al-Islāmiyyīn, 235, 324
al-Ashᶜari, Abu Musa, 28, 40, 46, 47, 152, 246, 351n173
 ḥādīth al-fidāᵓ, 56
 ḥādīth al-ruᵓya (attrib.), 29, 33–6, 38, 41, 56
Ashᶜarism, 2, 232–3, 242
Ashᶜarites
 and *aḥādīth al-ṣifāt*, 169–70, 247–8
 and *Asās al-Taqdīs*, 312
 and corporeality of God, 304
 Ibn Taymiyya and, 320–1, 322–3, 324
 and rationalism, 277–8, 364, 368–9
 and *ithbāt*, 166–7
 and *Kitāb al-Tawḥīd*, 86
 Shafiᶜite, 303, 316, 317, 324–5, 328, 329, 330, 337–8
 and *tanzīh*, 224, 229, 234
 see also traditionalists: middle-of-the-road
al-Aswad al-ᶜAnsi, 111n109
al-Awzaᶜi, 191, 202, 225, 336
al-ᶜAyni, Badr al-Din, 220, 221, 229–30, 231, 233

al-Baghawi, al-Husayn ibn Masᶜud: *Sharḥ al-Sunna*, 175n65, 301–2
Baghdad, 13, 83, 100, 134, 143, 164, 194, 235, 236
 Bab al-Azaj market, 269–70, 332
 Hanbalites, 11
 hospital, 277
 al-Madrasa al-Nizamiyya, 277, 340n10
 al-Mansur mosque, 2, 236, 275, 294
 Qadiri Creed (*al-iᶜtiqād al-qādirī, al-risāla al-qādiriyya*), 272–8
 riots (929), 13–14, 364
 scholarship, 1–2
al-Bahili, Abu 'l-Hasan, 241–2
al-Bajali, ᶜAmir ibn Saᶜd, 26
al-Bajali, Bayan ibn Bishr, 115n177
al-Bajali, ᶜIsa ibn al-Musayyab, 115n177
al-Bajali, Jarir ibn ᶜAbd Allah, 68, 73, 74, 89–92, 98, 366
 aḥādīth, 93–9; *ḥadīth al-ruᵓya* (attrib.), 94, 185, 186, 203
al-Bajali, Khalid ibn Yazid ibn Khalid al-Qasri, 90
al-Bajali, Malik ibn Mighwal, 97
al-Bajali, Qays ibn Abi Hazim al-Ahmasi, 94–5, 99, 102–3
al-Bajali al-Qasri, Khalid ibn ᶜAbd Allah ibn Asad, 90
Bal, Mieke: *Narratology*, 25
al-Baladhuri, Abu 'l-Abbas Ahmad ibn Yahya ibn Jabir, 111n109
Banu al-Muntafiq, 76, 77, 81, 83, 365
Banu Bajila, 89, 91, 92, 93, 94, 96, 98, 218, 365
Banu Murad, 53
al-Baqillani, Abu Bakr, 241–2
al-Baraᵓ ibn ᶜAzib, 163
al-Barbahari, al-Hasan ibn ᶜAli, 1, 235, 236, 237
 Sharḥ al-Sunna, 225
Barthes, Roland, 25
Basra, 8, 83, 88, 131, 134, 143, 148, 150, 351n173
Basrans, 92–3
Battle of al-Qadisiyya, 92, 95, 112n113, 113n133, 113n140
Battle of Siffin, 94
Battle of the Camel, 103, 113n145
Bayān Talbīs al-Jahmiyya, 255n108
al-Baydawi, Nasir al-Din, 9, 88, 124–5, 152, 231–2
al-Bayhaqi, Abu Bakr Ahmad ibn al-Husayn, 164–5, 169, 219–20, 255n100
 al-Asmāᵓ wa'l-Ṣifāt, 66n150

al-Bayhaqi, Abu Bakr Ahmad ibn al-Husayn (*cont.*)
Shuᶜab al-Īmān, 62n72
al-Bazzar, Abu Bakr, 175n72
Beaumont, Daniel, 22, 23, 24–5, 29, 128
Bedouins, 72, 73, 77, 80, 82, 102, 204
bi-lā kayfa, 187–8, 189–94, 207, 213–14, 224–5, 229, 234–5, 241, 267, 270, 286, 296, 300, 318, 324, 337, 368, 369; see also *kayfiyya*
Bible, 203, 254n91, 272
al-Birzali, ᶜAlam al-Din, 357n233
blasphemy, 143, 201, 281, 285
Bori, Caterina
Ibn Taymiyya, 356n230
'New Source for the Biography of Ibn Taymiyya, A', 354n212
'Theology, Politics, Society', 352n181
Bousquet, Georges-Henri, 121
Brown, Jonathan A. C.: 'Scholars and Charlatans', 176n87
al-Bukhari, Abu ᶜAbd Allah Muhammad ibn Ismaᶜil, 71, 74–5, 85, 106n21, 113n134, 131, 143, 153, 211, 289
Rafᶜ al-Yadayn, 313
Saḥīḥ al-Bukhārī, 208, 215, 216, 217, 218, 219, 220, 221, 223, 229
al-Saḥīḥān, 186

Cairo
Asās al-Taqdīs, 303, 312
Bulaq printing house, 223
Citadel Court, 327
kalām, 316, 324
El Calamawy, Sahair, 22
censorship, 210–11, 216, 218, 222, 223, 229
Chatman, Seymour, 27
Story and Discourse, 25
Christians, 2, 34, 35, 36, 37, 41, 43, 45
clothing, 127
Cook, Michael, 19n32
Cordoba, 350n164
corporealism *see tajsīm*
creeds, 226–7, 235, 237
Hanbalite, 368
Ibn Taymiyya, 317–18
Qadiri (*al-iᶜtiqād al-qādirī, al-risāla al-qādiriyya*), 271, 273–8
Qaᵓimi (*al-iᶜtiqād al-qāᵓimī*), 274
al-Sibghi, Abu Bakr Ahmad ibn Ishaq, 291–2

al-Dabbi, Quadama ibn Hamata, 44
Damascenes, 214
Damascus, 39, 43, 92, 298, 303, 312, 316, 322, 324, 325–6, 328, 329, 330, 332, 369
al-Daqiqi, Muhammad ibn ᶜAbd al-Malik, 7
al-Daraqutni, Abu Hasan ᶜAli ibn ᶜUmar, 3, 60n54, 97, 98, 360–1, 364
Kitāb al-Ruᵓya, 152, 175n67
al-Darimi, ᶜAbd Allah, 249n18
al-Darimi, Abu Saᶜid ᶜUthman ibn Saᶜid, 56–7, 107n31, 199, 353n198
Naqḍ al-Imām, 196, 225, 250n31
al-Radd ᶜalā al-Jahmiyya, 33, 180n141
Dawood, N. J., 341n11, 349n144
debate
public (*munāẓara*), 194–5, 280, 283
theological, 14, 72–3, 278, 280, 298, 301–2, 364
al-Dhahabi, Shams al-Din, 11, 74, 85, 95, 101, 103, 113n145, 131, 151, 194–6, 216, 268, 270, 281, 287, 322, 355n219, 365
response to Ibn Khuzayma's *ḥadīth al-ṣūra*, 297
Siyar Aᶜlām al-Nubalāᵓ, 17n5, 51, 66n146, 279, 292, 295–6, 343n44
Tadhkirat al-Ḥuffāẓ, 174n52, 255n103
Tārīkh al-Islām, 117n195, 346n100
al-Dhuhli, Muhammad ibn Yahya, 131–2
al-Dimashqi, Abu 'l-Hasan ᶜAli *see* al-ᶜUrdi al-Dimashqi, Abu 'l-Hasan ᶜAli ibn Ahmad ibn Muhammad ibn Salih
dīn al-ᶜajāᵓiz (the religion of old women), 299, 312
divorce, 5
dualism *(thanawiyya)*, 7, 10

Egypt, 131; *see also* Cairo

al-Faqih, Abu 'l-Walid Hasan ibn Muhammad, 282
al-Farazdaq, 46
Fatima (daughter of the Prophet and wife of ᶜAli ibn Abi Talib), 124
al-Firbari, Yusuf, 221
fiṭra, 252n70, 298, 299, 322
Frank, R. M., 229
free agents (*mutaṣarrif*): human heart, 308, 309

Gabriel, Archangel, 87–8, 89, 94, 148–9, 214
Genette, Gérard: *Narrative Discourse*, 23, 25
gesticulation, 123, 163, 164–5
  'iconic', 124
  muḥaddithūn, 157
  Prophet Muhammad, 129, 135, 146, 154–5
  transmission of Hadiths, 138, 161, 267
gestures
  in court, 155–6
  and declarations, 159, 164
  deictic, 123, 124–5, 154
  description of, 126–7
  forbidden, 161
  regarding God, 156, 189
  of Greeks, 123
  Hashwiyya and, 328–39
  human, 156–7
  iconicity of, 123, 369
  al-īmā᾽ wa'l-ishāra, 351n173
  al-ishāra bi'l-sabbāba, 313, 314, 327
  of Mary, mother of Jesus, 181n161
  meaning of, 122–3
  metaphoric, 123, 124–5, 128, 130, 131, 136–7, 154, 155, 169, 233, 334, 368, 369
  of narrators, 129, 132–3, 136–45, 147, 150–1, 153–4, 160, 225, 365, 367–8
  of the Prophet, 121, 123, 124–7, 130, 135–6, 137, 146–7, 154–5, 159, 163, 164, 165, 168, 169–70, 324, 327, 333, 335
  rafᶜ al-yadayn, 313–15, 327
  of Romans, 123
  and sign language, 120, 121
  and speech, 123, 124, 127, 128
  spontaneous, 160–4, 365
  trials of, 326–8
  types of, 123–4
al-Ghazali, Abu Hamid, 176n87
Gilliot, Claude: *Exégèse, langue, et théologie*, 18n10
Gimaret, Daniel, 139–40, 208
  Dieu a l'image de l'homme, 57n1, 279
God
  anthropomorphic descriptions of, 5, 14, 129, 188, 204, 226, 243, 244–5, 286–9, 290, 298–9, 305–8, 318–19
  attributes and actions of, 26, 72, 80, 130, 131, 135, 136, 137, 149, 162–3, 165, 166, 167, 186, 191–2, 195, 197, 198–9, 210, 226–7, 239–40, 274, 281, 311–12, 328
  corporeality of, 214–15, 303–4
  descent of, 30–1, 79, 159, 167, 193–4, 197
  dialogue with Muslims, 35
  gestures regarding, 156, 189
  hand of (*yad*, pl. *aydin*), 14, 48, 55, 56, 79, 124, 160, 163, 167, 168, 188, 198, 227, 237, 238, 245, 262n195, 299, 305, 306–7; two hands of, 197, 198–9, 226, 235, 238, 239, 240, 287–9, 307
  laughter of, 34, 35, 75, 130, 133, 134, 152, 190, 191, 192, 199, 226, 227, 244
  loin of (*ḥaqw*), 16, 208, 209, 215, 217, 218, 219, 220, 221, 222, 224, 226, 227, 228–9, 230–2, 310, 369
  mumāssa (physical contact or connection with creation), 79, 362
  perfection of (*kamāl*), 199, 239, 243, 251n46, 318–19
  personal invocation to (*duᶜā᾽*), 313, 315
  and the Resurrection, 75, 76, 79, 80
  seeing, 186
  situation of, 75–6, 159, 170, 204, 205–6, 237–8
  spatiality of, 186, 197, 314, 315, 322, 323, 324, 335, 336–7, 369
  taḥdīd, 204
  taᶜṭīl, 158, 167, 195, 238, 286, 292, 295, 312, 319
  transcendence of, 268
  utterance of the Quran, 327
Goldziher, Ignaz, 121, 123, 208, 220
  'Gestures and Sign Language among the Arabs' ('Ueber Gebärden – und Zeichensprache bei den Arabern'), 120, 121
  Der Mythos bei den Hebräern und seine geschichtliche Entwicklung, 171n6
  Die Richtungen der islamischen Koranauslesung, 17n10
  The Zahiris, 258n131
Graham, William A., 270, 271, 272, 276
Günther, Sebastian, 22
  'Fictional Narration and Imagination within an Authoritative Framework', 23–5, 27, 58n22

Haddad, Gibril Fouad, 358n251, 359n263
Hadiths
on the advent of the Prophet and the Hour, 125
al-akḥām, 23
akhbār al-āḥād, 240, 245, 246
of allegiance, 77, 82–3, 85–7, 240
Ashᶜarites and, 337
aṭīṭ al-raḥl, 152, 186
audiences, 24, 32, 38–42, 269–70
in Basra, 8–9
on beatific vision, 90, 94
of the black slave girl, 156, 158, 244
blasphemous, 201
coherence of, 24
al-Daraqutni on, 360
definition, 23
divine attributes, 162
of the divine fingers, 23, 29, 30, 48–57, 128, 152, 200, 227, 284–5, 308, 309
eschatological, 34
exegeses, 24
fabricated texts, 187, 204, 206, 207, 246; *see also al-mawḍuᶜāt*
al-fidāʾ, 38, 47–57; *fidāʾ al-muʾmin*, 44
gestures in *see under* gestures
God as a curly young man (*al-shābb al-qaṭaṭ*) 152–3, 186, 201, 204, 244–5
ḥaqw al-raḥmān see Hadiths: *al-raḥim*
ḥikāya munqaṭiᶜa, 340n5
Ibn Khuzayma, 314
isnāds, 47–8, 57, 83, 84, 95, 340n5
Judeo-Christian sources, 203
Kitāb al-Tawḥīd, 282–3
maghāzī (al-sīra), 23
manuals, 154, 162
matn, 47, 48
al-mutawātira, 353n203
al-Najjad's paraphrasing of, 5
narratology, 23–5
al-nuzūl, 30–2, 186, 197, 203, 227, 263n205
paratexts, 47, 48
al-raḥim (*ḥadīth ḥaqw al-raḥmān*), 208–10, 212, 213, 215, 216, 218–19, 223–4, 225–6, 227, 229–31, 232, 233–4, 310
role, 68
al-ruʾya, 29, 33–6, 38–43, 45, 48, 56, 68–105, 197; Abu Hurayra, 96; Abu Razin, 73, 75–87, 89–90, 104, 204, 205, 295; anthropomorphism, 33–4; audience, 74; Ibn al-Farraʾ, 330; Ibn Hanbal, 185–6
Saḥīḥ al-Bukhārī, 14, 62n71, 71, 97
al-Saḥīḥān, 33
al-shābb al-qaṭaṭ, 186
al-ṣifāt, 5–7, 8, 15, 21–57, 104, 238, 306, 365–6, 367–9; Abu Ya'la, 330; anthropomorphism, 129, 267, 364; Ash'arites and, 169–70, 247–8; al-Bajali's narrative, 73–5, 93–9, 186, 203; contextualisation of, 365; controversy of, 364, 369; dicta, 25–7, 28; earliest debate, 206–15; embedded narrative, 25, 27, 33–8; framing narrative, 25–33; gestures, 121, 128–9; Ibn Furak's reading of, 242–7; in Ibn Khuzayma's *Kitāb al-Tawḥīd*, 278, 282, 283–7, 292, 293, 294, 298; Ibn Salama's performances, 146–53; Ibn Taymiyya and, 317, 322; iconicity of, 186–7, 367, 369–70; *kayfiyya* (modality), 192; al-Khudri's narrative, 96; literal understanding of, 267–71; literary analysis of, 21–57, 366–7; paraphrases, 226; presentation, 368; public debates on, 339; rationalists and, 320; al-Razi's interpretations of, 309–10; settings, 32; theological debates, 72–3, 271–339; traditionalistic approach, 189–206, 367; transmission of, 100, 215, 245–7, 285, 361, 368
al-sīra see maghāzī
study of, 1, 2, 3–4
of 'the summit of the heavenly throne' (*qimmat al-ᶜarsh*), 159; *see also* Hadiths: *aṭīṭ al-raḥl*
al-ṣūra, 296–7, 301
al-taʾlīf bayna al-akhbār, 284
al-tashbīh (derogatory), 201
transmitters, 6, 98, 102, 103, 125, 130, 221
ṭuruq, 284
wajh (pl. *awjūh*), 203, 306
written, 147
see also aḥādīth al-tashbīh
al-Hakim Abu Saᶜid, 345n78
al-Hakim al-Nisaburi, Abu ᶜAbd Allah Muhammad ibn ᶜAbd Allah

Ma^c rifat ^c Ulūm al-Ḥadīth wa-Kamiyyat Ajnāsihi, 342n36, 343n44
Tārīkh Nīsābūr, 342n36
al-Hallaj, 343n36
al-Hamadhani, Mujalid ibn Sa^cid al-Kufi, 115n177
Hamat (Syria), 317, 321–3
al-Ḥamawiyya al-Kubrā, 354–5n212
al-Hanafi, Abu Bakr, 211
Hanafites, 156, 198, 280, 283, 300–1, 350n164
Hanbalism, 9, 33
Hanbalites
and *aḥādīth,* 2, 8–10, 12–13, 85, 87, 207, 223–4, 235, 239, 240, 247, 368–9
and anthropomorphism, 153, 237, 270, 361
creed of, 5, 226
and gestures, 130, 161, 162, 169
as Hashwiyya, 329
and Ibn Hanbal's *Musnad,* 139
and Ibn Khuzayma's *Kitāb al-Tawhīd,* 294, 296, 298
and al-Khallal, 11
and al-Najjad, 3
and Qadiri Creed, 276–7, 278
al-Razi and, 302, 303, 315
riots (929), 13–14
support for, 1
al-Tabari and, 18n10
and traditionalism, 343n43, 364
al-Harb, Sulayman, 153
Hashwiyya (*al-ḥashwiyya*), 161, 164, 187, 193, 197, 200, 201–2, 237, 248n1, 328–39
Heaven, 35, 37, 75–6, 91, 108n47, 133, 149, 155, 156, 159, 160, 167, 193, 203, 204, 210, 226, 238, 244, 262n195, 264n222, 281, 284, 288, 337; *see also* God: descent of; God: situation of
Hell, 34, 35, 36, 37, 38, 41, 43, 45, 47, 81, 108n47, 133, 156, 226
Herat (Afghanistan), 294
heresy, 285, 288, 289–90, 303, 310, 311, 318, 338, 370
heretics, 7, 13, 34, 37, 54, 201, 202, 204, 213, 273, 321, 322
Hijaz, 31, 154, 212
ḥijjat al-wadā^ᵓ ('the Farewell Pilgrimage'), 78, 169, 323–4
al-Hisni, Taqi al-Din, 331–3
Hoffman, Valerie, 118n211
al-Hudhali, Abu Ma^cmar, 142–3
al-Hudhali, Ghundar Muhammad ibn Ja^cfar, 258n131
human motives (*dā^cī* , pl. *dawā^cin*), 308–9

Ibadites, 118n211
Iblis *see* Satan
Ibn ^cAbbad, Muhammad, 217
Ibn ^cAbbad, al-Sahib, 242
Ibn ^cAbbas, ^cAbd Allah, 4, 6, 12, 26, 29, 49, 53, 84, 117n200, 141–2, 146, 284, 363
Ibn ^cAbd al-Barr, Abu ^cUmar Yusuf, 192
al-Tamhīd, 162–3
Ibn ^cAbd al-Hadi, Abu ^cAbd Allah Muhammad, 354n212
Ibn ^cAbd al-Rahman, Muhammad Jalal al-Din al-Shafi^ci, 326
Ibn ^cAbd al-Rahman, Sa^cid, 179n121
Ibn ^cAbd al-Rahman, ^cUmar Imam al-Din al-Shafi^ci, 326
Ibn ^cAbd al-Rahman, Wasil *see* Abu Hurra
Ibn ^cAbd Allah, Isma^cil, 217–18
Ibn ^cAbd Allah, Jabir, 179n119, 323
Ibn ^cAbd Allah, Tahir, 193
Ibn Abi Burda, Sa^cid, 41, 43
Ibn Abi Duwad, qadi, 101–2, 103, 104
Ibn Abi Khalid, Isma^cil, 94, 96, 98, 153, 366
Ibn Abi Muzarrid, Mu^cawiya, 211, 216
Ibn Abi Shayba, 113n134
Ibn Abi Talib, Ja'far, 363
Ibn Abi Ya^cla, Abu 'l-Husayn Muhammad ibn Muhammad ibn al-Farra^ᵓ, 3, 12, 235, 274
Ṭabaqāt al-Ḥanābila, 60n55, 191
Ibn ^cAdlan, 327
Ibn Ahmad ibn Hanbal, ^cAbd Allah, 85, 133n134
Kitāb al-Sunna, 42, 142, 144
Ibn al-Ajda^c, Masruq, 134
Ibn al-Anbari: *Nuzhat al-Alibbā^ᵓ*, 179n113
Ibn al-^cArabi, 126
Ibn al-^cAs, ^cAbd Allah ibn ^cAmr, 198
Ibn al-Asamm, Yazid, 117n200
Ibn al-Aswad, Dalham, 77–9, 83–4, 85, 107n35
Ibn al-^cAttar, Abu 'l-Hasan, 7
Ibn al-Fadl, Abu Tahir Muhammad, 293
Ibn al-Farra^ᵓ, Abu Ya^cla, 330, 349n159

Ibn al-Hakam, Shurahbil, 287
Ibn al-Hasan, 164, 166, 241–7, 318, 321
Ibn al-Jamil, Haytham, 145
Ibn al-Jarrah, Waki[c], 97
Ibn al-Jawzi, [c]Abd al-Rahman, 166, 168, 227–8, 330
Kitāb al-Mawḍū[c]āt, 139–40, 256n118
Al-Muntaẓam fī Tārīkh al-Rusul wa'l-Mulūk, 274
Ibn al-Khattab, [c]Umar, 88, 111n105, 112n113, 125, 127
Ibn al-Madini, [c]Ali, 100–1, 102, 103–4, 113n145
Ibn al-Mawsili, Muhammad *see* Ibn Qayyim al-Jawziyya and Ibn al-Mawsili, Muhammad
Ibn al-Mubarak, [c]Abd Allah, 211, 216, 295
Ibn al-Mu'tazz, [c]Abd Allah, 157
Ibn Na[ɔ]il, [c]Amir, 287
Ibn al-Sakan, Qays, 133
Ibn al-Tabari, Muhammad ibn Sa[c]id, 84–5
Ibn al-Walid, Abu Ali, 277
Ibn al-Walid, Khalid, 94
Ibn [c]Ammar, Hisham, 212, 213, 214–15, 216–17, 224, 255n103
Ibn [c]Amr, [c]Abd Allah, 210
Ibn [c]Amr al-Salmani, [c]Abida, 53, 55, 128, 366
ḥadīth of the divine fingers, 49–57
Ibn Anas, Malik, 127, 161, 162, 163, 164, 191–2, 202, 212, 217, 225, 336–7
Ibn [c]Aqil, 330, 353n194
Ibn [c]Asakir, Abu 'l-Qasim [c]Ali, 43, 84, 236–7, 268–9, 270, 340nn7, 10
Ibn [c]Asim, Nahik, 78
Ibn [c]Ata, Ya[c]la, 83, 84
Ibn [c]Ayyash, [c]Abd al-Rahman, 83–4
Ibn Ayyub, Muhammad (al-Malik al-[c]Adil), 302, 303
Ibn Batta, 18n14
Ibn Battal, 155, 156
Ibn Battuta, 330–1, 332–3
Ibn Bilal, Sulayman, 211, 216t
Ibn Bishr, Bayan, 116n178
Ibn Di[c]ama, Qatada, 136, 149
Ibn Furak, Abu Bakr Ahmad ibn Muhammad ibn Ayyub, 342n30
Ibn Furak, Abu Bakr Muhammad, 164, 166, 241–7, 275, 318, 321
Mujarrad Maqālāt al-Ash[c]arī, 239–40
Mushkil al-Ḥadīth aw Ta[ɔ]wīl al-Akhbār al-Mutashābiha, 242–3, 312, 320, 345n83
Ibn Ghazali, Abu Hamid, 353n194
Ibn Hajar al-[c]Asqalani, Abu 'l-Fadl Ahmad, 14, 125, 156, 220, 221, 229–30, 231, 293, 350n164, 356n229
al-Durar al-Kāmina, 332
Fatḥ al-Bārī, 155, 220, 221
Ibn Hamza, Ibrahim, 217
Ibn Hanbal, Ahmad, 2, 10, 17n5, 33, 41, 42, 43, 82, 96, 97, 100, 211–12
al-'Ilal, 101
creeds, 227
ḥadīth al-ru'ya, 185–6
Musnad, 3, 12, 33, 42, 43, 76, 84, 85, 139, 144, 152, 207, 212
Al-Radd [c]alā al-Zanādiqa (attrib.), 225
see also Hanbalites
Ibn Hani[ɔ], Muhammad ibn Salih, 281
Ibn Harb, Sulayman, 143, 144
Ibn Harun, Sahl, 150
Ibn Hashim, Yahya, 97
Ibn Hawshab, Shahr, 29–30, 56
Ibn Hazm, Abu Muhammad, 269
Ibn Hibban, Abu Hatim, 84, 165, 169
Ibn Husam al-Din, Abu al-Mafakhir Ahmad Jalal al-Din 325
Ibn Ibrahim ibn Muzayn, Yahya, 192
Ibn [c]Imran, Harmala, 129–30, 131, 133, 163
Ibn [c]Isa, Abu Isma[c]il Qurra, 145
Ibn Ishaq, Hanbal, 100
Ibn Isma[c]il, Hatim, 211, 216t, 256n119
Ibn Jahbal, Shihab al-Din Yahya Ibn Isma[c]il, 263n201, 334, 335, 338–9
Ibn Jabr, Mujahid, 3–4, 6, 7, 9, 14, 176n76, 360
Ibn Jahir, 275
Ibn Jinni, 351n173
Ibn Jubayr, Sa[c]id, 174n51
Ibn Jundub, Samura, 127
Ibn Kathir, [c]Imād al-Dīn Abu 'l-Fidā[ɔ] Isma[c]īl ibn [c]Umar, 13–14, 76–7, 354n212
al-Bidāya wa'l-Nihāya, 77, 110n85, 111n103, 342n29, 355n218
Ibn Khuzayma, Abu Bakr Muhammad ibn Ishaq al-Sulami al-Nisaburi
biography, 279–82
al-Dhahabi's criticism of, 297–8
Hadith compilations, 314
as a heretic, 303, 310, 311

Kitāb al-Tawḥīd, 33, 86, 131–2, 144–5, 175n67, 203, 207, 243, 249n6, 278–9, 280, 281, 282–9, 321–2
Hanbalites' response to, 294–7, 298
iconicity of, 282, 294
performative dimension of, 293
popularity of, 298–9
al-Razi's response to, 301–13
oral teachings, 281
rupture with former disciples, 292
semantic dimension of, 292–3
visit to Cairo, 343n37
Ibn Kullab, ᶜAbd Allah, 290, 345n81
Ibn Laqit, ᶜAsim, 82, 83
Ibn Mahdi, Ibrahim Ibn ᶜAbd al-Rahman, 147
Ibn Maja, ᶜAbd Allah Muhammad ibn Yazid al-Qazwini, 205
Ibn Makhlad, Khalid, 211
Ibn Makhluf, Zayn al-Din ᶜAli, 327
Ibn Malik, Anas, 29, 30, 33, 133, 134–5, 136–8, 141, 143, 144, 145, 146, 148
Ibn Manda, Abu ᶜAbd Allah, 85–6
Al-Radd ᶜalā al-Jahmiyya, 145
Ibn Masᶜud, ᶜAbd Allah, 29, 33, 41, 48–9, 50, 55, 56, 61n60, 94, 127, 133, 134, 157, 175n67
disciples, 51, 52, 56–7
ḥadīth al-ru'ya (attrib.), 37, 41
ḥadīth of the divine fingers, 152, 200, 284
Ibn Muᶜadh, Muᶜadh, 151
Ibn Muᶜawiya, Iyas, 141
Ibn Muhallab, Yazid, 46
Ibn Muhammad, Bishr, 217t, 218
Ibn Muhammad ibn Saᶜid, Yahya, 175n67
Ibn Musa, Bishr, 2
Ibn Musa, Sulayman, 90
Ibn Musᶜab, Muhammad, 8
Ibn Muslim, ᶜAffan, 143–4
Ibn Muzahim, Nasr, 93
Ibn Nasr, Ahmad, 104
Ibn Nasr, Asbat, 142
Ibn Qays, ᶜAlqama, 51, 53, 366
ḥādīth of the divine fingers, 49–57, 128
Ibn Qayyim al-Jawziyya, 14, 86–7, 174n51, 210, 320, 354n212, 358n248, 362–5, 369
Ḥādī al-Arwāḥ ilā Bilād al-Afrāḥ, 86, 99–100, 175n66
Iᶜlām al-Muwaqqiᶜīn, 105n7
al-Kāfiya al-Shāfiya fī 'l-Intsār li'l-Firqa al-Nājiya, 295, 333–4, 362, 364, 365
Zād al-Maᶜād, 86–7
Ibn Qayyim al-Jawziyya and Ibn al-Mawsili, Muhammad
Mukhtasar al-Sawāᶜiq, 60n55, 254n95
Ibn Qutayba, Abu Muhammad ᶜAbd Allah ibn Muslim, 188–9, 196–206, 239, 288, 318, 365
Kitāb al-Ikhtilāf fī 'l-Lafẓ, 196–7, 198–9
Kitāb Mukhtalif al-Ḥadīth, 284
Taʾwīl Mukhtalif al-Ḥadīth, 196–7, 200–1, 238
Ibn Rabah, Bilal, 127, 128
Ibn Rahwayh, Abu Yaᶜqub Ishaq ibn Ibrahim, 17n5, 193–4, 195, 196, 280
Ibn Rajab, ᶜAbd al-Rahman ibn Ahmad, 72, 317, 354n212, 355n216
Ibn Saᶜd, Muhammad al-Zuhri, 53
Ibn Saᶜid, Qutayba, 217
Ibn Sakan, 221
Ibn Salama, Hammad, 109n66, 134, 135, 136, 138–9, 140–1, 143–4, 145, 146, 159, 202, 246, 321, 366
aḥādīth al-ṣifāt, 147–53, 204
Ibn Shihab, Muhammad Abu Bakr al-Zuhri, 202, 224
Ibn Sinan, Suhayb, 28
Ibn Sirin, Muhammad, 51, 66n146
Ibn Sulayman, Khaythama, 145
Ibn Sulayman, Muqatil, 98, 161, 299
Ibn Taymiyya, Taqi al-Din Ahmad ibn ᶜAbd al-Halim, 151, 166, 362–3, 364–5, 369
Bayān Talbīs al-Jahmiyya, 210, 212, 263n201, 295, 316–17, 327, 362
bi-lā kayfa, 318–19
Hadith- *al-mutawātira,* 322, 327, 353n203
al-Ḥamawiyya al-Kubrā, 294, 316–28, 334–6
ᶜilm ḍarūrī (necessary knowledge), 322
ᶜilm yaqīn (certain knowledge), 322
labelling of, 328–9, 333, 338
repudiation of (according to al-Nuwayri), 328
trials of (*miḥan,* ordeals), 326–8, 329–32
Ibn ᶜUbayd Allah, Talha, 44
Ibn ᶜUdus (Hudus), Wakiᶜ, 82, 83, 84, 204, 205, 206

Ibn ᶜUtba ibn Masᶜud, ᶜAwn ibn ᶜAbd Allah, 41
Ibn ᶜUyayna, Sufyan, 39, 97, 191, 192, 321
Ibn Wahb, ᶜAbd Allah, 163
Ibn Yahya, Harmala, 163–4
Ibn Yaᶜmar, Yahya, 88
Ibn Yasar, Abu 'l-Hubab Saᶜid, 211
Ibn Yasar, Saᶜid, 211
Ibn Zafil (a derogative name of Ibn Qayyim al-Jawziyya), 358n248
Ibn Zahra', 331
Ibn Zayd, Hammad, 127, 128
Ibn Zubayr, ᶜAbd Allah, 82–3
icons, 276
ijāza (license to transmit a book), 346n86
Ikrima (disciple of Ibn Abbas), 26, 142
ᶜilm al-rijāl, 101
aᵓimmat al-hudā vs. aᵓimmat al-ḍalāl (Taymiyyan terminology), 353n199
infidelity, 296
infinite regress (*tasalsul*), 309
'innovators', 294
Iran, 147–8; *see also* Rayy
Iraq, 213–14, 365; *see also* Baghdad; Kufa
al-Isfahani, Abu Nuᶜaym, 72–3
al-Isfahani, Dawud ibn ᶜAli [ibn Khalaf], 160–1
al-Isfarayini, Abu Ishaq, 26, 183n184, 241–2
Islam
  and civilisation, 170n2
  public debates on, 194–5
  see also Muslims
al-Israᵓili, ᶜAbd Allah ibn Salam Abu 'l-Harith, 8
al-ishāra bi'l-sabbāba, 350–1n167
iṣṭilāḥ, 240, 351n173
ithbāt, 167–9
ᶜIyad, Qadi, 128, 220, 230–1, 344n59
  Ikmāl, 253n90, 344n59

Jaghan, Sayf al-Din, 325–6
Jāhiliyya, 81
al-Jahiz, 123, 151, 157
Jahmites *see* Muᶜtazilites
Jesus Christ, 181n161, 364
Jews, 1, 2, 43, 45, 163, 167, 246
  and Muslims, 34, 35, 36, 37, 41
  see also rabbis
Jordan, William, 69
al-Jubbaᵓi, Abu ᶜAli, 236
al Jubbaᵓi, Abu Hashim, 236, 240, 351n173
al-Juhani, Maᶜbad, 88
al-Juhani, Rifaᶜa ibn ᶜAraba, 31, 32
al-Jurayri, Abu Masᶜud Saᶜid ibn Iyas, 8
al-Juwayni, Abu 'l-Maᶜali, 300, 359n269
Juynboll, G. H. A., 98, 112n130, 116n182

kalām, 1, 2, 161, 198, 230, 236, 240, 241, 242, 279, 280, 288, 290, 300, 305, 306, 307, 309, 312, 314, 316, 318
Kalmar, Ivan: 'The Völkerpsychologie', 171n5
Karramites, 242, 243, 280, 302, 303, 315, 329
al-Kāshif ᶜan Ḥaqāᵓiq al-Sunan, 232
al-Kawthari, Abu'l Hasan Muhammad Zahid ibn al-Hasan ibn ᶜAli, 357n238, 358n248
kayfiyya, 192, 197
Kendon, Adam, 122–3
khabar literature, 23
Khalid ibn Makhlad, 217t, 218
Khalil, Ghulam, 101
al-Khalil ibn Ahmad, 179n113
al-Khallal, Abu Bakr Ahmad ibn Muhammad: *Kitāb al-Sunna*, 10
Khan, Dr Muhammad Muhsin, 223
Kharijites, 280, 283
al-Khatib, Abu Bakr, 4
al-Khatib al-Baghdadi, 3, 103, 157, 183n184, 247–8
  Tārīkh Madīnat al-Salām, 17n8, 102, 117n195, 118n209
al-Khatib al-Tabrizi, Wali Allah, 262n192
al-Khatmi, Abu Musa Ishaq ibn Musa, 132
al-Khayyat, Abu 'l-Qasim ᶜAbd al-ᶜAziz ibn ᶜAli, 9
al-Khudri, Abu Saᶜid, 31, 33, 74, 106n18
  ḥadīth al-ruᵓya (attrib.), 37, 97
Khurasan, 46, 85, 109n76, 131, 193, 242, 261n179, 282, 295, 315, 344
al-Khuzaᶜi, Ahmad ibn Nasr, 104
Khuzaymiyya, 280–1, 289, 291, 293
al-Khwarizmi, Abu Bakr Muhammad ibn Musa ibn Muhammad, 300–1
al-Kindi, Raja' ibn Haywa, 62n80
kinship, 208, 209, 233
al-Kirmani, Shams al-Din, 125–6
Kufa (Iraq), 52, 83, 92, 93, 134, 142, 145, 146, 350n164, 365
Kullabiyya, 290
al-Kushmihani, Abu Haytham, 222

al-Lalaka'i, Abu 'l-Qasim Hibat Allah, 160, 161, 162
language
metaphor, 16–17, 162, 232, 241
sign, 120, 121
theories of, 240–1, 351n173
see also Arabic
Laoust, Henri, 190–1
Laqit ibn ᶜAmir (Laqit ibn Sabira or Sabara) *see* Abu Razin al-ᶜUqayli
al-Layth Saᶜd, 182n179, 191, 225
al-Laythi al-Bukhari, Abu Muslim, 294
Lazarus, Moritz, 120, 121
Lecomte, Gérard, 196, 250n36
Leder, Stefan: 'The Literary Use of the Khabar: A Basic Form of Historical Writing', 25, 29
Levi, Rabbi, 179n119
liᶜān (oath of condemnation of the deaf husband), 154, 155, 158, 181n161
al-Lihyani, Ahmad ibn Saᶜid, 205
Little, Donald, 332
Lucas, Scott: *Constructive Critics*, 113n130

McNeill, David, 123, 124
Madelung, Wilfred: 'The Origins of the Controversy concerning the Creation of the Koran', 345n81
al-Mahalli, Jalal al-Din Muhammad ibn Ahmad and Suyuti, Jalal al-Din: *Tafsīr al-Jalālayn,* 361
Makdisi, George, 162, 352n180
al-Maktaba al-Shamela, 139
al-Malati, Abu 'l-Husayn, 176n85
al-Malik al-ᶜAdil, sultan (Muhammad ibn Ayyub), 302, 303
al-Malik al-Nasir, sultan, 328
Malikites, 155–6, 169, 192, 343n43, 350n164
Mallery, Garrick, 120
Mamluks, 369
al-Ma'mun, caliph, 100, 177n98, 273
al-Mansur, Abu Jaᶜfar, caliph, 84
al-Marisi, Bishr, 180n141, 320–1
Kufr al-Mushabbiha, 321
al-Marwazi, Abu Zaid, 221, 223–4, 228–9, 258n140
al-Marwazi (al-Marrudhi), Ahmad ibn Muhammad Abu Bakr, 9, 10–11, 12, 159–60, 169, 212–13, 214
al-Marwazi al-Sakhtyani, Bishr ibn Muhammad, 218
Mary, mother of Jesus, 181n161
al-mawḍuᶜāt, 181n151
Maymuna Bint al-Harith, 117n200, 211
Mecca, 32, 131
Medina, 32, 71, 72, 83, 87, 93, 211
Prophet's mosque, 78, 80, 95
Melchert, Christopher, 65n115, 226–7
miḥna, 99–101, 103–4, 185, 186, 237, 242, 273
al-Minqari, Hamza ibn Wasil, 149
al-Mizzi, Abu'l-Hajjaj, 293
Tuḥfat al-Ashrāf bi-Maᶜrifat al-Aṭrāf, 87
al-Mizzi, Jamal al-Din, 316
monotheism, 36, 166, 302
Moses, 135, 142, 222, 335
Motzki, Harald, 22, 64n114
Mount ᶜArafat, 202, 323, 333
al-muᶜammarūn, 95, 98
muᶜaṭṭila, 86, 281, 283, 286
Muᶜawiya, caliph, 71, 92, 93
al-Mughira ibn Shuᶜba, 71
muḥaddithūn, 86, 93, 136
and *aḥādīth al-ṣifāt,* 104, 146, 187
and anthropomorphism, 267–8
as educators, 190, 247–8
and *bi-lā kayfa* formula, 191
and createdness of the Quran, 100
evaluation of scholars, 51
and *ḥadīth al-ruʾya,* 41, 42, 57, 97–8
and heresies, 289
and Ibn al-Madini, 104
and Ibn al-Tabari, 84–5
Ibn Qutayba and, 196, 201, 202–6
ᶜilm al-rijāl, 366–7
narration of Hadiths, 24, 32, 128, 225–6
performance of gestures, 11, 125, 157–8, 367–8
praise for Ismail ibn Abi Khalid, 94
Qadarite, 88
and veracity of Hadiths, 9, 10
see also narrators
al-Muhallab, Abu al-Qasim, 155, 156
Muhammad, Prophet
aḥādīth al-ṣifāt, 32
Abu Razin's meeting with, 78–9, 80–2, 84, 93–4
appearance, 152–3, 163
authority, 215
and al-Bajali, 90, 91
and Banu al-Muntafiq, 77, 87, 89

Muhammad, Prophet (*cont.*)
beatific vision of, 22, 26, 28, 32, 33, 37, 56, 74, 90, 94, 99, 100, 101, 102, 104, 148, 159, 185, 190, 197, 203, 224, 237, 244, 245
cupping anecdote, 46
death of, 91, 113n141
dialogue with Archangel Gabriel, 87–8, 89, 148–9
on the divine throne, 363–4
'The Farewell Pilgrimage' (*ḥijjat al-wadāᶜ*), 78, 169–70
gestures (*ishāra,* pl. *ishārāt*), 121, 123, 124–7, 130, 135–6, 137, 146–7, 154–5, 159, 163, 164, 165–6, 168, 169–70, 313, 324, 327, 333, 335
ḥadīth ḥaqw al-raḥmān, 230
ḥadīth al-ruᵓya, 96–7
'honourable station', 360
intercessor role (*shafiᶜ*), 6, 7, 8–9, 13
laughter, 55, 128, 133, 134, 284–5
marriage to Maymuna Bint al-Harith, 117n200
meeting with rabbi, 48–9, 54, 55–6
and Moses, 222
noble virtue of, 5
preaching, 78
prophetic message, 2, 4, 73, 74, 75, 79, 88–9, 152, 167–8, 224, 319, 322, 323
and questions, 71–2
recitation of Quran, 214
reconciliation of Muslims, 208–9
supplications, 30
wives, 268; *see also* ᶜAᵓisha; Umm Salama
al-Mulk, Nizam, 277
munāfiqūn, 37, 71, 72
munāẓara (public debate), 194–5, 280, 283
al-Muqri', ᶜAbd Allah ibn Yazid, 131, 132–3, 138, 169
al-Muqri', Muhammad ibn Abi ᶜAbd al-Rahman, 175n67
Murad, Hasan Qasim: 'Ibn Taymiyya on Trial', 355n212
Mushabbiha, 161, 164, 239, 286
Muslim ibn al-Hajjaj, 75, 127–8, 131, 133n134, 143, 153, 255n105, 289
al-Ṣaḥīḥān, 186
Muslims
and beatific vision, 99
and Christians, 34, 35, 36, 37, 41
dialogue with God, 35
and *fiṭra*, 298, 299
and Jews, 34, 35, 36, 37, 41
as *Naturvölker*, 170n2
Umma, 71
al-mutakallimūn, 240, 246, 247; *see also ahl al-kalām*
al-Muᶜtasim Bi-'llah, caliph, 100, 101, 273
Muᶜtazilites
and *aḥādīth al-ṣifāt,* 7, 159, 164, 199–200, 248n6
and beatific vision, 237
and createdness of the Quran, 151, 273
and *ḥadīth al-ruᵓya*, 243
and Ibn al-Walid, 277–8
Ibn Khuzayma and, 280, 281–2, 283, 289–90, 295–6
Ibn Qutayba and, 197, 198
and *kalām,* 1
and language, 240
mistreatment of, 100
and ocular vision of God, 118n211, 158
and *taᶜṭīl,* 158, 167, 195, 238, 286, 292, 295, 312, 319
al-Tibi and, 232, 234
and transcendence of God, 268
muwāḍaᶜa, 351n173

Nahrawan, 95
al-Najjad, Abu Bakr, 1, 2–3, 4, 7, 19n32
narratives
embedded, 25, 27, 33–8, 47, 54, 54t, 130
framing, 25–33, 47, 54t, 76
instance of, 128–34
narrators, 24, 47–57
audiences, 128–34, 157–8
gestures, 128, 129, 132–3, 136–45, 147, 153–4, 160, 365
see also al-Juhani, Rifaᶜ a ibn ᶜAraba; *muḥaddithūn*
al-Nasa'i, Muhammad ibn Yunus, 174n54
Sunan, 85
al-Nawawi, Muhyi al-Din, 220
Nishapur, 131, 164, 194, 242, 279–80, 282, 289
al-Nuwayri, Shihab al-Din, 328

El-Omari, Racha: 'Accommodation and Resistance', 249n6
'Orient', 170n2

Postman, Neil, 69
prayers, 73, 74, 127, 315

Jewish Prayer for Food, 254n91
obligatory (*ṣalāt*), 313
predetermination *see qadar*
prophets, 167; *see also* Muhammad, Prophet

al-Qabisi, Abu 'l-Hasan, 221
qadar (predetermination), 88
Qadarites, 88, 150, 202
al-Qadir Bi-Allah, caliph, 273
al-Qa'im Bi-Amr Allah, caliph, 274, 275, 278
Qarqisiya' (Syria), 92
al-Qasim ibn Sallam, Abu ʿUbayd, 337
al-Qastallani, Shihab al-Din, 220, 221, 222–3, 230, 231
al-Qattan, Yahya, 103
Quran
anthropomorphism in, 14, 100, 190, 192–3, 196, 198
aḥādīth al-sifāt, 26
āyāt al-ṣifāt, 26, 160, 161, 187, 194, 239, 268, 270, 292, 317, 319, 320, 322, 332–3
createdness of, 100, 101, 214, 273, 282, 327
divine attributes of, 162
eternity of, 290
muḥkamāt (unambiguous verses), 70
mutashābihāt (ambiguous verses), 70
performative dimension, 273
Q. 2:115, 331
Q. 2:225, 273
Q. 3:7, 70–1, 105n6, 195, 247, 266n258
Q. 3:79, 66n135
Q. 4:58, 129, 163, 164–5
Q. 4:68, 163
Q. 4:164, 227
Q. 5:64, 163, 167, 198, 226, 238
Q. 5:101, 71
Q. 5:119, 167
Q. 6:91, 65n116
Q. 6:102, 262n201
Q. 6:103, 348n136
Q. 7:54, 317, 351n172
Q. 7:142–4, 135
Q. 7:143, 135, 136, 141, 142, 144, 146
Q. 10:3, 317
Q. 10:26, 26
Q. 11:37, 235
Q. 11:67, 382n1
Q. 11:94, 382n1
Q. 15:73, 382n1
Q. 15:83, 382n1
Q. 16:40–2, 345n81
Q. 17:79, 4, 9, 13, 18n10, 360
Q. 18:54, 124
Q. 19:29–32, 181n161
Q. 20:5, 234–5, 314, 317–18, 331
Q. 23:24, 382n1
Q. 26:23, 358n255
Q. 32:15, 29
Q. 33:32, 268
Q. 36:77–8, 344n70
Q. 38:24, 117n194
Q. 38:41–4, 116n194
Q. 38:75, 161, 235, 238
Q. 39:6, 308
Q. 39:67, 48, 50, 54, 55–6, 160, 226, 262n195, 288
Q. 40:36–7, 335
Q. 40:37, 335
Q. 41:11, 317
Q. 42:11, 166, 168, 195, 268, 303, 304, 310, 311, 319
Q. 47:14–15, 110n85
Q. 47:22, 208, 209, 219, 233–4
Q. 48:6, 167
Q. 48:10, 238
Q. 50:16, 263n205
Q. 50:30, 226
Q. 50:39, 74, 97
Q. 51:47, 238, 239, 264n222
Q. 55:26–7, 348n136
Q. 55:27, 167, 235
Q. 57:25, 308
Q. 67:16–17, 351n170
Q. 68:42, 36–7, 45, 61n66, 269, 341n11, 373
Q. 69:45, 238
Q. 89:22, 263n205
Q. 112:1–4, 214
sayings, 191
translations, 341n11
al-Qurashi, ʿUmara, 41–2
Qurashites, 81
al-Qurtubi, Abu ʿAbd Allah, 18n10, 85, 164, 181n161, 233–4
al-Jāmi, 105n6

rabbis, 48, 54, 55–6, 284, 285
racism, 121; *see also* anti-Semitism
Rahawiyya, 343n43
al-Rassi, al-Qasim ibn Ibrahim, 248n1
rationalism, 290–1, 318

rationalists, 150, 169, 186, 187, 197–9, 200–1, 243, 277, 319–20; *see also* Ash^c^arites; Mu^c^tazilites
rāwī (authorised Hadith transmitter), 125, 130, 221
rāwī (original narrator), 27, 31, 38, 49, 57, 69
Rayy (Iran), 164, 224, 242
al-Razi, Abu Hatim, 224, 369
al-Razi, Fakhr al-Din Muhammad Diya ᵓal-Din ᶜUmar Ibn al-Khatib, 262n201, 320, 321, 362, 363
  Asās al-Taqdīs, 302–3, 306, 307–8, 309, 311–13, 314–15, 320
  definition of *tashbīh,* 310–11
  and Ibn Khuzayma's *Kitāb al-Tawḥīd,* 301–13
  and *al-ishāra al-hissiyya,* 314–15, 323, 325–7, 351n173, 333
  al-ishāra bi'l-sabbāba, 313, 314, 327
  Mafātīḥ al-Ghayb (also the great *Tafsīr* of the Quran), 301, 303, 306, 314
  al-Maḥṣūl, 354n203
al-Razi, Ibn Abi Hatim, 132, 137, 224, 225–6
  Tafsīr, 177n93
Renan, Ernest, 121
Ritter, Hellmut, 179n118
Rosenthal, Franz, 17n10
El-Rouayheb, Khaled, 333

al-Safadi, Salah al-Din Khalil Aybak, 111n111, 347n125, 354n212
al-Saghani, Muhammad ibn Ishaq Abu Bakr, 11–12, 86
ṣaḥāba (sing. *ṣaḥābī,* companions of the Prophet), 3, 94, 147, 151
Ṣaḥīḥ Muslim, 38, 41, 127–8, 215, 216, 219, 220, 230, 323
al-Ṣaḥīḥān, 33, 74–5, 186
Salaf, 141, 169, 194, 195, 297, 300, 319, 320, 323, 338
al-salaf al-ṣāliḥ (the pious ancestors; Taymiyyan terminology), 353n205
Salah al-Din al-Ayyubi (Saladin), 302
Saleh, Walid, 262n193
al-Samᶜani, Abu 'l-Muzaffar, 300
al-Samᶜani, Abu Saᶜd, 347n107
al-Saqa, Ahmad Hijazi, 300, 347n122
Satan (Iblis), 148, 179n119
scriptures
  Arabic translations, 196
  Ibn Qutayba and, 196
  iconic, 271, 272, 276
  oral use of, 270
  performative dimension of, 272
  and questions, 70
  ritualisation of, 272, 275
  three-dimensional model, 272
  see also Bible; Quran
Senturk, Recep: *Narrative Social Structure,* 58n12
al-Shaᶜbi, 109n66, 115n176, 152
shafāᶜa (intercession), 6, 13, 14, 282, 360, 361
  Muhammad's role as intercessor (*shafiᶜ*) 6, 7, 8–9, 13
al-Shafiᶜi, Muhammad ibn Idris, 226
Shafiᶜites, 280, 292, 316, 343n43
Shah, Mustafa, 18n10, 19n43
al-Shahrastani, Abu 'l-Fath Muhammad ibn ᶜAbd al-Karim, 162
  al-Milal wa'l-Niḥal, 160–1
al-Shahwan, ᶜAbd al-ᶜAziz, 279, 346n86
Shakir, Ahmad Muhammad, 259n151
Shiᶜites, 1, 197, 280
Shuᶜba, 97, 125, 139, 202
Sibawayhi, 179n113
al-Sibghi, Abu Bakr Ahmad ibn Ishaq, 289, 291, 292–3
al-Sijistani, Abu Dawud, 3, 4, 17n5, 131, 143, 158
  Kitāb al-Sunan, 17n5, 85, 87
Sirach, book of, 70
Solomon, King, 181n151
Spain *see* Cordoba
speech, 123, 124, 127, 128; *see also* language
Speight, Marston, R.
  'A look at variant readings in the Hadith', 58n16, 171n12
  'Oral Traditions of the Prophet Muhammad: A Formulaic Approach', 171n12
Steinthal, H., 120, 121
al-Subki, Taj al-Din, 297, 334, 357n248
al-Subki, Taqi al-Din, 334
  al-Sayf al-Ṣaqīl fī al-Radd ᶜalā Ibn Zafīl, 358n248
al-Suddi, 142
Sulayman ibn ᶜAbd al-Malik, caliph, 39, 62n80
Sunna, 86, 225, 235, 263n205; *see also* Hadiths
Sunnism, 162, 196

al-Suyuti, Jalal al-Din, 219, 361
al-Durr al-Manthūr, 253n90, 361
Tafsīr al-Jalālayn, 361
Swartz, Merlin, 208
Syria *see* Damascus; Hamat; Qarqisiya'

al-Tabarani, Abu 'l-Qasim, 174n51, 175n66
al-Tabarani, Sulayman ibn Ahmad, 85
al-Tabari, Abu Ja^cfar Muhammad ibn Jarir, 4, 13, 18n10, 84, 208–9
*Jāmi*ᶜ *al-Bayān,* 20n49, 142, 219
Kitāb al-Rusul wa'l-Mulūk, 17n10
Ta'wīl al-Āyāt al-Mushkilāt, 229
Tārīkh, 111n103, 113n133, 126
*tābi*ᶜ*ī* (pl. *tābi*ᶜ*ūn),* 3–4, 98, 103, 147, 178n112
Tadhkirat al-Ḥuffāẓ, 340n7
tafwīḍ, 319, 333, 353n191
tajsīm, 14, 99, 189, 247, 303–4, 310–11, 328, 329
takyīf (modality), 195; *see also kayfiyya*
Talmud, 179n119, 253–4n91
tanzīh (transcendentalism), 167, 168, 195, 224, 229, 230, 231, 234, 238, 243, 244, 302, 304, 312, 313, 369
taqdīs, 302–3; *see* also al-Razi, Fakhr al-Din: *Asās al-Taqdīs*
Tarsus, 11
tasalsul (infinite regress) 309
tashahhud, 313
tashbīh, 5, 238, 247, 312, 368, 369
al-Razi's definition of, 310, 311
see also anthropomorphism
*ta*ʾ*wīl* (figurative interpretation), 166, 196, 237, 238, 241, 242, 243–4, 307–8, 319–20, 333
al-Tawil, Humayd ibn Abi Humayd, 135, 136, 138, 139, 140, 141, 143, 366
tawqīf (revelationist theory), 240
al-lughgha, 351
al-Tayalisi, Sulayman ibn Dawud, 75, 84
al-Taymi, Sulayman ibn Tarkhan, 224
Thabit al-Bunani, Abu Muhammad, 134–5, 136, 138–9, 140–1, 143, 144, 145, 146, 148, 366
al-Thalji, Muhammad ibn Shujjaᶜ, 153
al-Thaqafi, Abu ᶜAli Muhammad ibn ᶜAbd al-Wahhab, 289, 290–1, 344n73
al-Thawri, Sufyan, 109n66, 125, 127, 191, 202, 225
Thousand and One Nights, The, 25
al-Tibi, Sharaf al-Din, 232–3
al-Kāshif ᶜ*an Ḥaqā*ʾ*iq al-Sunan,* 232
al-Tirmidhi (unidentified *muḥaddith*), 9–11, 19n33
al-Tirmidhi, Abu ᶜIsa Muhammad ibn ᶜIsa, 10, 11, 85, 107n31, 138, 205
al-Tirmidhi, Muhammad ibn Ismaᶜil ibn Yusuf, 19n33
Toghril Beg, 342n30
traditionalism
curriculum, 151
discourse of, 234–48
and gestures, 130–1
Hanbalites and, 11, 12
Kitāb al-Tawḥīd and, 299–300
and rationalism, 187, 290–1
and tolerance, 369–70
see also Ibn Hanbal, Ahmad
traditionalists, 153–70, 207–8
and *aḥādīth al-ṣifāt,* 361–3, 367
and *bi-lā kayfa,* 224
discourse of, 189–206
elitist, 248
Ibn Furak and, 246
middle-of-the-road, 1, 5, 7, 12, 206, 361, 364, 367–8; *see also* Ashᶜarites
and Qadiri Creed, 273, 276–7
and rationalists, 152
Shafiᶜite, 316
ultra-, 1, 7–8, 12, 42, 86, 130, 134, 160–1, 169–70, 187, 194, 204, 206, 224, 238, 243, 298, 346n100, 353n203, 361, 364–5, 367, 369; *see also* al-Dhahabi, Shams al-Din; Hanbalites; Ibn Hanbal, Ahmad; Ibn Qayyim al-Jawziyya; Ibn Taymiyya, Taqi al-Din
transcendentalism *see tanzīh*
Tripoli (Lebanon), 145, 146
Turner, John P.: *Inquisition in Early Islam,* 18n10
al-Tusi, Mansur ibn Yahya, 289–90, 291

ᶜUmar ibn ᶜAbd al-ᶜAziz, caliph, 39, 40, 41, 42, 43, 44, 45, 92, 151–2
Umm Salama (the Prophet's wife), 29, 30, 56, 126, 199
al-ᶜUrdi al-Dimashqi, Abu 'l-Hasan ᶜAli ibn Ahmad ibn Muhammad ibn Salih, 331

al-ᶜUthaymin, Muhammad ibn Salih, 350n162
ᶜUthman ibn ᶜAffan, caliph, 92, 93, 95

van Ess, Josef, 19n32, 109n69
Theologie und Gesellschaft im 2. und 3. Jahrhundert Hidschra, 279
Zwischen Ḥadīṯ und Theologie, 64n115

al-Wahidi, Abu 'l-Hasan ᶜAli ibn Ahmad, 362, 363
al-Wajihi, ᶜUmar ibn Musa, 145
al-Walid ibn ᶜAbd al-Malik, caliph, 39, 43
al-Walid ibn Muslim, 224–5
al-Warraq, Abu ᶜAbd Allah al-Hasan ibn Hamid, 227, 228
al-Wathiq Bi-'llah, caliph, 100, 104, 273
Watt, William Montgomery, 260n168
Watts, James W., 271, 272–3
Weiss, Bernard, 240
Wensinck, Arent Jan: *The Muslim Creed*, 260n167, 264n215
Williams, Wesley, 65n115
Wundt, Wilhelm, 120

al-Yunini, ᶜAli, 222
al-Sulṭāniyya, 223
al-Yūnīniyya, 222, 223

al-Zabidi, Muhammad Murtada, 358n248
Zahirism, 161
Zahirites, 16, 208, 267–8, 269
al-Zamakhshari, Jar Allah, 232
Zaydites, 1
Zeitschrift für Völkerpsychologie und Sprachwissenschaft, 120–1
al-Zubayri, Ibrahim ibn Hamza, 82, 85, 211

EU representative:
Easy Access System Europe
Mustamäe tee 50, 10621 Tallinn, Estonia
Gpsr.requests@easproject.com

www.ingramcontent.com/pod-product-compliance
Lightning Source LLC
Chambersburg PA
CBHW052053300426
44117CB00013B/2111
* 9 7 8 1 4 7 4 4 5 2 6 4 9 *